Three Great Adventure Stories

Three
Great Adventure
Stories

One More River
Airline Detective
The Tartan Pimpernel

Collins
St James's Place
London

Three Great Adventure Stories was first published 1969
Reprinted 1971

One More River was first published 1965
© Gordon Hunt 1965

Airline Detective was first published 1962
© Donald Fish Ltd. 1962

The Tartan Pimpernel was first published by Oldbourne Book
Co. Ltd. 1957
A junior edition was first published 1961
© Junior Edition William Collins Sons & Co. Ltd. 1961

ISBN 0 00 192328 5

Printed in Great Britain
Collins Clear-Type Press
London and Glasgow

THREE GREAT ADVENTURE STORIES

Contents

ONE MORE RIVER
Gordon Hunt

AIRLINE DETECTIVE
Donald Fish

THE TARTAN PIMPERNEL
Donald Caskie

One More River

by
GORDON HUNT

SCALE OF MILES

0   5   10   15

Escape Route ▬▶▬ ▬
Camp Sites   X

N

B   U   R   M

IRRAWADDY RIVER

4ᵀᴴ ×

5ᵀᴴ ×   M

BHAMO
Japanese entered
3ʳᵈ May 1942   3ᴿᴰ MAY 1942

TA

Sinlumkaba

To Shan States
and Lashio

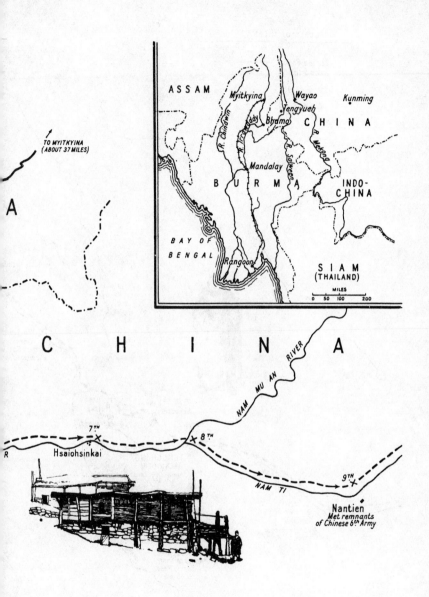

TO MYITKYINA
(ABOUT 37 MILES)

ASSAM

Myitkyina   Wayao   Kunming
Tengyueh
R. Chindwin   Bhamo   CHINA
R. Irrawaddy
Mandalay   R. Salween   R. Mekong   INDO-
BURMA   CHINA

BAY OF
BENGAL   Rangoon
SIAM
(THAILAND)

MILES
0   50   100   200

C   H   I   N   A

NAM MU AN RIVER

7TH
Hsaiohsinkai   8TH

NAM TI   9TH

Nantien
Met remnants
of Chinese 6th Army

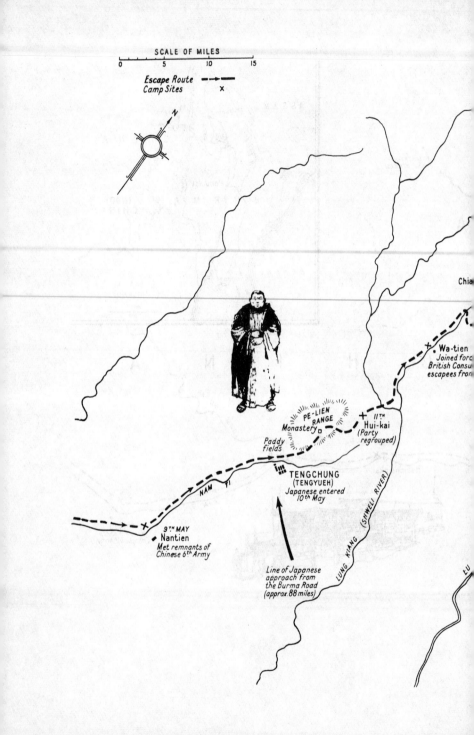

SCALE OF MILES

0   5   10   15

Escape Route - ➤ ➤ ➤
Camp Sites   x

N

Chia

× Wa-tien
Joined forc
British Consu
escapees from

PE-LIEN
RANGE
Monastery □
× 11ᵀᴴ
Hui-kai
(Party
regrouped)

Paddy
fields

NAM TI

LUNG KIANG (SHWELI RIVER)

TENGCHUNG
(TENGYUEH)
Japanese entered
10ᵗʰ May

9ᵀᴴ MAY
Nantien
Met remnants of
Chinese 6ᵗʰ Army

Line of Japanese
approach from
the Burma Road
(approx. 88 miles)

LU

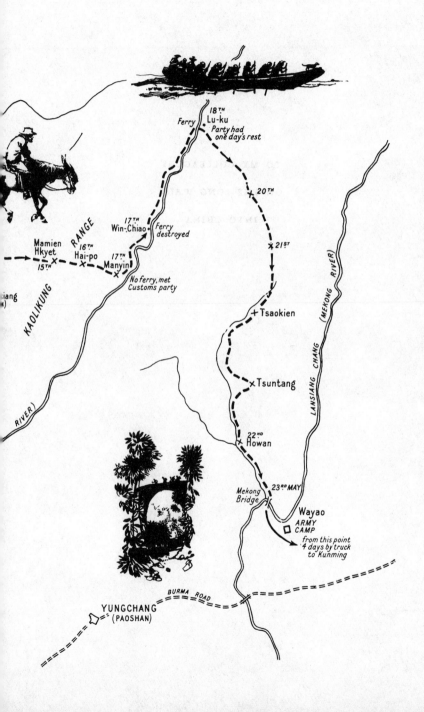

18TH Lu-ku
Ferry
Party had
one day's rest

20TH

21ST

17TH Win-Chiao
Ferry
destroyed

Mamien Hkyet
16TH Hai-po
17TH Manyin
15TH

RANGE

No ferry, met
Customs party

×Tsaokien

KAOLIKUNG

LANSIANG CHANG (MEKONG RIVER)

MEKONG RIVER

siang

RIVER)

×Tsuntang

22ND
×Howan

Mekong
Bridge

23RD MAY

Wayao
ARMY
CAMP
from this point
4 days by truck
to Kunming

BURMA ROAD

YUNGCHANG
(PAOSHAN)

TO MY COLLEAGUES

ON THE LONG WALK

INTO CHINA

Contents

CONTENTS

Preface

THIS IS THE STORY OF A HANDFUL OF MEN, OF WHOM
I was one, and Sheila, my dog. In order to avoid capture by
the Japanese, we travelled from the little river town of
Bhamo on the banks of the Irrawaddy River in Burma over
the Border into Western China and eventually as far as Kunming, from where we were flown to India. The first and
most dangerous part of our escape was a march from Bhamo
to the Mekong bridge. This long walk, which forms the
subject of the book, took about twenty-three days; but, at
this distance in time, I cannot be sure that my chronology
is exactly right. We were sick men by the time it was all
over.

The year was 1942. Most of Burma had been overrun
and the door was wide open to the invaders. But, away in
the extreme north, a few of us had stayed behind to help
with the evacuation to India of the thousands of refugees
who for weeks had been pouring through our station, making
their way to the Hukawng Valley and Assam. In that Valley
of Despair thousands of them were to die.

They were restless days, yet we found much to occupy us
keeping open the escape route, for all organised resistance to
the Japanese had ceased. But the more we saw of the remnants
of undisciplined servicemen and civilians of all races fleeing
into country unknown to them, the more convinced we
became that at all costs we must never get caught in this
struggling stream of humanity. So we decided to turn
eastwards into China, which was on our doorstep. Our
objective was Kunming, where there was an American Air

Force base which was already flying the famous "Hump" route from Yunnan to Assam.

Kunming was over 800 miles away, but that did not worry us too much. With our local knowledge—I'd been in the district twelve years, recently as manager of a teak company —we thought we were going to be clever. With a small party of fit men, bonded together by the determination to survive, we thought we could manage it quite easily. In my Bhamo house, which had become the headquarters of the "Last Ditchers," we laid our plans with military precision. We proposed to cross the range of mountains dividing Burma from Western China and, following the valley of the Taping River, walk the 120 miles to Tengyueh. From there we would cut down the forty-odd miles to the Burma Road and travel the rest of the way in the comfort of Chinese convoys to our objective.

We were completely unequipped, however, to climb to heights far above the snow line, and to tackle the great barriers of mountain ranges which in a hundred miles or so separate some of the longest rivers in the world—the Irrawaddy, Shweli, Salween and Mekong, flowing roughly parallel from the great watershed of Tibet down to the sea. In the event it was across this very country, in the upper reaches of these rivers, that we had to make our way to safety.

It was strange how we all came to be together. It started with the arrival at Bhamo of Dick Winter, an old China hand from Canton who appeared out of the blue one day to run his convoys of petrol and oil by the back door into beleaguered China. Then his assistant, Richard Weldon, came to join my household, which already included my last remaining Forest Assistant, a young man born in that country, who had elected to remain behind with me until it was useless to stay any longer. There was Angus the Scotsman, another teak man who, irritated by the lack of organised evacuation plans, took over from where the Government had left off. To complete our complement at that time there was a wild Irishman who, being naturally agin the Government, had thrown in his lot with us. Maybe we were a bunch of rebels, but at least we knew what we were doing, while all around us there was a swirl of confusion.

After fourteen years' service with one of the famous teak firms in North Burma I knew my frontier districts pretty well, and the hazards of a long walk into the depths of Yunnan did not worry me at all. Our party was fit and we were certain we would stand a better chance of survival by heading eastwards than by joining the mad rush along the westward route to India. The monsoon was about to break, and having been into the Hukawng I knew what that would mean to the ill-equipped refugees. Moreover, we had in Dick Winter a real leader.

Maybe our plans were too well-laid. Without warning there appeared in our midst a stranger, a large, fat man of academic distinction who was in need of help. His great bulk made him totally unfitted to climb into the high mountains of our private escape route, yet I had to decide whether to commit him to almost certain death on the westward road to Assam, or to make him one of us. I really had no choice, so Charles Ewing joined our number.

Of course, the Japanese came, and we just escaped their clutches. In Yunnan we almost met them again, evaded them, and it was there that our party grew to ten in number when a member of the Consular Service and a companion of his came to our rescue, having themselves escaped from the walled town of Tengyueh.

We certainly were a mixed bunch. A diplomat, two civil servants, two oil company officials, three tough men from the forests of Burma—plus Man Friday, as black as the Ace of Spades, and the humorist of the party. And, finally, Stuart Gracey, a man of God to whom we all came to owe so much. These were real men, and I was privileged to be in their company. Not all of them are alive to-day, I regret to say, but in deference to the living I have, in writing this account of our adventures in Western China, provided them with imaginary names. I am sure they would prefer it that way.

CHAPTER I

Escape from Burma

MAY 1ST-2ND, 1942

"AND THAT, GENTLEMEN, IS ALL I AM AT LIBERTY to tell you. As civilians I can appreciate your concern at the trend of events in the past few weeks, but I can assure you that the Army, although withdrawing, is doing so according to plan and, through the intelligence sources available to it, is watching every move of the Japanese forces advancing northwards."

The Brigadier took another sip of his whisky and soda, and by his supercilious manner indicated that we should mind our own business and not meddle in matters beyond our civilian competence to understand.

I sat back in my chair and waited for the pedantic monologue to resume. The year was 1942. Practically the whole of Burma had been overrun, and so fierce and sudden had been the onslaught of the little Nipponese that our own inadequate forces had been thrown back into India leaving behind a trail of blood, suffering and heroism as yet unchronicled in the annals of military history.

It had all happened so quickly, and now the scene had switched to the last remaining outposts of Burma, the Frontier Stations in the far north, of which Bhamo and Myitkyina were strategically the most important.

Bhamo, more than a thousand river miles from the sea, marked the navigable terminus of the Irrawaddy River, while Myitkyina, similarly located on the banks of the same river, was the railhead of the long line which for 840 miles wound its way through the great Central Burma Plain before discharging its passengers within sight of distant mountains, the higher peaks of which were covered in snow and at certain times of the year very clearly visible.

Bhamo was the gateway into Western China and Myitkyina opened the door into both Assam and Tibet.

For months now, through these riverine escape hatches, had been pouring tens of thousands of refugees of all races making their pathetic way towards India. The general order for evacuation of the country had been given; the Governor and his staff had departed and all organised military resistance to the Japanese advance had broken down. Government had long since ceased to function, in spite of the Herculean efforts and the example set by some of the older and more senior members of the Administrative Services who stayed until it became foolhardy to remain any longer.

The flood of refugees was now reduced to a trickle, and all but the last of the stragglers had been helped on their way. Just a handful of us remained. We still had jobs to do, even if they were no more than amateurish attempts to deprive the Japanese of some of the fruits of victory.

The most important thing of all, as we saw it at that time, was to give a breathing space to the refugees making their desperate bid for freedom. And desperate it certainly was, for on the route to Assam through the Hukawng Valley the monsoon was about to break in all its wild relentless fury. It required little stretch of the imagination to picture a struggling stream of men, women and children engulfed in a sea of mud, starving, fighting hand to hand with death to survive the appalling conditions in that valley of despair.

It was with this picture in our minds that Dick Winter and I had demanded an interview with the new arrival at Bhamo. The betabbed Brigadier had assumed command, over the head of the Commandant of the Frontier Force, of all that remained of Burma in the military sense. We knew perfectly well that within a matter of hours he would be gone on his way to Myitkyina and thence to Assam—unlike Rolly Jameson, the Colonel Commandant of our local battalion of Indian troops, who was of a different mould. Reared in the highest traditions of the Indian Army, Rolly had for many years ruled his domain like a benevolent rajah. He knew every hill and valley in the area of his command and, besides being a fluent linguist, he had a deep knowledge of the frontier tribes and understood their strengths and by the same token their weaknesses. But he was a sick man.

So it came about that we sat on Rolly's veranda that hot sultry evening and listened to the stranger talking to us as if we were a brace of subalterns impertinent enough to question the voice of authority. Perhaps, when younger, he had been a good soldier, but too many years of social life in hill stations had left their mark, and he seemed quite incapable of grasping the simple purpose which had prompted our request to see him. All we wanted to know was whether any plans existed to halt, even for a few days, the progress of the enemy approaching us from the south. To the refugees, waiting at Myitkyina, every day mattered. One bridge destroyed might save hundreds of lives. A few dozen large trees felled at strategic places on the narrow twisting hill road over which the Japanese were travelling could delay them for days. But we dare not do it in case, unknown to us, it cut off the escape route of men left behind to carry out demolitions.

We were getting nowhere and I waited for the explosion which I knew would result from our abortive talk with the Brigadier. Dick Winter had not reached his high position in the oil world for nothing, and he believed in straight talking.

" Christ all bloody mighty, man," he said, his face red with rage, " you haven't answered a single question put to you. Instead what do we get? I'll tell you. We came here to seek your co-operation and in its place all we have heard is the brand of cock-and-bull which died a natural death at Hong Kong and Singapore. My questions are simple ones.

Has the Shweli suspension bridge been prepared for demolition, and what steps do you propose taking to deny the Japs the stocks of fuel and oil stored here—enough, incidentally, to service an armoured division for a couple of months!

"Listen," Dick went on, "if it hadn't been for Gordon's foresight and the few chaps who stayed behind with him," and he indicated me, "hundreds of refugees would to-day be stranded and unable to reach Myitkyina, because in the mad rush to get out—and I'm sorry to say that the worst offenders were men in uniform—the long fair-weather bridge over the Mole River would have been broken beyond repair. Did your bloody army care? No. But a handful of civilians, ordinary chaps like me, have mounted guard over that crossing and made every convoy unload their vehicles and cross empty. At the same time repair material has been organised on site in case of accidents. At this moment there are two men there holding that bridge with orders to use force if necessary in order to keep that escape route open for any last-ditchers who may still be coming through."

Dick could hardly wait to take breath as he continued to tear into the soldier.

"Let me tell you something else," he said. "Yesterday evening at dusk I came over the suspension bridge and had to wake up the officer supposed to be in charge there. I crossed without being questioned, as did at least a dozen Chinese lorries. Yet I know for certain that within a day's run there is a Japanese motorised column awaiting only the order to move. And do you think that they will send an advance party to warn your people that they are coming? No, Brigadier, they will arrive in civilian lorries, seize the bridge intact and, followed by a couple of hundred men, will take this place without a shot being fired; and then move on to do the same thing at Myitkyina.

"It's as easy as that. And you're a bloody fool if you think otherwise."

All the bluster had gone from the Brigadier's manner, and

as Rolly recharged our glasses there was an embarrassing silence. I felt quite sorry for the man. Dick certainly had not minced his words.

Suddenly, the warm night air was chilled by an unearthly venomous chanting which rose in waves from the nearby prison in which were housed a hundred or so dangerous criminals, many of them known collaborators with the Japanese. There was defiance in every note we heard, and it sent shivers down my spine, knowing something of the evil habits of those inside.

"You hear that noise, Brigadier," said Dick in a quiet voice. All heat had gone from his words and he was deadly serious. "Let me tell you something. At least half of those foul creatures in there know far more about the Japanese plans than you do, or ever will do. For every man inside there are twenty outside waiting to slit your throat—and ours; and it is only a matter of hours now before their guards desert and throw open the doors of the jail."

Rolly nodded his head in agreement. The stark tragedy of all that had happened in recent months showed in the haggard face and bowed figure of this fine old soldier. Events had taken their toll of this doyen of our station; and he was now far from well. Mrs. Jameson was in England, where he himself would have been, enjoying retirement, but for the war. Months before we had cleared the decks and sent our families to safety; now we had only ourselves to think of, and time was running short.

With the defiant chanting from the jail still violating the quiet of the night, we took leave of our host and bid the Brigadier safe journey to Myitkyina.

As we were leaving Dick turned to him and said, "When you go over the temporary bridge, fifteen miles from here, imagine what chaos there would have been had it been broken beyond repair. Good night!" [1]

[1] The bridge, which is erected annually by local villagers in the dry season, spans a river nearly a quarter of a mile wide. In the rainy season

17

Dick was still seething with anger as we drove off in his car in the direction of the town where his precious fuel was stored. I knew the mood he was in, so we travelled in silence. As a very senior oil company executive he had come to share my house some two months previously after making a spectacular get-away, first from Hong Kong and then from Indo-China, as it was then known. More recently his job had been organising fuel supplies along the Burma Road to Kunming, the last remaining stronghold of the Chiang Kai-Shek régime in China.

Born and brought up in Canton and speaking its language as fluently as he did English, Dick Winter was one of the most dynamic personalities I have ever met. He must have been a man of just over forty, but his untamable hair was prematurely white and he looked older than his years. Of stocky build and with untold energy, he drove himself hard—and those who worked for him, relentlessly. He could do with little sleep and be as fresh as a daisy after a night out. Hardly a convoy passed into China without his personal supervision, and he would think nothing of driving his van all through the night in order to rendezvous with one of his consignments of fuel on its way to sustain what remained of the Chinese forces. The narrow mountain pass which he used so frequently on these expeditions into Yunnan was a nightmare of twists and turns, its surface apt to be strewn with great boulders dislodged from the cliff sides by a weight of traffic never intended for such a route. The road was in fact no more than an enlarged mule track.

Week after week the danger of meeting the Japanese on this road had become more imminent, yet Dick was never deterred from what he considered to be his job. He always travelled unarmed, relying on his own intelligence service of faithful Chinese to warn him in time if he

a ferry operates, but when the river dries up it is impassable because of dry sands and has to be bridged with timber and bamboos.

had miscalculated the risk he was taking on any particular journey.

Driving at speed into the town, Dick swerved into a side road where his main depot was located. Here, stored in drums by the thousand, was the fuel which was the key to a modern army's success. If some of this precious petrol could reach the Chinese within twenty-four hours it might mean the difference between the hasty withdrawal of the 6th Army then poised on the Border, or a rear-guard action of sufficient duration to give a further breathing space to the refugees then concentrated on Myitkyina and down the line of rail at Mogaung, the starting point for the long walk through the Hukawng Valley into Assam.

From what we knew from our sources of information it was the intention of the Chinese to withdraw gradually to the line of the Salween River where the bridge would be held; but Dick had great influence with the local commander and believed that, if given more supplies of petrol, he could be persuaded to hamper the Japanese advance on Bhamo which held the key to the escape of the refugees.

In our civilian capacity we had set a period of one more week to see them safely away and it had been to plan on these lines that we had approached the Brigadier in order to co-ordinate this effort. Had we succeeded in pooling our knowledge and " know-how " with his approval these vital days might have been secured. From Dick's silence on that short journey I knew perfectly well that he was determined to plan things his own way and " to hell and blazes with the Army."

I was not far wrong. The depot was in complete darkness for fear of attack from the air. We were within easy range of the Japanese, then operating from Lashio, and for all we knew they might by now have occupied the fighter base once used by the American Flying Tigers, just over the Border in Yunnan.

A whistle from Dick, and out of the shadows and into the

car lights came a powerful-looking dark man in European dress. This extraordinary figure carried what looked like a sten gun, had slung round his shoulders a carbine of ancient vintage, plus a murderous-looking sheath-knife which hung from his belt. Even more astonishing was the man's accent, for when he spoke I detected the drawl of the American Deep South.

"Mr. Winter, sah," was his greeting. "All well here, sah," and he stood at attention to receive his orders.

"Friday," said Dick, "I want you to round up every available lorry as we are going to run our last big convoy over the Border at dawn. I will be here at first light. See to it that every driver is a man you can trust as we may hit trouble on the way, and I want no collaborators in this party."

Then in terms of octanes and fuel oil specifications Dick designated the cargo to be loaded. "Man Friday," as I had already nicknamed this dark-skinned, jovial character, roared out orders to his subordinates behind the high wired security fence. I heard snatches of Burmese, Urdu and Yunnanese as the place sprang to life. What a change to see positive action after such a wasted evening!

As Dick was about to reverse the car I heard another bellow from Friday.

"One moment, sah, there is something to report. Thought you ought to know, sah. Abdul at our river depot says that this afternoon the Government launch left for Myitkyina with many sahibs on board."

"Just as I thought," said Dick as we drove away. "I bet the whole bloody lot has beat it without a word to anyone. Come on, let's go and check up."

"Oh, to hell with that bunch clearing out, Dick. That doesn't worry me," I told him, "but your going up the road does. God only knows you've risked your neck often enough, and now you really are sticking it out and asking for trouble."

But nothing would shake this man. If it was the last thing he did he was going to try and beat the Japs to the turn-off into China. Then it would be time for us to say our farewells to the country I knew so well.

The first house we called at was that of the Deputy Commissioner, the senior official at any up-country station. The place was in complete darkness, but at last an Indian watchman was roused from his slumbers and from him we learned that all the Government sahibs had departed.

We tried the houses of the policeman, doctor, forestry officer and public works man. They had all gone and the little residential area of Bhamo had become a ghost town.

I think that I was rather more tolerant in my attitude towards the Administration than Dick could bring himself to be. In any case Government, as such, had long since ceased to function, and with the remains of the country completely defenceless, it was now a case of every man for himself. For all we knew they may have been ordered to leave. But Dick wouldn't have it. To him, for these officials to have sneaked away without telling even the Commandant or me, in my capacity as Head of Civil Defence, was unforgivable. I knew these people better than he did, and I do not blame them for making their getaway.

The D.C. was a nice enough chap, a cultured, rather timid, Eurasian, as was the policeman. The others were either Burmese or Indians. We were a mixed community, typical of any small station in Burma at that time.

They were all of one pattern, with the club as the social arena. Normally there would be between six or eight fairly senior officials responsible to the D.C. Some of them would be products of English universities, others, of a lower order, recruited locally. In most places non-officials were in the minority, perhaps a handful of employees of the famous teak companies operating concessions in the area, or, farther south, civilians engaged in the various businesses on which the economy of the country depended. In the north it was slightly different, as the community was enlarged by officers of the Frontier Force or Burma Military Police and by members of the Frontier Service.

To me, as a teak man—I was my company's manager in these parts—life in the north was far more interesting than elsewhere, as we had the opportunity to play polo and to enjoy the company of a much wider and more interesting society than could be found at some of our headquarters. It was a full life and by good fortune it had been my lot to serve first in the Myitkyina district and then, on promotion, to become the head of our business at Bhamo.

The Commandant in each of the Frontier Stations, although complementary to the Civil Administration, was rather a law unto himself. He would have from five to seven Assistant Commandants scattered round the frontier, sometimes as much as a month's march away from base. The area was a vast complex of great mountains and rivers stretching away to the borders of Tibet and China; and it was not surprising that the Force held considerable attraction to young army officers anxious to escape the monotonous boredom of everyday regimental life in India. The pay was good and so was the fishing and shooting. To men of the right type, the life was an ideal one and if their mess debts in India weighed heavily on them, a few months on secondment to the Frontier Force would soon see them out of the red.

The Commandants, such as Rolly Jameson, were on a different basis. They were the men who years before had built up the Force and they belonged to a permanent and pensionable establishment—the old guard, in fact.

Each district was maintained at battalion strength, but so dispersed into small units that only one or two hundred men were available at one time at Headquarters. The troops were Indians including a section of Mounted Infantry who, because of their prowess at polo, rarely saw the lonely outposts in the far away hills!

The Frontier Service, as civil administrators, covered much

the same territory as their military counterparts and would disappear for months on end to their mountain fastnesses. Selected more for powers of leadership and manly qualities than academic abilities, their job was as watchdogs, so to speak, over Tribal Chiefs, of whom there were many. They were akin to the famous Sudan Political Service, now no longer, who used to be described, somewhat unkindly, as " a handful of Blues trying to govern some millions of Blacks."

Some of them were a wild lot, and when once a year or so they emerged from the depths of beyond and repaired to their home stations, it became a riot of fun. They certainly let off steam in a big way, and the more timid of our residents would decide it was time they went on tour, or if that was not possible they would take the precaution of locking up their daughters.

I shall always remember one particular episode which happened to me at Myitkyina on one of these Frontier Service invasions. It was ten o'clock in the morning and I was busy at my office desk when in came a couple of these cheerful beings to inform me that I could not go on working as it was Empire Day and officially a public holiday. Indeed it was, and I was immediately inveigled into a game of poker for stakes far beyond my means. But luck was with me. All through that day we played with food and drink being served at the table, and it was not until seven the next morning that the game ended and my hosts suggested we went for a swim in the Irrawaddy. By then I was £200 to the good. All this money I had won from one man, and, although I knew he had saved a great deal, I also knew that he had a son at Sandhurst and a daughter at one of the more expensive schools in England. So we cut through the pack for double or quits, and I lost. I had had my fun and it had not cost me a penny.

About five hours later, having had our swim and spruced up, we all joined up at the club for pre-luncheon drinks. I had not been at the bar for five minutes when my poker-playing friend appeared and handed me a cheque for £400.

" What in Hades' name is this? " I asked him.

" Your winnings, chum. Don't you remember we cut through the pack for double or quits and you won? "

I tore the cheque into tiny pieces and told him he could stand me a beer. For himself he ordered a double Prairie Oyster. It was a case of " the morning after " with him and even the ice cold waters of the river had failed to restore his memory. Somewhere in the back of his rather befuddled brain was the recollection of a debt of honour which he was determined to pay!

It was with such memories that I drove with Dick that night down to the river through the bazaar area, by then deserted. The Indian and Chinese traders had locked themselves in their shops and the only sign of life we saw consisted of half-starved pie dogs scavenging in the streets. Everywhere was darkness until we reached the Irrawaddy, where in the distance was the searchlight of a launch coming in, and we could hear the throbbing of its powerful engines as it came slowly upstream against the fast-flowing water.

Although it was a good half-mile away I recognised the chug-chug of our Mandalay manager's boat and was glad that Dick had insisted on taking a look at his riverine depot before setting out on his journey into China.

For some days I had been anxious about the fate of my colleague from Mandalay who was long overdue. I knew he was to come this way *en route* to Myitkyina bringing with him a party of last-ditchers. In fact, weeks before, I had drafted some fifty elephants over the hills to Mogaung to ensure that the remnants of my company's employees would have transport to carry their food and baggage through the Hukawng Valley.

As large teak forest concessionaires we had at our command several hundred trained elephants and when the situation became hopeless these had been sent to strategic points to give invaluable service on the refugee route to Assam. They had carried the Governor of Burma's staff to safety and to-day there must be many people who owe their lives to the foresight of the directors of my company who, ignoring assurances such as had been given to Dick and me that night by the Brigadier, had mobilised their resources and made their own plans, and carried them out. Not all the transport elephants we had sent overland for this purpose had reached their destinations, and the operation had cost the life of one of my young Eurasian assistants whom I had detailed to organise the trek. On his errand of mercy he had been murdered and robbed by his own men, who had then disappeared with their valuable animals. There was nothing to be done about it; no possible chance of bringing men such as these to justice, for the days of law and order were gone.

In all the turmoil my house remained an oasis of sanity and realistic thinking, thanks to the presence of Dick and some other stalwarts who had stayed behind to see the job through to the end. This small group of men had urged certain courses of action to stem the Japanese thrust northwards, but had been as good as told not to meddle in matters which were not their concern—by the very men who had now fled. So our plans had been laid without any proper authorisation, and we had done our best to regulate refugee traffic, had commandeered river craft and, to all intents and purposes, had taken over from where Government had left off.

As the powerful craft edged its way through the darkness I could see that it was full to capacity with the men who had remained until Mandalay had fallen to the Japanese. Thank goodness they had made the trip safely.

First ashore was John Henderson, my company's river manager. A Scotsman, many years my senior, he had been my predecessor at Bhamo and knew the area like the back of his hand.

"By Jove, Gordon, it's good to see you," he said as we shook hands. "I've been having kittens all the way here in case you had left and taken Mohammed Ali with you. I've been dreading the thought of attempting the defile passage without the old rascal to take us through. This chap is good enough in his way," and he pointed to a bearded old serang just clambering over the side of the launch, " but it would have been more by good luck than skill if he had got this tub through without smashing us all to pieces. Anyway, luck seems to be with us. I say, the river is unusually low for this time of year; the snow waters must be late coming down this season. . . . But tell me, where is Mohammed Ali, and why the bloody hell haven't you pulled out? You were supposed to have gone long ago."

I introduced Dick, and somehow we squeezed our way to a seat in this tiny overloaded launch; the other passengers being only too anxious to stretch their legs on the river bank.

John produced a bottle of whisky, and over a drink told us of the last nightmarish days before the Japanese came into Mandalay. It had been tragic, for many Burmese had turned against their British friends, or through intimidation by the pro-Japanese elements had gone into hiding to avoid being implicated. It had been a sad ending to the tremendous friendship built up over years between the two peoples.

We were soon back on the subject of Mohammed Ali, and I could see that John was surprised that the old man was not in evidence. As a rule he had only to hear the engine of a launch coming up river and he would be ready on the bank to greet it, as is the way with men whose lives are spent with boats. This old serang was a well-known character and had been with my company for many years. He was the only helmsman competent enough to take a launch through the turbulent waters of the Upper Defile, where he knew every whirlpool and rapid and how to circumnavigate them—provided the water-level was not too high. Many had been the occasions when, regardless of who might be aboard, he had turned the launch about, and, nodding his old grey beard, had indicated that he would take it no farther. Normally no

Government launch would attempt the passage without the old man as navigator, and needless to say his services were much in demand to take V.I.P.s through what must be one of the most spectacular defiles in the world.

I would say that the really treacherous stretch of water extended for not more than twenty miles; for at least seven months of the year it was impassable and one gave it a wide berth. I had actually lived within the defile itself, and on one occasion seen a build-up of water which rose nearly seventy feet in three days as it tried desperately to find a way through the narrow neck of the entrance as the snow waters from Tibet and China rampaged their way to the sea. But hemmed in and frustrated on either side by walls of rock two thousand feet high, all it had done was flood my camp site nearly two miles inland from the river bank.

I knew the time had come to tell John Henderson all about his " old faithful," for he was not only tired but worried.

" Well, John," I said, " Mohammed Ali is by now fast asleep in one of the servants' quarters of my house, because when I heard you were coming this way I took the precaution of moving him there so that he would not be open to bribes to take other craft through. I have told him that you will ensure his safe passage to India, and I know you will. He will be at your helm when you leave to-morrow."

" Wonderful, Gordon. You seem to have thought of everything. But how the hell are you going to get out of this mess? There isn't a square inch of room on my battleship, as you can see."

Dick nudged me as if to say, " Keep your mouth shut," and I told John that we had laid on our own escape route and not to worry.

By then the other launch travellers were coming aboard, having taken their exercise, and it occurred to me that they might like to come and eat at the house. To my surprise the invitation found little response. These chaps were dead on their feet and all they wanted to do was bed down and sleep, for they knew that for two more days they would need all their strength for the journey which lay ahead of them. Not so my colleague John Henderson. Bhamo was as much his home as Mandalay and above all he wanted to pay a call on his old friend, Rolly. In any case he had to pick up Mohammed Ali.

There was an ominous quiet hanging over Bhamo that hot evening. As we drove the three miles to my house not a light was to be seen, not a leaf stirred, and even the scavenging dogs had disappeared from the bazaar quarter. The whole place was airless, eerie and dead.

"Just like Mandalay a day or two before the Japs appeared," remarked John, "but I bet that behind those barred doors there is plenty going on and lots of plots being hatched." And he told us of how his faithful Burmese staff had insisted on hiding his launch in a village some distance from Mandalay in fear that it might be stolen. For with law and order on the way out the door was wide open to the bad hats, and in a large town such as Mandalay they existed by the thousand.

When we reached my house there must have been at least seven cars parked in the driveway, of which I recognised all but one, a large American Sedan with Rangoon number plates.

"Looks as if you have another guest, Gordon," said Dick, adding some sort of aside to John about this being the best hotel between Rangoon and Calcutta.

Inside my guests were in good heart, and seemed to be enjoying themselves, but towering above them all was a stranger. He was an enormous man of wide girth who somehow looked out of place in the company of the lean toughish men gathered over their drinks in the drawing-room. As we entered he came forward, as if recognising me, and in a deep voice, rich in the accent of Balliol, introduced himself as Charles Ewing of the Indian Civil Service on secondment from the Treasury in Delhi and now caught in the headlong flight into the unknown. Someone in his service—I cannot for the life of me remember who it was—had told him to seek me out if he was in trouble. In trouble he certainly was, but appeared to be quite unconscious of it, as he relaxed that night with a man-sized whisky in his hand.

My first meeting with this stranger was a brief one. Dick wanted to turn in because of his pre-dawn assignment with his convoy and John's main concern was to collect Mohammed Ali, have a brief chat to the Commandant and get back to his launch.

There was no time for formalities. Mine was open house and the servants were by then quite used to turning bedrooms into dormitories at a moment's notice.

Wishing Dick a safe journey to China, John and I drove round to the servants' quarters where we found the old serang fast asleep. He was overjoyed at seeing his master all the way from Mandalay, and within a matter of minutes his humble bedding roll was packed and we were away to the fort. When Mohammed Ali was told that he would go with John overland to India, all he said was, " May Allah guide our footsteps!"

The Commandant was drinking his coffee alone on the veranda, his guest having gone to bed ready for an early start with his escort to Myitkyina. Apparently Dick had put the fear of God into him with his stories of the jail-birds on the rampage and the possibility of finding the fair-weather bridge damaged beyond repair!

All the noise from the nearby prison had now died down, and we were able to sit and enjoy the quiet of the night. But Rolly was not himself and, although he talked more freely with his great friend John than he had done in the presence of Dick, it showed all too clearly that he knew it was only a matter of hours before the life he had known for so long was going to come tumbling down around him. He was bewildered and lost by the speed with which events had brought to an end his calm way of life. Rolly had become an old man overnight.

We learned that all his Assistant Commandants but one, who was due to arrive before morning, had been ordered to make for India with their men, unless they should come under the orders of a senior officer who some weeks previously had gone into the far hills beyond Myitkyina. Later, I was to learn that this charming Brigadier had died at Fort Hertz.

It was Rolly's intention to seek sanctuary in the hills when the time came, and to remain in hiding until the monsoon was over when he would then make his way to India. He knew that at his age and in his state of health he could never survive the march in the rainy season.

Whilst we talked the Commandant's faithful labrador slept with his head in the old soldier's lap to comfort him. I thought of the scores of times I had seen Dusty retrieving a bird to his master's hand, for Rolly was a wonderful shot and throughout the season had organised our Sunday expeditions after the jungle fowl for which the district was famous.

It was time to go, and the parting between these two men who were such close friends was a sad one. There was so little that could be said under such circumstances. John was responsible for getting his party to safety—ahead of them lay at least a month of travel and they were leaving late. Rolly was obviously determined to stay until the very last. I think both men knew they would never meet again.

I had to turn away, for there were tears in the eyes of this soldier old enough to be my father as he bid John God-speed and a safe journey to India.

I thought to myself as we drove in silence to the Irrawaddy how much easier it would be for us all if someone in authority ordered us to make a last stand on the pass, and we could be organised—probably die organised—rather than be forced to creep away one by one in the hopes of eventually reaching India by devious routes.

As we approached the river John again broached the subject of my own escape plans and urged me to leave while there was still time. By car I could make Myitkyina long before his launch arrived and from there onwards we could travel in the same party. I told him bluntly that having seen the exodus of refugees and the confusion at Myitkyina nothing would induce me to travel that way.

"Don't worry," I told him; "you have seen Dick and that resolute gang up at my house. We haven't been wasting our time, and I'll bet you a fiver that I am in the Calcutta office before you are."

"You're a bloody marvel, Gordon," said John, already beginning to nod, for he was near to sleep, "I suppose you have a special charter plane waiting somewhere to fly you to India."

"That's roughly the idea," I agreed, bluffing like mad; for Dick was most insistent that no one should know beforehand about the escape route which we had planned and organised down to the last detail.

There were a lot of things I could not tell John Henderson that night, but he made no attempt to put me under the pressure of his seniority with the company. Just as Government had ceased to function, so had the commercial concerns, and, having, in addition, seen the last days of Mandalay, he asked no further questions, for which I was grateful.

My last farewell that night was with Mohammed Ali. John was a typically unemotional Scot, and our parting was no more than a brief handshake before he went down the gangway to his overcrowded ark.

Not so the dear old Indian, who garlanded me with words, as is the way with his people. "Sahib," he said, pumping my hand and bending his old body in obeisance, " remember that at every going down of the sun and with every dawn I shall be praying for your safe delivery. May Allah take care of you!"

The old boy and I had journeyed a lot together and I was happy that he should be going in such good hands to his homeland. He followed his master down the plank into the launch he knew so well, and I was left alone.

All was darkness as I turned the car and headed for home through the blackness of a bazaar bereft of any sign of life. Just one light twinkled in the hillside to the south. This was our hospital and I was reminded that I had a job to do there the next day.

By now reaction had set in, and after a day packed with incident all I wanted was my bed. Fortunately my guests had all turned in and only Sheila, my lovely golden retriever, was awake to welcome me. Dick normally shared my bedroom when the house was full, but, apparently unable to sleep for more than an hour or two, he had gone off to complete arrangements for his convoy into China. I was not to see him again for more than forty-eight hours.

The sun was well up by the time I was fully awake. I had slept heavily. It was a lovely morning which promised to be a hot day. From my open windows I could see the gaily coloured honey-birds feasting off the pink and white blooms of the bauhinia trees which formed an avenue at the side of the house. The friendly chirruping of the pretty little birds as they flitted from branch to branch, so close that from my bed I could reach out to where they were feeding, made the events of yesterday seem like a dream, and such was the peace of my garden that I felt no sense of urgency or any desire to get on with the preparations to leave Bhamo.

Not a sound was to be heard in the house and when my Burmese servant, Tun Maung, appeared with tea I learned that all but my assistant, young Patrick Doyle, had driven off to the town but had left word that they would be back for luncheon. I guessed they were showing our new arrival something of the geography.

Patrick was the last remaining member of my staff. His father had been an Irishman married to a Shan girl. He was fair-skinned, highly intelligent and loyal to the core. Of medium height, he carried no spare flesh, but his wiry frame was as strong as his constitution. In every way Patrick was the ideal man to have at one's side in time of emergency. He had been living with me for some weeks and because of his knowledge of languages had been invaluable in keeping us in touch with all that was going on in the district. This intelligence experience was to stand him in good stead in the months to come. I suppose that at that time Patrick was about twenty-four years old; he had served with me since leaving school, and lucky I had been to have had him.

Downstairs the house was in chaos, littered with the abandoned belongings of evacuees. One extremely rich Englishman from the south, who had stayed a night on his way through, had arrived complete with a lifetime's collection of valuable Persian rugs, all beautifully sealed in metal containers. It must have been a lorry load. I fear he never saw them again and I have often wondered whether the silk Kirman I bought after the war came from his collection. Rugs were also my hobby and in a modest way I had bought one or two every year. Needless to say I lost the lot.

I found Patrick finishing off the last of our store boxes which he planned to take out that afternoon to our jungle hideout just over the Border into Yunnan. This was to be the rallying point should we be surprised or separated, since all of us felt confident that, given ten minutes' warning, we would be able to make our way there and avoid the Japanese.

Already one of our party was on the site making preparations for our departure. We were firmly resolved to avoid the Assam route, which left China as the only alternative. We knew it would be tough going and possibly dangerous, but we were fit and, above all, determined. I think we shared a common fear of being caught in a helpless and hysterical rush. There was nothing really courageous behind our decision to remain to the last and then head eastwards. If we were to survive it would be by our own efforts. The attempt was worth it.

For some years I had been in charge of a large forest area contained in the drainage of the Hukawng Valley and I knew only too well that if the monsoon broke early it would mean certain death to countless hundreds of poor souls caught in its path. The advent of rain would bring about panic. Supplies of food would be washed away, and disease would be inevitable.

That thousands were to die of disease, starvation and total exhaustion in this valley of despair is not surprising. But for the endurance and, above all, self-sacrifice of a few the death toll would have been far greater.

Any doubts I may personally have had about attempting the Yunnan route had been dispelled a few days previously when I had taken my four-wheel drive vehicle (a gift from the Americans) to Myitkyina to make a report on the situation as known to us through Chinese and other sources.

The airfield had already been attacked, and I had seen the beginnings of chaos as thousands of refugees milled helplessly and hopelessly in and around the township and on the Irrawaddy banks, as if waiting for something to happen. Every effort was being made to move them down the line of rail to the starting point at Mogaung, by then already dangerously overcrowded. The untiring work done by a handful of Government officials and civilians, some of them nearing retiring age, was a wonderful example of men at their best when faced with adversity. But in some cases men revealed themselves at their selfish worst. Morale was at its lowest ebb.

I was glad to come away. Driving back to Bhamo I had encountered lorry loads of late comers, many of them servicemen, the remains of units now in full unorganised retreat. It was a sight I shall never forget nor ever wish to see again. They were cheerful enough, but totally unaware of what lay ahead when the time would come to abandon their vehicles and leave them with nothing but their own feet to carry them to safety.

By the roadside I had stopped and chatted with several stragglers, who must have thought me mad to be travelling in the wrong direction, but being jungle trained and accus-

tomed to living alone, the thought of crowds filled me with horror.

There was another compelling reason for my feeling of exhilaration at the prospect of going deep into Western China. From my earliest days China had fascinated me; I attribute this to the uncle who had made a home for my mother when my father died at an early age. Uncle Hastings had held a senior position in the Chinese Maritime Customs; from him I had learned quite a lot about the Orient and the ways of its people. Perhaps it was the influence of this grand character that had guided my footsteps eastwards. Now I was about to penetrate the country he had loved, though my point of entry would be several thousand miles from the seaboard he had patrolled in and around the Yangtse.

My garden was looking particularly attractive that May morning, and I was in the mood to enjoy it. I knew there were last-minute jobs I ought to be doing, but I could not bring myself to do them. The garden occupied about three acres of lawns studded with shade trees and flowering shrubs and the long curving drive was flanked with beds of free-flowering cannas planted in solid blocks of colour.

My house was somewhat isolated, my nearest neighbour being the Commandant a mile down the road. The story goes that one of my predecessors, an Irishman, with a passion for fishing had persuaded the company to build its manager's residence three miles out on the road towards China in order to save himself unnecessary motoring when, of an evening, he would regularly go off to fish the river marking the Border between Burma and Yunnan. Mahseer, perhaps the gamest of all fresh-water fish, abounded in the rivers and streams only sixteen miles away, and there were pools and runs there which would make a salmon fisherman green with envy. The record for our district was eighty-seven pounds, but the really big fish lived in the Irrawaddy and its larger tributaries fed by the snow waters of Tibet. My home waters teemed with five to ten pounders, and I could sit for hours watching their bodies looking like shot silk lazing and playing in the ripples of water which flowed crystal clear from the hills.

My dreaming in the garden was interrupted by the appearance of U Sein, my head clerk, a charming Burman from the south who insisted in staying behind until I had departed. The office had been closed down a week previously and the staff paid off so that they could take their families to distant villages where they would stay in safety until the dust of the Japanese occupation had settled. But nothing would induce U Sein to leave, and every morning he would walk to the house and urge me to be on my way whilst there was still time. He had no fears for himself, and for some unknown reason was full of confidence that we would return to Burma and drive the Japanese into the sea. He had made me pack my more valuable possessions which he undertook to hide and keep safely for me; so into a box I had put my silver and a few other treasures.[1]

All the company's records had been sent overland to India by one of the earlier refugee parties. Later I was to learn that the parcel had arrived intact, but when opened the contents were indecipherable. Rain had reduced the ledgers to pulp.

U Sein, always immaculately dressed in his silken lungyi and with his gaily coloured headgear tied so decoratively, was full of news. He had seen John Henderson and his party leave at dawn, and he tried to tell me that John's last words to him had been an order that I was to leave at once! How he knew that the launch was leaving I do not know. It seemed that even the deserted bazaar still had ears.

As a Burman of the old school, U Sein had no time for Indians. He had heard the noise in the jail and predicted that the inmates would be free in a matter of hours as the troops were preparing to desert. How right he was.

On the subject of our escape plans, I was silent even with

[1] U Sein was as good as his word. Five years later he delivered the box to me in Rangoon, having carried it by devious means a thousand miles or more to his native village in Tenasserim.

this trusty Burman. From the beginning Dick had insisted that if we were to succeed absolute secrecy was imperative. Our plans had been laid accordingly, and not even my friend the Commandant knew of our intentions. Before long I would have to tell him, but it would keep for a while yet.

With U Sein gone to hunt out more news of what was going on in the town, Patrick announced his intention of loading up the stores and going off to the rendezvous. There was no question of eating first. He was like that and could go all day on a flagon of water and a dry biscuit. I knew him too well to argue, and soon he was gone, leaving me alone with Sheila and my thoughts.

The sun was now burning fiercely and I was forced into the shade of the house. I knew there was a problem to be faced and it worried me that I felt incapable of dealing with it or doing something useful instead of day-dreaming. One moment I was with Dick and his convoy, the next with John and his party seeing the beauty of the Upper Defile, or thinking of my family in India and of how my wife was coping with our English nanny, who before departing had become somewhat unbalanced.

But still the problem remained. It was this newcomer Ewing who was now on our hands. What were we going to do with him?

I had only seen him for a few minutes in a haze of tobacco smoke but it was long enough to realise he was in no physical condition to climb into the mountains of Yunnan without breaking down. Yet if all I had learned in the past few hours proved to be true—and in my heart of hearts I knew that it would only be a matter of hours before we had to go—then there could be no question of leaving him. He was one of us and there was no more to be said. Better to face up to it and accept the situation instead of worrying about what Dick would have to say. Stupid thoughts, anyway, as the last man in the world to ditch even a stray animal was Dick Winter.

It was time for a drink. A long cool shandy was what I needed and as I mixed it all ice cold from my paraffin fridge, I heard a car coming up the drive. From the window I recognised the stranger of the night before at the wheel of his large sedan. He was alone, which surprised me, as Patrick had said that he had gone off with the other two remaining members of our group.

Now for the first time I was able to take a good look at him. Rather like Toad of Toad Hall, when he entered the room he dominated it with his bulk and cheery presence.

"Hunt, old boy!" was his greeting, "I really must apologise for my intrusion last night, but to be quite honest with you I am not awfully good at all this escape business. Not my line of country at all." He went on, "You must think me a confounded nuisance and really I don't blame you."

Somehow my heart warmed to him. He was dripping with sweat from his massive domed forehead and jet black hair to his feet. Water ran in rivulets down his hairy chest and arms and he seemed exhausted by the effort of whatever he had been doing that morning. He must have stood all of six foot three in his socks and I am sure weighed a good two hundred and twenty pounds. He was enormous; rarely have I seen a man so out of condition.

"Come, Ewing," I said to him, "help yourself to whatever you want from the fridge and let us forget all about this escape frolic."

"Ah, marvellous; thank you."

"But tell me, what have you done with the others? I was told that you went off this morning with Angus and Richard. By the way," I went on, "as we are going to see a lot of each other in the next few weeks, we might as well start on Christian name terms. Mine is Gordon as you know."

The large man helped himself to a generous measure of gin which he topped up with tonic water, and, lowering his massive figure into a chair, took a big swallow before he went on.

38

" Good of you, dear boy; I am Charles to my friends, but I am not sure whether the chaps I went out with this morning will welcome our closer relationship. I have a feeling they resent my being with you. We had hardly got on our way this morning when some native chap appeared and said something about a bridge having been damaged during the night; and like grasshoppers they were away and gone in the second car. For hours I have been driving round this place of the dead, and but for meeting a charming Burmese gentleman who directed me here, I might still be lost in that frightful bazaar of yours."

I could picture U Sein in his Burmese-style Savile Row attire helping a stranger. " Of course, sir, Mr. Hunt is my manager." The old boy was an awful snob.

I did not like the drift of this conversation, and felt the time had come to take the bull by the horns and enlighten this man, so that he would understand once and for all his place in the scheme of things. I could sense that in his mind he was already building up a resistance to being in the company of my house mates, and this would not do at all. So I let him have it. Tactfully—at least I hope I was tactful—I explained that he had to choose between driving off to Myit-kyina and taking his chance on the Hukawng route, or joining us in our escape bid into China.

" Look at it our way, Charles," I said; " until a week or two ago we were all comparative strangers in this house, yet each and everyone of us has something to contribute to the chances of succeeding in what we know will be a hazardous journey. You might go so far as to say that we have been our own selection committee, bound together by the common desire to survive and with our minds firmly fixed on avoiding the Assam route, if we were to do the jobs here that somebody had to stay behind to do.

" Those grasshoppers, as you have described them, may have saved a few lives to-day by rushing out to the broken-down bridge. Dick Winter and his convoy of petrol trying to cross into China may be the means of saving hundreds of lives; and young Paddy McClusky, who for all I know may be in trouble, is living rough, possibly dangerously, out at our rendezvous, in order to save ours and possibly yours.

" Listen for a moment," I went on, now in full cry, " we are all pretty tough and there is still time for you to head up the road and take your chance. But, for what my advice is worth, I would say throw in your lot with us and see if there isn't something you can contribute to the pool.

" But there's one thing we must get straight: do you think that Angus McRobert and Richard Weldon enjoy repairing bridges, or that the Trinity, Dublin man is having a picnic in Yunnan waiting for us to join him? Don't start off by underrating them. You had better thank your stars that you have the chance to be put up for the Travellers' and forget all about the Athenæum, if you wish to survive. Come on, let's have another drink and then some food."

Poor Charles Ewing! I really had waded into him, but it had had to be done. He was very ill-equipped to join us, but I knew he would never stand an earthly chance of survival in the Hukawng. The Lord only knew what I had saddled our group with. But I knew I could not send him away by himself.

That afternoon there was a mild scare. A Japanese fighter aircraft flew low over my house and made a reconnaissance of the town and the deserted river moorings. In the garden was a slit trench, but I did not bother to take cover, and only Sheila got any real excitement out of the brief excursion of the enemy plane.

On its second circuit the aircraft made a run over the Frontier Force Headquarters, so low that one single well-directed burst of automatic fire should have been enough to have brought it down in flames; but there was no response. As it roared over my house at rooftop level I could see the begoggled pilot quite clearly crouched over his controls as he gained height to cross the hills on his way back to base.

I could have written his report for him; it would have read:

"Having been briefed at Lashio by Commander Sato, I flew a reconnaissance flight over the town and environs of Bhamo as instructed, and can report that the town is deserted and there will be no resistance to the triumphant entry of our Imperial Forces. There were no signs of shipping in the river and the Army Headquarters gave all the appearance of having been evacuated. I made two runs over the fort area at roof-level and not a shot was fired. As far as I could see all the approach roads are intact."

During this brief interlude I had quite forgotten my guest, who by all the rules should have taken cover. This was only the third time that a Japanese aircraft had ventured so far, but for weeks I had drilled the servants to make for the camouflaged trench—even the cars had special parking bays hidden amongst the bushes, so that in the event of a raid the house would not attract attention. The servants were by now emerging rather sheepishly from the trench, but nearby me on the veranda was Charles Ewing placidly smoking a cigarette.

"Brave little fellow, that chap," he said, "he could easily have had his guts blown out as he flew so low over the fort."

Clearly my guest had not been in the least frightened by the begoggled visitor, and he went up one in my estimation.

"But what were you murmuring about?" he asked. "I caught the word Sato."

"I must have been thinking aloud," I answered.

Mr. Sato had been rather a chum of mine; one of those charming Japanese to be found doing various jobs throughout the Far East before the war; I had always suspected that he was engaged on intelligence work for his country. When war came he had disappeared overnight, and with his going we lost the best mechanic in the north. His garage could not have been better placed to report on the build-up of routes into China and American efforts to bolster up the tottering remnants of the Chiang Kai-Shek Central Government.[1] It had always intrigued Mr. Sato that I had been brought up by an uncle who, before joining the Chinese Customs, had fought as an officer in the Japanese Navy.

Towards evening I began to worry about Dick and the other members of our group, all doing jobs whilst I twiddled my thumbs. The mood had been on me all day; I suppose the weeks of strain were now catching up. I came down to earth and spurred myself into action.

I thought then that this would be a good time to have a heart to heart talk with Rolly and to tell him of our plan to cross into China. I owed it to him as a friend, and, besides, it might well happen that during the night we would be forced to leave hurriedly, and I would never be able to look Mrs. Jameson in the face if I had to tell her that I ran out of Bhamo at the dead of night and never said good-bye to her husband. Rolly's family were friends of mine, whereas Dick himself had been a stranger to me until recently, and the others I hardly knew, apart from my young assistant.

Rolly sat in his usual seat on the veranda, his dog stretched out nearby, and I joined him with a cup of tea. He looked tired and all the fire and snap of the old soldier had gone.

The few sepoys I had seen seemed cheerful enough, but the place was quiet and it no longer had the air of a military establishment.

We were joined by Bertie Gresham, the young Indian Army Major whom Rolly had mentioned as being due the previous evening. I felt it prudent to refrain from mentioning the reconnaissance plane, which only an hour or so ago had passed over the barracks. The subject was not raised, and I guessed that such men as remained in uniform had been given orders to capitulate or pull out. There was to be no more resistance. The door was now wide open.

"You know, Gordon," Rolly said as he fed Dusty with

---

[1] Sato was in fact a Naval Commander, as I was to discover at the end of the war.

a biscuit from the table, " it's time you fellows pulled out of here: there's nothing left for you to do. Bertie and I will probably leave for the hills to-morrow. Why don't you come with us? "

When I told him of Dick's plan to travel eastwards towards Kunming and that our minds were made up and our arrangements complete, he did his best to dissuade me from joining in any such foolhardy adventure.

" It's utter madness," he said, " you will be lucky to survive twenty miles once you cross the Border. Come, Gordon, be sensible: join us and stay amongst friends."

It was difficult to explain to Rolly that between us we knew far more about the bandit-infested route into Yunnan than most people and had weighed up the chances of getting through with a military thoroughness.

Rolly belonged to the old school to whom Yunnan was a forbidden land. In all his service he had never been farther over the Border than was necessary for a courtesy call on the Chinese on the rare occasions of a Frontier Meeting when our local administrators camped on one side and their opposite numbers on the other. As for attempting to get as far as Kunming—that was simply ridiculous. But, when at last he saw that I was adamant, he became more his old self. I sensed that in reaching the firm decision to go on our own we had relieved him of any responsibility for our safety. After all he had been father of the station for a long time and he had come to think of us as children.

Now more relaxed, Rolly entered into the spirit of the adventure ahead of us, so much so that I tried to persuade him to join us, but he would not consider it.

" No," he said, " Bertie and I have our plans laid and you can have your Chinks and bandits. Jolly good luck to you."

I had not met Bertie Gresham before. He was a fine-looking soldier, but despite his strong exterior of calm I could detect signs of apprehension about the future. He had the look of someone badly in need of sleep. He was jumpy and every few minutes would find an excuse to leave us. To a man straight from a remote hill station it must have been a shock to walk into a headquarters already disintegrating with every moment of the day.

Having had a whisky and soda whilst we watched the sun dip below the hills marking the entrance to the great defile, and having promised to keep in touch, I was soon on my way back to the house.

It was a lovely evening and the reflection of the setting sun cast a halo round the highest peak in the immediate neighbourhood, the Kachin stronghold of Sinlumkaba, some twenty-odd miles away. It was my guess that this would be the first stage of Rolly's trek from the plains, and there he would certainly be amongst friends, at least until the Japanese consolidated their hold on the north. But India would still be far away, and I doubted whether Rolly would live to see it again.

There was no sign of Dick; all that his assistant, Richard Weldon, knew was that the convoy had left as planned. He and Angus had spent most of the day out mending the bridge and they had seen no one on the road. It looked as if the last of the trickle of refugees had gone on their way, and as soon as Dick appeared it would be time for us to leave this place.

Richard Weldon was a tall spare man of not particularly robust build. An Englishman of about forty, he was a complete stranger to the country, having arrived from farther east just in time to see the collapse of Burma. By profession he was an oil technologist, and indeed looked every inch the engineer. He had a pleasant quiet nature, coupled with a delightful sense of humour. Very much a family man, I would have placed a bet that in his pocket-book would be a picture of Mrs. Weldon and the children.

By contrast Angus McRobert had the build of a middle-weight boxer and moved like one. Aged about thirty-six, he was a senior member of another of the teak companies operating in Central Burma. After numerous adventures he

44

had, with several others, made his way north and had decided to stay and help with what we were trying to do. I think he had fallen under the influence of Dick's personality and they had become good friends. Angus had the typical fine features of a Scot. Though he got on well with us all, he was a man of few words, and could act quickly when the situation demanded it. Not a man to argue with.

Patrick had duly delivered our store boxes to the rendezvous. He reported that although Paddy McClusky had succeeded in buying four mules he was worried by the unexpected arrival of several Yunnanese traders at his camp site, also in the market for transport, and by all accounts rather ugly customers. His advice to us was to get moving as quickly as possible, as the sooner we could get clear of this crowd the better it would be.

I did not like the sound of this very much, for it was most unusual for mule traffic to be moving into China so long after the season had closed. Normally it opened in November and came to an end in mid-April. During these months of comparatively cold and dry weather there was considerable trade between Yunnan and Burma. Caravans would descend into the Irrawaddy Plain bringing walnuts and the oil of the tung tree, and return laden with salt, paraffin, vegetable oil and other necessities of life unobtainable in the hinterland of China. Sometimes during this period as many as a thousand mules would be encamped for a night or two in the caravan-serai only a few miles up the road from my house. Their arrival would herald the beginning of our cold weather and the shooting season, so much looked forward to after seven or eight months of tropical heat and the incessant rains of the monsoon. For Bhamo, although over a thousand miles up the Irrawaddy, is only about four hundred feet above sea-level. Its rainfall averages seventy-five inches, and the heat could be unbearable at times.

Charles Ewing, with his great bulk, looked even more out of place in the company he was in than he had the previous

evening. But I sensed that his relationship with the others
had improved, and he was going out of his way to be one of
them. This was not easy. We were all of us lean and tough-
ened by hard living, whereas this scholarly man, although
under forty, looked as if he had never walked farther than
from his London club to Whitehall. Yet he was a likeable
fellow, if a trifle pompous, but hardly the companion to
choose for a venture such as the one we were about to undertake. However, he was with us for keeps, and I was reminded
of this when he began to question me about our plans.

"You know, dear boy," he said, heaving himself out of
a chair to get another drink, "now that you chaps have been
so kind as to take me along with you, do tell me how we set
about it when friend Winter gets back to do his Pied Piper
act?"

"Well," I told him, "sixteen miles from here there is a
turn off the main road where the mule caravans from Tengyueh
come down from the hills. That's where Paddy McClusky is
waiting with his four mules. From then on we start to
climb into the mountains which divide Burma and Yunnan—
and I warn you they are very steep. Then we go down the
other side into the valley of the Taping River and walk the
one hundred and twenty-odd miles to Tengyueh. There are
a lot of bandits about, but we must chance that. From
Tengyueh, which is an important Chinese Customs Post,
there is a road leading to the main Burma Highway. This,
I believe, is about forty miles, so all together we have about
a hundred and sixty miles to do on foot. Then we thumb
a lift with the Chinese 6th Army and motor the three hundred
and fifty miles to Kunming where the Americans will fly us
to India. It's as easy as that."

"Sounds good to me," said Charles, thumping his large
stomach. "I need to lose a bit of weight." Then, as an
afterthought, he went on, "But how do you know the
Japanese won't have turned eastwards from Lashio to move
on this Tengyueh place? Do you think the Chinese are going

46

to fight? From all I've heard down the road, they spend their time in retreat."

I could only answer that to the best of our knowledge the Chinese would not move back beyond the Salween front. After all the Salween Bridge could be blown up and that would put paid to any further advance. The road we would take from Tengyueh meets the main Kunming highway miles to the west of the Salween River.

But Charles had made a point. God knows what we would do if the line of the Salween was abandoned. I wished that Dick would return and take over from where I left off. It was he who knew the Chinese plans, not me. With this sobering thought I went to bed.

CHAPTER 2

Across the Chinese Frontier

MAY 3RD

SLEEP DID NOT COME EASILY THAT NIGHT. IT WAS
hot and airless, and even Sheila was restless beside my bed
where she always slept; this was most unusual for her. I
tossed and turned, haunted by the idea that Dick and his
convoy had met with disaster and had been ambushed before
turning eastwards into China.

I had visions of him caught in a burst of automatic fire
and dying at the wheel of his van, cursing the Japanese until
his last breath, for he loathed them with a burning hatred.

Dick's presence during the past few weeks of crisis had
come to mean a lot to me, for he had infused into our diminished community a Pimpernel spirit of virility which before
his coming had been sadly lacking. Of us all he was the only
one with a definite job to do.

Maybe Rolly was right—it was time we went.

Sometime in the early hours of the morning, I must have
fallen into a deep sleep, and but for Sheila's cold wet muzzle
nudging me, as if to say " it's time for you to get up," I might
have slept on long after first cock's crow. My dog was like
that. From a puppy she had been above average in intelligence
and at the age of two years seemed to understand and respond
to my every mood. Rather large for a golden retriever and
with no pedigree, she was nevertheless one of the best gun-dogs
in the district and much loved by all.

The house was strangely quiet and not even the chatter of
the servants could be heard as I showered and made ready

for what I knew in my heart would be the last day in the home I had come to love so much.

There was something ominous in the air that May morning and I sensed that during the night things had happened. I had the feeling that I should be walking on tiptoe lest I break the spell which sat like a pall over the place.

I followed Sheila down to the garden and saw that under the trees near my stables were assembled a number of bullock carts, with the animals tied up nearby. In anticipation of my departure the servants had made ready to enjoy the loot which would be theirs for the taking once our backs were turned; and now they had decided that the time had come. I dare say they would have gone days before but for the temptation of having a free hand in the house. They had been good servants, but were a timid lot and I knew of their plan to disappear into remote villages as far away from the Japanese as their bullock carts would take them.

It was far from a nice feeling to be walking out, or rather running away, and leaving one's possessions behind. Ours was no panic exodus, such as had been the case in the south of Burma where the civilians were bombed and only too happy to escape and leave their homes. The thrust to the extreme north had been long in coming, with the result that our lives had hardly been disturbed. Perhaps we had even deluded ourselves into thinking " it won't happen here." But it had, and there was worse to come.

Walking down my drive towards the road I came on a scene I will never forget. Grazing by the roadside or cavorting about madly, as horses will when loosed from stable into paddock or meadow, were a hundred or more of Rolly's beloved ponies, beautiful well-bred beasts which were his pride and joy. I could see them on the golf course, the polo ground and the rifle range. Revelling in their new found freedom, they romped and played like schoolchildren given an unexpected holiday.

" Poor old Rolly," I thought, for I could picture his

distress, his mind numbed with shock by the tragedy which had befallen him during the night. From his house on the bluff all the land over which the ponies roamed could clearly be seen, and I knew that he would be pacing his veranda, sick at heart, with only his labrador to comfort him.

It was clearly evident that the Indian troops had disappeared in the night and men like my old bearded polo coach, Risaldar Mohamed Babadur, had opened the battalion stable doors so that their charges could fend for themselves. Men like these had lived for their ponies, and I am sure, knowing them as I did, that many a tear had been shed that night when the time had come for man and beast to part company.

Whether the troops had deserted or been told to disperse and make their own way to India, I never really knew for certain, but I fear they had taken the law into their own hands.

I found it difficult to drag myself away from the sight of the ponies, beautifully groomed animals which from foals had been cosseted like children. God knows what fate lay in store for them. My own two ponies I had given to the syce who had worked for me for years, and a week before he had ridden off to his native Manipur (the birthplace of the game now called polo).

It was time for action and I returned to the house to rouse everybody. Before going to bed we had agreed a plan for the day. I was to maintain contact with the Commandant, Richard with his oil depot, and the others were to stay in the vicinity of the house in case Dick appeared with bad news. The lethargy of yesterday had left me. There was no time now for lazing and dreaming, but the day of rest had done me good, and I was on my toes.

My car had hardly turned out of the drive when the familiar figure of my head clerk came into sight, and in his usual fashion he brought me up to date with news of the town. Yes, all the troops had gone, the jail had been thrown open and the shopkeepers had barred their doors in fear. Many families had taken to the jungle and rumour had it that the Japanese would arrive before nightfall. I really believe that U Sein was so curious to see the Japanese that it never occurred to him that they might be unfriendly and perhaps put him to manual work.

"Come on, jump in," I said to the faithful old Burman, "I am going to see the Commandant and then deliver some things to the hospital." For some time I had been a member of the Management Committee and all my company's surplus medical stores were in the back of the car to be delivered there.

The Frontier Force Headquarters were completely deserted. Not a soul was to be seen and the long lines of neat barracks stood empty and forlorn, the doors wide open in readiness for the new occupants.

Just as I had expected, I found Rolly pacing up and down the ramparts of his lost domain, his eyes gazing helplessly at all that was left of his life's work. His face was haggard from want of sleep, but it showed not a trace of fear. His khaki bush shirt and shorts were as neatly pressed as if he was going on parade, but I noticed a nervous twitching of his hands as they fingered the little swagger cane he invariably carried.

"I suppose you have seen what happened during the night," was all he said. I could do no more than nod my head in understanding. "Gordon, you chaps must leave here this morning, Dick or no Dick, as it's only a matter of hours now before the Japanese arrive, and it might be that Dick has met them on the road and will never return." He then rehearsed his own plan to leave for the hills with his Assistant Commandant.

Rolly's labrador hovered near his feet, and catching my glance at him he patted Dusty's head and murmured, "You are coming with us, old boy, aren't you? They're never going to part us." Dusty gave his master a typical look of confidence and affection; anticipating a question about Sheila I told Rolly that I was also taking her with me. I really had not thought about it, but had taken it for granted she would be at my heel when we left.

Conversation wasn't exactly easy that morning, and to tell the truth I felt rather an intruder into the private hell of the old soldier. We had said all there was to say and I was about to say good-bye, when I remembered I had a favour to ask him.

"Rolly, do you think I could raid your store and fit myself out with a pair of your army boots, as I have an idea that I am going to need a new pair."

"But of course, let's go and see what we can find for you."

As we descended from the house down the steps into the barrack area our way faced the prison. There, with its heavy doors wide open, stood the building from which we had heard the frightening noise two nights before. All was quiet now, and I knew that in our midst, perhaps even amongst our servants, must be lurking many of the cut-throats and spies it had housed.

"Yes, they went last evening," said Rolly, and I could imagine his state of mind as he had tried to sleep in the knowledge that he was alone and his men had gone. It could not have been a peaceful night for a sick man, and it is doubtful whether he had slept at all. Until then I had forgotten all about the prisoners and their defiant chanting. Now all I wanted to do was get away from this place as far as I could in the shortest possible time.

We found a pair of stout well-made army boots which fitted beautifully. The quartermaster's store was as spick and span as if ready for the colonel's inspection. Not so the armoury; the men had taken their rifles before they left.

I thanked Rolly for the boots and we shook hands wishing each other luck wherever we might be. I never saw him again.

My next call was to the hospital, which stood on high ground some distance from the town, facing towards the hills. From its second floor there was a clear view of the road over which the Japanese would have to travel, and it was possible to trace its course for miles as it snaked its way into the

Irrawaddy Valley from the Shan states and the turn-off into China used by Dick. From this vantage point would be heralded the arrival of the temporary masters of Burma. A cloud of dust would signal their coming should they advance by day and a flickering of headlights would give them away if they came by night, which was unlikely.

It was here I found my friend the Roman Catholic priest, who, as the doctor had gone, had taken over the hospital and, with the help of some Burmese and Shan nuns of a local Order, was quietly organising things in preparation for what was to come. His whole manner was serene, and looking at his ascetic face I knew that he had no fear for himself, only for those for whom he had assumed responsibility.

"Dear Mother of Jesus, why are you still here?" was the greeting I received from Father O'Donovan. He went on to reprimand me for being so foolish as to have remained so long, and bid me hurry on my way, scanning the distant hills for the tell-tale signs of what we both knew would soon appear there.

"Father," I told him, "for three days I have been meaning to bring you all our surplus medicines, but somehow never got round to it. U Sein is unloading them down below, and for you I have brought a few bottles of my own special prescription for your personal use." In the boot of the car was a case of whisky.

I knew of this great Irishman's decision to stay at his post, and some days previously we had discussed it. I had asked him what degree of freedom he could expect from the Japanese. He had explained that his church had sent him to us and he had not been instructed to leave Bhamo. The matter was as simple as that.

I stayed a while with Father O'Donovan, but he seemed worried for my safety and concerned that Dick had not returned. "Go now, my son, and have no fears for me as we shall meet again."[1]

[1] When the war was over we met again. Although banished to a

With these words in my ears I left this saintly man, and the last picture I had of him was with his hand held high in a farewell blessing, but his eyes still turning apprehensively towards the hills.

There was one more hand to shake, that of U Sein, who took his leave in the dignified manner of his race, and then I was alone driving slowly homewards with a lump in my throat. There was no question about it, we would be foolish to stay any longer; it was my forlorn hope that we would find Dick at the rendezvous, as we had planned, should something happen to prevent his return to the house by the main road.

I was just short of the Frontier Force Headquarters when suddenly I saw a cloud of dust in the distance and a car approaching at great speed. I braked hard and pulled over to the grass verge as the other vehicle with a screech of tyres drew up alongside. For a moment I did not recognise Dick or his van, but there was no question about his companion. It was Man Friday.

Dick was, in fact, practically unrecognisable. His white hair was red with dust, and with three days' growth of beard and the sweat running down his face he looked terrifying. Yet beneath his grimy make-up I could see the fire burning in eyes now half-closed from lack of sleep.

I knew at once that something had gone wrong.

" Christ, Gordon, for God's sake hurry or you will be wearing a kimono. I have warned Rolly who is leaving immediately but it's touch and go whether we can get out in time. The little yellow swines have been right on my tail."

With that Dick reversed and went like a bat out of hell up the home straight with me following as fast as my car would go. Only a few hours previously I had dawdled on this

---

remote place for the duration of the war, Father O'Donovan had not been treated unkindly by the Japanese. He is now a bishop.

stretch of road where the ponies had been grazing. Now all was dust as, with my foot hard down on the accelerator, I travelled in the wake of the car ahead.

At the house all was chaos. As I swung into the drive I could hear Dick's voice above the noise of his engine cursing the lot of them for being a dilatory bunch of bastards. He never got down from his driving-seat and within seconds the lot of us were driving like madmen up the road towards our turn-off into the hills. But not before Sheila had jumped in alongside me quite convinced that we were going on a shooting expedition, even if rather an unusual one.

Perhaps it was as well that I never had time to set foot in the house I had come to love so well. The only memory of it that lingers was seeing the servants loading up their bullock carts. The thought that the refrigerator was packed with cold beer to greet the Japanese fills me with rage to this day.

In this frantic rush to depart I had not even a blanket, but at the time it did not seem to matter. All I could think about was covering sixteen miles and seeing Dick turn away from the main road. As far as I can remember we had four cars in the convoy led by Dick, with my rather ancient jalopy in second place; and it was with a feeling of relief that I watched Dick swerve in to the side road leading to my picnic place beside the waterfall and the little bridge over the river in which the mahseer played. This was where Paddy McClusky was camped.

Once clear of the main road we should be assured of a breathing space, even if only of short duration. We had made it.

From what we learned later that evening we must have missed a head-on collision with the Japanese by a matter of minutes. Dick's timely arrival had saved our skins, but I knew that he had risked his own in order to warn us, for he could quite easily have made for the rendezvous instead of coming all the way into Bhamo itself—not only to save us but also Rolly and his companion. I was longing to hear all about his adventures with his convoy but that would have to wait.

By now the going was getting rough and the old car I had been driving that morning came to a halt, steam billowing from the radiator and a horrible smell of oil and burning rubber coming up from the engine. It had been driven into the ground in less than twenty miles. In a matter of seconds the expert, Richard Weldon, pronounced it a write-off, and without more ado it was toppled over a cliff into a deep ravine; its rusting frame is no doubt still there to this day. The operation was so swiftly carried out that there was barely time for me to grab the new boots I had collected from Rolly.

At least the interlude gave me a chance to light my pipe, and for the first time I was able to have a word with the other members of the party. Emerging from somewhere in the rear of our cavalcade, Patrick came to tell me that in his car was the assortment of guns and rifles which had accumulated at the house during the past month or so. He had loaded them into his vehicle to save them falling into wrong hands, but they would clearly have to be disposed of, as we couldn't carry them into the hills. And so it came about that the last few miles leading to the frontier between Burma and China became the graveyard for more than two thousand pounds' worth of aristocratic firearms. The collection included among others two pairs of matched Purdy's and a couple of Rigby 450-500's. Every one had to be smashed against rocks and rendered useless before being hurled into the valley beyond recognition or repair. The only weapon we retained was my Luger pistol which Patrick had rescued from the house.

Dick and I had discussed the question of carrying firearms and we had decided that it would be safer to rely on our wits rather than guns on the journey through Yunnan. Western China had for centuries been practically unadministered; much of its territory was unmapped and its frontiers and trading routes with Burma were dictated by a number of

56

ruling chiefs who were no more than bandits. These in turn had to pay toll to the Governor of Yunnan, an old rogue whose main source of income stemmed from the opium traffic he controlled. Straddling the approach routes with their armed levies, these gangsters charged so much per head for every mule which used them. There was no secret about the trade which went on as it had done since time immemorial.

It was into this unsavoury cauldron of organised banditry that we were about to enter, and the last thing we wanted to do was attract attention by a display of firearms.

I was now travelling with Dick in the van and Sheila had joined Friday in the back. The road had narrowed into no more than a track winding in and out of the great trees which covered the foothills. The heat of the day had given way to a damp cold for the sun had little opportunity to penetrate the heavy canopy of tropical growth which grew overhead.

Dick was in no mood to talk, being too intent on reaching the rendezvous and getting away into the hills. Things had not come out quite as planned, and it had been a near thing; but at last we were on our way.

Just short of my picnic spot by the waterfall which marks the end of the motorable section of the road, we came on Paddy McClusky looking like a bearded leprechaun in the half light. He was surrounded by a villainous-looking gang of Yunnanese who were waving their arms and shouting some kind of abuse at him. Paddy cursed us for being so long in coming; from what we could gather he was being accused of stealing one of these bandit gentry's mules.

The situation looked quite ugly until Dick, quick as lightning, jumped down from his cab and gave the Yunnanese hell in their own language, or rather, a mixture of the few words he knew of their dialect with the Cantonese he spoke so fluently. The gang backed away towards a fire they had burning beneath a nearby tree, followed by Dick now fully in command.

"Thank God you got here in time," said Paddy as the rest

of us ranged ourselves in readiness to cover Dick, "those bastards would have knifed me for two pins and they have put the fear of God into my muleteers."

He was clearly shaken, which was not surprising, as they were tough ugly customers and he was unarmed.

Our few belongings were soon offloaded and Richard Weldon and Angus McRobert set about immobilising our cars so that they would be useless when found by the Japanese. In deliberate and expert fashion they went about the job like enthusiastic schoolboys. We were all ravenously hungry and Patrick and Friday got busy with the store boxes; from one of these I took a bottle of whisky. Never was a drink more welcome.

"I don't like the look of those fellows," said Dick as he drank his whisky and we took stock of the situation. "My guess is that they are opium smugglers and with the Japanese coming, are getting out of Burma with as much of the filthy stuff as they can carry. Dark or no dark, let's eat and get cracking. What do you say, Paddy, can you persuade your chaps to travel in the night?"

Paddy thought it would be difficult, but we could but try. He had done a good job holding on to his four mules. During the week he had been living rough he had grown a beard and really looked the Frontier Serviceman he was. A man of about thirty, he disguised a keen brain beneath a façade of Irish blarney. I did not know him awfully well and cannot remember how he came to join our group in the first place. I wondered how he would get on with Charles Ewing, for Paddy wasn't easy.

Whilst we relaxed over our meal, the stillness of the evening was broken by the sound of an approaching car or lorry travelling slowly in our direction. There was nothing to be done but wait, rather apprehensively, for its arrival. It turned out to be a broken-down van with half a dozen Chinese passengers whose faces showed the relief they felt on finding no Japanese in sight. As usual Dick took command of the situation, and to him they poured out their story of having broken down on the main road, and from a hiding-place in the jungle had watched the Japanese go by. From all accounts the Japanese column had consisted of about thirty vehicles and it must have passed our turn-off only a few minutes after we left the main road. They had succeeded in getting their van back on the road and now all they wanted to do was walk back into China from whence they came.

Dick discovered that one of the younger men had been working for his company and would like to join us. In the party of Yunnanese by the fire he had recognised one of the men as a well-known bad hat and he was frightened. Dick agreed that he could come and work his passage to Tengyueh.

It took considerable persuasion and some threats to get our muleteers into action and it was nearly dark by the time we crossed the little bridge above the waterfall and entered China by the back door, leaving behind the ugly customers who scowled at us as we departed. Silently we climbed our way into the hills, our leading mule setting the pace.

Sheila seemed to think it all great fun and our party was in good spirits in the knowledge that every step was one nearer our escape from prison camp or worse.

The track was well defined and the going not too difficult even in the darkness. Now and again I caught glimpses of a young moon cradled in the night sky with a myriad of stars in full display as if for our benefit. I wondered how we would be getting on by the time the moon came to the full. But I was exhilarated and glad that at long last there was a definite objective ahead, a positive job to do, instead of the patchwork existence I had been leading, getting more and more frustrated as the stream of refugees I had helped became only a trickle.

Now I had the chance to talk to Dick and for the first time realised that all he had on his feet was a pair of fragile-looking tennis shoes. He always wore them on his motoring trips, but they were hardly the right footwear for the long walk

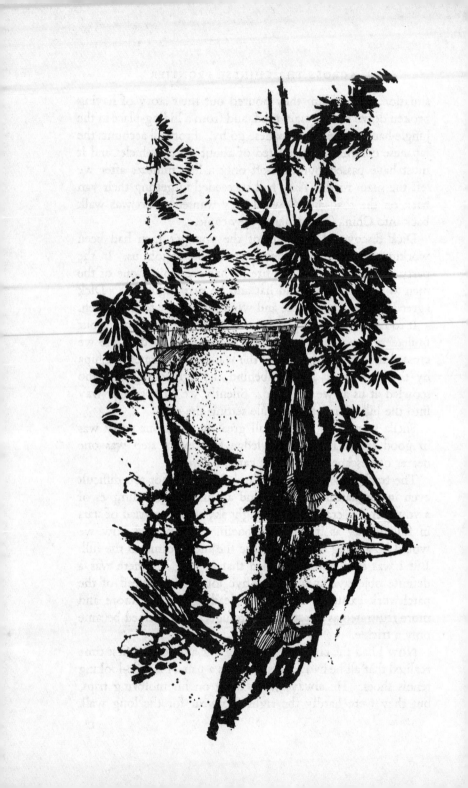

ahead of us. I had changed into my new marching boots throwing my shoes into one of the store boxes.

Dick told me that from the very beginning his convoy had run into trouble and finally ended in disaster. Crossing the first of the passes to be negotiated they had been delayed by a heavy rock fall blocking their way and he had slept in the back of his van whilst Friday organised the clearing operation.

At the suspension bridge over the Shweli River his suspicions regarding its preparation for demolition had been confirmed, and it was whilst following in the rear of his convoy at this point that he had come upon Friday running down the road to warn him that they had been ambushed and several men killed or wounded. The men who had not been hit had run into the jungle to hide. Dick then had an amazing stroke of good fortune. He had picked up Friday at one of the few places on the road where it is possible to reverse a car, and it was just as well, as before reaching the bridge he had found himself followed by a party of Japanese in one of his own lorries, no doubt the one in the rear which somehow they had managed to turn round. They had fired on him but missed, and with his much faster vehicle he had eluded them on the twisting winding road of hairpin bends leading down to the bridge. From there on he had driven like a madman to tell us to get out before it was too late. We had just made it.

"Christ, Gordon, doesn't it make you sick to think that the Japs took that bloody bridge intact riding in one of my lorries just as we told the Brigadier they would do. Just a handful of the bastards. Thank God they stayed there for a while to revel in their success, otherwise we would not be here to-night." And striding out aggressively into the darkness Dick voiced his opinions about the Army and the Administration and what a complete nonsense they had made of things from Hong Kong westwards. He was on his favourite topic and I marvelled that one who had done so much in such a short space of time still had the energy to talk, let alone climb into the hinterland of Yunnan in a pair of shoes more suited to the beach than a mule track of rock.

I was in good company and knew it.

It must have been well after two o'clock in the morning when it was discovered that in our hasty departure we had forgotten water-bottles. Everyone was complaining of thirst and in the darkness not a drop of water was to be found. Tiredness had hit us suddenly, so we decided to call a halt, try to get some sleep and wait until the dawn before continuing our journey.

I think we were all too mentally worked up to sleep and only five of the party had as much as a blanket to roll up in. The night cold of the tropics had set in; the rocky hillside was not the best of places in which to bed down, yet within minutes I could hear Dick snoring his head off. After what he had been through he deserved a few hours' rest.

Sheila became my blanket. With her heavy coat of fur she nestled close to my body as if it were her job to keep me warm. For some reason I was not tired but relaxed and eager to see the sun rise over China. We were free. What else mattered?

CHAPTER 3

Climbing

MAY 4TH

WITH THE FIRST RAYS OF DAWN IT WAS SHEILA WHO awakened us with her loud barking. Less than two hundred yards from where we had halted in the darkness she had found water, a glorious mountain spring gushing crystal clear from the rocky hillside whence it made its way into the valley below us. We must have climbed about four thousand feet since leaving the frontier. Sheila had already earned her keep.

How good that water tasted! We had our fill and then made a fire to boil water for tea. The sun was coming up and soon we had to be on our way. There was a long way to go.

We had certainly slipped up in our planning: never again must we be without a reserve supply of water. There was only one thing to do and I did it, hating every moment of it. Seven bottles of Dimple Haig whisky came out of the store boxes and I emptied them to the last drop, leaving the cupboard bare, as I had delivered the rest of my supplies to the hospital with the medicines. We would have to do without whisky, for it was no cure for parched mouths. But I made a big mistake. For the rest of our journey water was found in abundance and time and time again I had my leg pulled as the others reminded me, with their tongues hanging out for a drink, of the gallon or so of precious whisky which had been wasted that May morning.

It was Charles Ewing who produced the next sensation of the day when he came up to me and took me on one side:

"As you know dear boy, I am no authority on this walking into China business, but aren't we heading the wrong way? Surely, if I am right and the sun does rise in the east, then we must be travelling due north. Not quite the way I expected we should take, but maybe you jungle wallahs have short cuts."

Of course he was right. During the night we had missed the main mule track eastwards into Yunnan and wandered deep into the Kachin Hill tracts. We were back in Burma again, and in spite of our selection committee it had been left to the member of the Athenæum, the unwanted one, to tell us where we had gone wrong.

I could see that in his quiet way Charles was enjoying himself at our expense. Paddy was angry and roared abuse at the muleteers who had led us into the back of beyond, but all I wanted to do was laugh.

There was no option but to load up and go back on our tracks. The start of our journey had certainly not been a propitious one, but our troubles were soon forgotten as we breathed in the glorious mountain air and retraced our steps.

After the heat and dust of the plains everything about us was beautiful; long before midday we had found the right path and after climbing into the dividing range of hills we descended into the valley of the Taping River which would lead us to Tengyueh. At last we really were in China and I for one was revelling in it.

The pace was a steady one and we made good progress, but in the course of the morning Angus and I had a chat on the subject of how best to get the party into condition and safely through to our first objective. By training we had become the most experienced long-distance walkers and in this respect felt responsible for the others.

"You know, Gordon," said Angus in his practical down-right way, "there are only five of us capable of walking a hundred miles without difficulty, even if the route proves to be an easy one—and I have my doubts about that. Look at Ewing: he is keeping up, but he'll be dead on his feet by tea-time, so I think we should limit to-day to a short march and then perhaps gradually increase the distance as he gets fitter. Take Dick," he continued, " he's game for five hundred miles, but look at his shoes." I had, and it worried me. He had not even socks, and seeing him striding out ahead of us, he looked for all the world like a father on holiday at the seaside taking the children for a walk on the sands. Richard Weldon was equally ill-equipped in an ordinary pair of walking shoes.

" Then again," went on Angus, " our mules are far from being good ones and must be rested. No more night marches if we can avoid it, although I know that Dick has only one thought in his mind: to reach the Burma Road to Kunming and to get into a car to take him there."

I agreed with Angus. Dick's impatience must be curbed and each day's march planned, otherwise we would be asking for trouble.

We never saw a soul that day or even a village in the distance. It was like a no-man's-land, which of course it is— the great divide between two countries for ever engaged in border feuds.

Quite early in the afternoon we decided to call a halt and make camp on the banks of a pleasant river where the water flowed deep enough for us to bathe. There was grazing for the mules and the spot we selected provided an uninterrupted view both up and down the valley. By then we were in need of a proper meal and a good night's rest.

The water was ice cold but acted like a tonic and, in no time, feeling refreshed, we had a fire going and the store boxes open. At least we would not starve, even if there was no whisky to drink.

I had packed the usual camping foodstuffs—tinned sausages, baked beans, soups, bacon, rice, spaghetti, lentils, hard biscuits, cheeses, tinned milk, coffee, sugar and tea, to say nothing of two dozen bottles of Bovril and plenty of cigarettes and tobacco.

The party was beginning to sort itself out. Friday assumed quite naturally the role of chef, whilst Patrick, without being told, took on the responsibility for the stores. Paddy and Charles had paired off nicely and the rest of us just mucked in.

I asked Dick to tell me something of the dark man, Friday, who still carried his murderous knife round his waist. Apparently he was of Indian origin but had some European blood in his veins. He had travelled the world as a merchant seaman, which probably accounted for his deep Southern drawl—in fact I could see him on the waterfront of New Orleans. He was a most cheerful soul and willing to put his hand to any job, and he dogged Dick's footsteps like a shadow. What an asset that man proved to be in the days to come!

Sitting over the fire after our meal, I had a long talk with Dick on the course our journey was likely to take, pointing out that instead of setting off well provided with bedding and spare clothes we had little more than the clothes we stood up in. He knew no more of the road than I did, but we reckoned that seven days should see us at Tengyueh. Our letter warning the British Consul there had already gone ahead by a Chinese runner, so we should be expected. With riding mules and properly organised, I had known the journey done in five days by the Consul, but our party was in no shape to double march, and about twenty miles a day would be the maximum we should attempt, provided the weather held and the track was not too difficult. That should see us at Tengyueh on 10th May.

CHAPTER 4

Along the Taping Valley

MAY 5TH-8TH

THE NEXT FOUR DAYS WERE UNEVENTFUL AND WE made good progress, having settled down to a steady routine of covering eighteen to twenty miles a day. Our route along the Taping Valley was now taking us through a great plain, rather featureless and dull but in the far distance could be seen a high mountain range which we guessed must mark the drainage of the Shweli River. We had no maps nor even a compass, but all the time we were travelling more or less due east and from time to time picked up the tracks of caravans which had gone this way. Their old camping sites were easily recognisable.

The countryside was sparsely inhabited and the few peasants we did meet seemed friendly enough, even frightened of us, in contradiction to the general belief in Burma that no stranger should attempt the journey without written clearance from the Governor himself and an armed escort.

It was bitterly cold at night, but huddled round a fire we managed to get some sleep and there was plenty to eat. Actually I think we were all too keyed-up and eager to reach Tengyueh to bother about or feel the need for a great deal of rest. All members of the party were well and in good heart. Charles had lost a lot of weight and looked all the better for it. We all had beards but his was the prize growth, thick, bushy and black, whilst Dick sported a white halo which seemed to grow aggressively out of his face at right angles.

Sheila, needless to say, had been adopted by everyone including the sharp-faced little Chinese youth who had joined us. No dog could have been happier and it was a joy to have her company both on the march and at night round the fire.

The muleteers Paddy had engaged proved to be an unreliable, sullen, opium-sodden lot and would probably have deserted but for the fact that they were heading homewards under our protection and being well paid for their pains.

Tengyueh was getting nearer every day and with thoughts of reaching safety we were buoyed up and eager. We were not the least concerned about the forty-odd miles down to the main Burma–Kunming road—in fact our Chinese companion had told Dick that heavy lorries were now using it.

Not a single bandit had we seen, and by and large it looked as if the end of the journey was not far off.

CHAPTER 5

Bandits and Bad News

MAY 9TH

IT WAS ON THE SIXTH DAY OF OUR FLIGHT INTO China that the first hint of trouble occurred. It came on us quite unexpectedly and was all over in a matter of minutes.

The dull plain had given way to a rocky watercourse which the mules were having some difficulty in negotiating and, to urge them on, we had become grouped together instead of travelling to our set plan of having one-half of the party in front of the mules and the other following at their rear. This was to ensure that the muleteers were always in sight, a precaution we had adopted from the very beginning of our journey.

Suddenly, rounding a bend, we found ourselves surrounded by a party of Chinese who must have numbered about thirty men. They were a motley collection dressed in some kind of uniform and many of them were armed. Their manner was hostile, and in aggressive tones they ordered us to halt.

Uniforms they certainly had, but I could see no distinguishing flash or insignia such as the Chinese troops I had often seen in the past had always worn. One of their number was obviously the leader. As he came forward several of the men carrying rifles squatted in positions which covered his approach. So I nudged Dick, who of course would be our spokesman.

" Over to you, chum," I said. " I will cover you and if that so-and-so makes trouble I shall have a pot at him." With that, I felt for the Luger hidden beneath my shirt which I wore like a bush jacket.

Then the parleying began. Dick could make himself understood in Yunnanese, though with some difficulty, and, stepping forward, demanded to know the reason for the hold-up.

" He says he is a colonel and in charge of the area, and that we are not to proceed."

" Tell him I am the British Consul or that you are the Agent of Lung Yung, the Governor."

Then followed a superb example of quick thinking and bluff by Dick. Gesticulating with both hands and hardly stopping to take breath, he tore into the " colonel " with a torrent of words spoken in rapid and fluent Cantonese. Even if the " colonel " didn't understand a word, he must have recognised that he was dealing with someone in authority. Dick waved towards the squatting soldiery as if to say, " Tell your scum to get to hell out of here or there will be trouble," and we saw the " colonel " take a note pad from his pocket and write something which he handed over.

The " colonel " bowed to Dick and backed away. Dick bowed to the " colonel " and indicated that we were to proceed. I loosened my grip on the Luger butt. The party was over.

" Christ," said Dick when we had got on the road again, " that was a near bloody thing—let's get to hell out of this as quick as we can before those bastards have second thoughts and come after our mules."

It was only then I realised that the Chinese had no transport. We were all gathered round Dick, anxious to know how he had succeeded in getting us out from what looked to be a nasty situation.

" I told that bogus colonel that I was an American officer attached to the Cantonese Division of the Chinese 6th Army and that we were regrouping on the Burma Road beyond Tengyueh after consultations with the Governor of Yunnan."

" But what about the piece of paper ? " we all inquired.

" Oh, that nonsense. I spiked his guns by demanding that, as he was the colonel in charge of the area, he give me a note ensuring our safe passage to Tengyueh, to be signed with his name and rank so that I could express my thanks for his help. The Lord only knows what it says as I can't read his script, but I'll bet anyone a dollar that it isn't worth the dirty paper on which it is written, and that that bunch were deserters on the lookout for loot and trouble."

Trouble there was indeed, as we were to discover that evening. All day we pressed on to the limit our mules were capable of travelling, and by late afternoon, when it became apparent that Charles Ewing was developing a blistered heel, we decided to halt at the next camping site providing our simple requirements: a degree of shelter, abundance of water and fuel for our fire. By now we had learned how to bed down for the night but through experience had become somewhat selective in regard to the site chosen.

We found just the right place and the packs were unloaded and the store boxes opened. Friday got busy and soon we were huddled round the fire talking over the events of the day.

Dick's performance had been a magnificent one. He was neither tall nor imposing, and with his white beard and bare legs topped off by the tattered beach shoes he wore, he was outwardly anything but a person of importance. Yet the fire in his eyes and the fluency with which he spoke Cantonese had been sufficient to deter the bogus colonel from attempting to halt our progress. We were duly grateful and told him so, but Dick was one of those people far too big to wish his praises to be sung in this way, and our words of thanks were brushed aside in a typical Winter manner.

The site we had picked for our night's rest lay near the confluence of two small streams, one of which flowed out of quite rugged country to the west of us. Less than thirty miles separated us from Tengyueh. All was quiet and we felt satisfied that our forced march that day had seen the last of the bandit-like soldiery we had encountered.

This quiet was short-lived. Even before our meal was cooked, Sheila became alert and restive; moving out of the shadows cast by the fire, she stalked her way to the defile-like entrance of the stream to our west and came back to warn me that she had heard noises coming from that direction. Just a whispered instruction, and she was off again to watch, wait and listen. We could hear nothing.

Back she came and sat by my side and it was then that we heard voices approaching. It was not just one voice or those of half a dozen, but the chattering of a large number of men making no attempt to disguise their presence. There was nothing we could do but wait.

Then out of the shadows they came. Stumbling in the bad light poured forth a hundred or so Chinese troops, battle-stained and weary, the sick, wounded and dying being carried in litters of bamboo by their fellow soldiers.

In no time Dick was in the presence of an officer, to whom he explained the reason for our being in Yunnan; any fears we may have entertained were short-lived. We were amongst friends.

The senior officer decided that his men should bivouac at the confluence, and soon the night was full of the smell of wood smoke as fires were lighted and the troops settled down to rest.

They were a pathetic sight after a heavy engagement with the Japanese two days previously. Their uniform was in tatters and they looked half starved as well as weary. Yet these stoic little untrained men were carrying their wounded in the direction of home, and they had travelled through the most inhospitable of hilly country in order to seek a place of safety.

We discovered that this was a unit of the 6th Army which had been cut off when the Chinese Command decided to abandon the line of the Salween and retreat to the Mekong.

Now we knew the truth. Tengyueh was completely exposed and in all probability our escape route cut off. We were really in a fix. Perhaps more than the others, Dick and I knew what this meant. We would have no alternative but to take to the hills. What then?

Fortunately our minds were taken off our own predicament by the more important and immediate problem of helping the Chinese in their plight. As fast as our limited number of pots and pans would allow, so was hot sweet coffee brewed and shared amongst them and, with the officers gathered round the fire directing its distribution, we did what we could to help and feed these friendly people. Luckily my stock of Bovril was untouched, and this was given to the wounded. Never shall I forget the look on their faces as we plied them with cigarettes. Our stocks were too limited to allow one per man and only the wounded were given a smoke if they wanted one, but invariably after a few satisfying puffs it would be passed to the litter bearers.

The seriously wounded were in a terrible condition as the unit had neither doctor nor trained medical orderlies with it. From my medicine box I gave the officers all that would serve any useful purpose, but we could do little to succour so many.

Dick of course had been as busy as usual plying the officers with questions regarding the decision to retreat to the Mekong, but they could advance no reason why such a barrier as the Salween Bridge should be abandoned. Had it been destroyed? No, they didn't think so. Would the Mekong Bridge be held? Yes, they were certain on that point.

Did they think that the Japanese would bother to take Tengyueh, or would they concentrate on the advance to the Mekong down the main road? Yes, they were bound to occupy the Yunnan Governor's stronghold sooner or later as it was the Chinese Customs' Headquarters and would be full of loot.

Were any Chinese co-operating with the Japanese?

Most definitely yes in this part of China, where large numbers of civilians were bandits by occupation and owed no loyalty to the Central Government.

We were all gathered round listening to Dick and the officers. Dick was translating as the conversation went on.

Then from the darkness came the voice of Charles Ewing: " Why not tell them about our friends up the road and get the *laissez-passer* translated? "

Dick told the officers of our experience that morning and then produced the dirty piece of paper on which the bogus colonel had written: " These men are spies and should be arrested." The signature was apparently illegible and gave no rank. We might have bluffed our way through his little gang of bandits or deserters, as more than likely they were, but we could not help laughing at the thoughts of what might have happened to us if we had encountered a similar bunch of toughs and produced our letter of authority to enter Tengyueh. I suppose the old rogue thought it was the best way of getting his own back on Dick!

It was now time for serious business and, with the Chinese officers retired to their own fires, Dick summed up the situation and called for suggestions.

We had to face the fact that if the reports given us by the Chinese were correct, our line of retreat would be cut off, although if Tengyueh itself had not been occupied we might find some means of being smuggled through to the Chinese line of defence and reach the main highway. Much would depend on the speed of the Japanese advance; we took heart in the knowledge that from our experience they tended to consolidate a position once taken and not to move forward, unless cautiously, until a full appraisal of the situation had been made and orders received from at least divisional level. This had been a noticeable feature of their occupation of North Burma and the Shan States, which could have been taken much earlier had they wished.

One thing stood out quite clearly. If Tengyueh was occupied we should have no alternative but to strike in a northeasterly direction and head for the Shweli and Salween Rivers. I was able to enlarge a bit on what this would entail, as two years previously I had been host to a British expedition which had attempted to map the Upper Salween. Although backed by the Royal Geographical Society and blessed by the Chinese Government, this party had suffered terrible hardships and been lucky to survive. Yet the three men who led the expedition were highly trained and experienced mountaineers with some of the peaks of Tibet to their credit. I would not give our party a ten-to-one chance of crossing the Upper Salween even if properly equipped. It is one of the longest rivers in the world but even in the lower reaches, 1500 miles to the south, it is unnavigable. My company worked concessions there and many were the stories I had heard of conditions in the Lower Salween Valley. I knew enough to picture what the area would look like in the upper reaches to our north high up in the mountains.

Several suggestions were put forward, but it was left to Angus to come up with sound concrete advice on our next move. He was one of those practical people who normally have little to say, but when he voiced an opinion it was invariably backed by common sense.

In his quiet way Angus pointed out that, in the light of what we had now learned, it would be downright foolish for the lot of us to march in procession into Tengyueh the next day and, perhaps, into the arms of the very people we were escaping from. Why not a couple of us leave before dawn to reconnoitre the town or, at least, the environs of the place, leaving the others with the mules to follow in the same direction? The advance party could contact the Consul if he was still there and, if the worst had happened, we should arrange to rendezvous to the north-east of the town in the direction of the Salween which would then be our objective.

Angus was absolutely right. We had established that the town was not more than twenty-two miles from where we were encamped, at the most seven to eight hours' march to a couple of fit men. It could be reached by midday if an early start were made and, should it be necessary to regroup, we would have several hours of daylight left to make fresh plans.

Up went eight pairs of hands volunteering to do the job, although the choice obviously lay with Dick, Angus and myself. Dick because of his language, Angus because he was a powerful walker and ideally suited to such a mission, and I, because I was the only member of the party who knew the Consul and was also in top physical condition. Finally it was decided that the three of us should form the advance party leaving Paddy McClusky as O.C. of the remainder.

At this point we called up our Chinese companion, who knew Tengyueh, and from him obtained a rough layout of the place and the surrounding countryside. Apparently its walls were surrounded by paddy-fields which, in the direction we would have to take if the Japanese were already there, extended for about a mile before reaching the foothills which were heavily wooded. Somewhere in those hills, he was not quite sure where but knew it was within walking distance of the town, was a famous monastery. This we decided should be our rallying point if we were unable for any reason to rejoin the main group.

CHAPTER 6
The Abbot Regrets . . .

MAY 10TH

SLEEP WAS IMPOSSIBLE THAT NIGHT, AS SOME OF THE men who surrounded us were unlikely to see the dawn. With its first rays we were up and, as soon as the light was good enough to see our road, we were away with Sheila at my heel.

Friday as usual had given us coffee. I could see that he hated being separated from Dick. The others slept heavily, huddled together for warmth, and all around were the dying embers of fires round which the Chinese troops lay exhausted and quite unaware of our departure.

The morning air was chilly and, although we had not even as much as a pullover between us, it was good to feel the blood circulating as we set a smart pace towards Tengyueh. It was exhilarating to be on the move at a pace of our own making instead of being geared to that of the slow-moving convoy with which for nearly a week we had been travelling.

I had a feeling of freedom and was in the mood to sing as the sun rose directly in front of us. From deep orange and grey the horizon began to turn to a warm pink and the whole sky became alive with colours which changed with every minute, until the red of morning spread a canopy over the distant hills in the east, and slowly came to greet us on the plain.

My thoughts turned to a small book of poems which I had left behind and would never see again It was the work of one of Burma's greatest forestry men, a bachelor long since retired. I had met him as a youngster and for some reason he had taken a liking to me and given me a copy of his book which had been published privately. His name was Hewitt and in the service he was known as " Farmer " Hewitt. On tour this little volume had always accompanied me and, although quite untutored in the appreciation of verse, I could

detect in the works of " Farmer " Hewitt a note of melancholy stemming from the lonely life he had led—and would lead until he died. A few lines of my favourite poem came back to me, and as we strode out in silence I found myself trying to memorise more of them, but I could not get very far.

> So think not ye whose lot is cast
> In the teeming cities of men
> He's a heart of stone who dwells alone
> And a mind like a stagnant fen;
> That his blood has no force
> And halts on its course . . .

We were certainly treading a lonely road and never saw a soul all the morning. The plain was clearly narrowing, and with every mile the hills came nearer. In the far distance could be seen range after range of them, each one higher than the last. Forced marching at this pace came easily to Angus and me after our years in teak forests where twenty miles or so in a morning was nothing unusual, but to Dick it must have been something of a strain, although he never complained or suggested a slower speed. By now we were tanned with a mixture of sun and plain dirt. Dick from the beginning had been hatless. His white hair was long and with his bushy beard sticking out from his face he reminded me of a picture I had once seen of Ernest Hemingway on safari. Angus somehow always looked neat, probably because of his well-balanced figure. I am tall, and was in those days scraggy, my beard growing unevenly and in tufts in the fashion of a cabby of the Victorian era.

No one was in the mood for conversation. The miles seemed to fly past and by noon we were in sight of Tengyueh. Its walls could be seen clearly although the town must have been five miles off. There it stood as it had been described to us, and we wondered what exactly it held in store for us all.

About half a mile off we halted. Nothing was to be seen moving in the surrounding countryside. The whole place had the appearance of being deserted. We moved forward cautiously to within a few hundred yards of what we assumed to be the West Gate of this walled town and, from the shelter of some bushes, sat for a while studying the entrance.

Grubbing round the walls were several pigs, their snouts buried deep in the most filthy muck imaginable, the smell of which was already with us. This was my first experience of a Chinese town, and to this day I will never eat pork if I can help it, though I believe pigs are considered to be the cleanest of eaters. Not so in Yunnan, I can assure you. No more need be said. The smell was that of a latrine.

"Come on," said Dick, "there seems no point in staying here. Let's have a look through the gate."

A few pigs interrupted their feeding and gazed momentarily at the bearded and dirty strangers and then continued nosing in the muck. We moved into the gateway, the walls of which were the thickness of a small house. No one could be seen.

Then Sheila stood dead in her tracks as if pointing. She had heard something which we had not. It was the faint noise made by the opening of a peep-hole in a door, which had escaped our notice, and through it we saw a finger beckoning us to enter.

The door opened just wide enough to let us through and on entering we saw an aged bent Chinese with a long grey beard. The door closed as silently as it had opened and we found ourselves in near darkness as the room had no windows. It was tiny, like a cell, and cold after the midday heat outside. Still with his fingers to his lips, motioning silence, the old man in his blue robes indicated that we were to follow him, and he led us into an inner room where three other patriarchs were sitting cross-legged on the floor. The room was full of smoke from a fire burning wood on the floor. It contained no furniture. The whole atmosphere and manner of our reception was eerie, to say the least, but there must be some reason for it, I thought, as Sheila put her wet nose into my hand, as if to say all was well.

Then the silence was broken by the old bearded gentleman who had given us this shelter. He had no teeth and seemed to speak more with his hands and his eyes than his mouth. He was pointing and making signs to Dick who, I could see, was having great difficulty in understanding a word of what was being said. The conversation was in whispers. You could have heard a pin drop.

Then Dick said something which the old man understood. His hoary hands came out of the wide sleeves of his robe and his old head nodded agreement as he went on pointing in

81

the direction of a corner of the wall. His dear old face was now wreathed in a wide toothless smile. Clearly something had emerged from this strange conversation and at last he and Dick were on common ground. Angus and I edged nearer.

" What's it all about? " we asked.

Dick looked serious. " He says that at this very moment the Japanese are entering the town in force by the South Gate. The advance units have already occupied the Governor's residence and taken over the Customs building. There are also many bad Chinese with them intent on loot as their reward for helping the Japs. To enter the town would be suicide."

I reminded Dick about the Consul and he put another question to the old man. Again more head nodding and gesticulating, arms going to and fro, as if our host was explaining that he and the British Consul were blood brothers.

" He left yesterday," said Dick. " He must have been warned of the Japanese advance, as the Customs people also departed. Christ, this is a mess! We have this old chap to thank for stopping us just in time. A few more paces and we would have been wearing kimonos."

I remembered the last time he had used that expression, when his van came roaring down the Bhamo road in a cloud of dust to warn me of the dangers we were in.

Now the situation was quite different. All we had were our wits and feet with which to get away this time. We were as good as being in a cage stuck on the mantelpiece of a Japanese General. Yet for some reason I felt no fear nor feeling of being trapped. Beyond us stretched the whole of China. To escape was now a real challenge. I suppose being so physically fit made all that difference to one's mental approach in a crisis of this kind.

In the semi-darkness of the room which we shared with our host and his three mute companions, we sat down and began to plan. All the four were of a peasant type, judging

by their dress of dark blue, but the old man with no teeth and long grey beard carried the hall-marks of a leader in his community. For his age he was remarkably active and every few minutes would disappear into the outer room with the peep-hole into the West Gate entrance and come back to whisper to his companions.

By now green tea was brewing on the fire, and how welcome it was! We had walked all of twenty-two miles or more since sunrise and, apart from coffee and a biscuit, had not eaten. It was now about two o'clock in the afternoon.

How damned funny, I thought, to be drinking tea with the Japanese all around us: should make a good dining-out story one of these days back in London.

Our thoughts of course turned to the remainder of the party who, by now, should be within six to eight miles of Tengyueh. We should probably be hidden until darkness, but Paddy had to be warned and diverted into the hills with his mules to rendezvous at the monastery as we had planned. At least there was the comforting thought that the party had with them the Chinese boy who could act as guide and interpreter, and he seemed a sensible sort of chap and reliable.

Dick explained all this to the old man and there was more head nodding.

Yes, he would dispatch his own grandson with a message. No one would bother a small boy leaving the gate and we could rest assured that it would be delivered to our party. But as for us . . . the old hands came out of the wrapper-like sleeves once again and made signs which seemed to mean that we were to stay and then creep away like mice.

Dick wrote the message telling Paddy what had happened and how he must turn off the road and head for the monastery. We would wait for them there; but if things went wrong he must forget us and attempt the Salween crossing, which offered the only chance of escape now that the Japanese were in contro of this part of Yunnan.

Taking the message with him the old man disappeared

through yet another door. The place was like a rabbit-warren and somewhere, I thought, must be the living-rooms of a house. We were actually within the great walls of the town and I suppose that the other quarters were inter-communicating. They must have been, for within minutes our host was back to say that the note was on its way down the road over which we had travelled that morning.

I suppose it must have been an hour or so later when the old man came back from one of his periodic shuntings between the room we were in and his peep-hole. He was clearly agitated and distressed. Something had happened.

Dick listened to him, nodding his head in agreement every time the old fellow made himself clear—and then, moving over to the fire where Angus and I sat with the dog, he told us that we could be sheltered no longer and must go. Some-one had betrayed our presence in the town and at any moment the Japanese would be seeking us out.

There was no time for discussion, but later Dick told us our dear old friend had explained that he was not afraid of dying but, for the sake of his family who would be tortured and worse, he had no alternative but to ask us to leave.

To a Chinese, even of his lowly order, the comfort and well-being of a guest in the house is like a religion, and he had taken us under his roof and now was sending us away.

Speaking louder now, he gave Dick instructions as to the way we should go. Over the paddy-fields and up into the hills to the north-east and thence towards the Salween River.

As we were ushered into the cell-like room and before the door was opened, the old man remembered something and disappeared. We stood in darkness wondering what would be our fate when we saw the daylight outside. Soon he was back carrying a tattered old wide-brimmed coolie hat which he presented to Dick; and the next moment the afternoon sun hit us hard in the eyes and the door closed behind us.

There was no one in sight and we edged round the entrance gate into the shelter of the wall where the pigs were still going about their business. Grunts of disapproval at being disturbed came from those which happened to be in our path as we made our way unhurriedly down towards the paddy-fields which lay below.

The crop had been reaped and only bare stubble remained. It was full daylight. Dick led the way in his Chinese hat of straw. " Bend down and don't hurry. Pretend you are a peasant making his way home. Tell Sheila to look like a chow dog." With these remarks from Dick, and not a glance back, we crept away.

It was a charade-like manœuvre, but it succeeded. Not a shot was fired. Bending nearly double we did our best to blend into the landscape. Even Sheila seemed to know it was no game. Thus we left behind us the town we had never entered nor would ever see again.

We found a little shelter from a bund which gave us a measure of protection and which fortunately went in the direction we knew we must travel; after about half a mile this fell away into a dried-up water course into which we dropped somewhat exhausted. It was from this place of cover we heard the sound of rifle-fire coming from the town we had vacated. Looking cautiously back, it was obvious that our departure had been unnoticed. Not a soul was in sight. We had made yet another getaway from the Japanese.

Ahead of us lay the hills into which we would have to climb and go on climbing until many miles separated us from the enemy who, we guessed and hoped, were too preoccupied with looting to bother with us, even if our presence had been reported. Firing was still going on—for what reason we were never to know.

At the foothills we were forced to halt as the sole of Dick's shoe was coming adrift. Fortunately Angus had some string in his pocket and in his usual practical way carried out a running repair, binding Dick's foot into the rapidly deteriorating canvas in a bandage-like fashion.

" Damn it! " said Dick, " to think I had planned to buy

86

some new ones in the Tengyueh market. Instead, look at this mess."

Hungry and tired, we were yet in good spirits and Sheila showed no signs of exhaustion. The monastery was our objective. We knew the direction but could find no proper track leading from the flat plain into the hills. If there was a footpath, we had missed it, and all our searching was in vain. There was nothing for it but to press on, climbing blindly into the darkness which was now falling and praying that we should see sufficient of the moonlight to recognise a track if one existed. Up and up we went hauling ourselves hand over hand with the aid of the undergrowth, sometimes crawling on hands and knees in our struggle to ascend this unwelcoming peak.

At last we came to the pathway, a well trodden route, no doubt used by the pilgrims on their way to the monastery. We had taken a short-cut and come straight up the mountainside, but we had made it at last, though very weary through the effort. But still we had to move on and the path wound interminably upwards. For what seemed hours we dragged our weary bodies forward and when at last towards midnight we saw lights which proved to be the monastery, we were reeling like drunken men.

How we managed to stumble up the steps leading into the building I shall never know. All I can remember is being helped by priests who received us with that quiet courtesy common to the Chinese people and being bidden to enter.

Inside was a large courtyard open to the sky and surrounded on all sides by a series of cell-like rooms into one of which we were conducted.

Sanctuary at last, and the joy of water to drink ice-cold, while small novices were sent to bring bowls and towels so that we could wash off some of the grime which covered us from head to foot.

Our arrival had created quite a sensation in the place and the room seemed full of serious-faced little chaps who could not take their eyes off the three weird, bearded men who had arrived at the dead of night. Clustered round the door was quite a gathering of Chinese, peering in with inquisitive faces and chattering amongst themselves. Suddenly the crowd melted away and was gone. The reason was soon obvious. We were about to be in the presence of the Abbot himself.

Crossing the courtyard towards us we could see him in the light of the moon, now high and full above us. It was like a scene straight out of a Dulac fairy story. Round the perimeter of the quadrangle burned flares of some kind, presumably temple lamps, and from time to time the little procession approaching us was caught in the strange lights they cast. Leading the procession at a marked, dignified gait was the Abbot, a large man by Chinese standards, and in his wake followed several other priests.

"Looks as if you've got some explaining to do, Dick," muttered Angus. "Tell this old Lord High Executioner that all we want to do is sleep and how grateful we are for the wash and brush up."

But Dick, wise and versed in the ways of these people, motioned us to stand and be ready to receive our host. He stood in the doorway looking more like a stocky scarecrow than a man, yet his manner was that of someone accustomed to command. And so he received the Abbot, bowing as he did so.

Whilst they talked I took a good look at this priest and wasn't too keen on what I saw. He had about four chins and his belly was fat although largely hidden by the robes he wore. His head was shaven of course, but it was his small pig-like eyes I disliked and his manner was not exactly friendly. The remark Angus had made in fun about the Lord High Executioner fitted the Abbot perfectly. He was straight out of *The Mikado*.

Apparently the two spokesmen could understand each other though, very often, reference was made to the other priests. As usual much nodding of heads went on, but Angus

and I were used to that after our brief sojourn with the old
men in the Tengyueh gateway. More bowing, and the
Abbot tucked his hands into his gown and the procession
moved slowly back in the direction it had come.

" Well, Dick, what's the verdict? " I asked as he came back
into the room. " I wasn't too taken with your fat friend."

" Neither was I. And I'm afraid he insists that we must
leave early, as soon as it's light, in fact. Now that he knows
the Japanese have arrived he's scared stiff. It seems we are

the first here with the news and I'll bet a dollar that before we are asleep this place will be busting at the seams with townsfolk from Tengyueh. This is where they hide their worldly wealth. It's a sort of Monastery Inc. in these parts." And Dick started laying more bets in the dollar currency he was used to.

It was then that the most welcome sight of the day made its appearance. In came three small boys bearing hot steaming soup in a bowl of a size which even Oliver would have approved of. Accompanying it were small cups to dip into this inviting brew which was a form of bean soup made from soya. This indeed was hospitality at its best, and as we tucked in I forgot all about the little pig eyes of the Abbot, whom I had obviously misjudged. Not only were we being given shelter but also food, and it had been some thirty hours since anything but green tea and water had passed our lips. It was heaven, and Sheila seemed to think so too, as we gave her a generous helping of what remained in the bowl.

What a wonderful dog she was! Completely spoilt and used to her meat and evening bones, she had adjusted herself to the scraps of the tinned food we had given her each day. If she had lost weight it was not much and rather suited her figure, which in Bhamo had been becoming rather matronly. No, she was in fine fettle, even if, like us, completely exhausted after the day's adventures.

Exhausted we were and dead on our feet. The soup once inside us, reaction seemed to set in and within minutes we were asleep on the bare floor—out to the world. But this period of oblivion was short lived. I felt Sheila nudging me and with my long jungle training was immediately awake. The others slept on.

I saw a light approaching in the hand of a priest who made signs that I should wake the others. He was friendly enough but agitated, and then I realised that all the temple lights which had made such a lovely setting in the courtyard had been extinguished and only the light of the moon remained.

Little did I know then that we had only been asleep for half an hour.

Dick woke with a start, whilst Angus rubbed his eyes and had that bewildered look as if to say, " Where the hell am I ? " Whatever it was the priest said to Dick must have been brief, for in minutes we were being hurriedly ushered out of the monastery by then teeming with refugees streaming in from Tengyueh. The whole courtyard was full of men, women and children, like us, desperately tired after the long climb up the mountain to this retreat hidden away in the hills. Most of them, even the children, carried pathetic little bundles—a few possessions hurriedly put together before their flight from the town.

There was no question about the need for us to leave the monastery. The priest had told Dick that our presence was known to the Japanese, but this may have been just rumour.

And so we stumbled out into the night with only one thought in our minds—to put a few more miles between us and the Japanese.

The night air was keen, but the few minutes' sleep and the soya soup had given us a little strength although I expect it was more the power of the mind than the body which urged us forward. The moonlight was sufficient to see our way up the track which we hoped was taking us to the north-east, but by then we were beyond caring and intent only on moving farther and farther away from Tengyueh.

The path continued to climb steadily and for mile after mile we walked in silence. For nearly twenty hours we had been on our feet. We had not the strength to speak and by now Sheila was content to stay at my heels instead of exploring ahead and around as was her usual habit.

Suddenly we reached what must have been a high plateau in this range of hills and as we breasted the top we saw the first glimpse of a new day on the distant horizon. Before us stretched a panorama of grey-black peaks round which were creeping the strange, somewhat mysterious, aquamarine tints

which herald the dawn. I thought of all that had happened
to us since I last saw the sun rise over the plain. How many
miles we had travelled I shall never know, but now not even
will-power could take us much farther. Certainly Dick, with
his canvas shoe tied together with string, was in no fit shape
to travel, so we looked for a place to sleep.

Not far down the track was a belt of trees standing out from
the scrub and short grass of the plateau which now replaced
the dense tree-covered hillsides we had come through in the
night. To our surprise we found the belt to be a pine planta-
tion surrounded by a stone wall and then knew we were near
habitations as both the pines and the wall were the work of
man. In no time at all we were over the wall and asleep in
the welcoming bed of pine needles which lay inches thick
under the trees. The wall gave us cover, and for a time at
least we were safe.

CHAPTER 7

Disaster

MAY 11TH

THE SUN WAS HIGH ABOVE US WHEN I WAS WAKENED by Sheila, and it must have been nearing midday. Dick and Angus were beginning to stir so I thought I would " recce " the area before they were properly awake. I crept to the wall, motioning Sheila to stay at my heel.

No one was about, but a few hundred yards down the track I could see beyond another belt of trees a wisp of smoke which was possibly from a village fire. Cautiously I lowered myself over the wall to get a better view of our surroundings. I had been right, we were near a village, for I could see mules grazing. I crept back over the wall to tell the others.

" Thought you had had enough of our company and gone off on your own," said Dick sitting up, rubbing his eyes. " Where the hell are we ? "

I told them what I had seen and saw Dick conjuring up ideas about eating his favourite food which was, of course, Chinese.

" Come on, chaps. What's keeping us from good 'chow' ? "

" You," said Angus, pointing to Dick's dilapidated shoe. The string which had been tied was broken and the sole flapped loose as Dick raised his leg to present this forlorn piece of footwear for our inspection.

" That's what comes of wriggling your toes in your sleep," I told him. " You couldn't possibly have walked here with the string broken."

Angus felt in his pocket and produced all that remained of his reserve of precious cord—just enough for one more tying-up operation—and proceeded to bind the canvas and rubber with the remark, " Now you have had it, chum. You may not be wearing that kimono you have reminded us about so often, but you're going to look damned silly walking the next few hundred miles in your bare feet."

There were roars of laughter at this grim jest. Rested and relaxed after sleep we were now capable of speech which we certainly hadn't been for many hours during the previous day. It felt good to be alive and free even if our bellies were empty, but while Angus in his usual practical way dealt with Dick's shoes, we thought of the others in our party and pondered on their fate. Had our note of warning reached them, or had they walked straight into the arms of the Japanese? Then the horrifying thought: was our sudden expulsion from the monastery due to their having been caught at Tengyueh? We had certainly been evicted with what seemed now to have been undue haste.

" One thing they can be thankful for," said Dick, " at least they have my Chinese driver with them and he should be capable of guiding them in this direction if they got my note."

There was no doubt that we were heading towards the Salween; I guessed it must flow beyond the great ranges of mountains that could be seen in the far distance.

It was then that Sheila gave us warning that she had heard something. Her head first pointed alert in the direction we had travelled before falling asleep, then towards me, her large and beautiful brown eyes telling their own story. From a sitting position she lowered herself to the ground with her paws outstretched and her head moving slightly as her keen ears continued to pick up sounds which we could not hear. The three of us sat quietly watching the dog and speculating as to the reason for her alertness.

Probably no more than a few of the local inhabitants on the road, we thought aloud; and in any case we were well concealed by the wall and the close stand of trees. But for the repairs to Dick's shoe we would by now have been begging a meal from the village headman, our presence known. Yet Sheila's movements and the look in her eyes seemed to tell me that we should stay hidden.

Now we could hear a sound of voices coming nearer to our hiding place. They were indistinguishable to us, but not to Sheila. She got to her feet and looking towards the wall wagged her tail, then turned her head quickly to us as if inviting us to share whatever it was with her. It was clear to me that all she wanted to do was dash forward and over the wall and, but for her training, this is what she would have done. Instead her whole body quivered with excitement and, as she stood poised as if ready to bark out a greeting, we recognised the English voices of our companions.

As we rose to our feet, Sheila, her job done, cleared the wall in one bound. Our party was reunited, or nearly so, as the wall separated us and whilst we talked there seemed no point in scaling it.

Was it really possible that in such a tangled maze of wild hills and valleys we could meet under such circumstances, or had Divine Providence intervened to bring us together again? Maybe we should have offered up a prayer of thanksgiving to the God who had guided the footsteps of our friends to the place where we lay hidden. But amongst ordinary men, as we were, prayers are silent; however, I am sure that all eight of us in our own way acknowledged the debt to Him deep in our own hearts.

Our companions were in a terrible state of exhaustion and looked awful. Charles Ewing had already collapsed in a heap and Richard Weldon was obviously suffering terribly, as his face was ashen beneath his beard and he was dripping with sweat. Even Friday, so excited at being once more in the company of Dick and finding him safe and sound, was practically incoherent. Only Patrick Doyle and Paddy McClusky could stand full square on their feet and it was from them we heard of the disasters which had overtaken them and of their nightmare journey through the hills.

Somehow we managed to get them all over the wall and into the shelter of the trees where the casualties collapsed into sleep. Dick's Chinese driver was with the party but there were no mules or muleteers. All had gone, as we were soon to learn from Paddy as we plied him with questions.

Our message had been delivered to them by the small boy sent by the old man at the gate of Tengyueh and, taking our advice, they decided to head for the hills and the monastery, travelling roughly in the direction we had given them. This decision was easier made than carried out, as the muleteers were reluctant to leave the main route and insisted that they had contracted to travel to Tengyueh and would not take the mules in any other direction. A heated argument had followed with much shouting on the part of the muleteers. This I could well imagine as I have never in all my travels heard such a noise as when two Yunnanese caravan men have a row. With hands waving in all directions they shout abuse to heaven as well as to each other. They stamp feet and the air is blue with murderous threats as a kind of shadow boxing match is performed for the benefit of any spectators who might be present.

After quite a scene Dick's Chinese driver had persuaded the men to continue with the journey and to do what they were told with promises of extra rewards from his master. And so the party had turned off the main track towards the hills.

Paddy reckoned they must have been about eight miles from Tengyueh when our note reached them. Apparently Charles Ewing's blister had been troubling him and progress had been much slower than anticipated.

The route they followed across the plain presented no difficulty and all had gone well until the light began to fail as they reached the lower slopes of the mountain. Here they had lost their way but continued travelling towards the north-east urging the mules forward over rough and precipitous country where in places it took the strength of the whole party to make a passage for the mules. (I could see Friday with his large knife cutting away at the overhanging branches which barred their way.)

The route finally became quite impassable for the mules and the end had come suddenly and dramatically.

They were crossing what must have been a knife-like ridge when the leading mule panicked and, in its fright, turned about to rush back the way it had come. The mule next in line was knocked off its feet and fell headlong into a deep ravine, carrying with it one of the muleteers; whilst the leader stumbled in the opposite direction and disappeared over the other side of the ridge.

In the confusion which followed the remaining two mules and the three other muleteers disappeared, never to be seen again. It must have been terrible for five Europeans and one Chinese, already in a state of exhaustion, to be faced with a disaster of this magnitude. It was dark and the accident had come upon them with such suddenness. Yet something had to be done. It was unlikely that the muleteer thrown into the ravine had escaped serious injury. Paddy and Friday volunteered to climb down to find him, and Patrick started his descent to look for the other mule.

Paddy's face, as he told his story, showed all too clearly the agony and strain he had been through; for a moment the horror of what he had found on the rocks below was too much for him and he put his head in his hands and wept, great sobs choking his words. Then it all came out.

In the darkness he had stumbled on the mule still carrying its 120-pound load of stores. "Mother of Jesus, when I lit a match the first thing I saw was all that was left of a human head, smashed like pulp on the rocks. Friday also saw it and we were both sick. How we reached the others I don't know, for my legs gave way and I believe Friday dragged me out of that bloody ravine."

Paddy choked again and there was no need to tell us more,

as clearly the mule and its load had landed on the man's head and both must have died instantly.

Patrick took up the story of the tragedy. The other mule he had found dead, its load missing. It must have crashed into a tree which broke its fall and at the same time sent the store boxes tumbling into the valley below.

This part of the story told, we left them to sleep, saying that we were going in search of food.

Our suffering had been nothing compared with the ordeal they had been through and there would be plenty of time after food to hear how they had fared during the night and finally reached our hiding place in the trees.

The three of us, with Sheila eager to follow, climbed over the wall and out of the shade of the pine trees into the afternoon sunshine heading for the village.

"Well, now we know," said Dick stepping out at a brisk pace despite his patched up shoe. "Here we are sans every bloody thing but what we stand up in . . . still, who cares?" and he stuck out his chest and whistled a tune as much as to say, "To hell with the King's enemies."

We had no money, as even the silver I had packed to use

as barter for food if the worst came to the worst had gone with the rest, but I think both Angus and I caught Dick's spirit of lightheartedness. At least we were all together again.

The village, if it could be called that, consisted of one large house surrounded by a few small ones, the whole grouped within a compound of pine trees. As we approached, a few small children playing by the roadside took one look at our bearded faces and fled in terror, making such a noise that by the time we reached the larger of the buildings their elders were assembled ready to receive us. Whether they would be friendly and give us food remained to be seen.

Dick stepped forward and was soon in conversation with an elderly man who was obviously the headman and before many words had been spoken we could see from their faces that we were welcome strangers. It was as though they were expecting us and with much nodding of heads we were bidden to enter the house. The entire village seemed to be gathered there.

" What do you think, chaps," Dick said turning towards us, " the British Consul is camped seven miles up the road waiting for us. He passed through yesterday and told my friend here," indicating our host, " that he would wait for two days to enable us to catch up with him, unless the situation deteriorates and he has to flee."

It was such unexpected and wonderful news that I could have shouted with joy. But I was prevented by having pressed into my hand a shallow cup of green tea; it tasted of nectar. We all gathered round to hear what other news our friends had.

Apparently the Consul had passed this way once before and was known to the headman. He had a companion with him and three bearers but no mules, and was obviously intent on travelling light and fast. Knowing him and his capacity for walking, it crossed my mind that he would get a shock when he saw the condition of two of the party. However, that could wait. Of first importance was food and sleep for the five men now stretched out in the pine needles down the road.

Dick must have mentioned food, as there was some sudden activity, the younger women disappearing, no doubt to do some cooking. Not so two old grannies who were utterly fascinated by our appearance, particularly our beards. At first they had been shy, certainly modest, keeping well in the background, but now they came forward and for a moment I thought that one old crone was going to give my unruly whiskers a tug to see if they were real. Amongst their own people a beard generally signifies age, and he who wears one is entitled to respect. We could hardly be called old, even if we were travel-stained, hungry and tired. I could see one old dear nudging her neighbour and saying, " These strangers with beards must live far beyond Tengyueh." That would be about the extent of their knowledge of the world in which they lived. What happened beyond the hills was no business of theirs, and from birth to the grave the lives of these simple people centred round the few square miles which to them was home.

In all probability this granny had only seen a handful of men not of her race in her entire lifetime and then only in the distance—George Forrest, perhaps, the great botanical explorer whose grave is in the vicinity of Tengyueh,[1] or later Kingdon Ward on one of his plant hunting expeditions; Peter Fleming, who had once travelled this way; or Ronnie Kaulback and Hanbury-Tracy, the geographers who penetrated the Upper Salween.[2]

Refreshed by the tea and some kind of bean cake which came warm off the fire to be handed round by the grannies and devoured by us in our hunger, my mind began to work,

[1] Where he died before his collection was complete.

[2] I had met them all apart from Forrest, and strangely enough it was in Ronnie Kaulback's house in Ireland only a year ago that the outline of this book took shape in my mind—L. G. H.

and I turned to Dick deep in his description of how we had nearly walked into the Japanese in Tengyueh.

"Sorry to interrupt, Dick, but don't you think we should ask our host to get off a message to Desmond, telling him that we are moving towards his camp and should be there to-morrow before midday?"

"You're dead right—and it had better go quickly, so that it can get there in daylight. Will you write it, as you know him?"

My note to the Consul was brief. After thanking him for waiting to help us, I told him that our party consisted of the eight of us plus a Chinese whose home was in Yunnan. Two of the party were not in good shape, the others were. We would reach his camp as early as possible in the morning. I also thanked him for warning this friendly Yunnanese who was looking after us and was sending someone with the message.

Meanwhile Dick had arranged the runner with our host and by the time I had written the note he was ready for his seven-mile walk. He looked strong and reliable, and was soon gone on his errand.

The smell coming from the back quarters of the house was delicious. Sheila came through to me licking her lips trying desperately hard to remove the grains of rice which peppered her muzzle. She literally bulged with food after days of starvation and in her eyes was a look of contentment. Clearly she had flirted madly in the kitchen with good effect. It happened wherever we went. Although by no means a demonstrative dog she had a way of sitting and using her liquid brown eyes to attract attention. Or she would stretch out flat on the ground moving her large head just sufficiently in the direction where there was conversation to make a point. Then her eyes would drop and her head return to the pillow of her outstretched front paws; in this position she would stay for hours if the conversation was boring to her.

Dick had arranged that some of the youngsters in the

village should accompany us back to our hide-out to help carry the food, but when the time came to go the headman and three of his cronies insisted on joining us, no doubt curious to set eyes on the remainder of our party. In the language of dumb charade signs Angus and I said thank you and good-bye to the nice people who had been so hospitable and kind to us, and in procession we set off to eat our evening meal amongst the trees.

We had tea carried in ancient fire-blackened kettles, and a rice dish delicious with vegetables and flavoured with the tang of soya sauce. There were more of the little bean cakes to add to the rice, and plenty of water to make more tea should we need it.

Within minutes the small boys had a fire going at a safe distance from the trees and, as our companions, one by one, stirred from their sleeping, they awoke to the refreshing sight of a camp fire, friendly faces and the smell of food. It was simple peasant fare, but how good it tasted! The news of the Consul obviously put heart into even the most desperately tired amongst us, and our Yunnanese friends, noticing how tired we looked—even beyond talking—were soon on their way, leaving us to sleep.

Sheila curled up near me as usual and we slept like the dead.

CHAPTER 8

H.M. Consul in Western Yunnan

MAY 12TH

IT WAS BARELY LIGHT WHEN A SLIGHT MOVEMENT OF the dog told me that someone was approaching. I nudged Dick to wake him. It was the headman and he had disturbing news for Dick. During the night one of his neighbours had reached his house from Tengyueh with news that a mixed party of Japanese and collaborating Chinese had sacked the monastery where we had sheltered and were believed to be heading in our direction. He advised us to go as quickly as we could for it would be unsafe for us to stay and dangerous for the Consul who awaited our arrival at the next village. His friend would guide us, as he lived there. Hurriedly packing up the pots and pans and removing all traces of the fire, the old man busied himself whilst we roused the others, urging them to pour the remainder of the water over their heads and to get a move on. Once again we were fugitives with no time to be lost. Besides, we might be letting down the Consul who was risking his neck by waiting for us.

And so with the dawn breaking over the high plateau we bid farewell to someone who had gone out of his way to help us out of trouble. We could only reward him with our thanks—a nod of the head, a wave of the hand and a smile straight from the heart. I am sure that he asked or expected no more.

After a good night's rest I was feeling fine and glad to be on the move again. In fact the whole company seemed in fair shape after a night's rest and food. The road was an easy one, a long gradual climb with no steep gradients, but in the distance towering skywards were the hills which I knew we would have to cross. I took a closer look at Charles Ewing and Richard Weldon and dreaded to think what lay in store for them, as although they plodded on gamely they were not fit men and the ordeal they had been through showed in their haggard faces.

After the disaster on the ridge they had apparently managed to clamber their way up the mountainside for a mile or two and had then collapsed, unable to move another step. They had rallied with the morning and, just as we had done, found a proper track leading in the direction of the monastery. Some distance short of this rendezvous their Chinese companion had been warned by a fresh batch of refugees from Tengyueh that the monastery might already be in Japanese hands, and they had been given a route which by-passed it, eventually bringing the party out on the plateau where they had met us. It must have indeed been a nightmare, and they were reluctant to talk about it.

Towards the end of our short march to the village where Desmond Fortescue was said to be camping, it was decided that because I had met him a few times I should go ahead and prepare him for the shock he would get when he learned that we had no food or even bedding. Dick came with me.

All I had seen of the Consul I had liked, and Dick knew from his Kunming acquaintances that Desmond was held in high regard in the Chinese Consular Service, a *Corps d'Elite* which, alas, exists no longer. Officered by scholars and brilliant linguists, its members became men dedicated to the Oriental way of life, and they had a deep understanding of its peoples. The man we were going to meet had the reputation of being the most outstanding Mandarin scholar in the service.

A bachelor of about forty, it was known that he had a preference for being posted to the most remote stations in

China. It was said of him that he was a gourmet, a connoisseur of wine, and yet was quite content to be posted to Chinese Turkestan, provided the supplies he had sent from London by Fortnum & Mason and Berry Brothers reached him regularly and safely, together with his books. I couldn't help but ponder on Desmond's reaction when he found himself saddled with our mixed bag of humanity.

Just short of the village I saw him sitting on a high bank puffing his pipe, a tweed deerstalker hat on his head. At last I would get a fill of tobacco, the lack of which I had felt more than an empty belly. For years I had smoked two ounces of tobacco a day. My supplies were in the store boxes and for twenty-four hours I had not enjoyed a pipe.

Seeing us, Desmond's tall figure seemed to unwind and he jumped like an athlete down to the roadway to shake my hand. I introduced him to Dick. Compared with us he looked as fresh as a daisy and immaculate in his tailored bush clothes. His pointed red beard was as neatly trimmed as I recalled seeing it at a reception some months previously, and as usual an eye-glass dangled by a black cord round his neck. This was no diplomatic affectation; Desmond was nearly blind in his left eye.

Within minutes my pipe was filled and as quickly as possible we told our story and the latest news of the Japanese advance and the rumours we had heard. Desmond seemed quite unperturbed by it all, which filled me with confidence. Like Dick he was a born leader, and under the guidance of two such men I felt sure we would get the party to safety.

" Come over to my camp and meet Stuart Gracey and let's have a cup of coffee," he said.

The camp consisted of a couple of canvas groundsheets slung over the bough of a tree in Boy Scout fashion, the sides pegged in the ground leaving the tent open at each end. Desmond's companion was not in sight.

" You see that I am travelling very light," Desmond observed and, looking in the direction of the far hills, added,

" The chances are that we shall have to carry everything on our backs when we reach the stiff country, as porters may be unobtainable.

" By the way, did the old Chinaman at the West Gate send you in this direction? "

It was then we learned how it had come about that we had been welcomed at Tengyueh.

Desmond had heard of the Japanese breakthrough and the Chinese decision to abandon the line of the Salween River from Stuart Gracey, who had been one of a Friends' Ambulance team working amongst the Chinese troops on the Buma Road. Finding himself cut off from his Lashio base, he had walked to Tengyueh to warn Desmond. I gathered they were already friends. They had packed hurriedly, leaving the town the day before we reached it, but before leaving had told our old toothless friend to watch out for our arrival and direct us, which of course he had done.

How good that coffee tasted, after drinking nothing but water and green tea for what seemed like weeks! Time had ceased to have any meaning apart from the dawns which with monotonous regularity had seen us on another day's march.

Stuart Gracey, who had been in the village buying eggs, turned out to be a man of about twenty-six with the build of a rugby forward. Later we were to learn that he had in fact got his Blue at Oxford. If ever a man was good all through it was Stuart—and splendid-looking as well. In the days to come he was to exert a terrific influence on our lives. Although a non-combatant Quaker, Stuart had seen service in Finland and elsewhere in Europe before being sent to China. None of us will forget him. His cheerfulness and sincerity were an inspiration. Deeply religious himself, he seemed able to convey to us all the depths of his feelings and it was later from this young giant we gained courage when sometimes in despair.

By now the rest of the party had come straggling in to

drink the coffee that had been prepared for their arrival. Empty tins served as drinking utensils.

Having been introduced all round Desmond took stock of his companions to be and asked them if, after a short rest and something to eat, they would be well enough to move camp, suggesting that as it was only ten o'clock we march another ten miles in the direction of the Shweli River which would be our first objective.

Stuart had managed to buy a few scraggy fowls as well as eggs and the plan was to make camp early, have a good meal and plenty of sleep as the next day's going would be more strenuous.

Once again Dick's shoe was tied up with cord and soon we were on our way.

That evening was a memorable one. During the day we had descended from the high plateau down to about 5000 feet and found a camp site by a stream in which we were able to wash off some of the accumulated dirt which covered us, drying off over a fire. Friday was in his element, and, helped by Desmond's Chinese porters, produced the first proper meal of our journey. Yes, we even had a sip or two of whisky which Desmond sacrificed from his small stock. Fortunately, only half our number were whisky drinkers but even the thimble measure, which was to be our ration while it lasted, tasted wonderful. Desmond and Stuart had divided up their bedding, in spite of our protests, and this allowed one blanket to every two men. Thereafter we were paired off and I shared my covering with Dick all the way to Kunming.

Sitting over the fire that night whilst most of the party slept Desmond outlined some of the difficulties we would have to overcome. First, we must follow in a northerly direction the valley of the Lung Kiang (or Shweli) River, the crossing of which should present little difficulty. We would then be faced by the barrier of mountains known as the Kaolikung Shan which form the divide between the Shweli and the Salween. The Chinese call the Salween River, Lu

Kiang, which translated means, angry, and very aptly named it is.

The mountains between the two rivers are formidable to say the least. They range between 11,000 and 12,500 feet, the few passes which exist being closed by snow in winter. Fortunately it was spring. We were indeed venturing into a land of great rivers and into a country which Desmond told us was known to be hostile to strangers.

Less than fifteen miles as the crow flies divides the Shweli from the Salween at one point to our north. Fed by the snow waters of China and Tibet they both sweep and wind their tortuous way in a raging torrent and cascades of impassable rapids through China and southwards into Burma, and finally to the sea some 2000 miles distant.

Desmond's plan was clear-cut, and he had obviously given it much thought. Although he had no maps—if such things existed of this part of Yunnan—he knew exactly the route we should take. We had to reach the Salween and try to find a crossing. This might present difficulties, as they were few and far between in the upper reaches of this great river. Once over this obstacle we should make our way to the valley of the Mekong, a river which rises in the snows of Tibet and discharges its waters into what is now known as South Viet Nam. But first a way had to be found over the Kaolikung Shan where for days we might have to live at heights of nearly 12,000 feet without proper clothes and the added risk of starvation. Should the Chinese fail to hold the Mekong line of defence, our journey, even if successful, would have been in vain. Yet hold the Mekong the Chinese must, or Kunming, the last stronghold of the Chiang Kai-Shek regime would be wide open. That, at least, was our reasoning.

Yet looking round the shadows cast by the dying embers of the fire where our party lay huddled together in sleep, I realised the extent of the sacrifice Desmond had made so willingly by waiting for us to catch up with him. We had nothing to contribute and would, without any shadow of doubt, be a brake and a painful burden on his own road to safety.

It was an undertaking for a small hand-picked team of fit men welded together in the determination to survive. What had we to offer? Charles Ewing, sedentary by nature and by experience; Richard Weldon, already a sick man, although he would not admit it; Paddy McClusky, still badly shaken by what he had seen in the gorge; and Dick, who despite his indomitable will and physical toughness, might be shoeless in a couple of days.

It was not only physical handicaps that we were introducing, there would also be mental ones brought on by strain, as I well knew from my experiences in the lonely forests of North Burma. Even under those conditions I had seen men's morale crack. God knows how we would all react when the real test came.

It was with these thoughts turning over and over in my mind that I curled up next to Dick under the blanket we were to share, and Sheila found her place stretched out between us. Nearby I saw Stuart on his knees in prayer. For fully five minutes he prayed, as if at complete peace with the world and unconscious of all around him.

Sleep would not come. Instead I found myself repeating the words of " Farmer " Hewitt's poem on loneliness, and then, as though a chord had been struck in my memory, the last line of the first verse came to me:

> So think not ye whose lot is cast
> In the teeming cities of men
> He's a heart of stone who dwells alone
> And a mind like a stagnant fen;
> That his blood has no force
> And halts on its course,
> Forgetful of human ken.

CHAPTER 9

Across the Shweli

MAY 13TH

I AWOKE FEELING SO FIT AND WELL, IN HEART AND in body, that I knew I could have walked thirty miles that day had I been called upon to do so. For some reason I was in high spirits, anxious to get on the road to the Shweli, the selected crossing point of which was only a day's march ahead. I had seen the river on many occasions making its placid way through Burma. Now I was impatient to see it close up against the backdrop of the great mountain range separating it from the Salween.

Already the high peaks of the Kaolikung Shan dominated the view to the north and east of where we had camped for the night. In the clear early morning light of this spring day they were a glorious sight and in the far distance the rising sun picked out patches of snow, the remnants of a winter now fortunately long passed.

There was a smell of coffee in the air and it was mingled with that of burning turf. From the nearby village came a sound so familiar to my ears, the thud thud thud of rice being hand pounded by the womenfolk, and I could picture them with babies strapped on their backs going about the business of preparing to feed the family for the day. Gone was that sinister feeling of being on the run, of being wakened in the dead of night and of having to grope one's way into the darkness. No more dim lights and beckoning hands motioning us to be gone, nor the eerie murmurs of hushed voices saying, "you must leave this place or we will all perish."

At last we were really on our way in an orderly fashion. The road ahead was clear-cut, even if it was going to test our endurance to the utmost. To me it was a challenge; and I felt I was capable of seeing it through to the end. I think even the less robust of our party must have had their confidence restored and have been feeling rather as I did. They looked cheerful enough as they gathered round the fire where Friday was doling out coffee. What a difference meeting up with Desmond had made to our lives!

This was my first experience of travelling with porters, and as they busied themselves breaking camp and dividing up the loads, I watched, fascinated by the meticulous care that was taken to ensure that no one man carried more than another. Chattering like monkeys and, no doubt, arguing away, they were joined by children from the village who had to watch our departure. Everyone seemed to take a hand in the proceedings. I had yet to learn that Chinese porters cannot be hurried and will only do things at their own time and in their own way. Ours were cheerful ugly little chaps and I could see from their eyes that every one of them was an opium smoker. The contracted pupils of the eye told their own story. Pathetic perhaps, yet I had come to learn from my experiences with our elephant men what the daily pipe or two means to people who live and work under rough and sometimes appalling conditions. To them it is no more than a stimulant, in the same way as a glass of whisky is to us when dead tired after a strenuous day.

As a young Forest Assistant it had been part of my job to issue opium with the weekly rations. It was done under licence, the quantity varying from man to man according to his needs. Amongst the heavy smokers there would always be competition to ride a known "man killer" elephant as this carried danger money, which in fact meant more opium. How I had hated breaking up and weighing the horrible black, sticky, sweet-smelling stuff—but the Government insisted

that only the licence holder be permitted to issue it. I had once given evidence on the subject of opium usage before an International Commission and, although fully aware of its evil effects, had submitted that to certain workers it was a necessity of life which would only be eliminated when standards of living were raised.

It was good to be on the road again. At 5000 feet the morning air was chilly and I felt the urge to be on our way.

The village we had left behind us was called Chai Tien. It was quite a sizeable one and most of the inhabitants had lined the roadside to wave to us as we passed by. They were friendly people. In fact throughout the Shweli Valley we were greeted with smiling faces.

I was up ahead with Desmond and he was explaining that the porters he had hired would go no farther than the river. The other side of the Shweli we would have to hire more. Apparently this is the custom not only in Yunnan but throughout China. There are strict lines of demarcation which are rigidly adhered to.

"Tell me, Desmond, how are you off for money? We must square accounts when we reach Kunming. Luckily the company has an office there and I shall be able to settle with you. Dick, of course, can do the same."

Desmond rattled his pockets in which were a few coins. "The position isn't too good, I'm afraid. Stuart has a small supply of silver, and between us there should be sufficient until we catch up with the Customs people who are ahead of us. That is why I want to press on," he added. "But that chap Ewing of yours worries me somewhat. How did you come to pick him up?"

There was something in the way Desmond spoke that made me feel that these two were not going to make the best of travelling companions. I had already noticed a slight chilliness between them, which had surprised me, as, coming from the same official stable, so to speak, I had expected them to have a lot in common. Dick had also noticed it but we had put it down to Charles Ewing being dead on his feet. After all they were the two intellectuals of the party of ten and it was hardly possible that any jealousy existed between the Chinese and Indian Political Services.

I told Desmond about the arrival of Charles at my house and how overweight he had been to start with on a journey such as we had done. The poor fellow must already have lost about twenty-five pounds of fat.

"Don't worry," I said. "Give him a day or so to recover from what he's been through and you will find he has the guts to face all that is in store for us in the hills. It's his feet that worry me." And I told the story of Charles standing beside me on my Bhamo veranda, quite unafraid, as the Japanese plane flew low over the house.

"But what's all this about the Chinese Customs ahead of us?" I inquired.

"Well," said Desmond offering, me his pouch for my morning ration of one pipe, "the first hint I had that the Chinese might be abandoning the line of the Salween came two days before I left Tengyueh. The head of Chinese Customs, a nice chap by the name of Kiang Tun, whom I had come to know and like, appeared late in the evening at my house and told me that he was moving out his entire staff, and that they were going in this direction and over the Salween back to Kunming. He advised me to accompany them as the obvious route down to the Burma Road at Paoshan was by then unsafe.

He went on, "I suppose I should have taken this official hint and cleared out because the communications with Kunming had already been cut, but it was only when Stuart appeared that I knew there was no alternative. And here we are."

I gathered that the Customs party would be moving quite slowly as they had their wives and children with them. Although no doubt properly organised, right down to riding mules for the women and children, the progress of this caravan would of necessity be slower than ours, and within a day or two we should catch up with them.

Dick now joined us at the head of the column, going great guns in spite of his strange footwear bound up with string. Both soles had by now come adrift but Angus and Friday between them had made a good repair job and he was striding out like a two-year-old.

" Had you realised, Gordon, that this is our ninth day on this bloody picnic and we haven't really got started yet. But for that so and so, Chiang Kai-Shek, and his so-called defence policy we might have been in Kunming to-night. Jesus, what a party I would have given you! "

Dick was his old breezy self again, not in the least concerned about the towering mountains which drew nearer with every mile we covered.

" Do you see that tall chap over there, chum?" I said, pointing to a high peak showing through a gap and standing out like the Empire State Building as viewed from the end of Park Avenue. " Desmond has just told me that its name is Kaun-Ai-Shan, and it's all of 12,000 feet and right in our path."

" Listen," said Dick, " I've been learning something this morning from young Stuart Gracey. He's a bit of a geographer in his spare time and he tells me that we must have climbed from 5000 to nearly 9000 feet that night we hit the monastery. Hell, if we can do that in the dark and mainly on our hands and knees, that pimple over there will be a piece of cake."

This was quite true, as Desmond confirmed when we questioned him about the manner of our lucky break from Tengyueh and the route we had taken after our little charade act crossing the paddy-fields. He had more than once visited the monastery by the well-trodden path made by the pilgrims who travelled that way in search of the peace and seclusion offered by this place of retreat in the mountains.

" That short cut you took," he said, " probably saved you ten miles of walking, but how you got to the top in the dark, beats me. I would have thought it impossible without ropes. The Pe Lien range is one of the most difficult in the area."

Well, we had done it, I reflected, and I thought back to nine days ago when we had been living at only 400 feet above sea-level. . . . On the first night of our journey when we had lost our way in the Sinlumkaba hill tracks we must have climbed nearly 5000 feet before descending into the drainage-basin of the Taping the next day.

How easy our journey would have been had it gone according to plan! To-night we might have been enjoying the fleshpots of Kunming, the pipe would have been full, and reassuring messages sent to the family. I knew they had at least reached India safely, but for about two months or longer I had received no news of them. Their departure had been somewhat dramatic, and but for the link I had with the American Flying Tigers based at Loiwing it might have ended in quite a different way.

Having been assured that air transport would be provided from Lashio for women and children, we had arrived there to find utter confusion. Only through the intervention of an American Air Force colonel I had known in the Flying Tiger days had their passage been secured. They had taken off from Kunming in a Dakota bound for Calcutta. What a relief it had been to see them go after four frustrating days of waiting! Our English nurse was by then on the verge of a nervous breakdown, and my wife was far from well; only my young son enjoyed himself.

My thoughts about the recent past ended abruptly when I saw ahead of me the porters sitting down in their tracks shedding their loads. It was around midday and they had decided it was time for rest and a puff of the opium pipe. I was to learn that nothing would persuade these little fellows to carry on if they had decided to call a halt to the day's march. But they deserved a rest, and it provided an opportunity for the party to regroup and compare notes.

Sheila, as usual, was in her element, running from one to another wagging her tail as she greeted them before sitting down to pant. I was glad to see that Charles Ewing and Stuart Gracey had paired off and were deep in conversation. I think that in the nine days we had spent together we had all of us exhausted our small talk and latterly had tended to travel in silence.

This was, perhaps, not surprising, as none of us had a great deal in common. We got on well enough together, but there it ended. We were ten grown men thrown together by fate, each with our own thoughts and possibly fears as to the outcome of the journey. Some of us were better fitted physically than others to endure the strain of walking all day and sleeping rough at night. The real test of will had yet to come.

The porters, refreshed after a long pull at their pipes, were now gathering up their loads. I think a lot of their pleasure in smoking that opium must have come in the preparation of the weed: the ceremony of polishing the bowl of the pipe and filling it slowly, then the first puff. . . .

Anyway, we were soon on the road again, heading for the village of Wa Tien, where it was proposed we should camp on the west bank that night and cross the Shweli next day.

We were clearly now in the river valley, although some distance from its banks. The plain was quite wide and populated, and every few miles could be seen villages nestled away amongst trees a mile or so from our route. The few Chinese we saw, usually men and boys and a handful of mules, were going about their everyday business completely oblivious to the world at large. We would wave to them and they would wave back, and it was a nice feeling to forget the Luger which dangled from my waist.

Neither Desmond nor Stuart carried any firearms, but I was loath to part with my gun which constituted our sole armoury. Besides, it was an old friend. I had never used it in anger, but in my camping days in Burma it had been a constant companion and by long practice I had become a fair shot. Our camp sites in those days had always been by the sides of streams or rivers and one of the first things the servants would do once my tent was erected would be to put up targets on the opposite bank, if within pistol range. These would normally consist of empty bottles and tins arranged in a row on the ground or suspended from branches, and I was expected to knock off the lot in quick fire, as I sometimes succeeded in doing. I suspect that the servants used to have bets, such was their enthusiasm for this evening game, but in the process I became proficient, and later, more than once, had matched my skill at Loiwing with the Americans who had a passion for guns of all kinds. In those days we had often behaved like a pack of schoolboys, but it had been good fun. I even won a cup.

Wa Tien turned out to be a village of some size when we reached it at about 3 p.m. It sprawled along the banks of the river, then running at low water and some two hundred yards wide. In the immediate vicinity there was nothing of beauty but to our west ran a range of hills between six and seven thousand feet and to the east was a distant view of the mountains we would have to cross. Their foothills were two days' march away. Tier after tier they rose skywards looking glorious in the afternoon sunlight as they towered over the 12,000 foot level blocking our route to the Salween.

Our party was assembling by the river bank to get its first uninterrupted view of the Kaolikung Shan. The porters had shed their loads and Desmond and Dick had gone ahead to speak with the headman of the village.

I found myself talking to Charles Ewing who had struggled in. " There you are, Charles, all we have got to do is jump over that lot and we should be more or less home and dry. Kunming here we come! "

My lightheartedness seemed lost on the poor chap, already weary after what had been to me an easy day.

" Gordon," he confided, " don't tell the others, but I don't think I can make it. My heel is blowing up again and is as sore as hell."

One look was sufficient for me to know the mental as well as physical agony he must have been suffering all day. What had been an ordinary blister now had a red weal and if not treated and rested it would, within another day's march, develop into a suppurating mess. We would have to do something about it.

I felt mean, shod as I was in my good strong marching boots, raving about the beauty of the mountains to someone in pain who dared not look in their direction without flinching. Misery and despair showed in his face.

" Come, Charles, don't worry, we will buy you a mule and you shall ride like a lord."

The nod he gave me and the look in his eyes showed his gratitude even at the thoughts I had expressed without thinking.

He got his mule that evening.

Desmond rejoined us with news that the village school

was at our disposal for the night and that we would be sharing it with a small rearguard party of the Customs people.

"Gordon," he said, "do you feel up to a bit more walking to-day? I have located the Customs money, but it means crossing the river and climbing into those nearby hills where my friend Kiang Tun is camped to-night." And he indicated a group of lowish hills some six to seven miles distant. "I shall have to go myself but, if you are up to it, I want someone to help me carry the silver I am after. Dick will see to the party being bedded down for the night."

Dick appeared and I told him about Charles. "See if the Customs people have any Tiger Balm with them; and we must get him a mule to ride or he will certainly be a casualty to-morrow."

Dick nodded as if to say "leave it all to me," and Desmond and I left on our silver-hunting expedition, followed, of course, by Sheila.

We had need to hasten as it was late afternoon and a long climb awaited us over the river.

Our guide was a village youth who without hesitation waded into the Shweli. The water was cold and about waist deep in places but the crossing was an easy one. Sheila thought it great fun and on reaching the far bank found a pool in which she romped and swam about before climbing out and shaking herself.

As we climbed into the hills Desmond explained that the Customs party, fearing that they might be followed and robbed, had split up. The women and children had gone ahead, the money was being carried by a second party (the one we were seeking) and a few of the men remaining at Wa Tien would act as decoys and travel farther north up the Shweli before crossing to the high hills. The whole party had planned to meet on the Salween which they considered would be safe and beyond pursuit. It seemed a sensible arrangement.

Our guide took us straight to the head Customs man's

hideout; it must have been all of seven miles from the river.

Kiang Tun was overjoyed to see the Consul and only too pleased to act as our banker. The heavy hardwood boxes with their brass fittings were unlocked and the silver dollars counted carefully and checked by his assistants, whilst we sat and enjoyed a welcome drink of whisky. Not a thimbleful this time, but a drink in real Chinese fashion—half a tumbler and a dash of water. It was bliss and made every mile of the extra walk worth it.

Desmond signed an I O U. We bowed and, murmuring our thanks, returned the way we had come, both of us carrying a heavy bag of silver.

It was long after dark by the time the Shweli was crossed for the second time that day, and I was glad of a borrowed towel to give myself a brisk rub down over a fire built up on bricks on the schoolroom floor.

Dick had successfully negotiated the purchase of a riding mule for Charles Ewing and had treated his heel with Tiger Balm, that wonderful ointment manufactured in Hong Kong and universally used in the East as a panacea for practically all ailments. Charles was asleep, out to this world. The others sat with our new-found Chinese friends talking round the fire.

Strangely enough I was not tired, yet that day I must have walked at least thirty miles. Desmond was a wonderful walker. We were the same height, weight and build and would match each other's paces up hill and down dale, and it was possible that being so matched we had achieved a certain rhythm which had prevented any tiredness. Neither of us carried any excess weight and there grew up between us a sort of fitness or endurance contest.

The Chinese " Decoys," as they laughingly described them-selves in perfect English, were a nice and interesting bunch of chaps. I think there were five of them. They were educated civil servants of the Central Government in Kunming, all too well aware of the intrigues and machinations of Lung Yung, the Governor of Yunnan, and his opium-peddling son.

Conversation was interesting. We heard an account of how the Governor collected tolls from the Burma frontier onwards deep into Yunnan, and how they themselves were hated as Treasury agents and so collectors of revenue which by-passed the coffers of the Governor. It was this awful fear of Lung Yung's men being on their trail, not the fear of pursuing Japanese, as we had thought, that had led to Kiang Tun's decision to divide his party into three parts. All they hoped was that in the event the gangsters would head up the Shweli in their wake and, finding nothing, leave the other two parties to cross over the hills in safety.

That night I recall our Irish colleague, Paddy, being for once in full cry. He was as amusing as only the Irish can be, and for every story the Chinese told he would match it with one of his own; they were all about the frontier and the strange things that went on there.

Finally we prepared for bed. As Stuart Gracey prayed in his usual manner, regardless of everyone around him, I felt sure he knew that there was at least one member of our party who was in need of God's help to give him strength for what lay ahead.

CHAPTER 10

Bluffing the "General"

MAY 14TH

THERE WAS NO EARLY START THAT MORNING, NO sign of the porters who had been booked from somewhere east of the river by the kindly headman of Wa Tien. I could see that Desmond was anxious to be away and, on his insistence, we packed the loads as soon as Friday had produced eggs and coffee, in order that everything should be in readiness for the day's march. Our objective was the village of Lungchwankiang, quite an important place as we gathered from Desmond, who was by now pacing the river bank with Sheila at his heel; but it was a full day's march, and we would all the time be rising towards the foothills of the actual Kaolikung Shan range itself and the route might prove difficult.

Desmond and Sheila had become great friends. An attachment had grown between them in the short space of time we had been together. It was quite noticeable. She was a friendly creature at any time, yet already she lavished on him much the same special affection as she normally reserved for her master. Whether in the ordinary way he was a dog lover I never came to know, but he was there when, some years later, she died in the middle of China.

From the school building we were leaving I walked down to the river bank to join the others. Stuart Gracey and Angus were busy instructing Charles how to ride his mule and he cut a marvellous figure as, astride his charger, he tried out its paces exhibiting a total ignorance of the most elementary rules of horsemanship. Poor Charles was just plain awkward,

but at least he had his feet off the ground and his blistered heel was by then encased in bandages, which the Customs men had produced with the Tiger Balm.

"Come on, Steve," roared Friday, giving the mule a smart slap on the backside, which sent it careering down the road, out of control, with Angus and Stuart in hot pursuit; "I'll lay even money on the favourite for the Shweli Handicap." Friday was back in the Calcutta Silver Ring, revelling in his knowledge of the Sport of Kings.

Not so Desmond. He did not approve and it showed in his face as I came up alongside to discuss the non-appearance of the porters. He was rather grim and uncommunicative as the "horseplay" went on around us. Sheila had joined in by the time Charles managed to bring his mount to a halt midst roars of laughter not far from where we stood.

Fortunately, at that moment when I could feel tension mounting, our new recruits appeared on the far bank and waded in our direction. It was now I realised that there was more than an absence of sympathy between these two men. One of them at least despised the other, though for what reason I never discovered.

The new batch of porters were more ruggedly built than those we were leaving behind. They had the well developed legs of hill people, squat sturdy men who lost no time in gathering up the loads and marching off over the river.

Our cavalcade followed. The headman and our Chinese Customs friends stood on the bank waving us good-bye as we left the Shweli and made our way northwards by a route taking us inland towards the mountains.

It was a long day over uneven but not too difficult terrain. There is nothing worse than delays and a late start when distances have to be covered, and for the most part of that day I travelled in silence. Egged on by us all, the mule carrying Charles kept up a reasonable pace in spite of the weight it was carrying. But way out in front, sometimes even out of sight, as if wanting no part in the proceedings, stalked our leader wrapped up in his own thoughts.

The porters must have had their morning ration of opium before joining us, as they showed no signs of wanting to halt and rest. Each of them carried between fifty and sixty pounds of baggage on his back supported by a head strap of plaited bamboo. Their heads down and shoulders bowed under the weight they carried, they plodded on like pack animals, and as I looked towards the mountains I wondered whether it would be possible for man to travel that way over the route we would have to take in a couple of days' time.

It was early evening when the porters decided that they would go no farther. They had reached a kind of caravanserai and there they stopped. We discovered it was only about a mile from the big village of Lungchwankiang ahead of us. But stop and dump their loads they did. This was to be our camp for the night and they would not budge another inch.

By now we were all tired and could not care less. The previous evening's climb into the hills followed by the session of story-telling round the fire was catching up with me. Late nights and long marches do not go well together.

The camp site offered some shelter. There was a large roofed building with open sides, rather like a covered market, and several smaller structures on the same pattern. We settled for the main hut, where a fire was soon kindled on the floor of packed mud. But our period of relaxation was to be short-lived.

The news of our arrival must have reached the village in a matter of minutes; all through Yunnan we found a form of bush telegraph working most effectively, but on this occasion three Chinese appeared even before the water was on the boil. In the lead was a personage obviously of some importance in the locality, judging by the purposeful air of authority with which he approached us.

Desmond rose to his feet and bowed to the visitor, indicating to him to sit and join us over the fire for a chat and cup of coffee, as had the headman of Wa Tien the previous night.

But this man stood like a court bailiff delivering a summons or eviction order. His manner could hardly be called friendly. Nor did his two companions inspire confidence. They were sullen ugly men and their behaviour was that of bodyguards rather than village people come out of curiosity to greet and welcome the strangers. I then remembered Desmond's chance remark that once over the Shweli travellers were unwelcome, and I sensed that an unexpected and perhaps unpleasant situation was brewing.

Indeed it was, as a few minutes later the important gentleman turned and stalked away back to his village, leaving his companions standing by the building we were occupying, looking to all intents and purposes like prison guards. That these were no friends became obvious to me when I felt Sheila trembling as she put her head in my hand. She could sense an atmosphere long before we could, and I had come to understand her language. I could see by the way her fur had risen and the way her eyes moved that we must watch our step.

Desmond had become angry in the course of his conversation with the Chinaman from the village. There had been much hand-waving culminating in the "chief's" departure, when, even to us in our ignorance of the language, it became clear that the centre of all the trouble, if trouble there was, lay down the road. The hand pointing in that direction as a last defiant gesture left no doubt on that point, and the manner of the man's departure was by no means reassuring to tired and travel-stained men such as we were.

It was a grim-faced Desmond who rejoined us by the fire where we squatted impatiently to hear what had been going on.

Dick was the first to put a question. "What's all this about a place called Kaitou and some army general I overheard that overfed Chink bastard talking to you about? He was so bloody rude that if he had spoken to me like that I would have kicked him in the place where it really hurts and told him to go to hell."

One look at Desmond's face was sufficient to make Dick realise that he was off on the wrong tack, but Dick was ever quick on the uptake in spite of his explosive nature.

"Sorry, Desmond," he said, "I've spoken out of turn. Please forgive me. But I didn't like that so-and-so, and that goes for those two cheapjack gangsters of his over there," and he nodded towards the entrances to our shelter.

He stood up looking more than ever like a caricature of Ernest Hemingway, his aggressive white stubble of beard standing out like the back hairs of a Ridgeback, the lion dog of Africa.

"The trouble is," Dick went on, "I know just sufficient of the language you talk to these people to pick up a few words and that is all. This is a territory you know and understand, whereas I don't. And from now on I'm going to keep my great clap shut."

Dick took a pace or two forward and the two men shook hands. The understanding between them was even greater than it had been before this outburst. I heaved a sigh of relief.

We were all ears as Desmond explained the predicament we were now in.

"Kaitou," he explained, "is the local name for the village we know as Lungchwankiang, and from all I have gathered, I suspect that it is a stronghold of Lung Yung, the Yunnanese Governor. This is understandable, as it commands the entry and exit to Mamien Khyet, the mountain pass over to the Salween, which we will have to cross.

"The bumptious gentleman who came to visit us," he went on, "was one of the village elders who informed me that he came from the General responsible for the area who demands that we give reasons for our journey, deliver up all arms and report immediately to his headquarters for inter-rogation. I must go at once, Gordon, will you accompany me?"

He nodded to Dick in a friendly way as if to say, should we fail by diplomatic tactics that Dick must assume command, and by other methods bluster his way out of the situation which we now had to face.

Patrick came up with a cup of coffee, "Drink this, Mr. Hunt, you may need it before the night is over."

In his quiet and undemonstrative way this youngster would always give me confidence. To him, I suppose, I was still the boss, yet between us there was a relationship of unexpressed friendship. Perhaps it was only based on the fact that we " belonged " by reason of the company who employed us, and on a venture such as this were its representatives; I don't know.

I unbuckled my Luger and, unseen by anyone in the poor light, gave it over to Patrick. " Take care of it, and look after Sheila. We shall be back soon." One word from me, and the dog knew that it was to stay behind. I followed Desmond out into the night, the two Chinese thugs leading the way.

It was only a short distance to the village which proved to be the nearest thing to a town we had seen since leaving hurriedly from the outskirts of Tengyueh.

Our guides threaded their way through narrow thoroughfares, unlit and uninviting; finally to a largish building in the centre of the village. It was really no more than that, but compared with the settlements we had passed through it was, I am sure, quite imposing if viewed in daylight. It was double storied and for some minutes we were kept waiting at the foot of a wooden and rather rickety staircase which creaked and groaned as one of the guides ascended it, presumably to announce our presence, leaving us in darkness down below.

Desmond was silent. I wondered how he would play the hand about to be dealt to him on the floor above. If indeed we were to meet the Governor's agents, or whoever they might be, it certainly would be a game of bluff. As we waited I thought of our silver dollars and the nice Customs men and their plans to escape from the clutches of Lung Yung and his bandit army. . . . Ah well! we should soon know.

At last we were ushered up the stairs and into a large room dimly lit with oil-lamps. Behind a table presided an evil-looking character dressed in some kind of music hall khaki uniform, his fat breast, which seemed to droop over the table top, ablaze with multi-coloured ribbons and decorations sufficient to cover a Christmas tree. He wore a peaked cap and on each side of him sat his " aides," or at least that is what I assumed them to be, similarly clad, but minus the holly. We were in The Presence!

It was like a stage set; I could see them, minutes before, donning their fancy dress and arranging themselves so as to look important. They were utterly bogus, but very likely pretty dangerous and certainly obstructive.

Desmond bowed low, and for the first time I saw a British diplomat in China going into action. With each step he took towards the table he bowed as if before royalty, yet there was dignity, not humility, in the way his head and shoulders were lowered in the manner of his approach to within a few feet of where they sat. Then he stood erect, addressing them rapidly in Yunnanese.

His eye-glass firmly in place, and his red beard trimmed to a point, added a touch of theatre to the scene; yet it was clear to me that he was speaking with the voice of authority.

Meanwhile, I had done my somewhat clumsy best to imitate Desmond's approach, and now stood a pace behind him, slightly to the right so that I could get a better view of the proceedings.

Undoing his bush jacket Desmond produced an official-looking document which must have impressed the fat man, as he nudged the " aide " who appeared to be taking notes. It was, of course, all Dutch to me but I sensed that Desmond was not prepared to stand any nonsense, and if some form of *laissez-passer* was necessary to enable us to continue it was their job to produce one.

We must have stood in front of that table for a whole hour and I was really tired. On and on they talked, with Desmond refusing to budge an inch, yet never once did he show any signs of impatience. From time to time he would smile at the trio and once or twice I could detect a look of humour on their otherwise impassive faces.

Normally I liked the Chinese, and in Bhamo had represented their community interests as a Municipal Commissioner, but these men were of another breed. They looked sly and completely untrustworthy, as I am sure they were.

At last we seemed to be getting somewhere as the "aide" taking notes began to scribble characters as dictated by the

"General" who, with a flourish, added his name. It was then that for the first time he appeared to notice my presence. His hands fully outstretched, he raised his arms as far as the bulk of his bosom would allow—nodded his head in my direction, and made flapping movements which I took to be those of a bird on the wing.

I dared not look in Desmond's direction and could think of nothing else to do but simulate the flight of an albatross, which I must have done with some success as the "General's" peak

cap fell off as he put an excited arm round each of his "aides'"
shoulders, as much as to say, "I told you he was a bird
man."

"Maybe," I thought, "he is wishing me a good flight over
the Hump to India." But not on your life. He was bidding
farewell (it seems) to a distinguished major of the American
Air Force, so convincingly had Desmond told his story. He
had bluffed his—and our—way out of a situation which might
have been really dangerous.

By sheer weight of words and his remarkable command of
Yunnanese, Desmond had worn these Lung Yung bandits
down to the point where I think they were only too pleased
to see the back of us—but not yet!

As I was about to turn and make my exit in the normal
fashion, I was just in time to catch sight of Desmond moving
slowly backwards, bowing in a dignified manner as he made
his way to the door leading to the staircase and the street below.
To follow his example I did my act of bobbing and bowing,
but mine was far from being a polished performance and
I collided with the wall. Not until he reached the stairs and
was out of sight of the Chinese did Desmond straighten up.

My tiredness could have been nothing compared with his
after the long day and the ordeal of words he had just been
through, yet he set off at a fast pace back to our camp.

"They were Lung Yung's henchmen, as I suspected," he
said, "and I wouldn't mind having a bet that either the
Governor or his son has passed this way recently, leaving a
party here to cover their tracks and prevent anyone following
them over the Salween. They probably have a lot of loot
with them."

Desmond then told me briefly how he had been forced to
tell some tall stories to substantiate our presence in the area.
That is how I had become a flyer. He had of course been
able to prove that he was the British Consul and had satisfied
the "General" that, having been cut off, he was taking us
with him to Kunming.

There were lots of questions I longed to ask, but they would have to wait, as Desmond seemed wrapped in his own thoughts, which was perhaps not surprising. Anyway, I had received my first lesson in how to leave the presence of important Chinese.

How strange it is, I thought, that a range of hills should so completely mark the dividing line between two ways of life. China and Burma had been neighbours from the beginning of history, yet their ways and customs were poles apart. It was as if their common border saw the end of Western influences and served as a gateway to the real Far East. I must remember to ask Dick whether in Canton it was customary to leave a room backwards.

In Burma we used to shake hands in the manner of the West, although the traditional deep " Shaikoo " was still practised on ceremonial occasions. It had always rather embarrassed me to have someone prostrating him or herself at my feet, particularly when it was a pretty girl, as would happen when one of the staff presented his bride. It was all very formal. A time would be arranged and the couple would dress in their very best clothes. They would arrive carrying a small present of fruit or flowers which would be placed on the floor. They would then prostrate themselves with hands together, as in prayer, and would " shaikoo " three times. Then they would rise and the bride would present me with their gift. Tea would be served.

Some of my older contractors in the more remote districts would literally drag themselves along the floor, pushing their gift bowl of eggs or fruit in front of them as they made their shaikoos, but this generally meant that a request for an advance of money was about to be made.

Thoughts of Burma and the happy days I had spent there persisted all the way to camp, where the rest of the party were awaiting our return, rather anxiously, I thought, judging by their faces. They had already eaten, but Friday was there to take care of us.

" Hold on a minute," said Desmond to Friday, " we deserve a drink."

Although the whisky stock was down to little more than a bottle the two of us had a generous helping and felt all the better for it. We told them what had happened in the village and then turned in, as an early start was to be made in the morning. We would have to climb a couple of thousand feet in the direction of a village named Shantao. Also, the more miles we could put between us and the Governor's ruffians the happier Desmond would be. He knew their kind only too well to feel complacent just because of a piece of paper in his pocket, the so-called *laissez-passer* which had been handed to him that night.

CHAPTER 11

Bacon for Supper

MAY 15TH

OUR ROUTE THE NEXT MORNING TURNED TOWARDS the hills some distance short of the large village to which we had been summoned the previous night. I could not help laughing to myself as I thought of the " General's " peak cap falling off his head as he clasped his companions, wanting them to share his joke. The whole scene had been like a pantomime; looking back it occurred to me that at no time had we been offered anything to sit on.

Talk, talk, talk. How it had gone on into the night! I was afraid I would have made a poor candidate for Desmond's service, if this was an example of how matters with the Chinese were conducted.

Breaking camp that morning had produced the usual delays. Either the porters were missing when wanted, or something or other was mislaid. Charles's heel had to be dressed and his mule made ready for the journey. Paddy had assumed the role of medical and mule orderly, and he certainly stuck by his large blanket-sharing companion. Of the ten of us these two were the only members of our party slow to wake and get themselves up in the mornings. Some men are like that, and I could see that it irritated Desmond, who would simply ignore them and not say a word. Not so Dick. He would shout and curse them into consciousness and this had its effect, eventually. Friday was invariably the first to stir and with the first sign of morning would be up to tend to the fire and to scrounge from somewhere the bindings he needed to strap up Dick's shoes. He had become an expert at the job and always found something that would hold them in place for the day's march, and when we halted he would carry out running repairs.

At first we had all been worried at losing our toothbrushes, but I had introduced the Burmese coolie method of using a finger and wood ash, which is most effective, even if rather messy. By now we were used to it. Fortunately there was water everywhere and the absence of soap did not bother us.

Now that we were entering hilly country, progress was slowed down to the pace the porters could travel and I found it more tiring than striding out. I am a fast walker and the plodding gait we had to adopt came strangely to me. I said so to Dick. He was alongside me sucking a straw, a habit he had formed since the cigarettes were lost with everything else.

"I'm afraid it's going to get a damned sight slower when we really get started," he said, spitting out a piece of grass and looking to the distant mountains. "At this pace it is going to take us another week to reach the Salween, if we can make it."

Some of Dick's normal cheer seemed to have left him, so I inquired what was on his mind.

"Well, Gordon, if you really want to know, it's two things," and he spat out another piece of chewed grass. "In the first place, I wouldn't give that mule more than two days before it collapses under Charles's weight, and secondly, unless we can scrounge some food we shall be starving. Didn't you see me having an argument with Desmond this morning before we left? I wanted to go into Kaitou to stock up, or at least buy a few pounds of rice if they had it. But he wouldn't hear of it and insisted that it would have drawn too much attention had we offered dollars for such purposes. Maybe he was right, but I think we should have taken a chance."

It was only then that I heard something of what had transpired in the long-drawn-out session with the General.

Apparently Desmond had been questioned about the Customs money and had denied any knowledge of it or the whereabouts of his friend Kiang Tun. Rather than endanger him by going into the village, where such a large party would indeed have caused a stir, he had given it a wide berth.

Dick had suggested going alone to see if he could buy some foodstuffs but Desmond had been even more adamant in his refusal to allow such foolhardiness. I think, on reflection, he was right, but it must have been a difficult decision to reach. We were already eating only once a day, and frugally at that, and if the coffee and sugar ran out the mornings would indeed be bleak and inhospitable.

" Well, Dick," I said, my mind going back to the store boxes smashed on the rocks near Tengyueh and the care I had taken to provide a balanced ration, enough for three weeks if necessary, " I think hunger will dictate our next move and at the first village we come to we must stock up."

" In this bloody countryside," he replied, " we shall be lucky if we find one with as much as a fowl to sell. In fact I doubt if there is even an inhabited hovel between here and the Salween." Dick bent down and gathered another piece of grass to suck.

" But we are supposed to be heading for a place called Shantao. And there's always my Luger if we see any game."

The thoughts of a haunch of venison seemed to cheer Dick and to keep him in this mood I told him of all the animals mentioned in Ronnie Kaulback's recently published book on the Salween, omitting to add that Ronnie and his companion, John Hanbury-Tracy, had been exploring the river's source in south-eastern Tibet, a hundred miles or more to the north of us. The book had reached me a few months before the Japanese war and I had devoured every word of it, picturing myself climbing in the snow to perhaps the greatest watershed in the world. How I had envied them in those days! We had met when I was stationed at Myitkyina. It must have been early in 1935 when they had passed through on a journey which was to last for eighteen months. Sponsored by the Royal Geographical Society in London, they had done a wonderful job. In fact, Ronnie was awarded the Murchison Grant for the contribution he had made to the Society.

Now our pathetic little party was making its slow and painful way towards the " Black and Angry " River, the sources of which they had described so vividly in the books *Salween* and *Black River of Tibet*. As I looked down at Dick's bare legs and tattered gym shoes tied together with pieces of string, I thought of the seventy-odd porters the expedition had used and the equipment they had carried, and I recalled the muscular and intellectual giant of a man who had led it.

Nevertheless, I knew that Dick with his indomitable spirit would somehow find the endurance necessary to cross the mountains; but what if Charles Ewing was forced to walk on his blistered heel? The real test was still to come. How would Richard Weldon fare? He too had courage, but his complaint was getting worse and I had noticed that every mile or so he would disappear into the bushes to squat and suffer the agony of dysentery. And we had not as much as a roll of toilet paper between us.

I should probably have gone on working myself into a state of dejection, but my thoughts were rudely interrupted and I had to jump aside to avoid being knocked down by Charles and his mule which came up from behind, seemingly out of control, in a kind of mad desperate scramble to reach the top of the small steep hillock we were ascending. Paddy and Stuart Gracey were behind it urging it on its way as it stumbled weakly up the rough rock-strewn pathway. Charles was hanging like a sack of coals round the animal's neck. But not for long.

As the mule breasted the rise it gave a great snort, stopped dead in its tracks, and I am afraid we all roared with laughter as poor Charles went over its head and landed in a heap on the ground, narrowly missing Angus who had turned just in time.

" Now the ' Heaven Born ' [1] really has toppled," said Angus, helping Charles to his feet. He was not hurt, and he seemed rather to enjoy the joke. We soon had him back in the saddle.

It is funny how a silly incident such as this can put new life into tired people, but this it succeeded in doing, and I thought no more about the prospects of starvation for the rest of the day.

We failed to reach Shantao that night. Around five o'clock the porters decided they had gone far enough that day and we halted in a deserted settlement consisting of some half-dozen broken-down huts. I imagine that in this type of barren country the few peasants to be found practised the Taungya system of cultivation as I recognised the familiar signs. It is a most wasteful method of providing foodstuff, yet it is to be found everywhere amongst primitive peoples. Trees are felled and burnt, the land scoffled and not more than two crops raised before the village is moved to another site and the process repeated. Hill rice had probably been grown round this village. Maybe we would be able to buy some at Shantao. The evil of the Taungya system is that it leads to erosion. Come the heavy rains and what is left of fertile soil is washed away and finally carried into the sea.

We were soon busy collecting firewood. The nights were getting colder with every step we climbed towards the main range. One more day to travel and we should reach the foothills of the Kaolikung Shan itself. Firewood was in plenty, even if food was not. We were going to need it.

I was chatting with Desmond when one of the most exciting episodes of our whole journey happened; I can vividly remember every detail of it.

There was a sudden uproar: the whole area of the deserted village seemed to be in a turmoil, shouts and yells coming from every direction. I felt for my Luger.

The light was going, and from where we stood by the fire

[1] The Indian Civil Service was commonly referred to as the " Heaven Born."

it was impossible to see what was going on in the belt of trees skirting our camp some hundred yards away.

We could vaguely make out the figures of our companions running first in this direction and then in that, shouting as they went.

The porters who had parked themselves in a hut some distance from us were rushing to the scene. Desmond and I stood glued to the ground, fascinated by what was happening. Not so Sheila; she was barking madly with excitement as she raced to join in the fun.

Everyone seemed to be forming a wide circle, and from time to time we saw a shadowy figure throw himself to the ground. They were coming nearer and nearer. Then Desmond let out a bellow of laughter; and I, rather sheepishly, put my pistol back in its holster.

It was a pig—a real live porker being cornered by a dozen desperate men determined that it should not escape the human cordon they had thrown around it.

I saw Angus make a dive at its legs as it twisted and turned in a mad rush to break the barrier. He missed; and it was Patrick's and Paddy's turn to hurl themselves forward in a joint attack, which also failed, and the pig made for the

porters who, knowing no other rules, just closed their ranks and barred the poor animal's passage to freedom.

It was then that Friday, looking for all the world like a pirate carrying his sword in his teeth as he boarded a "prize," dived into the fray with a ferocious roar and succeeded in getting a hold of one of the pig's legs, but it struggled free and jinking and turning made one last gallant attempt to get away. It turned full circle and made for a gap in the ranks, as only a pig can, and I really thought it was going to make it, as did we all.

We had not reckoned on Dick. He hurled himself forward in a low tackle, like a scrum half passing out, and he held on.

Dick and pig rolled over and over, and then the scrum took command. Friday drew his long knife, and it was all over.

Clearly the animal must have strayed, or possibly evaded capture, when the village had moved on, and being used to its environment had stayed and foraged in the vicinity until found grubbing peacefully in the earth by Patrick who had been the first to spot it amongst the trees.

I think everyone had a different version of how it was finally cornered, but there was no question about Dick's great tackle. Our porker was a half-grown chap weighing about thirty pounds or perhaps a bit more. Village pigs in Yunnan which have to fend for themselves cannot be compared with the fatted sty variety, and they are pretty lean.

Tough as it was going to be, it was real meat and, in our predicament, a salvation, but the problem was how to eke it out after we had taken our fill for supper.

It was the ever-practical Angus who furnished the answer. "Eating is a matter of habit," he said, pointing to the dead pig lying near the fire. "Some people like to eat a lot at a sitting and some people prefer to take a bite when they feel like it. I suggest we make a barbecue, give the trotters to the porters and then divide the cooked meat into ten portions so that everyone can please themselves and have their ration when it pleases them."

There was universal agreement, and in no time Friday was busy making a roasting spit and we all joined in. Even Charles Ewing and Richard Weldon seemed relaxed and happy. We had had a lot of fun and now there was going to be something solid to eat.

I sat down next to Charles and pulled his leg about falling off the mule and the crack Angus had made about the "Heaven Born."

"Just as well you don't belong to the Jewish faith, old boy, or you would be in a real dilemma," and I sniffed as the smell of cooking meat rose from the fire. "You know," I went on, "I swore to myself after seeing the pigs around the walls of Tengyueh feeding off human excrement I would never eat pork again, but I am going to enjoy my few rashers off this beauty."

Charles was already licking his lips in anticipation, for he really needed food and I am sure under normal circumstances was a great trencherman. He then revealed to me that he belonged to the Roman Church.

"Gordon," he said, "even if to-day is Friday I'm going to enjoy my piece of pork and ask forgiveness at my next confession."

And it was a Friday. Charles had a diary and every day made a few notes in it. I had no idea what day of the week it was and cared less.

Dick, who had done his turn at the spit, came over and joined us. "Look at them; you would think they had never had a square meal in their lives by the hungry look on their faces," and he pointed towards the willing helpers over the fire.

"I'll tell you what, Dick," I said, "I'm going to smoke my ration and take it along like biltong after a bite to-night. Have you any ideas about smoking pork?"

He hadn't and neither had anyone else, although Desmond insisted that biltong was fresh deer meat, heavily salted and then dried in the sun. He had never been to Africa but was quite certain that was the way it was cured and dried.

Anyway, I was determined to try and when my ration was doled out by Patrick I was quite content to have a nibble, and with the rest of the meat I set about smoking it as I imagined ham must be treated. But first, of course, Sheila was to have her bite. Everyone was spoiling her and parting with bits and pieces of their tiny rations. She was thin but well, and her ribs, though one could feel them all right, were largely hidden by her thick coat.

It was going to be nearly a week before she had another reasonable meal.

CHAPTER 12

The Kaolikung Shan Range

MAY 16TH

I WAS PLEASED WITH MY HAM-CURING EFFORTS. I HAD tied the strips of cooked meat to stakes placed up wind to the fire near enough to catch the wood smoke but far enough away to be safe from the flames. They had dried out during the night, and although somewhat dirty I was satisfied and they were easily handled and could be carried in my pocket.

I asked Charles to sample my cured pork and he took a chew and pronounced it to be excellent. " Bloody good stuff, Gordon; wish I had done the same."

I did not like to ask him whether he had any of his ration left, but I guessed that Angus had saved most of his as I had done.

The beginning of a day's march was always a thrill for me, and this was a special one as it would bring us to within striking distance of the great mountains towering ahead to heights of over 12,000 feet. From the distance they looked magnificent, though threateningly formidable. Other people had climbed them and so could we.

That was my mood as we set out that morning, and I was looking for adventure round every bend in the pathway we followed. Gone was the awful depression of yesterday, and I think the meal of pork had put new spirit into even the weaker members of our party.

At about 7000 feet we reached the village of Shantao. The hour was long before noon and we had been climbing steadily since breaking camp. I was up ahead with Desmond and Stuart when the cluster of dwellings came in sight, and I was cheered to see signs of cultivation on the hillsides all around, which was a change after the barren and deserted countryside through which we had been travelling.

The place had an air of permanency, rather like a well-used staging post, which indeed it was, and as we approached the villagers could be seen going about their everyday business unaware of the arrival of strangers in their midst.

Bustling up behind us came Dick, puffing a bit after his climb, but determined to be in the forefront to see what was going on.

We were now in the village street and Desmond was soon making our wants known to what must have been the elders who, on seeing us approaching, had gathered as if to greet us. They seemed friendly enough and, encouraged by the sight and jingle of a few silver coins, their trading instincts were clearly roused and with much gesticulation the business of buying foodstuffs began.

It was not just a case of going to a store and saying, "I'll have ten pounds of this or that," for no such place existed. Instead, like everything else I had seen in Yunnan, it was a long-drawn-out procedure of talk, talk, talk; head nodding and a form of mime. Time seemed to be of no object. Our porters had discarded their loads and with loud noises, as though haggling over prices, were also bent on making purchases on their own account. To those of us who knew not a word of the language, nor their customs, it was an exasperating and exaggerated piece of time-wasting. Either these people had something to sell or they hadn't, and it seemed hours before bits and pieces of what they were prepared to part with were displayed for our inspection. It was like the ceremonial opening of a community chest, this time presided over by an aged wispy-bearded relic of the village, who from time to time would send youngsters scurrying back to their parents' houses to cough up an additional egg or tray of grain, intent no doubt on that extra bit of commission he was going to collect as soon as our backs were turned. He gave the impression of knowing down to the last detail what was contained in every house in the village and he obviously held a position of high authority, judging by the way his orders were obeyed.

Desmond and Dick took it all for granted, in fact seemed to be enjoying every minute of the proceedings; to such an extent that they might have " belonged," to judge by the smiles and words of encouragement they were giving to the Master of Ceremonies as he wheedled the last drop of marketable produce out of his neighbours' houses.

This was rural China as they knew and understood it, though the rest of us found difficulty in concealing our impatience. At last the old bearded " collector of other people's goods " indicated that he was satisfied that the last drop of blood had been drawn and we were invited to inspect all that he had rummaged for our benefit. It was not much, but even a little was better than none at all. The market was open, and we all gathered around, even Charles with his sore heel. But he must have been disappointed by what was displayed before us.

There was hand-pounded hill rice, sufficient perhaps to feed us two meals, if used sparingly. There was slightly more of a finely sieved whitish flour which I took to be ground millet. There were some two dozen eggs of doubtful age and a plate of sugary-looking stuff which I recognised as the crude jaggery made in the Burma hills by the Shans and used as a sweetener. Ranged nearby were quite a few rissole-like cakes which I later discovered were made from the soya bean, but what gladdened my heart most were some coarse turnips, complete with their blue-green tops as if they had just been lifted from the soil. Apart from my tobacco I had missed vegetables more than anything else.

The display was topped off by a fair quantity of walnuts in their shells and some tubers which resembled artichokes. There was no sign of meat or fowls.

With a wave of his hand Desmond bought the lot and probably paid a hundred times what the assortment was worth, but at least we had something to sustain us.

At this stage it was the porters who intrigued me, as they clamoured to take as their share of the purchases the artichoke tubers, ignoring all else. Later on Desmond explained that these were some form of edible root much favoured by coolies. This particular variety had in all probability been found at much higher altitudes, possibly above the snow-line, and they were believed to possess aphrodisiac qualities.

We were soon on the way, the porters refreshed by the odd pipe of opium they had smoked during our shopping expedition which must have taken up at least two hours of our precious time.

Watching the unsteady gait of the mule we had purchased for Charles to ride, I could see that it was nearing journey's end. Dick was quite right. It might be good for another twenty miles or so, but just at a time when it would most be needed I doubted whether it would be strong enough to walk, let alone carry any weight, particularly in the country we were about to enter.

To-morrow we should have to face the first stage of the ascent of Mamien Khyet, rising to nearly 12,000 feet, and in all probability we should have to spend three days in the mountain passes before descending to the Salween.

All that afternoon we plodded on along a rough track which wound along the hillsides, sometimes taking us steeply upwards and then, with surprising suddenness, leading us into valleys which blotted out all views other than the immediate landscape of sparse tree-clad, rocky and inhospitable slopes that closed us in, shutting out any remnants of the fast disappearing sunlight. We marched in silence, now in single file as the pathway narrowed and took us down into a deep gorge, where the air was chill and all around seemed mysteriously damp, dark and uninviting.

In places the pathway had become a series of stepping-stones taking us from one watercourse to another, and in the distance was the sound of water cascading from the hills above us into rocky pools hidden from our view by the tangled undergrowth which now blocked our way.

Friday had gone ahead to slash a passage through the overhanging vegetation with his machete-like knife, and Angus and I joined him to help clear the way for the porters and the rest of the party travelling slowly some few hundred yards behind us; this was the type of jungle we were used to. Overgrown as the track was it must be leading somewhere, as the stepping-stones had been laid by the hands of men, though clearly no caravan had passed this way for a long time.

Mile after mile we snaked our way along the foot of this seemingly unending gorge, tunnelling our way through the vegetation, until, rounding a sharp turn of the path, we knew that a matter of a few paces would see us clear of it. Shafts of sunlight lit the gorge exit and we hurried forward, eager to see what lay beyond.

Never shall I forget my first close-up view of the Kaolikung Shan Range as seen in the setting sun that late afternoon. The effect was dramatic, and I sensed that Angus felt as I did. He nudged me, and we stood speechless, our eyes held by the scene.

Stretching into infinity, as it seemed, these mountains stood stark and forbidding before us, and we had to raise our eyes high into the sky, so close were the nearer peaks to where we stood.

Frightening, yes, but magnificent. All aglow with fire, each range seemed higher and more formidable than the first; it was fantastically beautiful. While we stood in silence the sun must have dipped and disappeared behind us; we watched its glory of colour which contained our mountains to the east gradually fading and giving way to the more sombre hues of twilight. We were alone with our thoughts.

For twelve long days we had been travelling: facing us now was the real test of our determination to survive, etched sharply against an evening backcloth of a sky full of reflected colours. Was it possible for men to cross these mountains?

What a picture it would have made had we carried a camera! The gorge had brought us out on to a ledge which made a perfect setting for the panorama of mountains beyond. Sheila stood, as if posing, on the very edge of a cliff face. I saw her ears prick and I knew that the main party was approaching.

For some reason, I had no desire to share with the others what Angus and I had seen so vividly a few minutes earlier. I think he felt the same way, as he was strangely quiet all that evening.

The porters found a way down from the ledge with the uncanny instinct they possess and, sheltered under its protecting roof, we made camp for the night by the side of a stream.

Desmond was quite sure we had taken the wrong route, which indeed we had, although it had brought us to the mountain range we had to climb. The most intelligent of our porters, who claimed to have travelled this way before, insisted that he knew the path all the way to the Salween. He did, but not until later did we discover that through the gorge and upwards to Mamien Khyet, by his route, was far from being the one in regular use. It was, in fact, an old smugglers' track between the two great rivers, one that ignored contours and went straight up and straight down.

It had been a long weary day, and its effects showed on the faces of the party and in the lethargic way in which the chores of making camp were entered into. There were jobs to do, firewood had to be collected, boxes undone and many other tasks to be performed before we could finally rest and sleep.

The usual stalwarts, Friday, Patrick and Stuart Gracey, bore the brunt of it uncomplainingly, as they always did, and I fear the rest of us contributed little worthwhile.

Desmond and Dick were deep in conversation with the porters. Charles Ewing lay stretched out with his head against a rock, thankful to be off the back of his mule after a day in a saddle which was made of wood. Richard Weldon would disappear for a few minutes, return with a piece of fuel in his arms and then collapse from sheer exhaustion. The rest of us pretended to be busy but accomplished little. I was conscious of having retreated into a private shell of my own within which all was my business. I was not the least bit companionable, and all I could think about was the sight of the mountains and my urge to accept their challenge.

It was not a happy evening, and even Friday's complaint, that he had not the faintest idea how to cook and serve the fine sieved flour, brought forth little response.

We had food, yet not the will nor the wish to eat, and one after another we retreated under our blankets. I bit off a piece of my special biltong and chewed it and Sheila had some with me. Within minutes I was fast asleep with Dick, equally exhausted, lying beside me, and Sheila between us comforting us both with her warmth and her affection.

CHAPTER 13

The Mule Dies

MAY 17TH

DAWN WAS BARELY BREAKING WHEN I AWOKE STIFF with cold, and leaving Dick well tucked up in the blanket I set about making up the fire which had all but died during the night. I think this was the first time I had beaten Friday to his self-appointed task of being first up every morning and I was determined to exploit it to the full.

Sheila, who had given herself a good stretch and a shake, then trotted off on her own private affairs, but came back to rejoin me. Between us we planned a surprise breakfast for the bodies still dead to this world; Friday lay back snoring loudly, still clasping his knife even in sleep.

Only the mule, hobbled nearby, was awake to greet the dawn with us. The poor beast looked cold and starved, and my mind went back to my boyhood and the sight and smell of warm bran mash being served up at night in the livery stables which had been just over the fence at the bottom of our garden in Sussex. Early in the 1914 war the hunters normally kept there had been replaced by remounts preparing to go to France, but they had all been the same to me and over my tender years I had become part of the stables, escaping there whenever opportunity offered. It was there I had learned to ride.

Suddenly the answer to Friday's cooking problem came to me. Bran mash for the mule and porridge for us. That was how the millet flour could be used, and what better to start the day with!

151

Looking at the towering heights above our camp, I knew we should need every bit of extra energy we could muster. True that we had grown accustomed to climbing into the hills, but now the whole course of our journey had changed and we were faced with a mountaineering task calling for skill as well as endurance. Even at this altitude the morning air was cold and the occasional gusts of wind which swept the valleys tingled round my bare knees though my body was warm under the thick grey army shirt I was fortunate enough to be wearing.

By the time I had collected water from the stream our party was grouped round the fire seeking its warmth, and not far away the porters were busy with their own early morning tasks. Judging by the noise they were making, they were engaged in heated argument.

Everyone approved the idea of making porridge which could be sweetened with the sugary cakes we had purchased and Friday was soon busy with his pots and pans.

Desmond shouted to the Yunnanese telling them to make less noise, but as they took no notice he walked over to their fire, where by now it looked as if a fight was going to develop. We were soon to know the worst.

It was a grim-faced Desmond who rejoined us after about five minutes. "Bad news, I am afraid," he said, making signs with his hands as if to say, "I give up." "Only two of the men will go any farther and the others want to be paid off. There is nothing we can do about it. I know these people, and nothing will make them budge another inch—something to do with bad people and spirits in the mountains. Fortunately the old boy is game—the rascal who knows the way—and he has persuaded one of the others to go as far as the Salween with him."

I remembered Desmond's warning that this might happen, and I could see that the news came as no shock to him. He had started out prepared to carry his blanket and some food on his own back and now he was going to do it.

Dick swore, and his pugnacious bearded jaw stuck out. For a moment I thought he was going to say that no bloody coolie would disobey him, or that a stronger line on Desmond's part would have had a different result, but he restrained himself and shrugging his shoulders, spat out the grass he was chewing.

"Well, that's that, chaps," he said, "now we know the form, let's get cracking," and he made as if to walk away with a large empty pot on his shoulder.

That was typical of Dick and by this simple act of foolery he eased the tension that was building up.

"Breakfast is 'sarved,' gentlemen," roared the irrepressible Friday as he stirred the porridge. He had captured the mood of his master and was not to be outdone.

The meal was more akin to gruel than porridge though it tasted good, but what appealed to me even more was my first sample of the soya bean cakes which Patrick shared out amongst us. After a nibble I put the remainder with my "biltong" which fitted nicely into a handkerchief in my pocket.

Our start was of course delayed, and it seemed to take hours to sort out and pick and choose what should be taken and what should be abandoned. Finally it was decided that the two porters would carry the minimum in the way of pots and pans plus such stores as remained from Desmond's boxes. Each of us would carry, in bundles wrapped in blankets or canvas ground sheets, all that remained of the newly purchased food and the bits and pieces we had accumulated. All boxes and heavy items, such as cooking pots, were to be discarded.

It was left to Patrick to demonstrate how each roll should be carefully bundled and slung over one shoulder and secured at the opposite hip, or thereabouts. When the mule had been fed, and I had had a slight argument with Charles who would insist that he could walk and carry his share of the load, we set off, thus festooned, hardly daring to look ahead to what lay in store for us that day.

"Don't be so damned silly, Charles," I had said. "Even

if you can keep that heel of yours off the ground for another few miles, it's going to make all the difference and there's still a hell of a way to go." And I helped heave his bulk on to the wooden contraption that served as a saddle, and the mule staggered under the weight of its reluctant rider as it joined the queue making its way to the high mountains.

Poor Charles Ewing was no longer the fat, amusing intellectual of a fortnight ago. All the cut and thrust of his humour in conversation had been left far behind in our wake. To him every hour of our journey must have been purgatory, and the mental strain, coupled with his inability to endure the physical hardship which our daily routine demanded, had taken its toll. He was going steadily downhill and was by now near to utter despair. His whole appearance was mournful and melancholy. Even his great black beard had an air of sad unwashed neglect, and such was his weariness and so low his spirit that not even the sound of water, straight from the hills tumbling down into a rocky pool by our camp site would stir him into wakefulness after a night's sleep.

I knew that he was suffering the agony of mind of one all too conscious of the fact that he was a burden to his fellow men. His growing hostility towards Desmond and the latter's obvious contempt for his fellow intellectual made matters worse. Not that either of them ever spoke about the other; I wish they had and perhaps told each other what bastards they were. At least we would have understood that. Instead they ignored each other, and the gap between them grew wider every day.

So ran my thoughts as we set forth on the smugglers' path to which our Yunnanese guide had led us. Slowly we began to climb, nearly vertically in places, up a series of steps which seemed to have been carved out of living rock, though they must have been a natural geological formation.

Later on it was as if we had disappeared into the bowels of the mountain itself and were ascending a blind lift-shaft, groping our way upwards with the help of the trellis of vines which, dank and evil-smelling as they were, did at least provide the hand holds we needed to give us support. Water ran down the rock faces we clambered over and all signs of sunlight had been blotted out.

There was no question of forging ahead to reach the top in one wild burst of energy. The top was days away. This was the great divide between the Shweli and the Salween, and it had to be conquered rung by rung. First a step or two and then a pause to take a deep breath, gather strength and take a grip for the next surge upwards. Then a moment of rest before getting a foothold on the next " rung."

And so, leaving the comparative peace of the Shweli Valley behind us, we hoisted our way towards the mountain peaks which Angus and I had seen the previous day in the sunset.

Now it was all different. As if down a deep mine, we were climbing first one stope and then another with nothing in view but the bowed figure of whoever was in front, as he puffed, blowed and sometimes cursed his way upwards foot by foot, the unaccustomed load on his back now falling over his shoulder and seconds later trailing round his rump. At least that is what mine was doing. As I reached forward to take a grip of the undergrowth the bundle would slip and my free arm would have to be engaged holding it in place as I hauled with the other.

This was not too easy for me, as my right shoulder was a mess of tied-up sinews and some four and twenty stitch marks left there by a famous bone surgeon in London a few years before.

Those of us who had worked in the teak forests knew something about hill climbing but this was different. I knew that to hasten and tire quickly would be foolish. I would go up at my own pace. Already out of breath, I halted and leaning against a large boulder waited for the last of the party to catch up.

As soon as I saw them I knew that they needed help. Paddy and Stuart Gracey were literally pushing the mule from behind so that it could carry its burden another few paces forward. Charles was slumped over the animal's neck and I could see that Paddy was far from being in good shape. Fortunately at that moment Patrick appeared. I think he had waited to see how I was getting on. So leaving him to give Paddy a hand, I joined Stuart and between us we shoved from the rear with such force that the poor unfortunate animal had no choice but to move blindly onwards and upwards.

Stuart was superbly fit, but I was soon in a bath of sweat and could feel my heart beating overtime. Up and up we went for what seemed hours until I was on the verge of collapsing on the pathway. This might have happened had we gone much farther, but fate intervened. As we breasted a rise we came out at last in to a sunlit, grassy open space on the mountain side. There were the others stretched out beneath a wall of cliff face which blocked our way. It must have been all of a thousand feet high and there seemed no way up.

Somehow we hauled Charles off his mule, which tottered and then fell. At last we were lying in the fresh clear sunlight, recovering. Even Sheila was gasping for breath.

The glorious mountain air was like a tonic and it was bliss to be in the open again. Slowly we revived.

Far below I could make out the route we must have followed through the gorge the previous day, and in the far distance I could pick out the valley of the Shweli. I could see that we had left behind us the rain forest of the foothills and lower slopes of the mountain range and had ascended to a type of country with which I was quite unfamiliar. It was a mixture of bamboo and stunted pine trees, the presence of which indicated that we must be near the 10,000-foot level and the snow-line, although none could be seen on the surrounding peaks.

It was a new and exciting experience for me as before setting off I had never been higher than five thousand feet.

Stuart who had climbed in the Alps and in Scandinavia was in his element. Desmond was also an experienced climber and I could see them debating how best to tackle the cliff face which had halted us. All I wanted to do was laze and relax in the afternoon sunshine and when I heard the verdict that we would camp there for the night I was pleased.

Stuart and the old guide were to go ahead and reconnoitre while the light remained and they were soon lost to sight.

Making camp was now a simple matter, because apart from gathering firewood there was nothing to do but spread a blanket. What little food remained would have to be carefully husbanded. I was being like a miser with my " biltong " and soya cake and would only allow myself an occasional nibble and a bite for Sheila. Fortunately water was in abundance. Here on this promontory it flowed crystal clear, fed by the hill above, and while exploring, not far from where we had dumped our loads, I found a shower cubicle carved by nature out of the rocks. It was a perfect place to bathe but when I stripped the water was like ice and I was glad of the warm sunshine after the shock treatment of the shower.

This was the first day in our travels that we had halted so early and everyone was taking advantage of the relaxation. Patrick was busy showing the others how to make drinking cups from some large bamboos he had cut with Friday's knife, whilst Friday himself was busy weaving a new pair of shoes for Dick from thin strips of a pliant variety of cane he had found growing on the way up the mountain. If only Charles had been able to drag himself from his own thoughts and join with the others during this period of leisure. . . . Instead he brooded.

Dick and I wandered off together in the direction Stuart had taken and took stock of the position as we saw it.

" You know, Gordon," said Dick, now in one of his more serious moods, " at this rate it's going to take us a week to reach the Salween and after to-morrow there will be no food left." I sensed his impatience; under different circumstances,

I knew, he would have found a way over the barrier of rock in our path and marched on until the evening. He hated any form of delay.

"God knows how Charles is going to make out," he went on. "That poor bloody animal is dying and to-morrow he will have to walk. I suggest he goes ahead with Desmond and they sort each other out in Latin or Greek, or whatever bloody language these chaps argue in."

"Did you see the look Charles gave Desmond just now?"

"Why in hell's name can't they behave like ordinary humans instead of intellectual prima donnas? Maybe they will when they starve together," added Dick bitterly, and went on: "Sorry, chum, I shouldn't have said that, but they do get my goat."

Dick was back on his old theme about the difference between the business world and that of the diplomat or administrator. He had a phobia about the Civil Services, as I well recalled from our weeks together in Burma, but whereas he could tell a red-faced Brigadier that he was a fool, he knew as well as I did that Desmond had halted us this day in the full knowledge that Charles could not have travelled any farther.

This was the tragedy of the relationship between two men who might have been friends: every act of kindness or under-standing on the part of Desmond, our leader, was interpreted by Charles as a blow below the belt, aimed particularly at him. There was simply nothing we could do about it and I told Dick so.

"You are right, Gordon," said Dick, "they hate each other's guts for some reason. So the sooner we reach Kunming the better." And the very mention of the word seemed to transform Dick into a new person—his old self—and I visualised him sending cables to his family in India to tell them he was safe and well. Hard business man he might be, but thoughts of them seemed to drive him on to heights even beyond his normal capabilities.

I looked down at his bare legs and the pathetic bits of canvas which served him as shoes and knew I was lucky to be in the company of such a man. It was only on rare occasions as this that we scratched beneath the surface of our relationship. Friendly it was but neither deep nor destined to be lasting, yet between us there was perhaps something even more important —a sense of mutual trust and confidence.

Dick was a dynamic fellow; his strength stemmed from sources quite different from mine. I was the complete dilettante to his way of thinking and, although trained like an athlete and in far better condition than he was, I think he wrote me off as a dreamer more interested in the colour or smell of a wild flower, or the lights and shades of sunset or sunrise, than in the serious business of survival.

He was not quite right: it was from the very beauty of nature itself that I drew my strength and it sustained me in just the same way as Stuart found his comfort in prayer. This is how we differed and even as we stood there together I could hardly wait to see the shadows lengthen and the sun dip until we should be privileged observers of its going down.

Our camp site was magnificently placed to see to the fullest advantage the setting of the sun against a background of mountains. The view faced due west and from the bluff on which we sheltered only the hills and valleys in that direction could be seen as the cliff face above us blotted out all else to the north and east of us.

Already the sun was capping the higher peaks which had barred our way. I knew that never again would I see what Angus and I had seen in that brief kaleidoscope of reflected colour. Its sheer beauty had been unreal and now I was going to see the whole picture in reverse and I waited expectantly for what was to follow.

With startling suddenness the sky became so aflame that it hurt the eyes to look towards the west. It was sensational, but harsh and crude in its intense glare compared with the scene I had shared yesterday with Angus. Then gradually the fiery glow gave way to softer hues and Dick and I stood there and watched the end of another day on our way to freedom. It seemed that we formed part of the landscape and I felt near to Dick at that moment as never before.

"You know, Dick," I said to the man beside me who stood with legs apart and chest stuck out in a typical Winter posture, "I believe you may be quite wrong about it taking us a whole week to reach the Salween. Once over that hump we may find the going much easier. I have read quite a lot about these parts and if I am right we may find ourselves to-morrow in gently undulating countryside and be able to travel all day through lush pastures with soft turf beneath our feet instead of a rock path."

I even convinced myself that the picture I was painting was not a product of my imagination. "Here we are on the threshold of a botanist's paradise, and it's spring! Just think, expeditions from all over the world have been coming to these mountains for years at great expense to see the flowers which will be ours for the picking—and free at that. You and I are going to have fun gathering posies and posting them to our wives in every red letter-box we find between here and the Salween!"

My foolish remark hit the right note and Dick was still posting his bouquets to India when Stuart appeared with his Yunnanese guide.

"I have brought you a present," he said, not in the least fatigued by his exploration up the mountain. And in his hand was a bunch of gentians, some pale and others as dark as undiluted cobalt blue straight from the tube. In fact his hand looked like a palette with the flowers he had picked to show us.

"The route isn't difficult," Stuart went on. "About a quarter of a mile beyond here is a shoulder which leads to the top and the countryside gets easier beyond. I didn't like to go too far in case the light went, but it's attractive and quite different from this."

"There you are, Dick. It's just as I said!" And with this

welcoming news we made our way back to the fire. The sun gone, there was already a chilly feeling in the air.

Friday produced a strange meal that night of rice and tasteless turnips, but this was compensated by the smell of pine cones and the burning wood on the fire. Even Charles seemed to come out of his shell, and instead of a proper meal we told stories before turning in to sleep.

CHAPTER 14

A Rhododendron Forest

MAY 18TH

DICK WAS QUITE RIGHT. DURING THE NIGHT THE mule had died, and I think Charles was only too pleased to escape the torture of his wooden saddle and to be back on his feet. His heel was no longer sore; in fact both our invalids were in better shape than a few days previously. Whether it was our near-starvation diet that had cured Richard Weldon's dysentery or the altitude, I do not know. Unfortunately it was to recur in an even more severe form when we reached the Salween.

The night had been cold and so was our morning shower. We had neither tea nor coffee left, so no time was wasted getting on the road, but I must admit that I missed a hot drink even more than the absence of anything to eat but scraps.

Stuart led us over the traverse he had found, and climbing up the next thousand feet was less tiring than had been the ordeal of yesterday. Our pace was a slow one but it was steady going and within a couple of hours we were over the top and entering into more open country at about 11,000 feet.

The beauty of the high mountains acted on me like champagne; the very air was effervescent and I filled my lungs with it, breathing in and then out, rather like an old man doing his morning exercises. I thought of the horror of the Assam route, where by now the heavy monsoon rains would have set in, engulfing the struggling remnants of refugees I had seen at Myitkyina and down the rail at Mogaung; and

I wondered how my dear old Commandant and his companion were faring in the hills, whether they were better off than we were.

We might be verging on starvation but we were free; our light packs were our only burden.

The whole countryside was changing with every mile we travelled, alternating between stretches of pine woods and grassy meadowlands. It was just as I had described it to Dick and, seeing him ahead, I fear I boasted and reminded him of my forecast which had proved so correct.

"By God, you were right, Gordon," said the indomitable Dick, sucking away at his straw. "This is just the job for my brand of footwear," and he danced a jig on the soft turf under our feet.

Not many paces in front of us Desmond and Stuart were in the lead setting the pace for our party which I knew would have been a much faster one had they been alone. Yet this day I had no urge to race ahead. All round was too lovely, and the feel of spring was in the air. We were climbing again up an easy slope, and at the top of it I saw Desmond pointing, his arm outstretched. He turned and waved us on. There was a sense of urgency in his beckoning and we broke into a trot to see what was worth so much attention.

The hilltop commanded a glorious view of the valley below and there, stretched out before us and as far as the eye could see, was a breathtaking panorama of colour. We were looking down at our first glimpse of a rhododendron forest and it was one of the most fantastic views I shall ever see, for the trees were in full bloom.

Not a word was said. All we could do was stand and stare: Nature seemed almost to have arrayed herself to bid us welcome.

It was like a giant Persian carpet covering both sides of the valley; a riot of scarlet, creams, pinks, and varying shades of mauve mingled with white. A slight breeze ruffled the canopy of blossoms mixing one hue with another, and we were close enough to see that the slopes in the immediate foreground were scattered with flowers, like confetti thrown down at the feet of a bride. It was unbelievably beautiful and made every weary mile we had travelled well worth the effort, for it had been our good fortune to reach this place in time to see the trees in their full glory. They were not the shrubs of an English garden but a real forest of trees, and we were going to walk into it and perhaps sleep there.

This paradise belonged so much to Nature that I had a feeling of being an intruder. It was a private land which had deliberately been hidden far from men.

We gathered our bundles and in silence went down into the valley of flowers. The sight had affected us all.

The distant view of this parade of rhododendrons in their full dress was more than matched by what we found on descending into the forest itself. Beneath the magnificent umbrella of colour we had viewed from above, we discovered azaleas growing in all shades and colours, and beneath these was spread a carpet of pink and yellow primulas, bursting out of the soil to greet the warmth of spring after months buried deep under the snow. Blue gentians peeped out of rocky crevices, and here and there stood pine trees to add a touch of dark colour to an array so rich that it was almost embarrassing in its grandeur.

No artist's brush could have done full justice to this fairyland. There was too much on display at the same time; too many combinations of colour. It had to be seen the way Nature meant it to be and in no other.

We were privileged, and I am still grateful, that our journey, hard as it was, had brought us in the springtime to the high mountains of Western Yunnan. Now I know why some of the world's most famous botanists had described Yunnan as a paradise; why over the years there had always been money forthcoming to finance expeditions into this faraway place; perhaps why Forrest had died and lay buried at Tengyueh.

I felt woefully ignorant on the subject and my knowledge was so elementary that I could identify only the common flowers I have described. This was indeed a pity as every footstep we took seemed to uncover something new.

Only Desmond amongst us had previously seen the rhododendrons in bloom, and as we ceased to wonder and walked on he told me of a journey he had made through Kashmir into Chinese Turkestan to be Consul in that remotest of all outposts where the frontier of Russia marches with that of China.

And so finally we left behind us the blossom and the faint scent I had discovered as coming from the primulas (for the rhododendrons have no smell) and climbed out of the valley of memories into a countryside which was constantly changing.

With the going now reasonably easy it was imperative that we take full advantage of it whilst we had the strength, as it was most unlikely that any food would be found until the Salween was reached, and it was still a long way off.

One thing which had surprised me in the valley we had explored was the absence of bird life. I had expected to find masses of honey birds and the like feeding from the flowers, but there had been none, only bees which abounded and on one occasion a swarm had passed over, too close for my liking.

It had been different in the foothills of the range; there I had seen giant hornbills working amongst the tall trees and quite a variety of bird life which had helped while away the time in watching their flight and listening to their song. Now I was all set to catch my first sight of a pheasant which I knew had its natural habitat in these hills.

It was the excitement of hoping to see something new or interesting round every corner that helped me along our way and I was sorry for those who found no pleasure in such things and just plodded on and on in deep thought and, if one was to judge by their bearing, hating every footstep until camp was reached.

By now Sheila was beginning to feel the effects of lack of food, although she never complained. But instead of roaming off on her own to nose into a bush or chase some object, real or imaginary, she stayed at heel, keeping at the same time a wary eye on every member of the party. From time to time she would stop to make certain that everyone was in line, as if it were her job to round them up should they fall. In this respect she was like a working sheep dog, and with her eyes she talked to me and to Desmond who was her special favourite.

We were all losing weight rapidly, but for some reason I could join in a conversation about the food we would eat when the time came without feeling hungry in the least. Sheila and I still had a little of my bacon left in my pocket and this we shared in tiny nibbles. It did help sustain us but it was not much, and unless we found something to eat within the next day or so the situation would be desperate. Fortunately water was everywhere and I could drink it by the gallon when thirsty.

Towards evening the pleasant country we had been passing through came to an end and the scene changed from grassy slopes and pines to rock and stunted trees—in complete contrast to the beauty of the morning. We had travelled far that day in spite of the interlude amongst the rhododendrons and now everyone was tired. We threw down our packs by a mountain stream in which we bathed our feet in the cold water. This was a nightly ritual we had instituted from the first day of our journey and it had paid dividends—a kind of chiropodic shock treatment for weary travellers.

Gone now were the chores involved in the preparation of food which had previously set the party in motion to collect firewood and make ready for Friday's culinary efforts. There was nothing to cook, and as we were too weary to talk there was nothing in view but sleep, if it would come, and thoughts of to-morrow and what it would hold for us. A fire there had to be as the chill of the evening at more than 11,000 feet was already apparent and the night was going to be bitterly cold with only a rock for a mattress, half a blanket as covering

and boots or shoes for a pillow. It was a lethargic bunch of
men led by Stuart, Patrick and Friday who went in search
of fuel, but at last we had a blaze and a pile of timber in
reserve for the long night it was going to be.

Dick's shoe problem was now getting really acute, and in
spite of Friday's enthusiastic attempt at cobbling a new pair
from plaited cane the result had been disappointing, and Dick
preferred his tattered canvas. Unfortunately every bit of
string and cord had been used up and but for Patrick he would
have been barefoot. My young assistant remembered his
jungle training and the lessons he had learned from our
elephant men, who, selecting heavy bark from certain species
of trees, would pare it away and from the lower layers produce
the pads and thongs needed to keep their charges' harnesses
held tight to their bodies. On the march Patrick would keep
on the lookout for such trees and, cutting the bark away with
Friday's knife, would gather sufficient lengths of the under
fibres to hold Dick's shoes in place for the duration of yet
another day's march. He would leave these thongs soaking
overnight in a running stream and by morning they would be
strong and supple and ready for use.

As darkness gathered I crawled under the blanket I shared
with Dick, and Sheila, and tried to sleep.

CHAPTER 15

Over the Top

MAY 19TH

IT WAS SOON APPARENT WHEN WE STARTED OUT IN THE morning that we had reached the " great divide " between the Shweli and the Salween and the route took us up over rough country to around 12,000 feet. It was slow going and some of the knife-edged ridges we had to cross were frightening, particularly to me, as I have always had a horror of heights. They were less than two feet wide and on either side there was a sheer drop of hundreds of feet.

My first attempt to traverse one of these ridges, which was no more than fifty feet in length, nearly ended in disaster because half-way across Stuart, who was immediately in front of me, stopped to look at the view and I had to shout to him to hurry as the only way I could travel at heights such as this was to run with my eyes fixed rigidly straight ahead. To have looked down would have been fatal, as I could not cross a short twelve-inch-wide plank over a fenland dyke ten feet deep, without the urge to fall off it.

I decided that I must confess my fear of heights; it was the only thing to do. Thereafter, with Stuart ahead and Desmond behind, I managed, and they gave me such confidence that before the morning was through, I apparently insisted on walking quite nonchalantly over one of these obstacles. They did not seem to bother the other members of the party, but I was truly terrified and made no bones about it. Even my one act of showmanship left me with trembling legs once it was over and I made no attempt to repeat it. Fortunately these knife ridges were never longer than a hundred feet, generally much less.

It was at the end of one of these balancing excursions that we saw in a deep ravine a sight which for sheer beauty equalled our first sight of the rhododendrons in full bloom though in quite a different way.

The hillsides to the right and left of us were studded with dark-foliaged pines, and weaving between the trees ran rivulets of water, crystal clear in places and in others the colour of turbulent froth as they cascaded and tumbled over rocks and falls into the depths and darkness below.

Here and there shafts of sunlight found their way down the mountain, and in one place, as if a spotlight had been turned on them, there grew great clusters of tall blue and yellow irises, heads held high as if growing out of the water itself.

The scene at our feet was indeed a subject for palette and brush. The light and shade of dark trees flanking the banks of the valley; sparkling sunlit water, columns of spray as if thrown up from a fountain, and above all the two vividly contrasting colours of the flowers growing in profusion against a sombre background of rocky crags.

The temptation was too much. Stuart insisted that he must climb down to get a closer view of the irises, and as it was midday we decided to rest for a while. I went with him.

It was worth the little extra effort, and we had our reward. Starved of food we might be, but not of beauty, for here we found it in plenty. The plants were as virile and strong as the colours were brilliant. They grew along the stream banks grouped as irises should be in any garden, a clump here and there, a gap filled by water, rushes or plants, then a clump of bamboo and then more irises, this time covered in spray from a rock pool where the waters of two streams joined forces in their race to the river below.

" We must already be in the drainage basin of the Salween," I said to Stuart, puffing my way up the steep side of the hill we had descended. "What do you think of our chances of reaching it in a couple of days?"

His strong hand reached down to give me a pull up over some slippery rocks, and he paused for a moment before replying. "It's not going to be easy, Gordon. I must say that Charles's condition worries me a bit; but with God's help we will make it."

As he looked down towards me, his face had the look of serenity and confidence of someone who has absolute faith. For Stuart each day was a new adventure and whatever its pitfalls he would glory in it; in this he was unlike the others. To Angus, Dick and Richard the journey was no more than a means to an end and they were cheerful about it; Paddy tended to curse his bad luck; Patrick and Friday took it in their stride without thinking much about it; Desmond was sufficient to himself, even aloof when it came to expressing his feelings; and to poor Charles every day was purgatory.

I found Charles stretched out in the sunshine, rather apart from the rest, so I sat down beside him to recover from the climb.

"What about that for a bit of colour, Charles?" I asked him. "Aren't you glad now to have seen all this? I can see you now at the Chelsea Flower Show looking rather superior and saying to your chums, 'Well, yes, nice enough in their cultivated state, but if you had seen the rhododendrons, azaleas and irises as I saw them at 11,000 feet in Western Yunnan, you really would have seen something. Kew isn't in it'."

It was of no avail. Charles heaved his bulk into a sitting position and said, "Maybe you are right, old boy, but don't you think that the Creator might at least have matched the colours of the rhododendrons with equally exotic scents? And I don't suppose those irises you two madmen have been down to see have any either."

They had not, of course.

My attempts at friendly chaffing had no effect on Charles.

Perhaps I should not have been surprised: he was hungry, tired and mentally ill and certainly needed helping along, but it was not easy for him to accept the fact.

" Come, Charles, it's time to push on to the ' Black and Angry,'" I said, helping him into a standing position. " The others are already on their way. If we have luck we will be there to-morrow."

I do not know whether Stuart had offered up a prayer for help, but it came within a mile of the valley of the irises in the shape of wild raspberries. All along the wayside they grew in quantities; great big luscious fruits of fine flavour, ripe for the picking and sufficient to feed a company ten times our number.

The joy of eating again, even if it was only fruit! They were our salvation, for we found them all that day and the next, and although not to be recommended as an exclusive diet, they did serve their purpose; and they were good for our teeth. Or so my dentist told me when I told him of our days of starvation.

Unfortunately Sheila, who normally would take anything I offered her, refused to be a raspberry-eating dog and no amount of persuasion on my part would change her mind. It must have been agony for her to watch her companions —for she was very much one of us—gorging themselves with food. Her misery showed in her face, so I parted with the pathetic remnant of the dried pig meat which I had been carrying as a strategic reserve, wrapped in my one and only handkerchief. At least I could now wash it at our next halting place.

We had clearly crossed over the divide and were heading downhill towards the Salween. The going was far from easy and, noticing that Charles was limping his way amongst the rocks, I joined him again only to find, as I had suspected, that his heel was bothering him again and would be bound to get worse as the march dragged on. He did not complain, but I sensed that he was cursing under his breath. He looked ragged and unkempt, even compared with the rest of us, which I put down to the fact that he had started out on the journey badly in need of a hair-cut and, being one of those dark, heavily-bearded people, his hair sprouted in such profusion that the tangled mass from above reached down to meet the rapidly growing fungus round his face. To improve the effect, Charles wore a bush hat, an Anglicised version of a Stetson which did not suit his high domed forehead at all; and so, although we all looked like scarecrows, his appearance was quite outstandingly bizarre.

The Salween was now only one day's march away, thank goodness, but Desmond, ever cautious, had not raised our hopes of food too high, and had confessed to me in private that although he knew the valley to be populated, there was no telling what we might find. He knew his China far too well to make such predictions with any confidence.

Until late afternoon we forged our way ahead, but progress was slow, and going downhill seemed worse than climbing up. It was a terrible night, we were unquestionably too exhausted to sleep. Everything was an effort, even the washing of my handkerchief when we found some shelter. The wood some of us managed to collect for the fire was damp and refused to burn and, to add to our discomfort, and low morale, the wind got up and whipped around every corner of where we lay amongst the rocks. It was the first time we had experienced a strong wind after sunset; hitherto we had not met with anything more than a gentle breeze.

We had not the strength to move or even to talk. To make matters worse Charles began to moan as if in a fever. We were all restless, including Friday who I am sure could have slept standing up, had it been necessary. But this night he tossed and turned and joined Charles in an unearthly chorus of groaning. Even Sheila, who was normally so still and comforting, was unhappy. It was with a real relief that I saw the first rays of sunlight in the east from where I lay on my back, half awake, cold and miserable.

CHAPTER 16

The Customs Party

MAY 20TH

IT SEEMED TO TAKE AN AGE BETWEEN THE FIRST SIGN of dawn and its real awakening into a new day, but as soon as it was light I called Sheila and we went for our usual morning walk some few hundred yards from where we had made our fire and spent such an uncomfortable night.

Sheila had gone her way and I had gone mine, as was our custom on these early strolls into the woods, and it was whilst I was settling down for a few minutes' peace in solitude that I saw what I had been seeking. Less than fifty yards from where I squatted was a fully grown cock pheasant greeting the dawn in all his wild glory of colour and song. I was on one hillside and he on the other, and we were more or less face to face. I think he sensed my presence and it puzzled rather than frightened him as he strutted amongst the pine trees looking this way and then that, coming nearer all the while. There was no sign of a hen; just this lone old bird, looking as no reared pheasant can ever look. His feathers were brighter and more alive in their colouring, his movements more animated and his tail longer and seemingly more demonstrative as he paraded for my benefit. For fully five minutes I was able to enjoy this old cock's company, until Sheila picked up my trail and appeared on the scene. With the familiar squawk of his English relation the pheasant took flight and disappeared over the hilltop, and the last I saw of him was his tail feathers with their flaps up steering him well clear of the human who had disturbed his morning act of showmanship.

He was a beautiful bird with identical colouring to the pheasant we know at home, although perhaps slightly heavier. I believe the species is known as the "Blood Pheasant"; from it the European stock is descended. Farther to the north in Yunnan there are white ones, but their habitat is at much higher altitudes where there is perpetual snow.

That had made my morning. I forgot the sleepless night and all I wanted to do was hasten back to boast to Stuart that I was one up on him.

Somebody asked why had I not shot him for the pot. It had never occurred to me, I am afraid. In any case he was too beautiful.

A hot drink of tea or coffee was what I needed—I missed this more than food—but instead it was cold clear mountain water that refreshed us for our early start.

Charles was on his feet and insisting that he was well enough to travel, though obviously pretty weak. Dick's shoes received their running repairs, and, these completed, we were on our way again.

This last stage down to the Salween was utter hell, though it was not as bad as the original climb towards the Mamien Pass. Once again we found raspberries by the roadside which helped us along our way, but we were getting weaker and weaker and our progress was slow and painful.

Friday had to cut away part of Charles's shoe leather to ease the pain caused by his heel, now swollen as well as sore, and I think he was running a temperature judging by the great beads of sweat that ran down his face to form liquid cobwebs on his black beard which dripped as he struggled uncomplainingly down the track.

Richard was in trouble again with his dysentery and his anguished face told its own story. Possibly the raspberries had brought it on; whatever the cause, he was obviously in pain.

It seemed so unfair that these two should bear all the suffering. Apart from hunger the rest of us were fit. Not one of us had caught as much as a cold in spite of being so inadequately dressed and equipped for such a journey which had taken us to 12,000 feet or thereabouts. Personally I felt buoyed up at the thoughts of reaching the Salween and, given a little food, could have gone on for weeks.

All day we scrambled our way in procession over a countryside which had changed completely. No more the lush feel of meadowland and turf or the prospect of seeing a flower round the corner. Even the pines had been left behind and everything around us was drab, ugly and completely lacking in interest. We came on the river suddenly towards evening. Stuart, who had gone on ahead to assess whether we could make it that night or call a halt, returned to say that he had seen it in the distance and within half an hour we were lying on its bank recovering from the day's march.

Now I know why the Tibetans called it " Black " and the Yunnanese " Angry." The water had the same turbulence as the Irrawaddy in the Upper Defile, and from my knowledge of that river I knew that only in a few places could a boat get across and then only in the skilled hands of a local pilot.

Not a village was in sight. Both banks appeared completely deserted. The whole place was desolate and uninviting and I took an instant dislike to the Lu Kiang, as the Chinese called it. The river was only about four hundred yards wide but I could see that it was running deep with snow water from Tibet. Although by no means in full spate, I recognised all the signs of danger. Its flow was not smooth from bank to bank but broken up in eddies and whirlpools and I watched the effect of these on the flotsam of twigs and branches that from time to time came floating down from above. One minute they were on the surface and the next sucked under to reappear a few hundred yards downstream as if drawn under by hidden forces on the river bottom. There were no rocks actually in evidence, although I dare say they lay submerged in wait for the unwary. I did not like the look of it at all.

Desmond saw me scrutinising the water; I told him what I thought of it. I could see that he was anxious and it did not surprise me when he asked if I felt up to walking another few miles to see what happened upstream.

" Frankly I don't like it myself," he said, " and I did expect to find some sign of life on the river bank. Anyway, while it is light let's go and explore."

I left Sheila with Patrick. She was getting really thin, and I knew she would be happy with him as they were old friends.

We had not gone a quarter of a mile when I drew Desmond's attention to something which had caught my eye. He was ahead of me at the time, striding out like a greyhound let off the leash, for he hated marching slowly as much as I did,

and it was only on occasions such as this that we could match each other's prowess as fast walkers.

"Hold on a minute," I called to him, "let me go ahead." Sure enough, I soon found the traces I had seen a few yards back partly obliterated by Desmond's boots, now in a clearer form.

"Come and look," I said, rather pleased with myself. "Two men wearing shoes have passed this way within the past few hours," and I showed him their imprints, so fresh that the ridge marks on their soles still carried grains of dust which had not yet had time to settle.

"By jove! that's clever of you. Where did you learn all this tracker stuff?" Desmond was clearly impressed.

As we walked on for half a mile or so I told him of my days as a young Forest Assistant. Like most of my colleagues, I had been ambitious to shoot big game, and I had been fortunate enough to be trained to follow an animal's spoor by a wonderful Khanung hunter named Moh, who was a legend in the Myitkyina forests.

My story was cut short as there was a village right in our path and I saw smoke rising from the evening fires. At last we might find food and perhaps shelter.

It was indeed quite a sizeable hamlet, whose name we later discovered was Manyin, but instead of being occupied by the river peasants we were greeted in perfect English by several young Chinese, one of whom immediately recognised Desmond, and addressed him by name.

"This is a wonderful surprise, sir," he said, coming forward all smiles to shake hands and be introduced to me. "I am sure you have brought us good luck. You must meet my friends," and there was much handshaking all round.

It was the main Chinese Customs party from Tengyueh. Apparently everything had gone well on their journey until they reached the Salween, where they had found every village on the west bank completely deserted, and had so far failed to attract the attention of anyone on the far bank. They had encountered only one living soul near the Salween, an old fisherman who had told them that the Governor's son with a large caravan of mules said to be laden with opium had passed through, terrorising the villagers and burning all their boats so that no one could follow in his wake.

Two of the younger Customs men, both strong swimmers, had tried to swim the Salween to obtain help, but they had been swept away and never seen again. Only at certain points could the local dugouts make the crossing, but they were certain that Manyin was one of them and that some of the villagers on the east bank would return now that all was quiet. For this reason they had decided to stay in the village and wait for help.

Their party numbered about forty, mainly women and children, but it was not until later that we met them. The senior Customs man took us into his hut on the outskirts of the village and tea was brought to us. Weak as it was, the taste and smell was delicious and whilst we drank Desmond told him of our plight and how we had no food.

Then we learned the worst. Their own supplies were so meagre that even the children were rationed to one small meal a day. Perhaps the " luck " that our kind Chinese friend had referred to in his greetings to Desmond was conjured out of thoughts of the Consul travelling in official state with a train of porters bringing up the rear carrying all the things which someone of such importance would normally tour with.

It was the desperate food situation which had cost the lives of the two brave swimmers.

Not a trace of disappointment showed in the smiling face of our host as Desmond unfolded our sad story. Of course we were welcome and he would see that a meal was made ready for our return with the rest of our party, and meanwhile a room would be prepared for our stay.

No amount of remonstration would make this man change his mind. What they had we would share as his guests, and he was confident that all would be well in a day or so. As we left to walk back down the river bank Desmond told me that this was normal Chinese hospitality and there was nothing to be done but to acquiesce graciously. But I knew he was worried, and when he asked me to tell him more about my hunter, Moh, I supposed he was trying to put the matter out of his mind.

" You know, Gordon," he said, " I've never had the urge to shoot game, but the skills of a tracker have always intrigued me."

So I told him about the greatest tracker of animals I have ever met.

" Moh was the son of one of my most senior elephant headmen when I worked in the Indawgi Lake area before being posted to Bhamo. He had been born in an elephant camp and had grown up with the herd which his father had been responsible for, and at an early age had become an *oozie* (rider), eventually taking charge of the herd when I promoted his father to the very special job of training young elephants to work and obey spoken commands.

" We called it ' humane ' training, and humane it certainly was compared with the methods employed when I had first joined my company. The idea was simplicity itself. Instead of waiting until the calf was about five years old and then caging it in a ' crush ' where its lessons resulted in deeply scarred ears and feet, its education began from the time it was born. The idea was to encourage the children of the camp to make the new baby a pet and by the offer of rewards in cash there was much competition to see who would be the first to mount its back. As a rule the first substantial instalment would come when the animal was about six years old and would obey the simple commands of a child. This process continued until the day when the little chap would be ridden complete with carriage on its back and go through the full drill of a well-trained baggage elephant. It was then that the camp headman would receive a large bonus.

"Moh's father's job was to go from camp to camp to watch the results and teach the men and children how to talk elephant language. He was a wonderful old man and loved his 'babies,' but his son soon gained such fame for his skill in tracking down the occasional elephant that went astray that his services became in great demand; so much so that this became his role with the company, regardless of the district from which the loss had been reported. His knowledge of the ways and habits of straying elephants was uncanny; and he would invariably return astride the animal which had made up its mind to play truant, though some of them, being without fetters or tying chains, had joined up with a wild herd.

"I remember one occasion in the Indawgi Valley when a female of considerable value answered to the call of the wilds and disappeared, having shed her chains. The opium-sodden headman, too frightened to report the loss, had absconded, and it was ten days before a report reached me that the herd of fifty was minus Ma Galay, a beautifully proportioned old girl.

"To make matters even worse, all this had happened on the far side of the lake among hills to the north, where, according to the Game Department, there lived what was said to be the largest herd of wild elephants in Burma; it was believed to be about eight hundred strong. Ma Galay had obviously fallen in love and, when the opportunity offered, slipped away to join her boyfriend. This was only made possible by the negligence of her rider and the lack of discipline in a camp, of which I was going to have to sack every member in days to come.

"I called up my camp messenger and sent for Moh who reached me that evening having walked some eighteen miles during the afternoon. As he squatted before me under the canvas lean-to which served as my office I told him all I knew of the loss of Ma Galay and how the headman Tun Gyi had let me down.

"'We both have a problem, Moh,' I told him. 'You

may have to travel far to find her and I shall have to report the case to the head office. To make matters worse I am due to go on long leave in a month's time and this may be cancelled if Ma Galay isn't found.' With my company, to lose an elephant was to lose one's stripes.

" ' Don't worry, *Thakin*,' said Moh, puffing at the cheroot I had given him. 'Take me over the lake to Lonton for I am sure she has joined up with the wild ones around Wabum—I will find her.'

" The following morning we left early. I took only a bedding roll and one servant. Moh carried his blanket, knife and spear and a small bundle of bits and pieces slung over his shoulder. I would spend the night at Lonton with my contractor friend, Sein Lone, a Shan Toyoke (half Shan, half Chinese), and after seeing Moh on his way would return to my base camp.

" For use on the lake I had a converted lifeboat fitted with a powerful outboard engine and in no time we had covered the ten miles or so to the village. On many occasions I had dispatched Moh on expeditions such as this, but never before had the opportunity offered of actually seeing how he set about tracking down a beast. In this case the animal had been missing for eleven days.

" Moh always travelled alone, and this time he was going to take food for fourteen days which he would prepare at Lonton.

" Within minutes of our tying up Moh was deep in conversation with his fellow Khanungs from the camp from which the elephant had disappeared. Whilst I enjoyed the fish curry Sein Lone had waiting for me I knew that Moh was busy with his plans for her recapture.

" From the veranda of Sein Lone's house on its high stilts, I could see him questioning the men gathered round him in the compound below us, and before I had finished my meal he had made up his mind, for he appeared up the steps to where I sat and delivered his verdict.

" ' *Thakin*,' he said, ' I want you to take me back to the village of Thuyin,' and he indicated a point about seven miles down the lake, ' for that will save me much time. Ma Galay's *oozie* is coming with me to show me the place she normally grazed at night before she escaped, and I will follow her from there. I know that she is with the wild ones. Tun Gyi's men are useless,' he added, ' for they knew that she was behaving strangely at least a week before she got away and she will be up there,' and he pointed to a dense tree-clad range of hills which dominated the lake valley from its southern shore.

" Moh concluded by saying that he needed two hours to prepare his food and then he would be ready to leave."

I think Desmond had forgotten all about our own problems, for he urged me to go on with my story. " But how the blazes could he carry sufficient food for a fortnight? Or was he going to eat in villages on the way ? "

I was able to enlighten him as I had done an exploration in the very area Moh was going to seek Ma Galay.

" No, that would have been impossible," I told him. " Once away from the lake the interior is uninhabited for hundreds of square miles. On the far mountain tops there are settlements of Kachins, a very wild tribe who for some reason very rarely visit the lake, as they prefer going east into the Hopin Valley where more of their people live in the surrounding hills. But I am glad you mentioned Moh's food, as the way he prepared and stowed it for easy carriage was one of the most fascinating of all the proceedings for his lone job of tracking. It was so intriguing that I watched him do it from beginning to end.

" By the time I had finished my curry and joined the elephant men Moh was busy over the fire. He had sent off one of the group to cut lengths of a certain type of bamboo and four-feet sections of this wood had been carefully laid out for his inspection. They were about two and a half inches in diameter, and when I picked one up I found that the interior joints had been hollowed out from the inside to make an unbroken tube sealed at one end only.

" Moh had three pans on the fire. In one he was parboiling a form of hand-pounded hill rice to which, judging by the colour, much of the husk still adhered. In another he had pieces of pork sizzling away and in the third I recognised wild spinach chopped quite finely, soaking in what looked to be *ghee* (buffalo fat).

" He was as painstaking as a head waiter at Claridge's serving *crêpes suzette* to a duchess; not until he was finally satisfied did he mix his ingredients after straining away all traces of water from the rice. The tubes of bamboo were then filled, and I was amazed at the quantity they contained after being tightly rammed with a stick. The job done, the four tubes were packed and sealed with bamboo caps, and Moh browned them off over the fire.

" The sustaining mixture I had seen prepared has a special name amongst the Khanungs but I have forgotten it. Its merit, apart from its nutritious value, lies in the fact that all the hunter has to do is cut off a section and bake it over a fire. When really hot the bamboo splits and falls away, leaving the rice meal in an unbroken sheath of pith which is also edible. If there is no fire it can be eaten cold, will not deteriorate even if left buried in water, and a slice of four inches of the tube is sufficient for a whole day's supply of food.

" Sein Lone came with me in the boat and we saw Moh depart on his mission. The food tubes he carried slung from a bamboo yoke round his neck and this also supported several strips of dried and rather smelly fish. He didn't seem unduly laden and both his arms were free. As usual he carried a short spear, the tip of which was razor sharp, and his *dah* (long knife) dangled from his left shoulder in its wooden sling.

" It took Moh seventeen days to find and coax Ma Galay away from her wild companions. For more than a week he had kept up with the herd gradually getting nearer and nearer to her each night, so that he could talk to her as she grazed, and finally she had been persuaded to let Moh mount her back and he had ridden her home."

This is one of the greatest of all elephant stories—the more so because it is a true one.[1] I am glad to say that Desmond showed himself suitably impressed by it.

By now we were reaching the rest of our party and it was nearly dark.

It was ten very exhausted and dirty men who joined the ladies that night, for they had prepared our meal in the large room of a house where most of them seemed to be camped, and which served as a communal eating place for the entire Customs party.

Quite apart from the simple fare of cooked rice and some kind of wild vegetable, which to us in our starved state was a banquet, the very fact of being under a roof once again gave one a strange feeling. We really had gone wild in the past few days and it was quite a shock, almost an embarrassment, suddenly to find oneself in the presence of such lovely and charming people.

Sheila was in her element, as she adored children and I do not think they had ever seen a dog of her breed before. Shy at first of the frightening bearded strangers in their midst, the children clung to their mothers and hid their quaint little faces, but gradually they emerged all inquisitive to find out more about these hairy men.

The younger wives all spoke fluent English and one in particular I shall always remember. Everything about her was beautiful and she moved with the grace of a ballet dancer. Her raven black hair was dressed in two long plaits which

[1] Little did I know then as we walked on the bank of the Salween that Moh was gaining fame in another place. For it was he who rallied his fellow Khanungs and ran an elephant ferry-service through the hell of the Hukawng Valley carrying in food and bringing out the sick and dying. Maybe Ma Galay was there. I expect she was. When I told the story of Ma Galay to " Elephant Bill " after he had retired to Cornwall he believed every word of it. He also knew of Moh and the wonderful work that man had performed in 1942.

hung waist length below her shapely breasts. She sparkled, not only with good looks and intelligence, but also with humour, and her English was spoken in a fascinating deep husky voice with a slight trace of an American accent. Her twin daughters, aged four, were equally attractive, and the family made a lovely picture as they moved about the room now lighted with an oil-lamp or two. By her dress and bearing I think she must have been the senior of the ladies present.

What amazed me more than anything else about these nice people was their stoicism in the face of death by starvation. Admittedly, they had travelled over a much easier route than the one we had taken, but it must have been exhausting, particularly for the mothers of young children. Later I was to learn that one by one the mules had died and for days the children had to be carried. Yet, warned of our impending arrival, the girls had put on their prettiest clothes and dressed their hair. The children in their warm pyjamas and dressing-gowns were spotlessly clean. We were a family party, and I was quite sorry when the time came to say good night. Thanking them we repaired to an empty house which had been cleaned out and a fire laid on the floor. Round this we slept, comforted by the food we had so badly needed.

CHAPTER 17

The Black and Angry River

MAY 21ST

NEXT MORNING WE WENT INTO CONFERENCE WITH the Chinese who seemed anxious that we should stay with them. The position was a desperate one: the food situation was critical and we had two sick men on our hands.

Seeing the Salween in daylight it was clear that Manyin was a crossing point; but the opposite bank showed no signs of life, and it was only from that direction that help could come.

Far to the north, over a tortuous route, was the last known ferry crossing, and beyond this lay the Lushui country, peopled, according to our Chinese friends, by wild tribes given to dispatching strangers with the aid of the blow-pipe and poisoned dart. Beyond that was Tibet and the famous rope bridges over the upper reaches of the river.

The decision was not an easy one and for hours we debated what to do for the best. Desmond reckoned that it would take us two days to reach the ferry crossing at Lu-Ku, but whether it still existed was another matter. In any case the village was on the east bank and might be deserted.

Richard was in pain with his complaint which was now getting worse every day; and in spite of our friends' gifts of pieces of cloth with which to bind up Charles's sore heel, he would only be able to walk with difficulty. Besides he was acting strangely, and Stuart had at one stage to dissuade him from attempting to swim the Salween to get help for the Chinese. I was not present when all this happened, but apparently Charles had said that if he couldn't walk at least he could swim, and, but for Stuart restraining him, he would have made the attempt and of course died in the process. I can imagine the thoughts going through his head; the fear of another day's agony on the march, his loathing of Desmond driving mad thoughts of bravery into his brain. Perhaps, even worse, it was intended suicide. With Charles it was difficult to tell. He could not unburden himself unless it was done privately in the long sessions he had recently been having with Stuart. In their different ways they were both deeply religious, and during the past few days Stuart had drawn closer to Charles than anyone else, even Paddy.

I knew that Charles was full of guts. No man could have managed as he had without them. But for some reason he tortured himself, and I believe it was this mental torment that gave rise to his dislike of Desmond. They continued to ignore each other as if there were a tacit understanding between them. We all pretended not to notice it and it showed only at night when they bedded down as far away from each other as the fire would allow.

One thing was quite clear—and it was this that finally determined our fate in more ways than one—we could not accept further food from our generous hosts and must go, for there were ten of us and we would only be a burden on their party.

Stuart went off to tell Charles, who was resting in our temporary shelter. Dick, now rejoicing in a supply of leather thongs to keep his shoes in place, was in full agreement with the decision. In fact I think we all were, for it was unthinkable that we should deplete the small supply of foodstuffs they carried, and God knows how they would survive if help was not soon forthcoming.

Desmond paid off the old guide and his companion. They at least had kept their word and brought us to the Salween, but they would go no farther. We divided up the silver dollars between us and before the day was out I had come to hate my share. To carry a blanket and a few bits and pieces is one thing, but silver in bulk is hell.

It was a sad parting. Charles, heavily bandaged, was leaning on two sticks fashioned for him with great care by Patrick and Friday who, against his wishes, had taken his load from him so he could walk free and unencumbered.

We shook hands with the men and the girls cried quite openly. My last sight of that village was of the beautiful girl with her plaits, her twin daughters, hand in hand, waving their chubby little fists in farewell while their mother wept. I never looked back after that, and walked with a lump in my throat for quite a while.

For myself I was glad to be leaving that place. I hated the Salween and even more so Lung Yung's bastard of a son who had brought such misery on so many because of his filthy greed.

All I wanted to do was climb out of the " Black and Angry " valley of despair. There was something evil about it. Even the beauty of the high mountains seemed to have given place to ugliness and to me every twist and turn of the river gave me the shivers. It was like an evil cobra snaking its treacherous way, prepared to strike if one stumbled too near its path.

I realised that it was already midday.

At first we had followed a track of sorts, but now it had been eroded away and we were forced to clamber over huge boulders of rock in order to make any progress at all up the river bank. And to think I had once done this sort of thing for pleasure when I went fishing for mahseer at the famous confluence thirty miles north of Myitkyina!

We were travelling painfully slowly, and every yard must have been torture to Charles, but with the aid of his sticks and an occasional push and shove from behind he managed somehow. We struggled on and on with no other thoughts in our minds but of reaching the ferry—if it was still in existence.

This big question mark haunted us all and none of us

wanted to talk about what would happen if it operated no longer. Exciting as was the prospect of the rope bridges in Tibet, there was a limit to the endurance of Charles and Richard, and of us all. Richard could now only move for half an hour before the pain returned and he had to drop back to suffer alone behind a rock. Even the little food which was sustaining us was having another effect. It had sharpened our appetites and now our bellies were empty and we craved for more.

At this point the Salween runs at the 3000-foot level, and in the distance the mountains of the Mekong Divide towered even higher than those we had already negotiated and all the time they came closer and closer and ever more foreboding. Some of the higher peaks were in fact over 13,000 feet, although at the time we did not know it, which was just as well. But the frightening thing was the way in which they seemed to rise sheer from the valley to form what seemed to be an impenetrable barrier between the two rivers.

There was only one feature of this ghastly journey up the Salween that gave me any comfort. I knew that no mule caravan had passed this way, for it was impassable. This raised my hopes that even the Governor's henchmen had not penetrated this far to terrorise the few people who might live along the river banks.

All traces of a regular thoroughfare had disappeared and the whole valley had the appearance of being uninhabited, bleak and inhospitable. I was now sure that the opium-carrying caravan had crossed well below Manyin where the Customs people had hoped to find boats. No doubt, as an extra precaution, Lung Yung's son had sent his men to burn the Manyin ferries and the villagers had panicked and disappeared into the hills.

Quite early in the evening it became obvious that we were too weak and exhausted to travel farther, too weak in fact to make a fire. Fortunately it was much warmer by the river, and we spread our blankets on its bank, each resigned to the ordeal of a long sleepless night alone with our thoughts and fears.

As usual Stuart prayed on his knees, this time for rather longer than usual, and I knew he was asking that we be given strength and that the sick be healed. I expect we all said a few prayers that night but had not the courage to kneel in front of our fellow-men, as Stuart did each morning and before going to bed.

I found myself back with " Farmer " Hewitt as we lay in silence and I remembered a few more lines of his poem on loneliness.

> For he is not of your world,
> He lives in a world of his own
> Which he peoples at will
> With the thoughts that fill his mind,
> And he is never alone.
>
> .   .   .   .   .
>
> When he rides abroad they attend their Lord,
> And he sees them at night in the fire.
> But sometimes their persistence wearies him
> And he yearns to be truly alone,
> ' But until you die,' they make reply,
> ' You must reap where you have sown. '

The quiet of the night was broken only by the sound of the Salween's rythmic beat as its waters lapped against the banks on its long passage to the sea. I dreamed of the snows from whence it came and the great mountains of Tibet so beautifully described in Ronnie Kaulback's book. What a lot Ronnie and I would have to talk about one day. . . ! But first there was to-morrow.

CHAPTER 18

Across the Salween at Last

ON REFLECTION I BELIEVE THAT THIS WAS THE WORST day of the whole journey—our pathetic struggle over rocks, stumbling into black mud patches as we laboured on towards the ferry point at Lu-Ku.

Dick's shoes were now disintegrating in spite of their leather strappings and he was developing a sore heel. Charles was in a bad way and only sheer courage kept him on his feet. Richard was in a terrible state and I thought he might not last the day. Morale was low and all the time at the back of our minds was that big question mark: Would it all prove to have been in vain?

Sheila behaved like a sheepdog that day, shepherding her flock strung out along the trail. One minute she would be up with the leaders and the next back with the slower-moving members of her party as if to give them encouragement and hope. Ten men and a near-human dog making one last desperate bid to find a way over a river which seemed to defy them at every bend in its course.

In places Charles had to be supported, and by afternoon we were half carrying him. It could not go on much longer; I felt my own strength ebbing away with every mile we covered. Even Stuart, the most powerfully built of us all, was weakening and the strain showed on every face.

To make matters even worse we were forced to take detours to avoid great horrible stretches of impenetrable mud, and it was in the course of one of these diversions from the river bank that we came on a jungle track leading in the direction we had to go. We collapsed beside it and rested, for we knew now that there was some hope. Lu-Ku could not be far away. Could we reach it before dark?

It was decided that an advance party should go ahead to seek help and, as so often in the past, I went with Desmond leaving the strong to help the lame on their way. There was no question, as before, of matching our skills as fast walkers. We could get along but that was about all. Sheila came with us.

About three miles on we sighted the village of Lu-Ku on the far bank and Desmond quickened his pace until we were half trotting up the path towards where we guessed the ferry would be if it still existed.

There had been so many disappointments that I think we both feared the worst, but our luck had changed. On rounding a bend, there ahead of us was a large dugout-type of boat about to leave for the far bank. Desmond broke into a run hailing the Chinese in their own language as he raced towards them and, as they heard him and waited, I could have cried for joy.

I could tell from Desmond's face that all was well. For once his emotions showed and revealed the depths of his feelings of relief. All along I had known that he had assumed responsibility for our safety and now he had not let us down.

"Thank God for this ferry, Gordon," he said after pouring out a torrent of Yunnanese to the boatmen, who looked friendly simple people. "Do you think you could go back and tell the others the news? I had better stay and hold the fort."

I could barely wait, such was my excitement, and I refused to contemplate how we were going to climb the mountains which rose, almost vertically, immediately behind the village away downstream. The river was much wider at this point than we had seen it on our journey up from Manyin. It must have been all of half a mile across, though it was less turbulent in appearance.

I found myself breaking into a run as I retraced my steps down the path we had just travelled. My strength had returned, and I could not wait to share the good news with the others. As soon as they saw me they knew.

Dick pumped my hand, saying, " Gordon, do you realise that once across that pimple over there we shall be home and dry and on the road to Kunming? Think of that first beer we are going to have together! "

I am not sure whether Charles could understand our good fortune. His face was tortured with pain and I think it had numbed his brain. He dripped with sweat and so did Friday and Patrick who held him on his feet. We staggered towards the ferry and I walked with Richard, who was now reduced to skin and bone, though still as game as they come.

" Don't worry, chum," I told him, " these villagers are bound to have some cure for your trouble." And he gave me a wan smile. He had not the strength to talk.

The ferry could carry us all.

" Just close your eyes and hope," said Desmond, " for this is going to be an experience."

Indeed it was and not one I would care to repeat for fun. Hewn out of a single tree-trunk of large girth, it was a Heath Robinson contraption if ever there was one. But we were beyond caring.

It must have been fully thirty feet in length and, judging by its decrepit look, it had seen service for as many years. It was in fact a dugout; and into this ancient hulk we heaved our bodies, clambering over a miscellaneous assortment of oars, ropes, lengths of bamboo and gear of every description. Everywhere was the stench of rotting fish.

There were five boatmen and they were as weather-beaten as the craft we were about to set sail in—gnarled old sailors who would never see the sea, if they knew that such a thing existed, which is doubtful. But know their river they did, as we were soon to find out.

One toothless old boy, whom I took to be the captain, came to the rescue when for a moment I thought we were going to turn over. Gesticulating to Desmond and making himself heard above the constant loud chatter of his colleagues, he made it clear how we should seat ourselves and not until we had done this to his satisfaction did he give the order to cast off. By then we were crouched or stretched out like chessmen waiting for the hand of the master to make the next move. When it came I knew why the "Master" had been so meticulously careful in stowing his cargo; he had to be able to play the game his way.

Within seconds our cockle-shell was caught in a current which swept us down river at a speed which was unbelievable. Ignoring Desmond's advice to close my eyes, I watched fascinated as the paddlers fought to edge the boat in the direction of the east bank, where I could see a group of people awaiting the arrival of the ferry. It must have been a mile downstream, but at the rate we went hurtling down I had visions of walking back from Manyin and going through the horror of yesterday and to-day again. For it seemed that nothing could halt this frail old craft from sailing away into the night with us all aboard her. And soon it would be dark.

We were all too terrified to do anything but stay like statues, hardly daring to breathe. Already water was seeping up from the bottom of the boat and even forward where I crouched I felt it rising higher and higher until my shorts were soaked, and I could do nothing but wait for it to go over my knees. And nowhere at hand was anything with which to bale out; even to have moved half a turn might have meant disaster.

Suddenly the ferry shook from stem to stern and we were flung headlong below its bows, and there was the queer sensation of being on a turntable going round and round and round.

"Christ, we've hit something," I heard Dick explode from beneath a mass of bodies that engulfed him as he lay half submerged in the bilges, and he struggled to fight his way clear so that he could dive overboard and swim. "Let's get to hell out of this," and he cursed the Salween and all its ancestors, as only Dick could do.

But no such action was necessary. We had ceased to swing in a circle and were being hauled into calm water by the villagers who had caught a rope thrown to the bank by our skipper.

It was then we realised that the big bump which had thrown us into the bottom of the boat had been caused by its impact with the lip of an enormous whirlpool which swirled and boiled over some yards from the bank. We had been deliberately paddled into the outer circle of this treacherous cauldron, so that the ferry had swung in near enough towards the bank for a rope to reach the men who waited to haul us to safety. That is how the Lu-Ku ferry delivers its passengers.

All this had happened in a few minutes, but it seemed like hours.

At last we had crossed the "Black River" of Tibet, the "Angry River" of Yunnan.

Amongst those who awaited the arrival of the ferry was the village headman to whom Desmond introduced himself and explained our plight. I could see by the smiles and head nodding that passed between them that we were being made welcome and were amongst friends. The headman led us up the hill to his house which stood on stilts commanding a glorious view of the river below and the mountains above.

We were now safely away from the Japanese, and it was with a wonderful feeling of relief that we threw down our blankets and the weighty silver we carried, to collapse on the floor of the room which had been placed at our disposal.

The headman and villagers of Lu-Ku I shall always

remember with affection. Not so the Salween. Our experiences there made me hate it and when, months later, I learned the fate of my lovely Chinese girl with the plaits and her twin daughters I hated it even more.

It was the 21st of May and we had been travelling for eighteen long days. We certainly looked like a bunch of bearded scarecrows as we huddled in our new-found shelter, dirty, exhausted and starving, and too weak even to spread our blankets.

Our arrival must have created quite a stir in the village, and I think the entire population was gathered in and around our kindly headman's house, for there was much noise and bustle going on. Then came the big surprise. Our host appeared with a large pot which proved to contain home-brewed rice wine, of which very generous measures were poured out for us by his two young sons, who then sat down and joined us. I think it was more spirit than wine. It had a bite, and gradually I could feel a lovely warmth creeping up from my empty stomach which was bliss.

Desmond explained that the headman was having food prepared for us and he would also give us towels so that we could wash off some of the accumulated grime which covered our bodies. Meanwhile the party went on, and all joined in. Even the door to our room was packed with villagers as was the passage outside it. Everyone seemed to be talking at once.

We were the first to bring tidings of happenings in other parts of Yunnan. These simple people knew nothing of the Japanese invasion and Desmond had difficulty in keeping pace with the questions he was being asked. Dick was trying to help him tell of our adventures and, revived by the alcohol, we all joined in. Even Charles was awakening from his coma and getting some of the wine inside him. We were getting delightfully tipsy and I am sure it did us good.

Our meal that night was a banquet, though of the most simple fare, in which Sheila joined, needless to say. She had quickly made friends with everyone and was quite at home.

One moment she would be with us and the next gone to use her charms elsewhere in the house.

How we slept that night, comforted by the thought that to-morrow there would be no dawn awakening with the prospect of a long day's march without even a warming drink to see us on our way! Instead we could sleep for as long as we liked, having decided to halt and have a day of complete rest to give us strength for the next part of the journey, which we knew was not going to be easy.

CHAPTER 19

A Day of Rest in Lu-Ku

MAY 23RD

IT WAS NEARLY MIDDAY BEFORE ANYONE STIRRED.
It was strange to have a ceiling above one's head instead of
the stars; but the floorboards were hard and I awoke stiff
in every joint and with a nasty taste in my mouth.

There was no doubt about it; I had a hangover.

I crawled over bodies still huddled in sleep and went in
search of water to drink and a place to sluice down. I found
both. The ice-cold water piped with bamboos from the hill
above provided just the shock treatment I was in need of.

In the kitchen there was hot tea to drink—tasteless stuff,
but refreshing. Sheila had already explored the village with
Paddy, who must have been first up, so I joined them and got
my first proper look of the Salween's east bank as seen
from Lu-Ku.

The village proved to be no more than a cluster of huts on
a hill-top. To the north-east, clearly to be seen, was a peak
rising to well over 14,000 feet to dominate the ranges in that
direction; I thought I could see traces of snow still remaining,
but may have been wrong.

Immediately over the river the Lushui country stretched
away to the north-west in broken lines of hills from four to
about eight thousand feet in height, and in the far distance
stood three enormous peaks which Paddy reckoned must
mark the boundary between Burma and China. We thought
they must belong to the Hpimaw Range, a wild part of

Myitkyina District. It was thereabouts during my Myitkyina days that the Verney-Cutting expedition, guided by J. K. Stanford, had gone in search of the Red Tufted Deer and other rare animals and birds, collecting on behalf of the zoos and museums of New York.

J. K. Stanford had been Deputy Commissioner in my area,

and it had been in his house that I had first met Ronnie Kaulback. It had been a sad day for the station when J. K. (as he was affectionately known to us all) decided to retire from the Indian Civil Service; but his loss has been more than compensated for by the pleasure his books have given to so many in the years since then.

Everyone had chores to do that day in preparation for the attack on the high mountain so frighteningly close by. Returning to the headman's house I found Stuart acting as dresser to Charles's heel; Dick's was also being attended to. The former was looking much better after food and a long night's sleep. He was far more his old cheerful self.

" Morning, Charles," I said, " how's your hangover to-day? "

" Never had one in my life, old boy," came the reply, and I believed him. He was one of those large men with a capacity for food and drink so enormous that they could have no effect on him.

Desmond was less cheerful. With all our silver there was little or nothing to be purchased in the way of foodstuffs. The community was a strangely isolated one and desperately poor. They were a timid people, who appeared to have no contact with the outside world. How they existed, and why they chose to stay there had already baffled me.

As far as we could make out, not even the headman had ever seen the bridge over the Mekong which was our objective, though it was only four days' march away. The high mountain formed a barrier beyond which was a foreign country into which they would not venture.

Our only hope of replenishing our food supplies between the Salween and the Burma Road to Kunming depended on our finding a place called Maotsaoping, said to be on the route we had decided to take as the less difficult of the passes to the Mekong River. How far away it was seemed a mystery, as distances in Yunnan, as indeed throughout China, are judged in travelling time and not in miles. I never mastered the " *li* " method of measurement, particularly when applied to journeys in the mountains.

In contrast to our night of revelry to celebrate the crossing of the Salween our second night in this village was spent in a rather sober and restrained atmosphere. Everyone seemed subdued and apprehensive about the morrow and what lay ahead.

It was hardly surprising. Before sunset I had taken a good look at the towering mountain barring our way. It was like a wall of solid rock rising probably 9000 feet from my view-point at the 3000-foot level of the village. From the experience of crossing from the Shweli to the Salween I knew that the Mekong excursion would expose us all to an even greater test of physical endurance than we had so far encountered. Pushing Charles on his mule up the Kaolikung Shan was going to be child's play compared with dragging our way over the Mekong Divide. It was more formidable than anything we had yet attempted, and I had no illusions about it; nor indeed had the others.

This was quite obvious by the general reluctance even to mention the next stage of the journey. And so it was that ten very worried men put down their heads that night like ostriches burying their heads in the sand, and sought refuge in thoughts of anything but the realities of the situation. The prospect was frightening and, on reflection, I believe that the thoughts of living rough again and sleeping under the stars instead of a roof had induced a feeling of fear amongst us all.[1] We were all terrified of that mountain rising sheer into the heavens from the village of Lu-Ku. To a mountaineer I am sure the prospect would have been stimulating, but looking around me before I went to sleep, I began to wonder whether that day's rest in comparative comfort had not been a mistake

[1] When I eventually reached India I obtained the latest Survey Maps available. A large part of the area we traversed to the Mekong is a blank, but it was no doubt mapped later in the war by the Americans flying the now famous Hump Route.

and whether it might not have been better if, before the softening-up process had set in, we had pressed on in one last desperate effort. To stop at any stage meant to collapse.

For we had collapsed. After the nightmare of the march up the river bank, however, I doubt whether there could have been any alternative but to halt and try to repair the damage it had done to us all.

That night I dreamed of a great ship sailing down the Salween and being caught in our whirlpool and going round and round, all its deck lights ablaze and passengers in evening dress crowding the rails. I saw faces I recognised and waved to them and then they disappeared as the ship found its course down river and sailed on into my dream.

CHAPTER 20

A Long Haul

MAY 24TH

THE AIR WAS CHILL WHEN WE LEFT LU-KU SOON
after dawn, and the dull morning suited the mood of the
party. Thick mist shrouded the river and the mountains
were completely blotted out, for which I was grateful, as
the very sight of them the previous evening had given me
a sick feeling in the pit of my stomach, and I had no desire
to contemplate their threatening heights so early in the day.
The Salween I had no wish to see again. The memory of my
vivid dream persisted with such insistence that I had only to
close my eyes and the image of my ship was again passing by
and disappearing into space.

The village was just beginning to stir as we passed through;
we waved good-bye to the few peasants going about their
early morning tasks, and, moving slowly in a silent procession,
began the ascent of the mountain. Less than half a mile on
we bid farewell to the headman who with such kindness had
given us sanctuary. He had guided us to the path we had to
follow and it was now up to us. He had been well rewarded
in silver, but these poor people were so short of food that to
sustain us on our journey we carried barely sufficient to give
us two meagre meals.

We were now climbing step by step into the mist, following
a narrow path seemingly hewn through the course of centuries
out of a mountain of rock. It was so narrow that in places
we had to squeeze through sideways. Progress was painfully

slow. It was going to be a long hard day, and I knew that for most of it I would be alone with my thoughts.

Such glimpses I had of the countryside through the swirling mist that swept around us revealed little but uninviting rock and stunted tree growth. It was entirely different from the beautiful hills through which we had climbed on our way to the Salween. Beauty had given way to bleakness, and there was no longer that feeling of anticipation that the next turn in the path would reveal something of interest. Even Sheila seemed to understand that our way was going to be a grim one, every hour a struggle. Though she had eaten at Lu-Ku she was painfully thin, and I think the hard rocks worried her feet.

Dick, who had patched up his shoes, seemed to be managing quite well, and Charles was climbing without complaint, but it was difficult to judge how they would be at the end of the day. Climbing in this fashion was probably less damaging to their sore heels than ordinary walking, as every pace forwards and upwards had to be calculated and timed; feet firmly planted, then a heave, and one was another yard or two nearer the Mekong.

The headman had given Richard some native medicine which, temporarily at least, had eased his pain. So by and large we were away in reasonable order, if only our bodies could survive the gruelling test of four days in the mountains. Four days to a motor road and safety. We had been through hell before and survived, and would do it again, unless the mountain broke our spirit, which was not impossible.

Gradually the mist began to lift, and coming out on a shelf towards noon we emerged into bright sunshine.

Hardly a word had been spoken, and not once had we halted for longer than necessary to regain our breath. Now we could look back into the valley some two thousand feet below. The view was magnificent, but all we could do was to collapse amongst the rocks for half an hour. We had done well to climb that far, but the strain was beginning to show, and I doubted whether we would manage more than another thousand feet that day. Looking upwards it seemed that we had not yet scratched the surface of the mountain. To the west the three great peaks of the Hpimaw Range stood out clearly, and it was possible to see the Salween snaking its way for miles towards Burma and the sea.

Indeed it was wild country we were traversing. As I viewed it stretching away into the distance, the thought occurred to me that not one drop of rain had fallen since that mad rush over the Border which had avoided our capture by the Japanese. Yet between Burma and Assam the monsoon rains would by now have set in, trapping thousands of humans in the mud of the Hukawng Valley. I knew only too well how lucky we were, and I knew it perhaps better than the others, for I had travelled the other way.

"I suppose there's no chance of rain hitting us on this mountain?" I inquired of Desmond, who had joined me to look at the view.

He gave a wry smile before replying. "A hundred to one against, I should say. But if we get freak rains I wouldn't rate our chances of reaching the Mekong very high. In fact, they would probably be nil."

I doubt whether we could have survived such conditions; it is almost certain we would have died of exposure. Even in dry weather some of the going had been slippery, for water dripped everywhere amongst the rocks as it seeped down from above.

"Come on, Gordon, let's get moving before it does rain," said Desmond, adjusting his eye-glass. And he led the way on the next stage of the climb.

As the afternoon drew on the pace got slower and slower.

"Christ, this is bloody murder," muttered Dick, as he scrambled up behind me. His once-white shirt was wet with sweat; it hung outside his shorts, which were held up by string. We were all filthy and dirty from the moss and lichen-covered rocks and the white hairs on Dick's chest were matted with mud, which also plastered his bristling beard. Exhausted as he was the fire in his eyes remained, and his whole appearance seemed to say, " Get out of my bloody way; I'm going to the top of this ruddy pimple if it's the last thing I do!"

Clearly we could go little farther that day, for even the strongest of us had begun to stumble as if off-balance.

Patrick was my endurance barometer. Young, lean, hill-trained and superbly fit, if he said we had gone far enough I knew it was time to call a halt. He had been brought up in a jungle village, and from his Shan mother had inherited both stamina and an instinctive insight into the lore of untamed places in a way denied to the rest of us.

I leaned against a rock and waited for the rearguard of the party to catch up, leaving Dick to clamber onwards in Desmond's footsteps. One by one the sad procession of exhausted men came into view and it was painfully obvious that Charles and Richard were being driven on by sheer force of will-power.

" What's the verdict, Patrick? " I inquired of my young assistant as he came alongside. I thought he was looking pale and rather drawn but I expect we all were for that matter.

" Pointless going much farther to-day," he replied. " That heel of Charles is giving him hell and Richard's trouble has hit him again." The rest of the party were in agreement, and Stuart volunteered to catch Desmond and call it a day.

It must have been a full hour before we finally dragged our way to the site Desmond and Dick had selected for our night's rest on the mountainside. It offered little in the way of comfort apart from the shelter of some rocks, but we were beyond caring and even too tired to wash off the mud and dirt that covered us.

Everything was an effort, and it was somewhat grudgingly that the fittest of us gathered fuel for a fire. Dick's heel was now raw and Charles could only move with difficulty. Richard was in a bad way and getting weaker.

It was a grim prospect and the Mekong seemed farther, not nearer, with every mile we climbed. To make matters worse a cold wind got up after sunset. The little food we shared was impregnated with the flavour of wood smoke. I had no appetite nor even the desire to eat at all.

Hardly a word was spoken that night. An atmosphere of abject misery and a feeling of dejection had descended on us all, which boded ill for what was to come if we were to have any chance of surviving this vital last stage of the journey. When I think back I am sure that this feeling stemmed from the absence of Dick's normal cheerfulness and banter. Without it the seeds of despair were sowed in us that night. For though nobody had until this moment realised it, not even himself, his very presence had throughout been that of standard-bearer always ready to rally his men. Desmond had all the graces of chivalry and powers of leadership but he could not convey to others or give, as Dick could, that feeling of buoyancy which flowed so naturally from his every act. Dick's very impulsive and impatient movements were in themselves an effervescent stimulant and his loud curses a war cry to the weary. But now his spirit was low and so in turn was ours.

The night was long and I think everyone slept only in fits and starts, through sheer exhaustion. One moment all would be quiet and the next a biting cold wind would come howling round the mountain as if seeking us out to dislodge us from where we sheltered. Even Sheila was miserable and I could feel her whole body shiver in spasms as she nestled between me and Dick so that we could share the warmth of her thick coat, whilst she enjoyed the comfort of her human companions.

The words of Farmer Hewitt on loneliness haunted the hours of my consciousness and my mind revolved round the

theme of there being no escape from one's thoughts.　Suddenly
I remembered the last few lines of his melancholy words:

> So think not light of the Anchorite
> Nor rate his powers low,
> For his lonely brain bears a double strain
> Which yours will never know.

CHAPTER 21

Higher and Higher

MAY 25TH-26TH

IT ALL HAPPENED SO LONG AGO THAT MY MEMORIES of the next two or three days crossing the Salween-Mekong Divide are blurred, although I can clearly recall certain interludes in that period of utter torture.

Over the years I have perhaps erased unconsciously from my mind nearly all recollection of that period, and to this day have no wish to dwell too long on the final struggle to accomplish what at times seemed impossible.

The mountain all but won the last round.

For two days we fought it yard by yard, plodding on blindly more like broken down machines than human beings. With every mile we became weaker and weaker and at times our task seemed utterly hopeless. Morale was very low, and it hurt to see one's companions suffer to the extent they did.

Charles and Dick were in agony as the sores on their heels grew larger and larger, and Richard's condition deteriorated with every mile we travelled. He was in a terrible state, and how he survived at all is a miracle. For sheer guts, the way in which the three sick members of our party defied that mountain is something I shall always remember. There were times, it is true, when the fittest of us would help the others, to support them in their suffering. If there were any heroes amongst us, they were the halt and the lame and not the well shod better-equipped majority, of which I was one. How I blessed my Frontier Force boots and my mother's hand-knitted socks of heavy wool!

At one time we must have climbed to well over 11,000 feet, but once over the summit of this cruel range the going, fortunately, became easier and the country more interesting. But if there were things of beauty to be seen they escaped my eyes; I was blind to everything but the thought of reaching the end of the road.

In our physically and mentally depressed state doubts began to form in our minds as to our fate should the Chinese Army have retreated behind the Mekong River line back towards Kunming. Would our journey have been in vain?

Stuart had obviously been telling Charles of his travels up and down the Burma Road, for in one of our rare confessional periods in those strained days Charles confided in me that if he made the Mekong and found the Japanese in occupation he would ask to be allowed to go into retreat in a monastery in the Lake Tali area. Here a band of White Fathers were established, famous not only for the good work they did among the Yunnanese but also for the high quality of the home-made plum wine they dispensed to weary travellers. Charles admitted the attraction of the "*vin de maison,*" but also seemed sincere in his contemplation of becoming a lay brother with the mission of White Fathers.

Once again wild raspberries came to our rescue but they were of no use to poor Sheila, now reduced to skin and bone. She had now taken on the job of a real working shepherd dog for she would never leave her flock and never forget any of us. Time and time again she would draw attention to a member of the party who was falling behind. I wish I had a picture of her as I remember her on one occasion silhouetted on high ground waiting to make sure that the last straggler was safely on his way before she would follow a downhill path to join the leaders.

Our second night out of Lu-Ku was a repetition of the first, except that now we had no food at all. A bed of rocks—welcome enough to aching bodies—some sleep, and long periods of wakefulness and a longing for the dawn.

On the third day we began the descent into the Mekong Valley proper and, buoyed up with new hope, the invalids limped along uncomplainingly for hour after hour. Charles made progress with the two sticks Friday and Patrick had shaped for him; while Dick, using one stick, found that he could get along with a hop, skip and jump action which under different circumstances would have been funny.

I believe we did have a little private chuckle, if under such grim conditions it could be called that, for the fire had rather died out of Dick's normally pugnacious exterior. His face was fine drawn with pain beneath his white stubble of beard, and at every step he had to clench his teeth, wincing from the torture his heel was causing him.

There was no question any longer of the fit leading the crocodile, with the seniors and chaperones in front and the games mistress bringing up the rear to deal with any junior eyes straying from the straight and narrow route through the world of Men; instead we swayed about like a worn out and exhausted rugby scrum, first this way and then that, supporting each other morally and often physically. We were no longer strung out.

Everything was shut out of our world but the concerted task of finishing what we had set out to do. And if only we could keep the party moving no matter how slowly—the end was drawing nearer.

Each night, and every dawn, Stuart had gone on his knees and prayed, and in our moments I think we all drew comfort from his contact with the Almighty.

Banded together as we were, tired and sometimes in despair, the gulf between Desmond and Charles remained as it had from the very beginning. Nothing, even suffering, could alter the passive hostility between these two intelligent men. Each continued to ignore the other's presence, and I am sure both suffered in consequence. There was nothing we could do about it and no one tried. The position between the pair had been firmly established and was accepted as if it did not exist.

The strange thing was that though we were thrown together, the only close friendship formed on that long journey was between Dick and Angus, the extrovert and the introvert. We all got on well enough together, but there it ended, as is the way with men who, after enjoying a few drinks at the bar, go their separate ways home.

CHAPTER 22

A Night in a Coffin

MAY 27TH

HOW WE HAD MISSED THE VILLAGE OF MAOTSAOPING, where the headman of Lu-Ku had said we might find food, I do not know, except that throughout Yunnan we had noticed that mountain villages would often conceal themselves in folds in the hills, whereas those in the plains were clearly exposed. The hill people in Burma are much the same.

Since leaving the Salween we had not seen one solitary traveller—until late in the evening of the third day when Paddy spotted the figure of a man who, according to Paddy, took one look at us and ran for his life in another direction.

By then we were like a group of drunken men staggering home to bed. We were blinded with grime and sweat, for, quite apart from the effort of helping one another along, the country had become broken into small hills and valleys which, in our state, were moral as well as physical obstacles. Always it seemed that the top of the next hill would reveal our approach to the Mekong, but they all proved disappointingly similar mirages. One moment we would be full of hope, making that extra effort to reach the top, only to find yet another range of hills.

But the Mekong by our reckoning could not be far away and unless we had gone sadly wrong we should reach it within twenty-four hours.

It is not surprising that the man Paddy had seen had avoided our path, for we must have looked like people from another planet. Anyway, that he was there at all was a good omen, and the presence of human beings was confirmed when, breasting yet another rise, we saw a wooden structure rather like a temple standing alone on a small hill covered with bamboos.

The sensation of actually seeing positive evidence of human habitation, after the loneliness of the mountains, acted like a tonic, and we groped our way upwards, half-crawling to this sanctuary, thinking it might give us shelter.

Sanctuary it certainly was, but a sanctuary for the dead!

Stacked on one side of the temple were coffins which appeared to be sealed, and on the other, empty wooden crates of a familiar shape waiting to serve the purpose for which they had been built.

There was straw on the earthen floor and into this we collapsed more dead than alive. We were in good company for the night.

Not a sign of a village was to be seen, but even if there had been one within half a mile, I doubt whether any of us had sufficient strength to seek it out.

Even making Richard comfortable on a bed of straw was enough effort. We had reached the end of our tether and were beyond caring where we slept. And still there was the question whether we could travel yet another day.

Dick's heel was in a worse state than Charles's ugly sore. It was as big as a crown piece and beginning to suppurate in a most dangerous way. There was nothing with which to dress it or relieve the pain, which throughout the day must have become excruciating.

There was no water on that hill-top. Fortunately we had been swilling our mouths at every opportunity all along the route and drinking copiously from every stream we met. Starvation had brought on a continuous thirst, and had water failed us we would surely have perished.

After our experience in the hills beyond Tengyueh where we had found the monastery miles from the town, it would have been hopeless to have gone in search of food even if we had had the strength.

A cold wind was blowing outside and it bit into our emaciated bodies through the wide-open side of the temple.

The chance of villagers coming to the resting place of their dead after dark was ruled out by Desmond as unlikely, even if the man Paddy had seen had reported our presence.

So, reconciled to the company we were going to keep, we gathered up straw and sought refuge in some of the half-made coffins which offered a measure of protection against the chill of the night. We were too exhausted to worry overmuch where we laid our aching bodies. And we had a roof over our heads.

CHAPTER 23

Despair, Relief and the Mekong

MAY 28TH

THE SIGHT OF EACH MEMBER OF OUR PARTY DISEN-
gaging himself from the confinement of his coffin and shaking
off his shroud of straw, as if rising from the dead to greet
the dawn, will remain indelibly etched in my memory;
as I am sure it has to every one of us who is still of this world
and remembers the " long walk to freedom."

Near tragedy had been transformed into comedy overnight, and the ghastly mood of depression of yesterday had
given way to one of hope. We were alive again and ready
to meet the challenge of one more day on the road to safety.

Gone was that awful soul-destroying fear regarding our
fate on reaching the Mekong. " Of course the Chinese Army
will be there to welcome us," piped up Dick, much of his
old fire restored after a good night's sleep and the thought
that within hours he would be getting news to his wife that
he was safely back in China.

" Real chow to-night, chaps," he went on, " better practise
how to use chopsticks on the way."

It was from such thoughts as these that Dick drew his
strength and already at that early hour he was limbering up
mentally, quite forgetful of the handicap he carried in the
shape of a festering sore.

A feeling of expectancy prevailed that morning in this
harbourage of ghosts in which we had so unexpectedly sought
sanctuary for the night, too tired to be aware of such presences.
True, it had been strange sleeping in such company, but the

atmosphere had been friendly, and it was only when Richard made one of his periodic unhappy excursions into the night that I stirred, warned by Sheila that her keen ears had sensed something moving. Apart from that I had slept for hours in the utter bliss of a mattress of straw and a wooden box.

There was good reason for this renewal of hope and the urge we all had to be on our way. We were within striking distance of the motor road to Kunming where we would be amongst friends. The first sight of it would be a familiar one to Desmond, Dick and Stuart who had often crossed the Mekong Bridge on their frequent journeyings between China and Burma. For them it would be home territory, for the rest of us an adventure.

To each man it meant something different. As we were now so close to the realisation of our escape plan, my own mind turned to the future and what it might hold in store for me after I had found my wife and small son somewhere in India. I had no idea where they might be.

My company had lost everything in Burma, but I knew they would help financially as they had considerable assets in India and were renowed for their generous treatment towards staff. I would doubtless go into uniform and was fairly confident of a good job in Intelligence, as I had already been working for both the British and the Americans.

To Friday the road would be the gateway back to his native land; to Patrick, perhaps the birth of a new and fuller life far removed from the restricted environment of his village. He was only on the threshold of his career; he was an ambitious young man, and this might be his big opportunity.

Government would absorb its civil servants, leaving only Angus without a job waiting for him in India, for his company had also lost everything. Any further reflections on our futures were rudely interrupted by Angus himself.

"Hey, you chaps; come and give me a hand. I have lost my signet ring." He was rummaging through the straw which had lined his coffin and we all joined in, but the search was of no avail. Every inch of the floor was explored, but the ring had disappeared.

"Come, Angus," said Dick, "are you sure it didn't fall off on the march yesterday?"

Angus was positive he was wearing it and told us that it was his habit every night to turn it on his finger before going to sleep. Inside was engraved his wife's initials and the date of their marriage. We all knew he was deeply in love and this little nightly act was no doubt a symbol of the bond between them.

Poor Angus, the loss of his ring really worried him and nothing would shake his belief that it had disappeared during the night. Paddy put it down to the work of leprechauns being up to their usual tricks. Desmond suggested that maybe the ancient spirits of the Confucian faith had resented our presence among the dead and had demonstrated their displeasure. But I suspect that it had fallen from his finger on the previous day as he had lost a lot of weight. Anything could have happened as we had fought our way up to the sanctuary of the temple. The fact remains that it was gone, and there was nothing to be done about it.

We trailed out into the thick mist, leaving the ghosts and ring behind us. Who knows, perhaps it had been spirited away in the night?

Our path soon began to lose altitude and within a very short time Sheila found water. How wonderful it was! We drank our fill from a narrow fault in the rock where it flowed as clear as glass.

I was so exhilarated at the prospect of reaching the Mekong that I could have run. But it was not to be, and that day's march remains a painful memory. The enthusiasm of our cripples to conquer the last stage to freedom was short-lived and every step nearer the river became agony. Richard was so weak that he had to be helped on his way, and Charles and Dick were suffering in the most ghastly fashion.

We saw not a sign of a village throughout that long day.

Maybe we had passed near habitations obscured by mist early that morning. Round every bend and over every rise I prayed we might find help to carry our casualties, but fate was unkind and we stumbled on as if some hidden force had taken control of our movements and we had become mere marionettes dancing to a tune we could not hear.

It must have been after midday when we reached a place where the path diverged and we had to decide which we would follow. It was the meeting place of two ridges forming a low saddle with fairly steep slopes leading away in opposite directions.

There was little doubt that the left-hand fork was our road, the other track probably going up to a hill village—another good sign that we were nearing our goal. With luck, the Mekong might be sighted from the ridge top, about two miles distant.

Taking advantage of the breathing space, I gave Dick a hand in tying together the remnants of canvas that served as his shoes, taking care not to touch the open sore on his heel which by then was a nasty sight. His face, beneath the grime and beard, was grey with pain and, although he would not complain, I knew how much he was suffering.

I had not quite finished the shoe repairs when the party moved off, everyone anxious to sight the river. Dick and I, with Sheila of course in attendance, were left alone.

Dick managed to get to his feet, but had barely taken ten paces in the direction the others had gone when he faltered and, as if in a faint, collapsed to the ground where he sat with his head bowed between his knees. It happened very suddenly: one moment we had been chatting, and then this unexpected collapse.

Knowing Dick as I did, I left him alone to recover, for he would have resented my ministrations or words of sympathy. The others were out of sight and beyond shouting distance. All I could do was stand helplessly nearby, fearful that he was about to have a heart attack and might die on the hillside.

Not so Sheila. She did not like it at all. Burying her lovely great muzzle into his lap, she nudged his head upwards as if saying, "Please talk to me." And slowly Dick seemed to come back into this world. Lifting his head from his hands, he patted her and Sheila, satisfied with this acknowledgement of his affection, lay down beside him, her eyes asking all kinds of questions in the way that only dogs can do.

Dick broke the silence. "Sorry, Gordon," he said, wiping away great beads of sweat which, forming on his forehead, ran down his face half blinding him. "I've had it. I cannot move another yard. You go on without me and perhaps you will be able to get some help."

"Not on your bloody life," I replied, sitting down alongside him. "I'm staying right here and I'll bet you a dollar that your Man Friday won't go a mile before he realises you are not following; between us we will be able to carry you, don't worry. He will be here within ten minutes.

"But tell me," I went on, "what hit you so suddenly? Was it your heel or something else?"

"Christ only knows, Gordon. My legs have given way and my heel hurts like hell and I came over all dizzy just now and nearly blacked out for a moment. I'm all in, I guess. And to think that the Mekong is probably just over that ruddy pimple."

I knew how he felt. Home territory just round the corner, visions of messages flashing to India, proper food and medical attention. Yet here was the strong man, Dick Winter, stricken down so near to the end of the journey. His disappointment I could read in his sad face, racked with pain. He could no longer carry our standard and put heart into the weary with his loud curses. Looking down at the pathetic bindings which covered his feet, the thought came to me that they had survived more than three weeks of cruel treatment. We had all but reached the end of a long road and crossed from the Irrawaddy to the Mekong. And Dick had done that just in a fragile pair of patched-up tennis shoes.

How long we sat alone on that hillside I cannot recall, but we talked about our wives and families and life in general in a way we had never done before. It seemed to do Dick good to chat and take his mind off himself, and slowly he recovered.

It was not in Dick's make-up to moralise or search deep into his soul to find reasons for his own philosophy of life. He was a practical, clear-thinking man of action. But this day he unburdened himself.

" You know, Gordon," he suddenly startled me by saying, " if we survive the bloody mess we are in, let us make a solemn vow together that, if we are spared, nothing in our future lives will matter but happiness, come what may. Money, success and fame are meaningless without it. Marriage without happiness would be a mockery. Poverty doesn't matter if it goes hand in hand with happiness. Do you agree? "

I did.

And so it came about that with Sheila as the only witness we made that simple vow on that remote hillside. It has been my philosophy ever since and at times when I have been troubled and sore at heart, I have thought back to that day in China sitting with Dick waiting for help to come.

It did, but in a most unexpected way!

I saw Sheila's ears twitch and her head turn towards the place where the paths met and where we had halted not more than half an hour ago. She had heard something and I had to restrain her from rushing back up the track to investigate. Instead, with my arm around her, she lay full length at our feet with her head pointed in the direction from which it had come. She was quivering with excitement, yet we could see nothing unusual in the landscape of dreary hill and vale which had stretched before us for so long with such painful and monotonous regularity.

Dick was now sitting bolt upright and alert, his " black-out " forgotten. Sheila, with her front paws outstretched would from time to time turn her head towards me as if asking to be let go, but I held her back with soothing doggy words which she understood, and the three of us waited for something to happen.

Sheila must have heard sounds quite a long way off and her keen ears had been right, as usual, for descending from the hill path we had rejected came two peasant women, dressed in the familiar black unattractive costume of the Yunnanese, and on their heads they carried baskets.

For a moment I thought they were going to run away in fright as the man had done near the temple only yesterday. Motioning Dick to take hold of Sheila I rose to my feet and without any pretence of the language begged them to come nearer.

They were elderly women and the wrinkled old lady who was in the lead seemed to realise that we were friends, for she came forward and removing her basket from her head, squatted in front of me and poured out a torrent of words, not one of which I understood. Then it was I caught sight of what was in the baskets. It was eggs—dozens of them.

"Dick—an egg!" I bellowed, and picking up one of the baskets carried it to where he sat and laid it at his feet. It was too good to be true.

Never have I seen such a gastronomical performance as the one given by Dick that day. He was sucking them raw from the shell. One after another they disappeared and it was as if with each mouthful he devoured, back came his strength. His whole appearance transformed back into the Dick I knew of old.

His trouble of course had been nothing but starvation and it was that that must have caused his "black-out."

For the life of me I could not tackle a raw egg, but Sheila could and she went through half a dozen in as many minutes. It was wonderful to see her eat again; tail wagging, she ate shell and all.

By now Dick was questioning the friendly old lady from the village. The younger of the two was shy and sat at a distance from us, but "grandma" was in her element as Dick did his best to make himself understood.

"What do you know, chum," said Dick, now replete after about a dozen eggs. "The Mekong is only an hour's journey from here and the road comes out right on the bridge. There are many soldiers there and granny was taking the eggs to sell to them. She says they talk a strange language, but are Chinese from far away. What a stroke of luck if they are Cantonese!"

I filled the old lady's hand with silver, probably paying ten times more for her produce than she would have got at the bridge, but every dollar was worth it to see Dick back with us again, and to hear her news.

We were so busy with our girl friends that neither of us saw the approach of Friday, Angus and Stuart who were returning to investigate our failure to be with the rest of the party.

"For goodness sake!" exploded Angus when he saw the eggs. "To think we've walked all these ruddy miles in case you were in trouble only to find you sitting here making pigs of yourselves. The Mekong Bridge is just over the hill and we were waiting on the top of the ridge for you to catch up."

"Come on, chaps. Help yourselves to tea," said Dick, now on his feet and prancing about with his stick like a two-year-old eager to get away. "Tuck in and let's get cracking."

The rest of the party never knew what had really delayed us. There is no harm done in telling them now.

Stuart told us that from the viewpoint they had reached a lot of traffic could be seen moving on the road east of the bridge and there was a large military camp on the left bank. He assumed they were Chinese troops but could not be certain. We were able to reassure him on this point, and for some reason we all shook hands.

Everyone was in festive mood as we set off to sight the river. Our village women insisted on bringing the remains of the eggs, and no one would have believed that half an hour before Dick had collapsed. Hop, skip and jump, the agony of the past forgotten, he led the way, chest stuck out, his mane of white hair ruffled by the breeze. I knew how excited he was feeling and I shared it with him. Between us we had planned and organised this trek into Yunnan and now it was nearing its end.

We were soon at the top of the hill where Desmond and the others waited rather impatiently and crossly, but they were soothed by the sight of the eggs we brought with us.

Below us, maybe a mile distant, flowed the Mekong River making its way to Cambodia and the South China Sea a thousand or more miles away, there to form the great rich delta already occupied by the Japanese.

What a thrill it was to see a proper road and convoys of lorries moving to and fro! The bridge could just be seen. I could hardly wait to get a closer view.

" Well, Charles, here we are," I greeted the large man with his black beard spattered with yolk of egg. There must have been ten dozen of them in the baskets when the harbingers of luck had set out that day to market them. Very few were left now; Charles had taken his fill and looked all the better for it.

" Gosh, they were good!" said Charles, smacking his lips, rather as Sheila had done a little earlier.

Hungry as I was, the thought of a raw egg gave me a sick feeling and I was content to wait and then fill my belly and make a pig of myself with food I understood. Angus could not stomach them either, nor could Desmond, yet the others revelled in them. Poor Richard, who was by then just skin and bone, seemed to have forgotten his dysentery and tucked in with the rest.

And so, refreshed and thankful and full of good cheer we made our way towards the bridge.

As we neared this engineering masterpiece of steel spanning a chasm where the water ran turbid and deep, I recalled a visitor who had stayed at my Bhamo house a year previously. Bill Pawley had brought him down from Loiwing: he turned out to be a V.I.P. Chinese Minister of State in the then régime of Chiang Kai-Shek. Referring to the Burma Road, the Generalissimo's last remaining lifeline to the remnants of his beleaguered country, the Minister had extolled his Government's effort at pushing through the road with such speed in order to open up a vital supply line with Burma. With an expansive smile, revealing more gold teeth than I really think were necessary, he had told me that one hundred thousand men and women had died in the course of its construction. Rising in places to more than 8000 feet, every available man, woman and child had been put to work to hew a way through solid rock, regardless of weather, health or sickness. Conditions must have been appalling, and, needless to say, pestilence and disease plus malnutrition had taken their toll of the peasants " Shanghaied " into labour gangs and driven to work for a Central Government already corrupt. My guest had boasted of this achievement and at the time I had hated his guts. Now I was about to set foot on this monument to the unknown dead, and, ironically enough, to reap the benefit of their martyrdom.

There was no stopping our Dick as he swept down the valley towards the bridge, like an officer leading a cavalry charge in battle. It was his day and hour, and not one of us would have disputed his right to lead the way and we followed enjoying every moment of his performance.

Looking more hobo than hero, he waved his stick to attract attention when a hundred yards or so away a group of soldiers came into view. Heavily armed as they were, Dick charged on regardless, and by the time we caught up with him he was in his seventh heaven. They were Cantonese, using a dialect he spoke as well as they did; and judging by their manner of deference he might have been one of their reincarnated ancestors.

" What a stroke of bloody luck, chaps," he yelled at us,

" these boys belong to the 1st Division of the Cantonese Army and we are going straight to the General's headquarters."

Dick's face was wreathed in smiles. He was well and truly home, and fate had been kind enough to deliver him amongst a people with whom he had grown up since childhood.

It was a large, well laid out, tented camp we entered. Dick, accompanied by Desmond, was immediately taken to meet the Commanding Officer, whilst we, like a bunch of tramps feeling most incongruous in such surroundings, squatted outside the large marquee which served as the General's office. He must have been in conference, for out of the tent led by Dick came a party of officers all smiles and salutes to give us a proper welcome.

We really had arrived. Ten men and a dog. It had taken us all of twenty-four days and nights to cross from the Irrawaddy to the Mekong. It was the end of the road. We had made it—even if not quite as we had planned.

I think we were too exhausted and bemused to appreciate to the full the kindliness of those soldiers from South China. Nothing was too much trouble to them. We were to be their guests, a doctor had been summoned and transport to Kunming would be arranged for the next day. Meanwhile it was important that Kunming be informed of our arrival. We walked over to the communications centre, which was obviously the General's pride and joy judging by his eagerness to show it to us.

The wireless room was like a scene out of a comic film. Sitting on bicycles pegged to what looked to be railway sleepers, were little men in uniform pedalling away as if their lives depended on it. Apparently it was a means of charging the batteries. Other soldiers sat tapping furiously at their dispatching keys, whilst others with headphones took the incoming messages. This, at least, was the impression I gained. Only then did it occur to me that this was the front line and somewhere up the road to the west were the Japanese. There was a war on!

For the sake of brevity it was agreed that one signal to be passed to the British Consul-General at Kunming would suffice for the time being. In it we gave our names and designations, with the request that the Press be informed so that news of our safe arrival would be broadcast to India where the families of most of us were by then. Even had there been facilities for personal messages it would have been of no use to me. Months earlier my family had flown away to India and I had no idea where they might be. Communications had long since broken down—and they would certainly have no idea that on this day of May, I was watching a lot of little men in China practising for the *Tour de France* in order to generate sufficient current to start a chain movement of Press news, which we later discovered found its way from London to New York. We were news—particularly Sheila.

How the Chinese loved that dog! Long before they fed us, food was lavished on her. Dick and Desmond may have been V.I.P.s in their own sphere, but Sheila had a special place in her own right. She was a queen on this occasion, and being very female made the most of it that night.

My memories of the camp are somewhat scanty, but I do recall a shower bath where under water pumped from the Mekong we scrubbed ourselves with soap, a strange luxury after so long without it.

We had been allotted a couple of tents complete with stretcher beds and bedding. It was glorious to contemplate sleep in a bed and the thoughts of tucking blankets round one's body instead of lying like a statue frightened to turn over in case a sleeping companion might be exposed to the cold of the night. It was all too good to be true.

I found myself sharing a tent with Desmond, Dick, Angus and Stuart; clean, though as yet still unshaven, we sat on our beds and heard from Dick the news he had gleaned from his Cantonese friends. It was not very much and after nearly a month completely cut off we were not very much more enlightened than when we had set out from Bhamo.

The line of the Salween had been abandoned in favour of a safer and more easily defended front on the Mekong, but the Japanese had so far made no move eastwards, seemingly content to have cut the Burma Road.

General Stillwell, with his Chinese troops sent as a token force into Burma, had been pushed back into India. Beyond that it was all local news. Kunming was teeming with Americans and, according to our source, the cost of living had rocketed sky high; in fact to such an extent that even an empty bottle had become currency amongst the very poor.

Dick had gained the impression that the Cantonese, complete strangers in a foreign land, were far from happy in Yunnan with little heart in the job they had been given to do. All we heard was hardly complimentary to the Generalissimo and his lady. Looking back it is not surprising that the door was wide open for a new era in China.

Then the doctor appeared and told Dick that he had removed Richard to the hospital bay and had patched up the big man with the black beard. When he saw Dick's heel he was horrified. He had a few words of English which he interjected into the conversation he was having with his patient in the language they shared. "Hospital, hospital," I heard him mutter, so I could not resist pulling Dick's leg.

"Bad luck, old boy," I said to him as the doctor began to dress the suppurating sore, "looks to me as if we shall have to drink to absent friends when we reach Kunming. But don't worry, you will soon be fit enough to hobble down to the Mekong to fish."

"Not on your bloody life," came Dick's answer. "Tomorrow afternoon we are leaving on an eastbound convoy and my friend here," and he patted the little medico's head, "is going to fix me up—aren't you?"

The doctor sat back on his heels, and said in his best English, "Mr. Winter, you are a naughty man."

We sat round a fire to eat that night and some of the officers joined us. It was a simple meal, but to us a feast and prepared as only the Chinese know how to fashion food from scanty ingredients. The soup was perfectly delicious and the fried rice was studded with pieces of fish, sweet-sour pork and vegetables.

Tiredness soon hit us all. Heaven knows how we had stayed on our feet for so long that day. I suppose we should have been celebrating, but our thoughts of relief and thankfulness were sufficient in themselves. We had no need of any other stimulus. Had there been any form of alcohol we might just have raised a toast, but there was none, and it was not missed.

And so, without a care, we slept and slept and slept.

CHAPTER 24

Burma Road

MAY 29TH

DREAM I CERTAINLY DID THAT NIGHT, AND I WAS back in my Bhamo house. Early in the morning I heard the familiar sound of bugle calls from the Frontier Force barracks half a mile down the road; then the clip-clop of Rolly's ponies passing my gate on the way to the parade ground. I heard the fluttering and twittering of the honey birds busy feeding from the flowers of the bauhinia trees alongside the bedroom window. Soon the bells of Father O'Donovan's church would ring to summon his flock for early mass, and the day's routine would begin all over again. . . .

I suppose from time to time I must have been on the verge of wakefulness, but I was quite unaware of where I was and far from the world of reality. And in this state I remained until midday when consciousness gradually returned. My thoughts began to focus, dreams of Bhamo faded and, feeling rather ashamed, I jumped out of bed in an empty tent.

The rest of the party I found foregathered discussing the next stage of our journey to Kunming. Whether I am supersensitive to atmosphere I do not know, but somehow my companions seemed to have changed into different people during the night. During the next three days I realised that I was right. We had ceased to be the homogeneous body of men who had battled together for so long. Each of us seemed withdrawn into himself and mentally detached from the others. Reaction was at last setting in, which under the circumstances was quite understandable.

Maybe, quite unconsciously, we were reverting to normal individuals, our task as a team being done. From now on our fate lay in other people's hands and a joint effort was no longer required of us. Each one of us had personal problems to solve and his own future to think of. We were all undoubtedly preoccupied with these thoughts and already it was evident that the parting of the ways, so to speak, was not far distant.

To me it was like reaching the end of a voyage when the time comes to pack the night before the ship docks. Everyone disappears to go about his or her business and the whole mood of the passengers changes from a family affair into a private one. Close friendships nurtured on board begin to evaporate as if they had never existed. Tender romances fade into sweet memories of the sea. And when the gangway is lowered the voyage is over and one's companions become swallowed up in the arms of their families and friends.

One member of our party at least was in high spirits. Dick had been given a new pair of canvas shoes, similar to the ones I had seen the battery-charging soldiers wearing on their bicycles. He was only able to wear one as his heel was heavily bandaged, but he was very proud of it as he limped round the group, impatient to get on the road.

Apparently we were to travel by slow-moving convoy leaving at 4 p.m. that afternoon and it would take us all of three days to reach Kunming.

Charles was not satisfied with the arrangement, knowing full well that if Desmond had requested Consular vehicles we could have got there much sooner. He was already back in India where things were done that way, and he seemed totally unaware that petrol in China was a commodity as precious as silver. Paddy was inclined to back up Charles on the issue of the transport. I refused to become involved and wandered off with Sheila to the bridge, or at least as near to it as the defences would permit.

It was clearly wired ready for demolition, if necessary, but so strong were the surrounding fortifications that I doubt whether the Japanese would have succeeded had they attacked. The bridge spans a narrow, very deep gorge, the hills rising for hundreds of feet on either side. I guessed that on the other side the road would be heavily mined.

The Cantonese troops seemed cheerful little chaps and by the way they gazed at Sheila you would have thought they had never seen a large dog before. She was already looking fitter, although still very thin, and she was certainly enjoying the presence of so many attentive humans.

Richard had been pronounced fit enough to travel to get proper hospital treatment at Kunming, and in the late afternoon we left the camp having bid farewell to the Chinese officers who had so kindly sheltered us.

Ten men and a dog, we climbed into the backs of heavy American lorries already laden with miscellaneous military equipment, and as the convoy moved off we saw the last of the Mekong as we climbed out of the valley through which it flowed.

Standing clear in the afternoon sunshine stood the hills of the great divide between the Mekong and the Salween. Range after range, getting higher and higher, they extended as far as the eye could see; and viewed from the main highway it seemed impossible that man could traverse them and survive. Yet properly equipped I would like to travel that way again, if only for the rhododendrons, azaleas, irises and primulas growing with such abandon in the spring sunshine. Also, I shall never forget the breathtaking beauty of some of the dawns and sunsets we had witnessed in the high mountains. It had been a cruel journey but nature had provided certain compensations, and the memory of these I shall treasure always.

CHAPTER 25

Arrival at Kunming

IT WAS A LONG TEDIOUS UNCOMFORTABLE RIDE OVER the roughly metalled surface of the Burma Road to Kunming, and often a frightening one, with sheer drops into the valleys from the rock-strewn highway which had been hewn at such cost in human lives. In places the road reaches 8000 feet as it twists and turns on a course following the contours of the mountains. Over this we bumped our way, peering over the tailboard to look at the scenery or scan the villages through which we passed. Halts were frequent and on our second night we camped with the soldiers at a place overlooking Lake Tali which was like an inland sea at 7000 feet. Scenically this part of Yunnan is quite some of the most lovely country to be found anywhere in the world. The lake with its background of high mountains is majestic in its beauty. Its very remoteness makes it intriguing, and I wish I had seen more of it and that our timing had coincided with the Tibetan Fair which was held annually on its shores.

In spite of the discomfort of the lorries we all slept a lot. That is about all I remember of the journey until before noon on the third day from the Mekong Bridge, some fifty miles from Kunming, we came on a convoy of civilian cars coming from that direction.

Dick, with whom I happened to be travelling that day (needless to say Charles and Desmond never shared the same lorry), suddenly went wild with excitement for he had recognised his friends and colleagues who had travelled to meet him and take him back in triumph to his home base.

There was a tremendous welcome for us as we clambered down from our vehicles—bearded, gaunt and dirty but no longer starving.

The Press was also there in force asking all manner of questions, but what I remember more than anything else was the hamper of cool beers and the delicious food they had brought with them for us to enjoy before they swept us away to Kunming in their saloon cars.

This really was a joyous occasion, our first proper celebration, with the added comfort of knowing that by now our families knew of our safe arrival. No effort had been spared to have them traced in India or elsewhere. Apparently we were headline news, which all seemed very funny to us, as we had only done what a lot of others had done—run away from the Japanese. But in the process we had walked from the Irrawaddy to the Mekong.

The newspapermen seized on the names of these two rivers as if there was magic in them: "Eight Britishers survive ordeal of march from Irrawaddy to Mekong," ran one headline shown to me later in Assam. There were others on the same theme, and one accompanied by a ghastly photograph of unrecognisable tramps which had been taken on the wayside. I have a copy of it to this day. Needless to say, the story got a bit out of hand and over-dramatised. The impression was given that we had actually been caught by the Japanese and had succeeded in escaping, whereas all we had done was dodge from their clutches a couple of times. Admittedly it had been quite a near thing on both occasions, but we were not escapees in that sense, nor the heroes we were made out to be in the Press.

If there were heroes amongst us they were the sick; and the effort of Charles, Richard and Dick, particularly the two former who lacked Dick's terrific stamina, stands out. Physically and temperamentally these two men had started the journey totally unequipped to perform such feats of endurance as they had been called upon to make for all those days. Yet they had got through.

By this time even the strongest and fittest of us were pretty near wrecks. We were all gaunt and haggard-looking, apart from Dick whose solid squat frame still had a robust appearance which belied his real state of health.

The last fifty miles, reclining in the rich comfort of American sedans, was in sharp contrast to the first part of the journey along the Burma Road. Talk was unending and we were full of speculation as to when it would be possible to reach India, the next stage in our wanderings. Apparently passages in aircraft were not easily come by as the Americans had so many priorities for their flights. No doubt a lot of string-pulling would be necessary to get away quickly, or at least by those of us fit enough to travel.

We had reached the point when all we could think about was picking up the threads of the past and starting a new life in India. I had never been there, and more than anything else longed for news of my family, friends and colleagues, particularly those who by devious routes had made their way overland out of Burma.

The past two months had been lived in a vacuum, as, long before we had left Bhamo, all proper communications with the outside world had been broken. So much had happened, and now the end of our journey was in sight.

Excitement was running high as we approached the old capital city once known as Yunnan-Fu. Why such a euphonic name came to be changed I never discovered.

We got our first view of the town as our car breasted a steep hill and there below us stretched an enormous lake and beyond its banks stood Kunming itself basking in the late afternoon sunshine.

Flying low over the water with its shadow reflected on the lake's surface, a large transport aircraft was coming in to land and high in the sky were others, as if to remind us that this remote place in Western China had been transformed into a gigantic staging post by the Americans in answer to the challenge of the gauntlet thrown at their feet by the Japanese at Pearl Harbour not long before.

After the quiet of the mountains and the tragedy of all that had happened in Burma, the thoughts of which still lingered and hurt, here was something different. It was a new and stimulating world into which we were entering and I think it affected us all the same way.

We had been fugitives for too long. From now on there was going to be no more running away. The time had come to fight back and hit hard, to shave off our beards, cease to be hoboes intent only on saving our skins, and to get into uniform and " belong "—as most of us would have done long before had not the edict gone out from on high that we were specialists with expert knowledge and must remain as civilians as our contribution to the war effort.

With every rhythmic beat of the aircraft engines in the sky that afternoon came a new-found confidence that things were going to be different. I could not wait to get out of Kunming, and, although I dared not tell the others in the car, I knew that I would be the first away and in India within a matter of hours. I was.

Our convoy of cars was by now threading its way through the busy narrow streets of the town. They teemed with Chinese who stared in wonder at the bearded dirty occupants in their midst. To the Dicks and Desmonds of our party this was home ground. To some of us it was no more than a junction to be hurried through as quickly as possible for we had jobs to do elsewhere. We did not belong here.

I could think of little else than the joy of wallowing in a hot steamy bath, getting a change of clothes and drinking a long whisky and soda out of a glass instead of water from a cup fashioned from the stem of a bamboo. I needed a pair of scissors and a razor, and soon my Victorian cabby's fungus of a beard would be gone for ever. I was to stay with our company's representative who was still in residence winding up its affairs in China. He was a stranger to me and the idea was that he would collect me from Dick's mess which was to be our first port of call. We were to celebrate our safe arrival, and Dick was insistent that he be our host.

The party, I fear, was in the nature of an anti-climax and not quite what Dick had planned. Desmond excused himself as he had urgent matters to discuss with his Consul-General, and Stuart went with him. Already our ranks were broken and I felt sorry for Dick who for weeks had dreamed of the fun we would have on reaching journey's end.

There was a hollowness to this celebration which even the whisky could not fill, and one by one we melted away to the billets which had been allotted to us, never again to meet as the group of men who had battled together for so long and against such odds.

My host had a luxurious flat and he was kindness itself fitting me out with clothes from his own wardrobe which hung on my gaunt frame and gave me the appearance of a scarecrow. Shoes were a problem, so I retained the boots which had served me so well for nearly a month.

The first shock came when I had hacked away with scissors at my beard and then shaved off all that remained. Was the face I saw in the mirror really mine? Somewhat lean and hatchet-faced at the best of times I was now reduced to skin and bone. But I could not care: I was ready to go and only hoped that my contact in our Intelligence Service would recognise me and arrange my flight over the Hump.

I need not have bothered, for of course he did and by eight o'clock the next morning I was closeted with the Commanding General of the American Army Air Force who seemed to know all about me. Refreshed after a wonderful night in a real bed covered with a silken eiderdown, I was a new man. The General had an aircraft leaving that afternoon for Margherita in Assam and I could travel by it and he would arrange my onward flight to Calcutta.

It was one mad rush before leaving, and I am glad it happened that way, as I cannot bear partings. The Consul-General had put his seal to a document which was to serve as my temporary passport. There was just time to give Sheila a big hug and to shake her new master by the hand; I knew she would be happy with Desmond, and in fact she stayed with him until her death.

The gangway was down, the journey over, and from that moment we all went our separate ways, some of us never to meet again.

Epilogue

TWENTY-ONE YEARS HAVE GONE BY SINCE THE EVENTS
I have done my best to describe took place and, although my
memory is a good one, I may have erred as to the actual time
and place of certain incidents which highlighted our long road
to freedom.

No diary was available from which to draw material for
a book and I have not sought out my colleagues of long ago
to help me fill the few gaps that remain in my recollection of
our journey through Yunnan. Two decades have passed since
I saw any of them, except for a momentary chance meeting in
London not long ago. It gave me no more than the opportunity to congratulate Desmond on his knighthood and the
other honours bestowed on him since we had last met.

Fortunately, I treasured through the years the set of maps
I had acquired in India and which I had annotated to such
good purpose whilst the sequence of events was still clear in
my mind. On these I had traced the route we had taken from
the Irrawaddy to the Mekong, the places where we had
camped and where, from time to time, we had been in despair.
It is from these notes of mine, jotted down in 1942, combined
with my memory, that this story has been put together.

Of course, by rights, it should have been told by the more
able and erudite pens of Charles or Desmond, but for obvious
reasons neither of them would undertake it. Before leaving
Kunming I had suggested to the latter that he should write an
account of our journey, which I was sure would have been
welcomed by *Blackwood's*. "Not on your life," he had replied,
"I would have too much to say about that so-and-so, Charles
Ewing."

Months later I met Dick in India and he told me that whilst the main body of our party had been recuperating at Kunming he had prompted Charles to put pen to paper, only to be given much the same answer but couched in even more acid terms.

We shall never know what sparked off such a burning mutual loathing as existed between these two men. Something must have happened unknown to us on the day they met. Or did it have its roots long years before, when perhaps they had been at the same school, or perhaps in love with the same girl? If that was the case, fate had certainly played them a low trick, for their dislike of the other's company had dogged them for weeks on end and in consequence made them both unhappy men.

So, in the event it has been left to me to tell the story in my own way, and in doing so I have relived every day of our strange journey. Should, perchance, my companions of 1942 read this book, I think they will agree that in the main I have kept strictly to the facts. If I have embellished them here and there and done a little embroidery at times, I claim that as my right and the privilege of a chronicler.

Often I have thought back to those days and wondered what became of the men I had got to know so well and like. What, for instance, happened to Man Friday when he eventually reached his native India? If I judge him correctly, I am sure he had an exciting war for he was that sort of man.

Richard I shall always picture tinkering with the engine of his car in preference to playing a round of golf. He would be surrounded by a happy family asking little more of life than the peace of domesticity.

Paddy defeats me. Maybe he accepted office in the Colonial Service and retired young with a golden bowler after a few years in tropical Africa, hating every minute of it after his tranquil life in the Kachin Hills of Burma. Perhaps one of these days I will meet him at the Dublin Horse Show or some such place where Irishmen foregather.

Dick and Angus I was to meet up with again in India later in 1942, and they had become very firm friends. More than twenty years ago we drifted apart, as men do, and time has done the rest. Dick, I am sure, has scaled every " pimple " that has come his way in life and is no doubt in retirement like myself.

I wonder if Angus still insists that his signet ring was spirited away from his finger that night in the resting place of the dead? " Not on your bloody life," I can hear Dick telling him; " it fell off crawling up that ruddy hill in the dark."

One evening when my work had taken me to Calcutta I caught sight of the familiar figure of Charles dining alone like a lord in the Bengal Club, and I joined him over a bottle of wine. A few months of rich living and all traces of the ordeal he had been through were gone. We talked of everything but our days together, and once again it was " dear boy " this and " dear boy " that. Poor Charles, he was never intended to live rough. For all I know he has long since been honoured for his work with the Treasury. I cannot look him up in *Who's Who*, because to be quite honest his real surname escapes my memory.

Desmond went from success to success in the Foreign Service and ended his career as one of Her Majesty's Ambassadors. We happen to belong to the same London club and when I met him by chance not long ago he was hurrying away to luncheon, and I had dashed into Pall Mall to collect my mail before sailing to the Cape where I now live. Apart from greying hairs Desmond was unchanged. Give me this distinguished diplomat with Dick thrown in for good measure (provided he had a pair of boots!) and I would not ask for finer companions if called upon to undertake another long walk into the hills.

I was never to see Stuart Gracey again, and much of what I know about his career after reaching India came to me from a charming girl of a Quaker family who, but for the war, might have shared his life.

Stuart had seen more active service than most men of his age, but strictly as a non-combatant in accordance with the principles of his faith. But something came about to change this lovable young man's beliefs and attitude towards war, for he shed the uniform of the Friends' Ambulance and volunteered for a dangerous mission, from which he never returned. His convictions must indeed have been deep ones. If such a thing as fear existed in Stuart's make-up it would be the fear that anything he did would be wrong in the eyes of the God he worshipped so devoutly. He knew no other kind of fear.

Stuart trained as a parachutist, preparatory to being "dropped" as an agent behind the Japanese lines in Burma, where he was soon to die in tragic circumstances.

If ever a man deserved a special place in Heaven it was Stuart, for he belonged there, and I shall for ever remember him amongst the blue and yellow of the irises, and the confidence he gave me when hope of survival had dwindled to its lowest ebb.

After the sad chronicle of the passing of the man we had all come to love so much, I can turn to the story of my young assistant, Patrick Doyle, for his is one of success and his daring exploits during the war would, in themselves, provide material for a book.

This quiet youngster of mixed parentage was soon to come into his own when, after recuperating at Kunming, he was flown into India. Free of the restricted environment of the land of his birth, the war gave him the opportunities his keen mind must have been seeking and he seized them with both hands.

Patrick has the distinction of being the first parachutist to be dropped behind the Japanese lines in Burma, and strangely enough his companion on this intelligence-collecting-cum-sabotage mission was another of the youngsters trained in my teak forest stable. Their record is a brilliant one. After the briefest training they were back in the areas they knew so well and time and again until the war came to an end they operated in the Myitkyina and Bhamo areas. They lived to tell the tale as a brace of majors with a brace of Military Crosses and a high American decoration for bravery.

What a source of satisfaction it was to me to follow the careers of these men I had trained and then watched grow in stature with every challenge they had to face! After the war it was not easy for men such as these to identify themselves with the cause of Burmese Nationalism, although their roots were there. They were unwanted in the country of their birth and they had to seek new lives elsewhere.

To-day they are both successful business men somewhere in the Caribbean, which is now their home.

In India there was the formidable task of putting together the jigsaw puzzle of a past so rudely shattered by war. Bridging the gap in time was a painful process, for much of the news I learned was full of tragedy.

Of the five Englishmen who had comprised my peace-time senior staff only one was left and he was desperately sick. The others had been killed or had died on active service. Nearly all my closest friends were dead and the final roll call had yet to be published. War had indeed taken its toll in a big way. Meeting people who had reached India in safety one developed a set formula of guarded approach in conversation, for in some cases marriages had broken up or husbands or lovers were missing. So much had happened, and now most of us were strangers in a land foreign to us.

I was soon to learn that Rolly, my dear old friend the Commandant, and the younger man with whom he had taken to the hills on the same day that we had crossed into China were both dead. Had I not been adamant in my decision to travel eastwards I would have shared their fate. Yet Rolly had called me foolhardy and done his best to persuade me to accompany him.

They had been murdered as they slept by the very troops they trusted. The labrador, Dusty, must have been shot at the same time. All this had happened as we were struggling up the banks of the Salween towards Lu-Ku. Robbery was unquestionably the motive. Overcome by greed and covetousness of the cash box which accompanied the Commandant, the bodyguard had decided that in the turmoil of evacuation from Burma it would be an easy matter to do away with their two officers and then slip into India as rich men. This they did, forgetful that the arm of the law is a long one and stretches deep into far away places even during the chaos and upheaval of war. The four soldiers responsible for this terrible crime were eventually traced in India, tried and found guilty beyond any shadow of doubt. They were hanged in Delhi. Justice had been done.

Poor dear Rolly! I am sure that had he remained behind the Japanese would have treated him with the respect due to his age and rank. But it was not in this man's nature to bow to the invader and with his spirit broken by events beyond his control he had taken himself to the hills he knew so well, confident that he would be safe amongst the friendly people who lived there. But he misjudged the men who had formed his bodyguard.

During the months following the evacuation of Burma many strange stories were circulating, and in fact the fate of certain people who failed to reach India will never be known. But one of the strangest of all stories came out of China some time after I had been posted to Delhi, and I became involved in it.

A young English soldier who hailed from Berkshire had been found wandering alone and somewhat dazed in the vicinity of the Mekong Bridge. He was dressed in the rags of a Yunnanese peasant but still retained his identity disc and was able to establish his *bona fides* to the authorities in Kunming where he had been taken by the Chinese over the bumpy Burma Highway.

The boy was a corporal, a medical orderly, and after the usual preliminary interrogations he was flown to Delhi where, because of my knowledge of the area in which he had been wandering, I was asked to talk to him quite unofficially.

Smith, as I will call him, turned out to be one of those rather simple country lads who under interrogation become tongue-tied, but I gradually pieced together his story, and the more he unburdened himself the more fascinating it became.

With five other soldiers he had been travelling from Bhamo to Myitkyina but the vehicle had broken down somewhere on the road. He actually recalled seeing me driving alone in the opposite direction and admitted that at the time he and his mates had thought I was mad.

By the time these men had carried out repairs and got their truck on the road again it was deserted, and when they eventually reached the banks of the Irrawaddy opposite Myitkyina there was no ferry or boat in sight to take them over the river. They had slept in the truck and clearly taken no precautions to guard against being surprised from the rear.

Early the following morning Smith had gone some distance into the bushes by the roadside to answer the call of nature when he heard heavy automatic fire and, as he put it, he really was caught with his pants down.

The firing lasted several minutes while he crouched on the ground too terrified to move, and then there was complete silence.

For an hour or two he had lain hidden and when eventually he crawled back to the road he found his companions dead, shot by a Japanese patrol which must have been sent to reconnoitre as far as the river and had then returned to Bhamo.

Although suffering terribly from shock the young corporal had sense enough to gather up some food and, finding a jungle path leading towards the mountains, he had fled the scene. For two days he had travelled eastwards in a demented state, not meeting a soul.

It seems that he had then been found sleeping by a party of armed men, who, from his description, must have been a gang of frontier bandits probably on a foraging expedition into Burma. For some reason they had not killed him, and when he had demonstrated his skill as a medical orderly by treating the poisoned leg of the gang's leader they had taken him along with them and was made to work, although not treated unkindly.

Smith's story from then on became very confused and all he could recall was travelling east and climbing into high mountains. The gang had robbed and pillaged on the way and one of their number had been killed.

For months on end he had led this fantastic existence under the grimmest of circumstances, but with the resilience of a countryman he had survived. Before joining the army he had been a farm labourer. He was a man of very limited intelligence and to this day is probably following the plough on the Berkshire Downs none the worse for his temporary role as cook and orderly to a gang of Yunnanese thugs. He had actually learned a few words of their language.

With the help of my maps and his recollection of place names we traced his route to the Salween, and by a remarkable coincidence I found that he had crossed the river at the very place where our kind Chinese Customs friends had waited in vain for help.

My mind went back to the lovely girl with the long plaits, her twin daughters and her tears when we had left Manyin.

Smith had learned that the village had been the scene of a massacre of men, women and children a long time before he got there. From the tales he had heard the men had been butchered and the women, in order to escape being raped, had jumped into the river with their children in their arms.

None of this had come out in the official interrogation. Why should it? But it mattered a lot to me and I was sick at heart.

It was impossible to tie Smith down to dates or to relate the time of the massacre to the day on which Desmond had urged us to make one last desperate effort to reach Lu-Ku. I knew how anxious he had been at the time and how right he had been.

The Customs men knew that they might be followed by bandits, hence their plan to separate. Whether any of them survived I never discovered.

All this may account for my dislike of the " Black and Angry River." Our experiences there had all been harsh and cruel and the countryside ugly and uninviting. Only the kindness of the peasants at Lu-Ku remains as a pleasant memory of the Salween.

My seat in the aircraft which flew me to Assam was a bale of parachutes, which made a soft bed in the tail of the plane. This was just as well as we flew the Hump at more than 20,000 feet, and without oxygen my legs became like lead and I was incapable of any movement. Only as we circled Fort Hertz did the pilot descend to a reasonable level. He had been briefed to look out for any signs of Japanese activity there, following a report that it might be used as a fighter base to intercept aircraft plying between Kunming and Assam. The pilot was soon back high in the heavens, only too anxious to keep well clear of the towering mountains. Not that I saw anything of them and have no clear recollections of that flight until we touched down at Margherita high up amongst the tea estates. A friendly planter made me welcome and I remained his guest until an R.A.F. light plane came to fetch me. The next day I was in Calcutta.

I lost my bet with John Henderson thanks to our plans going wrong at Tengyueh. He had beaten me to it by ten days, and I stood him a night out in London where we were to meet again before the war was over.

Should they read this book my companions may be interested to hear that I was destined in due course to retrace my steps into the hills beyond Bhamo, not far from where our precious bottles of whisky had been poured away on that fateful night of 3rd May, 1942. I even bathed at the foot of the waterfall where Paddy had cursed us and Dick had put the fear of the devil into the suspected opium smugglers who would have stolen our mules but for his timely intervention. But this time I was alone and it was in the nature of a farewell pilgrimage to old haunts as I was leaving the Far East for good to take up an appointment in London.

The war had ended. Being convinced that the sands of time had run out so far as the European trader in Burma was concerned, I had long since resigned from the company which had taken me on as a youngster of twenty-two. Moreover, my heart was no longer in the job and I doubted whether many of the great forests we had worked so efficiently would ever be reopened. It was better that I sought fresh fields in which to earn a living.

Burma was then full of Nationalist aspirations and the day of its so-called Freedom was approaching. The newly-formed Government of General U Aung San was clamouring for the incorporation of all the Frontier States into a unified Burma under a Central Government directed from Rangoon.

The idea was sound enough, but to me, mixed up in matters of Political Intelligence as I was at the time, some of the problems seemed insoluble. I knew that the views of many of my friends and acquaintances, men who had devoted their lives to the well-being of the frontier peoples, went unheard or were written off as the prejudiced opinions of a bigoted race of old-fashioned administrators anxious to cling on to the past and afraid to face up to the new emerging Burma of U Aung San and his colleagues.

To the north, east and west of Burma proper and in pockets to the extreme south, lived the Karens, Kachins, Chins and Shans, owing allegiance to Britain. All but the last named, who are not a fighting race, had remained loyal throughout the war, whereas U Aung San had led his Burmese troops against us in his determination that Burma should for all time cast off the yoke of British rule. In the process he had quite cleverly double-crossed the Japanese.

The events, some of them bitter and tragic, that followed have no place in this book. Bold decisions had to be reached and the Labour Government then in power at Westminster set up a Frontier Commission of inquiry headed by Colonel Rees-Williams, M.P.[1] His task was to ascertain the true feelings of the hill tribes and, if possible, to draw up safeguards for them within the structure of a Central Government in Burma.

It was by no means an easy job, but he tackled it with vigour, intent only on reaching his own conclusions and taking evidence wherever it was to be found.

Lord Ogmore may recall the long journey we did together through war-tattered Burma, the pace of our small convoy of cars dictated by the speed of an obstinate armoured car which led the way for hundreds of miles like a tortoise— when its driver could persuade it to go at all. In this most frustrating fashion we had been guided to Mandalay and beyond into the hills, and there was nothing we could do about it as the Government had insisted that an armoured car escort was necessary. The weather was hot, the road was pot-holed and dusty, and the way to the northern frontier seemed interminable.

Of first importance, of course, was to set out and explain

[1] Now Lord Ogmore, the Liberal Peer.

the prospectus of a new and unified Burma to the few leaders who really mattered, and such men were far apart and burdened by problems of their own. Prejudices had to be overcome; prejudices born out of centuries of hostility between the men of the hills and those from the plains. They would take a lot of convincing that in the long run their people would stand to gain by throwing in their lot with the Burmese.

I was nothing to do with the Commission, but having lived for so long in close association with the Kachins I was deeply interested in the outcome of the referendum on amalgamation and hoped that Colonel Rees-Williams would succeed in his mission.

Thus it came about that, leaving the Commission in the Shan States, I set out alone to the Kachin country far beyond Bhamo; and as I drove my jeep into the town one afternoon I had the same feeling of exhilaration I had felt some years before when driving against the one-way traffic of the last of the refugees.

It could hardly be called a homecoming, and there were no familiar faces to give me a welcome. Dumping my bag in what had once been the Circuit House, I drove out to see if any traces remained of my house and garden. I was prepared for shocks as I had studied aerial photographs of the town when under Japanese occupation, and knew roughly what to expect, but I had not reckoned on having to search and re-orientate myself like a complete stranger before finding what I was looking for.

It had been sited where now stood an airfield, and at last I found it in a far corner of one of the parking aprons. All that remained to remind me of the past were a few of the bauhinia trees half obscured by new jungle growth. All else was concrete and rubble.

For a while I wandered round what had once been my lovely garden and I wished that U Sein, my head clerk, could have joined me, for he had been convinced that one day

I would return. It was on my return to Rangoon from this farewell visit to the north that he eventually found me. For some reason my name got in the newspapers and he immediately travelled there from his home in Tenasserim in order to hand over the few treasures he had so conscientiously guarded all these years.

It was the dilapidated state of Rolly's headquarters that depressed me more than anything else that day. Always so spick and span, like the colonel himself, the buildings now sprawled neglected and dirty with all the appearance of a shanty town slum. Where there had been trim hedges and flower-beds were broken bottles and heaps of refuse. Everywhere were signs of mildew and decay. Uncontrolled nature had done its work over what had once been the polo ground and golf course. There was no joy anywhere, so I left and made my way back to the town.

The main residential quarter and bazaar were little changed, and the hospital still stood on the hill to remind me of Father O'Donovan. Bachan Singh, my grocer, with the tenacity of his race, was still trading, as were some of the Chinese I had known in the past. I dare say more of them had co-operated with their new customers, for " business is business." News of my arrival soon spread and I had not the heart to tell the nice people who came to see me that night that I would soon be gone never to return. But this time I was not running away.

It was strange to be driving alone the next day over the road we had taken to safety at such speed five years before, and at the turn-off I halted a while and smoked a pipe, every detail of our hurried departure clear in my mind. The track into Yunnan was heavily overgrown and it seemed that the mule caravans no longer came through from Tengyueh.

Approaching the picnic spot at the foot of the waterfall I thought of Paddy cursing us for being so long in coming, and of the scene with the men bent on stealing our mules.

Leaving my jeep I climbed up to the old bridge and, sure

enough, there were the mahseer lazing near the surface of the water, enjoying the morning sunshine that filtered through the trees growing on the banks. War had not changed their breeding habits nor driven them from their favourite play-grounds.

I stripped and dived into the pool I knew so well of old, and then it was time to cast off my mood of nostalgia and get down to the business that had prompted me to travel so far. I had to take another road and climb to nearly 7000 feet to the mountain fastness of the man I had come to see and talk with.

Although little more than a mule-track it was just nego-tiable by jeep, and that evening I sat in the company of one of the most colourful characters of the war against the Japanese who, with his charming wife, gave me a wonderful welcome.

The exploits of Major Shan Lone, M.C., are legendary. If ever there was a man born to lead his people it was " Rusty," as he was affectionately known to us all: for years he had been a thorn in the flesh of the Japanese who had placed a price on his head. But time and again this fighting chieftain of the hills, trained in the use of modern weapons and well-versed in the art of sabotage, had eluded them and laughed behind their backs as he went about his Pimpernel acts and harassed the enemy from the rear.

Here indeed was a man to rally the Kachins, if he could be persuaded that it would be in the interest of his people to join forces with the new Government of Burma. Long into the night we talked and it was clear to me that many obstacles had to be overcome before firm decisions could be reached.

" Rusty " was not in the least concerned or nervous about any threat from the East. To him the Yunnanese were no more than crude bandits. Sinlumkaba was an armed camp, his men trained to the hilt by this ex-major of the Burma Rifles. But could the Kachins remain in isolation once Burma became a Republic and the last vestige of British influence disappeared for ever? Only a month or two remained before this would happen. What then?

Two days later I was none the wiser as I said good-bye to the comfort of the Shan Lones' remote home in the mountains. It was time to go.

As I was getting into my jeep Rusty gave me an invitation to return. "Come back soon, Colonel," he said, opening his arms wide as if offering me to share his whole domain. Then he added "And I'll guarantee at any time to give you the choice of four different brands of whisky."

Driving slowly down the steep hillsides towards the Irrawaddy plain, I speculated on what the future held for these wonderful fighting men who had fought side by side with us and often, at great risk to themselves, sheltered our parachutists and hidden our agents. Would Rusty be persuaded to enter politics and lead his people as a statesman, or would he turn bandit chieftain, defy the Burmese and take toll from the caravans which enter Burma from China through his homeland?

By the time a unified Burma came about and the Kachin people had agreed to form part of it I was back in London immersed in a new job which had nothing to do with the Far East. I suppose I could have found out from the Burmese Embassy whether Rusty had entered politics, but this I failed to do, and it was thirteen years later that the name of Major Shan Lone cropped up.

Of all most unlikely places in the world it was in the Katanga that I learned news of Rusty. The Burmese Government had sent one of their senior soldiers as a token contribution to the forces of the United Nations in the Congo, and on hearing of his arrival as Chief of Staff to Colonel Harry Byrne, then commanding the U.N. Forces in the Katanga, I sought out Colonel Ye Gaung in Elisabethville. He got the surprise of his life when I greeted him in his own language in a place so remote from his native land. Smoking one of his cheroots I learnt much of what had happened over the years

since I had sailed down the Irrawaddy, and he told me that
Rusty was indeed in the Government. Major Shan Lone,
M.C., was a Cabinet Minister and responsible for all the
frontier peoples.

Perhaps after all I may yet take up his invitation and travel
the long road again into the hills. Who knows?

Airline Detective

by
DONALD FISH

To the World's Airline Security Officers

I would like to record my thanks to
John Pearson, who has given me
invaluable assistance in the writing
of this book.

D.F.

Contents

FOREWORD

by Ian Fleming

One day in the summer of 1955 I was sitting in the innermost
sanctum of Scotland Yard—the private office of the head of
the C.I.D.—admiring, with Sir Ronald Howe, some forged
five-pound notes and gossiping about crime in general. It
was a chance, purposeless visit. I had had to do with Ronnie
Howe during my wartime years in Naval Intelligence and
the friendship had continued.

Ronnie Howe said that he would be flying to Istanbul
in a few days' time for the annual meeting of Interpol, why
didn't I come?

I had imagined that these meetings of Interpol would be
top secret affairs held in remote and heavily guarded police
headquarters. In fact it transpired that they were much
like the meetings of other international organisations in
smart hotels with banquets and speeches and open sessions
during which the top policemen of the world read learned
papers from flower-banked podiums. Their main object
was friendly contact and, if secrets were discussed, they
would be confined to private luncheon parties or hotel
bedrooms.

Ronnie Howe said that the only other journalist who
ever bothered to attend was Percy Hoskins of the *Daily
Express*, and it crossed my mind that if he, by far the most

brilliant crime reporter in England, thought these meetings worth while, so should I.

I was at that time Foreign Manager of the *Sunday Times* and, thanks to the kind heart of Lord Kemsley, more or less able to write my own ticket so far as foreign assignments were concerned. So I fixed things up and in due course flew off in the same plane as Ronnie Howe, Percy Hoskins and a man called Donald Fish who, it turned out, had something to do with airline security.

It was great fun in Istanbul and by scraping together fragments from official papers and speeches and tying them up with informed gossip, I was able to write two long dispatches on " The Secrets of Interpol " whose success was assisted by the Istanbul riots which took place conveniently over that week-end and on which I was able to give a scoop to my paper.

The next year I went again to the conference, this time at Vienna, but my " revelations " of the year before had put the police chiefs on their guard and, on this occasion, I was only able to produce a pretty thin three-quarters of a column. The learned papers read by the police chiefs had been more rigorously censored than before and were more carefully guarded, and the gossip dried up in my presence.

I skipped the next year's meeting in Lisbon, and that was the end of my acquaintanceship with Interpol.

At the two earlier meetings the British quartet saw a lot of each other and I was interested, and rather annoyed, to note that on no occasion was I able to extract a single grain of news or information from Donald Fish. Ronnie Howe was always generous in providing Percy Hoskins and me with snippets of background, though he was always careful to distinguish between what was secret and what might be published. In fact I think he cannily used me on one occasion to warn the British public about forged travellers' cheques. But at least he " gave," and he realised that Percy Hoskins and I had somehow to justify our existence at these conferences. Donald Fish couldn't have cared less. No amount of wheedling or badgering would persuade him to yield one word of information about the work of his little air security sub-committee, which got on with its business far from the madding throng of the conference hall. He ate and drank and chatted with us, this tall, rangy man with the poker player's eyes, but he revealed nothing, and both Percy Hoskins and I had to admire him for it, knowing what we had been able to extract from national police chiefs temporarily in their cups, or suffering from that suppressed vanity that affects men who know many secrets for which an audience is always forbidden them.

No, Donald Fish was one of the securest security men I have ever met, and now that he has retired and is free to tell some of his stories, the reader can be pretty certain he is getting the real stuff. There is nothing wishy-washy in these seventeen chapters, which are some of the best I have ever read in any language on police work.

Security, except when it becomes counter-espionage, is a dreary subject, and I have never envied the security men I have met in my life because so much of their work is of the " policeman on the beat " variety—testing door handles and window frames, and investigating mysterious noises that are always loose shutters. The reward for the work lies in the occasional scoop, and it is the hallmark of the true security officer that when the scoop comes along his mind is not so dulled by previous routine that he fails to recognise it.

Donald Fish and I had dinner together one evening at Sachers in Vienna at the end of the 1956 Interpol meeting, and he did admit that he had had exciting times with

B.O.A.C. in between stretches of drudgery. He was due to retire in two or three years' time and I urged him to think of writing his memoirs, but, like so many expert technicians, he admitted that he couldn't really distinguish between the wood and the trees in his job, and that anyway there was something magical about writing, and he couldn't master the art. This or that incident had of course been exciting, but he simply couldn't get it down on paper. I told him not to despair, but just to do his best and then find a professional writer to smooth the corners of his prose and prune out the irrelevancies and the libel.

In the event he followed my advice. Donald Fish teamed up with John Pearson of the *Sunday Times* to produce a text that reads true and yet is attractively written. A highly successful series in the *Sunday Times* resulted, a promising television series is in the offing, and there is this book.

Many people who have led exciting lives had talked to me, as they will with any author, about " writing something when they retire." Donald Fish's book, with its solid writing, unobtrusive background and local colour, is technically an example of how a man, himself untalented in story telling, can yet contrive a thoroughly expert distillation of some of the exciting things that have happened to him.

To say anything more about the book would be to write a review of it. This is not my task, and what I have written so far is merely to explain how I came to be asked to write this introduction. I will now leave Donald Fish and his book with my blessing and, quite out of context, tell two stories about " security " that have always stuck in my mind.

During the war one of the Assistant Directors of the Naval Intelligence Division in which I was employed was responsible for security—the physical security of ships and dockyards, the prevention of loose talk, the security of communications and so forth—thoroughly dull work that was often allotted to rather dull individuals. In 1942, Noël Coward had obtained Admiralty permission to use one of H.M. destroyers for the film *In Which We Serve* and he was naturally anxious to discover her name and when she would be available for filming.

Noël Coward, who told me this story, knew the Assistant Director of Naval Intelligence of that date and he frequently rang him up to find out when the ship would be available, but since the whereabouts of H.M. ships was deadly secret, he always received a dusty answer, until one day Coward was delighted to get a call from the Admiralty. The Assistant Director of Naval Intelligence himself was on the telephone, and immensely mysterious.

" I say, Noël, you know what they do in India, hunting I mean? "

" What the hell are you talking about ? "

" Well, you know people go on safari and they shoot things? "

" So I'm told."

" Well, now, the thing they shoot will be available at Portsmouth next week."

At last Noël Coward got the message. " Tigers! " he called excitedly. " You mean she's called *The Tiger*? "

" For God's sake be careful, dammit! This is an open line."

Those who were in the war will have their own stories along these lines, but I think the saga of Mohammed Ali, the green tea merchant, was probably unique in its example of security gone mad.

The political warfare experts, picking up the strings from the end of the 1914–18 war, began dropping leaflets over

Germany almost as soon as war was declared, and we all remember how asinine many of those leaflets were. For some idiotic security reason the leaflets were known by the code word of "Nickel," though why they should have a code word at all nobody could understand. Anyway, when the time came for the invasion of Africa, it was decided that a "Nickel" should be prepared to rally the North African Arabs to the Allied cause. Something simple was devised with a crude picture of Winston Churchill on one side and Roosevelt on the other, and some such slogan as "Victory rests with the Allies." In a "Top Secret" folder this project was put into the machinery of the Political Warfare Department, finally reaching, by devious routes and under a watertight cover story, the sole Arabic expert in the Political Warfare Department—a certain Mohammed Ali, a green-tea merchant from Casablanca who had rallied to the Free French and had come over to England after the collapse of France.

Mohammed Ali was instructed to translate the English slogan into Arabic characters and the finished product was then printed in its millions and trillions and shipped out to Gibraltar in cases marked "oranges" or "beer," and carefully stored in some top-secret depot in the Rock in preparation for the great day.

When the day came, fighters from the Fleet Air Arm were loaded up with consignments of the vital "Nickel" and took off again and again all through the day of the landings, sprinkling the whole of Morocco and Algiers with the leaflets.

After the invasion had succeeded, an American intelligence officer who had taken part in the landings came over to Gibraltar and found his way to the leader of the Allied Political Warfare group. He had a handful of the leaflets and he said to the propagandist in charge, "What

16

the hell's this stuff you've been dropping all over the country? "

Stiffly the political warrior replied, " Those are leaflets to rally the Arabs."

" Do you know what they say? " asked the American.

" Yes," said the propagandist, " of course I do. They say ' Victory rests with the Allies '."

" No they don't," said the American. " They say ' Buy Mohammed Ali's Green Tea '."

Well, those are two stories about " security "—the Evelyn Waugh model, so to speak. The Donald Fish marque is something very different indeed.

6th June 1961

CHAPTER I

A new dimension in crime

In the whole history of crime there is nothing quite like the way the organised criminal has moved in on the world's airlines since the war. It is not a thing the airlines themselves care to advertise, and little is known about it outside the ranks of the air security officers who exist to fight it. But during the last ten or twelve years, the immense expansion of the world's air routes has produced an international crime wave in the air that is still on the increase.

All this, however, lay very much in the future when I joined B.O.A.C. in 1946 to head the world's first air security organisation. We were expecting trouble, of course, but not on such a scale that within ten years practically every major airline in the world would need its own security organisation to deal with it.

As things turned out, I came up against the beginnings of this crime wave before I had been many months in my job. I remained in the thick of it for the fourteen years I was with B.O.A.C., and the organisation we built up to fight it became the model on which many of the other airlines based their own security services as they were formed.

These years were easily the most exciting and the most satisfying of my whole life, and it is only now they are over that I can see just how fortunate I was to have been in at the birth of air security.

I was nearly fifty when I joined B.O.A.C. By training and by inclination I was a policeman—one of the old school I suppose—with more than twenty-five years' service at New Scotland Yard and M.I.5 behind me, and throughout my time in air security I never ceased to regard myself as a " copper." Sometime or other during those hectic years, I must have caught the aircraft bug and caught it badly. Even to-day I cannot stop myself watching any plane passing overhead, and the one thing I really miss is the view from my office window at London Airport on a fine morning.

This office of mine faced right across the main approach, and I had a grandstand view from my desk of the liners that roared into London from every airport in the world. The view never changed much, but I never got tired of it.

When I was in London, I usually had a fixed routine. I would get to my desk just before nine in the morning, and already the big Boeing 707s would be thundering in from Idlewild and San Francisco. The D.C.7s from Montreal would arrive hot on their tails, and then a slight lull before the Comets and Britannias turned up from Tokyo, South Africa and Sydney.

I got into the habit of watching them out of the corner of my eye as I went through the morning's mail, for there was usually a pretty hefty batch of letters that had come in during the night from our airports and security offices scattered round the world. Whenever trouble occurred on our air routes, a report of it always turned up sooner or later on my desk, and then it was up to me to do something about it.

Most mornings there was enough to keep me busy until the tea arrived at ten o'clock sharp. Once the tea came,

my senior staff on the airport used to follow it in for their
morning conference, and that would be the end of watching
aircraft for that day.

Just occasionally there would be a morning when nothing
seemed to have gone wrong anywhere. The bullion flights
would have gone through without a hitch. The Far Eastern
routes would be free of narcotics trouble, and diamond
shipments from Africa would be going like clockwork.

Curiously it was on these mornings and on these mornings
alone that I ever actually worried about the background to
air security. For it was as I watched plane after plane flash
down the runway, some with up to a hundred passengers
aboard, that I had a chance to remind myself just how
complex the whole air security business had become
even in the short time I had been at it, and how easy
the high-speed modern airliner has made things for the
criminal.

There were times when my job seemed all but impossible.
Here was I Security Superintendent of just one out of
the many great national airlines operating across the
world. From Idlewild and Chicago to Rangoon and
Hong Kong, I had my men on the lookout, specially trained
to spot the sort of crime and racket that flourish under the
peculiar conditions of air travel, and sometimes we would
be lucky. Occasionally, as with the London Airport Raid,
or the great Indian Gold Smuggling Case, our investigations
would even hit the headlines.

Most air crime is unlike anything else. It is almost as
if the airlines have produced a new dimension in crime, and
I am still frightened at how little is really known about it.
For the majority of the profitable rackets being worked
across the airlines are also the most difficult to detect. Most
of them occur on normal scheduled services carrying

millions of ordinary passengers every year who never realise what is going on under their very noses.

Much of the time I was no better off than the ordinary passenger myself. Far too often I would know perfectly well that a certain racket was going on, but would just have to sit tight until the vital moment when one of the participants put a foot wrong. When some of our stewards, for instance, became caught up in a smuggling ring carrying many thousands of dollars' worth of illicit diamonds into New York, I had to allow it to go on several months before we could find sufficient evidence to secure a conviction.

No policeman enjoys working like this, and there were times when I used to pace that office of mine cursing the day the aeroplane was ever invented. But luckily there are few criminals or dishonest staff who are quite as smart as they think, and I found that sooner or later, they would usually give us the lead we wanted.

Then, of course, there were the times when I would get a tip-off from a security officer on another airline who had uncovered something on his aircraft before it had a chance of spreading to mine.

Crime knows no frontiers between the airlines. If one country's planes become infected with a particular crime, you never have to wait long before the rest are as well, and one of the most important developments I saw during my time in air security, was the way the security officers from the European, American and Far Eastern airlines were beginning to co-operate in attacking the air criminal.

There is still a long way to go in this, but I remember that the first hint I got of a possible Chinese immigration racket in San Francisco came in a query from the security officer on one of the American airlines that had already had its fingers badly burned over the whole business.

A new dimension in crime

It was in this way, one of the most important leads I received at the start of the continuous battle against the gold smuggling into India came in the course of a very casual drink in a pub off Piccadilly with John Drury, an old American friend, who was then my opposite number in T.W.A. He happened to mention that four crew members from his company's aircraft were having trouble with the Indian authorities for alleged gold smuggling by air into Bombay, and was only too pleased to give me all the facts.

I enjoyed every minute of my time as an air security officer, but now that I have retired and have nothing to worry about except improving my handicap at golf, I must admit that I am not sorry my old responsibilities are on someone else's shoulders. For every year the pickings on the air routes are becoming more tempting, and the life of the air security officer more exacting.

During my last five years with the Corporation, the departure of a bullion plane with three million pounds' worth of gold aboard had become a commonplace. I myself have travelled to New York many times with more than a million pounds' worth of diamonds in my charge. As for the strong room at London Airport, which was another of my responsibilities—Heaven knows how many million pounds' worth of gold, diamonds and other valuables it must have housed every year.

What worries me is that whileis th traffic has been increasing every year, and air crime has kept pace with it, I know for a fact that the really top-ranking international criminals still have hardly begun to nibble at it. Only in two cases—with the diamond thefts at Tehran and the great Indian Gold Racket—has there been a definite strategy on the part of the big international crime rings to prey on air traffic.

But I also know that the airlines would be unwise to rely on immunity from the big international operator much longer. Before I left B.O.A.C. there were clear signs that the international syndicates had realised the chances they had been missing, and were all set to make up for lost time.

What scares me about this is the knowledge that the normal forces of law and order are just not equipped to deal with the big-time criminal in the jet-age. Time after time while I was with B.O.A.C., I found myself taking on cases for the simple reason that there was no one else with the authority or the interest to deal with them. Local police could hardly be expected to investigate successfully a crime that had been committed when the aircraft was five countries away from the spot where it landed and the trouble discovered.

Nor are the powers of Interpol really sufficient to deal with crime in the air, despite the sixty-six countries that belong to it. For Interpol exists to pass on information from one national police force to another. It has no agents of its own, and no over-riding authority to enable it to act with the speed and effectiveness needed to combat the air criminal.

As a rule we had to work alone. Sometimes we were lucky. At other times, simply because we did not possess the powers of arrest and interrogation of a normal police force, people slipped through our fingers who should never have got away. And in a few cases, the sheer inadequacy of the law itself to meet crime in the air would lose us a case when it should have been firmly in the bag.

From the way the law books are written, you would imagine that the aeroplane still had to be invented, and so far, national law has just made little attempt to extend itself to cover even the most commonplace crimes if they occur in an aircraft outside the skies of its own country, or when it has landed on a foreign airfield. While an aircraft is in flight, the law still treats it as if it were a ship at sea, but whilst a ship's captain has powers of arrest and detention, no aircraft captain could ever use such powers, even if he possessed them.

Just to show what I mean, take a perfectly simple hypothetical case. Apart from the recent hi-jacking cases and the celebrated time-bomb murders, where aircraft have been destroyed and all the crew and passengers killed, there has never been a known murder committed aboard an aircraft in flight. But just suppose one was, and suppose, for the sake of argument, that it happened over mid-Atlantic on an Indian aircraft flying from Idlewild to Delhi.

Perhaps it was a *crime passionelle* with a French husband shooting his wife's German lover at the rear of the plane with only a pair of wealthy businessmen, one Italian and the other Japanese, as witnesses. The confusion aboard would be considerable, and the pilot would naturally make for the nearest airport, say Shannon in the Irish Republic.

What would happen once the aircraft touched down, I for one have not the remotest idea. The complications in establishing a venue for the crime would be so involved that I doubt if the Irish authorities could ever get the case presented to court. The crime had not been committed in their country, it involved none of their nationals and no doubt the Italian and Japanese witnesses, the airline and crew would soon be questioning any protracted delay in their departure from Ireland.

But if the Irish did not proceed with the case, who would? The Americans would not want to be saddled with it, although the plane had left their airport; nor, I suspect, would the Indians, although it was their plane, and under their jurisdiction. Only the Frenchman who had committed

25

the murder would have much cause for satisfaction. For he would soon realise that, thanks to the aeroplane, he had probably discovered the recipe for the perfect murder.

This is a hypothetical case, and so far the shortcomings of criminal law as applied to the international air routes have hardly mattered except to make things difficult for men like me, but towards the end of my time with B.O.A.C. I was seeing how these loopholes in the law were beginning to allow the really big-time criminal to get away with what he wanted. To-day, everyone in air security knows that once the really big trouble hits the airlines, there will be precious little help forthcoming and little the law will be able to do about it.

It is this weakness that long ago convinced me of the over-riding need for a code of international criminal air law. This on its own will not be enough, for the national police forces are not the people to enforce it effectively, even with the help of Interpol.

Instead, if the airlines are to meet the very real threat of highly organised air crime hanging over them at the moment, it is their own security forces who will have to do the work. Sooner or later, they will have to combine under some central authority, to form the nucleus of a really international Air Police Force, with full legal powers to attack air crime wherever it occurs, irrespective of local laws and national boundaries. There seems no other way.

CHAPTER 2

The Spitfire and the gelignite

It was the war that brought me into aviation. In 1939 I was a detective-inspector at Scotland Yard and had the good fortune to be among a small group of C.I.D. officers seconded to M.I.5 under Chief Inspector Len Burt, who was later to become head of the Special Branch.

Any secret service organisation is naturally strange to an outsider, but after Scotland Yard, M.I.5 seemed a very odd place indeed. It possessed every conceivable expert tucked away somewhere in its organisation, but for some reason we were the only policemen there. Officially we were " investigators," with the enigmatic title of " Civil Assistants to the War Office."

Our headquarters in those days were in Wormwood Scrubs Prison, and as soon as we arrived we were thrown into a group of cells, allocated a minimum of battered office furniture, and left to get on with it. During the next four years our anti-sabotage work took us to coal mines and islands in the Hebrides, to destroyers and radar installations. There were no recognised hours, and there were periods when I have never been so bored before or since.

But gradually I began to specialise in certain types of technical sabotage investigation. Fortunately, as a young man, I had been apprenticed for three years to a big firm of electrical engineers and my experience in their workshops had given me a feeling for anything mechanical that helped me time and time again.

If an aircraft engine was damaged suspiciously or the controls of a naval gun had been smashed, I was the chap they called in. Once I spent a week in an armaments factory where a ten-inch file had been dropped into the gearbox of a highly specialised milling machine, and a few days later I moved on to one of H.M. Dockyards where a mysterious explosion had occurred aboard an aircraft carrier.

I soon found however that the cases I enjoyed most were those involving aircraft, and the man who taught me most about my new job was a dapper, fresh-complexioned little man of about fifty-five called Harvey-Bailey. He was a senior official at the Rolls-Royce factory at Derby and one of the cleverest engineers in the place. He called himself " the Coroner " and his section of the huge works " the Morgue." For Harvey-Bailey's job lay with any Rolls-Royce aero-engine that went wrong. Whatever the cause, and whatever the circumstances, the engine would be brought back to the Morgue and the Coroner would hold a post-mortem to determine " the cause of death."

I worked with him several times, and the way he went about things always stuck in my mind. He would have the engine stripped down to each individual unit and split-pin before him on the bench, and point to it in the rather school-masterish way he had. " The answer's there, if you look " he would say. " Everything you want to know is in that engine, if you know your facts and what you're looking for."

It seemed easy for him, for somehow he always did know what to look for, but the emphasis he would lay on the word " look " was a lesson worth learning.

But there was one case where the answer was not in

the engine, at least not the whole answer, and Harvey-Bailey rang me up with a problem he thought must undoubtedly be enemy sabotage.

It was during a time when he was desperately overworked, for the Battle of Britain was at its height, and his experience was vitally needed to detect any engine faults that might have spread through the front-line squadrons. But he had been called away from his usual work to inspect a Merlin engine from a Spitfire based at Tangmere, which had been shot down and crash-landed in shallow sea on the South Coast some months before. There had been no engine failure but the aircraft was so badly smashed that it had been turned over straight away for scrap. The engine, corroded beyond repair by sea water, had ended up with a small firm of scrap metal merchants at Belper, to be broken up.

By the purest luck, this firm was run by a couple of ex-miners, and while they were breaking up the main fuel trunk-pipe with their sledge hammers, one of them noticed something. For melted all along the inside of the pipe, and down into the flame traps was a substance they recognised from their days in the pits. It was gelignite.

It may seem odd it had not exploded, but in fact gelignite can often be safely exposed to the very highest temperatures. As long as it is not actually detonated it simply melts, and can even burn quite safely.

But although this gelignite had not exploded, and had clearly not played any part in bringing the aircraft down, it was not something that could be ignored. Whole sticks of gelignite do not find their way inside Merlin engines by mistake. For the stuff to have ended up where the men found it, it must have been deliberately put inside the engine when it was partly dismantled for overhaul and, as Harvey-Bailey said in a grim aside when he was showing me the engine in his workshop, "The only people who place gelignite in aero-engines are deliberate saboteurs, and the next time they do it we may not be quite so lucky."

Although he had stripped the rest of the engine down there was little else he could tell me, and I was faced with a top-priority sabotage job with nothing to go on except the clear evidence that it had been committed.

When I began my investigations the next day this uncertainty seemed to continue. To start with, the squadron was no longer at Tangmere. It had been heavily shot up during the battle, and what was left of it had been withdrawn to rest and regroup at Prestwick. So off I went on the night train to Scotland, hoping at least that I could find someone who could remember enough of the squadron's activities at Tangmere to give some clue to the identity of the saboteur.

It is an odd thing about most investigations, but you can usually tell whether you are going to be in luck or not. From the very start of this one there was trouble. The first setback turned up as soon as I reached Prestwick. I had already discovered that the man who had piloted the plane on the afternoon it was shot down had baled out and parachuted to safety. He was obviously going to be one of my star witnesses, but as soon as I mentioned his name to the squadron's C.O., I saw his expression change and knew what had happened even before he told me. At this time the R.A.F. was even shorter of pilots than planes. He had gone straight back into action after the crash and been killed a few days later in a sortie over France.

Next I tried the Engineer Officer, but there was nothing unusual he could tell me about the plane, and since it had been written off, all its log-books had been filed away at the Air Ministry in London. After two back-breaking days at Prestwick questioning everyone in that squadron who might have been able to tell me about the Spitfire and its mysterious engine, I caught the train home about as wise as when I started.

But the case was far too important to consider abandoning, so I got the Air Ministry in London to trace the history of the plane and the engine, from the time of production until it reached its end in the sea. It had been delivered new only a few weeks before the crash, but had been flown for a while whilst the squadron was stationed on the East Coast of Scotland. This gave me the idea that the gelignite might have come from a local Scottish quarry that used it for blasting.

So I spent another week visiting every stone quarry within a radius of fifty miles of the Spitfire's old aerodrome examining their explosives records. Again I drew a blank, and it was not until I was actually back in Edinburgh having a last drink in the bar of my hotel before catching the train back to London that I had my first solitary stroke of luck. Although some of the sticks of gelignite had melted with the heat of the engine, others in the trunk-pipe had remained virtually intact in their original wrapping, and during my trek around the stone quarries of East Scotland, I had carried some with me, just to show the quarrymen what I was after.

I remember sitting in the bar wondering what to do next and for no very good reason had taken one of the sticks of gelignite out of my case. I was looking at it and wondering just where it had come from, when suddenly a large man with a red face barged up and asked me what the hell I was doing in the middle of Edinburgh with a stick of gelignite in my hand. The stuff was so discoloured that he must have been an expert to recognise it, and in fact he turned out to be the local representative of I.C.I., whose subsidiary, the

Nobel Company, had actually made the particular stick I had in my hand. I told him enough of the truth to convince him I was not an enemy agent trying to blow up Princes Street, and ended up by asking for his advice.

When he examined the gelignite he was puzzled. It had been made in the form of a three-quarter inch stick, and three-quarter inch sticks, as he hastened to tell me, had not been made by his company for six or seven years.

"All right," I said, "how does that affect the case?"

"It doesn't," he replied, "except for the fact that a few years after manufacture the chemical structure of gelignite changes. Now there are no signs at all of this stick having deteriorated, and I would stake my job as Edinburgh representative of the Nobel Company that this is nothing like six years old."

This was not much to go on, but it was better than nothing, so I cancelled my sleeper back to London, and on my new friend's advice, set out early next morning for the I.C.I. explosives factory at Ardeer in Ayrshire where the gelignite had been made. If nothing else I could at least establish whether or not the wrapper was a forgery.

At first the factory just repeated what the representative had told me about three-quarter inch sticks not being made for the last six years, but after a great deal of nagging and ferreting about in the office where the orders and requisitions were kept, I found one, just one special order for three-quarter inch sticks of gelignite which the factory had fulfilled eighteen months before. When I pointed it out, the old chief clerk was apologetic and said he was sorry it had slipped his mind, but it had been a very special order, and such an unusually small quantity that he had thought no more about it. It had been ordered specially for some out-of-the-ordinary combined operations attack on the coast of Norway, and there had been only three hundred pounds of it.

We spent the rest of the afternoon going through the records, and by the end of it I was satisfied that the sticks I had in my possession must have been in this particular batch.

At this point I suppose I should have started feeling optimistic about things but there really was something wrong about this case from the start, and as soon as I had traced the three hundred pounds of gelignite back to the ordnance depot near Gretna Green where it had been sent, I lost the trail again. I spent four days going through every solitary entry in the explosives record for the previous two years, but not one reference to it could I find.

There was no doubt that the small special order had been swallowed up in the bulk stock and all I was able to prove was that it had never been used for the specific purpose for which it had been ordered. Every one of the many small explosives dumps around the factory was searched and re-searched, but without success, so I set about compiling a list of all despatches of explosives to enable me to trace each one to the bitter end.

I even followed 14 lb. of the stuff I was looking for to a Home Guard Unit in Cornwall, but at the end of six weeks' hard work, I was really no nearer to discovering how the original sticks had found their way into the trunk-pipe of the crashed Spitfire.

In all investigation work there is a certain point where you have to realise that if you bang your head against a brick wall any longer, it will not be the wall that will suffer. So back I came to Wormwood Scrubs, and contented myself with writing as savage a report as I could on the shortcomings of the method of registering explosives in His Majesty's Ordnance Depots.

As a sort of consolation prize I had the pleasure of knowing that it was largely this report which led to a special committee on the subject being set up under Lord Swinton, which recommended a complete overhaul of the distribution of explosives. And as far as I know, there were no further outbreaks of gelignite in the trunk-pipes of Merlin engines, although, to me as an investigator, that was hardly the point.

CHAPTER 3

The Polish Wing-Commander

There is nothing very glamorous about investigating sabotage
during wartime. You need patience, and a mind that
enjoys detail for its own sake. You must be prepared for
long hours, abortive questioning, a great deal of boredom and
almost endless disappointments but, if you are to be any
good at the job you have got to have something else as well,
a sort of sixth sense that tells you for no reason you can
actually put your finger on, that such and such a thing is
simply not right.

It is this peculiar state of mind which enables an
investigator to reconstruct a crime and visualise what has
actually happened with such clarity that when facing a
suspect he can almost feel there was an eye witness to the
incident.

I had this feeling over a tragic case I came up against
towards the end of my service with M.I.5. It brought me
personally in touch with air travel across the Atlantic for
the first time through the famous Return Ferry Service that
operated between Canada and Prestwick and I suppose
that if subconsciously there was ever a point at which I
made up my mind to seek my future in aviation, this must
have been it.

It was a case that concerned a much decorated wing-

35

commander in the Free Polish Air Force. He was one of the Allies' top fighter aces, and during the Battle of Britain his photograph was always in the papers. It was one of those typically Polish faces, not exactly old-looking, but extremely lined, with a look of tension about the eyes, and a set to the mouth that seemed to combine toughness with unusual sensitivity. But there was nothing sensitive about his war record. He had shot down over twenty enemy planes, and by 1943 when I first met him, his bravery had been recognised by the late General Sikorsky, the Commander-in-Chief of the Free Polish Forces in Europe, by an appointment as Air Attaché in Washington.

The first time M.I.5 heard of him officially was when he suddenly emerged as the mystery man at the centre of a strange little melodrama played out in a Liberator of the Return Ferry Service, a thousand miles out over the Atlantic on the way to Montreal. It was particularly delicate since it involved the person of General Sikorsky himself.

The Return Ferry Service was organised to fly back to America the crews who had piloted American-built aircraft over to Europe. When weather conditions were favourable, the planes dropped out of the skies into Prestwick like a flock of starlings and then, after a short rest period, the crews would be bundled into a Liberator and flown back, a regular passenger service without any of the modern comforts. There were only a limited number of seats and the majority of the passengers travelled in flying suits, lying or sitting on mattresses in the fuselage; a thoroughly uncomfortable journey and one to be undertaken only from sheer necessity.

On this occasion General Sikorsky and several members of his staff were called upon to attend an Allied conference in Washington, and urgency demanded that they travelled by R.F.S. I do not remember how many were in the party, but the principal characters were our wing-commander and the general's personal secretary, a civilian. General Sikorsky and the secretary were allocated seats and the wing-commander a space in the fuselage on one of the mattresses.

For safety reasons these flights started at night with the aircraft painted black and the windows completely blacked out.

The plane was several hours out above the Atlantic, and most of the passengers including the general, were asleep, when the secretary saw the wing-commander go to the rear chemical lavatory. There was something furtive about him and he was seen to be carrying something in his hand. On his return the secretary had asked if anything was wrong and the wing-commander had told him that he had been sleeping when he was awakened by a smell of burning rubber from somewhere near his head and that he had found, wedged between the floor and the outer shell of the aircraft, a bomb which was so hot that he had thought it about to explode. It had all happened so quickly that he had not known what to do for the best, but in the excitement of the moment he had rushed it along to the toilet, broken it in half, and thrown the hot part into the Elsan fluid in the can. He had thought that the cool part of the bomb was safe, and so had hung on to that as some sort of evidence of what he had done.

There was a long and whispered discussion between the two men and it was finally agreed that for the sake of security they would say nothing about the incident until they reached Montreal. The captain of the aircraft was not to be informed, and in no circumstances must the general be alarmed. In fact, they were so secretive about the whole matter that nothing else was said about it until the party reached Washington. Then at last it was reported to the Intelligence Authorities who immediately went into action. Urgent messages were sent ordering a search of the aircraft in Montreal, and in particular to trace the part of the bomb which had been thrown into the lavatory. Every member of the crew was questioned.

But the delay had done nothing to help the inquiries. The remains of the bomb could not be found and the whole case was passed on to us in England. Top level arrangements were made for the portion of the bomb kept by the wing-commander to be sent to England by special courier, since nobody in America seemed to have the faintest idea where it could have come from. Along with it arrived a report setting out the facts in great detail and the case finally ended up on my plate, along with instructions to work with the closest possible liaison with the intelligence officers of the Free Polish Air Force.

It did not need much imagination to see why everyone had the wind up over this affair. During the time I had been with M.I.5 I had made a close study of the various examples of German sabotage equipment that passed through our section, and if there was any sabotage here, it had nearly been the sort of coup an enemy saboteur would dream about. For it is not every day an enemy agent gets the chance of destroying an aircraft without trace over the Atlantic with a passenger like General Sikorsky aboard. If an agent was involved, we had to find him before he had a chance to strike again.

From the start, there seemed something phoney about the whole case, but the first proof I had that somebody was lying came when the remains of the bomb turned up on my desk.

It was about four inches long, black and shaped like a

small cigar case. I knew at once that it was an incendiary bomb, and a very dangerous one at that. I also knew it was not an enemy one. I had seen several others like it before, and I knew that it was specially made in England for British and Allied agents dropped into occupied Europe. The problem was to explain how this one had found its way aboard an R.F.S. aircraft with the leader of the Free Polish Forces aboard.

There was nothing very complicated about the bomb. It had two tubes of a powerful incendiary material detonated by an acid and copper time fuse. I knew perfectly well that there were only two places from which it could have come, either the factory where it was made, or the school where the agents were trained in its use.

The extremely tight security regulations in force at the factory made it unlikely that it could have been smuggled out of there. On the other hand, the training school with agents of many nationalities always passing through, was a far more likely place for this sort of leakage to occur, so my first step was to get on to one of the Polish intelligence officers I was working with, and get him to trace every Pole who had been through the school.

My end of the investigation was still hampered by the fact that General Sikorsky and the whole mission, including the wing-commander, were still in America, but the crew of the R.F.S. Liberator who had carried them out to Montreal was back in Britain, so I took advantage of this and hopped up to Prestwick to see them. Rather as I had expected, none of them had anything very significant to add to the statement they had made earlier, but the one man I particularly wanted to see was the flight engineer.

One of the things that puzzled me in the wing-commander's statement was his reference to being woken up by the smell of burning rubber. There was no rubber, as far as I knew, in the bomb itself, and it was important to know whether he could be telling the truth. At first it looked as though he could not have been. The engineer knew nothing about it, and there was no reference in his log book which seemed to have any possible connection with burning rubber.

I kept questioning that flight engineer, and in the end he remembered something which could have explained what the wing-commander had been talking about. It seemed that at about the time when the bomb was supposed to have been found, a fuse had blown in the aircraft quite close to where the wing-commander was lying. There was just a chance that it might have made the sort of faint smell of burning the man had referred to.

Apart from clambering all over the Liberator, looking at an innocent fuse, and getting a final picture in my mind of where all the passengers had been placed, there was not much more I could do at Prestwick, so the station manager drove me down to the station in time to catch the night train back to London.

There was no question of a sleeper that night. I was lucky enough to have caught the train, and I remember having to sit up all night in a blacked-out third-class railway compartment.

A sleepless night on a train from Scotland in war time may not be much fun, but it is not a bad time for puzzling out a problem. There were still several possibilities I had to consider, and there was one important piece of the puzzle missing, but by the time my train steamed into St. Pancras early next morning, I had a theory worked out of what might have happened.

The piece of the puzzle I still needed was something that

The Polish Wing-Commander

would connect my wing-commander with the sabotage school. Once I possessed that, my theory had a good chance of turning into fact, and to find this last piece of the puzzle I was relying on the Polish intelligence officer I had left behind in London.

I rang him as soon as I arrived in my office, and learned that he had done his job well, for out of all the Poles who had been through the school he had found one who had served with the wing-commander. This was a young pilot officer from his squadron who had been grounded for medical reasons and had promptly volunteered for espionage duties. At this time he was nearing the end of his course at the school, and the intelligence officer had found out that on at least two occasions he had been visited at the school by his old Commanding Officer, the wing-commander.

The school was about three hours by car from London. I had had no sleep during the past thirty-six hours, but knew that sleep was impossible until I had the answer to one question, so with my Polish friend driving, we set off.

A quick check of the curriculum at the school showed that the young pilot-officer had been trained to use the type of bomb found aboard the plane, and we soon reached the point where we just had to see him and make him talk. He looked like the link we needed. He had to talk.

I am often asked how one sets about an interrogation. I don't know, even after all these years, but there is one essential—you must know the true answer to certain questions before you ask them. The reply you get decides the form from then on. The circumstances of each case dictate whether you play it rough or smooth, and on this occasion I decided to play it smooth.

I left it to my Polish colleague to make the introductions in his native language, but as the pilot officer had an excellent

41

knowledge of English, we continued the interrogation in English. To keep his suspicions down, we said we were vetting his friend, the wing-commander, for a top secret job, and it was soon clear that the young man worshipped him. His affection was obviously founded on hero worship and the fact that their families in Poland had been closely associated in happier days.

Questions on family background followed—occupation of relatives, education, financial position, and then suddenly we sprang the first important question, " Have you seen him since you have been at the school? "

" Yes, he has been up here twice to see how I am getting on."

" Now you know the security regulations here—have you ever discussed your activities with him? "

" Only in a general sort of way."

This was the first half-truth, and I immediately sensed we were home and dry, but this was not the time to strike so we switched to another subject. Then finally the moment came. I took one of the incendiaries from my pocket, and suddenly placed it on the table in front of him.

" When did you give him that? " I asked.

It was the one vital question, and we got the answer we needed. We also got the whole story.

It seemed that the young fellow had told the wing-commander a great deal about his work and the equipment he used, including the incendiary bomb. For some reason this particular bomb had interested him, and when he had asked for details about it, he ended up by asking the pilot-officer if he could get him one as a souvenir. It was an odd request, but the young man saw no harm in it, pocketed one of the bombs and handed it over the next time they met.

We could not tell the pilot-officer the real object of our

inquiry, but we had to be certain he did not talk or communicate with the wing-commander, so after obtaining a detailed signed statement, we had no alternative but to place him under close arrest for the breach of security regulations, and take him back to London with us in our car.

By now I was nearly out on my feet through lack of sleep, but I felt we were at least half-way home. There were many unanswered questions, but they would have to wait. When one is nearing a point of collapse through mental and physical fatigue there is only one way to sleep—strip to the buff and get in between the coldest sheets you can find.

Next day the Polish mission was due to return to Prestwick, so off I went again to Scotland by the night train, to tackle that wing-commander immediately he arrived. It was a dull, dreary morning when I reached the aerodrome and heavy black clouds hung over the hills of Arran. I waited anxiously until the Liberator broke through clouds, and taxied up to where I was standing.

The general came down the steps first, followed by his staff, but the wing-commander was not there. I soon got over my disappointment and decided to take no further action for the moment. I could easily find out in London why my suspect had not returned. So back to London I came.

It appeared that the wing-commander had been given a job of some sort which had delayed his return for four or five days, so I decided to take this opportunity of interviewing the general's private secretary and go through the statement he had originally made in Washington. There was always the chance that I could pick up some small point that had been overlooked and in any case he was more or less an eye-witness to the incident in the aircraft. However, I was certainly not going to tell him what else I had found out.

This interview with the secretary produced one additional piece of information. The wing-commander had not wanted a word of the discovery of the bomb to reach the general or any other member of his party or the crew. He had persuaded the secretary to say nothing about it on arrival in Montreal, and it was only when the secretary had insisted something must be done about it, that the wing-commander had agreed that the Intelligence Authorities in Washington should be told. The whole air of secrecy had been so well put over that even now the general had not been informed, and as far as I could see the secretary and the wing-commander were still the only members of the party aware of what had happened. There appeared no doubt that the wing-commander had done all this to make sure that the story did not leak and he was clearly trying to hush the whole thing up, but again, why?

To find this out I needed him alone and immediately he landed, so once more I packed my bag and went off to Prestwick to wait. I made my headquarters at the County Hotel in Ayr. The proprietor was an old friend who asked no questions when I asked him to keep a room always ready for me to interview someone.

For six long days I waited, watching the arrival of every R.F.S. plane, until early one morning I spotted the man I wanted. He was still in his flying suit, walking from the plane across the tarmac.

I introduced myself as an intelligence officer and, before he could think of any excuse, suggested we had breakfast together and took him over to a waiting car. During the three-mile journey to the County Hotel at Ayr, I purposely kept my mouth shut. He was worried already, and I wanted to keep him that way. He was the one who had to do the talking, for he alone knew the whole truth.

44

I kept this silence up during most of breakfast, and when I thought he had reached the end of his tether I pushed back my chair and said, " Come up to my room."

Despite the cold, there were small beads of perspiration across his forehead. His hands were never still but his eyes were steady. Here was a man who was worried but not afraid. It was not going to be easy.

I started by going through the statement he had made in Washington, reading it over slowly and deliberately.

" Anything you can add to that after thinking it over during the past ten days or so? "

" No, I don't think so," he replied.

Questions about the bomb, why the matter was not reported in Montreal on landing, did he realise the delay had hindered the inquiry and caused the loss of valuable evidence? Explanations given and accepted, and then, suddenly, " Have you ever been to ——" giving the name of the town near the Training School. This one shook him— and finally he answered just " Yes."

No explanation was offered, so to give him an opportunity to tell the truth, or to tempt a get out by a deliberate lie, I said casually, " Got a girl there? " and I was a little surprised when he accepted the bait with a wry smile and said, " Yes." He was only too pleased to tell me about his mythical girl friend, even admitting having stayed with her in the hotel, where he had in fact met the pilot-officer. He was now lying fast and furious to protect his friend, so I switched the questioning back to the bomb.

" Now I want a careful description of the thing— remember, you are the only one who has seen it." This was easy going, as he was only too glad to get away from the previous subject, and he went on to give a fairly accurate description of the article I knew only too well. He went

45

over how he had found it, and changed one word " hot " to
" warm." He had thrown away the " warm " part as he
suspected it to be a battery or something to explode the rest
of it. I let him talk without interruption, and when he
had again finished his well-rehearsed story, I said, without
any real motive, " Why didn't you tell the secretary about
it on your way to the toilet? He too would have seen it
then." The reply was spontaneous. " I thought he was
asleep. I wouldn't have told him anything about it at all
if he hadn't stopped me on the way back."

If this was true, and I felt it was, it ruled out any question
of staging an act of mock heroics, and I was quite sure by
now that he was just not the type to be a saboteur.

I had to think, to break up the carefully assembled pieces of
the jig-saw puzzle and start again. I had played the game
smooth all the way and our relationship was amicable, so
I had no difficulty in persuading him to take a bath and
snatch a few hours' sleep and to return to London with
me on the night train. He had already booked at a hotel
near Victoria, so as soon as I heard him splashing in the
bath, I phoned my Polish Intelligence friend in London and
arranged to have him shadowed from the moment we parted
company. I lived in Chelsea and would stick with him to the
hotel door.

Strangely enough, even with so much on my mind, I slept
through most of the journey back and, after dropping my
companion at his hotel, redirected the driver to the office.
It was Sunday morning, and I knew it would be quiet there.
I think I stared at the wall most of that day, occasionally
going through notes and reading over the available statements
and it was not until that evening that I was sure I had the
answer—so sure, in fact, that I took some foolscap out of the
drawer and wrote " Statement of Wing-Commander——

of the Free Polish Air Force," just as if he were sitting there in front of me, finishing it with the words "I have read this statement and it is true."

It was nearly 10 p.m. The night security guard had looked in twice during his patrols, and was obviously wanting me out of the way so that he could lock up the floor. I folded the sheets of the statement, put them in my pocket and found myself outside in the night air of St. James's Street.

It was all highly irregular, but I was going to play a hunch and blow this bomb story sky-high.

A taxi to the hotel at Victoria, a quick check from the man keeping the observation that my man was in and had not been out all day, and up the stairs to his room. I noticed he had not even unpacked his suitcase. No time for niceties now, so after acknowledging his courteous little bow, I said, "Wing-Commander —— I know and can prove that you have been lying continuously about this bomb, and I think I know why. I have put the reasons in this provisional statement. I want you to read it. If you want to, alter it. If it is not true, tear it up. If it is true only in parts, I will re-write it at your dictation. If it is true, sign it."

He took the document from me, sat on the bed without a word and began to read. At the end he let the pages fall to the ground, but still did not speak. I left him alone for a few moments, and then put my hand on his shoulder and asked if I was right. He nodded. Then he pulled himself together, picked up the sheets of paper, read them through again and signed his name at the end immediately below the words "I have read this statement and it is true."

This was the story. He had never wanted to leave his active service squadron and, long before the flight to America, had been pulling strings to get relieved of his job as Air Attaché so that he could get back into the air. For some reason the idea of the incendiary bombs from the sabotage school had fascinated him, and he set his heart on getting hold of one so that if ever he did fly again and had to bale out in enemy territory, he would still be able to carry on the battle. Once he had it, it became something of a symbol for him of the great day when he would actually fly again.

The news that he had been posted to America came as a shock. It put an end to his dreams of flying, and it also posed the awkward problem of what to do with the bomb. Perhaps he simply did not know how to get rid of it, or perhaps he had become attached to the thing in some absurd mixed-up way. But whatever the reason, he decided to take it with him, and actually carried it in the haversack he used as a pillow on the flight.

Like many pilots, he was a bad air passenger, and his nervousness increased as soon as he found himself inside the Liberator. But it was the blowing of the fuse and the faint smell of burning it produced which was the last straw. An obvious explanation leapt to his mind. He knew that the bomb contained a small thin glass phial of acid, as part of the timing mechanism, and it was more than possible that the altitude of the plane had caused it to burst. In his panic, the only thing to do seemed to be to break the bomb open and pull out the timing mechanism before it fired and killed the lot of them.

It was afterwards, when he knew that the secretary had seen him with the bomb in his hand, that he had made up the story about finding the bomb, and then tried to hush the whole thing up. When the story did come out, and the investigation started, he felt he had to stick to his original version, not only to save his own skin, but to protect his friend the pilot-officer as well.

48

The case was nearly over. I telephoned my office to call off the watch on the hotel, and then sat talking until the small hours of the morning. I had to get to know this man. His whole future would depend on my report and I wanted the truth about him as a person.

He was a brave man and a fine officer, but he was also very sick and what he needed was not a court-martial so much as a long holiday and a competent psychiatrist. In the end, I was able to get the British authorities to take this view as well, but the Poles did not see things like that—in a case such as this they were merciless, and although the matter was referred to the highest possible level and several very influential people interceded on the wing-commander's behalf, the Poles insisted on treating the whole affair as one of the utmost seriousness, and there was no alternative but to leave the matter in their hands. Finally we did wring one concession from them—there would be no court-martial.

Several weeks later I ran into him in Piccadilly late one evening. There was just time for a drink before closing time. He obviously knew what our people had done on his behalf and was profuse in his thanks, but he would tell me nothing of the final outcome beyond the fact that he had retained his rank.

We left the bar and went out into the blacked-out street. As we were parting, he put his hand in his pocket and took out a fountain-pen which he handed to me and said, " I want you to take this. In a day or two I am dropping into Poland —I shall not come back." With these words he turned away and I have never seen him again. I still have that pen.

CHAPTER 4

The legacy of the War

It was just after D-Day, with the end of the war firmly in sight, that I began worrying about the future. I was well into my forties, and because of my age, I knew there would be no more promotion for me if I went back to Scotland Yard. At the same time I had made up my mind that I was going to work with aircraft if I had the chance, and it was then that I got the idea of a career in air security.

I knew perfectly well that as soon as the war ended B.O.A.C., like any other transport organisation, would find itself vulnerable to a whole range of crime. I had no idea just how complex it was going to be, but on a sudden impulse I wrote them a letter putting myself forward to organise the Corporation's air security when the war ended.

I received an acknowledgment and a promise that I would be considered when the time came, and there, for many months, the matter rested.

At this time we suddenly plunged into one of the busiest periods of work we had had at M.I.5. With the closing stages of the war, the chances of sabotage in Britain obviously declined and our anti-sabotage unit was switched to a completely new type of inquiry. This was the study of the different traitors known to be working for the enemy actually in Germany or Italy, so that if ever they were caught the prosecution would have cut and dried evidence against them.

A lot of the work was routine, but it took a great deal of time, collating scattered pieces of information from a thousand and one sources. But gradually our dossiers built up, and soon we were able to list with certainty the names of quite a handful of unsavoury Englishmen working for the enemy in Europe, either by broadcasting propaganda, or recruiting among our P.O.W.s for our troops to join in the fight against the Russians in the *S.S. Freikorps*.

We were given the task of preparing the dossier against each individual top traitor and following every move he made until we were in a position to arrest him. Reg Spooner, now Deputy Commander of the C.I.D., took charge of William Joyce, " Lord Haw-Haw," and was the man who finally arrested him in Germany when our troops caught up with him. My responsibility was for John Amery, who was then Haw-Haw's opposite number with the Italians, and in the summer of 1945 I flew to Italy with Len Burt to follow up a report that Italian partisans were holding an Englishman who seemed to fit Amery's description. The report was correct, and after a two-day journey up to a village in the Alps where Amery had been in hiding, we formally arrested him, and later brought him back to trial at the Old Bailey.

I mention this, because it was just after I had got back from Italy that I had another letter from B.O.A.C. It was a brusque little note summoning me to an interview five days later with Brigadier-General A. C. Critchley, the Director-General of the Corporation.

I have never known anyone quite so formidably energetic as General Critchley. Although it was mid-July, it had been raining heavily that morning, and I turned up at B.O.A.C.'s headquarters in Berkeley Square with an army-type mackintosh over my uniform of a captain in the Intelligence

Corps. The first thing the general did as soon as I put my
nose inside his office was to tell me off for coming to see him
in uniform.

Then, without bothering to ask whether I still wanted the
job any more, or, for that matter, was even free to take it,
he told me I was to be ready to fly to Cairo at the beginning
of the following week to investigate a missing diplomatic
mail-bag. Feeling too dazed to reply, or even to ask any of
the usual questions about my pay and responsibilities I shook
hands and the interview was over.

It was only when I was walking back to M.I.5 across the
wet pavement of Berkeley Square that I realised it was going
to be easier said than done to join B.O.A.C. It was all right
for the Director-General to talk breezily about flying off to
Cairo at a few days' notice, but I was a very ordinary
policeman, not a general, and at this time was still officially
holding down three jobs simultaneously.

It was the sort of situation that can only arise in wartime,
but legally I was three people. I was still a detective-
inspector at Scotland Yard. At the same time I had been
seconded for special duties with M.I.5, and then just to
complicate matters further, I had been given the rank of
a captain in the Intelligence Corps. When I got back to
my office in St. James's Street, I telephoned B.O.A.C.'s staff
officer telling him all this, and decided there and then that
if the Corporation could sort out my peculiar status to get
me released by the beginning of the next week, the least I
could do was to agree to fly to Cairo for them.

I had reckoned without the great " Critch." Len Burt
took over the John Amery case and M.I.5 let me go back to
the Yard. They, by a short paragraph in Police Orders
seconded me to the Air Ministry (responsible also for civil
aviation) the latter loaned me to B.O.A.C. for " special

duties." The War Office gave me the swiftest demobilisation on record and sure enough the following week I found myself stepping aboard the B.O.A.C. morning flight to Cairo on my first job as an air security officer.

After the airfields I was used to in Britain, the dirt and disorder of Al Maza Airport just outside Cairo, came as a bit of a shock and then, just to put me in the right frame of mind, somebody picked my pocket on my first afternoon in Cairo. At the time I did not see the joke, and after my first day in Egypt I had decided that this really was not the place for me.

The missing mail-bag I had come to investigate turned out to be the least of my worries. As soon as I looked into the mail procedure, I found that everything—parcels, registered and diplomatic mail—were being off-loaded straight on to the tarmac, and left unattended for periods of up to three hours at a time. Quite casually I went on a little search of my own, and after poking round the untidy jumble of buildings along the tarmac, I actually found the mail-bag along with a sizeable stock of other mail lying in a disused hangar. I suppose that some member of the airport staff was not sure where it should go, and rather than take the trouble to find out, had simply slung it in the hangar to get it out of the way. This is the sort of thing that can happen very easily on an airline, and over the years neglect has probably been responsible for as many losses as crime, but on that afternoon when I found that pile of delayed mail I was appalled.

It was quite obvious that at Al Maza, already one of B.O.A.C.'s most important foreign stations, air security was a joke. It was also obvious that nobody minded very much that it was a joke. A few decayed local watchmen had been hired to guard the aircraft, but you could walk past them on to an aircraft and steal the engines if you were wearing a peaked cap, and although there was a strong-room, its most important function seemed to be to provide the cleaners with somewhere to store their brooms and floor polish.

It was only then that I got my first inkling of just how big a job I had taken on. For if this sort of thing was to be changed, I was the man who had to change it, but nobody on the station seemed very keen that I should, especially when fresh orders arrived from London telling me to stay on in Egypt, and begin reorganisation of B.O.A.C.'s security throughout the Middle East.

After a few more days in Cairo, I flew down the Nile to Khartoum and later to Tel Aviv and then on to Basra. Everywhere the story was the same. The makeshift atmosphere of wartime persisted, and everyone from pilots to airport managers seemed to regard me as an unnecessary busybody who had come out specially to interfere with the operational running of the station.

It happened that most of the old wartime rackets worked by aircrews and ground staff still flourished, but if currency offences occurred, or there were occasional outbreaks of cigarette smuggling or pilfering, the general attitude was that it was perfectly fair game and that no one in his right mind could ever get very worried about it—there was always the insurance company to foot the bill for losses.

But something that hardly matters in wartime becomes of vital importance to an airline in peacetime. Once you start carrying passengers and freight on scheduled services, their security is no longer something you can laugh about, and before I could get any further I had to make everyone security conscious whether they liked it or not.

This is not a thing you can do overnight, and a lot of this initial work in the Middle East consisted of the dull, everyday chores of security. Throughout the tail end of that sweltering Cairo summer I seemed to be travelling from one airport to the next, checking on warehouse security, and trying to reorganise the handling of mail and valuables.

While I was grinding away at this fairly thankless task, I had one stroke of luck. I met Buchanan. A lot of nonsense gets talked about investigators. I have never known one who was any good who looked remotely like the sort of detective you always see at the cinema, and, as I have said already, you need a methodical, painstaking sort of mind if you are to put up with the job five minutes. But it is a fact that the very top investigators always have a flair of their own which they are born with, and if you are in the business you always recognise them when you meet them. Whatever else I did while I was with B.O.A.C., at least I had the sense to recognise Douglas Buchanan and grab him while I could.

He was in Cairo at that time, a thickset young Scottish Flight Sergeant working for the Investigation Branch of the R.A.F. police. He helped put some order into the security out at Al Maza, and I hung on to him for several other jobs which turned up while I was in the Middle East. He was a quiet, tough, obstinate fellow, with spectacles and closely cropped hair, who always kept himself to himself, and was too much of an individualist ever to fit comfortably into any hidebound organisation. Working on his own he was unbeatable, and during the years he has been with B.O.A.C. he has proved himself the finest lone-wolf investigator in the business.

We did have one case together that summer. It occurred at Basra and concerned an R.A.F. officer, seconded to B.O.A.C., who had been caught smuggling 3,000 gold sovereigns from India into Cairo. Later on the traffic in smuggled gold was to flow exactly the opposite way and, incidentally, give me the biggest case of my career—the great Indian Gold Smuggling Case. But at the end of the war the inflated price of gold in the Middle East still offered considerable profits to anyone smart enough to smuggle the stuff into the Middle East in any quantity.

In his quiet way this officer was an extremely big-time operator, and must have made a tidy fortune before he was caught. Although he had been arrested with the gold in Basra, there was still a mystery about where he was hiding his personal profits on the smuggling. We suspected he was taking his cut in sovereigns and actually hiding them on the plane, but we could only prove this by finding them, and it was while Buchanan and I were at Basra, working over his aircraft that I learned just how many potential hiding places there are on a large passenger aircraft.

This was a lumbering old four-engined Ensign and it took us three days to search it before we found where the sovereigns were being hidden. There was an unusually long waste pipe from the galley sink, and when we unscrewed it we found fifty or sixty sovereigns still concealed in the bend. It was so long since I had seen any gold coinage that I was not sure when we found them whether they were sovereigns or half-sovereigns—but they were sovereigns all right and provided enough evidence to break just one of the rackets that B.O.A.C. had inherited from the war.

Shortly after this I took Buchanan officially on to my staff and sent him off to Karachi, already one of our most important foreign stations, to keep his suspicious eye on the whole of our Far Eastern routes.

By the end of that summer we had instilled some order into our security in the Middle East, but we still needed one really big case to make it plain once and for all that security in B.O.A.C. was really serious business. Quite by chance, the Augusta scandal provided exactly the example we needed.

Augusta was a wartime flying-boat base in Sicily which B.O.A.C. had recently taken over from the R.A.F. In those days it was a vital refuelling stop on our main service to Singapore, and by the time I was called in, the rackets going on there were so serious that they would soon have threatened the base's entire operations. B.O.A.C.'s business had become almost incidental, and the most important function of the Augusta base seemed to be to supply black market food and cigarettes for almost the whole of Southern Italy.

Duty-free cigarettes would be flown in from Malta by the crate-load. Food would be mysteriously diverted, and stores of every shape and size would be sold in the town, and actually delivered in B.O.A.C. transport. The whole set-up was like the plot of an Ealing comedy. The ring leaders were a likeable set of scoundrels, but things were becoming serious by this time. The Italian police had finally got wind of it and if I had not arrived, they would certainly have stepped in and created exactly the sort of international incident an airline has to avoid.

There were four of our men in the racket—one English and three Italian, and they were not difficult to spot. Almost from the moment I arrived I knew who they were, and they knew that I knew, but the niceties had to be observed whilst I built up a case against them. Everything remained surprisingly amicable while this was going on, and we even had our meals together.

After four days I had enough evidence to fix the lot of them ten times over. As usual we had dinner together, and then over a bottle of cheap Italian brandy, I told them the game was up, and asked them whether they were prepared to sign full confessions and let B.O.A.C. take whatever disciplinary action it felt fit. The alternative would be to turn the case over to the Italians, and an Italian gaol, as I was sure they realised, was hardly the place where they would want to spend the next couple of years if it could possibly be avoided.

So we finished the brandy, and got the confessions down in writing. When they had all signed we went off to bed and next day, the one Englishman, now only too anxious to resign, flew back to England with me. All the Italians were dismissed but knew they had been lucky to get away with it so lightly. At the same time B.O.A.C. was saved the bad publicity of having an international incident on its hands, and the Augusta flying-boat base remained from then on a model of propriety. Word soon spread along the routes that Security was on the ball.

CHAPTER 5

Trouble along the routes

In 1945 air security was still an idea that had to be sold, and sold hard. Nobody really knew what it would finally involve, and few people realised why it was necessary.

That first winter I had to share an office in a gloomy block opposite Victoria Station. I had no staff worth speaking of, and as no other airline in the world even had a security organisation in those days, I had no pattern on which to base my own. The rules of air security had to be worked out from scratch.

But before I could do that, I had to find a staff I could really work with. I already had Buchanan keeping an eye on things in Karachi and decided to get as many men as possible from the same source—the young fellows being demobilised from the services police. I knew that what B.O.A.C. and its world-wide operations needed was an active police force of its own, and by 1947 I had the bones of my organisation. My police force was actually in operation overseas and on the seven bases in Britain then used by B.O.A.C. I had also arranged that any crime occurring on a B.O.A.C. plane anywhere in the world was reported back directly to headquarters in London.

It is one thing to plan these sort of arrangements from an office in London. It is quite another thing to get them to work and we soon began to learn the hard way—by our mistakes. And we certainly made some.

Take the Cairo gold case early in 1947. For nearly a year there had been a series of minor losses, including gold, from shipments that had passed through London Airport for Singapore. They could have occurred anywhere along the route. They were covered by insurance, and compared with the immense quantities of gold we were already carrying, they were barely noticeable. But the regularity of these losses began to attract attention, and when a clue turned up making me sure the trouble was occurring in Cairo, I knew the time had come for me to catch a plane out to Egypt and do something about it myself.

Security at Al Maza had improved since my last visit and before I had been there a couple of days I thought I had a cut and dried case against a pair of Levantine maintenance engineers on the airport. They were not particularly good crooks, but with the number of small shipments of gold passing through Cairo at the time, there was never much difficulty in stealing a small consignment when you knew that the loss would not be discovered until the aircraft reached Singapore, six thousand miles away.

There was a good deal of circumstantial evidence against the two engineers and if I had been at home I would not have hesitated to apply for a warrant against them both. But in a foreign capital like Cairo I was in an awkward position. Of course I had no powers of arrest and all I could do was to drive down to the local Egyptian police station, swear a *proces-verbal*, and leave it to the law.

For two hours I laboriously went through the rigmarole of spelling out my complaint to the police sergeant on duty at the local police station.

To my surprise, the police took my statement sufficiently

seriously to raid the flat the following day where one of the engineers was living with a girl friend. But by now it was three weeks since the gold had gone adrift, and of course whoever had stolen it had had ample time to get rid of it.

There was nothing else I could do in Cairo and I got back to London cursing myself for wasting five precious days on a wild-goose chase and convinced I had heard the last about that shipment of gold.

I was wrong. My trip to Cairo had an ironic little postscript. A note arrived three days later, informing me that the Egyptian Customs were demanding £1,000 from B.O.A.C. By swearing that wretched *proces-verbal*, I had tacitly admitted that gold had been landed in Egypt without authority from one of our aircraft, and now the duty had to be paid. If I had said nothing, I would have saved the Corporation exactly £1,000 and myself five wasted days in Egypt.

After this, whenever any valuable dutiable article went astray, I never reported it to the local police unless I was absolutely sure that the men who had stolen it still had it in their possession. If they had had it long enough to get rid of it I would bide my time, and usually see that they were moved somewhere where they could do no damage in future. At the same time I would make sure that they knew that we had our eye on them, and that the next time they tried anything they would be in for trouble.

But it is surprising how often experience and common sense do help you to put your finger on the people you need. In air security you gradually get the same feel for the places round the world where crimes can be expected as a good policeman gets for the trouble spots on his beat.

Certainly I never stopped regarding myself as a policeman, even though I had officially left the police the day I joined

B.O.A.C. The habits of a lifetime stick, and there was one important habit I never managed to shake myself free from. This was the fixed belief that any crime I encountered was my concern. I carried this over with me into air security, and it became one of the unwritten rules of our organisation to take on at least the preliminary investigation of any crime that occurred on our routes. Often, if we had not tried to solve the majority of cases we took on, nobody else would have.

Legally a crime can be dealt with only in the area where it has been committed, so that with most air crime the local police have insurmountable difficulties collecting even the evidence to put the case on trial.

A good example of the inability of a national police force to deal with an air crime is the French perfume job early in my career as a security officer.

It began innocuously enough one Friday afternoon with one of my security men telephoning from the tarmac at London Airport to say that a £3,000 perfume consignment was missing from the plane that had just come in from Paris. There was nothing in that—consignments are always getting delayed or shifted from one plane to another, and almost always arrive on a later flight.

At this time B.O.A.C. were handling agents for all Air France's aircraft arriving in London, and as the perfume was being flown by Air France, I thought I had better put a call through to Paris just to make sure they knew what was happening. The man in Paris was apologetic and admitted that the perfume had not been loaded owing to a station error. It would be arriving by the next Air France plane from Paris.

But although we waited and waited, the perfume never did arrive. I stuck on at the airport until nine o'clock and saw two Air France planes land and unload, but my £3,000 cargo was not there. Again I telephoned Paris, and by the time I got through I had to put up with a bad-tempered freight clerk at Le Bourget who spoke about as much English as I spoke French, but who insisted that the perfume had definitely been sent. It was too late to do anything that night, so I drove home from the airport, knowing that there was nothing for it but to come in again the next morning and get down to the case over my precious week-end.

Next morning, the £3,000 shipment had still not arrived, and I found myself having to decide what to do about a mysterious consignment that Paris had insisted had been sent, London insisted had never arrived, and which presumably vanished into thin air somewhere over the English Channel. Since B.O.A.C. had not dispatched the stuff in the first place, I could not hop over to Paris to conduct my own investigations there, and I was faced with one of the classic problems which occurs time after time in air security—that of deciding exactly which police authority I could call in to take charge of a perfectly straightforward crime.

So just to see what would happen, I picked up my hat and coat and strolled over from the airport to Harlington Police Station to report the crime. The detective-sergeant there was an old friend of mine, and showed a great deal more patience than I would have done in his place.

He scratched his nose and said it was all very interesting, but what the hell did I think he could do about a crime that had presumably happened in Paris and was completely outside his jurisdiction. Later the French police gave a similar judgment and that is how the French perfume job has remained to this day, an undoubted crime that nobody, not even the insurance companies, who had to pay for it, has any intention of doing anything about. . . .

Not all the cases we tackled were as inconclusive as this, and the amount of crime on the airlines soon began to mount so fast that we had our work cut out keeping up with it. Nineteen forty-seven was a year when B.O.A.C.'s postwar traffic was only beginning, but 456 cases of pilfering from passengers' luggage were reported, along with another 403 cases where Corporation property was stolen, 150 larcenies from freight, and 29 from mail.

My job was not only detecting crime, but stamping on the weak points in the organisation where crime could occur. No sooner had we got one type of petty crime under control than another would crop up, and we would be back at the beginning again. Airlines are always a high security risk, and when an airline is changing as fast as B.O.A.C. was in those days, every change brings a fresh chance for the opportunist thief.

Even the aircraft designer can give the security man a headache as he changes the shape of his planes, and there was a mysterious epidemic of pilfering that broke out just after B.O.A.C. introduced its new, long-haul four-engined liner, the American Constellation on to the routes.

Until then things had been fairly quiet, but no sooner were the new planes in operation than we started getting report after report of luggage and freight being pilfered, and within a few weeks the situation had become really serious. From the pattern of the thefts I was certain that they must have been occurring at London Airport itself, but for some time we could not see how it was being done.

Now all my life people have been telling me that I am over-methodical and I suppose they are right. For some reason or other I have one of those twisted minds which enjoys information for its own sake. I like collecting facts and making lists, and although it often serves only to infuriate people, this was one occasion when it paid off. For one of the first arrangements made when I took over B.O.A.C. security was that records should always be kept of the loading teams who worked on every aircraft leaving the airport and as I worked my way through them I began to notice the one thing I was looking for.

In almost every case where losses were reported the same loading team had been involved. This was something to go on, but I had to have more positive evidence before anything could be done about it.

When you know what you're looking for, an airport is not a bad place for keeping people under observation, and for the next fortnight we studied that loading team during every second they were at work. At the end of it we knew exactly what they were up to and how they were stealing a great deal of other people's property from B.O.A.C. aeroplanes. It was a trick that several other airlines have suffered from since, especially in America.

What was happening was this. The new planes that had just come into service on our long distance routes all carried their luggage and freight in a long, narrow belly-hold running the entire length of the fuselage under the passengers' seats. It was reached by a hatch opening from underneath, and as the headroom inside the hold was never more than four feet, the only way to pack the luggage was for the loader to climb right inside the hold and have it handed up to him. Once inside he was practically invisible from below, and just to make things easier for themselves, these boys were starting to load each plane by handing the freight up too quickly so that a pile formed in the mouth of the hold. Behind this screen, the man in the hold simply could not be seen, and was free to do just what he wanted with the freight and passengers' luggage inside.

As soon as I had seen exactly what was happening I grabbed all four of them just as they had finished with one plane. I was very nearly unlucky, for the loader inside must have found the locks on the cases tougher than usual, and when we searched him all we found was a single jar of hair cream. But it was enough for the police, and on the strength of it warrants were issued to search the men's houses. I went on the search with my friend the detective-sergeant from Harlington, just to see what the four of them had really been up to.

From their houses you would have thought we had arrested a quartet of human jackdaws, and among them they had every imaginable object stacked away. One of the men, for instance, had 123 brand-new silk ties. I know that figure is correct, for I counted them myself. Then there were cameras and shirts and toys and fountain pens and field-glasses—enough to stock a flourishing London pawn-broker's!

But for me the most surprising find of all was to learn that they had managed to steal a neatly nailed-up wooden box containing a two-thousand-pound gold ingot. The fools must have taken a big chance or seized an opportunity when normal security provisions were relaxed, but being such amateurs had simply not known what to do with it, for it was sold at less than a quarter of its value. But that did them little good when they arrived in court a few weeks later, and it was a long time before any of that gang were around again to trouble B.O.A.C. and its passengers.

Another of the oddities about air crime is that sometimes you can get the clearest evidence that a crime has been committed, but can never find who has suffered. This happened in a most unusual case dating back to my very earliest days with the Corporation.

It began when the police at Kano in Northern Nigeria asked us if we wanted a £5,000 block of gold. It had been found in Kano quite by chance and nobody seemed to know who owned it.

There had been a run of pilfering from planes using the airport, and I had sent one of my officers out to investigate. He had not had much luck, although he slogged away at the case for nearly a fortnight. Then one morning, the local police arrived at his hotel to ask if he had lost a block of gold. It seems that they had had their suspicions about some local African on an entirely different matter. They had searched his house and found this gold that he swore was his own, but which they thought might have been stolen from an aircraft.

Naturally my security officer cabled me in London at once, and I spent an anxious couple of days checking up on all the gold shipments that could possibly have gone through Kano during the previous twelve months, just to make sure that no one had reported a loss or a robbery. No one had, and reluctantly I cabled back to the police in Nigeria telling them that the gold had nothing to do with B.O.A.C. There is no crime in simply possessing gold, even five thousand pounds' worth of it and since the Nigerian Police could find no one to claim the stuff they had to let the African keep it.

There was an unexpected postscript to this case. Three months later, a very worried police officer arrived in Nigeria and spent three weeks in Kano. He had come on behalf of one of the big European airways and was in search of a £5,000 block of gold stolen from one of their flights from Johannesburg. It had been lost nearly four months previously, but owing to the sort of muddle that occurs, all too easily with air freight, the loss had not been reported until an insurance claim had been lodged with the underwriters. It was the underwriters who had insisted on the inquiry, and I often wonder exactly how much the investigating officer told them in his report when he returned to Europe.

Despite this story, it would be entirely wrong to give the impression that airlines can never co-operate over their joint security. On more occasions than I can remember I would find myself telephoning my opposite number in New York or Amsterdam, and on several important cases it was this very ability we had to work together with security officers on other lines that made all the difference.

But there was no time when I was more grateful for the friendship and support of the security officers of the main American airlines than during the big American spares racket which suddenly blew up a few years after the war.

This was a fantastic business that must have touched almost every big airline in the Western hemisphere in one way or another. Certainly it hit the American lines far harder than it did ours, and they were estimated to have lost over four million dollars before the racket was squashed. It provides an almost incredible example of the way a ring of organised racketeers was able to muscle in on the aircraft industry.

The racket was possible for the simple reason that after the war almost every passenger aircraft in operation had been made in America. Dakotas and Constellations formed the backbone of practically every airline, and with the shortage of dollars outside America there was a virtual famine in American aircraft spares.

Usually the spares were available only in the States. Prices were sky-high, second-hand spares were almost as expensive as new ones, but an airline needs spares to live, and every year our purchasing mission in the States spent several million dollars on spares alone.

It was one of the spares the mission had purchased a few months before that caused me to make a hurried journey down to our repair factory in South Wales one cold January morning. This factory checked over every piece of equipment before it was used on our aircraft. The latest batch of American spares included a carburettor that raised the suspicions of one of the inspecting engineers and when I asked him what was the matter he said, " Have a good look. It ought to interest you and should be in your department rather than mine."

I had seen Spitfire carburettors several times during the war, but this was bigger than anything I remembered, and seemed to be nearly brand new. I fiddled with it for a minute or two, but could see nothing at all wrong with it.

" No," said the engineer, " there's nothing wrong with it. It works all right, and so it should. It arrived from America only the week before last."

" What's the matter then? " I said.

" Take a look at this," he replied, and turning the carburettor upside down, pointed to a spot on the casing which had been carefully wiped clean of grease. Engraved into the metal were several serial marks followed by a date.

" You know what that means? " asked the engineer.

I shook my head.

" It means that this new carburettor which we have just bought from America already belonged to B.O.A.C. a year before. Somehow the Corporation is buying its own property twice over, and someone in America is working a very nice racket on our buying mission."

At this stage we had no idea whether this was just an isolated incident. There might have been an innocent explanation for what had happened, so I informed our stores department at Idlewild, asked them to look into it, and suggested that if they were not satisfied they should report the whole matter to the New York City Police.

For a fortnight the matter rested. Then news arrived showing we were really up against something big. It was a report from New York. While our engineers were servicing an Israeli Airline's Constellation they had discovered it was fitted with another carburettor with similar B.O.A.C. serial marks to those on the one I had seen in South Wales.

Almost simultaneously officers from the District Attorney's office in New York arrested one of our own storemen at Idlewild. Under questioning he had admitted stealing $20,000 worth spares, not to mention thefts from two airlines before he joined B.O.A.C.

This was serious. There was no way of telling how much further the racket extended without investigating on the spot, so I caught the next aircraft out to New York myself and asked our stores at Idlewild to begin a complete audit.

This was soon in full swing, but with the amount of equipment carried by the stores department of a big airline, it was a fairly long-winded business, so I left the stores to get on with it and called at the District Attorney's office.

The officer in charge of the case went out of his way to be helpful. He showed me a copy of the confession made by our storeman. According to his confession, the $20,000 worth of spares had all been taken during the previous six months. This is not quite so enormous a haul as it sounds at first with the inflated sums American spares were fetching at the time. Still, it was enough to be going on with, and I thought I had better try to see the man myself as soon as possible.

Here again the police were more than helpful, and made

special arrangements for me to question the man when he came up for a preliminary hearing in court. He was a tall, good-looking young fellow who should have been playing in a college baseball team instead of finding himself mixed up in a racket like this. It was not hard to get him talking, and I steered the conversation on to the two subjects I needed to know more about. The identity of the people he was selling the spares to and the way he was disposing of such unusual loot.

It was here that we got our biggest surprise of all, for it was quite clear, from what he said, that the racket in stolen second-hand spares had become really big business, with connections spreading right across America.

He had been selling everything he could lay his hands on to a spares dealer with headquarters 2,000 miles away from New York in Miami, who made regular visits to New York to collect the stolen spares. The thief also made it clear that he was not the only one working on behalf of this racketeer, and that the man in Miami acted as receiver to a whole network of thieves operating in the maintenance sections of almost every big airline in the country.

The next day the result of the audit in our stores confirmed what had been told me for it showed an amazing variety of losses. These ranged from split pins and sparking plugs, to really large components like carburettors and fuel pumps.

From this point on, the case became immensely complicated, and passed into the hands of the New York Police. They worked quickly, and soon caught up with the man from Miami who had been doing the actual receiving. He was a tricky customer and before the police knew where they were, he had surrounded himself with a protective screen of lawyers, and had been released on bail. Despite this, the investigation went on, and what had originally been a very simple case from our point of view turned into one of the biggest joint airline security inquiries ever known.

I already had a good liaison with several of the security officers in the main American airlines and so, as soon as I had heard that the man from Miami was out on bail, I called on a couple of them. They were Bob Lynch and Ed Tucker, a pair of ex-F.B.I. agents who now worked in the Manhattan offices of American Airlines Inc.

Here I was in for another surprise, for they had already been working on the spares racket inside America for many weeks. One of their agents had already travelled thousands of miles and checked on countless second-hand spares dealers and aircraft employees in Miami, San Francisco, and other centres of the aircraft industry.

This agent had worked well and Lynch and Tucker were able to show me a dossier full of evidence of a conspiracy dealing in aircraft spares stolen from a hundred different places, that brought them on to the market with such cool effrontery that even B.O.A.C.'s buying mission in the States had ended up buying its own stolen spares.

Although the evidence was there in black and white, it seemed that it was quite another thing to be able to produce it in court and smash the racket as it deserved. Somehow the man from Miami and the rest of the spares racketeers have so far managed to bring up delay after delay to keep the case out of court. How much corruption and political intrigue have played in all this is anybody's guess.

Still, the hard work of the security officers of the Airlines had one result. Thanks to them the whole American spares racket came to a grinding halt and the airlines freed themselves once and for all from one of the most carefully planned conspiracies they have had to face.

CHAPTER 6

The London Airport raid

Nineteen forty-eight was a big year for British civil aviation. It was the year that London Airport opened on the site of the old R.A.F. station at Heathrow. It was not ideal, but it was the best spot close to London with enough room to take the great runways needed by the postwar giants coming on to the routes, and at last it meant that B.O.A.C. could begin to bring most of the scattered war-time operations together from the several temporary airports it had been using, and grow as a single unit.

This took time, of course, and my first memories of London Airport were not as cheerful as they might have been. They were of cold and wet and mud and still more mud, with the ceaseless rumble of the concrete mixers and the roar of the bulldozers as they tore up the flat market gardens of Middlesex for the twelve miles of runway the airport needed. It was a makeshift place then, of marquees and Nissen huts that were only slowly to give way to the great international terminal which London Airport is to-day.

But if 1948 was a memorable year for the airlines, it was an absolutely vital one for our Security Branch. Only a few months after we had moved into London Airport, the new airport was to become the scene of the biggest case we had yet had to face, a case which made everything that had

73

gone before look like chicken-feed, and which convinced even the most hardened sceptics that air security had its uses.

The case came to be called the Battle of London Airport. If it had succeeded, the crooks behind it would have pulled off one of the crimes of the century.

Although this case was to be so important for all of us, it reached our ears almost by accident. It was one of those periods when nothing spectacular seemed to have happened for months. The start of the new airport had presented us with a formidable security problem, and all my time was taken up organising the security patrols and keeping up with the opportunities this half-finished giant of an airport offered to any criminal on the lookout for easy pickings.

The traffic through the new airport was increasing every day, and by 1948 we had already started carrying the heavy shipments of watches, furs, stones and precious metals that have become such an important feature of postwar air transport. But inevitably security is almost the last thing anyone thinks of when they are struggling to make a new airport operational, and we had to make do with an old converted hangar as a combined Customs warehouse and strong-room. It was hardly the place I would have chosen to lock up so many of the valuables coming into the airport, but I had been promised a beauty of a strong-room when the new buildings were finished so we arranged for a security man always to be on duty in the warehouse, and hoped that no really determined criminal would try any tricks before it was built.

This arrangement worked perfectly until one evening early in July. We had been in the middle of one of those rare spells of really glorious July weather you sometimes get in London and on this particular day I had got home from the office earlier than usual and after dinner my wife and I had gone for our favourite walk along the Chelsea Embankment.

We arrived home to find the telephone already ringing, which usually meant trouble at that time of night. For the last couple of hours the security officer on duty over at the airport had been trying to get hold of me. There was something he had to discuss straight away and he hardly liked to trust it to the telephone.

It was a nuisance, but in the security business you ignore a call like this at your peril, and I knew there was nothing for it but to get the car out and drive down to the airport.

When I heard the security officer's story it seemed too far-fetched to be true. While he was on duty, he had been approached by one of the men working in the customs warehouse with a tale of a full-scale robbery that was being planned. Someone was supposed to have approached him with an offer of five hundred pounds if he would dope the coffee for the warehouse staff on the night a valuable bullion shipment was due into the airport. After this he said that he had been told that he was to let a gang into the warehouse so that they could get the keys of the strong-room from the drugged security warden.

The story was improbable enough, but the character of the warehouseman who told it made it seem less likely still and frankly I did not believe a word of it. For I knew the man pretty well. He had even worked for me once for a few months. He was an Irishman called Michael Gilroy who had actually been on my staff as a uniformed security warden. But he was an awkward customer who seemed to put everybody's back up, and in the end I received so many complaints about him that I had got rid of him.

I had always felt sorry for him. He was obviously something of a case. Sometimes he was morose, sometimes he was truculent, and I learned that a lot of his troubles had begun when he had been captured by the Germans during the war and imprisoned in a P.O.W. camp.

It was largely because of this that I had managed to stop him being sacked outright from B.O.A.C., and got him his present job in the warehouse. Remembering something of his mental background, I thought this story of his was either a pathetic attempt to prove what a good security man we had lost when we had got rid of him, or else final proof that he was in the grip of complete persecution mania.

Whatever it was, I had to be sure there was no possible grain of truth in his story, and I knew perfectly well that there was only one way of testing it. This was to make the man tell it over and over again until some discrepancy appeared. I made up my mind to see Mr. Gilroy the following morning.

When he came into my office there was an air of bravado about him I had hardly expected. He was obviously only too delighted to tell his story again, and I noticed he was doing it without hesitating or changing the facts from the version I had heard the night before. I was pretty sure he believed what he was telling me.

He had been describing the member of the gang who had made him the offer and telling me how he had first come to know him. It was during the war when they had both been prisoners in the same German P.O.W. camp, and this man had recently come from another camp called Genshagen near Berlin.

For a moment I let him talk on, and then it clicked. For I knew about Genshagen. I had even studied the place before I took on the Amery job at M.I.5. It was a special camp about five miles outside Berlin where the Germans had sent selected renegade British prisoners who had volunteered to fight the Russians in the *S. S. Freikorps*. In exchange, these prisoners had all been given exceptional treatment and even been allowed out to enjoy some of the night life of wartime Berlin. A character from Genshagen could be just the type to be mixed up in this sort of job.

From then on I could take no chances. It might perfectly well still have been a hoax, but the reference to Genshagen made it less likely so I told Gilroy to keep his ears open, do exactly what the member of the gang told him, and report back to me as soon as he had found out anything else.

For five days I heard nothing, and purposely kept right away from the warehouse and Gilroy. Then early one Tuesday morning I arrived at my office to find him already waiting outside. He was so excited that I had to make him sit down and have a cigarette before he could tell me his story.

For three days he had heard nothing from the gang, and then he had received a note fixing a date with them at nine o'clock the previous night in the public bar of a small pub in Epsom. He had gone, and met his original pal along with two other members of the gang. They had stayed until closing time, discussing the final details of the raid on the warehouse. He was able to give me a thorough description of all three men, along with the number of the black Vauxhall they had driven away in. He also told me that they claimed to have the warehouse under constant watch from an all-night café on the opposite side of the road from the airport gates, and that they had scheduled their raid for 1 a.m. on the night the next bullion plane arrived.

It was easy now to check whether the story was all a figment of the warehouseman's over-fertile imagination, and as soon as I got in touch with Scotland Yard's Criminal

Records Department, I knew the answer. The description of two of the men corresponded exactly with two gentlemen who had been on the Scotland Yard files for many years.

This was bad enough, but it was the car number that finally made me realise that I was sitting on a volcano. When Scotland Yard checked they had found that the Vauxhall was a car belonging to one of the most notorious names at the head of London's underworld. If he was mixed up in the case we really had to expect business.

It was then the strain began. Scotland Yard naturally came into the case in a big way, but during the days of waiting there was not a great deal they could do directly. For that matter, there was not a great deal any of us could do, and at the back of my mind there was always that warning from the warehouseman about the watcher in the all-night café. I knew that the slightest move out of the ordinary would rouse his suspicions and ruin our chances of catching the gang in action.

So, although I would have given anything for another peep at that strong-room, I kept religiously away, and left the normal security arrangements for the place exactly as they were. I also kept my future meetings with the warehouseman down to a minimum.

In the meantime I had found out about the bullion shipments expected through the airport during the next few weeks, and learned that the next big one was a quarter of a million pounds' worth of gold due in from South America via Madrid in five days' time. The stakes were bigger than I had thought, and we had precious little time to make our own arrangements.

According to Flight Control the South American bullion plane was due in late on Wednesday evening. It was now Monday afternoon and that very evening I drove up to

Scotland Yard for the first of the conferences we held to plan operations against the bullion gang.

I have never known time drag like those next two days. I could risk meeting the warehouseman only once to tell him what was going to happen, and what he had to do. To my surprise he was bearing the strain rather better than expected and confirmed that the gang had found out about the Wednesday night shipment from another accomplice they had working elsewhere in B.O.A.C. The raid was planned for sometime after one o'clock in the morning.

Wednesday dawned at last, and I was out at the airport early. Air Control had confirmed that the bullion plane was already on its way to Madrid, and should be reaching London Airport somewhere around nine o'clock that evening. I had a few minutes' chat on the telephone with Superintendent Bob Lee of the Flying Squad who was in charge of the police operations, and confirmed everything was in order at his end. The Battle of London Airport had almost started.

In a situation like this, the fewer people you have to tell the better, but it was too great a responsibility to carry on one's own shoulders. There was not only the chance that the raid might succeed in spite of all our precautions, but if a fight broke out some of our staff might get seriously injured or even killed.

Late on the afternoon of the raid, I saw the Administration Director, Mr. Temple Mellor, and gave him the details of the story. I know I left him with the feeling that I was over-dramatising the whole affair.

At eight that evening the warehouseman went on duty, with a packet of barbiturate in his pocket given to him by the gang. At nine the bullion plane arrived slap on time, was unloaded and the gold deposited in the strong room.

At ten a large B.O.A.C. van drove along the Western Avenue at about thirty-five miles an hour. It was the sort of van the Corporation used to carry valuables in, and as it drove up towards the airport the man watching from the all-night café opposite the customs warehouse must have noticed the uniformed security man riding in the cab beside the driver—a sign that something really valuable was arriving.

It was, but not quite in the sense that he would have wished, for as the van drove up to the warehouse and backed slowly against the main entrance, the tail-board came down and a large packing case was unloaded. Then, while it was still standing outside the warehouse door and blocking any view of the doorway from outside the warehouse, fourteen policemen climbed over the top of it from the van into the warehouse. I brought up the rear. The driver of the van and the security officer, both police officers dressed up for the occasion, trundled the packing case in after us, and then the doors closed and I heard the van draw away. The first round had gone to us, and we were inside the warehouse without being observed.

With the exception of Gilroy, the warehouseman, nobody could have been more surprised to see us than the other members of the night staff. I had purposely not told them we were coming and was determined that none of them should get mixed up in what happened next. So I explained what was up, locked them out of harm's way in a side office, and watched as four suitably dressed police officers took their places. The warehouse was pretty full and when the rest of the police had made themselves comfortable behind the bales and the packing cases, the wait began.

It was an eerie one. The warehouse was badly lit at the best of times, but I turned down what lighting there was to reduce to a minimum the gang's chances of spotting us and as I peered round in the dim shadows, and at the faint glimmer of light illuminating the strong-room door, I was grateful for those fourteen policemen crouched round me in the semi-darkness.

The hours ticked by. Nobody spoke, and although there was a strict rule against smoking in the warehouse, I would have given my soul for a cigarette. It was only now that I began to think what an uncertain business it all was. We did not know how many of the gang to expect or even whether they would be armed.

After an age I looked at my watch, thinking it must be long past one o'clock and that the gang had got the wind up and cancelled the raid. But it was barely eleven-thirty, and we had another hour and a half at least to wait.

What if they did not come? Apart from the fourteen men actually in the warehouse, there were another dozen police reinforcements who for the last hour had been waiting crammed tight in the back of a van parked for the night on a nearby car park. Then there were all the special arrangements we had made at the Yard. My hiding-place in the warehouse was in an office next to a telephone plugged straight through on an open line to Scotland Yard, and as soon as I gave the alarm, four squad cars which were waiting at different points about five miles from the airport would be called up by radio to race to the warehouse. If the raid was off, a lot of people would have lost a night's sleep for nothing.

From where I was sitting I could see only two people, both sitting at the table in a side office. One was Detective-Sergeant Hewitt, the man who had volunteered for the unpleasant job of taking the place of the security man who held the key to the strong-room. The other was the warehouseman. As far as I could see in that light, he looked perfectly composed, but if the gang did turn up that night, the hardest job of all still lay ahead of him.

Midnight struck, and still no one moved, although occasionally in the silence I could hear the rustle of someone stretching his legs to relieve the cramp of his hiding-place.

Then at last at about twenty to one there was a noise from outside as a van drove up and sounded its horn. It was the mobile canteen with the coffee for the night staff, and we all tensed, for this was the signal we had been waiting for. The game was beginning.

As I watched I saw the warehouseman get slowly to his feet, pick up an old enamel jug standing beside the table, and open the warehouse door to fetch the coffee. At the same time Sergeant Hewitt and the two other policemen taking the place of the night staff came round the table with their cups. I had never realised how good canteen coffee can smell at twenty to one in the morning.

Apart from the fact that the barbiturate was not in the coffee, everything else went exactly as the gang had planned it.

This was the crucial time. There was now no remote possibility of contact with the warehouseman. He was on his own. Would he carry out his instructions?

The minutes ticked by. Twenty minutes elapsed, and then I saw the signal pass between Hewitt and the warehouseman. Slowly he walked to the hangar doors, opened the wicket gate wide, letting out the light as a signal to the gang's lookout, left the door ajar, and re-entered the warehouse, where Sergeant Hewitt and the two other disguised policemen were slumped realistically across the table.

There was no noise now except the sound of my own breathing. Then out of the distance came the rumble of a heavy van being driven up to the gates of the warehouse. It stopped. There was a pause. Heavy boots crunched on the gravel outside. I lifted my telephone and just had time to whisper the code word to control room of the Yard before the gate opened and in filed eight men.

In the uncertain light of the warehouse their entrance was unnerving, for each of them wore a silk stocking over his head as a mask, and as they breathed, the leg of the the stocking filled with air and swung before them like some sort of trunk making them look like eight faceless men from another planet. To start with they were cautious and, signalling to the warehouseman, tiptoed over to the recumbent men round the table. One by one they shook them and lifted their eyelids to make sure that the drug had taken effect. But the police had strong nerves and none of the gang seemed to suspect them.

But it was Sergeant Hewitt I felt really sorry for. As he was impersonating the security man, he was the chap with the keys to the strong-room, and so had to submit while two members of the gang slapped him across the face, threw him on to the floor and then searched his pockets until they found the keys.

The evidence we needed was for those keys to be actually fitted into the strong-room lock, and we waited tensely as the leader of the gang moved over to the door. He reached it, his hand turned, and we pounced.

It was a bloodthirsty battle, for the gang had come prepared for trouble and fought like demons. They used crowbars. We fought with truncheons, and I shall never forget the dull thud of wood and steel on heads and bodies.

I have no idea how long it lasted. All I know is that it went on until all eight of the gang were out cold on the warehouse floor. It was only then we had a chance to pull those silk stockings off their heads and know for certain whom we had caught. They were not a bad haul for one night.

Then I gave the police a hand humping the eight of them into the back of a Black Maria and drove off to Harlington Police Station.

One by one I watched them being searched, patched up, bandaged and led off to the cells.

When all was over, we went back to the airport. Frank Wood, one of my officers who had nearly been knocked out during the fight, went off and got a couple of bottles of Scotch and some sandwiches, and we solemnly proceeded to break the licensing laws. B.O.A.C. paid for it on my expense account, but I felt we had earned it.

It was not until about eight in the morning that I got into my car to drive home and noticed a great deal of someone else's blood down the front of my shirt. It was then I remembered my interview with Mr. Temple Mellor, and on the spur of the moment I changed direction and went up to town, parked my car in Piccadilly and sat in it until the first editions of the midday papers arrived on the streets. The headlines were terrific, so I bought one, went straight to his office and blood-stained and unshaven, laid it on the desk before him.

As happens so often in this sort of case, we were never able to pin anything on to the man who planned it all, for the fact that he owned the black Vauxhall was the only definite evidence we had against him. He was far too smart and too important ever to have allowed himself to become personally involved in anything really dangerous, and although we knew perfectly well who he was, there was nothing we could do about it.

But he was the only one who got away with it. A few weeks later, I was sitting in the Old Bailey when the gang was given a total of seventy-one years' penal servitude for their part in the Battle of London Airport.

CHAPTER 7

The Bangkok watches

The London Airport raid was just the example I needed to prove the importance of air security.

Several influential people in civil aviation were shocked at the sudden reminder of just how wide open a peacetime airport is to anyone who wants to get on to it, and there were suggestions that entrance into London Airport should be restricted, and even that guard dogs should be employed to patrol the area after nightfall.

These ideas were fine in theory, but in practice there are four and a half square miles of London Airport, four bus services run right through it, and on a fine Sunday 20,000 sightseers visit it. No criminal could ask for anything much easier, and we all knew that there was nothing more vulnerable than a large modern airport with aircraft operating through it on regular schedules.

But the London Airport raid was the first sign that the really big-time criminal had turned his attention to the airlines. From now on the enemy was no longer going to be just the small-time nylon racketeer or the airport hand who pocketed half a dozen watches from a damaged carton, but the professional international crook who really knew his business, and would not be slow to exploit every weakness he could find across the 200,000 miles of B.O.A.C. routes.

Even then trouble was slower to arrive than we expected and the autumn of 1948 passed off quietly. A loader was convicted of stealing 1,600 cigarettes from a Stratocruiser and fined five pounds. A £250 watch was lost in transit from Manila. Three suitcases, one containing £100 in notes, disappeared from the passenger lounge of London Airport. It was all very small beer.

I was grateful for this, for by now I was reasonably satisfied with my organisation in Britain, and the time had come to perfect our defences across the world. The Western hemisphere rarely worried me. Occasionally there might be a few cases of pilfered cashmere twin sets from Idlewild, but otherwise American airports were surprisingly law-abiding and until the mid-fifties it was worth our while to leave our security there in the hands of a private American security organisation.

From 1950 on my real troubles lay to the East. To be exact, they began at Cairo. I have already made my feelings for that particular city clear, but it was not just that I happened to dislike the place. At this time, what was then called Farouk Field was the junction of the world's airways with our African, Australian and Asian services all stopping there to refuel and exchange passengers and freight. The opportunities there were endless, and as far as I was concerned there was no crime that could be ruled out.

Another important airfield that always seemed to attract more than its fair share of larceny was Drigh Road Field in Karachi. Gold consignments were always particularly vulnerable here, and it became an important embarkation point for opium and morphine being smuggled farther East. But here we had the advantage of being able to recruit a splendid group of Pathans to take charge of our airport security, whilst Buchanan was also there to keep his eye on the whole of B.O.A.C.'s Far Eastern network.

Although Cairo had a non-stop nuisance value, my biggest headache of all was to lie in Hong Kong, for to-day it has become one of the world's biggest entrepôts for smuggled heroin and opium. It is also the centre of the Far Eastern watch trade, a great place for the opportunist thief, and the home of the biggest gold-smuggling racket that has yet been worked on the airways.

Apart from the big places, the smaller stopping points for our aircraft formed a separate problem of their own, and several times during the spring of 1949, I found myself packing my blue suitcase and flying off for a five-day check on the security of some out of the way airport or other. One week it would be Rangoon, the next it would be Singapore, and, as the visas in my passport grew, I gradually began to feel reasonably confident that when trouble did strike the foreign routes we would have the men to meet it.

At the same time we introduced various security methods of our own, and it was one of them that in the summer of 1949 played its part in solving one of the first of the really expert robberies from our foreign routes that I had been fearing.

The security check in this case was one that we had been using only a few months, but which has since proved its value a hundred times over. It consists of a special steel strapping put round any consignment of real value and secured with an identifying metal seal. Each of our foreign stations had its own seal, and I made it standard practice for every valuable consignment being shipped from a B.O.A.C. station to be sealed immediately on acceptance.

This particular case concerned a box containing a hundred valuable watches flown in to Singapore from Switzerland.

The Bangkok watches

They had made the first leg of their journey by Panam as far as Karachi and then, as often happens with air freight, the watches had been transferred to a B.O.A.C. plane going on to Singapore. The box arrived. The lid, steel strapping and security seals were intact, but when the Customs opened it they found that every single watch had been removed, and the weight made up with three bricks and an old roller skate.

Buchanan was the first to hear of it, and sent me the news at once in a telegram which reached my desk just as I was about to shut up shop and go home for the night. As I puzzled over our next move, I realised there was not much I could do that evening, apart from cabling back to Singapore asking them to send me all the evidence they could lay their hands on. For I was up against the biggest difficulty any airline investigator can have to face at the start of an inquiry—that of deciding exactly where, across several thousand miles of route, the crime had been committed. This time things were more complicated than usual, since the first half of the box's journey had not even been in one of our planes.

It was not until two days later, when a large mail-bag arrived at London Airport, on the afternoon flight from Singapore, that the investigation could begin in earnest. For in that bag was all the evidence available, and as I emptied it out on to the floor of my office, I wondered just what it was going to reveal.

There was the strongly-made wooden box which had held the watches, the three bricks and the rusty roller skate, and there was the steel strapping which had been put round the parcel when it had gone through our freight department in Karachi. Apart from a short note from one of my security men in Singapore explaining the bare facts of how the parcel was discovered, that was the lot, and I scratched my head as I looked at this unpromising collection of airborne junk.

The first thing I examined was the box. It did not tell me much, beyond the fact that the nails had been drawn once already, presumably when the larceny took place, and then expertly replaced so as not to arouse anyone's suspicions until the box reached Singapore. There was nothing unusual about the bricks, and the roller skate was an old German model to fit a number eight shoe which could have come from anywhere.

But it was the security strapping which really attracted my attention. For according to what it told me, the watches should simply not have disappeared. The seal was intact and still bore the embossed " F " which was the code letter of Karachi and showed that the parcel was intact when it entered the Karachi Customs area, and had not visibly been tampered with after it left.

The crux of the case rested on that seal. From the way it was made, it was impossible for the criminal to have opened and then resealed it with the same seal. It would have been perfectly easy for anyone to have found the steel strapping and even to have fitted another seal if he had had the time, but not to have embossed the seal with the letter " F " of Karachi. To do this the man who stole the watches would have needed a special embossing tool, and only two of these were in existence. One was kept under top security by one of my officers in Karachi, and the other, an exact copy, was in my safe at London Airport. I just did not see how the job had been done.

I remember sitting at my desk and looking at that wretched seal until I was nearly blue in the face. I even tried imitating the heroes of the detective books, and peered at it through a magnifying glass, but it looked perfectly all right to me. But just to make sure, I thought I had better check it, so I opened up the battered old safe in the corner of my room, and took out the box in which I kept the duplicates of the embossing tools of all our foreign stations. I found the Karachi one, and when I held it right against the seal it was supposed to match, I noticed something. It was the lower arm of the " F ". The rest of the letter was all right, but just this part of it was the slightest fraction too long. This time when I used my magnifying glass it was to better effect, for when I examined the seal properly against the embossing tool, I could see that it was a skilful forgery.

This was almost all we needed to know, for it pinpointed the crime to the customs area at Karachi. The watches must have been stolen after they had been passed by customs and sealed for the first time by our people.

I cabled Buchanan the news straight away, and within a couple of days he had picked up the two men responsible. They had been employed for some time in our own bonded warehouse, where they had had ample opportunity to study the sealing procedure, and the evidence against them was enough to get them both convicted. But more important from our point of view was the fact that Buchanan had moved so fast that seventy of the watches were actually recovered from the markets at Karachi and nearby, where they were selling for about three pounds each. Whoever bought the other thirty certainly picked a bargain.

Another overseas case shortly after this gave us one of our rare opportunities to employ an outside expert on a mystery that had occurred over a thousand miles away, and which otherwise would never have been solved. It began when a small parcel of jewellery, a wedding present for the daughter of a wealthy South African banker, went adrift somewhere along its flight from Brussels to Johannesburg. From our point of view it was a tricky case for two reasons. Firstly, there had been a delay in reporting the loss so that it was now nearly a month since it had been sent, and secondly the parcel had been sent on rather a roundabout route from Brussels via London and could have been stolen at any of half a dozen airports *en route*.

As happens so often in a case of this sort, the only evidence we had consisted of the parcel which turned up at its destination. This time the small wooden box had been ripped open, and a handful of brick rubble placed inside as a substitute for the jewellery. But this brick rubble was surprisingly informative, for with a magnifying glass I thought I could just make out several tiny shells embedded in the mortar. It was a long shot, but we had nothing else to go on, so I sent the mortar along to the Natural History Museum at South Kensington with a note asking the Director whether he could tell me if the things I could see really were shells, and if so, where they would have come from.

It was three days before I heard anything, and by then I had almost given the case up as a bad job, when I had a telephone call from the museum. Apparently I did know a shell when I saw one, and the expert's identification was even more exact than I had dared to hope. For the shells came from a small mollusc which was found only in the waters off the coast of the African shore of the Mediterranean.

Although she probably does not know it, the daughter of that Johannesburg banker owes the recovery of her wedding present to that mollusc. For it fixed the larceny to one airport. Of all the places where the jewellery stopped on its way to Johannesburg, the only one within the area where the mollusc occurred was at Tripoli. When one of my investigators from London flew out there that evening, he found that the security men on the airport had had their suspicions about two local employees on the airport for some time, and when their quarters were searched the jewellery was found still hidden under one of the floorboards.

But the most expert job of all during this period was the Bangkok Watch Case and although I never met the man responsible for it, I still have a profound respect for his skill.

The case began one fine December morning at Northolt when a plump, bespectacled watch salesman turned up from Switzerland on his way to Bangkok with a large wooden box. He declared it at the Customs, saying it contained 500 valuable Swiss watches ordered by a customer in Thailand. It was the first time his firm had had such a large order from there, and he thought he had better go himself and keep the watches as near as possible to himself on the flight, just to be on the safe side. He was obviously acting in good faith, but it is illegal to ship merchandise like this as passenger baggage, so he was fined a nominal sum on the Customs bench, and someone had the job of telling the poor man that he would have to give up his precious watches and send them on to Bangkok separately by B.O.A.C. freight service.

He complained bitterly and the Customs officer tried to reassure him. The watches, he explained, would be as safe as the Crown Jewels.

Reluctantly the Swiss agreed. The watches were sent on and actually reached Bangkok four days ahead of him. Until his arrival the box was kept under lock and key in the Customs warehouse at Bangkok and checked three times a day.

On the fourth day the anxious Swiss arrived in Bangkok

and hurried over to the warehouse to collect his watches. Everyone was most polite, and when he produced his papers, the packing case was lifted down from its shelf. It was exactly as he had left it, with every seal and label in place. The warehouseman scrupulously placed it on the scales in front of him. The weight was correct to within two decimal places of the figure on the consignment note.

The Swiss was more than satisfied, and would probably have tipped the warehouseman and left straight away if it had not been for one of the local Customs men who appeared on the scene. The Swiss had had more than enough of Customs men by now, but the man insisted that the case had to be opened. Inside, instead of the neatly packed rows of small red boxes everyone expected there lay a pile of rubble, the torn remains of some of the boxes, several large stones, and an empty ink bottle.

Back in London, when I arrived in my office next morning, one of Buchanan's typically curt telegrams was already lying on my desk. He was still in Karachi but he had heard the news from Bangkok and as a matter of routine had already arranged for the packing case and its contents, to be flown to me direct at London Airport on the first plane from Thailand.

Everything now depended on that packing case, for it was the one thing which could tell me where the robbery took place along the 7,349 mile route from London to Bangkok. Until that was settled, it was impossible to know even where to begin our investigations, so I cancelled all other business for the afternoon and sat down to wait for the box to arrive. It was a long wait.

At six when the last of the secretaries left, there was still no news from Bangkok. Twice I rang the aircraft control desk, but there had been trouble with the plane and they were not quite certain when it would arrive. I shouted back something bad-tempered about what did they think their job was, and then made things worse by apologising.

By now the airport was quite dark. The blue pinpoints of the landing lights had flickered on down the runways, and I could see the hangars already lit up for the mechanics as the night shift came on to service to-morrow's aircraft. At the far end of the runway the airport's identification beacon turned endlessly against the wet night sky.

In the end it turned out that the aircraft had been delayed at Rome with engine trouble, and it was nearly nine o'clock before I saw it roar past the windows of my office and down the runway. Half an hour later the box, complete with rubble and ink bottle, was on my desk.

It is difficult to describe the sort of detached excitement you feel as an investigator when you finally get the evidence of a crime which has been committed a day or two previously on the other side of the world. I knew that the distance should make no difference and that evidence is evidence, whether it comes from Bangkok or Brixton. Certainly you go about the case in exactly the same way, but there was a thrill about this sort of case I had never felt at the Yard or even when I was working for M.I.5.

The packing case was exactly as the Customs declaration described it. Its lid was in one piece. The labels were clearly addressed from Geneva to Bangkok. The steel strapping and seal were complete except where they had been cut by Customs and at first it was difficult to see how the theft had been done. But when I looked closely at the packing case I saw that it was one of the neatest bits of work I had come up against. Instead of prising up the lid and leaving the box to attract everyone's attention, the thief had taken one of the large address labels off the side of the case. It measured about six inches by four, and was just big enough for what he wanted. For within the area where the label had been, he cut a hole just large enough for his hand to reach through. The job had been done with an extremely fine keyhole saw, and when the thief had pocketed the watches, he had replaced their boxes, added the rubble and then weighed the case just to make sure there would be no change in its weight to arouse anyone's suspicions. Then he finished the job off by replacing the piece of wood he had cut out of the hole, and neatly gluing the label over the top again.

So far, so good. I knew how the crime had been done, but what was still more important was to know where it had been done. Obviously no one could do a job like this in five minutes, but I had to have the timing of the crime a good deal more exactly than that. So I decided to perform an identical crime on a mock-up of an identical packing case full of watches.

As the case had been opened by Customs at Northolt and the number of watches counted, we were soon able to find out how they had been packed. The case had a layer of wood-wool in the bottom. The red cardboard boxes, containing the watches, had been stacked on top and the three-inch gap round the sides had been packed tight with wood-wool.

I had no difficulty in getting hold of a case and a keyhole saw. Although I am good with my hands the job took me a lot longer than I thought. It was not the case which was the trouble. What made it such heavy going was the way the watches had been wedged in with the wood-wool. Because of this, the saw had hardly any play, and only about six of the teeth could cut at a time.

Altogether it took nearly three hours before I had the

The Bangkok watches

hole cut, the contents removed, and the label stuck on again. This timing was important for it located the crime without a shadow of doubt. The one place where the packing case had remained on the ground for anything like three hours after it left London Airport was inside the Customs warehouse at Bangkok.

It was well past midnight before I had finished, but I knew now that I had done all I could at my end. From now on, the investigation belonged to Buchanan, and before driving home that night I cabled him in Karachi telling him what I had discovered, and handing the inquiry over to him.

This was exactly the problem to suit him. With his Scots canniness, he is the sort of man—obstinate and intensely methodical—who always works best when left entirely on his own.

This was how he worked now. For three whole weeks he watched that warehouse, night after night waiting alone in the dark after the staff had locked up for the night. Apart from the B.O.A.C. Manager in Bangkok, no one knew he was there, but if an extra cockroach had turned up one night, Buchanan would have been on to it. In the end, his doggedness paid off. At two o'clock one morning he heard a noise from the far side of the warehouse. Slowly a manhole cover lifted and a man with a torch crept out from the sewer below. He knew what he wanted, and he knew his way around, for the day before two more large consignments of Swiss watches had arrived. They were quite close to where Buchanan was hiding, and he watched as the man sat down by one of them, and got to work.

It went exactly as it had the time before. The label came off, a small hole was drilled, and Buchanan actually let the man spend half an hour on the case before revealing his

97

presence. I told Buchanan afterwards that he might have saved the poor devil half an hour's wasted effort, but he said that it was not every day you got a chance of watching an expert at work, and that after waiting three weeks for the demonstration, he had made up his mind to get his money's worth.

CHAPTER 8

Murder, hoaxes and Royalty

On the 9th of September, 1949, a Constellation of Canadian Pacific Airlines exploded in mid-air a few minutes after take-off from Quebec Airport, and crashed in flames on the banks of the St. Lawrence. No one aboard had a chance, and all twenty-three of them lost their lives.

We soon realised from the rumours reaching us in London that this was no ordinary accident. The first suspicions began when the Canadian authorities investigating the disaster examined the wreckage. The propeller blades were bent in such a way that it was clear that the plane's four engines had all been running when it hit the ground, so that the mid-air explosion could not have been caused by engine trouble of any sort. At the same time the panels from the rear baggage compartment had all been distorted, and bore the signs of a powerful explosion.

Baggage compartments do not explode of their own accord. The Canadian Pacific Railways Police and the R.C.M.P. were called in, and within a few days of the crash a full-scale investigation had started on the world's first time-bomb murder aboard a civil aircraft.

Although the number of people who could have slipped a bomb into the Constellation's passenger luggage before take-off was considerable, the police soon narrowed the suspects down to one man—a thirty-two year old jewellery salesman from Quebec called Albert Guay, whose wife had been aboard the plane. The couple had been living apart, but a few days before the flight, Guay had insured his wife for £3,500 and had actually seen her off at the airport.

By December the case against Guay was complete. His mistress, a waitress called Marie Pitre was also brought into the case as an accessory, along with Generoux Ruest, a crippled watch-maker, who admitted making Guay a special timing mechanism for his bomb. All three were ultimately hanged, Ruest being taken to the gallows in a wheeled chair.

The crime itself was bad enough, and fully justified the wave of horror which swept through Canada and the United States as the details of the time-bomb murder were released. There was something else about it that worried me. Time after time I had seen how a new departure in crime would give other people ideas, and I wondered just how long the airlines would have to wait for their next time-bomb murder.

Sure enough, a few months later a laboratory technician insured his wife heavily just before she boarded a plane from Los Angeles with a bomb in her suitcase, but at the last minute his nerve failed him, and he informed the police what he had done.

Then in November 1955 a trans-continental Skymaster of United Airlines exploded in mid-air " like a ball of fire " eleven minutes after take-off from Denver, Colorado, with the loss of forty-four people aboard. Here sabotage was suspected from the start, and a few weeks later twenty-three year old John Graham confessed to planting a time bomb in the luggage of his elderly mother whom he had previously insured for £13,000. Before he was executed, feeling against

him ran so high that a crowd threatened to break into Denver
County Gaol to lynch him.

These mass murders, terrible though they were, were not
the end of the story for the airlines. Before long they
produced another problem that soon became almost as
serious, for it threatened the entire pattern of air operations
across the world.

Some people have pretty strange ideas of a joke. A hoax
is a hoax, but I cannot understand why anyone in their
right mind should want to pick up a telephone and start a
scare by telling an airport that there is a bomb on one of the
planes. The Denver crash gave some practical joker the idea,
and from then on the anonymous bomb hoaxes spread like
wildfire across the world, until no airline could consider
itself immune.

Part of the attraction must have been that it was so easy.
There was no risk. It is almost impossible to trace a short
call from a public call box in time to catch the culprit, and
even if the hoaxer were caught, there was precious little
the police or anyone else could do about it. Even to-day
in England the only offence a hoaxer can be charged with is
that of " using a telephone to the annoyance of another
subscriber " with a maximum fine of £10.

In the United States the position became so serious that
a Bill was rushed through to make a bomb scare a Federal
offence with a maximum penalty of twelve months in prison
and a $5,000 fine. Despite this, the number of hoaxes
steadily increased.

All the hoaxer had to do was to ring the airport and say
" there is a bomb aboard an aircraft " and the trouble would
start.

It was really a war of nerves. It soon became apparent
that it was a thousand to one against a bomb being there.

People who go to the trouble of placing explosives in a passenger's baggage don't usually ring the airport to tell them about it.

However after the Quebec and Denver crashes, no one in the airline business felt like taking any risks. If they ignored a warning and then another bomb crash did occur, there would be all hell to pay. There were few airline people willing to risk another Denver on their consciences, and there was always the chance that a crash in no way due to a bomb might coincide with one of the anonymous telephone calls.

So, to start with, the bomb hoaxers had it all their own way, especially in the United States. Every bomb scare had to be taken seriously. Every aircraft on the runways would be delayed and thoroughly searched, and aircraft which had already left the airport and were airborne would be recalled and searched. On one occasion seventeen aircraft were recalled on account of a single telephone call.

All this, of course, was just what the hoaxers wanted. At practically no risk to themselves, they were causing the maximum inconvenience to everyone and costing the airlines a great deal of money into the bargain. For every hour an aircraft is delayed, it costs upwards of £250.

By 1957 the hoaxes had begun at London Airport as well, and suddenly the airlines found themselves facing a major crisis.

We had endless meetings to discuss the hoaxes with security officers from other airlines, but in the end all the arguments showed that a single decision had to be taken— whether to continue to take the hoaxes seriously or to ignore them completely. It was a decision which nobody was particularly keen to take.

Despite the cost and the crippling inconvenience, most of the Americans were in favour of continuing to take the hoaxes at their face value. It was understandable. They had already had two bomb murders in North America, and with public opinion in the state it was, no airline could risk a third.

All the same, I was sure that by taking the hoaxes seriously, we were actually encouraging them. They were getting publicity in the Press, radio and television, and I became convinced that as long as this continued the hoaxes would go on.

Nothing had ever been found as the result of an anonymous bomb warning, and as every air security officer knows, an aircraft is one of the most difficult things in the world to search properly. It has endless places where a really determined person could hide a bomb and, in fact, the sort of search which can be carried out following an anonymous call was simply not worth the time spent on it.

It was this that finally convinced me that the only way to fight the bomb hoaxers was to ignore them unless the telephone call gave specific information about the actual plane on which the bomb was supposed to be, or some other positive detail. In the long run, this decision proved to be right and to-day the number of calls received affecting London Airport is negligible.

Shortly after we had decided to ignore these calls, our decision was given just about the most nerve-racking test it is possible to imagine. It came when the Queen was flying back from Idlewild to London after her 1957 tour of America.

It was something I had been dreading all along, for this was the year when the bomb scares were at their height, and the plans for flying the Queen home could hardly have made things easier for a hoax. The Britannia aircraft in which she was returning had been flown out from Britain two days before, and for the forty-eight hours it was on the tarmac at

Idlewild it would be a sitting target for every bomb-happy lunatic and practical joker in New York.

To make matters worse, for those forty-eight hours the aircraft was my direct responsibility, so I had actually flown out to Idlewild aboard her with seven of my London staff to make sure nothing went wrong.

That afternoon, before departure, what I dreaded all along happened. Someone telephoned the New York City Police to say there was a bomb on an aircraft at Idlewild. Quite apart from our decision to ignore anonymous bomb calls, there was no question of delaying a Royal flight for a reason like this, but I knew that if anything did go wrong, I would be the man held responsible.

The only thing to do was to make absolutely sure that nothing could go wrong. For the long hours it was at Idlewild the eight of us lived with that aircraft. The fuel was checked and rechecked before it was put into the tanks ; the water containers were actually sealed at the filling point and every item of food and baggage had to be passed by us before it was allowed aboard.

It was October. We spent the first night actually on the tarmac guarding the aircraft ourselves, and I remember the lights of the taxis all night long weaving their way along the edge of the airport bringing sightseers out from New York for a glimpse of the Queen's plane.

The following night our vigil was over. When the Queen and the Duke of Edinburgh drove to the airport from their ball at the Armoury, I was as certain as anyone could be that not a single unauthorised person in the whole of New York had had a chance to get within a hundred yards of the plane.

Even when, shortly before 2 a.m. the Royal flight had roared away over the Atlantic, that anonymous telephone call was still at the back of my mind, and I knew there would be no sleep for me until I was certain the Queen was back in London.

So I stayed up, listening to reports on the plane's position as they came through to the Operations Room at Idlewild. Dawn was breaking as I heard the last message that the Queen's plane had landed safely at London Airport. Gratefully I went off to bed and slept the clock round.

It was the exception for Royal flights to be as worrying as this. Most of the time they were essentially relaxed affairs, and I used to look forward to them as among the most enjoyable duties that could come my way.

The year after the Queen's flight from Idlewild, for instance, there was Princess Margaret's tour of the Caribbean. On this occasion it was not bombs we were worried about so much as the over-enthusiastic crowds of admirers and souvenir hunters expected at every airport. Her plane became my responsibility each time it landed, so I flew out with her to Trinidad just to make sure that nothing went wrong. The airport authorities and the Colonial Police there knew their job, and it was soon clear that there would be little difficulty, but that evening something cropped up that landed me in an unusual investigation.

It started long after Princess Margaret had left the airport, and I had gone over to the bar for a quiet drink with the captain of her plane. I had flown with him several times before, and over his drink he admitted that he was a very worried man. When she left the plane, the Princess had been extremely complimentary about the flight but had complained that her bed had been so uncomfortable that she had hardly slept a wink. Naturally after this everyone had tried to find out what had been the matter with the bed, but no one had been able to discover the slightest thing wrong with it.

I had never had anything like this to investigate before, but obviously something had to be done about it, so we had one more drink and strolled over to the Royal plane together to take a good look at the offending divan. At first it was difficult to see what could be the matter with it. It had a brand new Dunlopillo mattress recently issued from the stores, and specially upholstered with a fitted cover so that it could be used for a day divan for the Princess's cabin.

It looked all right, but when I felt it I had to admit that it did feel much stiffer than the Dunlopillo mattress I had at home, so just to see what was wrong I carefully unpicked the stitches from one corner of the cover. Then I could see what had happened. In this sort of mattress, the underside of the foam rubber has a series of cavities like a honeycomb and, to my surprise I saw that each one had been carefully filled with fibre.

Presumably it had been done, with the best of intentions, by B.O.A.C. workshops when they were fitting out the cabin. They had placed the fibre inside to stiffen it for use during the daytime as an ordinary couch.

What they failed to realise was that the fitted cover was the same on both sides, and the stewardess in making up the bed, knowing nothing about the fibre stiffening, had turned the mattress honeycomb side up. Sleeping on it must have felt like lying on a bed of tennis balls.

So I had the job of unpicking the entire mattress, taking every ball of fibre out, and then sewing it up again ready for take-off the following evening. The rest of the Princess's tour was a great success.

The Caribbean in the spring was wonderful, but for me the most colourful Royal tour of all came the following year when I flew with the Duke of Edinburgh through India and Pakistan at the start of his round-the-world trip for the Geophysical Year.

The Duke has an easy informality that makes him the perfect V.I.P. to deal with. Because of this, I had many opportunities to enjoy the programme the Indians and Pakistanis had put on in his honour, including the wonderful spectacle of India's Independence Day parade and a journey through the Khyber Pass.

But the climax to the whole trip was the Duke's own idea, and was something that was not in the programme. It came when we reached Dacca. We were due to leave for Karachi by Comet at ten o'clock the next morning but at the last minute an order came through that, at the wish of the Duke, take-off time time was being advanced an hour.

On anything planned as minutely as a Royal tour, an hour's change on the programme causes no end of a commotion, and everyone wanted to know what the Duke was up to. We did not know until we got to the airport and heard that the Duke had applied for special permission to fly over Nepal along the Himalayas to Everest.

Even then, permission was late arriving, and it was not until we were airborne that official permission came through by radio from Nepal. When we were over Katmandu a radio message came up from the airport; " Your Majesty," it read, " we are pleased it is nice day so you can see our hills."

And a nice day it was, despite the hundred-and-eighty-mile-an-hour headwind we met over the peak of Everest. The whole Everest range was at its most spectacular for the occasion, with a long white finger of cloud marking the summit, and the sunlight gleaming on the snow beneath. I have always been grateful to the Duke for giving me the chance of seeing it.

CHAPTER 9

Diamonds in the air

There are only two things that have ever really disappointed me during my life. The first is champagne and the second is diamonds. I was a young soldier in World War I when I tasted my first glass of champagne. I did not particularly like it then, and I have found no reason to change my views in later life. Diamonds, I think, are gaudy things and the least attractive of the precious stones. I have never yet been able to understand their appeal.

Still, whatever my own feelings, diamonds are diamonds, and before I had been very long with B.O.A.C., I realised that a large slice of my working life was going to revolve around them. For to-day, by far the greater part of all international diamond shipments go by air, and any time you go into the strong-room at London Airport, you are almost certain to see at least one or two of the small tin boxes the diamond merchants use, sitting on the shelf and waiting for the next plane to New York or Amsterdam.

Not that you would notice them if you had not seen them before. A box of bullion is worth looking at, and if you try to pick it up it at least feels valuable, but diamonds make unassuming treasure. You can get a few thousand pounds' worth of them in a matchbox, but when they go by air they are generally wrapped in cotton wool, placed inside a tin

108

box and then sealed and addressed on a simple green label.

Often, with a particularly valuable shipment of diamonds, I or one of my security men would actually carry them ourselves, and although it may sound romantic to catch the night plane to New York with a million pounds in your charge, I found it the sort of excitement that soon wears off.

In fact, this sort of personal courier service is thought unnecessary for all except the most absurdly valuable shipments, and usually the diamond merchants simply send their stones by ordinary registered post.

This suited me perfectly. I had no direct responsibility for the mails. The Post Office never told me what was in the mail-bags we carried, and if anything did disappear B.O.A.C. had only the most nominal liability under the terms of the Postal Regulations. All the same, if a diamond robbery ever did take place from the mails, I had no intention of standing aside and letting the crooks get away with it on our planes. Whatever the regulations said about our liability was neither here nor there.

For some time the question did not arise. We must have carried many millions of pounds' worth of diamonds through the post without complaint. Then in the early summer of 1955 something went seriously wrong.

For years one of the regular diamond runs had been up from Palmeitfontein Airport, just outside Johannesburg. The stones travelled from there by air all over the world and I had never heard of any trouble. Then at the beginning of 1955 the new Jan Smuts Airport opened up, and no sooner had the traffic switched to there from Palmeit-fontein than diamond shipments started to go astray. Suddenly between March and May several parcels, worth over £50,000, disappeared from the mails.

One of the difficulties of starting the investigation was that there seemed no obvious pattern to be drawn from the places where the thefts were reported.

The first of the losses was reported from Hong Kong where something had happened to a £7,000 diamond parcel that should have been inside a registered mailbag. Buchanan flew straight away to investigate from Karachi, and was shown the cut bag which had held the registered mail. The G.P.O. seal was unbroken around the neck, and the rest of the registered mail was still inside and completely untouched along with the remains of the parcel which had held the diamonds. This alone appeared to have been tampered with, and every stone was missing.

Buchanan did what he could in Hong Kong, but found absolutely nothing more and a couple of days later returned to Karachi. He had been back three days when the second robbery was reported. This time the trouble was at Amsterdam. It seemed to have happened in exactly the same way as the robbery at Hong Kong, and was followed in swift succession by similar losses at New York, at Brussels, at Hong Kong again, and finally at London Airport itself. Long before the last robbery was reported, the G.P.O. and the insurance companies were both getting extremely concerned, and so was I.

Naturally I wanted the chance of seeing for myself what was happening, and as soon as the robbery had been reported from Amsterdam I had flown over to Schipol Airport to have a look at the mail-bag. The security people at the airport were old friends, and their hospitality was almost too lavish. There are very definite limits to the amount of Dutch gin I can take in an evening, and the restaurants of Amsterdam cater for men with heavier appetites and far larger stomachs than mine.

But before I had to worry about this, I had had my chance

to look at the mail-bag, and it had confirmed everything Buchanan told me in his report from Hong Kong. The way the robberies were being done was simple but surprisingly effective. First of all the thief selected out of all the mail travelling in the plane the one bag that held the registered mail.

This in itself may sound a remarkable piece of clairvoyance when you remember that he probably had at least twenty bags or more to choose from, but it was not really so difficult as it sounds. For that obliging institution, the Post Office, always gives the potential criminal a spot of initial encouragement by actually putting a clearly-marked identification label round the neck of every bag containing registered mail. Once he knew the mark, the criminal would have had no difficulty at all in picking out the most valuable mail of all.*

Now it almost always happens that the registered mail forms only an extremely small proportion of the total mail. Perhaps in a normal dispatch there might be a dozen or so items, so that usually the mail sack containing the registered mail is barely half full. The thief must have been an observant fellow, for he noticed this and turned it to good use. He always waited until he found a marked bag that was on the empty side with the seal tied a long way down the neck, and had found out that with a bag like this he could gradually edge the tightly-tied seal up to the top of the bag by tugging patiently at the folds of the canvas. There was a cord sewn into the neck of all British mail-bags

---

* On the 21st September, 1961, ten persons, all but two of whom were Airline employees at London Airport, were convicted at the Central Criminal Court of stealing from postal dispatches gold, diamonds and currency to the value of approximately £250,000. It was stated during the course of the trial that these thefts were made possible by the identifying labels attached to mail-bags containing valuable postal items.

that stopped the seal from being pulled right over the top, but once the thief had got it to the top it was enough for his purposes.

For once it was there, he would carefully slit the bag inside one of the folds towards the neck, and then put his hand in. It was something of a lucky dip, but if you feel inside a registered mail-bag coming from Johannesburg, slit it open, and your hand touches a small parcel heavily covered with official seals, the odds are that it is not cigars. It might be, of course. Then there is nothing for it but to wait till next time. But my man had struck lucky often enough to show that the risks were not excessive.

Up to a point he was showing himself slightly smarter than the run of common-or-garden mail thieves, and covering his tracks very neatly. When he had cut his bag and slipped the seal, he would take out the sealed packet, tear open one end of the wrapping and prise up one corner of the tin just sufficiently to allow him to pull out the cotton wool in which the diamonds were wrapped. Then he would pocket the stones, put the torn packet back inside the mail-bag and work the string and the seal back to their original position until the cut was completely hidden inside the folds of the neck of the bag.

In this way the robbery was not detected until the bag had actually reached its destination. If only he had used his imagination just a little more, he could have made things ten times more difficult for us. If he had taken not just the stones, but the whole registered packet, the post office at the bag's destination would have had a really complicated job on its hands, deciding exactly what had been stolen. The only information the Post Office records is that the registered mail-bag contains a specified number of registered items. If the thief had not put the opened box back into the bag, we would have had to wait until the sender complained that the diamonds had not arrived before we knew for sure what had been stolen. As I knew to my cost, you often have to wait so long for this that the crooks have had ample time to cover their tracks.

In this case the thief, whoever he was, was obliging enough to give us swift and accurate information of what he was up to, and it was quite clear from the start that the robberies were taking place in South Africa itself. As soon as I consulted the South African Police, however, they became absolutely insistent that the thefts could not possibly be occurring in the Union.

So once more the case hinged on the same old problem of fixing exactly where the trouble was occurring. I needed proof before I could reply to the South African Police, so to get it I turned once again to the old policeman's dodge I employed in the Bangkok watch case. I committed the crime myself in my own office in London Airport.

A great deal depended on this, so I spent nearly a whole day on it, timing myself exactly, going through it three times and then taking the average of my three performances. If anyone has tender fingers, I would strongly advise him against working a tightly-bound seal up the neck of a regulation mail-bag. Each time I managed to get it up, slit the bag and work it down again, it took me well over two hours. By the end of the afternoon my hands were stiff, but I had the information I needed. For I knew already that in no single flight from which diamonds had been reported missing had the aircraft even been on the ground for as long as two hours after leaving Jan Smuts Airfield. It would have been impossible to have committed a robbery of this sort actually in the air, and the only place left where the thief would conceivably have had time to perform his complicated trick would have to be actually within the area of the Jan Smuts Airfield, whatever the local police might say about it.

The London case gave a further clue to location. First on, last off, is a cardinal rule in aircraft loading. For obvious reasons it is essential the load should not be disturbed more than is necessary throughout its journey. In the London case the Johannesburg/London mail was loaded first, right inside the hold, and we found the cut mail-bag in such a position that it must have been almost the first bag loaded. What was more important was the fact that we found a small bag containing low-grade diamonds on the floor of the hold behind the slit bag. The thief had recognised them for what they were and had not bothered to go further with the crime, and had obligingly sent them on.

What really annoys me about this case is that even then, when we had evidence as clear as this, the South African Police would not budge in their insistence that the robberies could not be occurring within South Africa. I suppose they have their methods, but I know perfectly well that no police force in Britain would ever have refused to take notice of quite so obvious a crime when it was sitting on their own doorstep. Still without their help it was impossible for us to carry the case any further.

Although the number of men on Jan Smuts who could have had sufficiently close access to the mail to pull this job must be surprisingly small, and although one of them is presumably in possession of a lot of money made from diamonds pocketed from the mails, he has not so far made the slightest move that could give him away.

Frustrating though this case was from a security point of view, it did have one reassuring sequel. For it was partly because of strong representations following the case that airport security was taken out of the hands of the South African Police and reorganised under the South African Railways and Harbour Police, who had handled it most efficiently in the old days at Palmeitfontein. Since then there have been no more diamond robberies from Jan Smuts.

An even better example of the ridiculous disadvantages under which air security works with the present Post Office arrangements for carrying diamonds is the big Prestwick crash of Christmas 1954. For here, although it was our own plane involved and over a million pounds' worth of diamonds were aboard in the registered mail at the time, no one, not even the Post Office, took the trouble to inform us. Unbelievable though it may seem, that wrecked plane had been lying in the open with half Scotland clambering over it for several days before I got the first hint of what was hidden somewhere in the wreckage.

This Stratocruiser landing at Prestwick *en route* to New York in a low fog, had missed the end of the runway and crashed. As a matter of routine, I was always informed of any crash as soon as it was reported, and the news that the plane had caught fire and that twenty-eight people had died in the wreckage hardly helped to make that a particularly happy Christmas. In an airline, you are more involved in the operations of your company than in most professions, and although the million to one accident can never be ruled out, there is a strange way in which everyone feels collectively responsible when it occurs.

Still, from the first reports there did not seem to be a great deal I could do about it. There were no records of anything out of the ordinary in the cargo, and mercifully it has never been part of a security officer's job to deal with relatives after a crash.

It was five days later when I got my first mention of the

diamonds, and even then it was pretty vague. It simply consisted of an inquiry which came through by telex on behalf of a firm of New York diamond brokers about an important registered parcel of uncut diamonds sent from London more than a week before that had not turned up. There was obviously a good chance that they had been aboard the Stratocruiser, but there was no way I could tell except by asking the Post Office, and finally, as a result of most urgent inquiries, they did discover many packets of diamonds had been aboard.

Now in this case again, B.O.A.C. had absolutely no liability for what they had been carrying, and could have left the whole thing to the insurance companies to sort out. But I could not bear the thought of a million pounds lying around for anyone to pick up in the middle of the wreckage of one of our own aircraft. So, I rang up some acquaintances in the Diamond Corporation and told them what I knew. It seemed that the Corporation had come to the conclusion that the diamonds were on the plane at about the same time as the Post Office, and two of their men were travelling up to Prestwick on the night train to see what could be done about them. I arranged to travel with them.

It was a cold misty morning, very much like the one when the Stratocruiser had crashed, when the three of us reached Prestwick. We were met by Jimmy Jeffs, in those days still Commandant of Prestwick before moving on to take charge of London Airport. It was good to see an old friend whom I knew to be one of the sanest and most genial men in the business. If anyone could help us in this melancholy treasure hunt he would.

He drove us down the runway himself and out to the crash. It was a miserable sight, and none of us spoke as we looked at the charred wreckage. It must have burned like a furnace before the fire extinguishers got to work on it, and the sickly smell of burning still hung in the air. There was mud everywhere, with the cranes and vehicles still churning up the airfield as the Inspector of Accidents and his staff began dismantling the wreck. As I looked at the mess I thought we would have a better chance of finding uncut diamonds on Brighton beach than in the middle of all that mud.

News had reached Prestwick the day before that we were on our way and what we were after, so that a search of sorts had already begun, but so far without any results at all.

We had all brought gum boots with us, and as we squelched our way over to the wreckage I thought that despite the mud and the lorries and the search parties, we might still be in luck. For these diamonds had been uncut, and an uncut diamond is not a thing to attract anyone's attention unless he really knows what he is looking for. We did, but the others did not, and no sooner had I reached the tail end of the wrecked fuselage than my eye caught what looked like a small grey soda crystal lying in the mud. The first of the missing Prestwick diamonds had been found.

After this, the search hotted up as the three of us combed our way through the wreckage. By lunch-time our bag had already reached fifty, but we did not stop for lunch. The mist cleared but then the rain came in from the Atlantic and although we were soon soaked to the skin, our diamond hunt went on. The first finds had been easy, but it gradually became more difficult as many of the stones had been discoloured by the fire and their dirty brown colour was almost indistinguishable from the mud.

Nevertheless, by the time tea was brought out to us, the score had reached 150, and once dusk had fallen we arranged for arc lights to be set up round the wreckage and went on with the search. It must have been nearly eleven before we decided that we had done all we could for the time being, and next morning I caught the early train back from Glasgow with nearly two hundred stones for the Diamond Corporation.

As far as I was concerned, that was that. From here the Diamond Corporation and the insurance companies took over and carried out what must be one of the most intensive treasure hunts of the century. It lasted several weeks. Every scrap of debris was meticulously sorted. Then the ground around the wreck was bulldozed to a depth of two feet, and the earth washed and sifted. This was carried on also over open ground for half a mile to the hangar on the edge of the airfield where a lot of the wreckage had been originally taken, just in case any of the diamonds had become caught in the wheels of the lorries and then stuck in the mud.

The results of this mammoth operation were impressive, and in the end over ninety per cent of all the Prestwick diamonds were recovered. But I still think everyone concerned should count themselves lucky that out of all the men who worked on the crash there was not one who knew an uncut diamond when he saw one.

CHAPTER 10

Smuggling on the North Atlantic

I often felt that if diamonds had never existed the international crook would have had to have invented them, for they suit his purpose so ideally. They are light, they are easily concealed, they are infinitely negotiable and they never lose their value. There is no other currency for which you can say the same, and it is this combination of qualities which has often made the international smuggling organisations turn to diamonds when they need to transfer a lot of money across the world in a hurry without the law catching up with them.

Although several other airlines have had serious trouble with diamond smugglers in their time, we were fairly lucky, and there was only one occasion when a really serious outbreak occurred on B.O.A.C. It was a clever racket, and it was being worked on the one stretch of route I innocently thought was free from trouble—the North American flight to New York. If it had not been for the astuteness of a remarkable pair of Customs investigators we would probably never have got wind of it.

Late in 1952 it was really the Far East that had me worried. Narcotics smuggling in and out of Hong Kong had just started to touch the airlines, and although the few cases that had so far been discovered had all been on other people's aircraft, I had my doubts about how long it would be before B.O.A.C.'s planes would become involved. At the same time, as if this was not enough, Buchanan in Karachi reported that the Indian Government was getting the wind up over illicit gold being smuggled into the country by air. Again it was other airlines which were involved, but a security officer is paid to worry about trouble before it occurs, and neither Buchanan nor myself liked the way things were developing. For once we were to be right, although in our most pessimistic moments we could never have foreseen quite how big the threat of narcotics and gold smuggling was to become for B.O.A.C.

That autumn Buchanan was back in London for an informal conference on what was happening on the Far Eastern routes. The man is a walking filing-cabinet, and unlike me he really can remember dates and times and snatches of conversation from years before, so that these periodic conversations with him were almost the most valuable means I had of keeping up to date on the most distant parts of our routes. I would usually have him over to my flat at Twickenham after we had got through the official business in the office, and that would be where we would talk. He would have his doubts about such and such an engineer who had just arrived in Karachi. I would remind him that a steward who had been dismissed the year before for suspected morphine trafficking had been seen contacting some of our present stewards in Beirut only a few weeks before. He would reply with the news that a dealer we had suspected as the centre of a watch smuggling ring on B.O.A.C. planes a few years before, had just come back from Tokyo to Hong Kong and appeared to be in a prosperous line of business.

Once we got started on this sort of conversation we would

stay up half the night, and I remember that it was on a Sunday morning after one of these sessions with Buchanan that I was woken up by the telephone. I suppose it was about half past ten, but that was too early for me, so I grunted down the telephone and hoped that whoever was at the other end would have the decency to go away.

But when the voice replied I recognised who it was, and woke up immediately. For Sam Charles was the finest investigator the Customs Investigation Branch ever had the luck to possess and his speciality was diamonds. But he was very cagey over the telephone and simply asked whether he could bring his colleague Geoff Smith to see me first thing the following morning. This was proof something serious was up for Smith and Charles together formed a sort of double act and together they had broken up several of the biggest smuggling rackets in Britain since the war.

I was at the airport early next morning to see Buchanan off to India, but by the time I reached my office Charles and Smith were already waiting for me. One of the rules that was never altered in my office was that a pot of tea was brought in on the dot of ten o'clock, and it was while I was pouring them both a cup that Smith began his lecture on the financial difficulties of the oil sheikhs of the Persian Gulf. He talked very precisely, almost as if he were speaking from notes, and went on about the problems presented by suddenly acquiring an immense fortune. I said something about it being a problem I thought I would be able to cope with if ever I had the misfortune to face it, and asked what the devil this had to do with me at ten o'clock on a Monday morning.

" Of course," said Smith smiling sympathetically, " but I just wanted you to understand something of the background to this case." This was the first news I had had that there even was a case, but I said nothing.

"You see," he went on, "these sheikhs have an enormous amount of money, but none of them know how long it's going to last, and it has become quite a problem for them to salt away enough of their money outside the Middle East for a rainy day." "The point is," said Charles, butting in suddenly, "we've got evidence that these boys are getting their money illegally into the States, and we both thought you would like to know who's doing the work for them."

He went on to name three men at the head of one of the biggest and most efficient smuggling set-ups in Europe. Their headquarters were normally in Switzerland, but they often worked through London, and I had had several brushes with them in the past. They were real professionals, the members of this gang, specialising in only the very cream of international contraband, and they had an unfortunate weakness for making their journeys by air.

As far as I could make out from what Sam said, the gang was working for the sheikhs in the following way. The sheikhs were building up large currency reserves in London. This was easy and perfectly legal. What was not so easy and definitely illegal was to carry this money across the Atlantic, and to do it the sheikhs had authorised the members of the smuggling organisation to convert their money into diamonds on the open market in London. These diamonds were then being smuggled to America and passed on to a contact in New York who had no trouble in reselling them and placing the money to the sheikhs' private bank accounts in New York.

This was a fact which Smith and Charles had only just found out, and was the real reason behind their visit. For like most top international smugglers, the men he named did not do the dirty work themselves. Instead they entrusted it to a small circle of B.O.A.C. stewards who were working regularly across the Atlantic. As far as was known, six stewards were involved. They carried up to seventy thousand pounds' worth of stones at a time, were paid strictly by results, and had never been known to fail. This, explained Charles, was because the stewards were using an old smugglers' trick that we all knew was virtually undetectable. For they were adopting the unpleasant device of carrying the diamonds actually inside the body wrapped in cotton wool and concealed in a rubber contraceptive.

All this made the case more difficult than it might have been, since you obviously have to be pretty sure of your facts before you can insist on searching a man for anything hidden in this way, and Smith and Charles had so far failed to get any evidence strong enough to connect the smuggling with our stewards. All they knew was that the smuggling gang was buying large and unexplained quantities of diamonds in Hatton Garden every month. They also knew that they were having regular meetings with several of our stewards in pubs round the airport just before our planes left for New York. Somehow we had to get hold of watertight evidence to link the stewards with the diamond smuggling.

Put like this, it sounds a good deal easier than it was, for those smugglers really knew what they were up to. They were as slippery as eels and never seemed to give us a thing to go on, although Smith and Charles had them both under almost constant watch and knew practically everything there was to know about them. They were working from a large detached cream house in Belsize Park. It was the last place in London you would have imagined as the centre of a smuggling ring. An Austrian doctor lived on one side, and a middle-aged literary critic on the other. To them the three eminently respectable Central Europeans using the house were what they seemed—a trio of retiring business-men who used the house as an office and a place to stay whenever they were in London. For they were always coming and going, and often the dark blue Ford Consul they drove would draw up outside the house at two and three in the morning.

By now Sam Charles knew every diamond they bought and could even have drawn up a pretty accurate balance sheet of their transactions, and he soon realised that their buyings were increasing and their journeys into Hatton Garden becoming more frequent. The business was prospering and we knew we had to hurry if we were to stop the traffic before it spread any farther.

In any investigation it is never a bad rule to wait until your man thinks he is doing well, for confidence soon becomes over-confidence, and it is not long then before you find him becoming careless.

This was what happened now, for Charles found that after buying the diamonds in London the gang were making no attempt to disguise their movements and often drove straight down to London Airport the same night to deliver sixty or seventy thousand pounds' worth of stones to the steward on the night plane to New York. With the traffic at its height this was happening about once a week, and as soon as we had a full list of exactly which stewards were in the racket, I knew we were ready to strike.

The arrangement was that Charles would telephone me from Hatton Garden immediately the next purchase of diamonds had taken place. It was my job then to tell from the duty roster which of the suspected stewards was next on the Atlantic run so that we would have a hundred-to-one chance of picking the man up with the diamonds actually on him. Once we had decided that it was time to make our arrests it was an anxious time for all of us, for I had to rely entirely on Charles's information, knowing at the same time that there was always the chance up to the last minute that the duty roster would be switched and the whole operation postponed.

But it seemed our luck was in. We had arranged everything for the arrest, the rosters remained unchanged, and we knew that the steward who was catching the night plane to New York would have at least £20,000 worth of diamonds on him. Smith trailed the dark blue Ford down as far as the airport just to make sure that the diamonds really were on their way, and we picked up the steward according to plan just as he was walking up the steps and into the plane. The only trouble was that although he had the diamonds on him, he simply refused to talk. We tried every trick we knew, but there was no way of getting him to admit any connection at all with the organisation. He ended up by being imprisoned and dismissed from the Corporation, but that did not do us much good and the smugglers were obviously alerted by the arrest. We were right back at the beginning again.

But those smugglers must have been making so much money by this time that they simply could not give it up. There is nobody who becomes ruined by success quicker than a criminal, and this lot just could not take a warning when they saw one. Within a month the traffic was going on exactly as before with even the same car making its weekly journey to the airport.

This time we made no mistakes. We knew that the diamonds were being handed over in a pub on the edge of the airport, and so decided to make our arrests actually inside the saloon bar to catch the steward and the courier together. Our plans went like clockwork. We had several plain-clothes detectives at different places in the bar, and I was actually finishing a Scotch and soda with Smith and Charles when the member of the gang turned up.

I must say I admired the man's composure as he stood at the bar, a short, blue-chinned man in a dark blue raincoat, waiting for the steward to show up. He took longer to arrive than I had expected. In fact the stewards usually cleared Customs first, and doubled back from the plane to the pub, running through a wicket gate on the edge of the airport and then catching their plane a matter of seconds before take-off.

At last the steward did come in, nodded to the man in the blue raincoat, and gulped down a neat whisky which had been waiting on the counter for him all along. If we had not been looking closely we would certainly have missed the small package the man slid across the bar to him, but we waited until the steward had gone out through the back door before arresting the member of the gang. The steward was picked up a few minutes later on the tarmac with the diamonds on him.

This steward was not so reticent, and the arrests provided Smith and Charles with all the evidence they needed to expose the whole organisation. But although the police moved quickly and raided the house in Belsize Park a few hours later, the head of the gang moved swifter still, and got clean away. I have heard reports of him since in South America where a man of his talents is hardly likely to go unappreciated for long. But his two less fortunate sub-ordinates were caught, the steward and others turned Queen's evidence, and early that December the two members of the gang received two years' imprisonment apiece at the Old Bailey. The remaining stewards who were implicated were dismissed from the Corporation, and with Sam Charles and Geoff Smith, I shared the satisfaction of knowing that we had killed diamond smuggling on the North Atlantic stone dead.

After this case, the criminals we came in contact with seemed to lose interest in diamonds—the crime world is ruled by fashion quite as much as any other—and it was not until my last year in B.O.A.C. that I found myself with another major diamond theft on my plate. But this time it was a really big one, and it had been pulled with such consummate skill that I knew from the start that we were up against someone who really knew his job and who had an efficient set of international contacts as well.

The first we heard of it was at the beginning of January 1960. At the time we were up to our necks in the Indian Gold Smuggling case and then, just as I was wondering how on earth we were ever going to get through the work which that involved, I got a cable from Hong Kong which had nothing to do with gold smuggling.

It seems that a registered mail-bag from Tel Aviv had arrived off a B.O.A.C. flight. Superficially, it appeared quite intact and the Post Office seals were tied tightly around the neck. But when it had been taken along with the other mail, by launch from Kowloon to the main post office on Hong Kong itself, the Superintendent in the Registered Mail Section discovered that of the thirteen packages which should have been inside, one was missing.

An anxious telegram was sent off from Hong Kong to the Israeli Post Office asking for details of the thirteenth package. Five days later the reply arrived. The package had contained diamonds insured to the value of £70,000 and there was no doubt at all that it had been safely put aboard the B.O.A.C. flight at Tel Aviv ten days earlier.

The case was so similar to the epidemic of diamond thefts from South Africa of a few years earlier that I held my breath and waited for the next report of a perfectly intact registered mai-lbag turning up in some out of the way part of the world with more diamonds magically missing. But this time we were lucky, and it soon seemed that whoever had committed the theft was reasonably satisfied with his £70,000.

Still, a cool £70,000 was not something to overlook, and four days later Buchanan was able to find time during a lull in the gold smuggling investigations which he was carrying on in India, to fly in to Hong Kong, see the mysterious mailbag, and get some idea how a parcel could disappear from inside it while all the seals remained intact.

Buchanan is not the man to have much patience with conjuring tricks, especially when other people's money disppears, and after half an hour in the post office he had worked out how the trick had been done. It depended entirely on a curious fact about the mail-bags used by the Israeli Post Office for its air mail. Every other country has a thick cord sewn into the hem at the neck of the bag to stop the string and its seal from being worked over the top. For some reason the Israelis had dispensed with this, and Buchanan was soon able to prove that it was perfectly feasible to work the string and seal far enough over the neck to allow a hand inside. Afterwards it was simple to work the string back over the neck again so that the bag appeared completely sealed and unviolated.

It was obvious to us all that no one would have had the time to do this in Hong Kong, so that night Buchanan shoved his toothbrush and pyjamas back into his brief-case, bought himself a thriller to read from the bookstall at

Kai Tak Airport, and caught the night jet flight to Tehran with five minutes to spare.

Tehran in February has a great deal to be said in its favour—certainly a great deal more than London Airport at the same time of the year, and I particularly envied Buchanan his stay in the city, especially when he cabled me that he was working on the case with Colonel Ali Akbar Fahmy, the head of the Iranian C.I.D. I had already met him and knew him for an efficient and endlessly hospitable policeman.

But by all accounts, Buchanan had little time for the high life of Tehran, as there was still a great deal about the case that remained completely unexplained. The first thing of all he had to find out was just how the thief had had time to get anywhere near the bag during its transit through Tehran. It was here that he got his first surprise of the case, for it was soon clear to him that normally the theft simply would not have been possible. For all mail we carried from Tel Aviv to Hong Kong travelled up to Tehran on a normal Britannia flight connecting with only half an hour to spare with one of our Comet jets on the main flight to the Far East.

In this case, however, the Britannia had been late and so had missed the connection. Because of this, all the mail from Tel Aviv to the Far East had had to stay overnight in Tehran, and had been carried on to Hong Kong by the next available flight—in this case an Air France plane. Clearly the thieves were so well organised that they could afford to wait several months for the one occasion when the Tel Aviv plane missed its connection.

But as soon as Buchanan tried to find out exactly where the registered mail-bag had spent its one night in Tehran, he ran straight up against that wall of vagueness and deceit that you always find in the Middle East when a policeman wants some information he can work on. All he could discover was that soon after the aircraft landed, all the mail aboard was handed over to the local postal authorities who stored it for the night in the town Post Office and then delivered it by van the next morning to the B.O.A.C. office in the middle of Tehran. The job could have been worked almost anywhere during that time, and as always happens in this sort of case Buchanan soon found that almost everyone he came into contact with was a suspect of one sort or another. This even applied to the official airport staff for, as one of the local airline agents said to him " as soon as you take your eye off anything here you'd better start filling out your claim forms for the insurance company."

However, during two days of trying to keep his temper in the endless interrogations about the mail-bag, Buchanan did find one man who attracted his attention. This was a local Iranian called Moti—he was the man who worked for the post office and had driven the blue Volkswagen van which had been used to collect and deliver the mail-bags. He was about thirty-five, slightly taller than most of his race, well spoken, neatly dressed and falling over himself to be helpful. But there was just something Buchanan did not like, and somewhere at the back of that filing-cabinet brain of his, he made a note to find out a little more about Mr. Moti as soon as he could.

But before he could do that, two events occurred that seemed to change the whole face of the affair. The first was the arrival in Tehran of an English investigator called Miller who was working on behalf of the insurance assessors covering the loss of the diamonds. As soon as they met they realised that their interests were identical and agreed to work together on the case. They had a chance of doing this sooner than they had expected, for hardly had they finished their breakfast together in their hotel on the Avenue Suleiman than Buchanan heard himself being paged. Colonel Fahmy was on the telephone.

He said he had some information about diamond thefts from aircraft that he was willing to pass on to Buchanan if it would be any help. It was not a theft from the same aircraft that Buchanan was worried about, but there might be some connection, and if he would like the facts he was welcome to call in at police headquarters any time that morning.

Fahmy's office had a lot in common with Fahmy. A huge room in the police headquarters in the centre of the town, it was an unusually hospitable place for a policeman to inhabit, and half an hour after the telephone call, Buchanan found himself leaning back in one of the colonel's armchairs smoking one of the colonel's thin Turkish cheroots.

He had taken Miller along with him, and as it turned out it was as well that he had, for when the introductions were over, Colonel Fahmy rummaged a moment in a pile of paper beside his desk and finally produced a photograph of a European of about thirty-five, a good-looking man with a square jaw, closely cut hair, and a long scar running down his left cheek. Buchanan had never seen the face before, but he handed the photograph on to Miller before returning it to the colonel, and at once the assessor jerked himself up, staring hard at the colonel.

" Is he involved in this case? " he asked.

" How can one be sure? " replied the Colonel. " It is always difficult to pin this sort of case on as clever a man as this. But since you seem to know him, Mr. Miller, perhaps you would be good enough to tell Mr. Buchanan something about him."

" Certainly," replied Miller. " This character is one of the biggest individual diamond smugglers operating between Europe and the Middle East. He is a Frenchman called Duval, Jean Louis Duval. Is he here with his girl friend? He usually works with her. Blonde girl, Russian father, begins with a B."

"Bratski, " said the colonel obligingly, " Isobel Bratski. Yes, she was here too. A pretty girl. I don't know what she sees in a man like him. They were living together for nearly two months at the Park Hotel before they moved out."

Buchanan was getting baffled by the turn the conversation was taking, and finally asked what it was all about. For reply the colonel eased himself up out of his chair and crossed over to a large green safe in one corner of the room. He reached to the back and pulled out a small chamois leather bag.

"This, " he said to Buchanan, " is where your Mr. Duval comes in. We caught him and Isobel Bratski trying to sell these locally last November." He opened the neck of the bag and into the palm of his hand slowly tipped sixteen large cut diamonds.

"We knew they weren't theirs so we confiscated them. But even so, we could not prove anything against them. For I'm pretty sure that these diamonds must have been stolen from a mail-bag passing through the airport, but not a single airline during this period reported the loss of any diamonds to my Government, so there was nothing I could do to start an investigation. I've just hung on to the stones ever since in case an airline ever decides it's lost an odd ten thousand pounds' worth of diamonds.

"Now, if I'm right about where these diamonds came from, Mr. Buchanan, Duval and his girl friend may be not unimportant to you. Of course they left Tehran last November just after we confiscated these diamonds, but the strange thing is that they turned up again at the Park Hotel exactly ten days before your own diamonds disappeared. Then on 25th January, two days after that theft, Jean Louis Duval and Isobel Bratski paid the extremely heavy bills they had run up at their hotel and caught the morning Lufthansa plane to Frankfurt. If you want to see your diamonds again, Mr. Buchanan, I suggest Frankfurt is your best bet."

All the time he had been saying this, Fahmy had been absent-mindedly playing with the diamonds in his hand. Now he started pouring them back into the bag, but before he could finish, Miller leant across and stopped him, and asked whether he could look at them more closely for a moment. Fahmy handed them across to him, and there was a few moments' silence as Miller examined them.

" I think I know where these came from," he said at last. " You are quite correct, Colonel. They did come from an aircraft—they correspond exactly to part of a shipment of diamonds lost from an American plane last November on the way from London to the Far East. The insurance company who paid up are clients of ours, and will be very pleased to hear that you have still got some of the stones."

When he heard this, the colonel showed his first signs of annoyance during the entire interview, and asked why on earth the airline or the insurance company had not reported the theft straight away. I don't know what reply Miller gave to this, but certainly one of the gravest handicaps to any international air security work is the secrecy of many of the airlines about losses they incur. For this is a cut-throat commercial world, and many airlines would far rather soft-pedal their losses and let the insurance companies foot the bill, than risk the adverse publicity among their clients by so much as reporting it to the local police.

Still, thanks to Miller and Colonel Fahmy, this was one case where an insurance company was lucky, and the investigation had already brought to light ten thousand pounds' worth of diamonds nobody had ever reported as missing. But although Miller was happy, Buchanan came out of the interview not much better off. As he had thought all along, it was pretty clear that the men behind the theft were members of a far-reaching international syndicate, and if Fahmy was right he was just wasting his time staying on in Tehran when the diamonds were probably already safely back in Europe.

But although Buchanan cabled me straight away about the colonel's suspicions, and I actually sent a man off to Frankfurt that very afternoon, he had a hunch that the key to the whole mystery still lay in Tehran. With his usual obstinacy he decided to give himself another couple of days to prove his point. As it turned out, it was as well he did.

The first day he spent checking over once more every minute of the mail-bag's life from the moment it landed at the airport, to the next morning when it was loaded aboard the Air France Super Constellation, but at the end of a day's extremely hard work, he had still got nowhere.

But during these inquiries he again met Moti, the ever-helpful Iranian postal worker who had collected the mail, and once more he felt there was something wrong about the man. Perhaps it was simply that he seemed too good for his job. He dressed and spoke far better than most people in his position, and Buchanan actually discovered that he was driving a brand new Renault of his own.

There was nothing much else to go on in the case, so that evening Buchanan went back to the airport. He often says, " a good security officer spends most of his time wasting time," and he had no very clear cut plans for the evening. But on this occasion his time certainly was not wasted, for while he was at the airport a report came through of another missing mail-bag which had transited Tehran the day before. He set the wheels in motion to trace the bag and then decided to use this incident as an opportunity to have another go at Moti, although he knew there could be no possible connection in this case.

He telephoned Colonel Fahmy, reported the missing bag and suggested that Moti should be brought out to the airport to assist the inquiries.

When Moti arrived, Buchanan had a perfectly amicable interview with him, despite the presence of two of the colonel's detective-officers. He had a perfect alibi for his movements the previous night when the aircraft carrying the mail had transited Tehran, and there were a dozen people to back him up if necessary. But just before the interview closed, Buchanan asked whether, just as a matter of routine, he would mind being searched by one of the detectives. At this, Moti suddenly changed, and began to object violently, and when the policeman insisted and turned out his wallet on to the table, they all saw that it was bulging with bank-notes. In all there were 500,000 rials, in high denomination notes—about £2,500 in British currency—at least five times the man's legitimate annual salary.

When Moti was asked to account for so much money he tried to bluff it out, but Buchanan is not the man to be taken in with phoney stories about mysteriously acquired fortunes, and after several hours of really close questioning, Moti broke down and admitted the whole game.

According to his confession, he was the man who had done the actual theft, and he seemed quite proud of himself as he described how he had invented his own private method of slipping the string over the top of the Israeli mail-bags. The strange thing was that now he had been found out, he seemed to go out of his way to help Miller and Buchanan to clear the case up.

He even went so far as to tell them where some of the diamonds were. He claimed they were hidden under the bonnet of his Renault and, sure enough, when they went outside, Moti opened the car up, rummaged around for a moment or two in the tool-box and then brought out one of the missing packets with the original Israeli Customs declaration still wrapped round it. When Miller checked the contents through, he found that not a stone was missing from the packet.

Early next morning two of Fahmy's men found out that only a month earlier this poorly paid member of the Iranian Post Office had bought a house at Shemiran, one of the most expensive suburbs of Tehran, where his wife and parents were living at present. According to the agent who had sold the house, Moti had paid 2,350,000 rials—about £11,000 for it, and paid in cash.

Moti subsequently admitted that the whole of this money had been obtained from his diamond thefts, and it was not too difficult for Miller, acting on behalf of the insurance company, to arrange for the disposal of the property and take possession of the proceeds.

This, however, was not quite the end of the case for Buchanan; it was not Moti alone he wanted, but the people behind him. Through Moti he finally managed to implicate two Iraqi diamond merchants who had extensive contacts in Brussels and Tel Aviv. It was through them that Moti had been receiving detailed information of the diamond shipments passing through Tehran. This pair were also getting a tip-off inside the organisation of one of the biggest diamond merchants in Brussels whenever a shipment was coming their direction.

Some of the stolen diamonds were recovered from this source, and we were pretty sure they were using the two smugglers, Duval and Bratski to take the proceeds of the thefts back to Europe.

For some reason Moti and the Iraqi diamond merchants shut up like a clam when the name of Duval cropped up, but later Moti did admit that the diamonds Colonel Fahmy had confiscated from Duval were in fact part of the shipment stolen from the mail aboard the American plane.

This case had at least one unusual feature. We set out to find £70,000 and came back with £90,000. After this, we were perfectly happy to leave Colonel Fahmy with the job of sorting out the evidence to convict the people behind the robbery, for maybe the " Laws of the Medes and Persians " are different from those elsewhere.

CHAPTER 11

Passengers in distress

Unless I am extremely careful I shall be giving a one-sided impression of the world of air security. Of course there are the big-time criminals, the international syndicates, and the various gangs who have made a set at the airlines, but they are not the whole story. You always know where you are with crooks. They come and they go, and dealing with them is very much in the day's work.

Air security has someone more important than them to worry about, and often he is far more difficult to cope with. He is the man on the ordinary flight from Sudan to Sydney whose suitcase goes adrift somewhere between embarkation and arrival: or the middle-aged housewife on the tourist flight from London to San Francisco who loses her handbag while her Boeing 707 is being refuelled at New York: or the Australian businessman on a flying visit to London whose wallet disappears while he is washing at London Airport.

Crooks don't write letters of complaint or become critical of their treatment and so a bad advertisement. The ordinary passenger often does. He is with you day in day out, and unless he leaves your aircraft satisfied with the way he has been handled, the airline might just as well put up the shutters and find some less vulnerable way of making money.

Most of the time it is not so much crime you have to

protect the passenger against as himself, along with the normal hazards of modern jet-age travel. Passenger loads are increasing all the time. Quicker transits and turn-rounds are the order of the day, and passengers are constantly being transferred from one international airline to another.

Inevitably mistakes occur, even in the best run organisations, but in the air business you need make only one mistake and a couple of hours later a passenger and his baggage are a thousand miles apart. Once baggage has gone adrift it obviously becomes a sitting target for any light-fingered individual who happens to be around. And passengers are usually so keyed-up at the start of a flight that, if the slightest thing goes wrong there's often work for the air security officer.

It is checking and rechecking on minor complaints from this sort of thing which is the real bread and butter of air security. Every air security officer grumbles about it, but there is no denying its importance to an airline.

I was on the apron at London Airport one morning watching the departure of a flight to the Far East. All passengers were on board, doors closed and steps away, but there appeared to be some delay in starting the engines. Suddenly the passenger door opened and the chief steward signalled for the steps to be repositioned. Catching sight of me, he called me over.

A passenger was claiming that a valuable camera had been stolen from the rack over his seat and refusing to travel until it was found, saying it must have been stolen by one of the staff or a fellow passenger. I went on board, had a word with the captain, and walked down the gangway to the man who was complaining. He was an American, in his middle forties, and was standing by his seat with several small pieces of luggage spread across it, and loudly proclaiming his views on what he thought of British airlines and the staff in particular.

He had been one of the first passengers to board. He had put all his hand luggage, a book and the camera on the rack. With the request " fasten seatbelts " he had reached to the rack for his book and found that his camera had gone.

He quietened down a bit when I spoke to him. At first he insisted he had put the camera on the rack, but after a few questions he agreed he might have put it on the empty seat beside him.

" How many pieces of hand baggage have you," I asked.

He detailed the five items, including the camera, plus a coat he was carrying over his arm.

" Were you carrying the camera in your hand when you boarded or was it slung over your shoulder ? " was my next question. He wasn't quite sure, but he was certain he had it with him.

" Did the Customs Officer look at it ? "

" No."

" Where was the camera when you passed through the formalities? " Again he wasn't quite sure.

A few more questions and he began to wonder whether he had brought the camera on to the aircraft, but he was quite certain he had it when he boarded the bus which had brought him from the departure lounge.

" If it is not on the bus then it was on the aircraft."

Having explained that I could not delay the aircraft any longer, he insisted on being off-loaded—his camera was worth $300 and he was not going without it.

Two hours later his camera was found hanging up behind a bedroom door in the London hotel where he had stayed the night before. Here was a classic case of an experienced traveller losing something and then getting into a state of panic, so that he didn't know what he had got with him by the time he reached the airport.

The whole point about this is that if he had not missed the camera before departure but, say, at a transit stop a thousand miles away, and there was no one there with the time to spare to question him as I had done, we should not only have been faced with a claim for $300, but also with a passenger who would spread an unfounded story of a theft on B.O.A.C. when he got home. This sort of story loses nothing in the telling.

Another time I was flying to Karachi on a routine inspection of our security forces throughout the Far East, and found myself sitting next to a dapper little man from the Continent. We talked. He told me he was a director of a fairly big textile firm in Europe, but I managed to avoid telling him I had any connection with the air business.

After some while I asked him quite casually why he was flying on a British plane instead of on his own national airline, which also flew this route. His reply was surprisingly to the point. Never, if he could possibly avoid it, would he travel by his own airline again. He had learned his lesson about that. On one occasion when he had flown on it at the start of an important business tour of Africa, his baggage had been lost or stolen somewhere *en route*, and the airline had made no effort at all to trace it for him. As a result he found himself in a hot country at the start of the rainy season without so much as a spare pair of shoes or a change of underwear.

" You only need one lesson like that," he said, " and to this day I have never flown with them again."

I nodded and sympathised as well as I could, feeling slightly smug about the whole thing, but afterwards I thought to myself just how serious a single incident like this can be to an airline, and wondering how many more chance acquaintances like me had been told about his misfortunes. In the grimly competitive world of the airline business no one can afford this sort of publicity.

What makes it all the sillier is that from what I have learned since then, I should imagine that in the first place the man's baggage was never stolen. Probably all that happened was that it was wrongly labelled or just misdirected. The bags may then have arrived in the lost property office of some other airline or Customs bond, and have hung around for weeks, until somebody walked off with them, or perhaps they were eventually sold off to cover storage expenses.

On another occasion I went into the Customs controlled baggage room at Nassau Airport on a purely routine visit. I was really making a social call, but I happened to see three extremely expensive matching pigskin suitcases standing against the wall. Each had the owner's initials in gold by the handle, but it was the film of dust covering them and showing just how long they had been there that really caught my eye. They were unlabelled, nobody knew where they had come from or what airline had brought them, and there they had stayed, waiting for an official inquiry which never seemed to have come.

The stupid part of the story is that when I had the cases opened up, there was no difficulty at all in finding the name and address of the owner from the contents. As far as I remember, he came from Houston, Texas and had probably spent his holidays in the Caribbean. I know he got his cases back in the end, and I only hope for his sake that they went astray after his holiday rather than before it began.

Making sure that this sort of thing never occurs probably sounds a lot easier than it actually is, and when I look back

I am still surprised at the amount of time I spent inquiring into lost luggage, jewel cases and expensive cameras which had gone astray.

Then, of course, there is the passenger who will automatically exaggerate a loss. As one of my American colleagues once said: " All our passengers wear silk shirts, custom made on Fifth Avenue."

I remember a gentleman on a protracted business tour travelling with one suitcase. The suitcase was undoubtedly lost, but his subsequent claim for £400 aroused my curiosity. The claim form listed five suits, all recently made in Savile Row, at fifty guineas a time. What he didn't know was that every claim passes through Security.

He was seen by one of my officers, who pointed out that his claim omitted any description of the suitcase. What was its size? He replied that it was pigskin, 28 x 18 x 10, quite an expensive one which accounted for the £25 claim for the case itself, but he was a little dismayed when asked to explain how five suits, a dozen shirts, pyjamas and all the other items were packed in it.

A more important case involving mislaid luggage cropped up quite early in my career in air security. It was in the days when we were still operating a flying boat service from Singapore to Southampton.

It began with a telephone call to my office from an extremely worried surgeon at one of the big London hospitals. It seemed that one of his patients, a rich sheep farmer from New South Wales, had arrived from Australia by air the previous afternoon for an operation for some obscure heart condition. The operation was urgent if the man was to have any hope of pulling through at all, and the hospital was all set to go when it was discovered that all his medical records from Australia were missing.

The surgeon went on to explain that there was no time to send back to Australia for a duplicate set, even if they existed, and that as they included a series of highly complex X-ray photographs, he did not want to risk operating without them.

I could understand the urgency, but it is a tall order to try and trace one suitcase which could have gone astray anywhere between Singapore and Southampton. Surely, I said, there was something else the passenger could tell me about it. Anything that could give me a lead of some sort. Surgeons' minds don't seem to work like policemen's, and I could tell that he was already growing impatient.

" Well," he said briskly, " you know the plane he came on, and I can tell you that the records were in a black suitcase with the man's initials in gold on the outside. I can't see that it should be too much of a job finding them." Before I could even reply he had rung off.

The medical records were what mattered, and I moved our organisation into top gear, knowing that a man's life depended on the speed with which we could recover that black suitcase. Ten minutes after the surgeon had put his telephone down, an urgent cable was on its way to every station between London and Singapore where the flying boat had landed, giving a description of the case and instructions for a top priority search at once.

I had an idea that the suitcase had not really gone adrift at all, and that if there was an answer to the riddle it lay somewhere at Southampton or on the flying boat, which had brought the Australian to England. The aircraft was not due to leave again until that evening, and I knew that if I got a move on I could get down to Southampton and have a good look at it before it was on its way back to Singapore.

I'm not one for fast driving unless it's really necessary,

but this was one of the few times when it was, and I whistled down the main Southampton road a lot too fast for anyone's comfort, arriving at the docks just after lunch. Not that I had bothered about eating. Instead, I picked up the Duty Officer and drove straight out to the docks and there, comfortably moored like some old duck on the grey expanse of Southampton water, was the flying boat I wanted.

It was rather a business getting aboard her. We had to find the crew of the flying boat tender and then chug our way out to her through the strong swell which was running. I remember that the inside of the flying boat cabin was rolling like the deck of a ship as I began my search, and after half an hour of determined clambering around, I began to think that the whole of my journey had been a waste of time, but for some reason I still had a hunch that the suitcase just had to be somewhere on the flying boat, if only I could find it.

So I sat down in one of the seats and tried to work out exactly what would have happened to the luggage on every step of its journey from Singapore. I had been through the plane's documentation, checking on every piece of luggage which had come aboard, and at the end of it I was as puzzled as ever. That suitcase simply should not have disappeared.

And then I remembered something that the flying boat's captain had told me earlier that morning over the telephone. I had been asking if there had been anything unusual in his flight, and he had happened to mention that the freight which had been put aboard at Singapore had been particularly bulky. That sixth sense of mine began to tell me that this remark held the answer to the whole problem if only I could see how to use it properly.

So I went over in my mind the procedure which would have been followed at Singapore when a flying boat had to take on larger freight than it had bargained for. The normal freight holds would be filled up, but just suppose there were a few pieces of luggage still left over which somehow had to be got on to the aircraft. What possible place in the plane would there be where a loader might have stowed them? The galley, the rear of the cockpit, the mail hold? Unlikely, all of them, and anyhow I had already looked in each of these places, and there was no sign of the case there.

I had almost decided to give up when it struck me, and I could have kicked myself for not having thought of it earlier. There was just one place on the flying boat which none of us had thought of looking into, simply because there was no reason why the suitcase should have been there at all.

On all these flying boats there was a special locker under the floor in the middle of the passenger compartment. It was rarely used and could be reached only by lifting the carpet runner and then undoing a couple of Yale locks. This was the precious cargo locker, the nearest an aircraft ever gets to a safe of its own, and according to the plane's load sheets it had not been used on that trip. But I suddenly realised it might be just the place where some bright individual might have put an odd suitcase and then forgotten to record it on the aircraft's papers.

So I pulled up the carpet, unlocked the door, and peered in. At the bottom of the locker lay two small pieces of freight, and the missing case, embossed with the gold initials. As it turned out, all had been put aboard at Singapore and then forgotten about. That one suitcase was a matter of life or death, and once I had got it on to a fast car to London, I felt I had earned myself a quiet stroll and a cup of tea before driving back myself.

I learned later that the medical records reached the

146

hospital with several hours to spare, and a few weeks later we were actually flying one rich convalescent Australian back to Melbourne. I even got a letter from the surgeon, a very polite one really, thanking me in strictly formal terms for the efficiency with which we had tracked down the missing records.

I am digressing; for this investigation had a strange twist in its tail, and when I sat down in the tea shop near the harbour that afternoon feeling so pleased with myself I did not realise my work was by no means over.

I like my tea strong, and while I was leaning back in my chair waiting for the tea to draw, I realised that there was still something worrying me about that flying boat.

It was nothing definite. That was the trouble. If it had been, I would have known what to do. Instead, it was just that vague uncomfortable feeling at the back of my mind I have had so many times in my career as a policeman. It told me there was still a loose end somewhere which had to be tied up if I was to find any peace of mind that day.

So I drank my tea, ordered another pot to be on the safe side, and then forced myself to think back to every move I had made earlier that afternoon from the very moment I had set foot inside the flying boat. At first I drew a complete blank. The cockpit, the passenger compartment, the cargo hold—there had been nothing to worry about there. Then suddenly I stumbled upon the fact which was still worrying me. It was an absurd detail about one of the locks on the precious cargo locker which I had opened when I found the missing case.

When I had inserted the key it had been unusually stiff. That was all, but what was troubling me was why on earth a lock on a plane which had been in service so long should still be as stiff as that. It had no right to be, and neither I nor the flying boat were leaving until I had found out why.

The motor-boat crew must have thought I was off my head when I turned up at the quay for the second time that afternoon, asking to be taken aboard the flying boat. There was rain in the air and I felt the first chill of autumn as I huddled in the bows in my raincoat. The afternoon ferry from the Isle of Wight steamed in across the grey waters of the Solent, and I tried to forget that within a few days the flying boat ahead of us would be catching its first glimpse of the warm blue waters of the Indian Ocean.

Once again I performed the hazardous operation of swinging myself aboard from the dangerously rolling motor-boat and went aft for another look at the precious cargo locker. At first I could see nothing obviously wrong with either of the locks, except that one was certainly a lot stiffer with a key than it should have been. I thought this might have been caused by dirt or something which had got into the keyhole, so I took out my penknife and tried to prise the small blade in to see if I could find anything.

I discovered something, but it was not dirt. For the odd thing about that lock was that when I twisted my blade in it, it turned just as if the knife had been a key. The other lock was the same. The flying boat's precious cargo locker could be opened by anyone with a penknife in his pocket. It was only when I called a locksmith out to the boat that I discovered why.

It had been an expert job. For each lock had been expertly taken to pieces, and the spring plungers that engage with the teeth of the key had been drilled out. As a result, there was nothing to stop the drum turning and operating the lock quite freely.

That evening we alerted all our flying boats across the world, and when their replies came back next morning I

learned that five of them had had their locks treated in the
same way.

Somehow this is the sort of case where the man behind it
always manages to remain undetected. Of course, we made
our inquiries and found out enough to convince me that the
actual drilling out of the locks must have occurred while
the flying boats were moored on the Nile during the overnight
stop on the flight from or to the Far East.

I was also sure by the end of our inquiries that the whole
affair was part of an elaborate and extremely daring long-
term plan for robbing the aircraft of their most valuable
freight. If something had not jogged my memory about the
lock that afternoon in Southampton, we would sooner or
later have had our hands full with a serious epidemic of
precious cargo larcenies from our Far Eastern flying boats.

CHAPTER 12

The morphine in the suitcase

Drug trafficking has always been for me the one really unforgivable crime. Straightforward larceny is something a policeman gets philosophical about, but in my view this business is rather worse than murder, and the older I get the worse it seems. I shall never forget the first narcotics case I came up against before the war when I was a young policeman in Chelsea, and had to arrest a beautiful young woman who was already a drug addict at twenty. She was thirty-two when I next saw her and she then had the appearance of a woman of seventy. Whenever I have heard anyone talking about narcotics since, I have reminded myself of what they did to her.

But quite apart from my own feelings on the subject, narcotics smuggling is dynamite for any airline to become mixed up in. For as soon as there is any suspicion of it aboard one of your planes, not a single one of the countries through which you operate will leave you alone. Your aircraft will be endlessly delayed, passengers and crew alike will be subjected to the most rigorous search, and if the smuggling really catches hold, your line's entire operations can be threatened, and aircraft even impounded.

A good example of the way an airline is held responsible for any narcotics being smuggled on its planes is what happened last year to Pan American Airways in Hong Kong. A suitcase among the baggage unloaded from one of their aircraft was found to contain a large quantity of morphine and raw opium. The company knew nothing at all about it, of course, but because they were technically guilty of carrying unmanifested cargo, and Hong Kong was at the time in the grip of a severe outbreak of narcotics smuggling, the local magistrate decided to make an example, and the company was heavily fined.

Partly through luck, B.O.A.C. have always managed to avoid this themselves, but it was just because I knew this sort of action was possible on the part of the civil authorities that I got the wind up when the very first report of narcotics trouble came across the security officers' bush telegraph in 1950. A European airline had become involved with their flight from Bangkok into Hong Kong, and heroin had been found concealed inside two shipments of fruit. A few months later it was the turn of another airline. One of their passengers was actually arrested on arrival at Tokyo with five pounds of heroin in his luggage. From time to time other lines would have minor outbreaks, but B.O.A.C. seemed to be leading a charmed existence, and I began to tell myself that I was merely cultivating ulcers worrying about it so much.

But occasional scraps of information made me sure that something was going on, and then early in 1954 a rumour reached me in London that seemed to prove it.

For years, there had been a minor racket going on smuggling watches from Hong Kong into Tokyo. A few of our crew members were involved. Watch prices in Tokyo were just that much higher than in Hong Kong to make it worth their while taking a dozen or so expensive watches in with them when they landed. But since the amounts were not large and a case would have been difficult to prove I had always tended to turn a blind eye to it. I knew perfectly well what they were up to, but frankly I had more important things to do than go snooping after this sort of petty business.

Then I heard something that really made me sit up with a jolt. According to my informant in Hong Kong, the organisation I knew to be behind the smuggling had started taking the movements out of the watches, filling the cases with heroin and then giving them to B.O.A.C. crews for delivery in Tokyo without the slightest hint of what they were up to.

Now I know that a chap who smuggles a watch is legally just as much a law-breaker as someone who peddles a whole parcel of heroin, but as far as I was concerned there was all the difference in the world between the two, and I did not see why a gang of unscrupulous gentlemen in Hong Kong should be allowed to get away with such a double-cross involving such particularly dirty work.

Most of the B.O.A.C. people I knew felt the same way about it, for there is a very strong feeling against drug running among all airline people. So I published a notice to our people simply telling them what was going on. It proved sufficient. Almost all the watch smuggling stopped, and I know that where it continued, the carriers firmly insisted on having every one of the watches they handled opened in front of them, just to make sure that they contained nothing except the movements of an ordinary watch.

One of the odd things about crime is that you never seem to get a single case on its own, and in fact this one, inconclusive affair was important, for it was the signal I had been waiting for. The dope smugglers had turned to B.O.A.C. at last, and our immunity was over.

I knew perfectly well that if someone could be bothered

to use a long-established watch-smuggling organisation to get these small amounts of heroin into Japan, things must be pretty desperate. Obviously a new supply and demand situation was developing in the narcotics world, and somehow we had to find out what it was.

As usual when there was something important in the air, I called Buchanan back to London. We both knew how each other's minds worked, and I could usually get more out of an hour's discussion with him than out of six months reading official reports. I remember this visit of his well, because his plane was much later than anyone expected. It was gone eight before I saw his bulky frame bowling its way through Customs, so rather than keep him hanging about in an airport on a cold March night, I bundled him into my car, and drove him home to my flat in Twickenham.

Buchanan shares my feelings about food. He's not the sort of man for whom those delicate little meals on plastic trays are served on long-distance flights, and he looked decidedly happier once he had got the right side of a chump chop and a plate of my wife's chips. But it was not until we had reached the inevitable after-meal tea that we got down to the serious business of pooling what we knew of the threat of narcotics smuggling over the airlines.

We both knew the background perfectly well. The traffic depended in the first place on its raw material—opium grown in Turkey, Persia, India or the Northern Provinces of Burma. But raw opium as such is only of value to the habitual pipe-smoker. It was heroin which offered the smuggler the most astronomical profits if he could once get it to the drug-hungry shores of America.

Buchanan had picked up the current heroin prices on the black market in Hong Kong. One ounce was being sold there for anything up to seventy American dollars. Once it reached America, this single ounce would be adulterated with lactose to yield up to 5,000 shots selling to the individual addict at more than three dollars a time. It was these fantastic profits which were beginning to attract the real professionals of the international underworld, and both of us knew that the odds were heavily weighted in their favour.

That evening, as we settled down in our arm-chairs with a drink, I discovered that things were even more serious than I had thought, for Buchanan had received information that the trick of slipping heroin into empty watch cases was only part of a much bigger and centrally organised attempt to smuggle narcotics in every conceivable way in and out of Hong Kong. The Hong Kong Police were alarmed at the way things were going, for it was clear that the Colony was rapidly becoming a big-time clearing-house for narcotics. It was ideally situated for this, and we had good reason to believe that the gangs were turning to the airways in a carefully planned attempt to smuggle in their drugs from places as wide apart as the Persian Gulf, Bangkok, Singapore, Rangoon and India.

As the gangs became better organised, they were ceasing to handle raw opium at source, and were concentrating on smuggling compressed blocks of opium alkaloid with a high morphine content into Hong Kong. In Hong Kong it would be converted into heroin in kitchen laboratories, and would then take the next leg of its journey by air to Tokyo. According to Buchanan's information, the heroin would then be carried on to America, usually, it was thought, aboard U.S. Service craft crossing the Pacific to West Coast ports and aerodromes.

I am a late bird, but it was long past my usual bedtime before Buchanan stretched himself, drained the last of his drink and got up to go. But our night's work was not wasted, for at last we had a plan of action. We now had a pretty good over-all picture of the possibilities. For the time being we would be patient, but at the first sign that smuggling had reached B.O.A.C. we would strike so hard that it would never have a chance to get established.

That was the theory, at any rate, but of course in practice things don't work out quite so neatly as that, for Buchanan had hardly been back in the Far East more than a few days than I myself stumbled upon the biggest single consignment of smuggled narcotics ever found aboard a British aircraft. It turned up in broad daylight in the middle of London Airport.

I had just finished lunch on the day the case broke. It had been raining for weeks, but on this particular day the sun had come through. Spring seemed to be in the air and the airport was looking more cheerful than it had for months, and when my telephone rang and the engineering superintendent asked me if I could spare him a moment in the hangars, I was glad of an excuse to get out of the office.

The maintenance area at London Airport occupies several huge hangars on the far side of the runways, and as soon as I reached the one where the superintendent was working, I could tell that something serious was up, for a small group of engineers was standing at the rear of the wings of a big Argonaut aircraft which had come in for servicing. The plane had all its inspection hatches removed, and as I walked over to it, I was taken right back to the atmosphere of so many of the alleged sabotage cases during my days with M.I.5.

The engineering superintendent led me to a small panel in the fuselage and pointed inside. This hatch was the one the engineers used to get at the electric heater blowers which maintain the plane's heating system during flight, and the

inside looked to me like a hideously complicated tangle
of equipment. But then I saw what all the fuss was about.
Wedged tightly at the back of one of the blowers rested a
small blue suitcase covered in dust.

Someone asked whether it was a bomb, but I had never
seen a bomb in a case like that before, and even if it had been
it had obviously been in its present position so long that there
could not be much danger left in it. Although one of the
engineers finally climbed in and fetched the case out, I
had not the slightest idea what we were going to find inside
until we actually prised open the flimsy locks and lifted the
lid.

I know it is damned silly, especially as I had been doing
nothing but worry about narcotics for weeks, but I just did
not recognise what we had found. Inside the case lay six
neatly wrapped packets in green Cellophane, each about the
size of a two-pound packet of sugar, and to tell the truth,
I had no idea what they were from Adam.

It was only when we had taken the case back to my office,
carefully opened a packet and tipped some of the brown
cocoa-like powder across my blotter that I knew what we
had found. I would recognise that faint sour vegetable
smell anywhere, and it was that which told me we had
accidentally unearthed fourteen and a half pounds of high
quality opium alkaloid.

Then the fun started. Customs had to be brought into it,
and after I had telephoned an entirely disbelieving official
at the Home Office, a member of the Dangerous Drugs
Department came down to see just what all the fuss was
about.

It was only when I began a hurried check-up on the
Argonaut that very afternoon that I realised just how lucky
we had all been to find the case in London. The plane was

one of our Far Eastern fleet and was in for a "Check Four"—the complete overhaul every aircraft receives two or three times each year.

It was obvious that the suitcase had been there for several months, flying backwards and forwards from London to the Far East, neatly concealed behind the Argonaut's heating system. If it had been found anywhere else but in London, there really would have been hell to pay. For ignorance is no defence when you land an aircraft at a foreign airport with fourteen and a half pounds of illicit drugs on board.

As it was, the gentlemen from Customs and the Dangerous Drugs Department quietly confiscated the powder, and I was asked by Scotland Yard if I would investigate the Far Eastern end of the case on their behalf. Mind you, I think that the Yard knew what they were up to when they handed the case over to us, for I have never known a more frustrating investigation than this one turned out to be.

I was feeling pretty stupid about finding this stuff right on my own doorstep, and I really worked on the case. At first there seemed so much evidence lying about that I felt we were on to something big.

The facts of the case appeared simple. It had obviously been put aboard the Argonaut somewhere along the Far Eastern route, but for some reason or other had never been collected by the smuggling ring at its intended destination. Luckily the plane had always flown the Eastern routes, and from what we knew of the pattern heroin smuggling was taking, I was fairly sure in my own mind of both places which were involved.

Certainly, the most likely place where the stuff could have been placed aboard was in Bangkok, for Bangkok, unlike all the other stopping places of the Argonaut was smack in the middle of one of the biggest opium-producing areas in the Far East. There was no doubt at all that the suitcase should have been taken off again at Hong Kong, but more important still, I knew within very narrow limits who had done it. Nobody except a maintenance engineer actually on an airport would have had the skill or the opportunity to have opened that hatch, and hidden the suitcase behind the heaters. When I cabled this information off to Buchanan that night, I had few doubts that he would soon by typing me one of his highly businesslike reports which had marked the successful conclusion of so many of his investigations in the past.

Meanwhile there were several leads that I wanted to follow up myself in London. The actual suitcase in which the drug had been found was promising. It was a cheap affair, made of fibre and by a stroke of luck, the smugglers had left the maker's trade mark inside. It was an English firm, and after a morning's inquiry we actually traced it to a small factory in the East End of London.

There is always something oddly encouraging about establishing this sort of a link at the start of an investigation, and although the man who ran the case company was not able to tell me much when I drove over to see him, I kidded myself that we were getting somewhere when I could connect what had happened on an aircraft flying from Bangkok with a back street in Whitechapel. And there was one thing the case maker was able to tell me that was important. The suitcase had been one of a batch which had been specially made for the popular market in the Far East. As far as he knew they were never sold in Britain but they certainly were in Thailand.

This was a start, and then I turned my attention to a second piece of evidence which so far I have not mentioned. This was something that really should have settled the

investigation once and for all, for not only had the smugglers
been careless enough to send their goods in a clearly marked
suitcase, but they had also enclosed a message, laboriously
written in block letters in lead pencil on a sheet of cheap
paper, giving the receiver clear instructions about how much
he was to sell the contents for. The writing seemed fairly
distinctive and, more important, there was a spelling mistake
in one of the words. The writer had spelt the word
" guarantee " with two r's.

Now I know that men have been convicted on flimsier
evidence than this, and that in theory all we had to do now
was to find someone on the ground staff at Bangkok whose
writing corresponded to that on the message, and who spelt
" guarantee " with two r's. But as I looked at that slightly
yellowed paper on my desk, something told me that it was
not going to be quite so easy, and in fact it was not.

Poor old Buchanan worked away for nearly a fortnight
in Bangkok until half the airport must have written out
sentences in lead pencil containing the word " guarantee."
The examples of handwriting were all flown back to London,
but the comparison of writing in block letters is not easy,
and although the handwriting experts thought that there
were two people who might have written the original letter,
I had been a policeman long enough to know exactly how
some bright young barrister would enjoy carving up that
sort of evidence if ever it got as far as the witness-box.

It was this sense of nearly being able to prove the case, but
never quite clinching it that makes me annoyed, even when
I think about it to-day. I do not mind being beaten by a
case when it is impossible from the start, but this one should
have been solved, and I often kick myself and wonder if
there was something we should have done which was
overlooked. Buchanan feels the same way about it, except

that in his mind he is absolutely certain who the culprit was, although he was never quite able to prove it conclusively. He had the advantage of a personal interview with the suspects, so it is an odds-on bet that he is right.

At least I satisfied myself over how the suitcase turned up at London Airport in the first place. For checking back through all the flight movements recorded for Bangkok Airport during the previous six months, I found that there was just one occasion, four and a half months earlier, when two Argonaut aircraft, one of them the aircraft in which the drug was found, had landed at Bangkok at almost exactly the same moment. This was very unusual and only happened because one of the planes had been delayed, but it meant that two identical aircraft had been on the tarmac at the same time. The interesting thing about them was that they were flying in opposite directions, one to Hong Kong and one from it, and, if my theory is correct, the smuggler made the elementary mistake of not finding out which plane was which.

As I have said already, criminals are not always quite so bright as they think they are.

CHAPTER 13

A planeload of monkeys

For some reason I always hung on to that small blue suitcase in which we found the morphine at London Airport. I used to keep it stuck on a shelf facing my desk, and a single glance at it was usually enough to bring me to earth whenever I started feeling a bit too pleased with myself.

For me it had another significance. For that suitcase really marked the start of the narcotics war for B.O.A.C. By the end of 1954 Hong Kong had found itself in the middle of the heaviest shipments of illicit narcotics by air that it had ever had to face, and there was not a single airline operating through Kai Tak Airport that had not become involved. Seizures began to rise alarmingly, and although Customs and police at Hong Kong were kept on their toes in an attempt to keep up with the increasing ingenuity of the smugglers, we all knew the grim facts. The seizures were no more than a minute part of what was getting through. Heroin had been discovered in a shipment of small pictures, neatly pasted in between the picture and the cardboard backing; also in a hidden compartment in the back of a wooden doll. On another occasion, the stuff had merely been mixed with a shipment of rice. Buchanan's private intelligence system went into action between Hong

Kong and Bangkok. Security officers, in co-operation with
the Hong Kong Police began a discreet watch on passengers
and regular freight shipments in and out of the colony.

The biggest smuggling threat of all soon came to lie in the
simplest trick of the lot. It was an almost fool-proof dodge
that the narcotics smugglers discovered was particularly
suited to working on aircraft, and which caused us many
a headache before we succeeded in catching up with
it. It was a method which must have carried untold
quantities of narcotics past unsuspecting Customs officers
in its time and called for nothing except a large suitcase,
an iron nerve and a completely impassive face. The
Chinese have always been born smugglers, and the suitcase
job might have been invented specially for them.

The smugglers usually worked from Bangkok, Saigon or
Rangoon, and booked themselves as ordinary passengers
into Hong Kong. They would have a normal suitcase
containing their belongings taken to the airport in the usual
way and correctly labelled. Along with it they would also
take another suitcase. This one would be unmarked and
unlabelled and would be neatly packed with narcotics in
one form or another. Now, at the airport, the smuggler
would have someone in his pay, and this man would have
the simple task of seeing that the unmarked suitcase received
a normal passenger's flight luggage label and that it then
found its way with the rest of the baggage out to the plane
on which the smuggler was making his perfectly unsuspicious
way to Hong Kong. The one tell-tale difference between the
narcotics suitcase and the rest of the luggage was that this
luggage label bore a fictitious name.

Once the plane landed, the smuggler still behaved like a
perfectly normal passenger, passing through immigration
and into the Customs hall and presenting himself at the

Customs bench, making sure that his one legitimate suitcase was placed on the bench next to the narcotics suitcase. At the same time, he would keep an eye on what was happening and as the Customs officer moved along the bench, he would watch intently to see just how closely the luggage was being searched.

We all know there are times during peak hours when the Customs do not open all luggage and are rushed off their feet. If the smuggler was lucky enough to have struck one of these periods, he would quietly clear his innocent bag, pick up the narcotics suitcase standing with it, and walk out of the airport, maybe ten or twenty pounds of heroin to the good. On the other hand, if he saw that the luggage was being searched, or something went wrong at the last moment, he just walked away, leaving behind him one unmarked and completely unidentifiable suitcase full of narcotics to baffle the Customs.

By carrying out a minute examination of all passenger luggage labels before the baggage was loaded, we finally managed to persuade the suitcase smugglers that B.O.A.C. was not the line for them, but they were a smart lot of devils, and a few months later we caught them trying to pull a variation of the suitcase job which called for far more barefaced effrontery.

It all began when they woke up the fact that a V.I.P.'s baggage is usually given only the most cursory of searches by the Customs. I can only admire their thoroughness, for as soon as they had got the idea they worked out an elaborate routine by which they were able to send narcotics by air under the name of some perfectly reputable V.I.P. who was actually visiting the area. Somehow they got hold of the passenger lists and as soon as they found a flight which had departed with a V.I.P. aboard, they would deliver an innocuous looking suitcase full of narcotics to the airport. They would mention the V.I.P.'s name and quote his ticket number, explain that the case had been forgotten when the rest of the luggage had been delivered, and say that it must be sent on immediately.

The story was usually good enough to put the station staff in a minor panic, and willing to do anything to prevent a complaint by a V.I.P. Every assurance would be given that the forgotten suitcase would be forwarded on the next aircraft and that the receiving station would be signalled. The gang too, no doubt, sent their own signal.

The whole system of special treatment for V.I.P.s causes trouble for everyone. Things get out of normal channels and as a result often go wrong. In the case which brought this new racket to light the V.I.P. was a well-known bishop of the Church of England whose name was used as a cover for the smuggling of seventeen pounds of high-quality opium from Bombay to Singapore.

A little Chinese, looking just like a servant of the bishop's host in Singapore, was fussing at the airport ready to collect the missing suitcase which was so urgently required and would have got away with it but for an accident. One of the local officers of the Narcotics Squad happened to be at the airport with one of the specially trained police dogs. These dogs are trained to detect the scent of opium, they will find it among a ship's cargo, and this particular dog took an immediate dislike to the bishop's missing suitcase.

The vigilant little Chinese did not miss what was going on; he too knew all about the dogs, so he quietly disappeared. To this day the reverend gentleman is unaware of the use made of his name on that September day when he flew into Singapore to visit the faithful. We did some probing and soon found sufficient evidence to indicate that this trick had been worked before at other airports in the Far East, but it was easy enough to stop.

Closing loopholes against this sort of traffic was very much a matter of patience and routine hard work. There is nothing very exciting about air security when you are checking baggage labels and working your way through freight lists. Gradually I got the feeling that our work was paying off, and that the narcotics gangs were steering clear of our aircraft. They were, but as I discovered towards the end of 1955, their place was being taken by another and far more highly organised ring smuggling pharmaceutical drugs from U.S.A. across our Far Eastern routes. That's the trouble with airlines. You no sooner cure them of one disease than they seem to catch another. But this one really was particularly tricky and for a number of reasons.

It began for me about a fortnight before Christmas. As the routes seemed to be basking in a seasonal lull from crime, I had decided to take the morning off to skip up to London to polish off some Christmas shopping. I drove back to London Airport at about eleven thirty in the morning, to find that on top of everything else there was a scare on and that half the security staff in the place were trying to find me.

The cause of all the trouble lay in two urgent cables that had come through that morning from Buchanan in Rome. They were completely unexpected because he was supposed to be on his way back to Karachi after several weeks in London, but it seemed that he had stopped off in Rome for a day, and with that strange capacity he has for attracting trouble, had gone into a bar in the middle of the city and picked up evidence of what looked like a completely unsuspected new smuggling ring operating through Hong Kong.

In most capital cities there is one bar where airline people always do their drinking. I should have thought they would have wanted to get away from each other's faces when they are off duty, but they don't. In New York you find them in a bar on Third Avenue and in Hong Kong it is the bar of the Peninsular Hotel in Kowloon. In Rome they use the Quirinale Hotel on the Via Nazionale, and it was there that Buchanan bumped into one of our chaps who had just been posted to the Rome office of B.O.A.C. after a term of duty in Hong Kong. While they were talking, he happened to tell Buchanan about something which had never reached the pages of the security reports.

It seemed that about a month previously a large envelope had been discovered in a desk in the main freight office of B.O.A.C.'s agents in Hong Kong. It was unmarked and, when opened, was found to contain a cool four thousand Hong Kong dollars neatly done up in bundles of notes of fairly low denominations.

If it had not been for Buchanan that would have been that, and the money would have been forgotten, but although no one in Hong Kong seemed to realise the significance of the envelope, Buchanan had been long enough in the business to realise that that amount of money does not find its way into a drawer by mistake. It was as obvious to him as to me that it must be a pay-off to somebody for something, and as a result of his two cables I ordered an immediate investigation into every detail of the work passing through our office in Hong Kong.

The amount of paper work connected with every flight is staggering, and when all is collected at headquarters into what is known as a Ship's Papers File it can be anything up to two inches thick according to the duration of the flight. A lot of it may be unnecessary—at least some people think so—but ships' papers are invaluable when it comes to an investigation of the type on which we were about to embark.

The file contains a copy consignment note of even the smallest item of freight, its weight, value, description, name and address of consignee and consignor. The original is an international Customs document and travels with the items to which it refers throughout its journey. Another document, the cargo manifest, is a summary or abbreviated list of all consigned goods aboard the aircraft.

It was on these documents that Buchanan concentrated when he reached Hong Kong and it did not take him long to realise that his suspicions of a pay-off were right, and he began feeding me in London with details of his discoveries and suspicions, which could only be proved by a concentrated cross-checking of the documents on the master file.

My investigating officer at London Airport, Frank Wood, has been brought up on ships' papers for the past ten or twelve years, and he and I spent many weary hours checking the information coming from Buchanan. It was tedious work at both ends, but after many days and late nights, poring over thousands of illegible carbon copies we were able to prove that manifests and consignment notes were being altered and, in particular, those concerning shipments of antibiotics from a firm of manufacturing chemists in U.S.A. via London and Hong Kong, to Formosa. In each case there were specific routing instructions.

These shipments were extremely valuable and heavy, the total weight often running into hundreds of pounds. It was clear from our cross-checking of the consignment and manifest notes both in London and Hong Kong that the original goods were being switched in Hong Kong, and a consignment that started its journey as antibiotics arrived at its destination in Formosa as something entirely different, such as milk powder. It was significant that there had never been a complaint from either consignor or consignee.

There appeared to be *prima facie* evidence of a world-wide conspiracy. The specific incidents we had found covered many thousands of pounds' worth of goods, but the more serious aspect lay in the fact that all the items concerned were classified as " strategic material " by the American authorities, and their export was subject to the strictest control to prevent them getting into Communist countries. With the frontiers of Red China only a few miles away, it did not need much imagination to guess where the drugs were going after they had landed at Kai Tak Airport.

I don't know how Buchanan did it—that's his business, but a few days after we had found the discrepancies in the flight papers, he knew exactly what was happening and who was behind it. He practically took the freight department in Hong Kong apart, for it was obvious that whatever fiddle was being worked over the antibiotics, the men behind it had contacts actually within the freight office.

As I have said, one of the secrets of successful interrogation is to know at least half the answers before you start asking the questions, and Buchanan had the advantage of two extremely solid facts to work with. One was the $4,000 which had been found in the drawer at the office. The other was the certainty that the antibiotics were not reaching their destination, and that somewhere the official papers were being altered or reissued to cover the change from anti-biotics to milk powder.

The investigation eventually brought to light the fact that a wealthy Chinese trader had succeeded in corrupting the staff of the freight office from the European officer in charge down to the very porters. The cartons containing the drugs were being taken from the warehouse, whilst awaiting shipment to Formosa and sent into the town, where they were carefully opened and the contents extracted. Enough milk powder was then packed into the cartons to bring each one exactly to the original weight.

As I have said, the consignment notes gave specific shipping instructions, even quoting actual services on which the goods should travel. This was not too unusual, but its real significance became apparent when we learned that the freight office staff were being given advance notice of when the shipments were due, and so had ample opportunity to prepare all the false documentation.

The field over which this organisation operated was widespread, for we later discovered that not only antibiotics from the U.S.A. but strategic goods, such as radio transmitter valves and X-Ray equipment were also being switched.

The whole inquiry was so complicated and its venue so widespread that any question of a prosecution was impracticable, and we had to content ourselves with taking the necessary disciplinary action to clean up the freight office and report the facts to the various responsible authorities in the Far East.

I was due to visit New York almost immediately, so when our dossier was complete I went to the American Embassy in London and discussed the case with John Cimperman, the Legal Attaché. John was an old wartime friend and he was so interested that he immediately cabled the F.B.I. in Washington giving them the bare facts and the date of my arrival.

The matter was outside the jurisdiction of the F.B.I. in Washington and on my arrival in New York I had to make many inquiries before I eventually made contact with the right government department, and handed over the information.

I believe some action was taken, but as so often happens in cases of this sort, no one bothered to let us know the result. Government enforcement agencies rarely feel it necessary to acknowledge the work of any unofficial person such as an airline security officer.

It was only a few months later that I was brought back with a bang to the narcotics threat that still hung over the Eastern routes. I knew that two other lines had been having trouble with the suitcase boys, but I felt reasonably satisfied that we had driven narcotics smuggling off our aircraft for good. But that was before I had my conversation with Charlie Siragusa.

I should explain about Charlie. He is a short, dapper little American Sicilian with a taste for expensive Continental suits. He is also a man of great charm, an accomplished linguist, and as one of the top agents of the U.S. Treasury's Bureau of Narcotics he probably knows more about the international narcotics racket than any man alive.

I had known him on and off for years, but I met him again that summer quite by chance in the bar of a Lisbon hotel. The General Assembly of Interpol was being held in Portugal that year. I was attending, as I usually did, as the official observer for I.A.T.A., the International Air Transport Association, and when I met Charlie he was still directing his Bureau's highly successful attack on the Mafia-dominated narcotics network which had been smuggling enormous quantities of heroin from Europe into the United States. Largely as a result of his activities the American illicit narcotics market had begun to scream for heroin. Smuggling from Europe had been seriously curtailed and dope prices inside the U.S. were rocketing. Charlie suspected that to meet this new demand the established racketeers in America had begun to turn to Asia for an alternative source of

their supplies. Everything Charlie Siragusa told me confirmed that the amount of narcotics reaching America
across the Pacific by the West Coast was steadily on the
increase.

As luck would have it, proof that Charlie knew what he
was talking about came less than three weeks later. For,
suddenly, quite out of the blue, came information of a new
and flourishing narcotics ring out to the Far East on the least
likely of our regular flights.

One of the strangest by-products of the mammoth
programme of polio research sponsored by the National
Foundation in America was the international trade in the
many thousands of monkeys that were needed in the experi-
ment and production of polio vaccine. Since the early
fifties several sizeable fortunes have been built on monkeys,
and by the beginning of 1954 demand for the animals from
America had become so huge that it was clear that the most
humane way of carrying them was by air.

Monkeys make exclusive passengers. The smell they
leave behind them does not seem to worry other monkeys,
but it does make it difficult to carry human beings again in
a hurry in the same plane. So specially to meet this difficulty
the Corporation decided to charter several York transport
aircraft from an independent company, to operate a special
service along the monkey run. On the flight out, through
the Middle East, Bahrein and India to Singapore the aircraft
carried freight. On the return journey they called at Delhi
where they would be loaded with anything up to a couple
of thousand small monkeys bound for the research laboratories of America.

These aircraft always carried a special crew of animal
handlers aboard. They were not our personnel, although
as far as security went, I was responsible for what went on

during these flights, and when I heard a rumour that some of these men had started dabbling in opium smuggling, I decided to investigate at once.

As it happened, one of these freighters had arrived that morning, and as I looked out of my window I could see it standing on the edge of the tarmac. By this time the monkeys that had travelled on it had been transferred to another plane, and were more than half-way across the Atlantic. Just to see something of the background against which any smuggling would be taking place, I went down, strolled across the tarmac and poked my nose in through the rear doorway of the plane. I soon wished I hadn't, for inside that plane smelt like the monkey-houses of Whipsnade and the London Zoo rolled into one.

I realised that this very smell would in fact make these aircraft ideal for opium smuggling since the smell of monkeys was one of the few things powerful enough to drown the inescapable odour of raw opium, which is every bit as penetrating as garlic. At the same time, these slow old freighters themselves would be perfect for any sort of smuggling, for the simple reason that nobody ever seemed to take much notice of them.

According to my tip-off the trouble was beginning at Bahrein. An efficient little organisation had been built up there among a handful of the local airport staff, who were purchasing opium locally and handing it over to the aircraft personnel for delivery in Singapore.

Once you know what you are looking for, there is no real difficulty in keeping an aircraft under observation even if it is flying half-way round the world. In this case, I actually got a couple of my own chaps aboard these planes as relief animal handlers. I managed to get them a lightning course of instruction at the London Zoo beforehand, and they turned out to have quite a way with monkeys before the job was finished.

Of course they had to be careful how they behaved, so as not to arouse anyone's suspicions, and I did not see anything of them for several weeks. It seemed to have been so long since I had heard anything from them that I was beginning to get worried, and every evening I used to wait in at home in case they telephoned. The call finally came late on a Saturday night, and my officer confirmed everything I had heard and more.

He had certainly done his job well, for he was not only able to tell me that the smuggling was going on, but also to give me a complete blueprint of the organisation behind it. He knew the planes that were involved, the men who were on the payroll, and the actual leaders of the gang at Bahrein. The brain behind it was one of our own traffic clerks, an Anglo-Indian who had worked for us on the airport at Bahrein for some years. He had started in a very small way, smuggling gold into India, and had been building the business up for some time. But it was the starting of the monkey route that really gave him his chance. Although he was still mixed up in the gold racket, he had realised that the really big money lay in opium and was out now for a quick fortune to enable him to retire in comfort in a month or two.

Although it would have been perfectly easy to have caught him on the evidence of my officer alone, the organisation he had built up among crew and ground-staff along the monkey route was now so efficient that I knew I would have to smash that as well, unless I wanted the smuggling to continue under someone else.

By now I was in the delicate position of wondering exactly where and when to strike. I had all the information I needed to kill this racket completely, but if I bungled things, and gave them so much as a hint that we knew what they up to, we would be right back at the beginning again.

This is one of the few situations in air security that ever really starts me worrying. As a policeman, I have never minded launching an attack provided I am on the spot, but there is something peculiarly unnerving about ordering your chaps to go into action on a case five thousand miles away, on the strength of evidence filed in your office in London.

In this case, however, the very skill with which the smugglers were working made my job easier than it might have been. For I knew that they operated a first-rate information service. As soon as the aircraft they were using reached Tripoli on the flight out to Singapore, a telegram in code would be dispatched to the traffic clerk in Bahrein giving him the date the plane would reach there. It was all so neatly worked out that the smugglers never failed to contact their plane.

As soon as it came in to land, one of the ground staff at Bahrein would be waiting on the tarmac with a blue hold-all, and almost before the propellers had finished turning that hold-all would be taken aboard, for all the world as if it had been some important piece of official baggage. This hold-all would contain anything up to twenty pounds of high-quality local opium for delivery to another contact, who would be waiting on the tarmac at Singapore. The General Post Office itself could hardly have arranged a more efficient courier service.

Just because of this efficiency, I could be certain that the very next time the plane we knew to be engaged in the racket reached Bahrein, the opium would go aboard.

I had three days to wait. The plane at that moment was

on its way back from India with a full cargo of monkeys, and it would be another three days at least before it was in Bahrein again on its outward flight to Singapore. This suited me ideally. I knew that Buchanan was in Karachi, only a few hours' flying time from Bahrein, so I decided to give him the case cut and dried to finish off. As I dictated the telegram to him explaining the final details of the case, I remember thinking that this was one of those rare occasions where Buchanan was actually having a case handed to him on a plate.

Of course it wasn't. These watertight cases are just the ones to go wrong when you least expect it, and I should have known better than to have started counting my criminals before they were behind bars.

In fact Buchanan was not in Karachi, and what with the muddle and delay before my telegram caught up with him, it turned out that he arrived in Bahrein exactly half an hour after the plane he had been supposed to catch had left in the same direction from which he had just come. This was annoying enough, but we were so sure that the opium must be aboard, that Buchanan decided to set off in pursuit on the next Karachi-bound plane out of Bahrein. It did not leave until an hour and a half later, but with the slowness of the freighter, there was just a chance that Buchanan might be in time.

Buchanan is not really the worrying sort. Anxiety is not the sort of human weakness that he ever seems to betray, and for this reason alone I would give a lot to have seen him on that flight, as he had to sit tight with the plane he was chasing two hours ahead of him, and not a thing he could do about it.

As it turned out, he was a lot luckier than he had any right to expect. He was the first down the steps at Karachi, only to find that the plane he wanted was still standing silent and deserted on the far side of the tarmac. The luck of the game was with us. The plane had serious engine trouble, and the crew had all gone off for lunch into the town, so Buchanan used the opportunity to search the plane from end to end.

There is a right way and a wrong way of turning over an aircraft. Buchanan knew the right way, but even so he found nothing. He had rummaged the cockpit, searched the galley, and even peered into the well, in which the landing gear retracts, in case the opium had been hidden there. There was only one place which had defeated him.

This was the box at the rear of the plane where the monkey handlers kept their special equipment—the gloves, and medicines needed for the animals during the flight. It was carefully locked, so he called on the services of Sergeant Ali, affectionately nicknamed Khan Sahib, one of my longest serving Pakistani security officers in Karachi. Khan Sahib had a great way with locks, and after five minutes' work, the lock was opened and inside, hidden under the long gauntlet monkey-handling gloves, lay six five-pound packets of high-grade opium. Just to make doubly sure that the smell did not give the game away, the opium had been wrapped in a cloth which had had half a bottle of *Soir de Paris* tipped over it.

And that, as far as we were concerned, was almost that. For the opium was just the evidence we needed to break the ring wide open. Buchanan spent an afternoon in Karachi rounding up the crew member who was implicated, and handing him over to the local authorities. Later he was heavily fined.

Buchanan caught the night plane back to Bahrein and the evidence of the opium was enough to get the Anglo-Indian traffic clerk a jail sentence big enough to scare him off dope running for the rest of his life.

The contact in Singapore was a European with a responsible position. He admitted being concerned and was sent home. He was later charged with others in England. This was my one and only attempt to establish a venue in England for an offence committed on a British aircraft whilst overseas. Top lawyers in the country were briefed for the defence and the prosecution, and when the trial opened at the Old Bailey we seemed all set for a narcotics case which was going to make legal history.

Then once again the uncertain position of the law over crime in the air cropped up just when we thought we had everything straight. The prosecution was brought under the Dangerous Drugs Act, but on the first day of the trial after hours of legal argument, the Judge, Mr. Justice Devlin, ruled that whilst the Section of the Act in the indictment certainly covered the offence in a British plane while it was over Britain, it had no force once the plane left our skies. There was nothing the Judge could do except dismiss the whole case.

Naturally we all felt pretty sore that so much hard work should have this sort of anti-climax at the end of it. But at least the outcome of the case illustrated better than I could have ever hoped the enormous legal difficulties which at the moment surround any attempt at law enforcement on the international air routes. If anyone wants the case for an international code of criminal air law in a nutshell, he could not pick a better argument than the case of the opium on the monkey run.

Of course, it was not the end of the Far Eastern narcotics traffic, which was organised on far too big a scale for a single coup ever to stop it. Cases would always crop up again from time to time, but by now we reckoned we knew how to deal with the smugglers, and by keeping up the pressure we gradually found that the narcotics runner was tending to keep clear of our routes.

I cannot help feeling that the greatest danger of all now lies with the trans-Pacific routes that are becoming increasingly important connecting Hong Kong and Tokyo directly with San Francisco and the West Coast of America. There are tens of thousands addicts in the U.S. more anxious than ever to-day to pay three dollars a time for their shots of heroin. As long as this massive demand continues, the air security officer will have his work cut out keeping the smugglers away from the aircraft that offer them the quickest returns in the business.

CHAPTER 14

Fourteen pieces of gold

It was 1951, the middle of July, the time of the year when anyone with any sense or any money clears out of Cairo. But air security officers hardly fall into either category, and I had had to fly into Egypt that morning because of an incident that was threatening to hold up every one of our aircraft passing through Cairo.

The root of the trouble lay in fourteen smallish pieces of gold. Altogether they weighed just over twenty-five pounds, and according to the prices on the London Gold Market at the time, should have fetched around £5,500. The only unusual thing about them was their shape. They had been cast into small, thin, rectangular bars that would slip neatly into the pockets of a smuggling vest without attracting anyone's attention.

Unfortunately, for me and for B.O.A.C., this was exactly where they had been found by an over-inquisitive Egyptian Customs official two days earlier, on a couple of our stewards just before they stepped aboard one of our Constellations bound for Karachi, at Al Maza airfield.

It was the sheerest bad luck that they were ever caught. It is very rare for a steward to be searched, but on this occasion one of them had been careless. He had failed to fasten one of the pockets in the smuggling vest, and as he

179

bent down to pick something up off the floor of the Customs shed, a piece of gold had actually slipped out and landed at the feet of a surprised Egyptian Customs official.

By midday, Customs at Al Maza were holding up every one of our planes as soon as it touched down, searching the crews and turning over the cargoes. It was the sort of hold-up every airline dreads, and from the cables and telephone calls which started pouring into my office back in London, you would have thought Egypt had declared private war on B.O.A.C. It suddenly became my urgent task to fly to Cairo, attempt to sort out the case with the local police and Customs, and clear up the mess our two amateur smugglers had landed us in.

By the time I arrived, the two stewards were already cooling their heels inside the Citadel Prison. This is a huge, grey stone fortress in a part of Cairo where few tourists ever get to, and the taxi I took seemed to be driving for hours through a maze of alleys and Arab slums before we reached it. I had permission to interview the two stewards and when they were led into the visiting cell they were practically unrecognisable. Their heads had been shaved, they were filthy dirty and they wore ragged clothes made from what looked like old sacking. As they came through the door they cringed away from the warder like convicts who had been inside for years.

I was not feeling particularly sympathetic to either of them, but you could not help feeling sorry for the poor devils, and once they started talking they told me the whole story.

As I suspected, the gold smuggling was not their idea in the first place. They were just the mugs who happened to be caught. They had been offered one hundred pounds apiece by a couple of Egyptians to deliver the gold to an address in Calcutta on their next flight through India, and although they did not know who the Egyptians were, they were emphatic that they would recognise them again if they saw them.

When they had finished their story I had no idea what I could do to help them, and although I tried to be as optimistic as I could, I had my doubts about how co-operative the Egyptian authorities would be.

At first I thought we were going to be in luck. All airport security in Egypt at this time was in the hands of the Egyptian Frontier Police, and when I drove over to their headquarters at the Zaloum Police Barracks to meet the officer in charge, I was surprised at his affability and general helpfulness. He was a rugged pipe-smoking man of about thirty-eight, dressed in a light khaki drill uniform. His name was Neguib, and a few months later the world was to know him as the man who headed the officers' revolution that finished off King Farouk. On that afternoon, however, he just appeared to me as an unusually efficient high-ranking Egyptian army officer, and when he had heard the story the stewards had told me, he agreed that it had to be investigated at once, gave me all the help I needed and placed a staff car and one of his own officers at my disposal. More important still, he gave us official permission to get the stewards out of prison in an attempt to find the house where they had been given the gold and, if possible, to recognise the men who had handed it over.

It took the rest of that afternoon to make them even presentable. We bathed them, and fed them and dressed them and gave them tarbooshes to cover their sadly shaven scalps. Finally, at about eight o'clock, we set off for the Pyramids and began our search.

It was slow going. The stewards' memory was not so

exact as they had thought, and there are a lot of houses out towards the Pyramids, but the officer was conscientious, and when we had combed the area for more than a couple of hours, we found the house.

It was large, and obviously owned by people of substance. It stood in its own grounds behind a wall covered with bougainvillæa, and there were lights on in the room downstairs. A dog barked at us from behind the gate as we drew up, but there was no point in arousing anyone's suspicions, so we drove on, returned the stewards to their prison, and I said good-night to the officer outside my hotel, wondering just what would happen next.

In fact, quite a lot happened. At two o'clock the next morning Neguib's Frontier Police raided the house and arrested two Egyptians who corresponded exactly with the stewards' description. Shortly after I awoke, I had a call from Neguib's officer telling me what had happened and adding that an identification parade was being held before the stewards at the Zaloum Barracks at midday. Quite casually he invited me along.

Excessive punctuality is a habit I picked up as a young policeman and have never been able to cure myself of. On occasions it comes in useful, and this was one of them.

I arrived at the barracks at about 11.45 and asked for my officer. He was not in. I told the guard sergeant who I was and said I wanted to attend the identification parade of the two stewards. The sergeant was apologetic, but insisted that there was no identification parade. I have fobbed off enough people in my time to know when I am being fobbed off myself, and began to get annoyed. Surely I could speak to Colonel Neguib? The colonel, the sergeant insisted stonily, was not in either.

There was not much point in trying to battle it out, so I stepped into the courtyard, and waited a few minutes trying to make up my mind what to do next. It was while I was waiting that the police van drove up with the two stewards from the Citadel. They were back in their sackcloth, and were hustled inside with little ceremony. But then came the real show. The friends and lawyers of the two arrested Egyptians arrived. In all I counted six Cadillacs before the procession was finished. Most of the passengers were wearing the costliest silk robes, and had umbrellas held above them as they walked into the barracks, to shield them from the Cairo sun. By the time the last of them had disappeared into the building, I had a fairly good idea what the result of the identification parade would be.

I was not far wrong. The two Egyptians were released that afternoon and the stewards were whistled back to the Citadel, where they later served an eighteen-month sentence for smuggling. At the same time all restrictions on British aircraft at Al Maza stopped that very afternoon, although for some reason Colonel Neguib was never in when I rang to thank him.

I remember meeting one of the stewards a couple of years later when he was back in England after serving his sentence, and asking him about the identification parade. There was, he said, no question about it. The two men were the same pair who had handed the gold over to them in the house near the Pyramids two years earlier. He had always wondered what had happened to them.

I mention this here because, for me, the trafficking in gold was later to assume an importance out of all relation to the size of this case. It was the first occasion on which I had definite proof that gold was actually being smuggled by air into the Indian Subcontinent, and it turned out to be the forerunner of what was to be the biggest investigation of my entire career—the Great Indian Gold Smuggling Case.

But at the time I had no idea that gold smuggling by air into India was to build up the way it did. All I knew was that this was the first evidence I had had that the direction of the illicit international gold traffic had changed. At the end of the war, world prices were such as to make it actually profitable to smuggle gold out of India into the Middle East, and in one case I have already mentioned—the Basra Gold Case—the gold that the R.A.F. officer was smuggling originally came from Karachi.

But all this had been dramatically reversed in the autumn of 1946, and anyone who wishes to understand the real origins of the Indian Gold Smuggling Case has to go back to the Old Parliament Building in New Delhi one afternoon a few months before Partition. A coalition government was sitting, and with all the excitement of India's forthcoming Independence afoot, there was little interest in the complex details of the Currency Regulation Bill which the Member for Finance, Mr. Liaquat Ali Khan, laid before the House.

Years later, and just about the time when I had flown to Cairo and met Neguib, Liaquat Ali Khan was assassinated by the bullet of a Moslem fanatic. By a strange coincidence it was just about this time that the Bill he introduced on that November afternoon began to produce its first crop of unexpected and totally undesired results.

For by then its effect throughout the Indian Subcontinent had been to restrict gold imports and so raise the price of gold to exactly double its level on the free market. With one simple law the Government had made gold smuggling the sort of proposition that in the end would inevitably attract some of the cleverest and most unscrupulous brains in the international underworld.

I have always been slightly surprised that this took as long to happen as it did. To start with, the greatest part of all the smuggling went into India by ship or by land, and it was only as the Indian authorities became smarter at catching up on the conventional smugglers that the airlines really came into the picture at all.

Of course, several of the airlines with services across India realised what was occurring and became concerned over what would happen if their planes ever became caught up in an outbreak of really well-organised smuggling. As early as 1951 several of the security officers from the main companies who felt themselves threatened by this actually met in London to talk over the whole situation, and discussed it in some detail with Sir Ronald Howe at Scotland Yard. He said, quite rightly, that this was an international matter, and suggested we should take our trouble over to Interpol in Paris.

In those days the headquarters of Interpol's General Secretariat were still in a faintly decayed mansion at 37b, Rue Paul Valéry, but already the organisation had become the clearing-house for information on every imaginable and unimaginable crime committed in the fifty odd nations then belonging to it.

But even as our group of air security officers talked to Marcel Sicot, the plump, scholarly Secretary-General of Interpol, I appreciated some of the difficulties the airlines would be up against in taking action against any gold smuggling occurring on their routes.

Few countries really looked on gold smuggling as crime at all, and every nation seemed to have its own conflicting laws governing the export of gold. Certainly we would have our work cut out if we ever attempted to call in the local forces of law and order against any smugglers we caught because, as M. Sicot explained, shrugging his shoulders, almost every police force in the world regards gold smuggling as a purely fiscal matter rather than a criminal one.

And that, for the time being, was that. I remember how we arrived back from Paris feeling even more apprehensive about the possibility of gold smuggling than when we set out.

But for several years it hardly seemed to matter. The land and sea smuggling into India went on increasing every year, but apart from a few very minor cases Buchanan reported from Karachi, the airlines seemed to be leading a charmed life. Then gradually the ominous reports began to come in. They started about the end of 1956, when three passengers off a flight of one of the main European airlines were arrested in the Bombay Customs area with £15,000 of gold hidden among them. Then it was the turn of one of the American airlines, transiting through Karachi, to have a steward searched by Customs and discovered with three kilos of gold hidden under his uniform in a pair of swimming trunks. Our turn was still to come.

CHAPTER 15

Wan Fei and the missing bullion

On Christmas Eve, 1958, the Charing Cross Hotel had an unexpected guest. He had arrived late that afternoon from Beirut, and had originally come from Hong Kong where he worked and lived in some style. Not that there was anything particularly sinister about him. If you had caught sight of him sitting alone in the hotel lounge or setting out in the mornings with his overcoat collar drawn up against the winds of the Strand, I doubt if you would have given him a second glance.

A Chinese business man, you might have said to yourself; gold rimmed spectacles, rather undersized and obviously feeling the cold. But had your curiosity carried you a little further, as it did with me, you still would not have found out anything startling about him. He had signed the hotel register in his own name and given his correct occupation. He kept himself very much to himself, although he had had a few European visitors and had twice telephoned back to Hong Kong. There are always ways of checking on foreig.1 telephone calls. I checked but, as I expected, the number l.e rang simply belonged to his own watch-exporting company in the business quarter of Hong Kong.

But although he even kept his day-to-day expenses in a small black diary like any business man abroad on a straightforward commercial trip, there was something about him that was not quite right. For Wan Fei Liu was a very worried man. He was also rather a scared one, and his arrival in London proved to be the start of a case involving vast sums of money, which took many months to solve, and was to end with questions in Parliament and wholesale dismissals of B.O.A.C. staff.

That Christmas, however, neither of us knew that this was how his visit was going to end. For that matter, Wan Fei Liu himself did not know me, but I already knew him. Back in the security office in London Airport I had a file on him as thick as your fist, made up of reports from my security men across the Far East for the last ten years. For Wan Fei Liu was a smuggler, and a very good one. He had never been caught because his speciality lay in persuading other people to do his dirty work for him, and he was too smart to leave the evidence lying around. He was essentially an organiser, running his smuggling ring as a branch of his watch business, and running it with great success, since he had a natural talent for the work—sociable, adaptable, a born administrator, and a man who would never take unnecessary risks. Unluckily for me, he also had a strange weakness for using B.O.A.C. aircraft and staff.

He was a businessman-smuggler with a large reliable organisation that in the past had made its chief profits from its share of the regular watch smuggling that went on by air from Hong Kong. Right now in the middle of London, Wan Fei Liu was facing the biggest crisis of his career. He had recently started playing for higher stakes than watches, and just as things were starting to go really well for him he had treachery on his hands. One of his couriers had tricked him and he had taken it hard.

I had had a tip-off from Buchanan that Wan Fei Liu was

on his way, but until he had been in London a few days we were still uncertain of exactly what he was up to. It was only later when I began to piece together the full reason for his journey that I knew for certain what he was doing, and that instead of watches, his couriers were now carrying gold.

The courier he had come all the way to London to see was a very smart boy called Roynan who worked as a B.O.A.C. steward. I had had my suspicions about him for some time. Some people even said he took drugs, but I had never been able to pin anything on him. He was altogether too glib for my liking, good-looking, fast-talking, and a great man for the ladies. He was also a man of expensive tastes who dressed well—perhaps a little too well—and who liked greyhound racing and the best restaurants. Certainly he never made any pretence of living within his pay as a steward, and although I knew quite well that young Roynan was a frequent visitor to Wan Fei Liu's flat in Hong Kong whenever his plane was passing through, I was never able to prove that this was where he was picking up his extra cash.

In fact, as I later discovered, he was one of Wan Fei Liu's most experienced couriers, who had learned his job as a smuggler some time before, carrying watches for him on the Hong Kong–Tokyo run. When the organisation turned over to carrying gold in a big way it was natural that Roynan should have been one of the first boys Wan Fei Liu asked to carry the stuff.

This shows Wan Fei Liu to have been a far worse judge of character than I would have thought possible, for the temptations gold smuggling put on the courier were obviously more than a man like Roynan could bear.

The stewards were carrying up to sixteen pounds of gold apiece, cast into specially shaped flat bars, and carried inside a specially tailored garment next to the skin. They picked it up from Wan Fei Liu in Hong Kong, and delivered it when their plane arrived in India. The risks at this time were minute, as the stewards were rarely searched by Customs. The profits for Wan Fei Liu on the other hand were considerable. With Indian bullion prices now double those in Hong Kong he could well afford to fork out the £250 he was paying to every steward who carried a consignment through to his associates in India.

The only weakness in the whole chain was that the couriers had to be men he could trust implicitly. Roynan was not.

On the 14th of December, 1958, Roynan boarded his flight from Hong Kong bound for India with sixteen pounds of Wan Fei Liu's gold under his shirt. One of the other stewards on the flight also had a similar load, and just before the plane reached India Roynan promised the man as a favour that he would deliver the gold for him to the address in Calcutta, at the same time as he took his own. Neither consignment of gold ever arrived. When the aircraft left on the next leg of its journey for London, Roynan was there, serving the drinks and meals, as self-possessed as ever with eight thousand pounds worth of gold in his charge.

No sooner had the plane touched down at Beirut than he was through the Customs, and out into the town, where he had several unusual friends who found no difficulty in selling the gold for him on the open market.

By this time Wan Fei Liu, back in Hong Kong, had got the jitters. One of the specialities of his organisation which marked it out from the less professional smuggling rings was the amazing efficiency of its intelligence service, and two hours after Roynan had failed to turn up in Calcutta, Wan Fie Liu had been informed by coded cable. With a courage I would never have expected of him, he jumped on the next plane out of Hong Kong and set off for Beirut in pursuit of his gold.

At first he was in luck. Roynan's plane had had an overnight stay at Karachi and Wan Fei Liu actually caught him, early next morning in his hotel room right on the sea front at Beirut, just as he was getting up. Roynan, as I say, was a smart boy and the last person in the world to be rattled by a small Chinese like Wan Fei Liu, even if he did appear at seven in the morning after travelling half-way across the world to catch up with him. So although Wan Fei Liu tried to make as much fuss as he could, and even threatened to call in the police, Roynan called his bluff, told him to go to hell and slammed the bedroom door in his face.

The thing I have always admired about Wan Fei Liu is his doggedness. Wherever money is at stake he never gives up, and that morning no sooner had he made sure that Roynan had actually left his hotel and boarded his aircraft, than he booked himself on to the next plane for London and exchanged Beirut's winter sunshine for late December in the Charing Cross Hotel.

Soon after he booked in, I received an interesting piece of information from B.O.A.C.'s personnel department. As soon as Roynan had arrived at London Airport, he had stepped straight off the plane, handed in his uniform and resigned from the Corporation on the spot.

This complicated things, for Roynan was now completely in the clear. There was nothing I could do about him under the disciplinary regulations of the Corporation, and there was nothing the law in this country could do about him either. Smuggling gold into India from Hong Kong is no crime in England, and the law gives no protection to smugglers who are tricked by their carriers even if £8,000 is at stake.

By all accounts Roynan had an unusually happy

Christmas, whereas Wan Fei Liu must have had a very lonely one. It is clear that this really was a crisis for him and his organisation. Nothing less than the future of the gold smuggling racket on B.O.A.C. hung in the balance. If Roynan got away with the money it would almost certainly give Wan Fei Liu's other B.O.A.C. couriers ideas, and it would not need much to start a mutiny which would hamstring his whole organisation.

Wan Fei Liu knew this perfectly well, and was certainly not the man to give up £8,000 after travelling 7,500 miles to get it back, but short of threats or blackmail, I did not for the life of me see how he could ever get at Roynan now.

Christmas over, a waiting game began with Wan Fei Liu working patiently away in his hotel to recover the money, and Roynan working even harder to get rid of it. He had the time of his life, enjoying all the things he had dreamed of during the six long years he had been a steward. He ordered his suits from Savile Row, dined at the Caprice and drank at the Ritz. He had an expensive flat and an expensive sports car. But greyhounds were his speciality, and you can lose a lot even with the best bookmakers if you know how to go about it. Roynan did, and what with slow dogs and fast women, his £8,000 was soon looking pretty thin.

But, curiously, this never seemed to worry Wan Fei Liu, who stayed on at the Charing Cross Hotel as optimistic as ever through the first week of January. His first moves were to contact several of his old couriers who had worked for him in the past, left B.O.A.C. and now settled down near London. They all said how pleased they were to see him, and several of them even invited him to dinner. But they all knew Roynan and none of them felt like tackling him, even for an old friend like Wan Fei Liu.

I found out a lot about Wan Fei Liu's troubles at this

time purely by chance, for I had an old C.I.D. friend who was on plain-clothes duty in a slightly suspect night-club where one of our ex-stewards had taken Wan Fei Liu for a night out. They had got talking. Perhaps it was the brandy, or perhaps Wan Fei Liu was becoming desperate, but he told my friend a great deal more about his misfortunes than it is ever wise to reveal to a plain-clothes detective. He told him about Roynan, about the gold, and finally offered him a cool fifty pounds if he would help him to get his money back.

This was another occasion when Wan Fei Liu picked the wrong man, for the first thing next morning the C.I.D. man made it his business to ring me at my office and give me every detail that Wan Fei Liu had told him.

But Wan Fei Liu was indefatigable. Twice he actually went to see Roynan, but both times Roynan fobbed him off, and finally threatened to have him beaten up if he did not leave him alone. Typically, after this, Wan Fei Liu consulted the hotel detective about his safety and went on waiting. In the end it seemed as if his wait had paid off.

For just after midday, two weeks after Wan Fei Liu had arrived, Roynan telephoned him at his hotel. It was no longer the arrogant, blustering young man Wan Fei Liu had had to put up with on his previous encounters. This time Roynan sounded distinctly subdued, as well he might, for although Wan Fei Liu did not know it, he had already worked his way through a healthy portion of his ill-gotten gains.

A meeting was suggested. Wan Fei Liu guardedly suggested holding it in the lounge of his own hotel and at three that afternoon. As soon as Wan Fei Liu came down to meet him, Roynan was affability itself, explaining that all the trouble had been due to misunderstanding. I don't know what Wan Fei Liu thought of that, but he had so obviously set his heart on recovering his gold that he would have put up with anything to get it back.

It must have been this desperation of Wan Fei Liu's which enabled Roynan to pull his last and most outrageous trick of all. Heaven knows how he ever did it, but somehow he managed to convince Wan Fei Liu that he had never sold the gold at all, but had cached it with several of his friends in Beirut. He would, he told Wan Fei Liu, be willing to let him have it back again for a small consideration—£1,200 in cash.

In what happened then, Wan Fei Liu was not quite so stupid as it may appear in retrospect, for he agreed to Roynan's terms only on condition that the gold should be picked up in Beirut by a courier he could trust implicitly.

And so, over tea in the Charing Cross Hotel, this ill-assorted couple made their pact. Wan Fei Liu would instruct one of his couriers to call at an address in Beirut. There he would meet Roynan's friends and collect the gold. As soon as the courier had it in his possession, he would cable Wan Fei Liu in London who would then pay Roynan his money.

This courier was another B.O.A.C. steward, who had worked for Wan Fei Liu for many years, and I am certain that he was not trying to trick him. All the same, Roynan must have picked up some unusually efficient friends in Beirut, for somehow he arranged that when the steward called at the address he had given him, he was actually handed a parcel weighted to feel exactly like the gold.

The man took it back with him to his hotel, sent off the telegram to Wan Fei Liu telling him he had received his gold and would deliver it to a prearranged address in Delhi, and went to bed. In the middle of the night there was a knock on the steward's door, and three masked men pushed their way in, demanding the parcel of gold he had in his possession. They were armed and there was not much the poor chap could do except hand over, although curiously one of the men did agree to give him a receipt for the parcel, which he could show to Wan Fei Liu.

And that, as far as Wan Fei Liu was concerned, was the last he ever heard of his gold. Of course, the whole thing was a clever frame-up by Roynan. The parcel almost certainly contained lead, and the men who broke into the steward's room were probably the same people who had given him the parcel earlier in the afternoon. As far as Roynan was concerned, the cable from Beirut indicated that he had kept his side of the bargain and he received his £1,200 in cash. I believe he was with Wan Fei Liu when the cable arrived.

I once made a speciality of studying confidence tricksters, but this was one of the coolest confidence tricks I have ever come across. Still, although Roynan did get his extra £1,200, it hardly did him much good.

The bills mounted up, the greyhounds went on losing, and a few weeks later, when the last of the money had gone, he had one final night out, took a room in a Kensington hotel and ended it all with an overdose of sleeping tablets.

CHAPTER 16

The trap closes

It was the suicide of Roynan in his hotel bedroom in Kensington which really signalled the start of the Great Indian Gold Smuggling Case for me. In its complexity, its daring and its remarkable organisation the case is so far unique in the annals of air crime. It is the only time the airlines have been exploited quite so methodically for quite such high stakes, and it is important as a blueprint of the most profitable potential air crime of the future.

Anything up to one million pounds' worth of gold must have been smuggled by air into India, and when the smuggling was at its height at least sixty stewards on our airline alone were involved. Day in, day out, the gold would find its way by air from Hong Kong into India. The profits were huge, the traffic was as smooth as a railway time-table, and at one point these shipments of illicit gold were so serious that they had begun to threaten the whole balance of the Indian Government's financial policy. So much for the power of air crime when it really catches hold.

The incredible thing about all this is that up to the time of Roynan's death at the beginning of 1959, this smuggling had been going at full blast for nearly six months without anyone getting as much as a breath of what was happening. I still kick myself for this, and feel I must have slipped up badly to allow it to go on under my very nose for so long. But then, this is the sort of mistake you can make a lot easier in police work than in most jobs, and once the Roynan affair broke, what mattered was to make up for lost time and find out just how big Wan Fei Liu's operations really were.

At the beginning of 1959, none of us knew Wan Fei Liu as well as we were to during the months to come, and he was still something of a mystery man. It was only gradually that I discovered he was the effective power behind the Hong Kong end of the organisation, and in the end I had a considerable admiration for the man.

Without him the organisation could never have carried on on the scale it did. He was shrewd, he was businesslike, and he knew exactly what risks could be taken. But these qualities alone could never have kept him at the head of such a successful organisation for so long, and it was only towards the close of the case that I understood what else there was about Wan Fei Liu to account for his success.

It was quite simple, really, although most unusual in anyone at the head of an international ring of this sort. People liked him. He could be quite ruthless when necessary, but when it was not, he had the ability few top criminals have of knowing how to relax and enjoy himself. Most of the time he appeared a cheerful, easy-going family man with a large comfortable Chinese-style apartment in Jupiter Street, in the Chinese section of the Island. He was naturally hospitable, and through his endless parties he exuded an enormous charm which made people trust him, believe in him and be willing to work for him.

This apartment got the nickname of *Open House Hong Kong* and word went round, especially among the stewards, that if ever you were in Hong Kong and in need of a drink, a meal or even a loan, the place to go to was the flat in Jupiter Street.

It was here that Wan Fei Liu had first met Roynan. It was here that he met most of the stewards who were to act as his couriers during the hectic months when the gold smuggling racket was at its height. And it was here, as I was later to find out, that the gold would actually be handed over for smuggling into India and the receipts signed.

If it had not been for this air of casual hospitality with which Wan Fei Liu was able to surround the whole transaction, I don't believe he would ever have got a quarter of the men he did to work for him. But most of the stewards at Wan Fei Liu's parties were young chaps, few of them had much money or were used to living it up on anything like the scale Wan Fei Liu could offer.

At the end of a party with six stiff Dry-Martinis inside you, and a couple of your friends already in the racket themselves, the idea of earning yourself a quick couple of hundred pounds by smuggling a handy load of gold on your next flight out of Hong Kong probably seemed the most natural thing in the world.

And it would all be so easy. The gold would be in six narrow bars, and Wan Fei Liu would show you how to put on the light cotton smuggling garment beneath your shirt so that you hardly knew you were wearing it. Next morning, you might have a bit of a hangover, and find that some of the confidence of the previous night had evaporated, but you would think of that two hundred pounds, and remember that it was unheard of for Customs ever to search a steward. As you went aboard your plane at Kai Tak airfield with six thousand pounds' worth of gold tied neatly round your middle you would promise yourself that you would go through with it this time, and that would be that.

Once you arrived in India, things would go even smoother than before. Airline regulations lay down that as a steward you were entitled to a two-day rest period here, so a relief steward takes over your duties on the plane, and you have time to catch a local flight down to Calcutta, and deliver the gold to the address Wan Fei Liu had given you before you left Hong Kong. Two days later you would be back in London, and you would hardly have reached your home before an air mail letter with a Hong Kong postmark came through the letter box.

It would contain something that needed no covering note —a £250 cheque drawn on an account at a bank in the City of London, and payable in cash over the counter.

This would be the start. It is difficult for anyone to resist quite such easy money as this, but behind all the togetherness that went on at Wan Fei Liu's parties in Jupiter Street there was always one slightly sinister fact. Wan Fei Liu would drink, but he would never become drunk, and after every party he would keep an exact record of who had been there by making sure that everyone signed his visitors' book and gave their address in England.

There was also a tradition at Wan Fei Liu's parties that everyone had his photograph taken, for he was an enthusiastic amateur photographer and it was one of the highlights of the evening when he brought out his Leica and his flash bulb and took a group photograph of the party. At the time it seemed to add to the fun. What nobody realised was that afterwards, each name and address from the visitors' book would be entered on to a card, and Wan Fei Liu would carefully stick beside it the man's picture taken from the group photograph, before entering it in his filing cabinet. In this way over the years Wan Fei Liu had built up a detailed file on our stewards which our records department in London would have found it hard to beat. Every detail about the man would be there along with a short summary of his character, and details of every ounce of gold he had carried for the organisation.

It was partly this filing system that accounts for the silent efficiency of the smuggling, and also explains how Wan Fei Lui was able to build up such an immense traffic in gold over such a short period. For he always had at his finger-tips the exact information of what couriers were available, where they were going, and how far they could be trusted. As an example of how accurately Wan Fei Liu could schedule his shipments, we discovered that at the height of the smuggling every member of the three-man cabin crew on three successive flights from Hong Kong to Delhi was carrying six kilos of gold for Wan Fei Liu.

Once a steward had smuggled his first parcel of gold and earned his cheque, it was never difficult for Wan Fei Liu to persuade him to risk it again, and some of the regulars might almost have been on a steady payroll from Hong Kong. Roynan, I discovered, was earning nearly £3,000 a year from Wan Fei Liu at one time, and once a steward really got started, he generally became carried away by the excitement of making so much money and often decided quite openly to make as much as he could to buy a car or pay off a mortgage before giving up the game for good.

Between us, Buchanan and I picked up most of these facts during a few weeks of extremely rushed investigation following Roynan's death. I worked away in London and put an informant of my own on to the Far Eastern routes as a steward. At the same time Buchanan spent his time hopping between Hong Kong and India and preparing the ground for the fight with Wan Fei Liu's organisation, which we now knew could hardly be put off much longer.

The trap closes

It was a tricky time for both of us, and that spring I was torn between the desire to bring the whole thing to a head, and the need to exert the greatest caution in everything we did.

For it was not only against Wan Fei Liu that I had to be on my guard. Roynan's death had roused considerable interest in certain quarters, and in none more so than the Investigation Branch of the Directorate of Revenue Intelligence in New Delhi. By now the Indians were really out for blood over the gold smuggling, as it had grown steadily year by year. It had become a life and death matter for the Indian economy, and now that there was clear evidence that the gold was coming in aboard our aircraft, I was really worried about the steps they might take to stop it.

But then, of course, as always seems to happen when you grit your teeth to meet a crisis like this, the unexpected happened. There was a lull. The Indians decided not to move. Wan Fei Liu kept up his shipments but was careful to keep out of trouble, and I remember that I was so carried away by the general atmosphere of peace and goodwill along the routes that spring, that I actually went ahead and booked my summer holiday for the first three weeks in June. I should have known better.

Still, it was worth risking I suppose, and we nearly got away with it. An old friend of mine from Scotland Yard had recently taken charge of the C.I.D. in the Bahamas, and had invited my wife and me out for three weeks in Nassau. This was to have been the holiday of a lifetime, and both of us felt we needed it.

In fact some of our luggage had already been sent on to Nassau, when the first cable arrived from Delhi. I had set my heart on that holiday, and tried to kid myself that things

were not as serious as they sounded. Buchanan happened to
be back in England at the time, so I grabbed him as soon
as I could and bundled him aboard the next flight out to
India, hoping against hope that this was a false alarm. But
of course it was not. Within a few hours of Buchanan's
arrival in India, I had received my second cable. This time
it was from Buchanan himself, and I could no longer ignore
the urgency of what had happened, even for a holiday in
Nassau. So I cancelled the reservations, bought my wife a
large box of chocolates, and caught that afternoon's flight
to India.

What I had been afraid of ever since the death of Roynan
had finally happened. Quite by chance the Indians had
stumbled upon a couple of our stewards smuggling gold into
Calcutta, and it looked as though they were going to turn
nasty. Ever since Roynan's death the Indian Revenue
Intelligence had been quietly salting away every scrap of
information against our stewards passing through India,
suspecting that they might be involved in the smuggling.

Now, suddenly, the Indians were using the arrest of the
two stewards as an excuse to go into action against every one
of our stewards landing at their airfields, in a determined
attempt to wipe out the smuggling at one blow. As soon as
one of our planes landed, the unfortunate stewards would be
pulled off. By the time Buchanan reached Calcutta Airport,
four of our chaps were already in the bag and another four
were brought in while he was waiting.

Air security soon hardens you to shocks, but the fact was
that these goings-on were so serious that unless we managed
to do something in double quick time, we were going to see
the flights of all our jets and our biggest liners right across
the Far East threatened. For Buchanan discovered that the
Indians had blacklisted more than forty of our stewards on

the Far Eastern run. Most of these were chief stewards at that, and taking a chief steward off a plane in the middle of its journey completely disrupts the entire service. By the time I touched down at Calcutta, all our crews were being searched, transits delayed, and the situation was getting completely out of hand.

In the middle of all this confusion, however we had one bit of luck, in the person of the man the Indians had put in charge of their side of the investigation. His name was S. K. Shrivastava, Deputy Director of the Investigation Branch of the Directorate of Revenue Intelligence in New Delhi. I had known him on and off for years. He had even been to dinner at my flat in Twickenham during one of his visits to London, and as soon as I came down the plane steps and saw that this rather sombre grey-headed Indian was there to meet me, I felt an enormous sense of relief.

For I knew Shrivastava as one of the shrewdest and most conscientious investigators in the game, a man of almost frightening integrity and contempt for anything or anyone standing in his way. Still more to the point, I knew that if we played it straight we would not find him an enemy so much as an ally in the battle that had now started in earnest against Wan Fei Liu.

As it turned out, he had already done far more to help us than I knew. Buchanan had always got on well with him and had managed to persuade him to hold over the interrogation of the stewards until I reached Calcutta. At the same time, Shrivastava had given Buchanan a list of the forty stewards suspected of smuggling and I was able to avoid any further crisis on the routes by cabling this back to London in code along with a message emphasising that not one of these stewards was to be allowed aboard an aircraft flying across India.

This at least gave us a breathing space, but everything now depended on the course of the interrogation of the stewards, for none of us knew exactly what we would discover. Shrivastava was not a man for wasting time. He just gave me long enough for a drink and a quick wash before leading us over to the cramped little office he was using on the far side of the airport.

The first man to be led in was the steward who had started the whole scare by getting himself arrested with seven pounds of gold as he stepped off one of our Comet jets from Beirut. There was no difficulty in getting the man to talk. Like most of these people, he had never really thought of how serious the game was that he was playing. He was in his early forties, a fair haired fellow, slightly above average height, and I remember how he perched nervously on the edge of his chair and nearly talked his head off, as people often do when they have really got the wind up.

Although I knew the gold smuggling had been going on, I was mystified why this particular shipment should have come in from Beirut instead of from Hong Kong. But as the steward gabbled out his replies to Shrivastava's insistent questioning, I realised that it had been a thousand to one chance that he had ever been caught at all. For the first time, Wan Fei Liu's luck had deserted him. It was a good omen for the future.

What had happened was that Wan Fei Liu had been finding life so successful at Hong Kong that he had decided to extend his operations and build up a second ring with his stewards on the outward flight from Beirut into India as well as on the return one from Hong Kong. Not that this should have been much trouble for anyone of Wan Fei Liu's organising ability. There is an open market in gold at Beirut with no restrictions on its export, and this particular city has never been lacking in the sort of bright customers you need to set up a gold smuggling ring.

It was just luck that caught out Wan Fei Liu. For the ring had been set up, all the contacts made and this steward sitting before us now had been given the important task of carrying out the very first trial run of Wan Fei Liu's new gold route. Almost incredibly he had been caught.

I have explained that it is almost unheard of for a steward to be searched. This one had been because of the unaccustomed energy of one young Indian behind the Customs bench at Calcutta. Perhaps it was the effect of the monsoon, or perhaps he was just out for promotion, but the fact is that this young Customs officer had come on duty after lunch feeling rather more energetic than is usual among Calcutta Customs men at that time in the afternoon.

This energy soon showed results when he made one of our Chinese stewardesses just in from Hong Kong turn out her handbag on to the Customs bench. Inside lay a single-tael bar of gold. She tried to explain that it was the custom of Chinese girls to carry part of their dowry with them in gold, but whatever the truth of it, this small bar was enough to spur the young man on in his gold hunt, and he decided to give the crew of the next plane that landed the most thorough going-over of their career. Purely by chance, this plane turned out to be a Comet from Beirut, and by an even greater chance, on this one flight there was our steward with seven pounds of gold under his shirt.

It was late in the afternoon before we had finished with him. Interrogation is tiring work, especially in India during the monsoon, and I would have given anything for a good bath and an early bed. But there were still the seven other stewards being held on the evidence of the Indian authorities.

They had to be questioned as well, so we stuck at it most of that night and the following morning. By then we finally knew the full extent of the smuggling racket we were up against. Although we had known already what Wan Fei Liu was up to, none of us had dreamed for a moment that he was operating on anything like this scale.

I remember the end of the interrogation very clearly. We were all feeling tired and on edge as you do when you have been asking questions solidly for nearly twenty-four hours, and Buchanan and I were a little dazed at what we had found out. We had expected a battle with Wan Fei Liu, but this was a war. Everything now depended on the decision Shrivastava made over how it was to be waged. Up to now I had been hoping he would let us deal with it in our own way, but this hardly seemed possible after everything we had learned.

After the last of the stewards had been led away there was a strange silence in the room. Buchanan stretched himself and opened a fresh packet of cigarettes, and I looked across at Shrivastava wondering just what he was going to say. He is a funny fellow. One of his habits at moments of tension is to kick off his shoes, and I noticed now that sure enough his shoes were off, and that he was sitting barefooted behind his desk twiddling his toes with concentration.

When he did speak it was brief and to the point, and I knew that the case was still ours. On his own authority he promised to hold off any further action that could affect B.O.A.C. or its crews, provided that we promised to see that none of the forty stewards he had blacklisted ever flew through India again, and that we took appropriate disciplinary action against them when the case was finished. In return, we were together to carry on the fight against Wan Fei Liu in Hong Kong and wherever else it was necessary.

He would deal with the Indian end of the organisation, and we were to pool all our information.

It was a courageous decision for a civil servant to take, and as we shook hands on the agreement we all knew that from then on, apart from everything else, Shrivastava's career was in our hands. If anything went wrong now he would inevitably be criticised for not having taken the whole case to a much higher authority.

But Shrivastava is hardly the man to be influenced by things like that, and that evening when he joined us for dinner back at our hotel he seemed quite unconcerned at the risks he was taking. Although he is a vegetarian, he is the most cheerful one I have ever known, and we joked and chatted long into the night before he would allow us to call him a taxi to take him to his home on the other side of the city.

That dinner was important if only because it was the nearest we ever got to a battle conference in our private war against Wan Fei Liu. It was there that we worked out our plan of campaign and, incredibly, the events of the next few weeks followed almost exactly the pattern we planned that night around the hotel dining table in Calcutta.

CHAPTER 17

Wan Fei slips away

With forty of our stewards banned from the Far Eastern routes, the gold smuggling ring must have received quite a jolt, but I cannot imagine that Wan Fei Liu allowed this to disturb his imperturbability and good humour for long. He could not be directly involved in what had happened in India. He and the others in the organisation remained completely untouched and the ring could easily survive the loss of forty stewards.

I can just imagine the smile he would have had on his face when he thought of the clumsiness of the people he was up against for actually giving him such an obvious warning without really doing anything at all to harm him. For the time being he would take the hint and go carefully, but within a few months he would have repaired his organisation, and might even improve on the profits of the previous quarter.

For there was a very definite vein of conceit in Wan Fei Liu and this was one of the things we were counting on when we made our plans. We knew that his intelligence service was too good to allow him to remain in the dark over anything that had happened, but we also guessed that by now he would be so confident that if only we could let the panic die down he would soon be back at his old game.

Wan Fei slips away

And so, two days after our dinner with Shrivastava, Buchanan and I went into the main B.O.A.C. office in Calcutta and booked tickets to Hong Kong.

We spent several days there knowing only too well that everything we did would be reported back to Wan Fei Liu. We went openly to Hong Kong Police Headquarters, for we knew that would be expected, but what was more important was the knowledge that that was the one place where Wan Fei Liu would have no spies who could assist him.

The first person we saw at H.Q. was a Colonial Police Officer Buchanan knew called Roy Turner. As Assistant Commissioner of the Hong Kong C.I.D., he had a vital part to play in the events of the next few weeks.

It was there we agreed on further delaying tactics. Search warrants would be applied for but not executed for at least another four weeks, and in the meantime we would leave the Colony. We made a point of telling everyone how glad we were that we were getting back to England and even arranged for a paragraph to appear in the local Press saying that Donald Fish and Douglas Buchanan had given up their investigations in India and Hong Kong and were flying back to London the following day.

And sure enough, the following day we were at the airport with all our luggage in good time to catch the morning jet flight to London. It was a pleasant flight, and I only wish that Buchanan had been with me to share it all the way, but at Karachi he slipped out of the plane just before take-off and from there, unobserved by Wan Fei Liu's intelligence service, he caught a plane down to Bombay where he hid up for the next four weeks.

I was back in London by the end of May, and as things turned out I could easily have had that holiday in the

Bahamas after all. Come to think of it, that would probably have been the best place for me, as the next four weeks dragged interminably. Buchanan was hiding in Bombay, Wan Fei Liu was being lulled into a false sense of security in Hong Kong, and in London I had the uncomfortable feeling that I was sitting on a volcano with nothing in the world I could do about it.

It was not until the beginning of July that things began to move. Back in London my informant steward reported rumours that Wan Fei Liu was starting up his organisation again, and a couple of days later Buchanan registered under a false name on another airline, and left Bombay for Hong Kong.

From this point on we were fighting Wan Fei Liu on his home ground. The one thing we had learned in Calcutta was that it was no use trying to fight Wan Fei Liu with kid gloves. If we were ever to beat him we had to strike at the centre of his organisation and strike hard, and to this end we knew we had the help of the local police.

By now I knew of the existence of Wan Fei Liu's card index system, and that was one thing we would have given a great deal to have laid hands on, but knowing Wan Fei Liu and knowing the size of his operations, I was sure that there must be even more incriminating records than these if only we could find them. Even with only the card index in our hands we would be able to put tabs on every single steward who had ever smuggled an ounce of gold for Wan Fei Liu.

But we were also after much bigger fish than stewards or even than Wan Fei Liu himself. For the deeper Buchanan and I got into this case the more convinced we were that Wan Fei Liu was not the ultimate brains behind it all.

Don't ask me why we thought this. Perhaps it was little more than a hunch, perhaps it was something we both instinctively felt about Wan Fei Liu's character, but for all his cleverness and adaptability, he just did not seem to be the sort of person with the overall imagination to work out an operation of anything like this size. He was a brilliant technician, but I was sure that at heart he was essentially a small timer, whose highly efficient watch smuggling organisation had been taken over by some much bigger group. Otherwise I just did not see how he could ever have got the vast resources to switch his business almost overnight from a small watch racket into an international gold ring.

Somewhere Wan Fei Liu had to have his backers who were putting up the money, directing the overall strategy and taking a hefty share of the profits. And if we were right, somewhere within Wan Fei Liu's organisation there had to be evidence of some sort to show us who these backers were.

When you want evidence like this there is usually only one way to get it, and the more decisively you act the more likely you are to find what you want. So the search warrants were executed at six o'clock in the morning, two days after Buchanan arrived back in Hong Kong.

The actual raid was a fairly big operation, since Wan Fei's shop and his office in Hong Kong, his flat in Jupiter Street and about four other places owned or occupied by his associates all had to be searched simultaneously. Long before dawn Buchanan arrived in the police station to help brief the raiding parties and assist the police officer in charge of the raid. This was Superintendent Tom Cavanagh, a hefty and immensely energetic Irishman who headed the commercial crime department of the Hong Kong Police.

Everything depended on this raid. If we found what we wanted we would be able to smash Wan Fei Liu and his organisation and expose the people behind it, however powerful they might be. But if we drew a blank Wan Fei Liu would be stronger than ever. It would be almost impossible ever to get another search warrant if this one failed to produce the goods, and Wan Fei Liu's prestige would mount enormously if he could say he had made fools of the combined forces of the Hong Kong Police and B.O.A.C. security.

To start with, we thought he had succeeded in doing just that. Each place where the raiding parties called was deserted, and had been methodically stripped of anything at all that could be remotely compromising. Desks were empty, cupboards bare, filing cabinets stripped. It was obvious that once again Wan Fei Liu's superb information service had been at work, and back in police headquarters poor old Buchanan had the unpleasant experience of watching as one glum-faced search party after another trailed back with little to report.

It was a nasty moment. For nearly six months we had been working towards this showdown and now that it had come it had yielded precisely nothing.

But rather than let Wan Fei Liu get away with the whole trick, Buchanan and Cavanagh decided to have one last try, and drove over to Jupiter Street themselves determined to find something even if it meant pulling the whole flat to pieces.

What they saw confirmed exactly what the search parties had reported. Everywhere they looked there were signs of hurried but methodical flight. Even the wardrobes had been emptied and the clothes strewn across the beds, and while Cavanagh and Buchanan were actually in the flat, news came through that the night before Wan Fei Liu and his family had embarked hurriedly on a round-the-world cruise which had called at Hong Kong the previous night and left on the morning tide.

Everything seemed so hopeless that even Buchanan was in favour of calling off the search, and it was Tom Cavanagh who finally found the one vital piece of evidence from the entire Jupiter Street raid. Cavanagh is one of those men who seem physically incapable of ever giving in and after he had paced for the umpteenth time around Wan Fei's office he suddenly lost his temper. The one object that particularly seemed to infuriate him was Wan Fei Liu's empty safe standing with its door ajar in one corner of the office, and finally, just to show how he felt about Wan Fei Liu and the whole wasted morning, he put his arms around it and lugged it bodily across the room. In the place where the safe had been standing lay six long sheets of paper torn from a ledger.

Although neither Cavanagh nor Buchanan realised it at the time, those six sheets of paper justified the raids ten times over, and were ultimately to prove the death warrant of Wan Fei Liu's whole organisation.

When Tom Cavanagh and Buchanan got back to police headquarters and had time to go over the various items seized in the raids, the whole situation had changed. For as well as the six pages of Wan Fei Liu's ledger, a further search of the shop had also yielded results. These consisted of two of Wan Fei Liu's old diaries and address books along with a batch of the group photographs he had taken at his parties in Jupiter Street. By the time we had finished with them, the photographs and the address books between them gave us the names of more than 250 of our personnel who had had some contact with Wan Fei Liu over the previous few years.

But on its own, this information was obviously not enough, and it was here that those six pages of the ledger suddenly proved of such vital importance. At first sight they were difficult to understand. Most of the writing was in Chinese, and the figures seemed to have no particular rhyme or reason to them, but once some of the Hong Kong Police's Chinese experts had had a go at them, their importance suddenly became clear.

These six sheets were nothing less than the detailed record Wan Fei Liu had made of every ounce of gold he had sent into India by our aircraft during the three months from February to April, 1959. Nothing showed Wan Fei Liu's incredible tidy-mindedness better than these accounts. There were the names of the stewards being employed, there were the amounts for which the gold had been bought, along with the profits on its sale in India. Finally, and possibly most important of all, there were figures covering the proportion of the profit Wan Fei Liu kept for himself and the amount he passed on to someone else, annotated by a single code letter.

Our suspicions had been right after all. Wan Fei Liu was not the real head of the smuggling ring. The whole case had suddenly taken a completely unexpected turn for the better. If we could only discover the identity of Wan Fei Liu's mysterious principal we would have broken open the biggest international smuggling ring in air history.

But before we could get to him, a great deal of good hard slogging still needed to be done. The Hong Kong end of the investigation could safely be left to the local C.I.D. The next stage in the case needed to be worked out in London as quickly as possible, and so Buchanan with all the evidence he could gather, caught the earliest flight he could out of Hong Kong and was landing at London Airport thirty-six hours later.

I was there to meet him, and as we walked from his plane over to my office, neither of us particularly relished what lay ahead, for with the six pages of Wan Fei Liu's ledger we now had cut and dried evidence of gold smuggling against more than thirty of our stewards. A few of these names overlapped with those we had got during our interrogation at Calcutta, and this meant that we could now prove that nearly sixty of our stewards had worked actively for Wan Fei Liu.

If we had not had the evidence there in black and white, I still don't think I could have believed it, but there were the names written down in Wan Fei Liu's neat capitals on the photostat pages of the ledger which Buchanan unrolled across my desk, and as I ran my eye down them I felt slightly appalled at the upheaval those names were going to cause once we released them to B.O.A.C.

I was all for getting it over as quickly as possible. It is not particularly pleasant to discover that quite so many of the people you have worked with are rogues, but here we obviously had to take action, and there seemed a great deal to be said for speed.

Buchanan did not agree. He felt that so many people were involved, and that the whole case was so serious, that it was up to us to get hold of any additional corroborative evidence if it was humanly possible, and we spent the rest of that day arguing the toss over whether it really was.

I was not particularly hopeful about this. It seemed to me that Wan Fei Liu had covered his tracks so well that we were lucky to have done as well as we had. Even those six pages of the ledger had only been left under the safe, as far as we could see, because Wan Fei Liu could not afford to destroy his most recent accounts until he had cleared them with his principal. We had found them by a great stroke of luck, but I could not see Wan Fei Liu leaving anything else like that around in a hurry.

Buchanan finally seemed to agree with me, and late that night, after I had congratulated him again on a fine piece of work, I left him at the office and drove home to bed.

I don't know how much longer he stopped on at the airport. All I do know is that it was two in the morning when the telephone rang beside my bed. Buchanan was on the other end. I was feeling pretty bleary, and he was so excited I could hardly understand what he was talking about. All I could gather was that he had had a brainwave, and was catching the morning plane back to Hong Kong. He would be away ten days, and I was to hold over any further action until he returned.

In fact he was away more than a fortnight, and apart from one short and almost insultingly brief cable, I had not the faintest idea what he was up to, until the Thursday afternoon at the beginning of August when I strolled down to the tarmac yet again to welcome him back from Hong Kong. This is the one arrival of Buchanan's at London Airport that really stands out in my mind, for as soon as I caught sight of him standing at the top of the Comet's landing steps, I wondered what on earth he was up to. Over his shoulder he was carrying a bulging regulation size G.P.O. mail-bag. It was almost the only occasion I have ever seen him looking tired, and when I asked him where he had been for the last fortnight, he replied mysteriously, " General Post Office, Hong Kong. Great place for getting through a lot of hard work if you go about it the right way."

That was all I could get out of him until we reached my office and had closed the door firmly behind us. Then with a rush of triumph he dumped his precious mail-bag on to the floor, cut the string round the neck, and emptied the contents across my desk.

Although they were tightly rolled up, I recognised what

came out first. They were photostats of the six pages of
Wan Fei Liu's ledger. What followed seemed to be batch
after batch of photostat copies of G.P.O. registered letter
slips, and when I examined a few of them I saw that each
slip bore the name and address of a B.O.A.C. steward living
somewhere in England. At last I understood Buchanan's
brainwave.

He had remembered that each of the stewards who had
carried gold for Wan Fei Liu's organisation had been paid
in London by a cheque sent by registered post from Hong
Kong. Every registered letter sent from Hong Kong was
naturally recorded by the post office there, and it followed
that, if Wan Fei Liu's ledger was correct, every successful
transaction it contained ought to have a corresponding
registered letter slip somewhere inside the General Post Office
in Hong Kong, where the duplicates were stored.

The only trouble was that for the five months covered by
the ledger there happened to be a million and a quarter
slips to wade through.

Nothing illustrates Buchanan's methods as an investigator
better than the way he went about this job. I think I would
either have quietly forgotten about it or else have persuaded
someone else to do the hard work for me. But Buchanan
does not operate like that. For two weeks he practically
lived at the G.P.O. He managed to hire a few post office
clerks as part-time helpers when they were off duty, but the
bulk of this back-breaking task fell entirely on him. The
results of his labours were in front of me now on my desk.

Somehow he had managed to match every single entry
in Wan Fei Liu's ledger with a corresponding registered
letter slip from Hong Kong. As far as our stewards were
concerned, the case was complete. The evidence was
absolutely watertight.

Buchanan had done his part of the job. It was now my turn to act. The Chairman of B.O.A.C. had to be informed, and then I had to get down to the unpleasant task of interrogating every steward whose name was on Wan Fei Liu's ledger. Often it was heavy going, and there is not much fun dragging admissions from a never-ending stream of men all guilty of the same crime.

But the real strength of the evidence lay in Buchanan's registered letter slips. A steward could deny the evidence of the ledger if he wanted to, but the one thing he could not deny was that just after the date recorded on the ledger he had received a registered letter from Hong Kong. One by one every steward I interrogated broke down until I had a full admission in almost every case.

As I have already said, one direct result of the case was that fifty of our stewards were ultimately dismissed, and then there were a further twenty who had been blacklisted by the Indian Government and who formed a separate problem of their own. In the end they all had to have their contracts terminated as they were unable to complete the full terms of their employment.

There was naturally some sympathy for the stewards, especially those in the second category. A few weeks later I even had the unusual experience for a policeman of sitting in the House of Commons and hearing M.P.s actually debating the whole case, but although the debate produced several veiled criticisms of the way the Indian Government had summarily banned twenty of our stewards from their airfields, few M.P.'s mentioned the really remarkable restraint the Indians had shown while the case had been on, or the enormous trust Shrivastava had put in B.O.A.C. when he let us carry out the investigation on our own.

Once they had made their original bargain not to take

any more stewards off our planes, the Indians had stuck to it religiously. Their co-operation throughout was magnificent, and even when they were in possession of the ledger sheets and the statements indicating the size of the operation, there was never the slightest threat of any action against the Corporation under international Customs law to ban the use of any of our aircraft which had been involved in this large-scale smuggling through India. The ledger sheets alone proved that over £250,000 worth of gold had been smuggled into India by our staff and aircraft in a period of twelve weeks.

By the end of the summer of 1959 this side of the case was finished. For the time being at any rate we had swept our Eastern routes of the threat of gold smuggling into India, and by the sheer size of the dismissals that had followed the case, I knew now that any steward, whatever the incentive, would think twice before he boarded one of our planes with a smuggler's waistcoat under his tunic.

But although we had produced results of a sort, we had not successfully wound up the case. Wan Fei Liu had returned to Hong Kong from his cruise and had taken over the management of his watch business as imperturbably as ever. I even heard rumours that he was beginning his parties again in Jupiter Street—this time with Continental and American air crews as his guests. And more important than Wan Fei Liu, the principal was still at large, as anonymous as ever, and quite untouched by everything we had done, apart from a sharp drop in his annual income.

It is at this point that the real irony of the Indian Gold Smuggling Case begins, for here were Buchanan and I with cast-iron evidence of a gigantic international conspiracy which for many months had been worked across our routes. We had used this evidence to get at the couriers and punish them heavily for their pains, but already it began to appear that the people we could not get at were the real brains behind it all. Perhaps we had taught them to be a little more careful next time. Perhaps they would even fight shy of using anyone as well known as Wan Fei Liu, but clearly their power remained still virtually untouched, and the profits from smuggling gold into India were still so big that sooner or later they were sure to start their tricks again on some other major airline serving the Far Eastern routes.

I can only console myself that if this does happen, we at least did our level best to prevent it. For Buchanan and I spent the whole of that autumn trying to carry the case through to its conclusion.

Even Wan Fei Liu seemed to steer clear of trouble. We tapped almost every available source of evidence and prepared our case against him, but he is a wily bird and, as I half expected all along, he has so far found little difficulty in avoiding any legal attempts to interfere with his activities.

It was the identity of the principal which should have provided the real climax to this case, and we spent many months trying to find a lead from the evidence of Wan Fei Liu's ledgers and diaries to establish once and for all who he was. As this sort of thing has a habit of doing, proving the identity of the principal finally became an obsession for Buchanan and me. By Christmas of that year we had done it.

It doesn't matter how, but we had found out for certain who the principal was. He was a top-ranking international smuggler operating most of the time from Macao, the small Portuguese trading colony on the Chinese mainland in close proximity to Hong Kong. We had also discovered that the principal in his turn was financially backed and actively assisted by an extremely powerful financial syndicate with headquarters in Hong Kong, Geneva and the

City of London. This syndicate included several of the most reputable names of international finance, and there is no doubt that each member knew exactly what was going on.

But as soon as we tried to prove what we knew, we found ourselves hamstrung once again by the inadequacies of international air law as it stands at present. We had proved conclusively that our stewards had been exploited by a formidable gold smuggling ring. We had also proved that every steward had been paid through an account in a bank in the City of London, and that nearly £18,000 had been directly paid in this way for their services, on cheques sent by Wan Fei Liu on behalf of his masters. No cheque bore his signature. This huge sum we know was paid out over a twelve-week period. If only we could have found the details of that account and who was paying the money into it, it would have given us just the lead we wanted and helped us implicate the members of the syndicate itself.

Under the British Bankers, Evidence Act, a bank can be compelled to produce a customer's account only when ordered to do so by a court of law which considers it necessary evidence in a case. If we could ever have brought a case to court, I have no doubt that the magistrate would have given the order, but smuggling gold into India, even aboard a British plane from a British Colony is no crime under English law.

We could dismiss the stewards we had caught under our own disciplinary regulations, but we could never use this evidence to bring a court action against a single one of them in London and so enable us to get at that account in the City.

And in the City it remains to this day, probably hiding the names of several extremely wealthy international financiers who came near to being exposed as the men behind the most profitable air conspiracy of the century.

I have found that when you are dealing with crime, it is extremely dangerous to imagine you have ever heard the last of anything. As long as there is still any money in it, any crime you can mention will crop up again, and even in my last few months at B.O.A.C. I dealt with two more minor outbreaks of gold smuggling into India aboard our planes. One consisted of a small freelance smuggling ring started up by an ex-steward of ours who had once worked for Wan Fei Liu. He began buying gold on the free market in Beirut and actually had four stewards working for him smuggling it into Karachi. But this character was no Wan Fei Liu, and once we knew what he was up to there was no real difficulty in putting an end to his little game.

Then, a few weeks after this the Hong Kong Police helped us unearth yet another little gold smuggling racket, being run by a gentleman called Yau Mok Chi. He had once been a minor confederate of Wan Fei Liu and had worked out a cunning enough scheme to smuggle gold rods into India by sliding them into the frame of specially constructed suitcases. He might have got away with it if he had not tried to persuade one of our Chinese stewardesses to carry one of the suitcases through for him on her next flight out of Hong Kong. Unfortunately for him he picked the wrong girl, and when she had reported his offer to Buchanan, she actually helped us catch Yau Mok Chi red-handed. He was operating under the guise of an Import and Export business with branches in India, and my old friend Shrivastava came to Hong Kong at our request and spent many profitable weeks going through the books of the company and examining all the seized documentation.

Shortly afterwards one of the largest seizures of gold ever

made took place on a ship in Calcutta and this was followed by another on an American liner in New York—both lots originated in Hong Kong and were " Syndicate " gold.

Now that I have closed my files on the Great Indian Gold Smuggling Case and given up the active life of an airline security officer I have time not only to think of the years that have passed but to crystal-gaze a while into the future.

The liaison between the security officers of the various airlines is well established along with the exchange of information along the world's air routes. Active security organisation within an airline is slowly being accepted as a necessity, but there is much that has yet to be done. Some of the world's major airlines are still not convinced of the value of an established preventive service.

What is not realised is that often even the smallest theft or loss can have a serious behind-the-scenes effect that can cost far more than the actual amount of the loss or claim.

Because of the keen competition among the airlines there is still an unfortunate tendency to hush up serious thefts and losses, through a fear that a rival line might take commercial advantage of these incidents. For years the General Secretariat of Interpol have been trying to persuade airlines to report serious thefts of an international character, but even air security officers who do co-operate with Interpol on all other matters fight shy of the possible commercial consequences of publishing statistics like these.

This sort of reticence simply helps the thief, and now that there is increasing evidence that organised crime is moving in on air transport, an answer to the problem will have to be found.

The only logical solution seems to be the formation of an over-all security organisation, co-operating with national police forces, acting on behalf of all air operators, but entirely international and entirely independent. If the costs of this were only distributed between the airlines in proportion to operations it is obvious that the expense would be negligible, and the rewards unlimited.

Perhaps this is just a pipe dream, but I leave this great industry satisfied at having laid the foundations of what one day will be the world's first international air police force.

The Tartan Pimpernel

by

DONALD CASKIE

CONTENTS

CHAPTER I

SOMBRE DIMANCHE

I PREPARED for my morning service at the Scots Kirk in the Rue Bayard, Paris, with a heavy heart. The weather was beautiful and a slight haze that seemed to promise heat hung over the bridges. It could have been drifting smoke from the battles that were being fought around the city. German soldiers were driving up the valley of the Seine and the Wehrmacht, two millions strong and at the height of its power, was engulfing France. It was June 9th, 1940—a Sunday. Under a blazing sun, in their oven-like tanks, enemy soldiers, relentless and confident, smashed through villages, reduced homes to rubble and raced towards the French capital, jubilant in the belief that Paris lay defenceless before the might of their Fuehrer. So far, Paris was untouched, except by fear. It was a day when the avenues and boulevards should have been alive with gay and chattering Parisians, making the most of the Sabbath break from work. But Paris seemed dismal and dark. The sunshine, gilding the greenery of the trees in the gardens, mocked a people who knew but could not admit that defeat was imminent.

Rumour ran like wildfire through the city, false reports and tales that startled and struck horror. The Fifth Column was active and already a great exodus had begun. Cars packed with officials, private citizens, politicans and journalists made their way out of the city. Heavy lorries carried whole families and parties of neighbours, together with the pathetic conglomeration of household and personal oddments that human beings clutch in an emergency. A Siamese cat blandly grooming its whiskers sat on some luggage piled on a truck. Strapped to the back of a bicycle, ridden by a serious-looking girl, a doll stared unseeingly into space. An old woman laboured under a heavy, anonymous bundle.

Slowly in the heat, the endless snake of assorted vehicles moved on the jammed roads, all making for the ports, jerking into speed for a few moments and then halting, or returning to a sullen crawl.

Many more thousands of people, more than half the population, remained at home, clerks, working people, café proprietors, the great mass who had no other place to go. Some of them had been in the city in 1914 when the Boche advanced to within thirty miles of its outskirts. Faithful and fearless, a little obtuse and poignantly brave, they believed that another miracle would stop the new advance, that their Paris would not, could not, fall to the enemy. But the majority of Parisians knew they were imperilled, that Paris must fall, and they refused to be stampeded by Hitler's Wehrmacht. They were prepared for temporary occupation by the enemy. All around me that morning, as I made my way to the Scots Kirk in Paris—that little bit of France which is for ever Scotland—I felt the agony of France.

I chose the Psalm and the hymns and the readings with special care. As I sought out familiar faces in the congregation, my heart was full. Old, middle-aged and young friends were present. We needed the comfort of prayer, and we knew that trials and tribulations awaited all of us, especially the older members of the Kirk. But here, on that Sunday morning we felt at home—here was a happy place in this ancient European capital. We might so easily have been in Scotland.

For centuries the Hundredth Psalm has been popular with Scottish folk. Our Covenanting Fathers sang it before the Battle of Drumclog.

I suppose the appalling drama that was being fought out a few miles away made us tense as we worshipped. The threat was incalculable. The most fearful army of all time was marching towards us. My own heart lifted and was high when I read the New Testament lesson. Imminent peril strengthens faith and the words of the Gospel are always appropriate. I had chosen from the 24th chapter according to St. Matthew :

'And ye shall hear of wars, and rumours of wars, see that

ye be not troubled, for all these things must come to pass, but the end is not yet. For nation shall rise against nation; and kingdom against kingdom, and there shall be famines, and pestilences and earthquakes. All these are the beginning of sorrows.'

The service was nearly ending, and the walls of our little church had become like a strong hand confidently and happily holding us secure from the world. We closed with an item of praise that some have called the Scottish National Anthem. It was sung to the tune 'Salzburg.'

> '*O God of Bethel! by whose hand*
> *Thy people still are fed;*
> *Who through this weary pilgrimage*
> *Hast all our fathers led:*
>
> *O spread Thy covering wings around,*
> *Till all our wanderings cease,*
> *And at our Father's loved abode*
> *Our souls arrive in peace.*'

I commended my people to God. I committed to Him the Kirk where our kinsfolk have worshipped for nearly a century and then, outside in the warm sunshine, I said *au revoir* to my congregation.

On the table in the vestibule lay a bunch of white heather I had brought from my native island of green grassy Islay the previous year. That heather gave me an odd certainty that all would still be well for Paris. In my heart I was certain that I would see her again before I went westering home. I closed our church.

I had to leave Paris immediately. Out of the rumours one fact was clear. Within a few days the city would be occupied by the Germans. The heroism and strength of the French and the British armies could not halt this new type of military leviathan created by a nation that prepared for war, while our countries concentrated upon the crafts and arts of peace. General Weygand announced in one of his despatches that the enemy was attacking under great smoke-screens, and something of the kind covered news reports in and out of the city during those fateful days. But we knew that the majority of minor Government officials were packing

THE TARTAN PIMPERNEL

their bags, under orders to abandon the city. M. Paul Reynaud, we knew, was with the High Command, and it was a safe deduction that the Government soon must leave.

The British Embassy was evacuating. There was the hurry and flurry of departure around the buildings where our flag was still flying. Only neutrals remained. The U.S. Embassy flag was displayed and it was some consolation to know that a few friendly foreigners would be in Paris to remind Parisians that their city was not all German.

As I made my way to the manse in the Rue Piccini, I was thoughtful and preoccupied with plans for my own departure. Ordinarily, I suppose, a minister of religion, falling into the hands of enemy soldiers can rely upon their innate respect for the cloth. But my Scots respect for religion and human beings had prompted me to denounce Hitler, his works and absurd pomp from my pulpit. Hitler had elevated racial persecution into an expression of national and individual virtue, and corrupted the souls of his own people, especially the young. He lusted for power in a diabolical way, and his wicked pretensions and idolising of military 'might' appalled all decent men. When news of his concentration camps and atrocities reached us in Paris, I denounced them in the Scots Kirk in more than one sermon. In my first I chose the text from the Prophecy of Hosea:

'They have sown the wind and they shall reap the whirlwind.'

Like most texts the prophecy it contained was apposite, and as always, it was fulfilled in God's time. I could have chosen my texts more carefully for the Fifth Column was about, but my sermons had been delivered with no thought of flattering the master of the German 'race.' From every point of view it would be wiser to leave Paris, I decided, and make my way to the coast and from thence home to take stock of my future and render whatever service I could to my own country.

As the day went on it became apparent that I must go to Bordeaux. Our own soldiers had closed most of the roads out of Paris and stories were filtering through of enemy aircraft strafing

14

the routes taken by escaping Parisians. There were fantastic tales of parachutists disguised in the most improbable ways landing and attacking at the least expected places. I was to discover within a few days the meaning of this new type of air warfare. In the meantime I saw the French become refugees in their own country—a country which had given refuge in former years to many victims of the Nazis and Fascists. Mussolini had declared war on us now and beset on all fronts, poignantly fleeing—as their soldiers made a last hopeless stand—the French left their homes. The refugees were oddly silent; the old men and women who trudged along behind handcarts or sat on lorries, seemed curiously, nobly reconciled, so much more reconciled than the young, who know less of life's sorrows and so are more easily overcome by disaster. The old are surprised by joy but in adversity are more content. But one was sad for them above all, and I felt that the sunshine illuminating this most beautiful city was cruel in its warmth and comfort.

The afternoon was busy with preparations for my departure. I visited the older members of the congregation who would not be able to take flight, and bade them farewell, knowing that some I would not meet again. I deposited ten years' accumulation of sermons in manuscript in the cellar where later they were found by a German patrol which searched the manse. I never saw them again. My concierge reported that the soldiers were uninterested in my silver but seemed particularly interested in the matter of my preaching. I have no doubt they were aware of my opinions before they arrived, for a young person, known humorously to the congregation as 'the chiel' among us takin' notes,' had been present at most of our services, assiduously jotting down notes in a large book on his knees. I had hoped I was providing him with edification but, alas, events were to show it was evidence he sought. Time was to play a strange and consoling trick upon both of us.

To the ordinary citizen a Fifth Column is an especially sinister force. You may be aware of its agents and almost certain that you know some of them personally, but in times of war, when the powers they are pledged to support are victoriously advancing, one is powerless to deal with them. The German Fifth Column was strong and active in France before 1940. It was highly organised and efficient and like an iceberg, by far the larger part of it was unseen and unsuspected in its true dimensions.

I had locked the doors of the Scottish Kirk and to my very faithful friend, M. Gaston the proprietor of the café next door, given the key of the church for custody. With a bag on my back, and with a great sadness in my heart, I left the manse, and joined the great Exodus.

The guns at Mont Valerien, rumbling thunderously, were the accompaniment to a Paris which seemed to be entirely on the move. Unopposed enemy aircraft filled the sky and one felt they were extinguishing the light of the sun. Millions of refugees were marching, fleeing in all sorts of conveyances into the unknown, leaving the familiar places and escaping from the realities that had bounded their lives. To get within a mile of any of the railway stations south of the city, Lyons, Austerlitz or Montparnasse was impossible. A rumour that the French Government had moved to Bordeaux heightened the tension. Alas, the rumour proved true, and within a week Marshal Pétain had formed a new Cabinet. After that, the military authorities were given control of the capital and Paris was declared an open city.

The Germans marched in on the 13th, a Thursday in June. I have been told that they came as if from all ends of the earth, in every street, on every road, precise and correct in their grey uniforms. There were no French men or women on the streets to greet them. The open city was deserted, vast, silent, impersonal and uncommitted. The sun was shining and birds were singing as the alien soldiers marched through the suburbs.

They mounted anti-tank guns on the bridges and posted sentries on guard at the Tuileries. Their sense of humour did not equate their sense of history. They enforced a 9 p.m. curfew and a complete blackout, and, over the graveyard hush, the trudge of the boots of sight-seeing soldiers beat like mourning drums. Most of the theatres and places of entertainment closed. Only a few restaurants were open to feed them. Above the Eiffel Tower and over the Arc de Triomphe, the swastika was flying. One procession of French civilians was visible in public. It was under the Arc de Triomphe, quite oblivious of the flying swastika.

There at the Tomb of the Unknown Soldier dozens of women wept bitterly and prayed. The passing victors gravely saluted. Behind them they had left roads littered with dead, the towns they had passed through, had been reduced to a shambles.

At twilight on the 13th, the sky was red and as the sun faded, the swastika became enveloped in darkness and the Arc de Triomphe was outlined against a fiery sky. Trains had stopped running and the clock over St. Lazare had failed and stopped.

We refugees were on the march and Paris was behind us. On that early morning as I moved through the suburbs, which are so much more characteristic of a people than the centre of any great capital, I mourned for the little streets, the homes, factories, shops and cafés and the people who must endure.

The weather changed as evening came and rain began to fall. Because, I suppose, I am a Highlander, I remembered the white heather and was not too downcast. I knew that work awaited me wherever I went.

CHAPTER 2

LAST SHIP FROM BAYONNE

THE TRAIL of refugees struggled silently through the day. We wore an assortment of our most valuable or favourite clothes—summer finery and heavier winter garb, incongruously thrown on. A very few were practically and neatly dressed as for a hike in the country. None spoke to strangers such was the common fear of the Fifth Column. As evening fell thunder rumbled in the distance and rain began to fall, gathering force and soaking us. A few stragglers from the retreating army appeared; and the chastened civilians eyed them as if they were beings from another world.

The rain fell heavily, lightning flashed across the sky and I felt curiously relieved as if the violent weather somehow put the violence of nations into perspective, and brought humans nearer to human stature, small created creatures whose arrogant brutalities were being played out within their own small world. I halted late in the afternoon and gazed back towards Paris. The city was dead and silent.

The ordinary pains of life, such as being footsore and hungry, I gladly accepted, they seemed to be a cross for me to bear, but I was utterly exhausted when I arrived at the village of Sceaux near Chevreuse Valley. By my side an old woman pushed an infant in a perambulator; farther ahead a youth trundled a very old peasant in a wheelbarrow; a dainty girl sat on a pavement, her back against a wall, examining one of her feet, a light pair of city shoes lying by her side. In bundled ranks thousands of refugees lay on the village green trying to sleep in the deluge that poured down. I rested with them, sore and weary, but I could not sleep. Long before daybreak, only slightly less exhausted, I was on the march again. I knew the direction in which I was trudging, but the events of the past few days, the previous day's long walk and the night in the open under the rain had dazed me. Now, with the sun gathering in strength, my clothes began to steam. Many soldiers had joined us; they seemed to be sleep-marching, their eyes still seeing blazing buildings, the brutal onslaught of enemy armour, and dead comrades. They were under orders to make their way to the south, and had the right of way. Women, old and young, too tired to move out of their path, were roughly hustled aside. Many of their officers had deserted them, and there was no one in authority. Miserable, soaked in the dirt from days in the open, they struggled on, defeated and disorganised.

All through the day the dreary trek continued and at times I marched as if under hypnosis.

I covered thirty miles, and came to the town of Dourdan at nightfall. There I was slightly more fortunate than on the previous night. I found a roof for my head, in a dilapidated and half-demolished school. Into its shelter I crawled and—luxury of luxuries—found a bundle of straw, spread it carefully over the floor and stretched out for a few hours' sleep. The sun was rising when I awoke, and took the road to Tours.

Half conscious, but curiously alert to danger, I flung myself into ditches all through the day. It is impossible to judge the trajectory of machine-gun bullets striking from the air; sometimes when the aircraft seemed overhead they went wide, sometimes inexplicably close and once, I felt them thudding into the earth a few inches from my head.

The attacks ceased in the late afternoon and the sky was quiet again. I felt a wonderful sense of peace, I revelled in the freedom from the threat of instantaneous death. The road was under my feet and I drew deep breaths and enjoyed the air in my lungs. I was marching again.

There was no food to be found anywhere, and the days that followed were hard and hungry but I had a feeling of achievement when I reached Tours.

Before looking for a lodging for the night, I found a second-hand ironmongery shop and for a few pounds bought an aged and rickety bicycle. The shopkeeper was a kind and eager man. It was reassuring to notice how enthusiastically he subscribed to the adage —business as usual—solicitous, efficient and friendly, he was so eager to please and encourage me on my way that when I pushed the old crock into the street I felt all was well. The first bomb of the heaviest bombardment Tours was to receive landed at that moment, and I jumped on that rickety old bike and raced into nowhere. Close to the banks of the Loire I noticed people dodging into an opening in a wall. I followed them and plunging downstairs, bicycle on shoulder, came to rest in a nice dark anonymous cellar. My own kind, the refugees, were huddled about me, and in the darkness I did my best to comfort them, talking to them as the city rocked under the impact of high explosive. Not far away was a ruined castle, the scene of Sir Walter Scott's *Quentin Durward* which I had read as a boy and again as a young man. I hoped that it would not be hit. Bombs crashed all around us through the night and in the darkness we waited patiently. When the sun rose all was quiet and I left the cellar and pushed the old bike up the hill that lies on the south side of Tours and looked back at the city. It was enveloped in smoke, and in places tongues of flame curled through the shattered roofs. I turned my wheels towards Bordeaux.

The next night I slept in a byre with a pleasant old cow. A friendly creature and a perfect hostess. She did not disturb her guest, but philosophically munched the nourishment which, unfortunately, I couldn't share, and consoled me with her rhythmic champing. In the morning she awakened me with a cheerful ' moo.'

The following night I dined on grapes and had been so long without food that a fruit which might normally have made my dessert, satisfied me. Under the vines loaded with luscious fruit, I rested and felt secure. I looked up at the summer sky and considered the strange position in which the Rev. Donald Caskie was finding himself.

That night was heavenly. On such a night one recalls the goodness of life. My mind drifted over everything that had led to this interval in a long moment of universal peril. Parents and family love, school days and friends at Bowmore on my lovely native Islay and later at Dunoon on the bonnie banks of Clyde. Student days in Edinburgh, my first degree as Master of Arts and then the absorbing study given to theology and finally my initiation as Assistant Minister at the High Church on the Mound at Edinburgh. I remembered the companionship of friends and my thoughts were happy.

The next day I continued on my way and at nightfall I lay down behind a stone dyke and slept undisturbed.

On the following evening I arrived at a little village not far from Bordeaux, again tired and hungry. As I rode into the main street I was puzzled to hear angry shouts behind me. I halted and jumped from the bicycle and a turbulent crowd surrounded me.

'*C'est un Boche. Un sale Boche. Tuez le.*'

They seemed to mean it; angry hands stretched out at me and blows were aimed in my direction. I protested, shouting loudly that they were talking nonsense; I was no German! I was a Scot —an ally. Then gendarmes pushed their way through the threatening mob. I was handcuffed, and hustled off to the police station, vigorously demanding what charge was going to be brought against a friend whose country was in alliance with France.

'You are a German spy,' a gendarme said when we were inside the police headquarters. 'One of the advance guard sent by your criminal compatriots to prepare the way.'

My eyes widened.

'You carry the hateful symbols of Hitler and the Huns.'

He pointed to the bike that I was pushing awkwardly along with me, my hands constricted by the iron bracelets.

'Look on the back of it. Your identity card is there. That is proof of your mission, Boche!'

I could not turn the bicycle round but when we reached the police station and my hands were free I twisted old faithful about and peered at it. There on the rear mudguard was a miniature swastika which must have been stuck on before I bought the contraption. Furiously I ripped it off. I flung it far into the garden through the open window of the station.

Outside the mob roared and clamoured on the doorstep.

'Ask him for his identity card,' a man cried.

I handed it over. A policeman flung my bag on the table and the crowd quietened, those nearer the door standing on tip-toes, gazing in over the shoulders of their comrades.

On top of my personal effects lay two items that immediately protested my innocence—a Bible and a kilt. It was the latter, not the Bible, that did it. No German would have carried a kilt; only a Scot would pack one at a time when France was falling about his ears. My *carte d'identité* was handed back and all was now well. After profuse apologies by the gendarmes I was conducted to a comfortable room above the station where I slept soundly and next morning they gave me breakfast. As I rode out of the village to Bordeaux, people rushed at me again, but this time to shake my hand, and pat my back. I wobbled through them and friendly voices chorused:

'*Bon voyage!*'

When I reached Bordeaux I found it a maelstrom of rumour, fear and frustration. The last ships had left the harbour and were on their way to the United Kingdom. The first, loaded with refugees packed like herrings in a box, was torpedoed as she cleared port and sailed into the Gulf of Gascony. There were few survivors. The French Government, I was told, had left for North Africa and the Wehrmacht was at La Rochelle. Bordeaux would be occupied in a few hours. I lingered by the dockside, stunned by the news and then made my way to the railway station.

I was advised to go on to Bayonne, make another attempt to take ship and if that failed I could try to escape into Spain.

My spirits sank lower, and as I cycled slowly and hopelessly away from the port, I felt spiritually and morally exhausted. During the long trek to the south, hope had buoyed me up and the thought that I'd win through to join my own kind who, I knew, would hit back at the enemy and finally defeat him. Now for the first time, I felt completely alone, isolated from all I loved, even God Himself. Fatigued beyond endurance, my journey seemed aimless and futile. I could not even find a place to sleep and as my courage ebbed away, I sat down by the side of the road and instinctively reached for my Bible.

I opened it at random and there was the twenty-third chapter of the Book of Job. The words were applicable.

'Even to-day is my complaint bitter. My stroke is heavier than my groaning. Oh, that I knew where I might find Him, that I might come even to His seat. I would order my cause before Him, and fill my mouth with complaints. Behold I shall go forward but He is not there, and backward, but I cannot perceive Him. . . . But He knoweth the way I take.'

I closed my eyes, feeling comforted and my lips moved in fervent prayer; I felt God close at hand. When I opened my eyes two French soldiers were gazing down at me. They, indeed, I found were the answer to my prayer.

Their faces were covered with the stubble of men who had lived in retreat from discipline for days. They looked tired beyond human endurance, but they did not complain.

'M'sieur seems very tired,' said the taller, who even when in good condition must have been a gaunt man. He knelt and peered into my face; his eyes were red-rimmed but gentle and solicitous under the raw lids.

'When we saw you sitting here we felt we ought to speak. Can we help you?'

I told them I was exhausted. My only hope was to reach Bayonne and catch the last boat to Britain. I was a Scot.

They looked at each other and smiled without speaking. They seemed to be old friends, united perhaps by the dangers they had survived.

'Rest, M'seiu,' said the smaller man, his strong provincial accent seeming even more friendly than the quiet detachment of his comrade.

They moved toward the centre of the road. I sat back and watched. They held up their hands stopping cars, gazing into each, reassuring the drivers and passengers. But the cars were all full, even the rich limousines and then, hours it seemed, but, in fact, only about thirty minutes later, I was comfortably seated in a large car and chatting to a kindly gentleman, who turned out to be the owner.

I gave my bicycle to the soldiers who thanked me as I clasped their hands and bade them Godspeed. It seemed I had fallen among Good Samaritans. The car-owner passed me a rug and made me comfortable.

Escape was imperative for him, too, he explained, but he was not an enemy alien only. He was part of an older institution in history—a racial alien, a Jew. His whole race had been condemned to death by Hitler and the Nazis. Even worse, he was a journalist who had written of freedom, that ideal shared by all men west of the Reich. The journey to Bayonne passed quickly. We confided in each other and became friends. He drove into the town and I was grateful, but not surprised, when this generous refugee invited me to join him for the night at his cousin's home. Hospitality was a family trait and the Jewish household was full of refugees. I shared a room and a large bed with four other men, one of them being my friend whose name was Abraham. He smiled as I likened myself to the beggar in the Gospels who was carried by angels to Abraham's bosom.

The kindly soldiers, on the run from peril, and that gentle Jewish gentleman, self-sacrificing, uncomplaining, restored me to Christian contentment. When I set out for the harbour docks in the morning, I was reluctant to find a ship. Overwhelmingly I was aware that I should remain in France, that there would be work for me to do there for my country and countrymen.

The British Consulate was open, and I felt at home as I walked through the front door. I remember the feel of sea air on my face and the taste of salt in my mouth. I am an islander and the sea always suggests home and peace to me. I had friends in the Consulate, and they told me that the last ship for the United Kingdom would sail in a few hours' time. There was a place on board for me.

To my own surprise I told them that I had decided to remain in France. My friends were not quite as astonished as I by the refusal that had come almost spontaneously from my lips. When they urged me, frantically, even angrily, to reconsider, I am afraid my replies were not very satisfactory.

Here was escape and within less time than he had spent *en route* from Paris, he might be eating a good meal and listening to Scottish voices, and willy nilly, he refused to take ship.

I left the Consulate and walked through the dockside streets. The wind from the sea was kindly and consoling and the white gulls screeched as they wheeled and dipped over the harbour. Thoughts seemed to come into my head as if from some source apart from me. I could not take ship when so many wounded men sought transport. They should have that priority which is the right of the suffering.

The last ship steamed out of Bayonne. I saw it go. Scotland had been so near and now I was cut off from it forever maybe. My heart sank, but surely I was doing the right thing? At that time I was not entirely certain but I had chosen as a Christian minister should choose in duty to his vocation. Of that I *was* certain.

Throughout that day I wandered among the distracted and nerve-torn people, clustered on corners, talking in groups and in cafés, their voices muted by fear of the unknown. Here and there a man or woman would laugh loudly and for a few moments one could sense a feeling of relief, like balm pouring over their anxiety and easing the tense atmosphere. The docks always produced a few happy-go-lucky souls, incapable of fear, jesters who refuse to be intimidated and such men, when we feel that we are dropping down to hell, bring us back again to reality.

Night fell; a summer night when honest men might sit at their front doors and talk to their wives of the day's work, when wives might confide to their husbands little precious things they had done and left undone. It was the sort of night when God recompenses us for the trials we think we have endured. On such a night young people walk together and dream of the homes and families they will build. But the morrow could bring an invading army and I had to decide what to do.

My decision was to escape into Spain and I turned my back

on the harbour, walked through the town, and climbed up into the hills, walking in happy exhaustion along dark winding roads until I came to a tiny Basque village called Cambo les Bains. There I prayed for further guidance. I was sure that it would be given by Him who had promised to guide all those who put their hand in His, through each perplexing path of life.

CHAPTER 3

THE SEAMEN'S MISSION

THE LITTLE village where I rested was in the Basque country and
it seemed on that summer night a perfect haven. I walked along
the main street until I found an hotel, and was shown to a room
by the night porter. Before sleeping I prayed, as I had prayed now
for hours, asking for a sign. I slept well into the morning and
awakened at a late hour.

There was a new Government in Bordeaux which had surrendered to the Germans. The village where I stayed was not
peaceful, and there was no escape for its inhabitants. The traditional threat of the Boche had become an immenser reality. At any
time they expected its outriders to appear on the road.

The spokesman of the Bordeaux Government was Marshal
Pétain. His voice added the last touch of bitter irony to France's
tragedy. The Victor of Verdun, that invincible warrior who had
proclaimed 'They shall not pass' and kept his word at a terrible
price, had capitulated. He now led a Government of refugees, and
a decision to accept defeat was made after acrimonious debate at a
meeting held in a police station. There were men present who
would have died fulfilling the promise Churchill later made—'We
will fight in the streets and on the beaches.' The French knew the
Boche in a way that the British and Americans would never
know him. In the past he had marched into France, and the taste
of defeat lingered in their mouths and they hated it.

Beyond the village backwater, Frenchmen were still fighting;
companies severed from a great army, disorganised but brave, were
hopelessly struggling to keep the enemy from final victory. Ruthlessly the Wehrmacht stamped them out. The battle was soon to

27

be over and all that remained, the government realised, was to acknowledge defeat.

I lingered in the streets of the village that morning and felt a fierce and stubborn fatalism close in on me. History was being made, and the worries of ordinary men are of little account at such times.

After the first broadcast by the Marshal, the news spread rapidly, but so confused were reports, that people kept on the move, still trying to escape. We heard of German soldiers satirically showering refugees with looted foodstuffs and of the owners of marooned limousines being offered petrol, stolen from French units, by cynical Teutonic 'old soldiers.' People had taken flight in despair. They had built homes, had lived to the ritual of hour to hour, day to day, and year to year, jobs and careers; and now they were adrift, not knowing where to rest or where to go.

The new leader of the French people offered something like death. That he, Marshal Pétain, was the spokesman of defeat made their condition more appalling. The Marshal was old and senile and bearing a burden that should have been the responsibility of men half his age. Well-meaning, confused, confronted by complex problems when he was contemplating death, he was simply an old and tired soldier who thought he was saving France when he was sacrificing her. The free French were escaping to Africa and London. The fighting French had begun to rally, but the ordinary people of France, in that miserable hour, were aware only of defeat.

I was standing outside my hotel in Cambo les Bains, a few hours before the Germans marched into the village, feeling I must leave, impelled by a force that was inexplicable. The problem that perplexed me was, which way was I to go. If I went on foot towards the Free France side of the demarcation line, I would most certainly have been overtaken by the enemy. At that moment, two cars drove up and stopped outside the hotel. They both had British plates. There were two occupants in the first car, a French gentleman of Jewish extraction, and an English lady. The occupants of the second were a Russian princess, her son, and a very old lady, the princess's mother. I immediately recognised one of them. We had often met in Paris in social, artistic, and intellectual circles, and we both had mutual friends. While I was still staring at my friend in amazement, I heard him say, 'My God, Donald Caskie. What are you doing here, and the Germans only a few miles away? We're making for the other side of the demarcation line.' 'Then I believe you're the answer to my prayer,' I replied. 'Of course we are,' rejoined the Russian princess from the car behind. 'Come with us. We have room for you.'

Rushing back to the hotel, I paid my bill, ran to my room, grabbed my bag, stuffed my belongings into it, and in a few minutes I was in the company of friends in my hour of need. The cars hastened towards the demarcation lines which separated Vichy France from occupied territory. We were just in time, for a few hours later Cambo les Bains was occupied by the Germans, and the bed that I had slept in the previous night was occupied by a German high-ranking officer. After a long drive we reached Marseilles.

The Mediterranean port was in turmoil. All traffic was uncontrolled and converging on the water front. The streets around the docks were crowded with British soldiers and airmen, the remnants of Dunkirk who had escaped and with incredible ingenuity and bravery made the journey south. Among them were merchant seamen who had been torpedoed in the Atlantic and escaped while on the way to prison camps in Germany. The plight of these men was pitiable. All were hungry, some weak with starvation, others wounded; and their wounds, rudely dressed, were often dirty and gave them intense pain. A number were crippled. For a variety of causes there was not a man to be seen in the crowds who should not have been in bed receiving attention. In groups on the pavement and dockside, they huddled, worn out and totally exhausted. Yet they were held up by a grim spirit of utter determination that drove them on towards survival.

France had surrendered. Public services were at a standstill. France had fallen, and there was no one to help the British soldiers. It was distressing to see them waiting around in their unrelieved misery after the hell they had come through in defence of the common cause.

I wandered around the docks, speaking to them, trying to console the wounded, but feeling helpless before their need. Here indeed were sheep without a shepherd. I prayed for relief for their agony, for some way in which I could bring help to them.

I had said good-bye to my friends who had brought me here and now I had to find somewhere to stay. I knew of a colleague in Marseilles and I went off to see him. He was a French pastor and he found me cheap and good accommodation. My landlady was the widow of a French pastor and she was delighted to have me in her house. She had spent holidays in Scotland and spoke wistfully of the happiness of those days in our lovely warm-hearted country. Strangers are always welcome when they visit Scotland. We are interested in foreign countries, and the viewpoints and customs of foreign peoples, and try to make our guests feel perfectly at home.

I moved into her house and prayed for enlightenment as to my next move. We Highlanders have the gift of second sight which admits us to dimensions of the unseen world which are closed to races other than the Celtic. I had been moved to pray on the road to Bayonne and two weary 'poilus' had placed themselves nobly at my service. I turned my mind to God, praying for a sign and a way to help my countrymen. Several days passed and I was feeling more and more dispirited until one morning when I was at my devotions, an unmistakable call came. Immediately I knew why, when at Bayonne, 'I had essayed to go into Bithynia, and the spirit suffered me not.'

As I knelt in that house in Marseilles all things became clear. The city outside the window was remote. Its noises diminished, and I was secure in the embrace of God. My new vocation came with the clarity of crystal. The words of the Prophet Isaiah sounded in my ears. 'And thine ears shall hear a word behind thee saying: this is the way, walk ye into it; when ye turn to the right hand, and when ye turn to the left.'

In that plainly furnished and unpretentious little room, cut off from my own people and the happy normality of my life as a minister, I was alone in an alien world, but not alone in the infinitely larger world of God. Distinctly a Voice spoke from behind me in an unmistakable tone of urgency.

'Comfort ye, comfort ye my people. . . . Feed the hungry, clothe the naked; bring deliverance to the captives, and the opening of the prison to them that are bound. That is your task. Arise and go.'

Immediately I rose from my knees. Instinctively I looked around the room. I had heard the Voice so clearly that I thought I surely should see someone. Unseen but not unknown, God had shown me that I was not isolated, nor were my comrades, the soldiers on the waterfront.

The little apartment now became as impersonal as a railway waiting-room. The objects in it, the bed with its home-made quilt, the table, chair, and mirror over the dressing-table, became things that had their uses, but made no impression. I had an important job to tackle and I was aflame with its urgency.

I have only one recollection of my walk to the American Consulate. The sun was blinding; I could feel the heat penetrating the soles of my boots; and I knew my destination instinctively. I did not hesitate.

The door was open and I walked up the stairs to the office until I was restrained by a hand laid on my shoulders. I heard an English voice.

'Padre, we've been looking for you."

I turned, and the speaker regarded me intently.

'We need you to help starving soldiers and airmen from Dunkirk,' he continued. 'My name is Dean. I'm the former British Consul from Nice.'

I did not answer for a moment. Insistently, he said, 'Can you do anything to help these chaps, Padre? I feel sure you can.'

I grasped his hand and told him that I had received my instructions. Hurriedly I blurted out my experience of that morning, and of the Voice I had heard.

He was a quiet, serious man. He looked at me with new confidence and at that moment we saw into each other's heart.

'We must go then, Padre, for God has spoken.'

We went out into the sunshine and talked as we went through the streets. The first thing was to find accommodation for the men. We must open a House of Refuge. I decided to call upon the police and ask their aid in my search for a house. Audacity offered the only hope of a permanent solution.

I asked my friend to return to the Consulate and gingerly I approached the police station. Recent events, the atmosphere of distrust and fear, and the Fifth Column which lurked in my mind like a phantom, had made me wary. Despite the confidence I felt in my mission, I knew the task facing the British in France seemed impossible. We must trust in God and hope to make the best of every opportunity given us to save our own afflicted men and work for our country's cause.

They were polite and sympathetic at the police station, but the Gestapo, with its machine-like efficiency, had already issued its instructions. The French officials directed me, reluctantly I felt, to the special branch where I made no apologies for my request for aid. After establishing my identity, I demanded accommodation for stranded British subjects.

The detectives sitting around in the office of the special branch listened carefully. I was not yet aware that these men had received more detailed and peremptory orders, than their colleagues, in the less subtle departments of the Marseilles police force. They too were under surveillance. We were being caught in the web of the functionaries of a police state, something outside our experience; something so remote from the character of French civilisation that to these policemen their world must have become something like a nightmare.

'Padre,' the senior of the men said, 'we know you are the only member of your calling now at liberty in France. We can arrange for you to go home if you wish.'

'There's nothing I'd like better,' I answered, and hurriedly added, 'But that is impossible. I cannot desert my own people in such a dreadful hour of need. I am a minister. How *could* I leave them?'

'No?' Quizzically, he smiled. 'Then you stay here. You have permission and complete liberty to find accommodation and to help British civilians, but give help to one British soldier and you will be interned.'

I rose to leave, bowed and walked towards the door. As I

opened it my inquisitor bent over his desk and another detective followed me. We walked downstairs together.

'Understand, m'sieur, now, alas, we must obey our new masters. Do not reproach us. . . .'

I told him I understood the position in which they found themselves. It was none of their doing.

Quietly he said: 'I advise you to take over the British Seamen's Mission at 46 Rue de Forbin. But let no soldier be found hiding there. And trust no man, m'sieur. You will be watched. I know it. You must beware of paid agents, and of sudden raids.'

He stopped, and caught my arm.

'My best wishes go with you, m'sieur.'

Before I could thank him, he had turned on his heels and raced back upstairs.

I made my way through the evening streets to the Rue de Forbin near the old harbour. The Mission was deserted. When I opened the door one glance was enough to tell me that it had already been looted. I searched around for evidence that would lead me to some of the people who had worked there. There was nothing. I wandered through the empty rooms, working out my problem but the only decision I reached was to be especially discreet. From my old lodgings I fetched my bag and after a rough-and-ready meal made my way back to the British and American Seamen's Mission near the Joliette.

Three sailors stood outside gazing at the building. Here were my first charges. Their pleasure at finding a padre was equalled by mine at finding them.

I invited them inside and we immediately set to work to get the place into order. Before I retired that night I prepared a notice. The seamen helped to pin it over the door.

'Now open to British civilians and seamen ONLY.'

My tongue was in my cheek as I hammered home the nails. I had a job to do for servicemen and already plans were formulating in my mind.

CHAPTER 4

LE VIEUX PORT

I THREW OPEN the doors of the Seamen's Mission with a flourish. Almost immediately travel-weary visitors began to arrive. Their stomachs were empty. Gaunt, sick from exposure, unshaven and ragged, many were almost unconscious on their feet. Marked men, aliens in a country to which they had come as allies a few months earlier, they were now sought by the police who would intern them like animals. To all save I, who existed to serve them in Marseilles, they were an embarrassment. They were starving. They had no documents that were of any use and no ration cards. Not that ration cards in Marseilles in 1940 guaranteed food; but they did ensure a place in food queues. I set to work to welcome the men, making them feel at home in the traditional way of the British Army by putting the able ones to work. We set out to get our house in order as an escape hatch for Allied soldiers, airmen and sailors.

The old harbour district, *' le vieux port,'* close to the Mission was a rather different spiritual bailiwick from the one to which I was accustomed in the Rue Bayard. It was a labyrinth of narrow winding streets where the poor of many nations, human flotsam of the Mediterranean, had settled. The majority of its inhabitants were decent, working folk who struggled to raise large families, and feed and clothe their many children. Lithe, grimy, sun-tanned boys and girls swarmed, racing, skipping and dancing, tumbling on the cobbled lanes and alleys. So congested was the district that it became an ideal place for criminals hiding from the police. There was always a substratum of crooks in the old harbour, dope pedlars, agents for the indescribable brutes whose livelihood is vice, smugglers, dealers in international currency and stolen property, in effect, all the villainy that is part of the traffic of cities.

These criminal elements had increased in Marseilles with the fall of France. From all parts of the republic, especially Paris, they had escaped with the facility of old practitioners of the art of making the quick exit. Now they coagulated in the cafés, garrets and remoter hide-outs of the district.

Rogues were safe enough in the new Vichy France. The government, rigidly directed by the Gestapo, was urged on pain of further invasion, to concentrate the police on rounding up their former allies—much to the distaste of some members of the force. The refugee evil-doers who joined their brethren in Marseilles were left in peace to establish themselves in the old harbour district, and get organised to exploit war irregularities which usually are fruitful for the wicked.

A little more than two years after the mushroom rise of Vichy, the Pétainists and the Nazis had cause to regret this myopic drive upon Allied soldiers. At the end of 1942, when the Wehrmacht marched into the city, both the maquis and the criminals were so snugly organised, so craftily hidden in ' le vieux port ' that heavy armour had to be sent in to root them out. Even then, they escaped, and at no time was it safe for a German soldier to venture into the quarter. At any moment a bullet fired from a window or rooftop might despatch him out of this world. If he was accompanied by friends, so much the better from the viewpoint of the experienced sharp-shooters. There was no safety in numbers for a man in alien uniform in the old harbour. They merely ensured that the soldier did not go alone to death, and the sniper could congratulate himself on a bigger ' bag.'

After nightfall, the maquis and the crooks (one never knew which—different in most ways, they had a common zeal for killing Germans) did their work even more efficiently and at close quarters. Silently and neatly they struck and then laid out the bodies on the pavements where the morning patrol would find them.

The old harbour became the province of the underground army and the scum of the republic. The latter especially resented Teutonic intrusions.

In August 1940 they had not yet organised the Black Market. It was still possible to purchase food if one had money and was prepared to work at the task of hunting it out.

I enlisted foraging parties. Rising at four in the morning, we paraded, in a most unmilitary way, I and about half a dozen of the men. We had contacted nearly every possible source of supply when the time came to postpone the hunt until the next morning. Everything was rationed; but we soon found friends, the best of whom were Greek and Cypriot merchants in the harbour. As soon as they heard that I was a Scottish clergyman, that my companions were servicemen from the U.K., and that we sought food for a houseful of refugee soldiers, mariners and airmen, they went to extraordinary lengths to find us provisions. Without them I could not have fed the men.

With every train from the north the escapers poured into the city and quickly sought out the Mission. Many arrived foot-sore and bleary-eyed from days and nights on the road escaping from Dunkirk. So many crowded into the Rue Forbin and I was kept so busy that invariably some time passed before I questioned new arrivals, asking them how they had known, before they reached the town, that help might be waiting at the Seamen's Mission. Surprised at my ignorance, they told me they had received orders from British Intelligence operating in Northern France. Make for Marseilles, find the Seamen's Mission and ask for Donald Caskie. That was all. It seemed I had been already put on the active list by my countrymen who were engaging the enemy in the north.

My first task with each new arrival was to hide him. The Mission was under constant surveillance and I had to walk cannily. My only armour was the grace of God and my native gumption. Everywhere I went I was being watched and followed. In retrospect, I believe that the Gestapo must have given the Mission a high place among the priorities they listed for the Vichy police. Raids on the house began a few days after I arrived and requisitioned it. The first came at six o'clock in the morning. Fortunately the raiders caught no one in uniform or without papers. But they solemnly warned me again that I must not give aid or hospitality

36

to soldiers or airmen. According to international law, Vichy France had a duty to intern all alien combatants. Wagging an admonitory finger they conveyed an unmistakable impression that they would return.

I could now ' go underground ' with a clear conscience and this I did. I believed that my ministry on behalf of these men was actuated by my sense of duty and was righteous.

We went to work in the house, the men making hiding places with the utmost ingenuity; finding, for example, that the extraordinarily shallow space between floor boards can contain a man, we gently prised boards up all over the building, fitted them so that they would slide out and into position without trouble, and thus created ' holes ' in which our men could shelter.

This precaution was taken quickly, and luckily we managed to utilise floors, spaces behind cupboards and under the roof. Doors, entrances and exits for these hiding places were disguised and smoothly fitted into their places before the police could notice any signs of men.

Regularly at six in the morning they raided us. There was no need for an alarm clock in the British and American Seamen's Mission on the Rue Forbin during those months. The early morning raid became routine.

We stacked garments in the cellar, behind heaps of coal. To keep the bundles clean we wrapped them in old blankets. Men, on arrival, were refitted, if necessary, with clothes, and tucked into tiny compartments until I could furnish non-combatant papers and prepare them for despatch to Spain.

Getting forged papers for the travellers presented problems which the clergyman of a few months ago would have believed impossible to solve. The minister in charge of the Seamen's Mission discovered that put to it, as they say, he found resources that hitherto he had not thought existed. The Americans, ostensibly neutral, were especially helpful. Nothing was too much to ask of their Marseilles Consul who took incredible risks, protected, of course, by his ' neutrality ' coupled with Vichy's elaborate and pompous approach to this, its sole justifying principles.

Under international law, the American Consul was now handling British affairs. He did so with an affectionate enthusiasm and a disregard for 'red tape' that I found wholly admirable. If a British 'civilian' had lost his papers, passport, etc., the American representative provided new ones. He had an apparently inexhaustible supply of identity cards and, most wonderful of all, a magnificently imposing American seal, red, heavily embossed and ornate. This decoration on an identity card reduced the Marseilles detective force to solemn and silent respect. Show them one of these and only the strongest self-discipline restrained them from touching their forelocks.

I should mention, perhaps, that this gentleman, the most kindly of all the generous Americans I have met, was named McFarlane. His name may, I feel, have had an influence upon his attitude to a British outpost run by a man named Caskie and a Highlander.

Identification papers were only part of our problem and it was essential that I should get pocket compasses, materials for disguise, maps that could be copied and, most important of all, guides to lead the men over the Spanish frontier at the most inconspicuous places. The task was doubly difficult to a Scottish minister with little local knowledge.

In the meantime food was becoming even more scarce. The amounts I measured out to my guests were shrinking daily. If something were not done to solve the problem of a quick 'turnover' in the Mission, we would become overcrowded and before long the raiders must catch me unprepared for their arrival. The shortage of food was especially worrying, for men weakened by lack of nourishment would be in no condition to dash to the border —a perilous enterprise at best.

I was racking my brains in my office one afternoon, as close to despair as I ever have been, when from the corridor outside I heard a Cockney voice raised in cheerful song. Alfred, I thought, sounds cock-a-hoop. Corporal Alfred Smith was one of that irrepressible species, the Londoners: the memory of his insouciance in the most depressing situations is quite enough to make me understand the dimensions of the task Hitler set himself when he decided to defeat the Cockney city. Nothing daunted Alf: he was as cheerful as a sparrow and as tough as a hawk. Loudly he bat-

tered upon my door. When I called out, he positively burst into the
room, beaming with joy, exploding glad tidings.

'Padre, Padre, I went out in my nice new suit to look at this
lovely town. And look what I found!'

One at a time, like visiting cards, he placed seven ration cards
on the table before me. Grinning from ear to ear, with his chest
stuck out, he must have been the happiest soldier in the world
that morning, even if he was disguised as a sailor. Obviously he
believed the cards were a gift from above. I was not so sure.

'They would be very welcome, Alf,' I said. 'But where did
you find them? Seven ration cards! The person who dropped
them must have been an hotel-keeper or——'

'But Padre, it means seven less mouths to feed.'

I picked up the cards and read the names upon them. My
gloomy suspicions were justified. The spontaneous delight quickened by Alf's news was ill-founded. These cards were owned by
poor people and only one bore the signature of an adult. The
name was 'Jeanne Tillois (41)' and the woman was a widow. The
other six were obviously her children and Madame Tillois, I knew,
would be very, very unhappy this morning.

Alf was chattering on as happy as the widow must have been
sad.

'There I was, Padre, stepping out like the Brigade of Guards,
not a care in the world, the sun shining, and not a Jerry in sight,
nothing but the birds and the children and lots of French people
and suddenly there they were—lying in the gutter, neat and
comfortable-like. I grabbed them and ran home as fast as I could.'

It was nice to know that Alf felt at home in the Mission and I
hated to deflate his joy.

'I'm awfully sorry, Soldier,' I said.

'What's the trouble, Padre?"

His face had fallen but I knew it would smile again very soon.
He was as resilient as a rubber ball.

'We can't use these, old man.' I pointed to the names, which
he had not read. To him they were just foreign documents.

'They are the property of a widow and her children. I must

39

return them as soon as possible. Our work here would never prosper if we were to take advantage of your find."

Alf smiled, ruefully scratched his head and looked at me.

'Of course we can't, Padre. Now, why couldn't they have been the property of some Vichyite?'

More than an hour passed before I could leave the house to take the cards to their owners. Shortly after that I climbed to the heights of a Marseilles tenement. The door was slowly opened by a small child, opened just enough to show me a little round face with great round eyes staring up. I smiled, the infant opened the door wide and in I walked.

Madame was kneeling by the bedside in the room and her face was wet. Poor soul, she had been weeping, broken, I suppose, by this final misfortune. At the best of times life must have been difficult for her and now she was at her wits' end. A lump came in my throat as I handed over the cards without a word. She clapped her hands and embraced me. She had been praying and weeping at the same time, she said, and now the precious cards had miraculously been returned. She was beside herself with joy, rushing hither and thither around the room, hugging the children and saying:

'A miracle. A miracle.'

Another miracle, which was as welcome to me, emerged from our subsequent conversation. When I had waited for the lady to calm down and told her how I acquired her documents, she questioned me about my presence in Marseilles.

I explained that I was a pastor and now in charge of the British Seamen's Mission in the Rue Forbin. This impressed the good soul even more than my, to her, brilliant talent for finding other people's ration cards and genius for returning them. She insisted on taking me to meet her own pastor, M. Heuzy.

Without waiting for my consent, which would gladly have been given anyway, she put on her coat and hat, admonished ' les enfants ' to be good until the return of ' maman ' and ceremoniously ushered me out. Only M. Heuzy could adequately give thanks to me for the service I had rendered. Her gratitude was poignant and, God knows, the terror in which she found herself in Marseilles 1940 with six children and the prospect of no food, would have struck fear to the heart of the strongest person.

When we arrived at M. Heuzy's home I found myself confronted by a modest-looking gentleman who listened patiently to Madame's pæans of gratitude. Before I could intervene, he turned and thanked me in English that was, in his lips, so quaint and touching that I nearly became as incoherent in my joy as Madame Tillois had been earlier.

'Ah'm verry grateful to you, sir,' said the French pastor, in accents that would not have raised an eyebrow in Sauchiehall Street, Glasgow. 'You would be welcome in this house at any time. You are doubly welcome in these days. The kindness you have done Madame is verry great.'

I told him that the ration books had been found by another Briton, not me. I had only returned them.

He smiled widely.

'Ah, yes. I have heard of your Mission,' he said. 'It is close to the old harbour, is it not? You are a verry busy man. We must talk for a bit. Maybe I can help you, in fact I would be verry glad of an opportunity to do so.'

I had contacted a pocket of resistance—of moral resistance.

M. Heuzy had been French pastor in Glasgow for many years and that accounted for his Caledonian accent. A Glasgow man by adoption, he was a true Christian, a minister whose assessment of the new forces in Germany was detached, balanced and shrewd. 'They are wrong; they produce professional evil-doers.' His friendly eyes held mine and in a few moments we felt we were old friends.

'You have many enemies,' he said.

I had suspected that although I had found friends—one always knows one's friends—there might be enemies. The French pastor spoke with simple candour.

'I also loathe the Nazis.'

I suppose I hesitated and he chuckled, looking me in the eyes.

'I know a lot about your work in the Rue Forbin,' he said clearly, curiously emphasising his accent in the way of Glasgow men when they wish to make their point without ambiguity, without the possibility of confusion or misunderstanding.

'I wish to render you and your people any help that lies within my power.'

Pastor Heuzy was a working minister and he brought me face to face with the moral strength of France. Alf had done good work when he found the ration books of the widow Tillois and her children in the gutter. The widow had led me to a congregation of French Christians. During the next few days their minister and I became close friends and he told me of the patience of his people. Each Sunday they gathered at Christian service and prayed to God to sustain them in difficult days and for guidance in combating the evil that had befallen their country.

Like all congregations they were varied, some accustomed to prosperity, others living carefully on small incomes, paying their way, finding their pleasures with their families and in their homes, strong in their faith in God. Professional men, factory workers, intellectuals, old and young, a diversity of French Christians, they had their humanity in common and the supreme gift of faith in Christianity. Believing in God, they knew that the wicked men who directed the German invasion and conquest of their country would be defeated in God's good time. They prayed and were confident.

Pastor Heuzy and his people became a vital link in the 'escape route' that was in process of being created from France into the free world. Never, never in my life has an honest action brought such a wonderful reward as my return of Alf's treasure trove of documents to the widow. The minister discussed our task with some of the 'elder statesmen' in his congregation and arrangements were made to lodge the overflow of our guests in selected homes where they were carefully and safely hidden. The French Christians were brave people and kindly in the modest way of the truly religious. They gave shelter to our men in their own homes and all they had, not only their own lives but the lives of those they held most dear, were risked apparently without a moment's hesitation.

This hospitality was only part of their work for us. They marshalled their resources to accumulate compasses, maps and other escape materials. Regularly, neat packages of precious goods began to arrive at the Mission. The parcels were delivered unobtrusively and quickly hidden.

One problem remained; we could not find guides and Pastor Heuzy could not help us over that difficulty. The 'underground railway' was perilous and our men were forced to take deadly risks alone.

A couple of nocturnal callers solved my problem.

CHAPTER 5

NOCTURNAL VISITORS

THE SECRET POLICE knew that the Seamen's Mission was becoming a clearing house for British soldiers in flight out of France. As yet they could not prove it. We had not been caught, but the enemy did not despair. Apart from the regular raids, suspicious-looking men hovered about the building throughout the day. By peeping from a window with heavy curtains, I often saw them keeping an eye on the Seamen's Mission from across the street. Fortunately soldiers coming to the Rue Forbin were warned to move in quickly and stealthily under cover of darkness. But we had narrow escapes, some comic, some eerie, all nerve-racking. Our task was to transform the men quickly and efficiently into civilians, and then despatch them out of France. With the help of Mr. McFarlane at the Consulate, documents were acquired without delay and M. Heuzy's congregation was accumulating a nice little stock of equipment for the travellers. But clothes and money presented a nagging difficulty.

Major X was the first official visitor who called on me, after I found myself, willy nilly, on the active list. A tall, fair-haired young man of about twenty-five, he did not so much make an entrance to the Mission as manifest himself in my room. The men were in bed asleep, or impatiently lying awake thinking of home. I was bending over my desk, working under a hooded light when I heard a polite little cough from behind me. Turning my head towards the sound, I saw a tall slim figure immaculately dressed. For a moment I was a little nonplussed by the presence of my nocturnal visitor, for this was the hour when I usually pulled my

44

private notes from their secret repository, and arranged my programme for the next day. However, a hand was held up, a quick
apology uttered, and my momentary anxiety was allayed.

'Please forgive me, Padre,' said my young visitor, 'for disturbing you at this unearthly hour, and for entering your room without
being announced. I hate publicity, and very specially at this time.
The work in which I am presently engaged compels me to be very
cautious. My name is——'

I raised my hand, and halted him peremptorily.

'Don't tell me your name now, please. What is your business?'

A visiting card was held out. I looked at it and saw a familiar
signature.

'Padre,' he began, and in less than a minute gave me a detailed
report of all my activities since I had first arrived in Marseilles.
Quickly, but unemotionally, he gave me a résumé of my ministry
in Paris.

'I'm happy to meet you, Donald Caskie.'

A hand was held out, and I took it.

'The fewer names I know, the better,' I said as I shook his
hand. For I knew that sooner or later, the time would come when
I would be arrested in connection with my work, and questions
would then be asked. 'I'll think of you as Major X. It is a name
which balances theology and science in decent proportions. Now,
how can I help you?' I added.

The Major grinned. 'May I be permitted to sit down?"

I apologised for my lack of hospitality, and nodded towards a
chair.

'I am an Intelligence officer,' he continued. 'I collect and
transmit any and all information that can help at home. Will you
assist?'

'Of course I'll help. But what can I do? I am a padre. And
I'm extremely busy pushing to safety as many as possible of these
good lads who have come to Marseilles.'

'I know exactly what you are doing, Chaplain, but you could
also use your resources to find out certain things I wish to know.
Such information is vital. I'll tell you exactly what we need.'

He approached the desk, smiled at me politely as he took up a pencil and produced a roll of very thin paper. On it he wrote a short list of words, tore off a piece and held it out to me.

'Memorise these words and whenever possible discuss the subjects they suggest to you with the men who arrive from all parts of France. You may glean something that might also bear upon these matters from the civilians you meet.'

I ran my eyes over the page. What he had written was self-explanatory. Before I could speak, he continued: 'Please memorise this material *now*, Chaplain, and then destroy the paper. Forgive me for putting it this way. It is an order.'

'I understand,' I said.

'You may or may not see me again but our representatives will call. They will be pleased to talk to you.'

His smile was slightly mischievous and he moved over to the doorway. With a wave of the hand, half-salute, half-salutation:

'No, don't get up. Thanks for offering your help. Please forgive me for disturbing you at such an hour. Good-night.'

Major X was wrong about his visit disturbing me. Paradoxically, I was heartened, feeling myself part of the large force which was fighting for freedom. I memorised the writing on the scrap of paper, and then I devised my own simple method for deluding the enemy. I began my 'Book of Words' which I wrote in my native tongue. The Gaelic is a most beautiful language, but it is more than that and I was not the first Scot during the war to put it to a practical use.

I was still harried by the problems of feeding and clothing the hungry. Intelligence officers, I suppose, made history. Clergymen are obsessed by souls, but faith solves all problems. Would it, I wondered, bring me hard cash? Money might solve most of my problems.

Money came to me at first very slowly and in small amounts and then a sum arrived which rather confounded me. To be handed money by an apparently casual caller is not an experience with which I am familiar. I needed all the money I could raise. Goods of all kinds were in short supply and illicit traders, I learned, work on the principle that a fair profit consists of all the customer has in his pocket.

One morning a dapper gentleman called to see me. He greeted me in the hallway into the Mission in quiet English:

'Good morning, Padre. I have business with you. May we talk?'

I invited him into the office where he pulled his coat about him and without ado said, 'You need money, I know. I have brought you a little contribution.'

'That is kind of you, sir, but I don't know you.' His hands spread out in a deprecating way.

'It is not my money, Padre. I am a mere messenger. I come from Monte Carlo.'

My visitor was a very charming person, but I had become a very wary clergyman and I did not allow him to leave at that moment.

'I insist, sir, before I accept money, I must know more of *you.*'

The blue eyes glittered in the dark, tanned face. His obvious amusement was slightly irritating. In one short sentence he calmed any remaining fears I had.

I handed him a cup of coffee, and between sips, he recounted his story. Thanks to the intervention and interest of business men whom I had known in Paris and were then in England, money was released to assist me in my work from French branches of British industrial concerns on the Continent. I followed his story and checked it carefully. He mentioned names that were well known to me. Some of them had been most faithful members of our church on the Rue Bayard in Paris, and still are; others were friends of mine, living then on the Riviera, who were supporting me, loyally and liberally, in my work at the Seamen's Mission in Marseilles—Lady Robinson, Col. T. and Major E.S. Lady Robinson has passed away, but the other two, true-blue Britishers, are back again in their homes, by the blue waters of the Mediterranean, and have rendered me great service in the rebuilding of our Scots Church on the Rue Bayard.

For several reasons, I will not mention the French branches of British industrial concerns who assisted me, but I must say that they contributed generously to the winning of the war. Another name that my friend mentioned was that of the late Sir Benjamin Guinness—of stout fame—who came to see me some weeks after the visit of the man from Monte Carlo. He said that any time we needed money for the Great Cause, I was to write to ' So-and-So,' and a given address, and that financial help would be forthcoming. Sir Benjamin also gave me the wording of the code letter I should write to this person when we needed cash. We did not need to tap this resource, but it was good to know that the money was there, if we needed it.

After my visitor from the Riviera had mentioned all these names of good friends in France and in the homeland, I felt more confident. I was greatly encouraged by the thought that my friends at home in the United Kingdom had instructed their representatives in France to ' thaw out ' some of their ' frozen assets ' to help my work in Marseilles.

' And now, Padre,' said my friend, ' I must take leave of you, as I have further business in Marseilles. I shall be leaving for England immediately, but shall return very soon. Van Gogh has been very helpful.' Van Gogh, I knew to be Arles, where the famous Dutch painter Vincent Van Gogh lived for a time. When he mentioned this name, I felt still more confident that he was altogether *bona fide,* for between Arles and England there was a thriving clandestine air service. ' You must excuse me now, I must be away.' As he left he paused and said:

' Ah, our little contribution to your Mission, Monsieur le Pasteur. With it comes our good wishes and prayers.' He placed an envelope upon the ragged pad of blotting paper on my desk. ' And now, au revoir.'

We shook hands, he bowed and, refusing to permit me to show him out, left. I poured another cup of coffee and sat back in my chair. These visitors were welcome, but interviews with them were exhausting. The previous night I had worked late with a squad of tired and harassed men; I had got up from bed about 5 a.m. My eyes drifted to the thick envelope. I picked it up, burst the seal of plain red wax and turned it upside down. A fold of bank notes fell out; there was no message. Mechanically I counted the money. It was £5,000 exactly, in French currency.

This vast sum, a fortune indeed, intimidated me and I dashed around to my friend Heuzy and placed it in his safe keeping, luckily, as it turned out, because that very week we were raided and the house was searched more thoroughly than usual.

Other donations of cash trickled into the Mission from good folk, retired Englishmen and women living abroad and French resistance friends who had heard of our work.

Sister Brigid, a member of an Irish order of Roman Catholic Sisters, brought clothes. How she learned of me, I do not know, but mendicant orders, I suppose, must hear gossip. Just how this healthily happy lady and her colleagues interpreted the neutrality of the Irish Republic is also a mystery that I would not care to try to elucidate. They were Christians and knowing that my men needed clothes, they naturally played their part. One cold morning she came bustling into the Mission followed by a retinue of soft-voiced Gaels, their eyes sparkling from sable headdresses. Sister Brigid did most of the talking.

'Ah, now, Chaplain, I hear you are doing grand work for the poor sailors in this part of the world, God help the boys.'

I admitted I was doing what I could.

'I am a chaplain, a Scotsman, Sister, God knows these lads need more than a wee bit of help.'

'Ah, there, Chaplain, of course they do, poor boys. Would some old clothes help them? Sure everywhere we go they give us cast-offs and very fine some of them are—just the thing, maybe, that would help your boys.'

A fraternity of Christian men and women exists throughout history and throughout the ephemeral place we call the world. I was deeply moved, not for the first time, by the Christian spirit, nor for the last. But I was suspicious.

'Sister, where do you come from?'

One of the richest chuckles I ever have heard bubbled from the well-worn habit.

'Sure I come from Dublin, dear dirty Dublin. Wouldn't you know it and you a chaplain?'

There was a demure chorus of giggles, and I knew who I was dealing with—real Christians. All they cared about was helping people. In the department of other-help, which is quite distinct from self-help as all Christians know, Sister Brigid and her ladies joined the organisation.

They brought us clothes, and when they could they brought food. They also brought Captain Janek.

The lads who passed through my Mission on the Rue Forbin were not all of the Protestant Faith and, I suppose, with the eagerness that is an essential part of my work as a Minister of God, I was irked by the thought that the Roman Catholics should not receive what they felt were the complete consolations of their religious faith. They wished to confess their sins to a priest. Captain Janek was a priest, a Polish padre in hiding with other Polish officers and men in the city. He heard their confessions; and he gave them Holy Communion. One morning a message came by word of mouth to me that he had gone to England with his party to carry on the good fight I was trying to fight in Marseilles. His country was in chains, and mine was free. It was good to know that the men he served would find a base from which they could fight, and he could serve them.

When Janek left, a Franciscan priest took over his work. Ecclesiastically, the Mission in the Rue de Forbin presented no more than the many problems that are presented by any cross-section of any Christian community.

The refitting problem was perennial until we found our own rather sleazy Bond Street, and then we purchased most of our necessary clothing in the Arab quarter of Marseilles, a bazaar of a place where everything traded was secondhand. After nightfall I would escort my protégés in groups of five or six to the merchants where they were fitted with suits, shirts, socks and shoes. The journeys to these peculiar tailors were trying. We would keep to the darker streets, and walk close to the walls. I soon found doorways into which we would dive and linger while one man reconnoitred before the platoon moved on its away again. The return to the Mission was more leisurely. The men were usually hilarious in a very subdued manner; their new appearance in job-lot 'civvies' invariably struck them as extremely funny.

We would go back by different routes, each man carrying a

bundle of the rags of khaki or air force blue in which he had arrived at the Mission. It was necessary to dump these. The Arabs naturally feared to have them in their premises even to burn, and so long as a thread of service cloth was in the Mission it imperilled each one of us, and the whole organisation. It was the evidence the police needed. We made our way to the walls of the old harbour and dropped the outmoded wardrobes into the blue Mediterranean.

There were times, however, when we had to work too quickly to organise the refitting department as efficiently as we would have wished. We were part of a very big machine which was uninterested in our immediate problems, and an element of comedy entered our work when this happened. Two young Irish doctors were the occasion of one of these interludes. They never, I am sure, discovered the facts of their cases.

They were officers in the R.A.M.C. and they arrived late one Saturday night. They had escaped from a Paris prison attired as nurses. Now they were in tattered army denim overalls. Tired to the point of blindness, famished for lack of food, their clothes rancid on their backs, they staggered into the Mission. They could not be placed in lodgings until their rags might be changed for garb less conspicuous in the Vichy dispensation, and at such times I billeted men in my own room. It was imperative that their presence be kept secret from the guests in other parts of the house until they were more discreetly attired. If we had been raided and caught, only I could be accused of harbouring soldiers. None but I knew these men were in the house.

I gave the doctors hot drinks and they dropped off to sleep like clocks stopping. They were beyond their powers of ordinary converse. After wrapping the poor lads in blankets I settled on my couch which I had set up behind a screen.

When I wakened they were still asleep and I left them to take my morning service. After leading my congregation in prayer I looked in on the new boys and found Dr. Malachy awake.

'You had a visitor, Padre,' he informed me. 'He left something on the desk. He seemed a taciturn sort of bloke.'

The something was a message, a sign that only I could read. It instructed me to have a party ready for despatch that night.

'He was a friend of mine,' I told the doctor, 'and now we must waken John and have some breakfast. You need it.'

I turned away from them to go to the kitchen for warm food, and the problem he and John were violently presented itself to me. They were doctors; they were priority passengers. They must leave that night and I must reclothe them before nightfall. I wandered along the corridor to the kitchen, prepared their food and took it to the office. All the time I brooded on the problem of the clothing shortage. While the lads settled happily to the first decent meal they had eaten in days, I scrounged around the house assembling 'civvy' clothes. By mid-afternoon, a complete 'new' outfit was available for each man—complete except for one suit of underwear. Up to a point I had been fortunate. Malachy could put aside the stinking rags which covered his tired body but what about John? I felt miserable thinking of John going home without underwear.

I sat in the room and looked at those boys whose life-long task was to heal bodies. They talked cheerfully. They felt at home with me. I found that it was imperative to my peace of mind that John's undershirt and shorts should be clean. He must be refitted completely. I scrutinised Dr. John intently. He was about the same size as the padre. I fear I deceived him.

'Excuse me, gentlemen,' I said suddenly. 'I must do just a wee bit of bookwork.'

Rudely leaving my guests, without more ado I darted behind the screen and bending over the desk, wriggling in a most undignified way in his efforts to make no noise, the Rev. Donald Caskie did the first 'quick-change act' of his career.

A few hours later, the doctors were on their way through the Pyrenees, bathed, fed and in clean clothes. They were ready for the journey home, and I was content. Around midnight I sallied out, took their uniforms to the harbour-side and triumphantly dropped them in the sea. Next morning, they were in Spain and I, philosophically, I hope, washed my other, now my only suit of underwear. I learned that a small wardrobe is an unconscionable time a-drying.

I lived constantly on the alert; my senses attuned to danger; my racial faculty of second sight sharpened until I could read men's characters in a frightening way. The times were out of joint and, I suppose, mind and body adapted themselves. I lived by faith and prayer, and an overwhelming affection for those of my countrymen who came to the door of the Mission demanding aid. I was aware that the stream of refugee Britons would not lessen and I was ready at all times to receive them. I lived in the moment, and found satisfaction in succouring the needy. Once, indeed, time seemed to flicker, I was projected a few hours ahead of the moments in which I lived and I saw them before they came to me.

After retiring to bed one night, I lay for some time in a state of blessed ease, my mind drifting in reveries. Whether I fell sound asleep or dozed I cannot say, but suddenly I was fully conscious and wide awake. My body was heavy with perspiration, my pyjamas soaking wet. I felt cold. It was one o'clock by my watch and I was intensely aware that I must be up and preparing for a party of men who were on their way to the Mission. I had seen them in a vision; gaunt, tattered, starving, they held out their hands, stretching their arms to the fullest extent, appealing for help. The dreadful silence of their request moved me beyond words and my eyes filled with tears. I knew they were coming to us and immediately made ready for their arrival.

I rose, hurriedly dressed and went to the kitchen. At the rough catering which satisfied our guests I had become expert, and in a very little time a meal for twenty was spread on the table. All was ready when I heard the measured knocking on the street door that told me of a new intake. Outside in the darkness there were a score of men who had escaped from a German camp in the north. They were the men I had seen. I recognised them; they had been with me earlier in the evening. As if it had all been organised like a church social I welcomed each with a hurried word as one by one, they filed into the hallway. When all were assembled I led them to the kitchen. The table laid out, the food ready, the atmosphere of an arranged thing surprised them, but they were less amazed than their host.

One man managed to overcome his astonishment.

'Padre,' he said, hesitating, stumbling. 'Were you expecting company?'

They looked at me, waiting by the table laid before them. I faltered before I answered, but the words came to me.

'Yes. I expected you.'

'Us?'

'Yes, you. The company I expected is present. Come on now, sit down and eat. You must be famished.'

They ate ravenously, clearing the table in less time than it took me to prepare it. As each man relaxed he sat back in his chair and turned his eyes towards me.

I felt compelled to tell them of my experience; but for it the meal would not have been prepared and laid out. They listened with the rapt concentration of men who had endured much and suddenly found comfort. The kitchen with its twenty-one inhabitants was quiet. We were tired, they after their forced march, I still bemused by my experience.

A Cameron Highlander from Fort William rose to his feet.

'Ach, sir,' he observed. 'We Highlanders are most uncanny.'

CHAPTER 6

LINES OF DEPARTURE

EVEN A life of constant peril, I was beginning to find, eventually becomes routine. After the first gruelling initiation, one becomes canny by instinct; living like a hare in the heather one's ear becomes attuned to suspicious noises, and one's eyes seek out essential truth which is revealed by the tiniest, carelessly displayed detail. We ordinary people, for the most part, lived civilised lives, our days dedicated to service of a Higher Good. We work and earn to purchase the material needs of those who are dependent upon us, to keep the fulfilment of our happiness, the homes in which we find the joy of loving those dear to us, secure. But how quickly we men adapt ourselves to an existence of war which is something alien to all we strive to achieve, indeed all we experience in peace. Twice in little more than forty years men like us have been plunged into the barbarism of warfare. Somehow God has protected us, and humanity has survived.

When in the busy days at the Seamen's Mission in the Rue Forbin, I cast my mind back to the equally busy days in the different setting of the church in the Rue Bayard, the present seemed unreal. The two lives of Donald Caskie had only the great and blessed fact of God, and the discipline of prayer to give them shape.

Men came and departed, but their departures were not quick enough to satisfy me. Guides remained the perennial problem. And it was never solved to my general satisfaction. Brave men risked their lives organising escape routes, and they were intensely aware at all times that many of the professional guides whom they used were dubiously faithful to their trust.

It was my friend Captain G of the Seaforth Highlanders who

accelerated the development of the line of departure from the Seamen's Mission. At three o'clock one morning he called and gave his host a disturbing moment.

I had fallen into a deep sleep. Quick, sharp knocks on the door jerked me into consciousness. Captain G was the last soldier I expected to see in the Rue Forbin. Some time previously he had passed through the house after escaping from the Germans at St. Valery. I believed he was safe, at least in Spain, and I hoped he was in England.

But this officer had a taste for in-fighting, as boxers say, and he had an interesting story to tell.

On the road to the frontier it had occurred to him that he might be more useful here in Vichy France as a British agent working with escaping servicemen. His French was perfect and he knew the country. He decided to become an escape expert and place his craft at the service of soldiers 'on the run.' His minute knowledge of Southern France helped him to make contact with the British secret service which charged him with the building of an organisation, beginning in the north with M. Wood, the English-speaking Mayor of Calais and to include John McLean, a Highlander who had lived for fifteen years in Arles; in effect to span all France.

Rapidly these intrepid men built up their 'underground railway' establishing it link by link, until now it reached the Marseilles area. Men could be brought to the south even more quickly and much more safely than in the past. What Captain G needed now was the last link, an organisation to take his comrades on across the Pyrenees.

Would I help him? There was only one answer to his question. He then told me that he had employed a number of guides and the following night I must be prepared for company.

They arrived without a hitch and Pierre accompanied them. I did not like Pierre: not to put too fine a distinction upon it, I considered him a rascal.

Pierre's fees for his professional services ranged from £25 to £30 a party. I have no moral scruple about a man asking a fair price for his services. The road through the Pyrenees is not easy on foot, at best of times. When France was ruled from Vichy, which meant the Gestapo always overseeing the police and taking their own precautions—neutrality was a convenient fiction for the Germans as long as it lasted. Pierre was entitled to his hire, but his demeanour made his attitude plain. If something went wrong with our finances and his pay was delayed he would not hesitate to recoup himself by claiming rewards from the Germans. He had the savage, introspective loyalty to his own material security that is characteristic of the congenital traitor. In an emergency, I asked myself, could we trust this sort of man? Working out the answer to the question did not take prescience of a high order. I was unhappy about Pierre. The men passing through the Mission in the Rue Forbin were not mere units to me. I had schooled myself and been schooled by my parents and teachers to see each man I met as a soul and a body, a being who loved and was loved, precious to his Maker and to those with whom he lived. Although they passed rapidly through that extraordinary church-cum-manse on the fringe of the criminal district of Marseilles, I knew them all. Each I loved like a brother. Pierre's single principle of twenty-five to thirty pieces of paper for the preservation of ' a batch' of souls was repugnant. I pitied the poor fellow, but he was set in his ways, and I feared him on behalf of the men I could see only as a congregation of the faithful.

For the first few months of Captain G's new order all went smoothly. In those days one learned quickly and did not make mistakes twice. I hated employing Pierre, a feeling complicated by the thought that I might be doing him an injustice, but there was nothing else for it. I was nagged by a conviction that, sooner or later, he would reveal himself in his true colours and we would not like them.

I made one mistake arising out of eager pleasure at sending the men home, and the naïvety of inexperience. A few hours before the guide was due to arrive I announced that we were sending a group into Spain that night. After the party left I felt happy about them, anticipating their joy on arriving home, and I found the house clamorous with men asking me when their turn would come to follow their comrades. I hated telling them that I could give no definite news. I was a mere cog in a machine and must await the development of arrangements made elsewhere.

After that I became canny when arranging my procedure. When instructions came, I had already mentally listed the men for despatch with the next party. But I gave no hint of my intentions to anyone. Two a.m. was starting time. At midnight I wakened the travellers and whispered orders to them. They acted quickly and on their stockinged feet followed me to my room.

Each man had been told to bring his complete gear. When the party assembled I thoroughly searched them. It was essential that if captured no one should be carrying evidence that might incriminate not only the Mission, but the whole escape route. We had become the H.Q. in the South of France. I then made each pledge himself that if he were captured he would not involve the Mission in any way no matter what happened. It was a harsh instruction, I knew, but I lived with the knowledge that hundreds of men making for Marseilles, from all over France and even Germany, would be mortally endangered if the enemy discovered us. The Rue Forbin was a springboard to freedom for those men, their sole hope, and must be preserved as long as possible.

These preliminaries preceded a briefing of each man. I explained the escape route in detail, and gave them knowledge that I considered a sanction on the guides.

Before the tap on the door that announced the coming of the guide, we offered a short prayer. A quick reconnaissance followed and then, if the coast was clear, I bade them Godspeed. The system functioned perfectly during those months and twenty to twenty-five men each week were sent to freedom.

The escape route was now functioning with the smoothness of a well-oiled machine. Men were moving out to the U.K., and I made arrangements that ensured their next-of-kin learning as soon as possible that they were alive.

When a man arrived at the Rue Forbin he was thoroughly interrogated. I took (1) his name, (2) the name of his next-of-kin, (3) his regiment and (4) his address in the homeland. I entered these details in a ledger, and when times became very perilous I placed this book in the hands of a heroic French friend, Henri Thebault, who guarded it carefully. To-day it is one of the most precious possessions in my manse.

After entering this information in the register I questioned the new arrival, gleaning as much information as I could about the activities and movements of the enemy in German-occupied France. All this material was passed on to my frequent nocturnal callers from the Secret Service. The men's names were sent through Lisbon to the U.K. In that first year I despatched some hundreds of pounds worth of telegrams to Britain by way of the Church of Scotland offices at 121 George Street, Edinburgh.

For months this telegram service and the 'underground railway' worked with routine efficiency. And then the Germans tightened the frontier guard, became more fiercely on the alert and we were endangered.

Harassed by the new conditions, cut off as we were, I was beginning to despair when one of the most remarkable men I have ever met came into my world.

He was young, cool and humorous in demeanour but almost surgically business-like in conversation. He gave me the password which proved he worked for the organisation. I gave nothing away. I listened carefully and said nothing.

'You are wise to be careful, Padre,' he said in a jesting way. His accent was vaguely foreign although his English was almost pure 'B.B.C.'

'You must check on *me*. I know your work so I can trust *you*.'

I said nothing.

'The name,' he continued, a good-humoured smile playing about his face, 'is Pat, the rank, Lieutenant-Commander, Royal Navy. I bring orders from Whitehall.'

Lieutenant-Commander Patrick O'Leary, R.N., was one of the bravest men I have ever known. Gay and fearless, his sense of humour led him to enjoy situations so nerve-racking they might have stopped the stoutest heart. But he was strict, kindly and protective to those under his command: fighting the enemy he was entirely ruthless. He knew the methods of the Gestapo and hated

59

them. A cultivated man, one felt he had set everything aside, the things he enjoyed and loved in peacetime, all that makes life worth living, until victory was won. But Pat was not languishing for peace. The O'Leary's of County Cork are a fighting family, worthy descendants of great Irish warriors. They can have no complaints about the underground warrior who bore their name in the Southern French sector of World War II.

At first sight Pat seemed slight and frail. I think the clothes he wore contributed to this impression. He was not a tall man. He moved with uncommon grace and agility. As he moved one noticed the powerful shoulders, the brawny thrust of the legs, the steady, almost machine-like grasp of the muscular hands on objects such as coffee cups, pencils, documents. Pat, I suspect, could have strangled a strong man as easily as I might stick a stamp. His efficiency was awe-inspiring. All arrangements for his operations were worked out to the minutest degree. Each man knew his task thoroughly. Pat was a disciplinarian, steel under a jaunty manner, a perfect expression, I thought, of the training of the Royal Navy. Pat, drolly and unmistakably, knew all. He was a man born with all the characteristics of a romantic hero. He spoke English with near-perfection, a touch of accent colouring his vowel sounds. The lilt in his voice giving an odd inflection at times which might have been a curiously musical expression of a brogue. He would talk with fine appreciation and understanding of music and the arts, but there was a hint of the bizarre in the cut of his jacket, the design of the tie, its knot and the tilt of the hat. In the most grave conversations a sudden grin would hint at civilised scepticism, which is not to say that Pat was anything but an idealist. He merely distrusted human motives when they were expressed too solemnly; self-righteousness he found ridiculous; a man did a job and he should not dramatise it. He never showed anger. In Marseilles and beyond he was a tower of strength to us. He was 'Pat,' at first an agent, and later a leader.

Among the papers that Pat showed me were letters signed by Very Important People.

'I am working,' he said after I returned his credentials, 'with Captain G. Tell me about your work, Padre.'

I told him and he listened carefully, the quick smile coming when I mentioned my Book of Words.

'Alas, Padre,' with a deep chuckle, 'I do not understand the Gaelic.'

I gave Pat the most thorough report I made to any visitor in those days. He had listened carefully and said:

'I am a traveller, Padre, and shall leave town to-morrow. The branch is expanding rapidly, so rapidly that it is difficult to keep track of everyone—but do not worry.'

Captain G's organisation was increasingly efficient. Like Pat, the gallant Seaforth was a man born to this hazardous trade. They both enjoyed danger without losing sight of their objective, which was to avoid peril as much as possible, and win victories. Victory to them meant soldiers deposited in places where they could be used to fight, and information sent to an H.Q. where it would be used to harass the Nazis. They were single-minded officers and the pleasure they got from their task derived from the knowledge that it was important if the values they held dearest were to survive.

Agents were coming more frequently to the Rue de Forbin and among them was a young man named Bruce Dowding with whom I struck up a very close friendship. Bruce's brother was a minister of the Presbyterian Church in Australia. This boy and I had common things to discuss. He was a Christian with the out-spoken frankness that is part of the Australian national character. He had supreme faith in our cause, and was quite fearless. Bruce Dowding's friendship was a consolation to me when I was ex-hausted by my dual tasks of minister and agent. His visits were of necessity fleeting. I passed on the necessary information I had gleaned, and Bruce passed on my orders.

On the Christian front I had my own agents. These were old friends of my Paris days, links with the place where I had set down roots, the Church on the Rue Bayard, and the intense happiness in the social life of my people at the manse on the Rue Piccini. Henri Thebault was one of the closest of these friends. In 1938 I had married him and his wife Antoinette at the Scots Kirk.

Henri had been transferred to Marseilles by the great firm of merchants he represented. His aid became indispensable to the

Mission. His company had branches in all foreign countries and he knew his colleagues abroad. Through them he could disseminate information for me. On my 'Operation Telegraph' by which I sent to Edinburgh the lists of missing soldiers whom I had found —or who had found me—Henri played a vital role. He was adviser and reconnaissance officer, testing out post office departments and police for me. He was an ally and friend. More than once he risked his life on my behalf, and my war debts to him only began at the Rue de Forbin. At a moment when my family might have despaired of my survival, Henri brought them news that I was alive.

I needed friends during that winter of 1940-41. The mistral blowing down on Marseilles from the valley of the Rhone was scorchingly cold. On its breast it bore snow and sleet. The Old Harbour froze under a white pall that thickened as the weeks passed. In this frozen cocoon our men might have sickened and died so near, but yet so far from release. An epidemic of influenza, for example, would have crippled the link which I controlled on the escape route. Men would have piled up on us but for the stealthy friends who brought us aid. They included natives of Marseilles, some of them of British ancestry, and seamen, especially Americans who, with the impulsive warm-heartedness characteristic of their race, silently and rapidly got on with the job of relieving need at the Mission.

It was named the British and American Seamen's Mission, and because of this it was well known to American as well as British seamen. My friend McFarlane the Consul gave us helpful publicity among visiting U.S. merchant marine officers and men.

They would drift into the house in the evenings in twos and threes and fours, after their ships had docked, and they had worked their shifts. Casually they would ask for a cup of coffee and place a large can or bag of the ' makings '—enough to last a large family for a month—on the table in the dining-room.

' D'ya think you can make five cups of coffee from that, Chaplain? We'd be deeply obliged.'

The total request always amounted to the exact number of men

in the company, plus one cup for the padre. They'd sip my
'makings' judiciously, nod their approval and perhaps comment.

'Could do with a little more sugar, Chaplain. Nice though.
French? Eh? I never met a Scottie who could make coffee except
you, and you're a French Scottie.'

I would reach for the sugar bowl and they'd halt me, winking
largely.

'Oh, no, Parson. We're slimming. But your coffee is good. All
it needs is something to be added—a new flavour, maybe. Must
see what we can do to bring you out. You sure are a promising
coffee-maker.'

They would sit talking, joining in the general conversation for
an hour or more, and then respectfully bid us adieu.

When I awakened next morning, sacks of potatoes, rice, boxes
of sardines, cases of tinned food, bags of sugar, boxes of butter,
even bags of coal—something from such a list (dependent on ship's
stores)—would be heaped inside the building. They did not wait
to be thanked, and I never met any of those kind American lads
again. But I shall not forget them. To-day in every part of the
U.K., in Ireland and in the Commonwealth there are happy,
healthy men working and living with their families who might
have starved and frozen but for the generosity of those American
mariners. In the post-war reveries of the minister who was in
charge of the Mission in the Rue Forbin, they play a warm part
and they are remembered in my prayers.

Every good work, I wryly was finding, brings its own reward.
In Marseilles was a community of old people who were British
citizens; cut off from their kin, unharried, because of their age by
Vichy or the Gestapo, they were left in 1940 without help of any
kind. Whenever I had a moment to spare I would escape from
the Mission and visit these old folks. It was on one such visit that
I met Henri Thebault again and I nearly broke my neck in achiev-
ing that meeting. I had taken the bus and I saw from the window,
Henri Thebault. I shot up from my seat, dashed to the platform,
and yelled at his vanishing figure. He did not answer and I
launched myself into space. Clerical gentlemen are not trained for
space travel. Luckily the good Lord took over that snowy day

and I landed on the least vulnerable portion of my anatomy. Some minutes later, I overtook Henri, who was striding along intent on reaching a business appointment.

I walked with him and arranged a further meeting, after I told him my task for the day.

'By the way,' he casually mentioned as we parted, 'do you know Mr. Arckless, Donald? He is truly British but has never lived in his own country. Born here, I believe, but keeps in touch. He's a member of our church. He'd be glad to see you.'

Mr. Arckless's house was on my way, and I cut my time carefully to ensure that I could visit him. The old gentleman, dapper in his French suit, benign in his French whiskers, was as British as steak and kidney pie. He gave me a warm welcome and, instead of asking my help, begged me to let him help us. Mr. Arckless, I discovered very quickly, was a retired coal merchant. He knew every coal merchant, big, medium and small, in Marseilles. They were difficult times and coal was scarce. The poor of Marseilles were huddled in their houses and scraped for fuel. But from that day forward we at the Rue Forbin received a share of the fuel that was available. Wood and coke were added so that we might eke out our days above survival level at least.

The men were now moving in and out of the Mission at a better rate. We might have relaxed our vigilance but for Pat and the omnipresent threat of the Gestapo which hung over the city. Captain G's representative on the road, as he called himself, appeared when he was needed, skilfully clearing up problems and good-humouredly dissolving gloom. Obviously he was a man who was enjoying life with all the hilarity of a Glasgow apprentice *en route* to Rothesay on Fair Friday. We were aware now that the Mission was under almost incessant surveillance.

We suspected we were being watched from windows on the Rue de Forbin and I was warned that on various points of the route to the Mission men had been noticed lurking at certain times. Accordingly I worked out time-tables which, while dominating our movements, were arbitrarily changed from day to day. My arrivals and departures must have seemed very haphazard to the chiels taking surreptitious notes behind window sashes and in cafés.

Our work intensified as the organisation strengthened. Pat's orders were pressing the necessity of transporting larger parties of prisoners. They fitted exactly Pat's personal inclinations. The Mission was not the only point upon the escape route where surveillance had been increased. We had information that more and more Gestapo agents had been drafted into the area. Our contacts reported that frontier guards had been trebled and the route was becoming more hazardous. O'Leary flung himself into the task of mass escapes with characteristic enthusiasm. The day-to-day work increased in efficiency and rapidity of movement. Pat elaborated schemes which were characteristic of the artist in him. One of these was to seize a ship and transport something like a battalion at one ' go '; another was to hold up the Marseilles-Perpignan train for a sort of excursion dash into ' sunny Spain.'

He knew that London would not back him on such projects. An ' outrageous ' incident might provoke further trouble with Vichy and might bring the Boche marching into the city. But it contributed to Pat's gaiety to work out such schemes.

I should add that I am not by any means sure that he would have failed on those seemingly grandiose undertakings. Pat's audacity paid high dividends when the stake was his life. He took chances with a cool head. He had established himself in many places as a citizen with roots, and the number of personalities that were Pat O'Leary, but accepted as different characters by shrewd, hard-headed and sometimes vicious men, were and still remain a mystery to me.

CHAPTER 7

DEATH AND A TRAITOR

I HAD AN appointment to meet one of our agents, known as 'Le Patron,' outside Jean's Café on the waterfront near the old harbour of Marseilles. As I walked from the Mission in the early afternoon I felt winter waning and spring stirring. The sun was high in a clear sky and a shabby little sparrow hopped in the gutter; I stopped to watch it. I thought of Edinburgh, the city of my student days. On such a day, Auld Reekie, loveliest of towns, is at its best. The lads and lassies from the university come running helter-skelter down the braes, scarves flying behind them, books uncertainly held under their arms. They would be laughing. Another two weeks and March would come to Edinburgh, and I allowed myself to feel nostalgic. There would be holidays soon. A lad might go home to Islay and be, for a few days, the centre of a happy home. This, however, was Marseilles and I had an appointment with an agent. I sighed. To-morrow night would be an ' operation ' to the frontier.

I was soon outside the café and I pulled my wintry coat around me as I sat down. The day was chilly. A man sitting near to me, came to my table.

'Coffee, Donald? Nice and hot.'

I nodded and smiled. My mind was still in pleasanter places.

The waiter brought coffee and my companion sipped his drink slowly. I remember the red wine in his big glass; I watched it tilt and find its level again as he put it down on the cold marble-topped little table for two.

'Cigarette?' The paper packet came at me. I took one and lit it, feeling curiously withdrawn from my friend and ruefully

66

thought, 'This must be a spring mood. Come alive,' I urged myself, 'forget it.'

'Donald, nine men will arrive to-morrow night. Be ready for them at 22 hours. They are coming from the north by train.'

'By train?'

'Yes, by train. They have nice clean papers. It's all sweetly laid on. They have an escort too.'

'An escort? Who?'

'Fellow named Cole. An N.C.O. with a good mob. Old Scotland Yard man.'

'How old is he?' I asked. 'And he's an N.C.O. on active service? Sounds fishy to me.'

'Oh, he's not decrepit. He bailed out of the police to join up.'

'How do you know?'

'Look, Donald, you're becoming very suspicious in your old age. Cheer up, this isn't a funeral service.'

He went on to explain the whole operation.

'All right. All right. But this job seems to be too well-organised for my liking. What's this man going to do after he delivers the men? Go out with them?'

'He's too useful for that, old man. He's for the north again and more visitors for you. Now, don't worry, Donald!'

We parted then and we were not to meet again. A few months later the Gestapo shot him.

I had a premonition about 'Cole.' It was strengthened by his demeanour when we met. In meetings with agents, one was always aware that there was, of necessity, a missing dimension to their personalities, something withdrawn. We did not talk about our private lives. The less we knew of each other, the less could be extracted, under torture, by the experts of the Gestapo. But we were not on our guard against each other. The suppressed dimension had become an instinct. Cole lacked that instinct and to me he was insincere. The missing dimension worried him. He was always on the defensive, the difficulties of the journey he had made were as nothing, he proclaimed. That was untrue, as I well know. Lounging into the Mission at the appointed time, he delivered the nine men and then went off to contact one of our agents. I prayed that the lad would not talk too much to him and I wondered if I were doing him an injustice.

I could not free my mind of these suspicions. Cole was, I felt, a half-man and when the unresolved half was defined he might be a traitor. I spoke to Pat and told him of my fears, but he would not listen. He laughed and, very reasonably, said:

'My dear Padre, we have no evidence that the chap is a risk. On the contrary his first job was an extremely profitable one. Nine blokes at one " go " is pretty good you'll admit. I know he's not the sort of chap one takes to—he's a bit of a loud-mouth. But he doesn't shoot anything that matters out of the cavity."

I could not disagree with Pat. He was right and just. He took the line that, as a good officer, he was compelled to take. The man did his duty. But I was still unhappy.

In retrospect I believe that my Celtic gift was the source of my uneasiness. It enabled me to ' see through ' Cole. Essentially, ' the second sight ' is a spiritual faculty. Highlanders of my generation, those who went before us, and to a great extent the present generation, live simple lives, close to God and nature. We are a strictly God-fearing people. We find our intellectual pleasures in social gatherings with our own people. Our vision remains fresh, undistorted by channels of mass entertainment. We live in the open more than most of the other inhabitants of the British islands. All men are a mixture of good and bad. A wicked man has an existence, secreted among his other lives, that is evil and egotistical. In this way I sought to analyse the conflict I sensed in Cole. The evil he did pushed itself through the surface of his disguise, betrayed itself in small indefinable things, and I felt it. But there was nothing I could do. As Pat said, the man seemed honest enough. I pushed my worries into the background of my life and plunged into work, trying to make the good soldiers happy during their stay at the Rue Forbin and bringing help and the solace of religion to the men in the internment camps.

Suffering, adventure, bravery were part of one's day-to-day experience in the Rue Forbin and in the prisons. One reached that state of mind where nothing was astonishing.

My nagging suspicions of Cole, and the possible infiltration of the organisation by a traitor still worried me. I was feeling very despondent but one evening my heart was lifted by a very simple gift from God.

About nine o'clock I was reading for my next service, feeling the contentment that comes after a busy day when a young pilot, highly qualified as an R.A.F. officer, arrived at the Mission.

I interviewed him and gathered that he must be given high priority as an escapee. He was worth his weight in gold to his service. But his clothes were in rags and so filthy he might have been sleeping in sewers since his escape from a plane shot down by anti-aircraft fire. I told the lad to plunge himself in a hot bath; as I walked the floors frantically puzzling about his departure I could hear him splashing about, enjoying his new luxury. My problem was clothes. Two men were going out in that next morning and I had spent the previous day working on their 'case.' He could join them, but he must have clothes and I had none in the house. In daylight he could not have travelled a mile in the rags which were burning in the dining-room fireplace. I could not go to the Arabs; no appointment had been made and to take, as it were, suit-luck with them was too dangerous. My guest was tall and lanky. I am short and uncommonly broad-shouldered. I could think of nothing and so I turned the matter over to God. 'Dear God,' I prayed, 'You think this one out for me. Please. I'm beaten.'

I dropped on to my knees and prayed intently, pouring out my heart to Him. I was interrupted, in a most irritating way, by a loud knock at the door. I jumped impatiently to my feet and heard a female voice coming upstairs with one of the lads in attendance.

I opened the door.

'Good-day, Madam Hamel. Are you in trouble? A visit so early.'

'No, no, Monsieur le Pasteur. I have been thinking of you all night and I have come to see you.'

She carried a large flat cardboard box, tied with string. Dropping it on my table she continued:

'I had a feeling that you need clothes for some poor Tommee

69

so I brought these. Please forgive me for disturbing you, Monsieur le Pasteur. It is very foolish.'

'Foolish. My dear lady, you are an angel, sent by the good God Himself. You are a direct answer to prayer. Please take a seat. Coffee?'

Madam Hamel was one of Pastor Heuzy's parishioners. The dear soul was ecstatic.

'Ah, you do need clothes. I knew it, Monsieur le Pasteur. I knew it. But I must go now.'

She grasped my hand and bade me good-bye.

I approached the box as fearfully as if it had contained dynamite. A gift from God must not be taken lightly. Its contents took my breath away. The suit and overcoat were beautifully cut. Madam Hamel's husband was a rich Marseilles business man. Her eldest son was something of a dandy. The shoes were hand-made, the shirt and tie of silk and the underwear new. All that was missing was a hat.

Allan, the R.A.F. boy, walked in on me at that moment, a towel wrapped around his naked waist.

'Hello there, Padre. Just about choked the old pipes I fear. I feel a ton lighter and want to go to bed. I am beastly tired.'

I turned to him.

'Try this lot on first.'

The boy scrambled into the clothes and then stood contemplating himself in a rather short mirror in my corner.

'By George, Padre. I've never been as well dressed in all my life. They won't know me when I get home, I'm such a toff. Must say, your service in these parts is pretty good. I'll recommend you to all my friends.'

I gazed at him happily marvelling.

'I am so sorry, Allan,' I said, 'I cannot supply you with a hat. We're all out of them and our outfitter did not send one for you.'

'Oh,' he said, 'don't worry about that, Padre. I wouldn't have used it if he had sent one. I've never worn a civvy hat in my life.'

Quietly I packed Allan off to bed and, on his behalf and my own, thanked the One, ever above all, who protects us in His own infinitely loving and omniscient way. Early the next morning

Allan and two new friends whom he had just met set off for the frontier.

All went well that time but a few days later when I had sent another party off to the frontier a traitor struck and the ring closed in, shooting down the helpless before it reached those of us who could fight back.

CHAPTER 8

DARK SPRINGTIME

THE GUIDE returned to the Mission ten days after the hapless party had departed for Spain. He told me that one boy had been shot and was dead. One other soldier, he said, had been severely wounded. The remainder of the party were in prison. Only his experience of the district, and his realisation that the game was up, had saved him.

'Monsieur le Pasteur,' said the guide, 'all would have been well if we had followed your original plan. But I received your letter at Perpignan; and we walked right into a trap.'

'My letter? What are you talking about? I sent no letter,' I said. 'I rarely write letters these days. If I have an important message, I usually send it by word of mouth. You *must* know that. Experience has taught me to be cautious.'

The man insisted, and he was telling the truth. A letter ostensibly sent by me from the Mission had altered the route he was following. He had destroyed it, according to orders, but it was a fact. It was now evident that there was a traitor among us, conversant with our activities, and our escape route.

My mind focused on Cole. Obviously we had been tricked by someone inside the organisation, someone who was aware of the original route and had diverted our guide and his party to a point where the frontier guards would be certain to intercept them. He knew where and when the enemy patrolled. He must have known the inn at Perpignan where the party would halt; he must have been well-briefed in the methods of both sides.

That evening, I reported my suspicions to another agent and he pointed out that Cole had an alibi. On the night of the captured party's departure the ex-Scotland Yard man was *en route* for Paris and Lille. He could not possibly have known of our operation.

'One of your chaps must have talked out of turn, Padre, before leaving. It takes only a word in the wrong place and you know what happens.'

'That is extremely unlikely and you know it. Cole might easily have discovered the operation before he left Marseilles. If he is, as I suspect, a Gestapo agent, a traitor, *he would make it his business to find out if there were parties ready for escape.*'

'Look, Padre, Cole is bringing down a party of R.A.F. men, every one of them worth his weight in gold. It was not him, I know.'

I accepted the agent's judgment. I was a padre, after all, and not the man to fight a superior's orders, but I never have ceased to regret that I was persuaded against my will. Had we relied on my instinct, we would have been spared the most shameful betrayal of our experience.

A few days later, I had a meeting with friends of our escape route in a little village on the outskirts of a forest, thirty miles or so from Marseilles, not far from Auban. After the interview was over, I wanted a breath of the country, and I walked in the nearby forest. As I strolled aimlessly among the trees, I felt that I was being followed. Turning quickly round, I caught sight of Cole, watching me from behind a clump of bushes. I continued my walk as if nothing had happened, but now I was perfectly sure that my instinct or second sight had not led me astray. At that moment, from information I had received from our agents, Cole was supposed to be at Roubaix near Lille in the north of France. Yet here he was following me through this forest, like a detective on the track of his quarry.

Signs began to multiply that we were betrayed. It soon became apparent that I was not alone in my suspicions of the efficient agent who moved so freely between the north and the south. Other members of the organisation became edgy and harassed. The weather changed as spring came, and I moved freely as ever but under increased surveillance. In April I was taken to Vichy headquarters for interrogation. Complaints had been received that I was 'an agitator against the State.' I was warned in a friendly but firm way that I was in danger. That night I told the men in the house that I was suspected of being 'an undesirable alien.' They, God bless them, thought it a marvellous joke. When a padre establishes himself with servicemen, he can do no wrong. The thought that even the enemy might suspect me of being anything other than their chaplain struck the lads as funny. The padre saw their point of view. Their affection was one of the consolations that kept him going. But his sense of humour failed to see the joke.

I lost many friends in the dark springtime of 1941. It ended in a blood-bath. Only a handful survives of the brave band who lived in peril, their lives dedicated to their Faith, their God and their countries.

The forged letter which brought death in the Pyrenees was quickly followed by two more betrayals. First Captain G was arrested and taken to the Reich, and Pat became the officer in total command. Then our top contacts inside Spain were arrested and imprisoned. One of our men brought the bad news to me from the Pyrenees. I had not spoken to him of my suspicions of Cole.

'It's treachery,' he told me. 'It must be. I have been told you are uneasy. Tell me, Donald, whom do you suspect?'

I hesitated to answer. I had been told so often, and God knows with truth, that I was 'an unworldly minister,' and that I had no proof that my fears of Cole were justified. Yet I felt from the beginning that the man was not to be trusted. He was, as we say in Scotland, 'aye speirin''—trying the work information from me. The tales he told of his resource and daring were supported by the dozen or so escapes from the north he had organised but why, I asked myself, tell them? There was not an agent in the organisation who had not risked his life often. It was their war work. They did not talk of it.

The man from the Pyrenees watched me.

'I think,' he said bluntly, 'it is No. 11.'

No. 11 was Cole.

'Our wonderful No. 11,' he continued, 'spends too much

money on his girl friends for my liking, and they are all aiding
and abetting him in his double dealing.'

'Then there's only one thing you can do,' I told him. 'Report
your suspicions to Pat. I don't know what to think. Pat will have
a special investigation made into No. 11 and his off-duty behaviour
and contacts. We cannot go on like this, suspecting each other.
We'll never prosper without mutual trust.'

The report was made to Pat, but he would not listen. For
reasons which were entirely sound, Cole had his full confidence
and we were moved only by our suspicions. Cole had been
thoroughly checked again and again. Escaped soldiers sang his
praises; so did the Secret Service. London had complete confidence
in him and Pat was not alone in his faith in the man's loyalty. I
was silenced because I had been constantly harried by the knowledge that it is evil to speak ill of anyone without absolute proof,
and we who suspected had no proof, only our instinct and that
might be at fault. Confirmation of Cole's baseness was to come
from an unsuspected source.

A few days after the report was made to Pat, security officers
circled the Mission and entered to search the house. Every man in
the place was interrogated and his papers thoroughly checked; the
walls, floor and cupboards were tapped in search of hiding places.
Nothing was uncovered that compromised us, and it was with a
feeling of relief that I showed the officers to the door. But before
they departed, one drew me aside. One of the many French detectives who had shown goodwill to me, his sympathies were with
the Allies.

'I want to ask you a question about Monsieur ——', he said,
using the name Cole had chosen as his alias. 'I know you have
met him several times.'

Immediately I went on the defensive.

'I have met the man, but I know nothing of him.'

'Has he a wife and children in England?'

'Why do you ask?'

'Because, mon cher Pasteur, he is very much too friendly with
a certain pretty little Parisienne, and she is in league with the

Gestapo. And I am friendly with a certain Scottish pastor which is my reason for asking questions.

'You will understand, M. le Pasteur,' he went on, 'that to trust such a man is to invite disaster. In your case, my dear friend, the danger is very, very great.'

He took my hand and shook it warmly, bowed and departed.

The heart sank in me. This was confirmation of our suspicions with a vengeance. It might mean the end of all our good work. Already the organisation, without G and the Spanish agents, had been weakened. Pat and his lieutenants were working at full stretch. Time was needed to replace the gaps made in our ranks. Cole could ruin everything—if he had not already done so.

After dark, I slipped out of the Mission and, by a devious route, made my way to Pat and placed my report before him. He acted promptly.

Cole was due in Marseilles two days later, bringing down airmen from Belgium. As soon as he arrived, he was invited to a room and there confronted by Pat and three other agents, Dowding, Prassinos and Duprez. Pat immediately challenged him, throwing the accusations clearly and unambiguously in his face.

To my knowledge, O'Leary had decided to kill him that night. Pat and his lieutenants were certain that the case against Cole was complete. His movements in certain areas coincided with betrayals or were close enough to make it likely that he had been more than a possible traitor. All other members of the organisation had been checked. Only Cole remained ambiguous. The friendly man from Vichy Headquarters had put his finger on the suspect—Cole, he revealed in his oblique way, was the Gestapo agent. O'Leary decided to strangle him.

Heatedly he denied his guilt. Pat, losing patience with his self-righteous indignation, beat him into a condition of stupidity. But still he asserted he was innocent. True, he admitted friendship with a girl in Paris; but when he heard she was consorting with Germans he refused to meet her again. He demanded an investigation at the Northern Headquarters of the resistance. He demanded an apology. By this time O'Leary was again undecided and was reluctant to kill the man.

He agreed to ask Paris for a report. He ordered Cole to proceed to Madrid, pending its arrival. England, he reasoned, could be radioed, and Cole arrested by our agents in Spain and smuggled home by plane. There the matter could be finally and justly decided.

That night Cole was despatched through the Pyrenees with the R.A.F. men and the wretched creature led them into a Nazi trap. Afterwards he fled north and joined the Gestapo. We did not see him again in Marseilles.

The news of his final treachery reached us on the day we heard from Paris that their investigation of his mistress proved beyond all doubt that he was an enemy agent, a professional betrayer of his country and countrymen. Now it was clear that we were all in the gravest danger. Pat contacted me without delay and gave orders to burn all papers in the Mission that might incriminate me. All activities which might place me in any danger whatsoever were to be discontinued. I must take cover and function only in my vocation as a chaplain to the men in the Mission. He and his three chief lieutenants would leave immediately to warn all other agents in the organisation. Alas, it was too late.

Cole's report had been thorough. The four British agents walked into separate gangs which were lying in wait upon their routes. Only O'Leary escaped to carry on the battle and later in the war to endure torture most horrible. He became, as a prisoner, a centre of hope and bravery in a concentration camp.

Pat's escape was due to the heroism of a schoolgirl who cycled for many miles through a long night to intercept him before he moved on the final stage of his journey. He went into hiding. The great enemy round-up continued, with him as the prize object of the search. Over 100 of our more than 150 agents were arrested and within a few days thirty of these were shot out of hand. The rest, including housewives and nuns who were moved by charity for the hunted men they had helped, and young French members of the resistance, were sent to gas chambers in Germany from which there was no escape.

The tale of Cole's treachery does not end with the deaths and imprisonment of these heroic men and women. More than 500 of his own countrymen, British soldiers, were secreted along the escape route. They too were captured. Some were shot as spies because they were wearing civilian clothes.

Among all these heroes let me tell the story of one man who lives in my memory. He was a priest, another clergyman who was not of my Church, but of the same Christian Faith, the Abbé Carpentier, a gentle little curé whose parish was in Abbeville.

Like so many French priests and nuns the Abbé thought little of his life when he balanced it against the liberty of La France, which is more than a country to its sons and daughters. It is a personality, mother, father and ancestor, the great reality which surrounds their humble lives.

Like the Apostle Paul, who sat at the feet of Gamaliel, the Abbé was a craftsman. Paul was a tent-maker; the Abbé in the days of peace had made himself a fine printer. Whenever he was free of the manifold duties that are part of a clergyman's day he retired to his little printing press. He became an artist in that gracious craft. He printed and bound rare copies of the classics. He became an expert in photogravure. And then the Boche came and the Abbé ached for his youth so that he, priest as he was, might take up arms for France. But France was defeated, and he was old so he carried on with the holy tasks of the day and waited for God to call him. His prayers were answered. The resistance was organised and, before long, the Abbé received an appeal from its leaders.

They had learned of his craftsmanship, they said, and they appealed to him to use it for the cause. Would he set up a press for the printing of passports, ration cards and identity cards for soldiers of the British ally who were trying to make their way across France so that they might rejoin their army and prepare for the Liberation? It was the moment for which the good little man had waited. He set up his press, and through the night hours worked with patient, meticulous skill carrying out the orders of the patriots. The papers he prepared were perfect down to the smallest detail, and were prized by the man in control. But, like his senior officers, the modest little man was known to Judas.

There is something classical in the history of Christianity in his ending.

Cole brought him three exhausted R.A.F. men one night. The priest was alone in his study when they arrived, and he gave them food. The agent told him that his guests were part of the air-crew of a British bomber that had been shot down over the coast. For ten days the lads had been on the run. Would the Abbé help them? They wished to reach Marseilles and there strike out for Spain, but they needed papers issued by the occupied zone of France. The three men produced proof of their identity. One even showed burn marks he had received when the plane went on fire. The Abbé was convinced.

He took them to his secret workroom and assembled his press. After testing it, he brought out fresh cards and was about to start on the first job when he heard a noise behind him and turned. Three revolvers were pointed at him. He was in the hands of the Gestapo. He made only one comment, and we know what it was; turning to Cole sorrowfully, he said:

'In all my life I have met many Englishmen. You are the first I have known who would sell his country, for gold, I suppose. I am not likely, thank God, in the short time I have to live, to meet another.'

The Abbé was taken to Paris, secretly tried and sentenced to be beheaded. Like many of his countrymen he met friends in prison among the gaolers, and it is to one of these, who smuggled out a letter telling the story of his arrest, that we are indebted for the facts I have set down. The priest-printer was taken out early one morning and modestly as he lived, he died.

From that moment, the Resistance took oath to seek Cole out and kill him. He became a marked man and fled to Berlin to work there for his German masters. Before he died as squalidly as he lived, they were driven from France.

Meanwhile in Marseilles I carried out Pat's orders. Most of the men in the house were scattered through friendly homes in the city, quickly, surreptitiously and, I suspect, under the blind eyes of certain friendly Vichyites. I burned all incriminating papers apart from my books of names which Henri Thebault took from me and planted, as I later discovered, at the bottom of a disused well. I bade farewell to my friends. I was never to see Pastor Heuzy again. He too was arrested.

They silenced his pulpit and the Gestapo shot him. So his life ended, but not his witness, which is remembered by his congregation and told to their children in Marseilles.

They came for me one morning about 8 a.m. I was taken from the Rue de Forbin in a Black Maria.

I was angry as the Black Maria left the door. There is something unreal about being arrested by the police; one is irrationally indignant. Most of my life I had been a law-abiding man; the laws I could not abide in 1941 were wicked and stupid. I thought of the men left in the Mission and became more angry. What was going to become of them now? Not one of the poor lads knew his way about the town. The journey was very short, but by the time we arrived at Fort St. Nicholas, which lies at the mouth of the old harbour, I was in no mood to be trifled with.

I was given a seat before a long table in the Salle de Tribunal in the old fort, and the Vichy Military Tribunal studied me. I bowed before taking my seat. The Juge d'Instruction leaned forward, rested his elbows on the table, pursed his lips, and said:

'You are English?'

'No, sir,' I answered sharply, 'I am Scottish.'

The lips flickered. My reply seemed to amuse the old gentleman. He sounded more friendly as he proceeded.

'We have arrested you,' he announced, 'because we have proof that you are agitating against the interests of unoccupied France. You are in touch with the British Intelligence Service. You are helping soldiers, airmen and civilians to escape from France across the Spanish frontier. You are spreading pro-British propaganda among our own people, and urging them to join the Resistance.'

He paused and looked at me.

'I have no counsel,' I replied. 'This, I take it, is a Court of Law.'

He shrugged and held up his hands.

'May I take it that I must act as my own counsel? If so I should like to hear the witnesses for the prosecution.'

He smiled and went into a long vague dissertation on my work in Marseilles; nothing definite emerged from the story. No witnesses were presented and again I challenged the court on that point. The interrogation began, and I answered questions without incriminating myself. The farce irritated me more and more. It was much later that I realised that the court was more embarrassed by it than I.

They were in a difficult position. They must have known of my liaison with Edinburgh. I was a clergyman. My work in Marseilles was known to all the priests in the city. The nuns were among my friends and helpers and, God knows, they must have been aware that Sister Brigid's neutrality was of a distinctly Hibernian type. She was a neutral, enthusiastically against Hitlerism. If I were handed over to the Gestapo and shot, Vichy would be in extremely hot water. Every Christian church and convent in Marseilles had contact with foreign countries, foreign missions, and any violence to me could not have been kept secret. The French, God bless them, had not acquired the diabolic skill of the Germans in covering their misdeeds, nor did they aspire to it.

For five hours the interrogation continued. I became very hungry. Hunger reminded me of the poor lads in the Rue de Forbin. What would they do for dinner? My anger became insupportable and for a moment the quiet hum of the court was upset.

'I have told you,' I snapped, 'that I am a Scot and you say that I am an enemy of France. My record in France proves that accusation is nonsense. The history of our two countries shows it to be demonstrable rubbish.

'I love France next to my own country, which is France's ally now as ever.'

Then the balloon went up. The court was in an uproar when I shouted across the table:

'When our troops liberate France from its present undignified position, with the help of honest Frenchmen who are, thank the good God, by far the greatest number of Frenchmen, you will discover again how much we love this land.'

The Juge d'Instruction remained cool and withdrawn. With a

smile he watched me, and then thumped on the table. The court came to order.

'Will you explain to us, Monsieur le Pasteur, how it is that many of the men who have been arrested on the frontier had passed through the British Seamen's Mission?'

'Sir,' I answered, 'those men had identity papers which were checked by members of the Sûreté Nationale, experienced security officers who expressed themselves satisfied that they were in order. I am a pastor. Can I be expected to detect something that professional police officers have missed in their systematic investigations?'

I was becoming very tired. The events of the past weeks had placed an agonising burden upon all of us. Comrades whom I had loved might be dying as this trial proceeded. Hope was draining out of me. The court withdrew and I waited. About an hour passed and then they filed in again.

'We find the prisoner guilty.'

The judge paused, and I watched him assemble his papers.

'You are sentenced to two years' imprisonment. But '—I wondered what was coming next—'your sentence will be *avec sursis.*'

'Pardon me, sir,' I said, 'what does that mean?'

'It means,' he replied dryly, 'that you will be temporarily released—put on probation. You will close the British Seamen's Mission within ten days. You will leave Marseilles and go to another place. I suggest Grenoble. And I warn you that if you are caught again, engaged on any clandestine activity whatsoever, you will be arrested and thrown into gaol without further trial. You are, I repeat, sentenced to two years' imprisonment and are released on probation.'

They escorted me back to the Rue Forbin, with great courtesy, in the Black Maria. I found a house full of disgruntled men who came to life when I entered the front door. I could hear them spreading the word through the house, and from all parts they ran to meet me. The poor lads thought that I would never return to them. Already, I was told, they thought I had been shot.

We had a celebration dinner that night. Not even the news that the Mission must be closed in ten days worried them. It was a pleasant dinner, but my thoughts were elsewhere. Where would

I go now to carry on the work which I had pledged myself to do nearly a year ago when France was falling?

A few days after my trial at the Fort St. Nicholas, a young Englishman arrived at the Mission. 'Padre,' he said, 'we know all about your trial, and condemnation, and we feel sure that your life will, from now on, be in danger. A plane will take off from an airfield near Arles in a day or two, and I have been commissioned to offer you an air flight to England.' 'Thank you,' I said, 'it's most kind of you, but I feel that wherever I go from here, I must continue my war work. I have been called to this work, and I feel confident that all will be well with me.'

CHAPTER 9

SECOND STOP GRENOBLE

THE HOUSE had quietened into the silence which a marauding mouse can shatter, and to me the future seemed as empty, as enigmatic, as the dark noiseless night beyond the Mission walls. I lit a cigarette, tried to read but could not settle to my book. Restlessly I wandered through the rooms of the Mission and then I lay down in my room and tried to sleep. But my mind would not rest. It careered over immediate problems. More than sixty men were still at various addresses in Marseilles, soldiers and airmen whom I had vowed to succour. Only ten days remained to me. If they were left here they would be defenceless. I was exhausted physically. What more could I do? Soon my thoughts were pursuing each other in circles until I reached a fruitless stage of worry but, before oblivion came, I stilled my soul with a prayer for the dead and fleeing comrades whose plight was the true cause of my agony. It is not easy for a man to live when those he has served with are in danger, and he is in comparative safety. It is a sorrowful experience to see the good work of many men who have risked their lives brought to nothing by a traitor.

The bright sunshine of the early summer morning instilled courage in me. I heard the birds singing outside my window and I prayed for help and contemplated the problem that faced me. The men must be cleared out of the city without delay. The stores in the Mission must be placed in the hands of Christians who would put them to good use.

The days that followed were happy. I found golden loyalty among my friends in the southern port. Guides seemed to spring from nowhere, men who had already escaped death only because their professional services were occasionally rather than regularly employed by us. My French comrades were embittered by our betrayal. My contacts among the Christians spread the news of the difficulties at the Mission and the battered remains of the escape route were inspired to heroic action. I suspect that during those ten days the Sûreté winked, knowing that my work in Marseilles was ending. They were content to be rid of me. As I have recorded, I had friends in the police, French Christians who did their duty to Vichy and were ashamed of it.

I visited the men in their hiding places and I made arrangements with guides to escort parties through the mountains as soon as the frontier hysteria quietened and the guards slackened their attention. We had little time for farewells, but the old routines were maintained. I briefed each man on the hazards of the journey that faced him; counselled each to give absolutely no information to the enemy if captured; and prayed that they would find a way home to work and fight for our country.

The Quaker Mission in Marseilles solved the problem of liquidating the material resources of the Seamen's Mission. Donald Lowrie, an American who was attached to this centre of Christian endeavour, had helped me enormously with food and francs for my work. A fellow student at New College, Edinburgh, Donald Stevenson, was another of the Quaker officials. I gave all that was of value in the house on the Rue Forbin to these good people when my work was completed and the next day I took train for Avignon which, I thought, was far enough from Marseilles to satisfy the Sûreté that I would be immobilised there, and near enough to the city to enable me to establish communications and continue my work.

The journey was long and tediously uneventful. The French train service had not been improved by war conditions. On arrival at the City of the Popes I was bedraggled. I hoped that the Pontiffs found more hospitality there than the twentieth-century padre who made his way to a police station to report his presence. I must go in the morning, I was told, to Central Headquarters. My case would then be considered.

I found a hotel and tumbled into bed in a room I cannot

remember. Next morning I made my way to the Sûreté where polite and deferential officials received me. They were kind but slightly embarrassed. Perfunctorily they scanned my papers, which were in order. I became aware that they knew all about me and I was still an 'undesirable alien.'

'Alas, M. le Pasteur, you cannot remain in this city.'

'But why not?' I asked, hopelessly. 'My papers are in order. I complied with the Marseilles Sûreté's instructions and left the town. You will appreciate, gentlemen, that I am a clergyman and I cannot continue to wander over France. Much as I love your country, I need some place where I can live.'

The inspector smiled with sincere regret and spread out his hands.

'Please forgive us, M. le Pasteur, and let us hope that sometime we in Avignon will atone for our apparent lack of hospitality. But,' his voice became intensely serious, 'we have had orders. Avignon is not far enough from the city where you have been found guilty and sentenced. You understand.'

'I understand, my friend,' I answered. 'But where am I to go?'

The inspector smiled very broadly and I began to like him more than I had done until that moment.

'I suggest Grenoble, Monsieur, a congenial city I assure you, with a fine university. You are a pasteur, a man of learning. You will be at home there, I assure you. There you will find compatriots in need of you and your colleagues in scholarship.'

He arose from the desk upon which my papers lay. Very smartly his assistants followed his example. The inspector offered me his right hand and I shook it.

'You will escort M. le Pasteur to his hotel,' he instructed, 'give him the courtesy due to him, and see he suffers no inconvenience before his departure.'

He bowed gravely, shrugged impatiently, threw out his arms in the traditional gesture of Gallic irritation.

'Forgive us, M. le Pasteur,' he muttered, and with a quick turn on his heel left us.

The subordinates stood looking at me. I held out my right

hand to one of them and they relaxed. They were good lads, doing a duty as distasteful to them as it was to their superior officer. As we walked out on the broad boulevards to the hotel I felt happily elated. Avignon could not offer the Scottish outcast hospitality, but it revealed friendship.

I settled into the train with a parcel of food, fell asleep and wakened from time to time as we steamed through the night. The carriage was dimly lit and crowded with uneasily slumbering figures. Bending towards the light I took out my scriptures, and lost myself in the story of the Master and His disciples until sleep came again. After many halts and intervals we pulled into Grenoble. I walked from the station to face a new phase in my adventures, wondering what awaited me there.

In the Sûreté in the University City I found the police as agreeable as their colleagues in Avignon and more accommodating. My papers were scrutinised and I was directed to the university where I might find counsel and assistance. There I was sent to the Hôtel de l'Europe where I settled down to my first war-time night in the city I came to love next to Edinburgh and Paris.

There was a place for my vocation in Grenoble. I had arrived in the Gaullist country. It is a source of some amusement that I was sent to such a place by the police. What motivated certain officials in the Vichy Sûreté in sending me there? For Grenoble was the capital of the intellectual world of the Resistance. The most popular and brilliant student at the university was Pierre, nephew of Charles de Gaulle, and his uncle had no better soldier. The surrounding country was alive with maquis. Planes were landing by night in nearby valleys, escapes were being made into Switzerland, information was flooding out of France and here the young heroes of the maquis were preparing for battle.

There was great need for a British Protestant pastor in Grenoble. The city had become a refuge for aged British citizens who were eking out their meagre existence on miserable allowances. Tired, sick, hungry, bereft of spiritual guidance, they dragged out their days. I realised as my first day winged away that I would not be unemployed in Grenoble. There was a job here for me, I thought, but I was modest in my estimate of the possibilities. There were many tasks waiting for my hands.

I spent nearly two years in Grenoble; they are among the happiest years of my mission as a clergyman. At the university I was greeted with warm kindliness and generosity and met old acquaintances and friends of my friends at Edinburgh University. From medieval times European universities have been linked by travelling scholars; professors, lecturers and dons keep in touch with colleagues they have met abroad; war divides these men. They yearn for peace so that they may interchange knowledge with scholars in other countries. They think wistfully of the days when they may spend their 'sabbaticals' in the colleges of their choice and when they can invite professors from abroad to instruct their students. Fortunately for me, Grenoble decided almost as soon as I contacted the Senate that a visiting Professor of English was required as an attachment to the Faculty.

To a man, the Senate was Gaullist. Many had taught at Edinburgh University. A few professors were neutral; they were old and tired, with memories of 1914-18. It would be foolish to condemn them self-righteously. Like the sad old Marshal, they had been valiant in youth and middle-age; the wickedness of the new world in which they lived defeated them. Had they felt strong enough to choose they would have chosen to support their old ally, but they believed the cause hopeless and had capitulated in their hearts. They were a minority. The university hummed with democratic discussion and the senators and students knew just what democracy meant.

I settled in to the Hôtel de l'Europe to prepare my lectures and found in English and Scottish literature a source of relief from more exhausting duties. We Highlanders are natural born bookmen. I always think with pleasure of Barrie's Highland ghilly in *Mary Rose* who, discovered reading Sophocles by a visiting British officer, was congratulated on his ability to read Latin. 'It is good of you to say so, sir,' he answered, 'but in these parts we call it Greek.' Of course, the ghilly became a minister as the play developed.

The students came from all parts of France, and among them

were youths from Luxembourg, these latter even more enthusiastically pro-Allied than their comrades. I made friends with them without delay, having discovered during my life in Marseilles the perfect drink to loosen men's tongues and keep them contented. I made them tea. I pride myself on brewing tea, not perfect tea—that is something I hope to achieve in my old age—but tea that one can roll on the palate and savour. They enjoyed my tea. It melted the ice between us, so much so that one lad shouted from the throng:

'Teach us to make English tea, M. le Pasteur.'

'I'll teach you to make Scottish tea, my lad,' I answered. 'The sort of tea we make in Bowmore, Islay, where I come from.'

I had to tell them about Islay before we settled to the practical task, and then, with kettle and teapot, the former bubbling on its fixed perch, the latter under escort, I inducted them into the ceremony of tea-brewing. Carefully I measured out the exact, as I then thought, amount of leaves. They watched solemnly while I heated the pot, added the carefully balanced spoonfuls of tea, let it brew, then dexterously poured.

'Tea, gentlemen, is an acquired taste. You may add, if you are a beginner, sugar, but I warn you, it is not advisable. Cultivate a palate, my dear friends. You will not regret it.'

They drank. We discussed the nature of tea and its wonderful properties. My tea-making classes began that night. They became hilarious interludes in the sessions in which I lived again my boyhood, prowling through Cheapside with Falstaff, through the Western Highlands with Allan Breck and David Balfour, listing with Baillie Nicol Jarvie in Glasgow for 'thae Hielan' diels.' We became friends.

My work as a clergyman with the British in the city was more difficult, but it was infinitely rewarding. Old and infirm, tired and friendless, they needed someone to write letters for them to the authorities in Geneva, explaining their hardships and asking for material assistance. Some died without the benefits of the Church, some indeed of starvation, for their doles were small, prices were rising and, in the past, they had learned nothing of how to buy in the market place and spend their money so that they might get value for it. They hung on to life grimly, sometimes it slipped from them, and their friendless corpses were buried almost anonymously.

In the morning queues began to gather outside my room at the Hôtel de l'Europe and, at first, I was a little perturbed by them. I did not wish to become a conspicuous person; already the Resistance had contacted me. But I was aware that the authorities were pleased by my work as chaplain to the aged. As it piled up they assumed that it kept me out of mischief. My heart lightened and I plunged into the work, finding ready helpers among the younger British ladies in forced residence. The lot of the old and often infirm was made easier, but tragedy still lurked where we could not find it in time. Sometimes too late it came to my hotel room. One Monday morning, for example, I opened the door and noticed, about third in the queue, a tall, pleasant-faced, emaciated French curé, a Catholic priest. Hastily I apologised to my other guests and drew him into my room.

'M. le Curé,' I asked, 'you wish to see me? Can I help you?'

He sat down, wiped dust and sweat from his face, and told me his story. He was parish priest in a village farther south, a small community of shop-keepers who served the local peasantry. Soon after the German invasion of France an old lady, *une Anglaise,* he said, had arrived and taken a room in the local inn. She had no servants. She did her own meagre shopping and he called upon her. A gentle old soul, she welcomed him and apologised because she had no tea to offer.

'I am not of your religion, Father,' she said, 'I am Scottish and a member of the Scottish Church, but I am most happy to meet you and grateful for your visit.'

They became friends and Père Raoul visited her on his normal round of parochial visits, once triumphantly bringing her a few ounces of tea he had managed to scrape up somewhere.

'You understand, M. Caskie. It was nothing. We do not drink tea.'

She was delighted with the gift and insisted he share it with her, which he did. The weeks passed until a few days before his visit to me he was interrupted in the confessional by a frantic woman of the village. The English lady was dying. Would the Curé come to her? Raoul rushed out of the church to his friend, but she was dead when he arrived. In Grenoble he had heard there was a Scottish priest of her religion. Would I bury madame? Would I officiate at her interment the next day? He must leave very soon; he was getting a lift on a lorry. Could I accompany him?

I told him to wait and then I explained to my parishioners in the hotel hallway why I must leave them for a day. They should return on Wednesday and I would continue my work for them. They almost thrust me back into the room to my colleague.

The lorry was waiting near the hotel. Crouched on the floor Raoul and I were driven deep into the country, discussing the tiresome problems war had brought to our people, comparing methods of dealing with them and our mutual experiences of the 'authorities.' I remember we talked of mission work abroad and wondered how our brothers among the heathen were faring in these days, cut off from their home directors; laughing aloud as we thought that they were safer and more secure in the twentieth century than clergymen in more 'civilised' lands. So much for the dreams of our youth when we wished to work in perilous places for our faith. Raoul and I became comrades in Christ that day for we were serving Him; with our sins upon us, we knew that we had one Master.

Early next morning, with the sun warmly rising, I read the burial service of our people over the poor coffin and grave of the English lady who was Scottish. Raoul stood by in his shabby black cassock, his eyes cast downwards, his hands clasped in prayer when he was not handing me the requisites for the office of burial.

When the last shovelful of earth was smoothed on the grave we walked back to the village square, for the lorry left early and I had to hurry back to the city. The Christian faith, love of God, our God, binds men into warm friendship with an ease that, in this world of ours, seems miraculous. Love is the enduring miracle of our God. Raoul was my friend. I stood looking down at him from the floor of the lorry that morning and he smiled that wise, happy smile, as he clasped my hand.

'Dear Donald,' he said. 'Remember in Grenoble, wherever you are, if I can help you, I am ready. Send for me; I am at your service.'

The tasks God sends us bring their own rewards. On that rolling lorry during the dusty three-hours' journey back to the city, I was happy and I prayed for my friend and the exile we had laid to rest. All three of us were in the Hands of God.

When I arrived at Grenoble about midday I did not go straight to the hotel but made my way to the church which was mine to use when my two staunch friends, M. Westphal and M. Cook, Protestant pastors in the city, were not using it for their own services. There I recollected myself and offered a prayer of thanksgiving for the work that had been entrusted to me and the kindness of Raoul who had brought me news of the dead woman to whose grave I had brought the prayers of the church to which she had been loyal. I felt wonderfully happy. I must have been in the building for nearly an hour and a half. When I walked into the blinding sunshine with a smile on my face, I was confronted by M. Brachon, the beadle.

'Good afternoon, M. le Pasteur,' he greeted me. 'You look very happy to-day.'

'I am very happy,' I answered. 'I've just been to a funeral in the country.'

The poor man's jaw dropped inside his long beard. I suppose he judged me just as mad as the other Britishers; I patted his shoulder and went back to the hotel to eat.

M. Brachon was a true friend and was always on duty on Sunday afternoon when I held divine service for the British. He was to prove himself an ally in the more hazardous cause of assisting our boys to escape.

I had been restricted from prison-visiting during the first few months of my stay in Grenoble, but within a few days of my arrival, I received a charming visitor.

She was a lady from the south who called at the hotel where I received her in the dining-room. Over coffee, she leaned forward and whispered to me that the Intelligence knew I was in the city. I must establish myself as a member of the community and as soon as my permit came through I must resume my visits to the men imprisoned in Vichy France. After coffee she left and I did not see her again.

My work in the university and for the folk in forced residence filled my days. I appealed to the Red Cross in Geneva for food and other necessities for the old people. They had neither the means nor the craft to use the 'Black Market.'

Shortly after the day Raoul and I buried the Scottish lady, I returned to the hotel to find that eleven large cases of food had arrived. That night, with help from British ladies, willing assistants, I broke it up into fair parcels for all the people I knew who were in need. Some of it we delivered by hand, trudging through the streets to people so old they could not help themselves. The others called at the hotel and I distributed the precious food to them. The hall became more thronged. Soon we became unpopular with the *patron* of the establishment, a dubious personality, who was to prove a villain in the end. A member of the dread and obscenely cruel *milice,* those French who had sold their souls to Nazism, he was afraid, in those first days, to move against me. The Resistance was stronger than I knew at this time and the proNazis were careful. I believe he kept me under observation throughout my stay. I gave him nothing to report back to the Gestapo.

CHAPTER 10

THE VISITING PADRE

I WAS granted permission to visit prison camps as a chaplain and I set off one day for St. Hippolyte du Fort. The secret agents once more conscripted me. It was the early autumn of 1941.

We made our Communion Table from beer boxes covered with a white cloth, and the Union Jack. I set up a picture of the King, His late Majesty, and the Queen, now Queen Elizabeth the Queen Mother, and led the officers and men in prayer. I preached a short sermon and we sang hymns. The relative peace of Grenoble, with its familiar undertones of scholarship, study and services in a proper church seemed somehow unreal.

My days again became balanced between the rounds of a chaplain and study, and the perilous deliberations of the Intelligence Service. In La Turbie, St. Hippolyte and at Chambarran, evidence of the great battle that was spreading across the whole globe confronted one. There were the happy-go-lucky men who studied their guards and the means of escape at their disposal. To them escape was a game they would play to win. And there were the sick in mind and body, the unhappy ones who worried about families, often with very real cause. The 'old soldiers' sang and baited the Germans, the students, thinkers, the innocently guileless, all talked the many dialects of home. Those prisons were cross-sections of the best in British manhood. I was glad to get back to them.

Once each month I visited the camp at St. Hippolyte du Fort near Nimes. Before each of my journeys, which took seventeen hours by train, I had to procure a pass from the Sûreté in Grenoble. I had no difficulty. *M. le Pasteur Ecossais* was established. I would travel through the night and as my destination approached my mood would lighten for the men gave me a wonderful welcome.

I carried the tools of escape. On my first visits the guards passed me into the prison after carefully scrutinising my papers. No attempts had been made to search me and I had received instructions to co-operate with the officers inside all the camps I visited and do all I could to assist them. Stowed about my person, I carried strong scissors for the cutting of barbed wire, files which, properly used, would sever iron bars, forged papers to further the British 'tourist' on his way and concentrated rations, all of which I passed to the officers in control of escape committees. To a great extent at the beginning of my prison visits I worked in the dark. Security, I knew, had been intensified. Pat I thought dead with the others and, with the recollection of the traitor Cole burdening me, I was glad to work with as little knowledge as possible in my head. All I needed to know for this job were the elements of the escaper's craft and the most useful type of information I could assemble to pass back along the Intelligence routes. The less I knew of the organisation the better. I had become a true professional.

The phase of determined ignorance did not last for many weeks. A message came that Pat was alive and was rebuilding the organisation with characteristic speed. All who might help were conscripted to the service, life for me again became exciting.

At the prison I conducted two communion services. A special dispensation had been granted me by the Bishop of Gibraltar to dispense Communion to the men of the English Church. Afterwards I gave Communion in our simple Scottish fashion, with six of our soldiers, three on each side of me acting as elders.

Even in the chapel we were under surveillance. A French or German officer, who had a smattering of English, was always in attendance, to ensure that I did not convey information to my flock. Fortunately, they did not understand the Doric, so by quoting our national poet, Robert Burns, I was able to tell the lads all I wished, pleading against the supervisor's angry protests that I was quoting their national poet. This, alas, particularly angered one Frenchman and, I believe, he was seen by one of our officers after an especially irate altercation, brooding over a copy of Rabbie's works in a corridor.

The 'quotations' were necessary. I was compelled to find a language in which to talk privately to the men assembled in the chapel for in many of the prisons morale was low. Until the escape route was reorganised, men breaking out of military gaols had not got far before they were arrested. I had been instructed to hearten the inmates for the task ahead of them—return to the U.K. The contents of my pockets helped to rebuild morale and soon a trickle of men began to move out.

Suffering, adventure, bravery, were part of one's day-to-day experience in the prisons. One reached that state of mind where nothing was astonishing. I met men who had wandered out of the social register into the maelstrom of war and found them tough, inspiring and as careless of their own safety as the heroes in boys' adventure fiction.

There were over a thousand men at St. Hippolyte du Fort, near Nimes. I always anticipated my visits to them with pleasure. I held a service, brought them whatever comforts I could find and among the hymn books smuggled in compasses, files and ropes. St. Hippolyte was run efficiently. It was not easy to escape from it, but it had happened in the past and would happen again. My visits opened with a service and after that I got the men to open their hearts in song. I had reason to believe that even the irreligious enjoyed the break from the soul-deadening routine of ordinary prison life. I enjoyed being with them and, I confess, loved the welcome they gave. I talked with the officers and received news of fresh arrivals which, in due course, I passed on to Pat.

Under orders I sought out in the camps 'important personalities' and officers and men of special qualifications and training. It was thus that I met a man, then an American and now a British subject, named Whitney Straight. Had the Germans managed to penetrate his true identity, they would have considered him a first-class prize. But Mr. Straight, an officer in the Royal Air Force, was not the type who gave anything away to the enemy.

A member of the best society in London and a friend of the Royal Family, Whitney Straight was famous as a motor racing driver and an airman. During the Battle of Britain he became an ace flyer in the service to which he had volunteered. His disappearance on a sortie over Le Havre had created a sensation in England. Reported missing, no further news of his fate had come to the authorities. All that was known of his 'end' was that suddenly he had ordered his flight to return to base and then, very quickly, before his crash:

'I have been hit. I am going to land here.'

His capture by the Germans had not been reported. I met him at St. Hippolyte du Fort, in the country of the Gard.

On this visit I was introduced to an officer in the R.A.S.C., a crisp, business-like gentleman, whose face was familiar. I was sure I had seen him somewhere. His name, I was told, was Captain Whitney. I knew no Whitney but I found myself puzzling over the feeling of having met this officer when I was once with one of our trusted contacts.

'On no account let this secret out to anyone but the officers in charge of the route, Padre,' the contact explained. 'Captain Whitney is Whitney Straight.'

I whistled softly to myself. Of course, I had seen Whitney Straight's photograph in magazines, at social gatherings and in the overalls of a contender for car racing honours.

'Jerry hasn't a clue to his identity,' my confidante continued. 'If he did know, Straight would be whisked to Germany before you could say Jack Robinson.'

As soon as I reported to the Organisation that Whitney Straight was in the prison they set out to release him. He was a valuable property and it was decided that he should be 'invalided out' with the assistance of a Polish pastor. A series of tiresome misadventures began. The Polish chaplain brought the prisoner aspirin tablets in sufficiently large quantities to make him sick. Once in hospital he could escape more easily. As I have already explained, 'the medical swindle,' given a certain amount of luck, was a useful device. But at first, it seemed, luck was against Whitney Straight. On the night of the planned escape, his comrades of the R.A.F. carried out a bombing mission that was so successful it aroused antagonism in the authorities and the invalids were marched back from hospital to gaol, presumably to punish the airmen, who by that time were back in England. During the following weeks Straight made various attempts to escape and then he was transferred to La Turbie prison. Here I again met him and our luck improved. This time we were successful. We again chose the 'medical swindle' and dope was brought to him. He swallowed it. The symptoms looked very bad and he was moved out to hospital for treatment and this time he got clean away. I shall never forget his courtesy and thoughtfulness. Immediately he was free he sent me a charming message giving the news of his success and inviting me to visit his home after the war.

Naturally, his arrival in England leaked out, but no one, apart from the proper authorities, ever learned how it had been accomplished. Whitney Straight knew, better than most men, just how many others remained behind whose hopes of escape would be wrecked if the Boche got on the track of the escape organisation.

His departure enraged the commandant at La Turbie and the whole prison came under intensified surveillance. A number of men working upon an escape came under observation and search revealed that they had tools in their possession. Fortunately I was dramatically warned or I might have joined them in a dungeon.

It was a bright morning and I was exhausted after my night's journey from Grenoble as I came to La Turbie behind Monte Carlo. Borne down by a sack containing Communion vessels, hymn books, cigarettes, files, chocolate, forged ration books and passports, and a few small crowbars, I felt like Atlas bearing the world on his shoulders as I climbed a hill on the road to the gaol. But I was not apprehensive. The entrance to La Turbie I still thought 'a piece of cake.'

As I staggered up the narrow climbing lane I heard a goose cackling and turning around saw a lad of about fourteen years of age struggling with a very bad-tempered bird. Having experienced in my boyhood something similar, I knew how he felt, so I put down the sack and made towards him to help. He was about twenty yards away. As I approached he seemed to let the bird go half-loose from him and I hurried. It cackled like a fiend, louder, shriller and louder. I reached the lad under cover of the goose's sinister warblings. He whispered:

'Keep walking, M. le Pasteur. I beg of you.'

I grasped the bird firmly by its threshing feet, regretting, not for the first time, that the skull of a goose is constructed in such a way that a man cannot give it a healthy slap on the ear, while its anatomy in general precludes a lusty clout on the place where it sits down. The lad grasped her firmly. I went back to the sack and set out on my way. He followed. We moved between low hedges, he paddling in the rear, until the lane dipped in a way that cut us off from possible viewers in the prison.

'You are the Scottish chaplain?'

His eyes were eager. He was breathless.

'Yes.'

'I knew it. You are M. le Canard.'

The words shook me. Only Pat O'Leary called me Donald le Canard—Donald Duck. His sense of security disliked the label Donald le Pasteur, his sense of humour dictated a name linked in sound if not sense with the earlier label. He used a nickname given me by an old friend—Le Canard.

I had become more security-conscious, more obsessed by my remembrance that I had suspected Cole and yet, even under orders, stilled my suspicion and left him exploiting his treason until my friends died, killed by it. The use of this nickname irked me. It was known to this boy yet the Gestapo had not pounced on me. I looked at the village boy who, apparently in innocence, used it. I wondered if a new threat was hanging over us.

'What do you want of me, my boy?' I asked.

'I have a message from M. Wood,' he answered.

A bright lad, he smiled up at me. I remained silent, looking, I suppose, like a tiresome schoolmaster. Wood was a friend, the interpreter for the prisoners at St. Hippolyte du Fort, an agent on the escape route and the organist at divine service in the gaol. He was one of O'Leary's most trusted accomplices.

'Well?'

'M. Wood,' the boy went on, 'says you must be careful what

you bring in the sack to-day. You will be searched. He says to tell you it is an order from M. Pat.'

'How do you know M. Wood?'

'My name,' he said, 'is Jean Morel. My father is a patriot and so am I. He sent me. He says we always will help Le Canard. There is much trouble in the camp, he says, and the commandant believes you are bringing tools in the sack. Now I must go or the guards up there, if they have been watching, will wonder what delays you.'

Dragging the goose, the little Jean turned back a little way and watched me for a few moments. Then I reconnoitred. Below me, over the hedge, a burn rippled along the hillside. Quickly I pulled the bag after me through the leaves and down I plunged until the water was at my feet. In a matter of seconds I hid the incriminating goods in the undergrowth. Then, puffing and panting, I began a zigzag climb back to the lane.

The move was lucky for suddenly before my eyes I saw what might be a way of escape from inside Fort de la Revere La Turbie. Almost hidden by a large overhanging bush, the exit to a sewer was to be seen overlooking the burn. I gazed into the fetid aperture, shone my torch and recognised its obvious route. It must come from the camp. In a flash of joy I saw its possibilities. We might run an excursion from this exit, if my delay in the dip of the lane had not been noticed by the guards. I had been out of sight about ten minutes. Apprehensively I approached the gates of the Fort.

I was out of breath when I entered, still staggering under the load in the sack. The guards were smiling and I noticed one brash blond youth wink at his comrade. The mouse, I thought, seems to have walked into the trap.

An N.C.O. took my papers and shouted an order. I found myself surrounded.

'You will follow me to the commandant,' said the sergeant.

Under escort I was led to an office where a short man, in the uniform of a colonel, open at the neck so that his jowl protruded, sat at a desk, his boots propped on a blotting pad, a short thick cigar slobbering in his mouth.

'Ah,' he sneered. 'The man of God.'

I remained silent.

'Turn around,' he yelled.

I obeyed. He came to my side, hands on hips, looking both brutish and ridiculous. The guards stood by at rigid attention, holding their breath in an idiotic way. This was one of the Vichy prisons where Nazi methods were used. One of the weaknesses in the German military machine derives from an imbecile vulgarity that raises officers to the level of godlings. This Vichy commandant might have studied under Himmler. I stood respectfully awaiting the next move.

'The sack,' he shouted. 'Where is the sack? Ah, yes. Let us see what the man of God has brought his children this time. Empty it out. Let us see what he has brought.'

The blond youth stepped smartly forward, grasped the sack by its 'ears' on its lower end and cascaded the contents out before 'Simon Legree' as I was beginning to think of this absurd officer.

Bibles, hymn books, a couple of cans of beef, cigarettes, chocolates, some safety razor sets and paper-back thrillers lay in a heap at the toes of the glistening boots. All were recognisably innocent. His consternation was comical.

'Let me see,' he yelled, and down he went on his knees to scramble through my kit and the gifts for the men. But there was no evidence that suited his purpose.

'Put these things back in the pastor's sack,' he snapped to the sergeant. 'And get out of here, all of you, except the prisoner.'

They left and I waited until we were alone.

'The prisoner, M. le Commandant?' I said.

'Yes, the prisoner, until you leave here. Men have been tunnelling from this camp. Maps, compasses and ration books have been found in their cells. You smuggled them in.'

This was ridiculous. If he had evidence against me, I should have been arrested at Grenoble. The comedy of the search would have been superfluous.

'You will have no further communication with the British prisoners in this camp,' he snarled. 'I know your reputation.'

'M. le Commandant,' I answered, 'if you handicap me in my

duty I shall insist upon an investigation of conditions in this prison. I cannot tolerate your manners nor your interference with me in bringing relief to these men. I have the authority of France, I must remind you, and I have international authority. Has there been inefficiency among your staff? Are you trying to make me the scape-goat? If so, I demand immediate release and I shall report you to the Sûreté in Grenoble.'

His bluff was called. He composed himself quickly. The boots which had resumed their place upon the table-top came back to the floor. He sat straight up, the thick fingers adjusting his uniform collar.

'You may take the service to-day,' he said slowly, 'but I warn you, M. le Pasteur, I believe you to be responsible for the unrest among the men. I shall investigate you thoroughly before your next visit.'

I bowed and a few minutes later, flanked by two English-speaking officers, one German, one French, I greeted my parishioners. I had been given two minutes to speak with the senior officer, Squadron-Leader Higginson; my escort kept within earshot and I had to confine myself to social enquiries.

Mr. Wood, ensconced at the harmonium, gave me what is called an 'old-fashioned look.' I kept my eyes averted. I pulled the Union Jack over the beer crates and as I brought out the picture of Their Majesties, an idea came to me. I could irritate the enemy, I decided, even if they handicapped me in my job.

They were hard-working lads those interpreters. They did not give me a chance of even the most stealthy word. Wood even faked a breakdown in the harmonium and I dashed to his assistance. The officers moving on each side of me, forestalled us at every point and grew more irritated by our pranks. When the service ended the moment for revenge came.

'Gentlemen,' I instructed the congregation, 'we will close this service by singing the National Anthem, which is a prayer for our beloved Sovereign and our country. It is a hymn of supplication to our God and in praise of Him for his goodness to us in making our country great and enabling us to defend the good.'

The men stood quietly to attention. Our overseers lounged half-deferentially. I turned to them.

'You, sirs,' I snapped, 'have insisted upon intruding upon divine service, fully participating, to use your own phrase. Now I must insist that you stand to attention when we sing directly to our God who is, presumably, your God too. If you do not join in, after honouring us so far, I shall construe it as a deliberate insult to our religion, my office, which is above wars, and to international agreements.'

The long ferret face of the Frenchman on my right grew longer and I thought his eyes would pop out of his hatchet head. To my left I heard furious spluttering noises. Their heels clicked as they stood to attention. The harmonium began and the men joined in, some of them, alas, smiling, others looking too serious to be convincing. I turned my head and noted our nurse-maids; their lips were moving soundlessly. Their agony was gratifying. The English service ended and the Scotsmen moved in to take their places for the second, Presbyterian service.

I forgot about the spies as it progressed. I remember recalling to our men places we all knew, telling them that in little kirks, in the Govan Road, off Leith Walk, in towns and villages, in the sunshine and the rain, their wives, children, friends, were being led in prayer by their ministers for them. That God remembered them and in Scotland those who loved them clamoured to Him to protect and bring them safely home. I came to the end of my talk.

'And now, lads, we'll sing our national anthem, asking God to protect our earthly ruler's graciousness.'

There was an angry grunt on my left. The German snarled at his French comrade and strode from the room, the latter following. We sang alone. Wood played loudly on the harmonium and I passed on the news to him.

'The prison sewer leads out on the hillside. It is a perfect escape route. Check on its position inside. This will be followed up and outside arrangements made. Higginson must not let many men into this confidence.'

My departure from La Turbie was made under formal escort to the gates. The guards were stiff and no winks passed between them. When I came to the dip in the lane, I halted, looked about me in the dusk and plunged through the hedge, down the hillside to the burn, collected the tools and papers and quickly stowed them about me. A few lines on a sheet of paper fixed the point where the sewer emerged and I scrambled back to my road. That night I descended the hill to Monte Carlo. Next morning, at a meeting with men of the French resistance, I asked them to arrange an appointment with O'Leary and to plan refuges for the men who would, I knew, escape from the camp.

Within the façade of my formal work which I had erected to take me around the country, I moved carefully until a message came for me to go to a certain café. Pat was waiting; the reunion was brief. I told him of my discovery and when I concluded he smiled, shot to his feet and nearly danced with joy.

'We'll run an excursion to the U.K., Padre,' he gloated. 'You carry on with your job. I'll check on the route taken by the smelly tunnel and pass back routes for the men to follow when they get out. Next time you go to La Turbie, brings tools as usual, but linger in the "dip" for a few moments. If there is danger, you will be warned there.'

We planned to take 150 men out of the prison fort behind La Turbie on that operation. It was the most magnificent opportunity that ever came to us and Pat planned it nobly. By radio he contacted England and asked how many men could be picked up at the coast and taken home by submarine. His one worry hinged not on the escape but on the number of lodgings the French could arrange in which we might hide the tourists. This problem was solved by radio messages from England which dashed his immediate hopes. Only thirty-six men could be accepted by submarine. But his plans were only halted by this discouraging report.

'You will tell Higginson,' he ordered me, 'the exact truth. He must choose the thirty-six lucky ones. But he will instruct the others that if they are prepared to take a chance upon reaching the frontier under their own steam, we will provide maps and places where they can find food and shelter.' He continued, 'Donald, after you see Higginson, meet me at the inn in the village. It will be safe for you to report to me there.'

It proved extremely unsafe. When I passed through the village on arrival, I found Morel's brother walking by my side.

'Beware of the inn, M. le Canard,' he whispered. 'The Boche is too interested in it. Many Boche are in the prison, Monsieur. You must be careful.'

I asked for a light for my cigarette and as he bent towards me I whispered, 'I have an appointment at the inn with a fellow-countryman. Watch for him and warn him. It is important.'

Inside La Turbie the escape was organised. The sewer had been penetrated with the help of Jean Morel, father of the goose-boy, who under orders from Pat had drawn a map of the sewer showing exactly where it ran under La Turbie, in fact beneath the gaol's boiler-house. He passed this map to Wood who brought it to Higginson and work was soon under way. Labouring in relays, prisoners made contact with their singularly noxious 'Jacob's Ladder.'

It was my task to convey to Higginson the good news that the escape had been fixed for a few days after my visit and the bad news that only thirty-six men could be accepted for submarine excursion.

When I entered La Turbie all seemed normal and I was brought to Higginson immediately. The place, he told me quickly, was alive with Germans, but he did not know the purpose of their visit. He was disappointed by my news, but he had chosen his party. The men who would not find places on the submarine would be given an opportunity to try to escape on their own account. Connection with the sewer had been made. Given reasonable luck—and the absence of the Boche—the escape operation would be successful.

I wished him good luck and afterwards led the men in prayer, edgily wondering if Morel's brother was on the watch. The gates of the prison were clearly visible from the village and I had told him I would signal with a white handkerchief if there was danger when I emerged. I prayed the man was vigilant.

As I left La Turbie I found myself surrounded by five courteous Germans who volunteered to help me with my bag down to the inn. They said they would like to drink a glass of wine and wished me to accompany them. Scared out of my wits I had the hand-kerchief out in a jiffy. It was seen by Morel's brother who dashed to the inn and told O'Leary. When we arrived he had gone. After a rather nervous session of conversation with the Germans I took leave of La Turbie's environs with relief.

The zero hour came and the escape plan went into operation. Eight men went to the boiler-house and quickly overpowered a French worker in charge of the boiler. Six of them opened the tunnel and made their escape into the sewer. Two remained to take control of the traffic. In parties of six the men moved out until, within ninety minutes, the chosen thirty-six had gone into the night, met their guides, and were on the way into Monte Carlo and their hide-outs.

Another twenty-two men followed them, each ready to take his chance on making a solo getaway. Still more would have escaped but for a tragi-comic miscalculation involving a fat man, a squadron-leader from the R.A.F., who stuck in the tunnel.

The poor man struggled furiously to get through the aperture. He succeeded only in becoming more tightly wedged. His com-rades sent down a small fellow in the role of human ferret to try to dig him out, but the task was beyond him. Infuriated by the delay, the men in the boiler-house began to whisper instructions and then to call louder and louder until at last the French were disturbed. Within a few minutes the boiler-house was surrounded and the would-be escapers were escorted back to their quarters. The alarm went out for those who had gone. But the organisation had arranged their departure efficiently. Fourteen of the solo escapers were recaptured, eight got clean away. Not one of the submarine passengers was lost; all returned to England to continue the fight.

Within a few days of the operation I was placed under arrest and interrogated by the Security Police. There was no evidence against me. Again I was released.

CHAPTER II

THE LADIES OF CHAMONIX

WINTER CLOSED in and travelling became more arduous. Grenoble was an enclave in which learning, espionage, and death were strange companions. We were cut off from the great movement of the allies that was taking place all over the world. At home, soldiers from the British countries were gathering and Britain had become an armed camp. Confidently the British leaders were concentrating industries for the final battle and, I know now, that our people were sustained by faith in its outcome. Sir Winston Churchill's massive oratory and bronze-like honesty had created an atmosphere of expectancy in Britain. However, out there our nerves were tautened by the perils of each passing hour; we had become accustomed to living as citizens of the underworld which the Germans had made the only place where a man might honourably exist. An opaque curtain of secrecy cut us off from the free world and news of home.

Christmas came and I brought food and the little seasonable oddments men cherish at such times. I even managed to obtain more than one goose for my interned compatriots to be roasted and eaten on the Christmas day. They made paper hats and they played games. When tired of that they relaxed and talked of home. I led them in prayer and loved watching them lose thought of themselves as they remembered and celebrated the birth of the Child. Christmas is a time when all men remember God.

Winter passed and 1942 emerged from its icy grip into the gentle season of spring. Summer came with life dragging on in the camps. August brought word of the landing at Dieppe and there was a resurgence of confidence through the camps. Guards looked at us more grimly. Dieppe seemed to us the turning point. Our armies were at the ready. We knew they would strike when the moment was propitious and soon we would be free.

Our escape organisation was moving smoothly but slowly. We lost men, it is true, but we expected that death might come to any one of us. The important thing was that the traffic of information and escaping prisoners should be maintained and that the disaster Cole had brought upon the escape route should not be repeated. In Grenoble I had my problems but I was surrounded by friends. The manager of my hotel I knew to be an enemy, but I did not wish to move out because I could watch him while he thought he was checking up on me. My old friend M. Brachon, the beadle, was one of my great consolations. His assistance in the church and his practical approach to his duties were a perpetual reminder of the normal work of a pastor in peace-time, work that must continue in war. He was heart and soul in ' *La Grande Cause.*'

Brachon was quite fearless and his detached assistance in my more dangerous work was given as if it were part of the ordinary duties of a beadle. As befits the office, he moved with imposing dignity; he addressed everyone with measured courtesy. The great beard which spread over his chest slightly intimidated me. Our Scottish beadles too, are dignified men but in my generation the beard had gone out of fashion, and the French language always sounds more ceremonious than my own homely Scottish tongue. When Brachon escorted me one morning to a very dark cellar which, unknown to me, lay beneath the sanctuary of the church and formally confronted me, I was not quite prepared for the little speech that followed.

'Voilà, Monsieur le Pasteur. Consider this excellent cellar. Surely here is a safe hiding-place for your men. Here you can conceal them in an emergency. Have confidence in me. This place is secure.'

I was startled at first and then began to thank him. Majestically, he raised his hand.

'It is a privilege, Monsieur le Pasteur. And it is one of the few ways in which I, Brachon, who am too old to fight, can serve. Please do not thank me.'

Obediently I followed him without another word, my emotions stirred to that embarrassing point where a man does not know whether to laugh or weep.

Within a few weeks I was compelled, much against my instincts, to make use of the cellar and Brachon's suggestion. The thought of endangering the church where my people had been given divine hospitality terrified me. But prisoners-of-war on the run are men in danger of death. Two entered my room one evening and I had no other place to secrete them.

They were tough cheerful lads and I did not doubt that we could get them through to freedom. I led them to the church cellar where they settled down for the night.

Next morning, which was Sunday, I brought them food. We sat talking while they exercised healthy appetites, washing down great mouthfuls of bread and sausage with draughts of vin blanc. When they had finished they rested, opening the tops of their trousers to let their stomachs expand because they had eaten, I suspected, rather more than their fill. As I got up to leave I told them that service would begin in less than a half-hour and they must keep quiet. I did not want my flock to be worried by mysterious noises coming from the floor under their knees.

'But we want to come to church, Padre,' one of them protested. 'Don't we, Johnnie?'

Johnnie agreed that he was as eager as his friend and reluctantly I took a chance. I led them to the church gallery, told them to lie on their stomachs throughout the service and promised no one would intrude upon them. Outside I found Brachon and asked him to stand guard at the stairway and forbid anyone to enter the gallery.

The service proceeded in the ordinary way. Not a sound was heard from my stowaways. At lesson-time I chose, as is my frequent custom, at random the Old Testament lesson. The large pulpit Bible opened at the 27th Psalm and I began to read:

'The Lord is my light and my salvation, whom shall I fear? The Lord is the strength of my life, of whom shall I be afraid?' I continued until I came to a passage that was a veritable word in season for the soldiers prostrate on the floor of the gallery.

'For in the time of trouble, He will hide me in His pavilion; in the secret of His tabernacle shall He hide me.'

I glanced for a second at the gallery. They had raised their heads. Two pairs of sparkling eyes gazed down at me, two ruddy faces were grinning. Two weeks later those lads who heard the service in hiding in the French church were strolling down Piccadilly in brand-new battledress blouses and uniforms, on the way to their homes for leave before rejoining their units.

My second winter in Grenoble began and the grip of the Germans upon France grew more cruel. The landing at Dieppe had alarmed them and too many men were escaping from French prisons. The Nazis knew that a large number of French guards were divided in their allegiance and that their sympathies were with the British. They issued new and brutal orders that all men on duty at the time of an escape would be transferred to forced labour camps in Germany. We knew then we could expect no quarter. Even the most friendly official would not accept the suicidal consequences of turning a blind eye upon our activities in gaol. I was banned from visiting. I protested, sent letters to Geneva, stating my case, knowing these would be opened and read on the way. I said all I could—and I had comprehensively learned the methods of embarrassing the authorities—to make things awkward for our persecutors. Eventually I was reinstated.

But Grenoble became an inferno of wanton cruelty and violence as the Allies intensified their air attacks on the Reich. The enemy became more and more dominated by hatred. The *milice,* his French collaborators, were diabolical in their conscienceless brutality. M. Hullier, the manager of the Hôtel de l'Europe, was one of that unsavoury band. I knew the time would come when he and his accomplices would strike at me.

In the early spring of 1943, with the Allies coming closer to Italy, the landings made in North Africa, the enemy became more and more like an evil beast. On impulse he struck, blindly but fatally. I suppose the strain began to tell upon me when I was banned again from the camps. My fight against the authorities irritated them; and exhausted me. A message came from London that the escape route through Spain was becoming so difficult that

we must try to find another way. The agent who brought it advised
me to go to Chamonix, the winter sports resort which lies at the
foot of Mont Blanc. My health was poor and when I applied for
a permit to visit this innocuous place I was granted one without
fuss. The medical certificate enabled my friends in the Sûreté at
Grenoble to grant the visa quickly.

Chamonix is a very beautiful little town at any time of the
year, an international meeting place of climbers and other sports-
men. I came to it on a Saturday and wandered through its streets
drinking in the beauty of the country, spiritually relaxing in its
peaceful atmosphere and revelling in the cheerful voices of the
men and women walking its streets on shopping forays. I strolled
to the graveyard attached to the Anglican church and stood before
the statue which has been raised to British climbers lost on the
lovely but dangerous mountains. I was very tired. During the
nine hours' journey from Grenoble the train had been boarded
repeatedly by examining officials, stupid, pompous and selfish men
who had asked us the same questions more than once, varying their
form each time. A man with the most extraordinary squint travelling in my compartment was, I knew, shadowing me. He had
booked in at the Hôtel de la Gare where I had taken a room and
the atmosphere of that pleasant place was now marred by his
unsavoury presence. The climbers' statue stood above the snow. I
remember the exalted beauty of the Alps around the town that
day. I felt grateful for it all. It was with reluctance that I dragged
my feet back to the hotel, ate a very small meal and went to bed.
I did not awake until eight o'clock had struck next morning, and
the sleep and the air of Chamonix had revived me. Feeling a new
man I set off for the little Anglican church.

The building was crowded with the townsfolk. None of my
countrymen or women seemed to be present and I felt disappointed,
at the same time chiding myself ironically with the thought that in
Britain the winter sports season had been postponed for a few
years. I lost myself in prayer until the singing began and I heard
voices, singing in French, but unmistakably English voices. I did
not manage to isolate them from the rest of the singers until we
were crowding into the centre aisle after the service. Two neat little

English ladies, precise, delicate and as sure of themselves as miniature guardsmen, were walking with their fellow worshippers. I was
sure they were English. When I reached the entrance of the
church I waited. They returned my bow in a dignified way.

'Pardon me, ladies. May I ask are you English?'

'We are, Monsieur.'

'Then may I introduce myself. I am the Rev. Donald Caskie,
Minister of the Scottish Kirk in the Rue Bayard, in Paris, presently
chaplain to the British people in the city of Grenoble.'

They bowed again, almost curtseying. Their right hands advanced and I shook them, watching the ladies all the time in a
way that must have seemed rude. They were so English. The hats,
the little veils, handbags, longish tweed coats, the blouses with
beads embroidered up to the necks, the frills, the determined little
chins, might pass anywhere at home unnoticed. They spoke French
with the fluency of old residents.

'My name is Miss Forrest,' said the smaller of the two. 'This is
Miss Wood. We, of course, have heard of you and your work,
dear Mr. Caskie. Alas, we are the only English persons remaining
in Chamonix, but we are safe and contented. M. le Maire is our
friend and most kind to us. We have nothing but friends in the
town. May I invite you to our mission this evening?'

'Your mission, Miss Forrest?'

'Yes, dear friend. We were trained to be missionaries by the
Faith Mission in Edinburgh. I do not need to tell a student of
Edinburgh what that means. We shall never forget the excellent
training we received from J. G. Govan who founded the Faith
Mission. But perhaps you will join us for a meal this evening.'

They smiled at me with that curiously strong, paradoxically
frail, charm of old ladies who have seen much of life and sur-
mounted all its difficulties doing the work they believe to be
sacred.

'I know your mission very well, dear lady. I shall be happy to
come to you this evening and enjoy your hospitality. But please
do not expend much on my entertainment. You must have big
demands made upon you.'

My remark seemed witty to them for they looked at each other and giggled aloud.

'Yes, we have uncommonly big demands made upon our stock of food at present. But to entertain you will be a great pleasure to us. We warn you we shall insist upon you eating a good meal.'

The moon was up when I plodded through the snow towards their mission that evening. The valley was that wonderful stainless white which stretches like a lunar landscape in Switzerland in winter, challenging, awe-inspiring, its whiteness tinged with blue under the evening sky and the white globe of the moon. One feels close to God in the moonlight on such a night, in such a place, and I thought of the Faith Missioners. They had been founded in Edinburgh by J. G. Govan; their motto was 'Seek Ye First the Kingdom of God.' By it they lived. Their little mission halls were built in the most unexpected places but surely Chamonix, centre of cosmopolitan society in the season, world-famous as a climbers' testing place under the most invulnerable of Europe's Alps, was their strangest mission. Did Miss Forrest and Miss Wood expect to convert the local people to their branch of faith? They were so English, so self-assured in their modest way. I could find no answer.

The mission hall at the foot of the mountain could have been set down anywhere in the world from Manchester to Bombay and it would have looked as odd. Practical, unadorned, strong; hundreds of buildings of the kind are to be found in the U.K. From the interior I heard the sound of a harmonium. Respectfully I opened the door and timorously gazed into the hall.

'Come in, Mr. Caskie. Do come in.'

Miss Forrest, a Bible held confidently in her hands, confronted me from the far end of the room. Miss Wood, seated at the organ, bowed, and continued playing. The congregation filled the seats, men and women, all local people who turned and gazed at me with the expectant look of a congregation of established church members contemplating a new boy.

'Please sit down, Mr. Caskie.' Miss Forrest was firmly and courteously in control. I wasted no time in taking a front seat which obviously she had reserved for me. The service began.

The sermon was concise and practical, its message, perhaps the most important in Christianity, that we exist by God's love, are brought to life, sustained and saved by it. Miss Forrest's French was lucid and fluent, and her delightful Northern English accent gave it a flavour which made one conscious of each word she enunciated. She halted after making a point and gazed at us, allowing it to sink into our minds, as automatically she adjusted the frills on her blouse. She did not speak for more than a quarter of an hour; the congregation listened raptly, hanging on her every word. When she ended, she raised her hands, looked at me and then steadfastly at her flock.

'And now,' she said, 'let us pray for our poor brother, Dr. Donald Caskie, here present, a servant of God who has been working so very hard for British lads imprisoned by our enemies and who has been himself unwell in health.'

They prayed and then Miss Wood's organ pealed out, Sankey's hymns filled the little hall there on the side of the mountain so remote from the places where they had first been sung. Not far away the armies of the Nazis surrounded the humble hut where the old ladies carried on their work and across the seas men and metal assembled from all the four corners of the world, were gathering for the greatest battle of all time. Unafraid, unconcerned Miss Forrest and Miss Wood in that Swiss enclave sought first the Kingdom of God. I know all things were added unto them.

The Sankey hymns, even rendered into French, filled me with nostalgia; as the little organ pealed out and the rough peasant voices blended into their fervour, my mind strayed to city square, street corners in working-class tenements, the spaces in public parks, all those open-air meeting places where simple people pray and sing to their God on Sunday throughout our island. The singing stopped; the organ lingered for a moment and there was silence in the hall. We stood up and I joined the ladies in the porch where they bade the members of their congregation farewell until the next meeting. We walked slowly back to their little house adjoining the hall.

A fire burned brightly in their kitchen-dining-sitting-room.

The table was neatly laid, the modest silver glittering by the side of shining blue plates. We might have been in Huddersfield.

'We hope you are hungry, Mr. Caskie?' Miss Wood was smiling with that good humour which is the mark of a born hostess.

'Ladies, I am so hungry, I shudder to think of it in these times.'

'Do not speak of it,' Miss Forrest broke in. 'We always have a few tins set apart for emergencies. To-night we shall have a feast.'

They gave me a splendid meal, a feast indeed, although I suspect that in better times few families would have considered it more than a makeshift repast. A soup made from stock they had hoarded, laced with a small tin of broth, a hotpot made from canned meat and potatoes, with lots of gravy, and a sweet created from cake, dried fruit, saccharine and cream, whipped from milk that had stood for a day, and then a good piece of Swiss cheese. We finished with the greatest luxury of all, two cups of tea each. And then we sat back and smiled at each other.

'Alas, in better times it would have been roast beef and Yorkshire pudding,' said one of the good ladies.

Miss Wood's hands rose in mock sorrow and dropped to her lap again. 'But we do hope you found our poor hospitality appetising.'

'May I give thanks for the table, ladies?' I asked. 'I am grateful for a delightful meal, beautifully cooked and for your kindness to me.'

We stood up and my eyes wandered around the homely room, the brass gleaming before the fireplace and on the walls, the fire reflecting in its sheen the photographs of family and friends, I suppose, the pictures, mostly Bible studies, the books, china, the dear knick-knacks old ladies assemble in every town in Britain. I said our thanksgiving with great fervour.

'Tell us, brother, about your work.'

Miss Wood was leaning towards me and I began describing to her the work of the church in Grenoble and our order of services. I spoke of the social side, the meetings, concerts, tea-parties I arranged and the work we were trying to do for the aged.

'And then,' I continued, 'there are the soldiers in prison. I visit them as you know. But sometimes they visit me.'

Miss Forrest looked at her friend and both smiled. Miss Wood spoke.

'You mean you help prisoners-of-war to escape?'

'Yes, ladies. I'm afraid I am considered a dangerous man. I help prisoners-of-war to escape.'

'So do we. Don't we, Elizabeth? That is why we laughed so rudely at church when you spoke of demands on our food. Boys come to us and we send them across the mountains to freedom. Not as many as come to you, but some.'

The room was swinging around my head. Miss Forrest had given me the biggest surprise I had received since war began. Hands on lap they gazed, sweetly smiling, into my face.

'You send them across these mountains.'

'Oh, we don't send them all by themselves. The best guides work for us. This is Chamonix, you know. We have quite a reputation here for our guides. Haven't we, Charlotte?'

'You know the guides?'

'Why, of course we know the guides. We know everyone in Chamonix. They are our friends. We often have them to tea.'

During the next few days I met those friends and Miss Forrest and Miss Wood agreed to become a regular link in the underground escape route. Until then, bravely and haphazardly, they had helped the stragglers who came to them. They saved many lives. From that day forward the traffic on their line became a steady flow. They handled it with workmanlike efficiency. Selfless in their attitude to life, profoundly intelligent, shrewd in their estimation of character, there could not have been better agents in all France or Europe, nor more unexpected. They were without vainglory and when, after the war, those of us who knew their work tried to ensure that they were honoured for it, we ran into one and only one insurmountable difficulty. Neither Miss Wood nor Miss Forrest would hear of it. In peace-time they preserved a united front of modesty as they had done during the dangerous years.

My remaining days at Chamonix were pleasant when I was

working with these ladies. But the man who had travelled from Grenoble in my compartment revealed himself more obviously to be a spy. A medium-sized, fat fellow with a yellowish face, oddly red on the cheek-bones as if touched with rouge, his terrific squint coupled with big, broken, nicotine-stained teeth, constantly bared in what I assume was meant to be an ingratiating smile, made him a disturbing object to confront at every turn.

A few moments after I sat down for breakfast each morning he would enter the dining-room, bow smoothly, his head coming down and forward to greet me so that he looked like a duck about to dive. More than once as I opened my bedroom door to retire for the evening, he passed me in the corridor. I never saw him in the street except reflected in shop windows or mirrors. He had a gift for disappearing. He never spoke to me except in greeting. The squinting eyes were unsmiling and, darting about above the flabby smiles, created a hideously sinister effect.

In the evenings when I set out for the Faith Mission I knew he followed me. Somewhere along the route he hovered waiting to pick up my tracks when I returned to the hotel. I have mused often on that peculiar agent's possible reactions if he came close enough to the mission hall to hear us singing, in French, *Hold the Fort for I am Coming* and *There is a Gate that Stands Ajar*.

On the morning of my return to Grenoble I moved quickly out of the hotel. My bag was packed. I paid my bill and reached the station with only a few moments to spare before the train moved out. In my pocket I carried a map of the new link in the escape route. Before the first stop was reached I saw my friend M. Squint-Eyes as I called him, move along the corridor. Quickly he turned his head away from me and hurried onwards. But I was not mistaken. When the train halted at the next stop I saw him dismount further along the platform and scuttle across it into a refreshment room which was filling up with travellers. The engine started up. Within a few minutes a tall, quietly dressed man sat down opposite me. I tried to read but whenever I raised my eyes I saw this newcomer carefully scrutinising me. He was one of the Deuxième Bureau, the French Scotland Yard. I was under observation, I was sure, by the French as well as the Gestapo. The map in my pocket began to feel heavy. Before we reached the next stop I hurried to the *toilette* and there I memorised it carefully. Fortunately the document was drawn on very thin cartridge paper. Carefully I chewed it up into pulp. One became absurdly careful, reacting I suppose against the heady risks we had to take from day to day, in tasks of that kind. Piece by piece I flushed the pulp down the lavatory pan. Slowly I walked back to my compartment.

Before I reached Grenoble I was searched three times on that journey, methodically, politely and each time by the French.

The ending was in sight but I was curiously confident, and while with a half of my mind I knew that capture was imminent, another part was aware only of the tasks to hand and oblivious of the dangers that loomed before me. My friends among the young men in Grenoble were being thinned out by arrest, deportation and death. When I moved from the hotel I was always followed. I kept on working at my task because I thought that only one thing was inevitable, that I should not return home until France was freed and my fellow-countrymen and women in France and my dear neighbours the French all liberated.

Before the end it would have been easy to go. One night an agent from England arrived and sent an urgent message ordering me to meet him in the home of a friend. He was one of those anonymous men, thin, tough, friendly, rationing his breath and his words to the minimum.

'Caskie, you are going to be arrested.'

'I think you may be wrong about that.'

'I know I am right. You've had it as far as work is concerned in this part of the world. You've had a good innings, Padre.'

I remember feeling mildly irritated by his confidence and yet smiling at it. There is something comic about a man who blithely prophesies another man's ending as all part of the day's work, and something charming when the speaker accepts probable death as his own wage.

'I hope you are wrong about that.'

'Caskie, you must go home.'

'Can you arrange it?'

'Yes.'

The answer, I confess, staggered me, but I knew I could **not** agree to accept his offer. The road into Bithynia still stretched **out** before me and, unlike that day in Bayonne when I was tempted **to** return to Scotland, I had no doubts whatsoever in that dark room in Grenoble. I thought of the prisoners and of the old people, who needed coal and food and a minister in Grenoble. But it seemed discourteous to refuse the offer without discussing it.

'You are kind. What do you suggest?'

'I am not kind. I have my orders. A plane is landing above the town to-night. We must move quickly. We leave now. You will be in England before breakfast.'

'I am afraid I won't, my friend. Forgive me for wasting your time. I shall not be a passenger on that plane. I must remain where I am needed. Grenoble is my parish until someone arrives to take my place.'

He smiled at me and shrugged his shoulders.

'Good luck, Padre. I hope we meet again.'

I left him and went back to the hotel. As I moved through the foyer Germans stood around calmly watching me. They did not hide their interest. Even the fat corporal did not bid me good-night.

CHAPTER 12

THE FEAST OF THE PASSOVER

I WAS AWAKENED by a quiet knocking on my door. It was so quiet that I lay for a moment thinking I imagined it. Hesitantly the tapping began again. I turned back the bedclothes and reached for my dressing-gown.

'A moment, please. I am coming.'

Outside the doorway one of the older servants stood. His eyes were cast down so that I could not see them.

'M. le Pasteur. . . .'

'Yes, Pierre. Is something wrong?'

'M. le Patron demands to see you as soon as possible.'

'Is that all? But he must be in a great hurry.'

'We are sorry, M. le Pasteur. We are your friends.'

Before I could speak he turned on his heel and shambled off, moving with all the speed his old bones could muster until he disappeared out of sight.

I dressed without delay and made my way to Hullier's office. He was seated at a desk littered with papers and he swung round on a swivel seat as I knocked and entered. Without greeting, he began :

'M. Caskie, you have abused the hospitality of this hotel. You will pay your bill and leave immediately. We do not wish your kind here. I do not wish to discuss the matter further.'

He swung away from me and picked up a newspaper. I gazed at the broad glistening black back of his waistcoat.

'What does this ridiculous behaviour mean?' I began. 'How dare you speak like——'

'Get out.'

The monosyllables were measured. I think the man was afraid and, on reflection, he had much to fear whether the Germans were victorious or not. In a terrible way the French were to take vengeance upon their traitors. The maquis lived for that day of revenge—but even if the Allies had lost the war the wages paid by the Nazis were seldom to the taste of their quislings. One needs a long spoon to sup with Satan. Hullier was trembling. Resolutely he kept his face turned away from me.

'Get out.' Intensely he whispered the words. 'Get out. Get out. Get out.'

'Give me my bill.'

A hand reached into a pigeon-hole above his head. Over his shoulder a sheet of paper was passed to me.

I counted out the money I owed him and flung the notes on to the table.

'I'd be obliged if you would give the change to my friends in your employment. I expect you know them.'

The sun was shining as I walked out on to the pavements of Grenoble and strolled through the avenues to a café where I ate breakfast under the trees. Spring had come again and the two years I had spent in the city had made me one of its citizens. I came to love that graceful centre of learning, knowing that here were cradled honest scholars and brave men who longed to live for learning and when the time came were ready to die for freedom. I ate slowly, wondering what the future had in store for me.

After breakfast I telephoned my friend Harris Rudowitch and told him that I was homeless. Immediately he gave me the name of de Verger, a boarding-house in the suburb of La Tronche. Before lunch-time I was settled in a pleasant room. I then set out to collect my few belongings and inform all my friends and contacts of my new address. Throughout the afternoon I was shadowed but in the evening I gave the sleuths the slip and made my way to a secret meeting place where I encountered an escaped prisoner-of-war who will always have a special place in my memories. William Nash of Whitburn was his name. William was the last 'tourist' I helped escape to Britain.

The farce of neutrality was over in France. William was one of those who used his intelligence to make the most of an opportunity the new dispensation presented to him. Chambarran on the Isère near Grenoble where he was imprisoned was, until the Italians and Germans invaded Vichy France, not a bad camp. True, the lads were held behind barbed wire; the French kept them prisoners and went through the motions of strict discipline; but they gave their charges an easy time. Live and let live was their motto. Their attitude to the Germans was cynically correct.

We had one extremely good friend in Chambarran, the French interpreter whom I shall call Jacques. Jacques's grandfather was a Methodist clergyman in England. The lad was reared a staunch Christian. When I conducted divine service for the prisoners he accompanied the singers on the harmonium. A witty man, with a sparkling and generous sense of humour, Jacques helped me on numerous occasions in ways which might have led to his death had he been detected. He was a great morale-builder among the prisoners. Through him I knew all that went on in Chambarran and he kept us informed as to the moods of the officials in charge. Jacques was a favourite among the men.

There were 1,000 men interned in the camp when the news spread that Italians were coming to transport them to captivity in Italy. The British did not like the prospect, but most of them had to reconcile themselves to it when Italian lorries, guarded by men armed with tommy-guns, arrived to escort them to their new homes. William refused to reconcile himself to the journey and planned his escape with a nice sense of timing and a shrewd knowledge of the lay-out of the medieval château in which he was held. Early on the morning of the day the prisoners were to leave, he crawled from his bunk, dashed across a court and into stables which adjoined the house. There he climbed as high as he could into a loft and covered himself with hay. Though buried in that comfortable substance, he still could watch the court through an open window. His compatriots lined up for inspection by the Italians. Approvingly William noted that they moved very smartly.

A roll was called. His name was unanswered and he lay very quiet in his hiding place expecting a search to begin. There was much excitement down below. Roars of rage from a stout Italian officer, much rushing about on the part of N.C.O.'s and then, in the midst of this upheaval, the officer consulted his watch. Transporting 1,000 men is not a simple task. Trains are scheduled and must run to time-tables. A whole operation can be drastically delayed by even a brief pause, and officers consequently censured, if a general hold-up ensues. William deduced that Fatty had to get his contingent to the train so quickly that he could not halt and form a party to search for the missing man. Fatty began to issue brisk orders.

The prisoners marched out of the camp. William watched until the courtyard was empty. Stealthily he crept to the window, stuck his head out and looked all around him. The place seemed deserted. And then Jacques strolled out of a doorway, a cigarette in his hand and a blithe song on his lips. William gave him a low whistle. The interpreter looked up, laughed and said:

'Why, there you are. Naughty, naughty boy. And all your friends gone to sunny Italy worrying about you being missing. They were heartbroken. Naughty boy.'

William hurried down to the court, clapped his friend on the shoulder, and the little man continued, 'But why don't you go to Italy? Don't you like spaghetti? It is very pretty.'

William knew exactly what he wanted. His tastes were chauvinistic. He came from West Lothian.

'No, I don't like spaghetti. I want a good plate of broth. Scotch broth if you want to know, Jacques, my lad. None of your fancy French or Eytie stuff. And that's why I remained behind.'

'Mon Dieu,' said Jacques. 'You, Écossais. All you think of is bagpipes, broth and whisky. I don't blame you, either. Maybe I too am Scotch, eh?'

'Maybe you are, Jacques. But you can help me.'

'Come with me.'

Jacques took William by an arm and led him down into a cellar under the château.

'Stay there until I come for you.'

The Scottish lad waited, crouched against a stone wall, peering at an aperture until the daylight faded. When eventually Jacques whistled and he crawled forth to see the irrepressible organist grinning down at him, he was famished by hunger and cold.

'Would you like a bowl of spaghetti now, Scotch boy. Here are sandwiches. Drink this.'

William took a bowl of broth, French broth and very good, in his hands and gulped it down. The sandwiches disappeared under his coat.

'The nice Italian mans are all gone home. Now listen to me, William.'

His face now serious, Jacques described the route to Grenoble and when he finished he handed the lad a few hundred francs. He had told him where and how to contact me in the city.

'Go to M. Donald, William.' With a broad smile, 'Is he not a Scotch boy too? He is a good mans and will see that you go straight home to your Scotch broth. Good luck, my dear friend.'

William was outside the prison and on the road to Grenoble. Rain drizzled down and dusk had spread a blanket across the land. Next day we met and I saw him safely on our branch of the underground. I hope the broth was ready when he reached the end of the line.

My commission as an underground conductor ended with him, although I did not know the future when we said good-bye. My next few days were preoccupied with a project to speed up the delivery of food to be parcelled for our old people, and in visiting the sick. Then one of the wickedest acts of the Gestapo was attempted, a blow directed at these aged and physically failing invalids.

As a security measure the Germans who now controlled Grenoble announced that all British and alien subjects and known Gaullists in the city would be shipped to the Reich for internment. I knew what this meant and so, God help them, did the threatened innocents. They would be sent to the horror camps, to the gas chambers, for many of them were too old to be used as the beasts of burden that the Nazis made of their physically strong prisoners. I dropped all other work to fight this hideous measure.

From morning until night I waged a one-man war against the

authorities. Before I slept each night I beseeched God to help us and I thanked Him for the guidance that stopped me accepting the offer to return to England made by the London agents. Here I could do something to defend the poor from the miseries that the Godless new order was heaping upon them.

I wrote letters to friends abroad and had them smuggled across the Swiss frontier. I bombarded, through the same channel, the Red Cross and our own Government with pleas and protests. I charged into every relevant office in town threatening the day of justice and, I now realise, taking the most appalling risks. Most of these offices were controlled by that time with cowards and craven place-seekers. The Gestapo had rooted out the better Frenchmen. Those who survived were keeping quiet, waiting for the liberation. The traitors sat in the chairs of authority. One of them had me kicked out into the street. I realised then that I must take a final chance. I went to see the new commandant of the city who was an Italian.

Signor Commandante was a self-important man, beautifully groomed, good-looking in a plump way and like most vain men incorrigibly stupid. Left to himself, he would have been, I believe, a harmless sort of creature, efficient enough as a small tradesman and skilful enough on a suburban bowling green. Left to himself he wouldn't have made a big mark in the smallest parish in the world. But he had taken the Duce's nonsense about Cæsar's Rome surviving in the new Rome of the twentieth century, the façade raised by Mussolini himself, very seriously. Signor Commandante, I could see, had a prophetic vision of himself wearing a laurel wreath and returning to the Eternal City to burn sacrifices before gods that died with Constantine. He had flattered his way to success. He struck attitudes. He brooded. He looked magnanimous. He looked stern and pompous, and every so often he looked in the mirror. He was very handsome and quite ridiculous.

'Signor, these people are innocent!'

'M. le Pasteur, they are enemies of the Italian Empire and dangerous.'

'Dangerous to you, Signor Commandante! Forgive me, it is ridiculous.'

The manicured hand ran over the thick, shining black hair. He was thoughtful and clement. He smiled.

'You do not understand, M. le Pasteur. We fight a total war. All enemies are dangerous until they are subdued.'

'Life has subdued these people, Signor. They are old. They are ailing. They are women. Does Italy fight the aged and sick? Do your soldiers war on women?' and, taking a risk, 'Such battles make the Italians look ridiculous before the world.'

'You forget yourself, Pasteur. Our allies, the Germans, have investigated these people. Our allies wished them removed to the Reich. They will go.'

Leaning back in my chair, I grinned as offensively as I could, reached for a cigarette and when he stared at my effrontery I said with as near a leer as I could manage:

'I understand, Signor Commandante. You take orders from the Gestapo. I have been wasting your time, and my own. Forgive me. I'll see your commanding officer at S.S. Headquarters this evening. And I'll put a kind word in to him for you. You have been generous.'

I stood up to go. He jumped to his feet, pulling at his collar. Here it comes, I thought, now is the end. He pointed a shaking finger at me.

'Sit down,' he shouted. 'How dare you talk to me in that way. You forget yourself. If you were not a priest I'd have you shot. I'd have you shot now, this instant.'

'Forgive me, Signor,' I apologised. 'I know you are a humane man and I feel that only under duress would you agree to the brutish treatment that my poor compatriots are receiving. They will be killed in Germany. Now, if they were being sent to Italy, they would be happy. The Germans are not a cultured people, like your compatriots. These people, believe me, are too weak to menace anyone.'

'My information is that they are dangerous elements.' He was composed again, hand brushing the sleek hair. 'I shall investigate to-night. They do not leave until the morning. If there is truth in what you say, they will remain in Grenoble. The Germans, as you have noted, M. le Pasteur, are not civilised in the high Roman manner.'

With a flick of the hand he dismissed me. I left the office in low spirits. The poor silly man meant well, but I did not doubt that he would forget the matter or succumb to the bullying of some German, and my friends would be lost in a death camp.

Early next morning, I watched as they were herded out of the prison and on to lorries which had no coverings and looked filthy. Each of them carried a suitcase which was all the luggage permitted by their persecutors. They brightened when they saw me and called out. I spoke with each, offering words of good cheer that sounded hollow in my ears. The lorry filled and pulled a few yards up the street. As it started one or two shouted in despair:

'Good-bye, Padre.' The others waved their hands and wan faces struggled to break into smiles. Tears ran down my cheeks. I heard sobbing from French men and women who had come to watch their friends taken away. They had no doubt that they would never return. The scene was heartbreaking. But there was a respite when the lorry halted a few yards up the street and another drew in to the pavement opposite the entrance to the gaol. Immediately another party of victims filed out and again the good-byes began. I clasped their hands and told them I would keep on fighting on their behalf which, to me at least, seemed poor consolation to them. But even those few words of kindly intention pierced their sorrow and they brightened a little. The S.S. commandant looked on. His face unmoving. He was silent except for an occasional quiet instruction to a roaring sergeant of the Gestapo.

Four lorries filled and were lined up in the sunlit street and the fifth was drawing in when I heard the screech of a motor siren, the sort of thing that is used for dramatic effect in the more violent types of cinema entertainment. The screech turned into an agonising squeal of brakes as a luxurious Italian saloon car pulled in before the lorry. A young officer jumped out and shouted to the driver of that shoddy vehicle to withdraw. The German driver roared back until a second, less ornate car pulled in behind the limousine and a huge Italian N.C.O. leapt out, followed by a platoon, each bearing a tommy-gun. The young officer spoke to the giant very quickly. The latter turned round, focused his eyes on the Aryan lorry-driver and yelled so loudly that the old ladies on the lorries started with fright. Another Italian car arrived at that moment. Another platoon was disgorged from it. The lorry withdrew. Then and only then Signor Commandante stepped out from the limousine. With a wave of his hand he called over the S.S. commandant who stepped forward briskly and saluted.

With rapid, florid gestures the Signor Commandante began to speak to his ally. The latter seemed to answer sharply. The Italian patiently listened and began again. The German answered as sharply and there was a roar of anger from the signor. His arm shot out like a railway signal; and obviously he was ordering his racially pure friend indoors. There was going to be trouble and to a man in his position he may have felt that a fish-wives' squabble on the street of Grenoble would not bring prestige. The laurel leaves might have wilted. He spoke to the young officer who in turn addressed the sergeant and then followed his master indoors.

The Italian men-at-arms moved along the pavements, stringing themselves out beside the lorries. The German guards eyed them dubiously.

Nearly a half-hour passed before Signor Commandante emerged with his lieutenant. Again the latter spoke to the sergeant. Their car drove off and the S.S. commandant appeared. Italians and Germans sprang to attention as he gave orders. Then, to my relief, they started to clear our people from the lorries. Those exhausted victims of more than three years of war descended and again filed into prison. There still was hope. That evening some returned to their homes, again on parole; within three days all were freed. I sent a letter of thanks, full of operatic praise for a noble enemy, to the signor. God bless him wherever he is. The poor man was just a victim of the sort of nationalist superstition that irreligious dictators can fasten on simple people.

April, 1943, was a month of sunshine, a golden month of heat cooled by pleasant breezes from the north. During the week after my friends escaped from the German transportation plan, I constantly visited them and tried to readjust the older and the ill to the sense of security which had been rudely disturbed by the threat of removal from Grenoble. I wrote letters and with my assistants parcelled up into generous rations consignments of food that came to us from the Red Cross. I was elated by the victory won with God's help over the Germans and began to feel that the fears of my friends about the future were exaggerated. My confidence was strengthened by a visit from some of the more active members of my flock.

'Padre,' they said, 'we have arranged a social meeting of all your friends to take place on April 17th. We wish to make a small presentation to you as a token of our respect and gratitude for all you have done for us, especially your intervention when so many of us were about to be transported last week. You saved our lives.'

So long as a Minister of the Gospel has a congregation he has a home. I listened to those good folk that day and felt I might be in Scotland. I forgot for the time being that their lives had been endangered just a few days earlier; and it was release from that danger that had inspired their gesture of affection. I felt secure in their love and even now I know that the feeling was not misleading. A man exists by the love of God and he lives out his existence best when that greatest love of all is reflected into his heart by his fellow men and women.

I told them that I was grateful and that truthfully I was more indebted to them than they to me. We were all infinitely indebted to our Redeemer, the Master who saved all of us from wicked men and I agreed to come to their celebration. The tree-lined streets of Grenoble were alive in the sun that April day and I was happy going from British home to British home in the city, seeing love blossom again with fear cast out and watching our French neighbours' relief from the agony, knowing now that their allies and friends were safe again and next door to them. So the days passed away until April 16th, the day before the presentation. That evening I was invited to the home of a friend, Harris Rudowitch, which he shared with his father-in-law, Abraham Korn. It was the feast of the Passover and I rejoiced that I was going to be a guest of the Jews and would pray with them.

Condemning the anti-Semitic laws of the Nazis, outraged by them, a famous churchman once said that we Christians are all, in our Faith, Semitic. I pray that some day all of us will come to understand exactly what he meant. Until we do so we cannot be wholly Christian. Our God when He chose to walk the earth as a man, became a Jewish man and so the promise made to Adam was fulfilled. The Jewish scriptures are part of our Bible. The psalms we sing are Hebrew, as are the lessons we read and the texts of so many of our sermons. The Cross was raised over the world after the Feast of the Passover. The time is holy.

In that Jewish home on that April evening I was present and broke bread with my friends, representatives of the perennially victimised race, in a ritual older than the Europe which is Christian; Europeans had gone to their land as conquerors. It was Jews, the Apostles, who, invading Europe, brought us, in return for persecution, Christianity. There is an infinite tenderness in Jewish family relationships. The patriarch Abraham presiding, the neat ritual caps giving authority to the occasion, curiously isolating this family, strong in its faith, from the warring nations beyond the walls, had the atmosphere of eternity.

I listened to the ancient words and was moved by the simple undemonstrative way I was brought into the family circle as part of it. These people were intellectuals of the finest and most sensitive type in Europe and they had survived partly because France provided pockets of silence where a man might find a retreat and wait for better times. But at any moment now jack-boots might strike echoes from the road outside and father, grandfather, his children, their children, might be consciencelessly taken away and blotted from existence, liquidated as if they were worthless and malignant things. They simply were good. They were masters in the arts of elaborated goodness. They gave to the poor, the sick, the dispossessed; to unhappy Christians who had fallen victims to political persecution they gave friendship and compassion. They kept open house for all who came to their door.

As their guest on that blessed evening I found myself caught up in the old ritual, passed down from generation to generation, prayers elaborated and refined to a point of wonderful complexity yet so simple when offered by these men and women who spoke from their hearts.

When the time came for us to part I took the two hands of each member of the family in mine and wrung them warmly. I walked from their door in the state of high exaltation that close communion with God brings to a man, the words of the scriptures recurring in my mind as I made my way home. I thought of my own flock who would gather to-morrow to show their love for me and I felt grateful. They had part of their Bible in common with my Jewish friends and they had suffered in common with them for the same things.

When I reached the boarding-house it was in darkness. The whole world seemed asleep. The garden was silent with that whispering silence which comes on a warm spring night. My mind steeped in prayer found the world infinitely beautiful. I opened the front door with my latch key and tiptoed upstairs to my room, halted on the landing for no reason at all and then opened the door and walked towards my dressing-table to switch on a bedside lamp. Behind me a switch clicked over. The room was full of light. I turned around and found myself looking at five pointing revolvers.

I could have laughed aloud but surprise mingled with shock and I was silent. Five armed men had come to arrest the little minister as some of the Scottish lads called me. I must have made a considerable reputation. I must be reckoned a desperate character. The faces behind the guns were stern and unsmiling, solemn as only the faces of those who have the temerity to point guns at a man can be. It seemed ridiculous.

'Pastor Caskie, you are under arrest. You must come with us. Now.'

I asked for a few minutes and collected my Bible, a cigarette case, a pen and a razor. I put on a coat and they put handcuffs on my wrists. The manacles were too small and cut me. I winced and held them out.

'They'll do for you,' I was told.

As I walked downstairs between my captives I realised that I would miss the presentation party of the following afternoon. But already that part of my life seemed very far away. I hoped the old people would not miss me too much.

CHAPTER 13

IN THE VILLA LYNWOOD

THE CASERNE HOCHE in Grenoble is not the best of prisons. The cell into which I was flung was filthy. The wall against which I fell was hard, the guards violent. My face was bruised. On the floor, the bedding, a bundle of rancid straw, gave off a poisonous smell. Brutally the guards twisted me around until I faced them. They removed my braces, tie and shoelaces. The Italians were not as efficient as the Germans but they were more cruel. Their prisoners have been known to hang themselves with accessories of the kind that they took from me. They treat prisoners like vicious cats playing with mice; but they lack the final savagery of cats. They do not kill without orders. Their absentminded vindictiveness degrades the prisoner.

For two weeks I was held in the Caserne Hoche, adjusting myself to a new small world of darkness bound by damp stone and uninhabited by anyone who saw me as a human being. I asked to see the *commandante* and the guards did not answer. I asked for a trial and they guffawed. I asked them to tell me the nature of the crime I was accused of committing. They told me to ' shut up.' It was a strange, isolating experience, desperately humiliating, in which a man might have collapsed into despair. But my knowledge of the Scriptures saved me, and my recollections of the imprisonments of the Apostles and later Christian martyrs gave me a rule by which I lived during those weeks and the months that followed. I existed in memories of good days, and in prayer.

They took my Bible from me and the few possessions I had brought from de Verger. When I protested, an official answered with a sneer. 'You are a priest. You should have this book in

132

your head.' I had it in my heart and head and it preserved my faith and sanity. Each day I was given a small crust of bread and a flat tin containing less than a half pint of water. After the second day I felt no hunger for food. Imprisonment was my torture. During the first long hours I wandered around the cell like a mouse on a tiny tread-mill, but I was a man and I hated the limitations of the place and the frustrating bounds it set upon me. I thought of my family in Scotland and I resented the misfortune that had halted my work. I worried about my friends in Grenoble and wondered if I had left evidence that might compromise them. The Italians did not interrogate me and this led me to suspect that I might be only one victim of a wholesale round-up. But when despair threatened to engulf my soul the voice of Christian reason asserted itself and I prayed. The knowledge came back to me that I and my persecutors were in God's hands. In His time he would make everything just again and I was consoled. In the darkness my heart lifted and joy surged through me.

Years later I learned that I was the only person arrested that day. My imprisonment was not a signal for an outburst of persecution. When I did not arrive for the presentation party my friends, British and French, investigated my absence and were told of my imprisonment. They asked for permission to visit me and this was refused. They were told, in the words of the Italians, that M. Caskie was ' being treated with all the honours of his rank as a Protestant clergyman.' My rooms were searched and two friends, Miss Ethel Davidson from Aberdeen and Mlle. Suzanne Creton of l'École de la Légion d'Honneur were visited by the Gestapo and interrogated, but not arrested. They were faithful friends and brave women. They both helped me, encouraged me, and inspired me in my work. Some time before my arrest they agreed to hide documents of considerable importance to the organisation. These were secreted in a wooden box in the toilet of their flat when the Germans came. Fortunately for the ladies, no search was made, but the danger did not pass immediately. Later when I had become a memory in Grenoble an epidemic broke out in the school and the Gestapo transported pupils and teachers to the Château des Combres near Voiron. The ladies were not searched on the journey.

The epidemic may have done them good service in this respect for they were not even approached by officials. A very cursory inspection of the travellers would have revealed that Miss Davidson carried the documents on her lap under the travelling rug she held about her knees to keep her warm in June. Caught with that evidence, I cannot but believe that those two courageous women, Ethel and Suzanne, would have been shot or sent to a death camp in the Reich.

At the end of April, I was taken from the Caserne Hoche and transferred to Cuneo in Italy, where I remained for a couple of nights sitting on a stone floor without bedding of any kind in complete darkness nursing raw and bleeding wrists. The handcuffs used on the journeys were again so tight that I cried out when they were forced on to my wrists. Rusted, crudely finished, dirty, I thought at first they had crushed the wrists to pulp and I would be crippled when the implements were removed. But when blood forced its way back into the blanched hands that were hanging limply by my side I knew that soon I would be able to use them again.

Time was one long unending night and when they came to take me to the Villa Lynwood at Nice I blinked like an owl as the door opened and light struck my eyes. The guards sniggered as they dragged me outside. They did not use handcuffs that time but wound heavy iron chains around my wrists, leaving the ends hanging so that they struck against my heels as I walked. Thrust upstairs and, with carabinieri walking behind me carrying rifles with naked bayonets attached, I reeled into a courtyard where a lorry stood. The sun hurt my eyes. I fell to my knees and struggled to my feet again. Shuddering with shame at my condition, dirty, unkempt, weak from starvation, I rocked on my heels. I ate no food at Cuneo. They did not give me any. The guards heaved me on to a lorry and during most of the journey to Nice kept me standing. Light-headed, half delirious, I gazed sickly about me, seeing nothing and aching to scratch my face where my beard, under the hot sun, was itching in a painful way. Sweat ran down my face and nausea nearly overcame me. Before we reached the villa in the evening, after numerous halts, during one of which

I was given a crust and a pannikin of water, I was allowed to sit. When the lorry pulled into the avenue leading to the big house, I was barely conscious.

The Villa Lynwood, in peaceful days on that beautiful coast, had been the property of an English lady. It was large and beautifully proportioned, standing in about an acre of ground. The gardens had been cultivated with the good taste in gardening for which the English are justly famous. Happy sunlit holidays had been spent in it by the English lady and her friends and they must have taken grateful memories home. In May, 1943, it was a house of torture isolated in a garden that had degenerated into a wilderness. Barbed wire enclosed it. An air of sadness and the sordid hung about its walls. Heavily armed men guarded every entrance; dogs wandered loose in the garden through the night. Many prisoners suffered torture in the Villa Lynwood and the maquis believe that many murders were committed in its dark and gloomy cellars.

When the lorry jerked to a halt that evening I lay still upon the floor; my face pressed against its rough boards. Suddenly my mind was feverishly active. My limbs remained leaden. Two carabinieri caught me by the heels and dragged me to the ground, catching me as I fell and thrusting me to my feet. With hands under my armpits they heaved me through the house, down into the basement and along a corridor. We passed a door of bars leading into a cell and I saw a woman gazing out, on her face a look of desolation that spoke of suffering and privation. It was Odette Churchill, the heroic woman who was the centre of one of the epics in the annals of the Resistance. I forced my head up and tried to smile at her and I saw her face light up before a heavy blow drove me onwards to the end of the corridor. I never saw Odette again and, indeed, it was later when one of her comrades was imprisoned with me, that I learned the identity of the lady in the cell in the villa, but her tired bravery impressed me during those few seconds outside her cell.

A door clanged behind me and I sank on to the floor into a deep sleep or coma. When I wakened the morning was advanced and a broad shaft of light lay across the cell. Above my head was a window on ground level and by standing on a bucket which had been left to supply sanitary conveniences I could see out into the deserted courtyard. About noon, as I reckoned—it may have been later—a piece of very hard bread and a pan of water were thrust through the bars at me. By dipping the bread in the water I was able to eat it. The Italians, I realised, had attained a certain efficiency in their arrangements for dieting penal establishments. They simplified it.

During that day I saw no one but a silent patrolling guard who gazed through the bars every hour as if checking on a peculiar, voiceless beast. When I spoke to him he did not answer. He did not so much look at me as through me, as if I were part of the not very lavish furnishings of the place. When evening came he opened the door and took out the sanitary pail. My food he always put through the bars. Another day passed during which I lost myself in a world of memories, separating myself from the cell, recreating my own life. I meditated upon the Scriptures and found that while gaol lacked the amenities penal reformers in my country took for granted, it offered wonderful opportunities for meditation upon the mysteries of my religion. When the hours of torture began I prayed quietly, stilling my angry and enraged compassion for the bodies and souls in hazard in the rooms above. I came to think that maybe my vocation lay there in the villa, offering prayers for the lost ones of the patriot organisations. The padre to the prisoners had been chosen by God to follow those whom he could not contact in other days and live with them on the brink of death.

In my cell there was evidence that the Villa Lynwood had become a projection of hell upon earth. The plastered walls were covered with the names of men and women who had halted there on the road to death or the camps. Among them I found signatures of old comrades of mine who had disappeared. Some I knew were dead, others had just vanished.

The sound of feet dragging in the corridors beyond my door brought me away from my meditations on the second day, and a few minutes later a man came into view marching blindly. I rushed to the bars and gazed out at him. A guard carrying a rifle and bayonet marched behind. The victim did not raise his eyes but staggered the few yards to the outside walls and leaned against them. The naked bayonet prodded him. He did not cry out but turned heavily on his feet and moved away out of sight again, passing my door. I saw he was young. The dark face gaunt, unshaven, sagged. He staggered as he walked. A few minutes passed and again I heard the dragging feet and saw him move towards the wall at the corridor's end. The guard now carried the rifle resting in his armpit and again he prodded the poor body that automatically rested against the stone. This ghastly patrol continued all through the day. Whenever I stood by the door the rifle bayonet was turned towards me significantly. I lay awake throughout the night praying, but all through the next day the march went on. It continued for four days. Then it suddenly stopped and I heard no more of the man who marched.

For hours I sank in misery, praying for him who had gone and feeling miserably futile, realising as never before the bonds that can be put upon a man's soul when his body is held in prison. My every instinct, all my training for the ministry, all my service to God and His flock urged me to help that shambling broken man. A bayonet held between us stayed me. When the guards rattled the bars of my cell and I went forward to take my crust and pan of water, I saw in the latter a fly scrambling to get out. I picked it out and set it on the floor where its legs flickered like tiny thin black lines. I watched it begin to move. It crawled across the floor and I followed it to one of the walls where former prisoners had inscribed the honours roll of those who had passed through the Gethsemane of the Villa Lynwood. I was one of them. My nails were long and uncut and I recall the irony that filled my heart as I considered the claw on my right thumb. Carefully I inscribed my name and rank in the Church of Scotland in the hard plaster. The task finished, I observed my handiwork. It was, I flattered myself, quite a neat job. The roll was up-to-date. But I was the padre. Choosing a largish space on the plaster untouched by names, I wrote:

'Thus saith the Lord. . . . Fear not for I have redeemed thee . . . I have called them by name. Thou art mine. When thou passeth through the waters, I will be with thee, and through the rivers, they shall not overflow thee. When thou walketh through the fire, thou shalt not be burned, neither shall the flame kindle upon thee . . .'

The light had changed when I completed my task. Slowly I had prayed the words as I cut into the plaster, sending them out to the man whose tired soul maybe was at peace as I wrote. I stood back to study the verse and heard noises outside the window. Climbing on the bucket, I pulled myself up and gazed through the misty pane. The light was still good enough for me to see a figure that was familiar standing outside, his hands bound behind him. He turned his head and I recognised Gerald Hakim who had been an agent in the South of France when I was more actively engaged with the organisation. He bent and peered at my window and then I knew he had recognised me. With an effort I managed to hold on with one hand while I placed a finger on my lips to silence any demonstration from him. The effort was too much for me and I tumbled backwards into the cell, banging my head against the hard floor.

Long into the night I lay thinking of Gerald. The slightest disturbance of prison routine, I discovered in gaol, unleashes all sorts of memories and associations in the mind of a human being who is a prisoner. The figure in the garden outside my window brought to mind events that led me back to my experiences. I wondered how the enemy had captured Hakim and if he had been submitted to torture; if he was fit and what they would do with him. At last I fell asleep. When I awoke, two guards were standing over me. They took me to a cell on the other side of the house where one of them motioned me to enter. I was very tired as I walked mechanically through the door. One develops in gaol an instinct for obedience to guards. I looked around me. The place was just another cell, but a man was in it. It was my friend Gerald Hakim. Trembling I held out my hands and he grasped them.

'Padre, Padre, what are you doing in this place?'

At first I did not answer but just looked at him. To measure the joy I felt seeing Gerald and hearing his friendly voice I should have to recapture the feeling of having escaped from that dreadful vacuum of pain again. He clapped my back gently and put an arm around my shoulder. We sat upon the floor and talked throughout the day. I told him of my arrest and the events that followed but neither of us lingered upon our experiences in the villa. I spoke of Scotland and he of England and we compared notes on our memories of home. We spoke of our wartime professions. He told me his story and revealed that the woman I saw on my first night in the villa was Odette Churchill.

Gerald was one of those amiable men who undertake perilous duties with the absentminded savoir-faire of a clerk going about routine tasks. The Intelligence Service employed him to travel around the South of France collecting information and he knew the terrain well, was a brilliant linguist and well-trained to exploit a talent for recognising every relevant movement of traffic, troops, supplies and people. Using no disguise and the minimum of forged papers, he toured France on a push-bike. He cycled into towns and villages, spent a night or so observing and drifted on his way, all the time gathering details of enemy activities which formed parts of a vast jig-saw puzzle which, at Whitehall, was being constantly assembled into a moving picture of Europe under the Nazis and Fascists. When Odette was arrested at Sevrier on the lovely lake of Annecy in the Savoy, the Gestapo knew of Gerald's work with her. They sought him too but he was gone and they arrested all the inhabitants of the little village, herded them together and drove them through the interrogating rooms they had established in a little villa Gerald had occupied in 1939. He had escaped on his push-bike and his work continued. They did not betray him.

A traitor betrayed him in the Nice district. This man was an old friend, Carlo Monferrino by name, whose treachery puzzled Gerald. They had been close to each other for nearly twenty-five years and had shared a common passion for ski-ing and rock climbing. They had endured much as comrades in the latter sport. The betrayal seemed inexplicable to Gerald but it was a fact. He was a prize the Gestapo reasonably sought. His apparently absent-minded progress on that push-bike had brought him to places and people a more conservative agent would not have attempted to reach.

His 'star turn,' as he called it, deserves a note, at least, in the annals of those years. Pierre Laval's secretary was stopping at Thonon-les-bains in the Haute Savoie and Gerald decided to call upon him. The secretary was a busy man and by collecting a little information about his background, Gerald casually convinced him that his caller was an old friend of his family. They drank coffee together and talked for more than an hour. M. Hakim departed with his head crammed with valuable information. He chuckled like a boy when he told this story. It was a hard blow to me when the door of the cell opened again and I was taken out and escorted back to my first cell. But I felt happier in soul and body when I lay down to sleep. My day with Gerald Hakim restored to me a feeling of human companionship, and I knew that I was not alone.

Early on that first morning of my return to the private cell I scrutinised the wall. Another name had been inscribed upon it. It had been occupied in my absence by another guest. I looked at the verse I had cut with my thumbnail and began to cut it deeper into the plaster. I became engrossed in the task. 'The rivers shall not overflow thee . . .' When I reached these words I was interrupted by guards dangling handcuffs. They told me to come with them.

They had come to take me to the fortress of St. Remo in Italy.

CHAPTER 14

THE FORTRESS BY THE SEA

LIKE A great sprawling rock the prison at St. Remo was almost surrounded by water, from some angles it resembled a man-made island. When clouds obscured the sunlight it loomed darkly like a charnel house of the living.

Many centuries have passed since it was built. A multitude of men and women have lived in chains within its massive walls, never feeling the ocean breeze on their whitened skin and never the touch of the blessed Italian sun. A mournful heritage of age-old cruelty gives the place an atmosphere of doom. For centuries there was no hope for those held in its black, remorseless bowels. It is an ante-chamber of hell, a place Dante might have imagined. Water drips from the four-feet-thick cell walls as though the sea beyond, in beating against it, had turned malignant and slowly penetrated to play its part in the tortured isolation of the inmates. The dungeons are foul, encrusted with the filth of centuries. I believe they have never been properly cleaned at any time since the place was heaved into existence. Poor sanitation is part of the Italian tradition and no attempts were made during World War II to improve it. A bucket was left in each cell. Sometimes it was not emptied for a week or more; even then it was slopped out and not rinsed with clean water. Sometimes it was taken away for a few days and returned still stinking to the prisoner. The stench of St. Remo symbolised the moral evil done within its ancient walls. But the diet did not leave material for nausea to exploit and the sickened body writhed in physical frustration.

I was brought to the fortress on a May evening when the sun was sinking and the Mediterranean winds were fresh. The gates closed with the ponderous movement that prisoners had heard from ancient days. The guards awaiting grasped me as if I had been a dangerous beast or a lunatic likely to attack them in a homicidal way. They were of the Neapolitan breed of prison attendants and, I believe, the worst in the world.

Through narrow winding passages I was shoved, downwards on uneven stairways and along passages until it seemed we must be approaching the pit. All around us was darkness. We halted and a torch was flashed. Its beam steadied on a narrow iron doorway, rusted into the deep stone. Laboriously it was opened outwards, creaking with age, and I was pushed inside.

I found myself in a medieval ' bottle ' cell. There are, I suppose, special chapters in the history of penology treating of these diabolical apartments. I do not wish to read them. The ' bottle ' cell in my experience is ingenious, easy for the torturer to operate and guaranteed in time to drive the strongest victim insane. Shaped like a man, it is a bottle-shaped cell of stone big enough to contain one human being but short enough not to permit him to stand upright and narrow enough to restrain him from lying down. It tapers at the top so that the face is never more than two inches from the walls that encase his head.. He cannot move his knees more than a few inches. If he rests on his shoulders the strain on his legs becomes agonising. The flow of his blood and cramp will deprive him of consciousness so that he hangs in stone bonds; his body deformed by them, until consciousness wrests him into pain again. It is, I conjecture, the most vile instrument of torture ever devised by men.

They left me for only twenty-four hours in the ' bottle.' Then I was picked out and taken to a cell where I was flung upon the floor. When my wits were assembled I found bread and water lying beside me. I drank the water and fell asleep.

When I awakened I was exhausted, so tired that the flesh seemed to hang upon my bones with a dead weight, the bones felt curiously dry. I have never felt so conscious of my body. There seemed to be thin sand in my veins and life was draining away. There was no sound in the place, no light. I might have been entombed. How long I lay there I cannot tell. In absolute darkness and silence time is immeasurable. Sometimes I crawled on the

floor, perhaps a few yards, until my head found a wall. After a
moment of rest I stood up with a movement between a push and a
crawl. Erect I leaned my head against the stone, which was wet.
My fingers moved across its rough surface and found water
trickling in the crevices. How long I stood there I do not know. I
must have slipped to the floor again and dropped into sleep. For
the second time I awakened, but now I was slightly refreshed and
my mind began to work, my eyes became accustomed to the darkness. Dimly I saw that the dungeon was bigger than the cell at
the Villa Lynwood but the iron door was solid. Beside it a bucket
stood and there was a plate on which some crusts of bread lay and
two pans of water. Without interest I gazed at the objects and
saw there were two plates and two pans of water. I was hungry
and thirsty. Ravenously I rent the crusts with my teeth. They had
the texture of charcoal and were tasteless. I dipped them in water
and they tasted good. One pan I drained, the other sipped, and
with a little water I rubbed my eyelids. Again I slept.

I do not know how long this state of mind and body continued
but I remember awakening and lying watching the door and hearing it squeak softly, like a frightened mouse. I watched, there was
a fumbling noise and it opened. My eyes moved downwards and I
saw a plate slide in and a gloved hand being withdrawn. And
then I knew I was in solitary confinement. I was weak and I did
not mind being alone. I lay back and rested, unthinking, un-
worried, barely alive. I began to pray.

The hours became long and I waited for the hand at the door
to reassure me that I was not dead and walled-up, that they had
not entombed me and left me to die, my flesh to rot and then my
bones swept out into the sunlight, anonymous, forgotten by all save
those who loved me and were praying even then in Islay, Paris,
Grenoble, Marseilles and beyond the sea. Thinking of my loved
ones steadied me and I remembered the religion we held in
common and thus after an unending night of darkness and brooding I began to live again. I yearned for my Bible and the words of
the Apostles filled my head. I began to murmur whole chapters
of the Bible aloud to myself, not chanting but whispering and
reflecting, my mind moving over the words as it did in peace-time,

and as it still does when I work on sermons or seek advice or solace in sorrow. The book might have been open before me. I saw its pages in my mind's eye. Strangely this vision came to me as I meditated on the blessings of recollection and I thought of my school in Islay and the schoolmistress who taught me French and was in charge of our Sunday school.

Miss Jessie Marshall is one of the persons to whom I shall be indebted throughout life and eternity for she gave me the language which was the means of my work in Paris, and she was one of those, next to my dear mother who taught me to pray. I was not an easy pupil, sometimes lazy like all healthy boys who wish to be off in the heather when they should be at their books. Oh, those French verbs! In the dungeons of St. Remo I thought of her in my distress and found myself smiling, for Miss Marshall has become one of the legends of the school at Islay and I, her recalcitrant pupil, am part of the legend. Carefully I led my mind into the past. I had rebelled one day when she chided me for not working as hard as she would have wished.

'Why must I study this wretched language?' I stormed. 'It's no use to a Scotsman. I hate it.'

'French is a great and wonderful language and you will be grateful for it some day, Donald,' she answered.

Reluctantly I took her instruction and thus she made me a citizen of Europe and enabled me to contribute a little of Scotland and our religion to life in Paris. When I was called to church in the Rue Bayard she was overwhelmed with joy. Our Scottish people hold the ministry in great honour; for one of Jessie's boys to achieve the pulpit in the Rue Bayard was an achievement crowning her teaching. In the years that followed whenever a boy or girl was absentminded about homework, she would raise her fingers and say:

'Once I had a pupil who, like you, asked why he should learn this foreign tongue and to-day that boy . . .'

She told the story so often that there came a time when the class chorused to her:

'We know, Miss Marshall, the Reverend Donald Caskie, the Minister in the Paris Kirk.'

More than a month passed before I saw a human being apart from the silent guard. The dungeon I made a world of memory and prayer. For hours I continued to recite the Scriptures. Whole days would pass while in reverie I reconstructed my past life. I would end a Bible session with a thought of my family and my mind would drift to Islay. The dungeon walls would disappear and I would see again the Paps of Jura, the view across the water, the blue hills and green fields, the lapping water on the beach. I heard the voice of my mother call me at seven-fifteen on a winter's morning and I smiled as I remembered driving my grumbling body from between the blankets. As memories filled my mind I stretched out on the stone floor and luxuriated in them.

The days stretched behind me. I lost count of time. I felt reconciled to my fate, I was relatively happy but physically I had weakened considerably although I was then unaware of it. A daily crust of bread and pan of water were rather less than the diet my body had been accustomed to absorb.

Days, weeks, more than a month passed. On the Sundays I devised for myself, I projected my soul to Islay and the mid-morning Gaelic service when the blessed words are spoken in our native language and then at another service at noon in English. I attended both.

So I lived out my solitary days filling the dungeon with the laughter of my family and friends until the day came when the dungeon door opened and a figure was hurtled through to fall beside me. Almost timorously I touched him and then helped him to his feet. One can live almost too long in a world of one's own devising. The prisoner was dazed and bruised, but he was real.

'Vallet's the name,' he murmured. 'Captain Vallet. Je suis Français. I'm glad to see you, Monsieur. I've been in solitary. Nearly killed myself. It was at Nice, in the Villa Lynwood.'

His eyes were red-rimmed. His whole body trembled. After he had spoken he lay down and slept while I sat by his side.

Captain Vallet had been wounded and crippled for life in the 1914-18 War. In 1940 he became a soldier of the Free French Army. In St. Remo he became my friend for life. He was not young, but he was a singularly brave man. I confess that when, in retrospect, I think of the engagements in which he and many of my friends took part during those years, I wonder any of them survive to-day, to sit and talk over old times after dinner in the manse with me.

'I was terror-stricken when they took me,' he said. 'I knew too much. Under torture I might have betrayed some of our friends.'

His task, I learned, had been supremely important to the organisation. He had been in control of the despatch of officers of very high rank escaping from the Boche. Their route, I was startled to hear, ended at Cap d'Antibes where a submarine surfaced at certain specified times and the V.I.P.s were taken aboard for transport home. Fortunately Vallet had been free of company and papers when he was taken. It seems uncertain that the Italians knew how important and useful his work had been to the Allied cause. They flung him into the Villa Lynwood at Nice and there his experiences weighed on his mind to such an extent that he contemplated suicide. All this he told me and he added the words that bind us in friendship to this day:

'I was on the point of cutting a vein and killing myself when I looked at the wall of my cell and saw words that stayed my hand and brought me comfort, consolation and strength. I am no longer afraid. I'll never forget those words.'

He relapsed into silence for a moment and then slowly he quoted the text from Isaiah I had carved into the wall of the cell at the Villa Lynwood.

'I am Donald Caskie,' I told him. 'I wrote those words on that wall.'

He did not speak and both of us sat quietly. I looked at him and saw tears running down his face. He took my hands in his and then we ate our bread together and talked until we were exhausted. During the days that followed, my friendship with Vallet deepened by our exchange of common memories, opinions, ideas, hopes and fears. I had learned the worst of the prison at St. Remo and although weeks of discomfort and starvation lay ahead of me I was not left alone again for more than a few days.

Vallet remained in the cell for about a week before his transfer to another camp. Some days passed and then I was joined by

Pierrugues of the Brigade of St. Jean. Pierrugues was an old soldier of the maquis who would have been at home in the Grand Armée of Napoleon. Soldiering was a trade to him. He would work out plans and maps in the dust on the floor and use the plates and pans on which our food and water were delivered as objects illustrating his themes. He had no doubt of victory. To this day he continues to be my friend, still the staunch lover of France.

He was a liaison officer of the underground; one of the men who distributed orders and intelligence to units scattered through France. When he first told me of his duties, he smiled a little crooked smile as he said:

'I was compelled to take Holy Orders, Monsieur Donald, to carry out my task. I got myself a cassock from the curé of our village, a good man who did not like his parishioners to go without clothing fitting to their day's work.'

Pierrugues's term of duty before his capture had been long. He worked for over two years without detection and his disguise as a priest was more than adequate. He could tour the villages without arousing anyone's suspicion. Late in the evening he would come to a village church, he told me, and install himself in a confessional apartment. There the local maquis lieutenant would meet him and receive his briefing.

'But, my friend,' I said, with a shudder, 'supposing a true penitent came first. What did you do?'

The brown face broke into a broad grin. Prison pallor had not taken the sun out of Pierrugues's skin.

'Pasteur, Pasteur, it was simple. I merely said that he or she must see M. le Curé since I was using the "box" to shrive certain people who were all known to us. No one questioned my reply. No sacrilege was done and God forgave us, I am certain, when we used the Church as part of our plan, for He knows we did not invite the Boche to invade our country. Let the Germans get back where they belong and you will be able to return to your place in the pulpit and I to my job during the day, the café in the evening and my church on Sunday. That is where we belong.'

I learned much from Pierrugues and Vallet as I talked with

them and the two men who followed them, Raphael and Ribout, a Jewish father and son who had fought tenaciously and relentlessly before they, like Pierrugues, were betrayed by the one Judas who occurs in a thousand patriots, on whose head may be laid the guilt of betraying hundreds.

Thin, wiry men, in appearance a curious blend of the purely Hebrew and the French townsman, they were strikingly alike, like an old and newer version of the same man. Radicals of an old, tough and honest kind, they knew nothing of their own religion. Their Jewishness and native good taste, I suspect, kept them from the excesses of anti-clericalism that have marred and distorted the Radical movement in France. Perturbed to find themselves gaoled with a *clerc*, not out of distaste for the cloth, but because to see one in prison affronted their very Gallic ideas of dignity, they soon engaged me in discussion of the Idea of God, the Jewish and Christian religions and the Churches in general. Their approach to these subjects began with inessentials, continued with the repetition of anti-clerical gossip and ended with rather inflated ideas of the advantages 'the revolution' would bring to the poor. It was easy to dispose of their rather obvious assertion of the truism that all priests and pastors were not saints and the extraordinary deduction they made from this fact, that there is no God and consequently all churches are frauds perpetrated upon the simpletons of this life. I reminded them that all revolutionaries were not loyal. They were in gaol because of a traitor who certainly was anything but a priest. But what absorbed me most was taking them through the Bible and explaining the theological arguments upon which we base our faith. They would listen, question me, agree or disagree, argue and so our days passed. I began to feel almost at home in St. Remo. When the morning came that I left I was sorry to say good-bye.

The brute-guard who brought us food opened the door of our dungeon and motioned me to get out. Raphael and Ribout had lightened the burden of my days. I think I had taught them something of my religion and their ancestral Judaism. They were good companions, those Jewish comrades, father and son and, like Good Samaritans, they gave comfort to at least one Christian. I grasped their hands and left them, so touched by their kindness that I did not know where I was until the guard led me into the *commandante's* office.

Brusquely the Italian officer behind the large desk told me to stand up straight. I was weak and my sudden release, after months of incarceration in the dungeon, disconcerted me. My wits did not so much wander, as fly in all directions. What was going to happen now? The officer issued quick orders to an N.C.O. sitting at a smaller desk and this man went to the door and called in a middle-aged sergeant who snapped handcuffs on to my right wrist, leaving one cuff dangling at my side. An envelope was handed to him and he motioned me to the door. Outside in the courtyard I was helped into a truck and there the other cuff, with me attached, was locked on to a pallid young man who sat on the floor. The lorry moved out of the prison precincts and that was the last I saw of St. Remo. I sat on the rumbling lorry and did not attempt to look back at the place. It was the worst prison I ever entered.

It was July, 1943. All round the world the armies of the free world were being marshalled. In Asia, Europe, from West to East, millions of people were slowly dying in camps. In peace-time this would have been the height of the season on the Mediterranean. The sun was high and the air from the sea was fresh in the truck. My companion was silent and the miles were quickly covered, past beaches, villas, casinos and wayfarers.

At last the young man chained to my wrist spoke to me. Another underground fighter, he was on his way to possible death and torture. I tried to comfort him until the road became familiar and I knew we were approaching the Villa Lynwood. I said good-bye to my travelling companion when we reached the sinister building. I prepared myself for the worst. In my cell I prayed for strength to face the morrow.

I was awakened early and without formality brought to the courtyard and placed on another truck. We drove off and Italy receded. I was being returned to France. The villa behind us, my heart lightened. It is good to go home and France is my home— even in chains. We reached Toulon and I was handed over to a German corporal with another soldier in attendance. Both were very solemn in their attitude to the Italians and very 'regimental' in their attitude to me until we reached the station and I heard the older one mention Marseilles. He winked when he spoke and handed me a bundle of sandwiches.

'Prisoner's rations, sir,' he said. 'Hope they are up to Italian standards.'

When we settled down on our seats in a train compartment the corporal was smiling. Blandly he stuck a 'reserved' notice on the door. He leaned towards me and took my hands. The hand-cuff clicked and came off.

'We'll forget about these things in the meantime, Pastor,' he observed. 'So this is the way they treat the clergy in Italy. Now make yourself comfortable. You can feel at home with us. I go to church, your church I think. My name is Hans and that's what our pastor calls me.'

The square face, under a thinning thatch of hay-coloured hair with white streaks in it, broke into a wider grin and in my weakened condition I could have wept. It was a decent, working-man's face. It would not have been out of place taking a parade of recruits at Maryhill Barracks at Glasgow, the Gordon Barracks at Brig o' Don or the Black Watch Barracks in Perth. I had helped many men who might have been his brothers to escape from Marseilles. Hans noticed that I was emotionally moved.

'Tell me, Pastor, are you English still singing that song—now, how does it go?' He had loosened the collar of his tunic; his legs in the jack-boots stretched out across the floor. In a raddled bari-tone he sang:

'*We're going to hang out the washing on the Siegfried line,*
Have you any dirty washing Mutti dear . . .?'

The heavenly choirs, if I am blessed to hear them sing, will sing no sweeter than Hans sounded in my ears in that shabby compart-ment. I found myself joining in and when the chorus ended we laughed aloud, he, I and the solemn young soldier who was his comrade.

'Pastor, it looks as if they will hang out that washing before much time passes.'

Hans was looking at me very seriously. Throughout the journey

to Marseilles he brought me up-to-date with news of the war and
I was heartened. The tide of war was running our way. German
soldiers, I learned, like the French civilians, were devoted listeners
to the B.B.C. 'We are *kaput*, Pastor.' When we reached my old
parish I was primed with encouraging information.

Outside the station Hans took me to a café and there he and
his comrade ordered the best meal the place could provide and I ate
it while we talked. Over coffee he said that I must prepare to be
handcuffed again.

'It is our orders, Pastor, and it will not help you if we arrive at
St. Pierre without the bracelets.'

I held out my hands when the meal ended, thanked both men
and received their good wishes. I parted from them in the orderly
room of the Prison of St. Pierre at Marseilles, which was thronged
with arriving prisoners. Part of a long queue, I stood in a corridor
beyond which lay an interrogation room. The door was never
closed and my heart sank during those hours. The inquisitors were
not gentle. They stormed at their prisoners. I heard the sound of
blows being struck, and then I was pushed through that door.

CHAPTER 15

HOLIDAY CAMP

THE GESTAPO OFFICER was tall, his uniform fitting sleekly to his slim, unbelted waist. The boots gleaming black. In his mouth he held a thin brown cheroot as he stood over the desk, scrutinising the papers which had been placed before him. About a dozen members of the corps stood around or sat on chairs. There was only one desk. All the subordinates wore gloves. A prisoner was hustled half-conscious from the room as I entered.

The officer found the papers interesting. He read very carefully, taking the cheroot from his mouth, absentmindedly picking a piece of tobacco from his lips with finely manicured hands. He was very handsome; the fair hair shampooed to a fluffiness, the long tanned face with that finished shaven look that only a valet can impart. On his wrist a gold watch shone, held in place by a thin tracery of gold threads woven into a strap. I stood for about five minutes waiting. He put the papers aside and motioned to a sergeant. A chair was placed behind me. I was told to sit down and the officer sat down also, laid his elbows on the desk top, bent his head forward, smiled in the most kindly way and burst into song:

> ' My heart's in the Highlands
> My heart is not here.
> My heart's in the Highlands
> A-chasing the deer.
> A-chasing the wild deer and following the roe,
> My heart's in the Highlands, wherever I go.'

Around the room the underlings sat up in their chairs, admiration on every face. I gazed stupidly, fearing at first that he was

152

mad and then thinking this was one of the famous Gestapo novel approaches to torture. He continued until the ending:

  '*My heart's in the Highlands,*
   Wherever I go. . . .'

Applause broke through the room. He waved it down with a magnanimous hand.

'Alas, Mr. Caskie. I am saddened to see you here in this place. It grieves me to hold you under arrest. I have orders, but you will find that here in St. Pierre you will receive treatment worthy of your position. But what do you think of my knowledge of your folksongs? You are surprised, I expect.'

'You are a very fine tenor, Herr Commandant,' I stammered, truthfully. 'And I know your people often have knowledge of our Scottish music. I have heard it sung, and sung it myself in Germany for friends, in happier times.'

'Ah, you have visited the Reich. But of course. All men of education know our country. Let me tell you I know England and Scotland well—very well, especially Clydebank and Coventry.'

He arose from his desk and began to pace up and down the room, blowing thin columns of smoke from his pursed lips. I could not forget the treatment I had heard meted out to my unfortunate French fellow-prisoners. I watched an interesting and uncommon type of monster.

'I, Pastor, am an engineer. I mentioned Coventry and Clyde-bank because they were some of the many places I visited just before September 1939 in England and Scotland. Coventry and Clydebank! Alas, so many fine engineering plants. Those machine-tool manufacturers. All gone, you know. Such a pity but it was necessary. The Luftwaffe is ruthless and it must be so. But I know all those former great centres of engineering. And now they are no more. I expect you knew the magnificent Clyde ship-yards. Alas, you will never see them again. War is ruthless and we were forced to act. It grieved us, you know, and none more than the Fuehrer.'

The thought of the Clyde destroyed sickened me; I had no means of knowing that he lied or was a victim of Goebbels's lies. I remained silent, utterly sickened. He continued, diverting on to folk songs. His knowledge of the subject would have been remarkable in a Scotsman. Even I, a man with a lifetime of study in music, given to a great extent to the folk music of Scotland, had to keep my mind alert as he touched on aspects of the subject, traditional and contemporary. Burns set to music seemed to fascinate him. He quoted the lyrics, sang them, hummed Gaelic airs and obviously enjoyed himself. He stopped his singing abruptly.

'Alas, we must stop this interesting conversation, Pastor. I hope you will be comfortable here. I shudder to think what you must have endured in the hands of our vulgar Italian allies. Here you have nothing to fear. But I must warn you. Accept discipline. Do not attempt to escape. Keep to our orders and we will be kind. Good-afternoon.'

The blue eyes contemplated me almost tenderly. It would hurt him to discipline me. A package was pushed across the table.

'Take this, Pastor. It is yours.'

As I followed two members of the corps to a cell, I opened the little parcel and inside found the cigarette case, Bible and other things commandeered by the Italians in Grenoble months earlier. In the cell a little shopkeeper from Toulon greeted me with a question about the commandant.

'He was polite,' I said. 'But isn't he a strange man? Before I was called into him I heard the sound of beatings and torture. They were treating the other prisoners like cattle. All he spoke of to me was music.'

The thickset figure was hunched on the floor, resting. The fleshy, red face suddenly emitted a spittle which shot across the cell.

'Music. Sale Boche. Music. He is the most cruel swine I have ever met. He kills by the centimetre and is polite as he does it. But they are vain, my friend. They are vain. He found in you an audience and tried to impress you. The flattery of the fools under his command he knows is worthless. But you are a foreigner and a man of education. Besides, we will win the war and your people and the Americans will be here. He fears the French and thinks you British and the Yanks, who are sentimental, will protect his fancy skin.'

He helped me as he spoke to arrange the meagre bedding provided, which was clean, and I thought over his words. Later experience and conversations with other prisoners were to convince me that he was a good judge of the prison O.C.'s character. My first fears were reasonable. The dandy engineer was a professional torturer of skill, a man who gloried in the terrible trade. It was reasonable for him to fear the French; for they had vowed vengeance for the wrongs done to them, wrongs outside the experience and beyond the range of the imagination of the British and American forces which were commanded by humanitarian soldiers. Eisenhower, Montgomery, etc., represented a unique breed of officers to the Germans. But the O.C. kept his word in one important respect. After the Villa Lynwood and St. Remo, St. Pierre was like a holiday camp to me. There I met other prisoners at exercise in the prison courtyard, talked with them and exchanged ideas and opinions with a French pastor to whom I lent my Bible. I managed to throw a message over the wall into the garden of a man who had been a well-wisher of the congregation when we worked in the Rue Forbin.

I was worried about my mother. When I sent letters home to Islay from Grenoble I was always uncertain that they would reach their destination. For the past four months I had been gaoled and without contact of any kind with the Christian organisations which might have kept my family informed that I was alive, at least. Word of my arrest, I was certain, had been sent home and Mother would fear the worst and perhaps, as time passed, come to believe I was dead. Adjacent to St. Pierre there was a house and garden which, two years earlier, had been the property of a man known to Henri Thebault. I had a stub of pencil and just enough paper to wrap round a stone. We were not under surveillance all the time. I wrote the words: 'Inform Mother I am safe and well, Donald,' addressed the paper to Henri and in the yard wrapped it round the stone. Watching for an opportunity I waited and then quickly flung the little object over the wall towards the friendly house.

Throughout the next day I worried, feeling that I had taken a foolish risk, but as nearly a week passed and I was not challenged, I assumed that the paper had either been found or had now been washed or blown away from the prison walls. The truth was that

I had been extremely lucky. The paper was delivered to Henri Thebault and he wrote to a colleague in his firm who was stationed in North Africa. This kindly man sent a message to a mythical personage he described as Monsieur le Lord Maire de Bowmore, Islay, Écosse, asking him to inform Madame Caskie that her son, Donald, was alive and well in Marseilles. So by a strange chance the message flung over the prison walls of St. Pierre in Marseilles was transmitted to an unknown friend in Casablanca, from there to the Highlands of Scotland and one mother's worries were stilled.

My heart lifted in St. Pierre for more than one reason. After the nightmare months in St. Remo the companionship of Christian men brought me back into something like normal human society, even if we were gaoled. The Germans watched us closely; but their very efficiency was protective after the brutal medieval methods of the Italians. All was order and while the food was sparse it was clean and the sanitary arrangements seemed luxurious. I was given the use of a razor and my face assumed its more normal clerical appearance. I sympathise with my fellow-men who cultivate beards but when conditions force a man to grow hair on his face and at the same time forego washing, the consequences are not to be recommended.

Some days before I was removed in mid-August I received food parcels, a consequence of my surreptitious correspondence with Henri Thebault. They were addressed to me and in themselves were evidence that someone knew I was alive. I was to find out later that my friends had been unremitting in their inquiries and unsuccessful. One lady, Mrs. Schroeder of Schroeder's Bank, London, and Dunlossit Castle, Islay, had approached the Vatican Commission which did admirable service on behalf of prisoners-of-war and their dependents and the Roman Catholic authorities in Rome set out to find me. But they met a blank wall. Donald Caskie was unknown to the Italian War Department. My message to Henri brought those parcels.

Cheerfully I distributed the contents of the parcels delivered to me by the German guards, and the cigarettes, tins of food, magazines and soap were accepted by my fellow alumni of St. Pierre. I felt happier when I was taken under guard to a railway station in

Marseilles for despatch to the prison of Fresnes on the southern outskirts of Paris.

The train journey was long and, I suppose, hazardous, but to a Scot abroad in time of war the danger was invigorating. The Allied air forces were, almost literally, making hay of the French railway system. For days we were diverted, shunted, held up for hours. Although I encountered no raids on the way, I was told all about them for I had company, the nicest kind of companions, poor soldiers, Germans who had been 'crimed' and were travelling under light escorts to the Reich's equivalent of our 'glass-house.'

My own guards, the customary corporal and one other rank, were easy-going old soldiers, if not so talkative as Hans and his companion of my journey from Toulon. We settled comfortably into our compartment and when, a few moments after the train moved, a young soldier put his head through the door and asked if he and his fellow-travellers might join us, the corporal agreed. I was, he observed, a chaplain and could do only good to the criminals in the next compartment.

There were about six of them, nondescript, happy, neat, scruffy, talkative and silent, a pretty ordinary lot of recruits. They tumbled beside us singing, their guards standing back in the corridor laughing at them.

The prisoners, their guards and mine, I learned had accepted defeat. The invasion of the Reich they expected would come within one year. Hamburg had been destroyed, I was told, and the British and U.S. Air Forces were devastating German war factories. The Italians had collapsed. Germany was at the end of its tether—*kaput*—and still new armies were massing against her. They and all their comrades knew that victory was a dream which would not be fulfilled. The Fuehrer went in terror of his life and only the most fanatical members of the 'party' believed he could save the country. I listened and felt happy. Whatever lay ahead of me I knew that the efforts of every man who had died in 1940 and those who lived to fight on had not been in vain. The dead ones who gave their lives and the traitors' victims were justified. In that noisy compartment surrounded by happy prisoners I rejoiced and sent up grateful prayers. Through nights when we lay in sidings and moved cautiously along side-lines I sat awake feeling exalted.

We sang together during the hours of daylight and shared our rations. I did not want for cigarettes on that journey. The young soldiers, I learned, longed for defeat. Years of inactivity had killed the illusory zeal for soldiering instilled in them by the Nazi propaganda machine. The facts of Germany's devastation could not be hidden from them. I parted from my German friends when we reached Paris and came to Fresnes in good spirits, my hopes aroused by their information of the Allied victories and their prophecies of future defeat for their country. Nearly four years had passed since I locked the church in the Rue Bayard and left the manse in the Rue Piccini. Even in handcuffs it was good to be back so close to my parish.

The Prison of Fresnes lies about five miles south of the centre of the capital. Fifty years ago the ground on which it stands was a pleasant place of rolling green fields marked off by tall chestnut trees, their colours changing with the seasons, their tones as subtle as music. The young Impressionists must have found their inspiration there. One can imagine them on their picnics and week-end excursions, visualising the masterpieces they painted and which now are treasured throughout the civilised world. The fields on which the *maison de correction* is built are not far away from the main road. Often they have been invaded by the rollicking trippers from the Left Bank. To-day they offer a grim and forbidding aspect to the passer-by.

Fresnes is the biggest and most spacious prison in Europe. Much younger than St. Remo, nevertheless it has had a sorrowful history. In its half-century of existence hundreds of thousands of men and women have been incarcerated within its walls. There have been hundreds of suicides in its cells. Fresnes was one of the first places commandeered by the German S.S., after their triumphal march down the Avenue des Champs-Élysées and under their command the dark and dismal building became still more dark and more dismal. Most of the British residents in the city were rounded up, arrested and brought to this gaol before being taken to the Caserne de St. Denis, north-east of Paris, for internment. I, being a criminal, was brought to Fresnes.

I was exhausted when I lay down in my cell that evening, travel-sore and hungry, dispirited by recollections of the stories I had heard of the *maison de correction* and apprehensive of the morrow. There was a dreadful silence in the great building, I yearned for company, and it came to me from an adjoining cell occupied by someone who was, I assume, for I never met him, Scottish. He began to sing and I listened:

> '*Maxwellton's braes are bonnie*
> *Where early ja's the dew*
> *And it's there that Annie Laurie*
> *Gave me her promise true.*'

The familiar words were clear in the silence and they filled my heart with solace. In a measured, cheerful way he sang the ballad right through and then began again. I joined in with him. We sang it to the last note and were silent and then, with a joyful note of irony, I heard him begin:

> '*Should Auld Acquaintance*
> *Be forgot*
> *And never brought to mind*
> *Should Auld Acquaintance be forgot*
> *For the days of Auld Lang Syne. . . .*'

The duet continued and again we sang the song twice, were silent for a few moments, and my unknown companion closed the recital with the National Anthem to which I stood to attention and added my quota.

We slept on straw in Fresnes. The floors were stone. Before I rested that first night I thought of Luke's story in the Acts of the Apostles relating how Paul and Silas imprisoned in Philippi sang together in a cell and the other prisoners hearing them felt happier. I was the prisoner in the cell. I thanked my Master for the ministry of song and praise. My spirits rose slightly and I slept soundly.

The tramp of jack-boots through the corridors wakened me one day at 5 a.m. and the roaring voices of the S.S. sergeants:

'*Raus! Raus!*'

My eyes still filled with sleep I forced myself to the alert. They passed my door and I did not see anyone until a guard brought bread and water. He did not speak when he entered. Plates were put on the floor. The days of solitary confinement were over and I received cell-mates but I returned to my St. Remo meditations, relying on my Bible and my past life to further populate my cell. I had become a gaolbird-contemplative. When at last I was taken to exercise I was steady on my feet. My spirit, I am grateful to write, was serene in that dreadful place.

Fresnes was not, like the Villa Lynwood, a house of torture, not like St. Remo, a place where men and women were left to rot. It was a slaughter-house. It was crammed with Gaullists, maquis of all colours and the perpetual victims of the Nazis, Jews.

At five o'clock each morning the silence of the great gaol was broken by those shouts I had heard on my first awakening and the thud of jack-boots. It was part of the S.S. routine of death. Paris is a free city, and the tyrants devised a system for keeping it at bay while they prepared to kill the free world. In 1943-44 when they were fighting off the friends of France they applied their system ruthlessly. They took a batch of ten men from each district and imprisoned them. If any German was attacked in the area from which these men were taken the hostages were shot out of hand. There were no trials and vengeance was taken on the innocent for the actions of the men who fought to liberate them. They were freedom's scapegoats.

My remaining physical strength began to ebb away in Fresnes and though my spirit remained serene I think I came to accept death as inevitable. I knew that our armies would be victorious but I thought that we in the *maison de correction* would be butchered before the S.S. took flight. I ate my meagre food and prayed and lived apart. Under the tuition of my cell-mates I learned how to use the prisoners' grape-vine, to tap out messages on my walls and receive them from the inmates of nearby cells. It was always the same report we received, death, death, death, and always the innocent.

I prayed for them and when they came for me on November 26th at the customary hour I was ready.

'Pastor Donald Caskie?'

'*Ja.*'

'*Folgenden.*'

I followed them down the corridor and waited while they brought me a companion from another cell. He was a thin-faced, very young man, stricken with fear and trembling. We were led out and ordered into a Black Maria.

'They're going to shoot you, Monsieur?'

'I do not know,' I answered. 'We must be of good heart and pray. All will be well with us. We have done no evil and war was forced on our people.'

'They have told me I shall die to-day, Monsieur. Pray with me.'

I had come to the end of hope that morning. I was resigned to death. He spoke of his wife and children. They were young and my heart ached for him and that girl and those babies. When the van stopped, he tried to leave it ahead of me but the guard motioned him back.

'Not you. The pastor dismounts here. You are for the Rue des Saussaies, Pastor. The other one is for Mount Valerien!'

'May I say good-bye to him?'

'You have two minutes.'

The pale face turned to me blankly. It was deadened by despair. I put my hands on his shoulders and spoke to him, telling him that his children would be safe and soon the Allies would be here and peace would come. His children would be protected. Tears streamed down his cheeks. I told him to remember the One who died on the Cross for love of him and for his children.

'He is with you now, mon cher. It is He who has brought us together this morning. He has sent me to tell you this. You die in His company. You are secure in His care, and you must pray for all of us who remain.'

The young face was serene and at peace before he took my hand and I jumped from the Black Maria. The door closed and the engine started. I knew my own destination now. The Court of the Gestapo, in a building in the Rue des Saussaies, was strangely enough a few hundred yards from the British Embassy in Paris.

CHAPTER 16

THE RUE DES SAUSSAIES

A CLOCK HUNG on the wall over the long table where the judges sat. It was eight o'clock to the minute. I was marched to a chair opposite the table and told to face the court. There was no other furniture in the room which was big, oblong in shape, with low ceilings, the walls painted a drab colour. The place was bleakly institutional. My judges gazed at me without interest.

There were a dozen of them, ten men and two women. The latter were blonde, heavy-faced German types, one seemed about forty years of age, the other a little older. The younger woman had a strong jaw, a good forehead, thin mouth and cold hard eyes. Her colleague peered out of shrewd, vicious eyes, blue and small. The mouth was curiously curving as if ready to spit. The men were strong and brutish, thick-set in their uniforms, on first glance seeming exactly alike in physical appearance. The president was thin and tall, his face and eyes oddly bright. A bundle of documents lay on the table. These were carefully separated and passed from hand to hand. The silence in the room was broken by the ticking of the clock which seemed to grow louder as the seconds passed. In a leisurely way they read the papers. One of the men achieved identity by turning his eyes towards me with a blank stare and adjusting gold-rimmed glasses as he read. About ten minutes passed and an awful tiredness began to fill my veins. Suddenly an apoplectically red face turned to me and barked words.

'Your name is Donald Caskie. You are English.'

'I am British, by nationality Scottish.'

My interrogator waved a grey-gloved hand. I remember wondering: why do they always wear gloves? Answering the question

in my head, I thought, they want to keep their hands clean, and I
formed a picture in my mind of Pilate to meditate upon.

'You are a civilian, a clergyman.'

'I am a minister of the Church of Scotland, formerly incumbent
of the Scottish Kirk in the Rue Bayard in this city. In recent years
I have ministered to my own folk in various parts of France.'

'You are a spy, agitator, agent for escaping soldiers, prisoners-
of-war, and friendly disposed towards that hated race the Jews.'

The last accusation brought me out of my exhaustion.

'May I ask you to be a little more explicit,' I said.

'You are an ally of the Jews. You are their friend. We have
the evidence.'

Anger drained out of me, and my tiredness went with it. The
classical Nazi accusation had been brought. I had committed their
favourite crime. I smiled and knew that there was now no hope. I
was quite prepared for death and I wished only that it would be
soon.

'I do not know what you mean by being an ally of the
Jewish people, sir,' I answered. 'So far as I know they are at war
with no one. But then I have been in gaol awaiting some sort of
trial for many many months. If you mean I have Jewish friends, of
course I have. Every civilised man in Europe has friends among the
Jewish people. Are we all going to be tried for our friendships?'

'You have aided Jews against the Reich.'

'I have aided Jews because they are human beings and because
of your country's policy they are in need of help. But I never have
aided them *against* anyone.'

My questioner leaned back in his chair and spoke in German to
his colleagues. The trial was in French and I had noticed bewilder-
ment on most of the faces lined up across from me while I spoke.
In my years in France I have become as close to a native speaker
of the language as any man who is not a native can come and I love
the French tongue. In friendlier atmospheres I had used it as an
instrument of debate. Debate is a Franco-British sport. It had no
place in the *kultur* of the Third Reich.

As the day progressed I knew that much of the meaning of
what I said was lost on the verbal butchers I confronted. My

German was not as good as my French and their private conversations eluded me. Voices were dropped. Accents were varied. Deliveries were quick between them and they deliberately excluded me from their colloquies.

The president spoke:

'You deny being a corrupter of youth! Did you not conduct systematic agitation among the students at Grenoble during your term at the university? Did you not infuriate them against the Reich, abusing the hospitality of the professors?'

'I taught the students to make tea,' I answered. 'And I instructed them in English literature. If you wish to know my methods, they were simple. I chose good books, masterpieces of the English written word that I knew would appeal to young people and lead them to more complex works.'

While I spoke one of the men was watching me closely, his pasty face flushing.

'You lie.' The voice was screaming.

'I am telling the truth.'

Another voice ripped out of the silence. It was one of the blonde women, the older one.

'You deluded the professors at Grenoble who gave you hospitality because they are fools. You organised the students into bands of murderers.'

She was a hard, merciless creature. The little eyes screwed themselves back in the blotched face.

'This accusation would be silly if it were not wicked,' I answered. 'I ask you to bring one person from Grenoble who will support this hotch-potch of charges. What sort of court is this?'

'Be silent.'

A man at the extreme right of the table shouted at me. The papers were assembled before the president and the *sotto voce* Teutonic deliberations began again. About fifteen minutes passed and then the interrogation, mostly by assertion, began. It continued until eleven o'clock, with questions and accusations being fired from all parts of the table. The most vicious of the pack were the women. Their hatred was terrifying. Some years later I was to see those faces again in a news photograph. According to the picture they were being tried as two of the Belsen murderers. That morning they were my judges and from minute to minute and hour to hour hounded me with their poisoned, irrational charges until the big hand on the clock touched twelve. Then the R.A.F. gave me a respite. Across Paris the air-raid warnings sang their moaning song. My judges stood quickly to their feet. Without a word they left the room and I heard the lock on the door click behind them. I stretched my legs and waited, feeling ridiculously elated. 'The good old R.A.F. is on the job,' I said aloud, and waited for explosions praying that a bomb would fall on this place. For about twenty minutes I was left alone, pacing in the silence, waiting. And then the 'all clear' sounded and I sat down.

They entered again, talking angrily among themselves. The visitors from across the Channel had not amused them. The younger woman reopened the inquisition. With something of the air of a schoolmistress giving a good impression of Judge Jeffries, she began :

'You consorted with the notorious spy Picault. You met him in a café in Marseilles on December 18th, 1940. The following night a dozen British spies escaped across the mountains to Spain.'

'I do not remember what happened on the date you mention. I know Picault but was not aware that he was a spy or notorious. I have never met a dozen spies in my life nor consciously seen so many, outside a moving picture.'

'You lie.'

The lady's method of cross-examination was simple. It left no opportunity for discussion. A charge was delivered with cold, arrogant deliberation. The answer was heard impassively. The subject was closed with the phrase, 'You lie.'

I watched the clock move around as I sat there under the endless barrage of questions. Its round white face seemed the only contact with the realities outside the courtroom. When the clock was twinkling out the stroke of the hour, I heard the president give an order to one of the men who rose from his place, went to a side door which he opened, and I found myself for a moment gazing into the face of Pierre, a guide used during my days in the Rue

Forbin in Marseilles. Briskly he stepped into the room and took up a place before the table, keeping his face averted.

One of the women stood up and pointed to me.

'Do you identify this man as Donald Caskie, a clergyman who abused his status to act as an agent for the British?'

He glanced at me unsteadily and I tried to look into his eyes. They flickered over my face avoiding any communication with the man behind it.

'Yes. This is Pasteur Caskie. He was in charge of a mission which was a centre of English spying.'

The president directed ferret eyes towards me.

'Do you know this man, Caskie?'

'I know him?' I answered. 'I should think I do know him. Even before I suspected him of being what he has now proved himself to be—a double agent—I regret to say I associated him in my mind with Judas Iscariot. His purse was his god. His every word and action sought to magnify it alone. He had no other aim in life. May I continue?'

Ferret Face nodded.

'He is the first witness brought into this court against me. I suggest he is hardly one that will assist you to be just. In all our dealings he asserted he was pro-British, not pro-French—although he is, in his strange way, a Frenchman. Perhaps his purse predominated over his patriotism. Perhaps he thought the British paid better. He swore allegiance to us and he used to say—I remember the words exactly—he would give his right arm to get the " sale Boche " out of France. You may agree that he is a most interesting witness. Someday he may give evidence against you. He is a professional.'

The president spluttered a mouthful of German oaths as I finished. He brought his fists down with a thump on the table-top, and shouted at Pierre:

'Tell us what you know of the prisoner.'

I forgot the clock as he spoke. His hands grasped the lapels of his heavy jacket and he shuffled his feet. The voice was eager, so quick that he had to be halted from time to time. The accent was rural and some members of the court, I am sure, could not understand more than a few words. But to the Germans he was a faithful servant; I found myself thinking he told a convincing tale.

In detail he explained my methods of despatching parties. One description of how seven lads had been despatched soon after Christmas 1941 aroused moving memories in me, emotion not unmixed with amusement that Judas should touch the heart of his victim while betraying him. He knew, he observed at one point, that I was a British Intelligence officer.

'How do you know?'

Pierre halted and looked around the room in a puzzled way. The tale had been interrupted, something disconcerting to any artist. He began again.

'Yes,' he said. 'Sir Samuel Hoare told me. Sir Samuel is the biggest Englishman in Spain.'

'Sir Samuel Hoare,' the president observed, 'is British Ambassador to Spain, as you say the biggest, most important Englishman there. What did he say to you?'

'I am a guide, Monsieur. And I was told that Sir Samuel Hoare would help me to find work. I went to him in Madrid. He told me if I wished to work for the British Intelligence in France I must go to Monsieur Caskie, the Scottish pastor in the Seamen's Mission in the Rue Forbin in Marseilles. Monsieur Caskie would put me into contact with agents who would employ me.'

The younger woman took over his interrogation. Waspishly she interrupted each time he strayed from what she conceived to be the point while he expanded his recollections of my espionage, all of which were pure invention, based upon the conjectures of a naturally suspicious man of little education. His stories of the escaping parties were substantially true. The fables he invented about espionage were nonsense and the Germans must have been able to see them as they were. But he rambled on. He was in court for forty-five minutes when he was suddenly halted and told to leave the court. Pierre bowed and let himself out of the room, closing the door very quietly behind him. He did not look at me.

'You *are* a spy.' The words were roared by the older woman. I denied this and the cross-examination began again and so it continued until the clock registered 2 p.m., when the court came to a stop like a machine. A fresh-complexioned member of the junta had begun to harangue me about my elaborately fancied plots with Jewish monsters, wholly of his own or some other fabulist's imagining, when suddenly, inconclusively, he halted, looked along the table, reached down to the floor and produced a leather brief-case. His comrades followed his example and then, *en masse,* they stood up and solemnly left the room. Again the lock clicked and I was left pondering this enigmatic exit. It had all taken place so mechanically that nearly fifteen minutes passed before I realised they had gone off for something as human as luncheon.

Waiting for food to be brought to me, I patrolled the room again but I heard nothing until three-thirty when the court filed in again, this time talking more loudly among themselves, but of matters that did not concern me. French cooking, I was interested to learn, did not agree with one of them and I regretted that he lacked my experience of German and Italian fare.

Throughout the morning they had smoked, cigarettes and cigars, and I, a moderately heavy addict of that amiable vice, occasionally yearned towards the fumes that filled the room. After lunch some chain-smoked, lighting one cigarette after another until the place was rancid with the fumes of nicotine. Now they moved around the court and their questions came at me from all angles, sometimes three of them shouting from different corners with the women interjecting while I tried to listen. They had lists of agents' names and I was glad that I had told my contacts to keep their names from me. I became dizzy as the light faded and although I felt no hunger became light-headed. But still I stuck to my defence.

'I have committed no crime. I have done what any patriotic man would have done in my place. Would a German have abandoned his fellow-countrymen? Your single witness is a knave, a double agent, a professional betrayer. I am a Scot. Would you have me abandon my people?'

'Where did you get the money to run your spy organisation in Marseilles? Did the Americans not help you?'

It was the young virago who spoke. That flat, metallic voice began another story, into which she mingled some facts of my

168

friendship with McFarlane, the American Consul. A black-out screen was placed over the window. The voice continued in its clipped way. Now she spoke more in German than in French and the mongrel monologue filled my ears until the scene confronting me became dreamlike. And then there was silence for a time and I looked about me. The room was empty. The clock showed me that it was a few minutes past five forty-five.

I slumped in the chair, turning myself to rest my head on an arm propped on the chair-back. I was exhausted, the day was ending and I yearned for my own people far away at the blessed hour when they were returning to their homes. Sweet memories crowded upon me in the courtroom and my mind filled with prayer:

> Be it granted to me to behold you again dying
> Hills of home! and to hear again the call;
> Hear about the graves of the martyrs the peewees crying
> And hear no more at all.

The plea of the gentle R. L. Stevenson who died so far away from the land we love was in my heart and in that place of evil farce I forgot my judges. I was prepared to accept my fate whatever that might be. I knew that the whole Nazi conception was doomed. Our God, loving and kind, was watching and His children were safe in His hands. My comrade of the morning journey was dead at Mount Valerien by this time and God's love was being lavished on him. It would be thus with me and with his other children too when their time came. At six-thirty when the court returned, I faced them with pity in my heart.

The young woman began her rambling story of my complicity with the Americans in Marseilles. Now she was refreshed and used little German. I listened. At seven o'clock she sat down and the court conferred. The colloquies were carried on very quietly in whispers, with intervals during which the members consulted their notes. A half-hour and more passed and the clock was moving away from half-past seven when the president stood up. The ferret face was composed and his words were enunciated with legal precision.

'Have you anything to say for yourself?'

Placing my hands on the sides of the chair I pushed myself to my feet and I think I swayed. I was very tired and hungry. I moved behind the chair and held it tightly to steady myself. A dozen pairs of eyes were turned in my direction.

'Yes,' I said. 'I have one thing to say. Before God I have only done what any true man would do for his country.'

They waited, but I had nothing to add to my statement and I sat down. The president placed his hands flat on the table before him and spoke.

'Guilty.'

The words came quietly. He looked along the table to his right and then to his left. He raised a hand and his fellow-judges in a rambling way chorused their agreement.

'Guilty.'

He got to his feet.

'The court finds you guilty, Caskie.'

I nodded my head and they began to file out. Within a few seconds I was alone. It was seven forty-five. The room was cold now and the light went out. I sat in black darkness at peace and waited until there was a click from a switch. The light blinded me as it struck across the room. Two guards beckoned at the door. I gazed at the clock before I stood up. The time was eight-three. For more than twelve hours I had been in court. I was guilty. They had omitted to tell me what the sentence would be.

Sleet was falling on Paris and my face was wet when I entered the Black Maria to be driven back to Fresnes. In my cell I slept heavily. After the five o'clock rally for the firing squad passed my cell I lay down to sleep again. But one of my cell-mates wakened me. I learned that it had been presumed in the gaol that I was dead, shot the previous morning at Mount Valerien.

Carefully, slowly, I gave them my news.

'I was taken to a Gestapo court and tried and found guilty.'

Lying on straw I waited and my neighbour answered.

'What are they going to do with you? Are you to be sent to Germany?'

'I do not know. They did not say anything about punishment. I think it will be death.'

'It is to be expected.'

It was to be expected, always, and during the morning I prepared myself for its coming. When the guard brought me my food I spoke to him. Little time, I felt, was left to me and I did not wish to die without speaking with another minister.

'Please tell the commandant that I wish to see a pastor.'

The man looked surprised.

'A pastor?'

'Yes. I am, as you know, a man of religion and I wish to confer before I die, with a pastor.'

I could see that he was puzzled. He scratched his head and then shrugged his shoulders.

'Oh, well, I'll tell them.'

When he left me I dipped the bread in water and began to suck it, feeling despondent. It seemed unlikely that my request would be granted. The guard seemed to think it improbable. But finally it saved my life.

Next morning the cell door opened and a gentle little man in the uniform of a German chaplain entered and bowed.

'My name,' he said, 'is Peters, Hans Helmut Peters. I have come at your request.'

'Hans Peters?' My memory stirred. The name was familiar.

'But surely, I have heard of you—many a time,' I said.

He took my right hand and smiled.

'I think that is likely,' he answered, 'for we are ministers and I have heard of you, Herr Caskie, very many times. But perhaps our dear friend, Herr Lamb, is the strongest link between us.'

When he mentioned Lamb's name I recollected all I knew of him. Before the war they had been friends in Nice where Peters served the Lutheran community. Later this German had been a pastor in Paris, at the German church in the Rue Blanche.

'Herr Lamb is one of my strongest friends,' he said. 'Alas, this wicked war which involves us men of God. When first I came to Nice, life was very difficult for me. We Germans had no church and I had to wait very long for accommodation of our own. Do you know, Herr Caskie, I should not have had a place to gather our people but for our friend Herr Lamb?'

The earnest grey eyes gazed into mine and I forgot that I was in a death cell in Fresnes. We were two ministers talking of church affairs.

'No. I was not aware that Mr. Lamb had helped you, but it does not surprise me. After all, we are Christians.'

'That is true. But I was desperately worried and he saved me much trouble. He gave me the use of his church, the Church of Scotland in Nice. Yes, he placed the building at my disposal and we never wanted a place in which to hold our services.'

'I think,' I told him, 'you would have done the same thing in his place. I know I should not have hesitated.'

He got to his feet and walked across the cell away from me, turned quickly and we stood face to face.

'I know what you would have done, Herr Caskie. To me you might be the Rev. Lamb, here in this cell. What can I do for you? You are in a dreadful place and, I fear, you have yet to learn the worst.'

'It is death?' I said.

'So you know? I shall do all in my power to save you. But we pastors have no power in the Reich to-day. I shall try with all my strength. I promise it.'

'Will you give me the sacrament, now, Hans?'

He stood over me and patted my shoulder, his hand falling very gently.

'Yes, Donald, and you must pray while I prepare.'

With wonderful reverence he conducted the service and gave me the sacrament. Afterwards he left me, promising to return soon and to spare no efforts for a reprieve. I had little faith that he would succeed. But Hans had strengthened my faith in the more important life. He left me sustained and greatly comforted.

CHAPTER 17

SILENT BELLS RING OUT

THE DEATH SENTENCE had been confirmed, said Helmut Peters at our next meeting. I must expect to be ordered to the place of execution at any time, but Peters had applied for permission to put forward a plea of reprieve. I remained undisturbed for some days when Helmut went to Germany on leave and there he carried the case to Berlin, emphasising that I was a clergyman and that the evidence against me had been largely based upon the testimony of a double-agent, a man who betrayed the Germans with the British and the British with the Gestapo.

How Helmut's plea would have worked out a year earlier it is difficult to say. In 1943 it had the effect of the Berlin authorities sending to Paris for my dossier. I heard that the dossier had been lost. The most likely explanation for its disappearance, I believe, is that it was delivered when the Berlin Gestapo was in process of being reorganised by the butchers who took revenge on Hitler's own minions after the attempt on his life. It is a fact that the Nazi officials who were handling my case disappeared after the unsuccessful assassination plan and were not heard of again.

For about six weeks after the trial I remained in Fresnes, at first anticipating the death call every morning and then as Christmas 1943 approached, hoping that there might still be a chance of life for me. Helmut delivered parcels to me and life was easier. News filtered into the prison and passed along the corridors that the Western Allies were ready to leap into France and before the New Year ended the country would again be a battleground. The maquis were organised, planting men and arms in places where the Germans, now on the defensive, could be harried when their retreat began. Hope strengthened and began to warm even despairing hearts. But still the death squads came at 5 a.m. Still new prisoners arrived in batches. Still my neighbours were dragged away to the place of execution. I would pray for them, and with my cell-mates face another day.

Relief came on January 7th, 1944, when the last entry was made on my *carte d'identité*. The death sentence was lifted. That day I was taken to the Caserne St. Denis and my future seemed to be assured. I suppose the gateway to St. Denis and the barbed wire that enclosed the camp would have looked grim two years earlier. But I never shall forget the unutterable joy that filled my heart when I came to that place which housed over two thousand of my compatriots whose only punishment was to wait and pray for the tramp of friendly feet through the streets of Paris and the sight of the fleeing enemy.

After Fresnes, St. Denis brought me the feeling of being resurrected. The place was alive. Men were intensely aware of the outside world and news poured into our enclosure. Naturally, radios were forbidden. Naturally men made radios out of parts smuggled into the place. One was the property of Major Horsford, the extremely capable and versatile medical officer, who to his professional skill wedded a bedside manner that would have given a lunatic the confidence and poise necessary to pass the Bar examination. The major kept his radio secreted in his medical supplies and through this channel came a steady service of Allied news to St. Denis. It was amusing and consoling to hear the inmates of my room in the caserne discuss the latest intelligence from the B.B.C., with all the confidence and almost sporting interest of a group of men in a St. James's Street club, amusing and consoling. Major Horsford was not the only ' B.B.C.' reporter in the camp. There was a radio, I know, secreted somewhere near the sanctuary. The great thing about St. Denis was that it was a civilised community. A man can be very happy in a barracks surrounded by true comrades.

There were inconveniences. One could hear them. Indeed, they only emphasised the differences between the caserne and Nice, St. Remo, Marseilles, Fresnes and that first caserne at Grenoble. There were the radio raids, aiming to find our sets. From the German viewpoint the raids proved useless. They did not find anything. There was the routine of prison life and its inconveniences but I was alive again and living with British men. I found myself planning services, meditating on the conditions I would face when I was free and making my way to the Rue Bayard. I joyfully saw myself setting out on Sunday mornings back to our dear church and those friends I had left nearly four years ago.

There were talks with other clergymen in the caserne and these gently brought me back into the mainstream of life. Scholarly White Fathers of the Roman Catholic Church in France who had ministered to the maquis were among my comrades in gaol. We talked on the common points and the differences we held. And Helmut Peters kept in close contact with me.

He had believed, he told me, in the early days of Nazism that Hitler was truly the saviour of the German people and he, Helmut, a German patriot, had given him his support. He was not a Nazi. Indeed, like many German Christians, and not a few of our own people, he was profoundly ignorant of the realities of Nazism. The Reich had been in a chaotic condition, politically, socially and legally. There were riots, unemployment and moral degeneration. The Fuehrer had brought order, he believed. It was only later that the dreadful truth of the nature of the New Order penetrated his consciousness. Helmut Peters was, and is, a man of God, married, with a good wife and a large family, a pastor who saw his flock as a part of God's family to which he was a religious foster-father. The horror of the world that Nazism had imposed upon God's creation wounded him and he turned to his religion for consolation. The cross became the symbol of his life, and his faith his sole driving power.

Easter 1944 came and with it a card from my German ally on which the Risen Christ was shown still crucified and a message written to me his 'brother under God.' I cherish that card. It is still in my possession—a link with the friend who is now incumbent of a poor parish near Hanover where his lot was lightened during Germany's hungry post-war years by allied soldiers who, sent by the padre Donald Caskie of the church in the Rue Bayard, left him supplies for his family and flock.

Easter passed. Spring ripened into summer. In June the caserne was illuminated by joyful news that sent us into a riot of happy talk that was not to be surpassed even on the day of liberation. The Allied Armies had landed in Normandy.

I had just conducted early morning service in the chapel, which was on the top story of the building. About sixty men were present. The singing had been especially lusty. Afterwards I chatted with each of them, listened to the customary stories of what had happened the previous day, the jokes, the hopes, the anticipations of what might happen any day now and eventually found myself alone and free to go downstairs and prepare another sermon.

I was descending the stairs when I found myself facing Major Horsford, who had achieved the broadest smile I ever saw on his face or any other.

'Padre,' he said. 'The great day has arrived.'

'What do you mean, Major?' I answered, my mind far away.

'I mean that the great day for which we all have been praying has come. This morning the Allies made a landing on the beaches of Normandy, not far from Bayeux.'

'Oh, God be praised and God be with them,' was all I could say.

'God be with them,' he echoed. 'I feel sure they are having a tough time. We must remember them in prayer.'

Rushing back to the chapel I sent a messenger to gather the boys who had been at service, to spread word all over the camp. Quickly the chapel filled and we knelt down in prayer, raising our hearts to God, begging him to help our comrades who, even as we prayed, were fighting and dying as they reclaimed France inch by inch, foot by foot and mile by mile from the Boche.

Throughout that day the caserne hummed with joyful, excited discussion of the news and I prayed with fervour for those who had come to succour all of us and let light, happiness and God's freedom into Europe again. When darkness fell we lay awake in our rooms scarcely whispering to each other but knowing that each of us was awake and the thoughts of each were enough to keep him wakeful until dawn. Our loved ones were close to us for the first time in years.

Throughout the following day we prisoners were excited and I, suddenly conscious that our moment of joy was the beginning of a campaign in which a multitude of our brothers would fight their way over roads and fields, prayed and arranged services of prayer. The camp leaders reminded us that the battle was still in process of the fighting and while victory was inevitable men were risking their lives for our country and for us now helpless and frustratd in the caserne. We prepared our comrades for freedom and the problems it would bring, for we were making ready in our hearts to take up our tasks again.

In talk with Helmut I learned that he was making ready to face the perils of retreat. His wife and family were returned to the Reich. German women were being cleared from the city. None knew just what course the great battle, soon to gain ferocious momentum, would take and the Germans were preparing to salvage what they could from the débris of their imperial dreams. My friend, like my soldier friends of the journeys from Italy and the south, had expected this day for many months. But there was sadness in contrasting the hopes that had stirred his heart in the beginnings of the Third Reich and the evil thing it had become. That sadness, I knew, was minimised by a new hope, that Germany repentant might work out her days of retribution and that his Germany, the Christian Reich, might rise again and play a decent and honourable role in the intercourse of the nations. Our conversations were tinged by joyful anticipation. Soon there would be peace and Sunday morning again would be the culminating point of the week's work when we would lead our flocks to face another week.

June passed into July and the radio kept us close to the fortunes of the fighting men.

During the following few weeks the atmosphere in St. Denis grew joyfully tense. I saw Helmut once or twice and then I did not see him and sensed he had joined the retreat. From the caserne we could see that in the most ironical way the exodus of Paris had been reversed in 1944. Vehicles of all shapes and sizes, tanks, heavy artillery, limousines carrying, presumably, officers of considerable rank, crowded the road. The staff of the caserne began to thin out. We knew that our imprisonment was now a matter of days, and at night we lay, our ears cocked in the silence, waiting, waiting, waiting. Only air-raid warnings had broken that silence during recent years, and for many nights before sleeping we listened for them.

And then one night as I lay on my upper berth in the big barrack-like cell I shared with thirteen others, I heard the far-off blessed noise. It was an impossible sound; I doubted my ears. But faint, sweet and clear it came again and I cried out to my cell-mates.

'Listen, listen. They are here. A bell is ringing. It is the sign of liberation.'

From their beds they moved close to the window. Without a sound, in their bare feet, they stood listening and waiting. And then far away, the bell rang again and then nearer we heard another. But still we waited in silence. We were afraid we might disturb the music of freedom ringing from the churches of the city.

That first eager tinkle called more and more bell-ringers to their posts and it was drowned in the rising tide of sound. The bells of Notre Dame St. Sulpice and hundreds of other churches in the French metropolis were ringing out the glad news on that memorable August night in 1944 that the Allies had entered the city and that Zion's captivity was at an end.

CHAPTER 18

A TANK ON THE CHAMPS-ELYSÉES

PARIS RESOUNDED with the rejoicing of the free. The music of the bells echoed throughout the air. We waited, our hearts full of gratitude. Then a man in another room began to cheer and like the bells of Paris the prisoners of St. Denis followed the leader. A great roar of happiness bubbled from the caserne. One of my comrades rushed to the door of our room, flung it open and ran downstairs. The place was thronged with men. There was not a German in sight. Our guards had fled. Offices and German living quarters were deserted and a thorough search was made by the responsible officers for documentation that might prove useful to the incoming command.

We wandered through the caserne, talking freely to each other, rejoicing in the absence of guards. Some of the younger men were restrained with difficulty from rushing out on to the roads. But already fighting was going on in the streets and before many hours passed a thin, tough youth with a tommy-gun in his grasp arrived to instruct us—for our own good—to keep off the streets.

'Messieurs, the temptation is strong to get out of prison,' he said with a quick, tense smile in the tanned face, 'but be patient. Far from ensuring your safety, we will only add to your peril, for the military have not quite arrived. This is a Free French rising. We are fighting our way. At any moment the Germans will strike back.'

He hustled out and we were left to wait. He was a wise mentor. Through the night we huddled in our rooms, listening to explosions, the crack of rifle shots, random shouts, the noises of guerrilla warfare. Morning came and we scraped together meals from the supplies that our fleeing hosts had left behind. During that second day we had a few more visitors, each a hardy youth with tommy-gun or rifle and each repeating the warnings to stay off the streets. Towards evening, one of the young men broke under the strain of waiting and flung his life away by disregarding the guerrillas' advice. He slipped from the barracks and was not seen again alive. His body was found later lying in a gutter, the head pierced by a rifle shot.

The second night of freedom from German supervision was spent even more ironically by the liberated guests of the caserne. Some time soon after ten o'clock shells began to whistle over the building and we retreated to the basement to await death or the dawn, wondering if we had been wise to follow the counsels of the young maquis. Would it have been easier to dodge bullets in the street than shells in the gaol? Better, someone observed, to be brought down on the leg than to be a sitting pigeon. Dust descended on us in clouds, the walls shivered and seemed about to split. The roar of the exploding shells nearly shattered our ear drums, but there were no casualties. The men with the tommy-guns spoke wisely. None died in St. Denis after liberation apart from that solitary one who could not wait for the gate to open for him.

Throughout the day and into the night the shelling continued and we remained disagreeably safe in our basement, listening to the shells bursting and gloomily still wondering about the wisdom of the F.F.I. On the fourth day a Red Cross car arrived with supplies and the official in charge invited me to leave with him.

The journey into the centre of the metropolis convinced me of our wisdom in staying put since the night the bells rang. No one who was absent from Paris in those few days can envisage the running fight through the streets, the winding lanes and squares, the rifles firing from high windows and shops, the bodies dropping on the cobbles, the feeling of a myriad of one- and two-man battles that spat from the very pavements. My Red Cross friend had the genius of the French for making a car behave like a greyhound. The vehicle positively leaped through the city. I crouched down close to the floor conscious of the rifle bullets that buzzed about us on every few crossings. He dropped me by the Place de la Concorde and for the first time since 1940 I was back in my beloved city, free to put my hands in my pockets and stroll up the Avenue des Champs-Élysées, which is exactly what I did. I walked through scurrying men bearing rifles, citizens rushing towards businesses or what passed for business during the hectic time of liberation until I came to the Rue du Colisée and there made my way to the Hôtel Avenida, praying that the patron, a dear friend, had survived the occupation.

As I crossed the threshold I heard a frantic yell of joy.

'Monsieur Donald Caskie. Monsieur le Pasteur, welcome home to Paris.' Tears were streaming down her face, her arms around my neck and she was vehemently embracing me in the French fashion. 'Oh, cher Pasteur, we were told you were dead.'

Madame was overcome by emotion and I was so moved to see my old friend in the Avenida that we both collapsed into chairs and spoke incoherently for a few moments, trying to express our happiness in a Paris miraculously free of enemies. The British and the Americans had arrived. The familiar friendly khaki could be seen from the windows.

'Oh, Monsieur, to see again our friends and to know those soldiers out there do not menace us. The Americans throw sweets and chewing-gum to the children. The British bring food.'

She was half-weeping, half-laughing and not until a servant brought us real coffee—'A gift from an American visitor'—and we drank together did she relax and sit watching me with a twinkle in her eyes.

Suddenly, majestically, she stood up, with an air of mock pomposity, belied by a smile.

'Follow me, Monsieur Donald and the Scottish Pasteur will see how his French friend keeps trust.'

She led the way downstairs, deep into the basement, past the intriguing scents that come from a French hotel kitchen and into a cellar.

'Voilà, Monsieur Donald. You see the goods you deposited here for safe custody before the Germans entered Paris.'

Neatly stacked in a corner were books, furniture and other materials from the various offices I had used in my work as a minister in the old days, among them the Toc H lamp, for before the war, as now, I was Toc H padre in Paris.

Proudly Madame looked on and I thanked her. The possessions which surround one in work become precious to a minister; they are not his property but they, as the years pass, become something like helpers. There was and is something personal in that Toc H lamp; it is a material object that is an old friend.

Madame agreed to lodge me in the hotel until I straightened out my affairs and investigated the condition of the church and the manse. I set off across the Avenue des Champs-Élysées to the Rue Bayard which is about ten minutes' walk away.

When I turned the corner of the Avenue Montaigne into the Rue Bayard my steps slackened and I began to fear what I might find. Gaston's café came into view; I could see him setting the tables. I hurried past and there it was, our church. Thankfulness filled my heart for it seemed untouched. I stood outside and gazed at it for many minutes, my eyes devouring the blessed place which I had not seen for more than four years. And then I returned along the street to find Gaston clearing a table that stood outside his café on the pavement. He threw up his hands in recognition.

'Monsieur le Pasteur, a thousand welcomes. Monsieur le Pasteur, where have you been?'

I took his hand. He chuckled and shouted his pleasure at seeing me. My homecomings were assuming something like gala proportions in their effects on myself and my friends.

'Come in, Monsieur Donald. But wait, I have something for you.'

He disappeared into the rear of the café and a few minutes later appeared holding out the key of the church.

'See, Monsieur. It is here. I did not give it to them. I am a French Catholic but I have kept the key of the Scottish Church safe for you.'

The theological aspects of his charge seemed to give Gaston tremendous pleasure. He roared with laughter as he spoke the words and dug me in the ribs.

'Perhaps the key has converted me just a little, Monsieur Donald, to your Protestant faith, eh?'

To see his joy was touching and his pride in keeping the key of the church and the building inviolate lifted my heart.

'It may be, indeed, Gaston,' I said. 'But whatever the cause, how can I thank you?'

Gaston had the French feeling for dramatic occasions. The smile faded and he stood straight, a little absurd in his pride and quite wonderful in his generosity.

'You shall not thank me more, Monsieur le Pasteur. Are we not neighbours and friends? Now let us forget the past. Dear friend, they are gone and now '—he laughed aloud—' it shall be like it was before they came. Will it not be so?'

'We will make it so, dear Gaston,' I told him. 'We will make it better. The good God has kept us, you and me, safe, and we must be happy now for so many have died.'

'You will have coffee and when you have seen the church you must return for luncheon.'

Over our drink he told me that the Germans had asked him for the key of the church and he denied having it.

'But, Messieurs,' he said. 'There is nothing there. It is a church no more and it is closed. Le Pasteur left when you became our guests and no one comes now. They went away and I was not again approached for the key.'

It was exactly as he said. There was no change in the church except that the key was stiff in the lock and when it turned with a grinding click and I flung the door open, dust lay heavily on the interior. Motes danced thickly in the sunshine that flooded into the porch. The sound of my footsteps echoed in the empty building. On the table by the doorway the sprig of white heather I had left behind me in June, 1940, lay withered and welcoming. I was home; my fingers were gentle as I touched that morsel of Scotland. Before I returned to Gaston for luncheon I prayed again in our own church and thanked God for my deliverance. I remember the words of Abraham Lincoln came to my mind and I thought, ' these will be my guide in the days to come. . . .'

'With malice towards none, with charity for all; with firmness in the right as God gives me to see it, let us strive on to finish the work we are in; to bind up the nation's wounds; to care for him who shall have borne the battle and for his widow and his orphans . . .'

And then I moved around the familiar building, opening windows, noting the work that must be commenced immediately to make the building clean for Sunday's service. The air and sunlight touched the dear walls and the happiness of the minister grew until he fancied choirs of angels were singing as he moved about his task.

The days that followed were busy with our late summer cleaning. From my window in the Avenida I watched Paris liberated take revenge on its traitors and celebrate the arrival of the liberators. There were the wretched women who had befriended the Germans. For their punishment they were paraded shaven-headed through the streets. There were the members of the *milice* hunted into corners, and summarily shot by the maquis. There were the Germans who in their turn had become prisoners-of-war being led in pride of conquest by the F.F.I. to places of internment. For a few weeks Paris was berserk but I was busy, first in the Hôtel Avenida preparing to take up my old life and then from the manse in the Rue Piccini.

Before I moved back to my own home I received a visitor from British Intelligence, the customary polite officer, his deferential approach bringing a quick poignant recollection of the nocturnal callers at the Rue Forbin.

'You are Donald Caskie of the Seamen's Mission in Marseilles and later a member of the staff of Grenoble University?'

'I am Donald Caskie minister at the Scottish Church in the Rue Bayard.'

'I have been instructed to find you, sir. You are required at Intelligence Headquarters. Please come with me.'

He was an agreeable young man and I had no reason to suspect him but the habits I had acquired in the war were not easily put aside.

'I cannot accompany you now. Please give me the address of this place and I shall find my way there to-morrow morning.'

He bowed and handed me an envelope and we parted.

I did not wait until morning, but in the later afternoon of the same day went to the place, which was a large villa on the edge of the forest of Boulogne west of the city. As I neared the building two British soldiers challenged me.

'I am a padre, lads,' I said. 'Donald Caskie is the name.'

'Come this way, Padre,' one of them answered. 'We have orders to take you to the boss as soon as you arrive.'

I met 'the boss' on the steps leading to the villa and he knew me.

'Donald Caskie, I presume,' he observed, using Stanley's words to Livingstone when they met in Africa.

'Yes,' I answered, 'here I am—at least what is left of me after seven prison terms and the internment camp.'

My host was, in the way of the Intelligence Service, just as polite as the junior members of his corps with whom I had worked.

'Do come in, Padre,' he said, 'and please excuse the dreadful aroma of the place. We moved in only yesterday and there are still some German corpses in the cellar. We have been so frightfully busy, just haven't had a moment to spare to bury the fellows. Must get round to it this evening.'

In his office we sat down and he turned and looked hard at me.

'We know all about your war work, Padre. How are you off for cash?'

"I am penniless. At present I am living on—tick—isn't that the word—with old friends in the Hôtel Avenida.'

Automatically, it seemed, his hand flicked open a desk drawer; he extracted a bundle of French notes and handed them to me.

'Take this stuff,' he said. 'It should tide you over your present difficulties.

'Now,' he continued, 'I suppose you want to go home at once and see your family after all these years of separation. That is what any man would wish and I hate asking you to sacrifice your hopes. But the job here is not finished, Padre. Not by any means. A tricky time lies immediately ahead. Will you remain in Paris as an officiating chaplain and help us with your knowledge of the city and, most important, experience over the past four years?'

Without a pang, much as I longed for Scotland, I agreed to wait until my services were no longer urgently needed in the city and so I settled into work again. My days were busy; we opened a canteen for the R.A.F. at Le Bourget, the first British canteen in liberated France, and when called upon I aided the Intelligence Service. My friends began to appear in the town, arriving at the manse in the Rue Piccini to share a cup of Caskie's tea.

I became visiting chaplain to our men in various camps, and to military offenders in the prison at Port de Lilas, on the outskirts of Paris, and one day the camp commandant from the latter establishment sent for me. I was feeling rather low in health at the time and physically was little more than skin and bone. Major Macdonald, the commandant, opened characteristically by warning me to rest more and then continued.

'I've got a new chap here, Padre. I want you to see him. He's British all right, but he was picked up disguised as an American colonel. A tough case. He refuses to talk. We don't know yet just who he is.'

The major went on to tell me about this taciturn prisoner. It was apparent that he was an interesting specimen. For three months, it was known, he had attached himself to a special unit engaged in recovering art treasures that had been sent to Germany. He was a popular and efficient officer. Then an inquisitive man had discovered that he was doing a little private looting on his own account. He was arrested and the Americans, having discovered he was not one of their forces—something for which they could be thankful—handed him over to the British.

'He is a crook, all right,' said Major Macdonald. 'I'd like you to have a chat with him. We'll find out who he is soon enough, and for his own sake the sooner the better.'

He was Cole. As soon as I entered the cell I recognised him and saw that he knew me. But quickly he pulled himself together.

'Hello, No. 11,' I said. 'We meet in interesting circumstances. So many of our friends have been in gaol, rather worse gaols than this, you will understand.'

He had the effrontery of the born confidence man.

'Name of Smith, Padre,' he countered immediately. 'You've made a mistake. What's more, preaching's not wanted here. Get out.'

The brazen falsehood of the man enraged me. Thoughts of Pat—whom I again thought dead—my comrades of Marseilles, the Abbé Carpentier, boiled in my head and I shouted at him.

'You lie. You disgusting traitor. Are you quite without shame? You deserted your country. You sold your friends for money, accepted money from the Nazis—God help you. And you abandoned your wife to——'

'Leave her out of it,' he yelled back across the cell. 'If you are a gentleman and a Christian you'll tell no man's wife of his mistakes. Soon I'll be gone. Leave it at that.'

But he insisted he was not Cole and I was touched by the spark aroused in him by mention of his wife. I left the cell.

Major Macdonald was waiting for me. I reported what I knew of his prisoner. He whistled and told me that I would be summoned later when a check had been put on my information.

I left the prison that day with a heavy heart. Seeing Cole had reminded me of the dead ones, the bright lives extinguished by his treachery. Comradeship in war is such that while one always feels cut off from the friends who die, somehow one always remains part of that fellowship of death. Always they live in one's memories. In the manse that night I prayed as I had learned in prison, thanking God for those who died that we might live. Next day the authorities sent for me and, in the course of that meeting, I learned news that lifted my spirits again. Pat O'Leary was alive. It was the first news I had heard of him, except that he had been taken by the Gestapo in 1942.

'I have heard nothing better since the night the bells of Paris rang and we listened to them at the Camp at St. Denis,' I told my informant, and he smiled and clapped me generously on the back.

'Your friend is alive, Padre,' he said, 'and he will survive. He's not the kind that dies easily. But he is in pretty bad shape. At present he is in hospital in Bavaria, where they are trying to put flesh back on his bones. We will have to wait some weeks before we can bring him to Paris where he will check on your identification of Cole.'

'Pat will make no mistake,' I told him. 'But—pardon me for saying—don't you make one! Cole is one of the trickiest scoundrels that have exploited this war. The devil is in the fellow. Watch him night and day.'

They watched him but he escaped. A great hunt began for him. But Paris is a city in which it is easy to hide. Time passed and I was warned not to venture out alone at night, for he had sworn to kill me. There is comedy even in evil. Cole apparently believed my identification of him was a betrayal. I am not of the stuff of heroes and I remained home in the evenings, or went out with friends, except when an urgent call came from one of my people who was ill. And then one evening the telephone bell rang in the manse.

Cole had been located in a flat on the Rue de Grenelle. Would I stand by to identify him when he was arrested? The building was surrounded by armed men. It was expected that the traitor would put up a desperate fight for freedom. It is curiously true that those who sell the liberty of their comrades always cherish their own. If Cole were taken alive, my caller said, I would be summoned immediately. I agreed and hung up.

It was an evening shortly after the heart-warming news that 'Pat O'Leary' had been awarded the George Cross and I remember walking the floor of the drawing-room thinking on those extraordinary extremes, the Belgian hero with the Irish name, and the Englishman, and the forces each had represented in the European conflict. The Belgian hero, a professional healer in peacetime, who, in his gay and unegotistical manner—indeed, he deprecated his own efforts—had given his all for freedom. There was the English soldier, in times of peace a policeman, who had consciencelessly sold the lives and freedom of so many good men and women. The chapter was about to end. Pat had emerged on the side of victory and his courage had been recognised by the King of the country whose side he had espoused. The French were closing in on the poor wicked animal who had sent the Abbé to his death, and many other members of the Resistance.

The telephone bell jangled through the quiet house. I picked up the receiver.

'Is that Donald Caskie?'

'Yes.'

'He's dead, Padre.'

'God help him,' I replied. 'May God have mercy on his soul.'

'We sent half a dozen men in after him. The door was locked and they had to break it down. He got two of our men before the others filled him with bullets. Our two chaps are wounded but they'll be all right in a day or two. He's as dead as ever he'll be.'

I hung up the receiver. I suppose if the troops had waited for a few days, keeping Cole under observation, he would have been taken alive. But I think they did the right thing; he would have been executed anyway after a fair trial. But a fair trial would have brought agonies on his innocent family, for the story of his sordid treachery would have been revealed to the world. The French have a logic of their own. He was in the Hands of God the omniscient and merciful Judge and his life was over.

My only difficulties now were of a practical nature, for there was much suffering in Paris during that first period after the liberation. Again I found myself distributing to the needy the contents of food parcels from charitable organisations in Britain and America. Even among the newly imprisoned Germans one found work and this had the healing force of charity and was part of that 'binding of wounds' that Lincoln spoke of so many years ago and far across the sea.

It was a strange time and work was complicated by an incessant need to forage or, in the dry language of soldiers, scrounge. Autumn came. Fuel was a very trying problem. I mentioned this to one of the Intelligence officers in the villa on the edge of the forest. He advised me to approach a certain major in the British Embassy who would, he felt sure, help us at the church. Next day I presented my card at the British Embassy in the Rue du Faubourg St. Honoré and asked for this officer. The official at the door was not hopeful that I would be given an interview.

'He is extremely busy, but I will present your card immediately.'

A few minutes later the major appeared and, taking my hand, drew me into the hallway.

'Donald Caskie,' he said, 'I have been looking forward to meeting you.'

I must have looked as mystified as I felt for he laughed and continued:

'Do you remember X?'—using the name of that agent I knew but never by name—'I am he. We were on the same job, you know. You sent our men across into Spain. I arranged the rest when they reached Madrid. Now, what can I do for you?'

'I need coal, Major,' I answered. 'The church is too cold for the old people in the congregation—indeed, in normal times we would consider it cold enough for polar bears.'

He chuckled and answered:

'Coal you shall have, Padre. Can you be at the Rue Bayard by eight to-morrow morning? I'll see the Army brings you four tons which should keep things hot enough for your people for a bit. When you need more come and see me again. You shall have it.'

On the following Sunday the Kirk was cosy and, I know, the most comfortable place my flock had been in for weeks.

Not many weeks later this same officer helped me again. I heard that all the German property in Paris was about to be confiscated by the French, a move which had my complete approval until it dawned upon me that among the German materials were the family possessions of Pastor Helmut Peters, my friend. In desperation I called upon the major and found that he knew all about Helmut's intervention on my behalf; the whole story of how he had striven to protect me was on record in the British Embassy where the authorities agreed that he saved my life.

Major X wrote to the French Minister of the Interior, explained the services Mr. Peters had given the British chaplain, and requested that his belongings should remain intact and be placed under British protection. With great courtesy the Minister granted the request and a few weeks later a British lorry delivered Helmut's furniture to the vicarage in a little village near Hanover. With it went a large parcel of flour, tea, sugar, canned goods, powdered milk and cigarettes. So the Christian international continues to work for its members in peace and war.

The church in the Rue Bayard was open again and services had become as regular as in the old days before 1940. But my happiness on the first Sunday after liberation can only be imagined; it cannot be described.

When I looked out on the congregation that morning it seemed that victory had already been achieved. The building was crowded with men in khaki, British soldiers of liberation and members of the Control Commission, among them the remnant of my scattered flock. I was assisted by Professor E. P. Dickie of St. Mary's College, St. Andrews, who had been my teacher of Greek. The happy faces of the soldiers were turned to us and surely I have never led a more joyful service to Almighty God our Father, Protector and Leader. And never have men more fervently raised their voices in the Psalm which had been sung thousands of years past by others who had known the bitterness of bondage by the rivers of Babylon :

'When Zion's bondage God turned back,
Like men that dreamed were we,
Then filled with laughter was our mouth,
Our tongue with melody.'

The service ended and I had my moment of silence after leading my congregation in prayer.

I walked out of the church and was hailed from a tank which stood on the Rue Bayard.

'Jump in, Padre,' a brown-faced man, in the khaki and black beret of the Tank Corps, shouted. 'Cheers for the Seamen's Mission on the Rue Forbin.'

The tall sergeant whose head protruded through the turret was one of the chaps I had sent out of Southern France more than three years earlier and his grin extended from ear to ear. He was laughing at my astonishment. After that happy first service this new and joyful shock brought me near to tears but in a twinkling I was by his side and the tank, crew shouting hilariously, rumbled on its way towards the Avenue des Champs-Élysées. The August sun beat

down on us and I stood beside my old comrade and from the
pavements of Paris the people shouted greetings and we shouted
back to them. Down the long, broad, noble avenue we rumbled
in triumph towards the Place de la Concorde and I knew in that
moment what victory meant, peace, love, happiness and freedom—
the luxury of holding one's head upright marching with friends
under God's own sun and sky.

THE END